Second Edition

Automotive Electronics and Engine Performance

Davis N. Dales
Frank J. Thiessen

PRENTICE HALL
Englewood Cliffs, New Jersey   Columbus, Ohio

Library of Congress Cataloging-in-Publication Data

Dales, D. N.
    Automotive electronics and engine performance / Davis N. Dales and
Frank J. Thiessen. — 2nd ed.
        p.   cm.
    Includes index.
    ISBN 0-13-350547-2
    1. Automobiles—Motors—Maintenance and repair.   2. Automobiles—
Electronic equipment—Maintenance and repair.   I. Thiessen, F. J.
II. Title.
TL210.D28   1995
629.25'04—dc20   94-26855
                                                                       CIP

Editor: Ed Francis
Editorial/production supervision and interior design: Tally Morgan, WordCrafters
    Editorial Services, Inc.
Cover design: Thomas Mack
Prepress/manufacturing buyer: Deidra Schwartz

This book was set in Palatino by The Clarinda Company and was printed and
bound by Semline. The cover was printed by Phoenix.

 © 1995, 1984 by Prentice-Hall, Inc.
A Simon & Schuster Company
Englewood Cliffs, NJ 07632

Printed in the United States of America

10 9 8 7 6 5 4 3 2 1

ISBN 0-13-350547-2

Prentice-Hall International (UK) Limited, *London*
Prentice-Hall of Australia Pty, Limited, *Sydney*
Prentice-Hall Canada Inc., *Toronto*
Prentice-Hall Hispanoamericana, S.A., *Mexico*
Prentice-Hall of India Private Limited, *New Delhi*
Prentice-Hall of Japan, Inc., *Tokyo*
Simon & Schuster Asia Pte. Ltd., *Singapore*
Editora Prentice-Hall do Brasil, Ltda., *Rio de Janeiro*

Contents

■ CHAPTER 10 COOLING SYSTEM DIAGNOSIS AND SERVICE, 268

■ CHAPTER 11 HEATING AND AIR CONDITIONING SYSTEM DIAGNOSIS AND SERVICE, 281

■ CHAPTER 12 LIGHTING, INSTRUMENTATION, AND POWER ACCESSORIES DIAGNOSIS AND SERVICE, 327

■ APPENDIX, 361

■ ANSWER KEYS, 367

■ INDEX, 373

Preface

This second edition of *Automotive Electronics and Engine Performance* details the diagnosis, service, and repair of today's sophisticated electronic engine controls, engine support systems, emission control systems, lighting, instrumentation, power accessories, and driver information systems. The easy-to-read style and much greater emphasis on "how to, hands on" information make this a valuable source of information for those already in this field and for those desiring entry. The information may be used to prepare for ASE certification tests in the following areas:

TEST A6, ELECTRICAL SYSTEMS
TEST A7, HEATING AND AIR CONDITIONING
TEST A8, ENGINE PERFORMANCE

The content area for each test area is as follows:

ELECTRICAL SYSTEMS (TEST A6)

Content Area	Questions in Test	Percentage of Test
A. General Electrical System Diagnosis	10	20.0%
B. Battery Diagnosis and Service	5	10.0%
C. Starting System Diagnosis and Repair	5	10.0%
D. Charging System Diagnosis and Repair	6	12.0%
E. Lighting Systems Diagnosis and Repair	6	12.0%
1. Headlights, Parking Lights, Taillights, Dash Lights, and Courtesy Lights	(3)	
2. Stoplights, Turn Signals, Hazard Lights, and Back-up Lights	(3)	
F. Gauges, Warning Devices, and Driver Information Systems Diagnosis and Repair	7	14.0%
G. Horn and Wiper/Washer Diagnosis and Repair	3	6.0%
H. Accessories Diagnosis and Repair	8	16.0%
1. Body	(4)	
2. Miscellaneous	(4)	
Total	50	100.0%

HEATING AND AIR CONDITIONING (TEST A7)

Content Area	Questions in Test	Percentage of Test
A. A/C System Diagnosis and Repair	11	27.5%
B. Refrigeration System Component Diagnosis and Repair	10	25.0%
1. Compressor and Clutch	(4)	
2. Evaporator, Condenser, Receiver/Drier, Etc.	(6)	
C. Heating and Engine Cooling Systems Diagnosis and Repair	5	12.5%
D. Operating Systems and Related Controls Diagnosis and Repair	14	35.0%
1. Electrical	(7)	
2. Vacuum/Mechanical	(4)	

3. Automatic and Semi-Automatic Temperature Controls   (3)
E. Refrigerant Recovery, Recycling, and Handling _____ _____
             Total   40   100.0%

ENGINE PERFORMANCE (TEST A8)

Content Area	Questions in Test	Percentage of Test
A. General Engine Diagnosis	19	24.0%
B. Ignition System Diagnosis and Repair	16	20.0%
C. Fuel, Air Induction, and Exhaust Systems Diagnosis and Repair	21	26.0%
D. Emissions Control Systems Diagnosis and Repair	19	24.0%
1. Positive Crankcase Ventilation	(1)	
2. Spark Timing Controls	(3)	
3. Idle Speed Controls	(3)	
4. Exhaust Gas Recirculation	(4)	
5. Exhaust Gas Treatment	(2)	
6. Inlet Air Temperature Controls	(2)	
7. Intake Manifold Temperature Controls	(2)	
8. Fuel Vapor Controls	(2)	
E. Engine-Related Service	2	2.5%
F. Engine Electrical Systems Diagnosis and Repair	3	2.5%
1. Battery	(1)	
2. Starting System	(1)	
3. Charging System	(1)	
Total	80	100.0%

*The 5-year Recertification Test will cover the same content areas as those listed. However, the number of questions in each content area of the Recertification Test will be reduced by about one-half.

The information in this book is divided into chapters as follows:

I. Introduction

1. Engine Performance Factors
2. Drivability, Performance Diagnosis and Tune Up
3. Electrical System Diagnosis and Service Principles
4. Computer Control System Diagnosis and Service Principles

5. Battery, Starting, and Charging Systems Diagnosis and Service
6. Ignition System Diagnosis and Service
7. Fuel Supply and Fuel Injection System Diagnosis and Service
8. Intake, Exhaust, and Turbocharger System Diagnosis and Service
9. Emission Control Systems Diagnosis and Service
10. Cooling System Diagnosis and Service
11. Heating and Air Conditioning System Diagnosis and Service
12. Lighting, Instrumentation, and Power Accessories Diagnosis and Service

Each chapter includes the following features:

- *INTRODUCTION*   Introduces the subject matter covered in the chapter.

- *LEARNING OBJECTIVES*   A list of the major areas of *skill* and *knowledge* that the student is expected to acquire during completion of the chapter.

- *TERMS YOU SHOULD KNOW*   A list of the *automotive terms* used in the chapter. Tells the student what to expect in the chapter and the terms the student is expected to be able to use in discussing the operation and service of the automobile.

- *SAFETY CAUTIONS AND PRO TIPS*   These appear throughout the text to emphasize potential *problems, safe procedures,* and the avoidance of *accidents and injury.*

- *REVIEW QUESTIONS*   Short-answer, fill-in-the-blank, and true–false questions. May be used by the student and the instructor to review comprehension and progress.

- *TEST QUESTIONS*   Test questions of the type used in certification tests. Provides practice for writing technician certification tests.

Answer keys are provided at the back of the text.

These features are designed to make it easier for the student to understand the technical language commonly used in the automotive service industry without which effective communication in the shop is not possible. They emphasize the terminology that must be understood, the potential hazards that may be encountered, and the safe work habits that are essential to productivity and profit.

Acknowledgments

Special appreciation is hereby extended to Ed Francis and Prentice Hall, Tally Morgan and Word-Crafters, the many vehicle and equipment manufacturers, colleagues, and educational and training institutions across the United States and Canada for their most valuable assistance. Their help is what makes this book possible.

■ IMPORTANT SAFETY NOTICE

Proper service and repair are important for the safe and reliable operation of motor vehicles. The service procedures described in this book are effective general methods of performing service operations. Some of these operations require the use of tools specially designed for the purpose. These special tools should be used as recommended in the appropriate service manuals.

This book contains various general precautions that should be read carefully to minimize the risk of personal injury or damage to the vehicle being serviced. It must be noted that these precautions are not exhaustive. The authors could not possibly know, evaluate, and advise the service trade of all the conceivable ways in which service may be carried out or of the possible hazardous consequences of such methods. Accordingly, anyone using any given service procedure, tool, or equipment must first confirm that neither personal safety nor the safety of the vehicle or equipment will be jeopardized by the service method selected. This book is not a service manual and should not be used as such. Always refer to the appropriate manufacturer's service manual for specific procedures and specifications.

Second Edition

Automotive Electronics and Engine Performance

Davis N. Dales
Frank J. Thiessen

1 Introduction

The performance and drivability of today's automobile depends on the engine and its support systems. The comfort and convenience experienced while driving depend on the performance of the heating and air conditioning systems, power accessories, and the various information display systems. This introductory section reviews the principles of engine operation and design, introduces the systems required to support engine operation, and provide comfort and convenience to the driver and passengers. Good performance and drivability are also defined. Problem diagnosis, testing, service, and repair of these systems is described in the chapters that follow.

LEARNING OBJECTIVES

After completing this section you should be able to:

- List basic engine components
- Describe how engines produce power
- List basic engine design types
- Describe four stroke cycle engine operation
- Describe two stroke cycle engine operation
- Describe the relationship between cylinder numbering and firing order
- Define engine bore, stroke, and compression ratio
- List engine classification methods
- Describe rotary engine operation
- List engine support systems
- List passenger comfort, convenience, and information systems
- Define good performance and drivability

TERMS YOU SHOULD KNOW

Look for these terms as you study this introductory section and find out what they mean.

energy conversion
engine power
air/fuel mixture
combustion
four stroke cycle
two stroke cycle
diesel engine
cylinder numbering
firing order
bore
stroke
square
undersquare
oversquare
displacement
compression ratio
engine classification
engine systems
passenger comfort
passenger convenience
information display
performance
drivability

■ BASIC ENGINE COMPONENTS

The basic engine consists of a cylinder block, a movable piston inside the cylinder, a connecting rod attached at the top end to the piston and at the bottom to the offset portion of a crankshaft, a camshaft to operate the two valves (intake and exhaust), and a cylinder head. A flywheel is attached to one end of the crankshaft. The other end of the crankshaft has a gear to drive the camshaft gear. The camshaft gear is twice as large as the crankshaft gear. This drives the camshaft at half the speed of the crankshaft **(Figure I–1).**

■ ENERGY CONVERSION

The internal combustion engine is used to convert the chemical energy of the fuel into heat energy and then to convert this heat energy into usable mechanical energy. This is achieved by combining the appropriate amounts of air and fuel, and burning the mixture in an enclosed cylinder at a controlled rate.

An average air/fuel ratio for good combustion is about 15 parts of air to 1 part of fuel by weight.

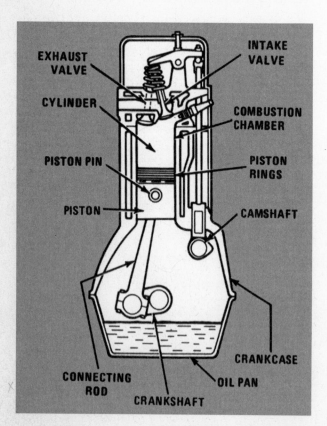

■ FIGURE I–1

Basic engine components. (Courtesy of Chrysler Corporation.)

This means that for every gallon of gasoline burned, the oxygen in about 9000 to 10,000 gallons (34,000 to 38,000 L) of air is required. Air is about 20% oxygen and 80% nitrogen.

Diesel engines operate on a much wider air/fuel ratio, since air intake is not regulated on most diesels. Ratios may range from about 20:1 to about 100:1. This fact, plus the high compression of the diesel, makes it a very fuel efficient engine.

■ PRODUCING ENGINE POWER

Engine power is needed to move the vehicle. To do this the engine converts fuel energy to usable power. It does this by burning the appropriate amounts of fuel and air (air/fuel mixture) in the cylinders. This is called combustion. As each piston moves down, a partial vacuum is created in the cylinder. Atmospheric pressure entering the throttle body and intake manifold runners forces the air/fuel mixture into the cylinders past the open intake valves. When the appropriate amount of air/fuel charge has entered the cylinder the intake valve closes trapping the air/fuel charge in the cylinder. This occurs shortly after the piston starts moving up in the cylinder. As the piston continues to move up the air fuel charge is compressed to about 12% of its original volume. A spark at the spark plug ignites the air/fuel charge at exactly the right instant for best operation. The air/fuel charge burns at a controlled rate even though it appears to explode. This results in a rapid buildup of heat and pressure in the cylinder **(Figure I–2).** High pressure in the cylinder forces the piston downward. Piston movement is transferred to an offset on the crankshaft via a connecting rod causing the crankshaft to turn. When the piston nears the bottom of its travel limit the exhaust valve opens. Upward piston movement forces the spent exhaust gases past the open exhaust valve into the exhaust system and from there into the atmosphere. This sequence of events is repeated in each cylinder again and again as the engine runs **(Figure I–3).** Combustion takes place in alternate cylinders at evenly spaced intervals to provide a smooth flow of power. Power output is increased as the throttle is opened wider allowing more air/fuel mixture to enter the cylinders. Only about one third of the energy of combustion is usable. The other two thirds is lost through the cooling and exhaust systems **(Figure I–4).** The vehicle manufacturer decides what type and size of engine to use in any particular car model. Larger cars generally have larger engines. The same engine is often used in several different models with minor design differences. In some applications a turbocharger or supercharger may be used to increase power output. See Chapter 8 for details.

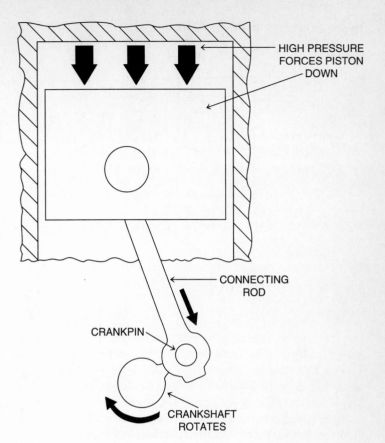

■ **FIGURE I–2**
Combustion of the air–fuel mixture in the cylinder creates the pressure needed to force the piston down and rotate the crankshaft.

■ GASOLINE ENGINE OPERATION

Four-Stroke-Cycle Engine

The movement of the piston from its uppermost position (TDC, top dead center) to its lowest position (BDC, bottom dead center) is called a stroke **(Figure I–5).** Most automobile engines operate on the four-stroke-cycle principle. A series of events involving four strokes of the piston completes one cycle. These events are (1) the intake stroke, (2) the compression stroke, (3) the power stroke, and (4) the exhaust stroke. Two revolutions of the crankshaft and one revolution of the camshaft are required to complete one cycle. **(See Figure I–3.)**

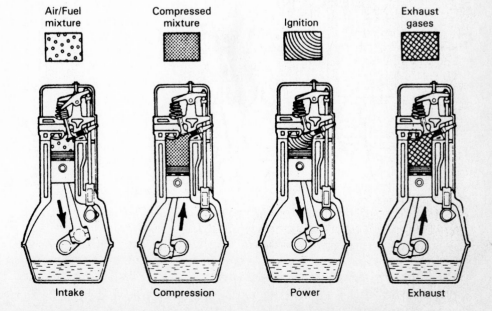

■ **FIGURE I–3**
Four-stroke-cycle engine operation. (Courtesy of Chrysler Corporation.)

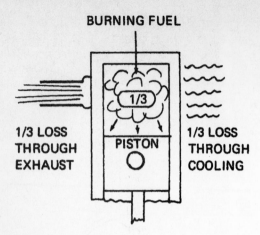

■ FIGURE I–4
Of the available heat energy in the gasoline, only about one-third is usable energy in the internal combustion engine.

On the intake stroke the piston is pulled down in the cylinder by the crankshaft and connecting rod. During this time the intake valve is held open by the camshaft. Since the piston has moved down in the cylinder, creating a low-pressure area (vacuum), atmospheric pressure forces a mixture of air and fuel past the intake valve into the cylinder. Atmospheric pressure is approximately 14.7 psi (about 101.35 kPa) at sea level. Pressure in the cylinder during the intake stroke is considerably less than this. The pressure difference is the force that causes the air–fuel mixture to flow into the cylinder, since a liquid or a gas (vapor) will always flow from a high- to a low-pressure area **(Figure I–6).**

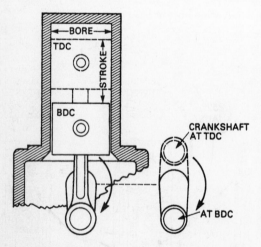

■ FIGURE I–5
The distance the piston travels from its highest position in the cylinder (top dead center, TDC) to its lowest position in the cylinder (bottom dead center, BDC) is known as the stroke. The length of the stroke is determined by crankshaft design and is twice the crank throw dimension.

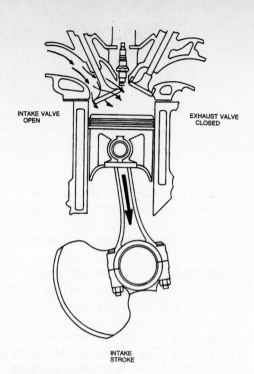

■ FIGURE I–6
Piston, connecting rod, and valve action on the intake stroke. (Courtesy of Chrysler Corporation.)

As the piston is moved up by the crankshaft from BDC, the intake valve closes. The air–fuel mixture is trapped in the cylinder above the piston. Further piston travel compresses the air–fuel mixture to

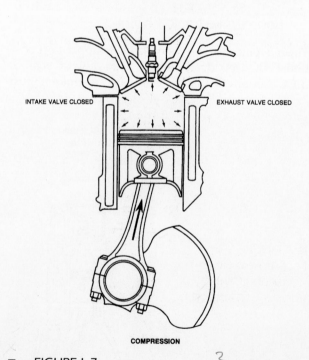

■ FIGURE I–7
As the piston moves up on the compression stroke, both valves are closed. (Courtesy of Chrysler Corporation.)

approximately one-eighth of its original volume when the piston has reached TDC. This completes the compression stroke **(Figure I–7)**.

When the piston is at or near TDC, the air–fuel mixture is ignited. The burning of the air–fuel mixture (combustion) takes place at a controlled rate. Expansion of the burning mixture causes a rapid rise in pressure. This increased pressure forces the piston down on the power stroke, causing the crankshaft to rotate **(Figure I–8)**.

At the end of the power stroke the camshaft opens the exhaust valve, and the exhaust stroke begins. Remaining pressure in the cylinder, and upward movement of the piston, force the exhaust gases out of the cylinder **(Figure I–9)**. At the end of the exhaust stroke, the exhaust valve closes and the intake valve opens, repeating the entire cycle of events over and over again **(Figure I–10)**.

To start the engine, some method of cranking the engine is required to turn the crankshaft and cause piston movement. This is done by the starter motor when the ignition key is in the start position. When sufficient air–fuel mixture has entered the cylinders and is ignited, the power strokes create enough energy to continue crankshaft rotation. At this point,

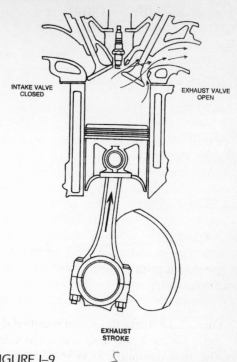

EXHAUST STROKE

■   FIGURE I–9

The piston rising in the cylinder forces the exhaust gases out past the open exhaust valve on the exhaust stroke. (Courtesy of Chrysler Corporation.)

the ignition key is released to the run position and the starter is disengaged.

Sufficient energy is stored in the flywheel and other rotating parts on the power strokes to move the pistons and related parts through the other three strokes (exhaust, intake, and compression). The

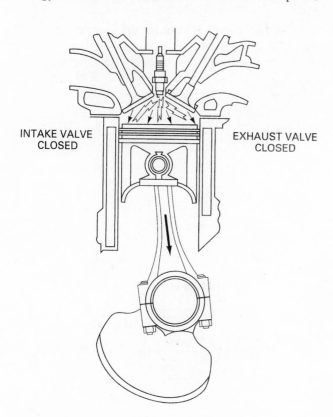

POWER

■   FIGURE I–8

When the air–fuel mixture is ignited, the expanding gases force the piston down on the power stroke. (Courtesy of Chrysler Corporation.)

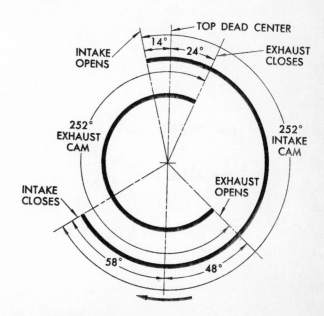

■   FIGURE I–10

Example of valve timing diagram indicating the duration of each stroke in degrees of crankshaft rotation. (Courtesy of General Motors Corporation.)

amount of air–fuel mixture allowed to enter the cylinders determines the power and speed developed by the engine.

Two-Stroke-Cycle Engine

Two-stroke-cycle engine operation, as the name implies, requires only two strokes of the piston to complete all four events: intake, compression, power, and exhaust **(Figure I–11).** There are several types of two-stroke-cycle engines. One type uses ports and a reed valve to perform the function of the intake and exhaust valves of the four-stroke-cycle engine. A specially designed piston head helps to control the flow of intake and exhaust gases. This type of engine is used mostly on small engine power applications. A mixture of air–fuel and oil in correct proportion is used. There is no separate lubrication system. The oil in the mixture provides the lubrication required.

Orbital Combustion Engine

A more efficient two-stroke engine has been developed for use in automobiles by Ralph Sarich of Australia. It is called the orbital combustion process engine. Compressed air is used to inject fuel through the transfer ports after the exhaust port is closed. This results in no fuel loss through an open exhaust port as is the case with other two-stroke designs. The engine is more compact, lighter, and cheaper to produce than four-stroke engines of the same displacement. It also has fewer moving parts and lower emissions.

Comparing Two- and Four-Cycle Engines

It could be assumed that a two-cycle engine with the same number of cylinders, displacement, compression ratio, and speed as a four-cycle engine would have twice the power since it has twice as many power strokes. However, this is not the case, since both the power and compression strokes are shortened to allow scavenging to take place.

■ DIESEL ENGINE OPERATION

Four-Stroke-Cycle Engine

The diesel engine is easily recognized by the absence of such components as spark plugs, ignition wires, and coil, common to gasoline engines.

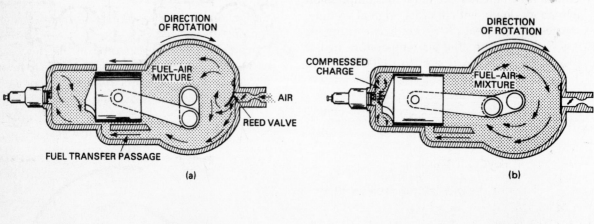

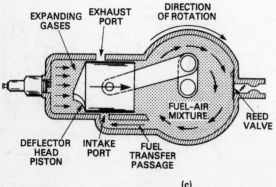

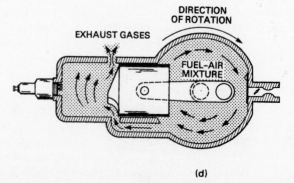

■ FIGURE I–11
The two-stroke-cycle engine requires two strokes of the piston and one revolution of the crankshaft to complete one cycle of events: a) intake, b) compression, c) power, d) exhaust.

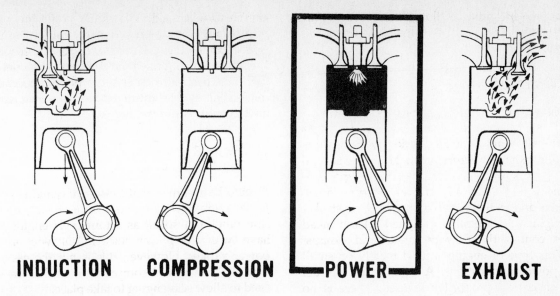

INDUCTION   COMPRESSION   POWER   EXHAUST

■ FIGURE I–12
Four-stroke-cycle diesel engine operation. (Courtesy of Ford Motor Compony.)

In the four-stroke-cycle diesel engine the four strokes occur in the same sequence as in the gasoline engine described earlier. However, only air is taken into the cylinder on the intake stroke. The air is compressed to a much greater extent on the compression stroke to about one-twentieth of its original volume. This creates a great deal of friction between the air molecules, which raises the air temperature in the combustion chamber to about 800 to 1200°F (425 to 650°C). This is hot enough to ignite the diesel fuel when it is injected near the end of the compression stroke. Consequently, no spark ignition system is needed **(Figure I–12).**

Two-Stroke-Cycle Engine

The two-stroke-cycle diesel engine completes all four events (intake, compression, power, and exhaust) in one revolution of the crankshaft (or two strokes of the piston) **(Figure I–13).** A series of ports or openings is arranged around the cylinder in such a position that the ports are open when the piston is at the bottom of its stroke. A blower forces air into the cylinder through the open ports, expelling all remaining exhaust gases past the open exhaust valves and filling the cylinder with air. This is called scavenging.

As the piston moves up, the exhaust valves close and the piston covers the ports. The air trapped above the piston is compressed since the exhaust valve is closed. Just before the piston reaches top dead center, the required amount of fuel is injected into the cylinder. The heat generated by compressing the air immediately ignites the fuel. Combustion continues until the injected fuel has been burned. The pressure resulting from combustion forces the piston

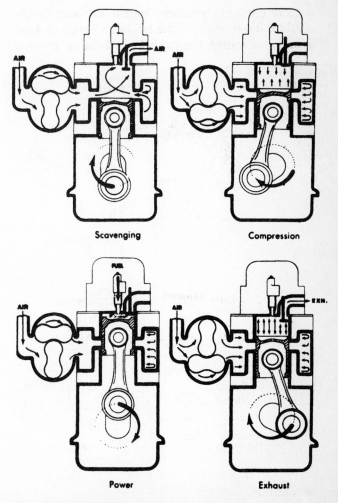

Scavenging   Compression

Power   Exhaust

■ FIGURE I–13
Two-stroke-cycle diesel engine operation. (Courtesy of General Motors Corporation.)

IN-LINE 4

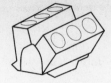

V6

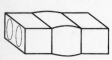

OPPOSED 4

NARROW V4

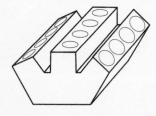

W12

■   **FIGURE I–14**
Various cylinder block designs. (Courtesy of F T
Enterprises.)

downward on the power stroke. When the piston is
approximately halfway down, the exhaust valves are
opened, allowing the exhaust gases to escape. Further downward movement uncovers the inlet ports,
causing fresh air to enter the cylinder and expel the
exhaust gases. The entire procedure is then repeated,
as the engine continues to run.

■ ENGINE CYLINDERS

Engines may have 3, 4, 5, 6, 8, 10, or 12 cylinders.
In general, engines with fewer cylinders have less
power, other factors being equal. Engine designs
may be in-line (all cylinders arranged in a straight
line), V-shaped (two banks of cylinders arranged in a
60, 90, or 15 degree shape), or opposed (two banks of
cylinders 180 degrees opposite each other). Another
design uses the W-design (three banks of cylinders
arranged in the shape of a W). The in-line and V
designs are the most popular **(Figure I–14 to I–15).**

■ CYLINDER NUMBERING AND FIRING ORDER

The engine manufacturer arbitrarily decides on the
cylinder numbering method and firing order of the
engine during engine design. The sequence in which
the cylinders are fired (firing order) is designed to
distribute the load of power impulses along the
crankshaft as evenly as possible. In-line engines usually have the cylinders numbered in order from the
front (end opposite to the flywheel) to the back. On V

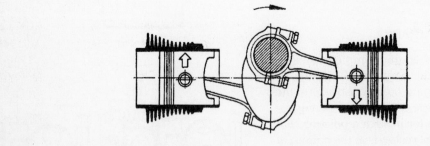

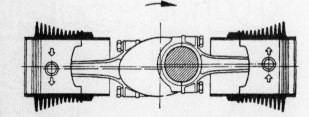

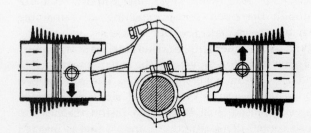

■   **FIGURE I–15**
Finned cylinder pots are used on this horizontally opposed air-cooled engine.
(Courtesy of General Motors Corporation.)

① ② ③ ④
Firing Order
1-3-4-2
1-2-4-3

① ② ③ ④ ⑤ ⑥
Firing Order
1-5-3-6-2-4

② ④ ⑥ Right Bank

① ③ ⑤ Left Bank
Firing Order
1-6-5-4-3-2

② ④ ⑥ ⑧ Right Bank

① ③ ⑤ ⑦ Left Bank
Firing Order
1-8-4-3-6-5-7-2

① ② ③ ④ Right Bank

⑤ ⑥ ⑦ ⑧ Left Bank
Firing Order
1-5-4-8-6-3-7-2
1-5-4-2-6-3-7-8

■ FIGURE I–16
Typical cylinder numbering methods and firing orders.

engines the number one cylinder may be at the front on either bank of cylinders. On some engines all the odd numbered cylinders are on one bank and all the even numbered cylinders on the other. Another arrangement is to number the cylinders in order down one bank and then continue in sequence down the other. See **Figure I–16** for examples of cylinder numbering and firing orders.

■ BORE AND STROKE

The engine bore (cylinder diameter) and stroke (distance piston moves in cylinder) are major factors in engine power and performance **(see Figure I–5).** An engine where the bore and stroke dimensions are the same is called a square engine. An engine with the stroke larger than the bore is called an undersquare engine. An engine with the bore larger than the stroke is called oversquare. An oversquare engine provides rapid acceleration (rapid rpm increase), is quite responsive at higher engine speeds but lacks low speed torque. This engine requires a lower overall drive train ratio to take advantage of its higher rpm. An undersquare engine is less responsive (slower in gaining rpm), is a slower engine, but has good low speed torque. This engine requires a higher overall drive train ratio for better fuel economy. A square engine compromises between low speed torque and high speed power.

■ ENGINE DISPLACEMENT

The displacement of an engine is determined by cylinder bore diameter, length of stroke, and number of cylinders. It is the amount or volume of air pushed out of the cylinder (displaced) by one piston as it moves from BDC to TDC, multiplied by the number of cylinders in the engine.

Displacement is calculated as follows:

$$\pi r^2 \times \text{stroke} \times \text{number of cylinders}$$

where $\pi = \dfrac{22}{7}$ (or 3.14)

$r^2 = \text{radius} \times \text{radius}$ (radius $= \dfrac{1}{2}$ of cylinder bore)

Therefore, a six-cylinder engine with a 3.800-in. bore and a 3.4-in. stroke would have a displacement of

$$\frac{22}{7} \times (1.9 \times 1.9) \times (3.4 \times 6)$$

$$= \frac{22}{7} \times 3.61 \times 20.4$$

$$\frac{22}{7} \times 73.644 = \frac{1620.168}{7} = 231.45 \text{ (cubic inches of displacement)}$$

In metric terms, a six-cylinder engine with a 100.0-mm bore and a stroke of 80 mm would be calculated as follows. First, since metric displacement is stated in cubic centimeters, it is necessary to convert the bore and stroke dimensions to centimeters.

$$100 \text{ mm} = 10\text{-cm bore} \quad 80 \text{ mm} = 8\text{-cm stroke}$$

$$\frac{22}{7} \times (5 \times 5) \times (8 \times 6) = \frac{22}{7} \times 25 \times 48$$

$$\frac{22}{7} \times 1200 = \frac{26{,}400}{7} = 3771 \text{ cubic centimeters of displacement or 3.771 liters}$$

The power an engine is able to produce depends very much on its displacement. Engines with more displacement are able to take in a greater amount of air–fuel mixture on each intake stroke and can therefore produce more power. Engine displacement can be increased by engine design in three ways: (1) increasing cylinder bore diameter, (2) lengthening the stroke, and (3) increasing the number of cylinders.

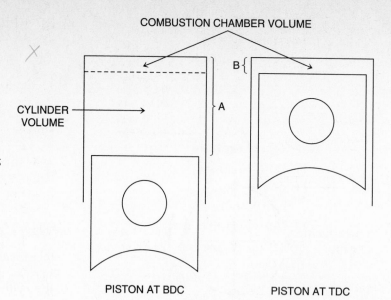

COMBUSTION CHAMBER VOLUME

CYLINDER VOLUME →

PISTON AT BDC   PISTON AT TDC

■   FIGURE I–17
The engine compression ratio is the combustion chamber volume plus cylinder volume compared to combustion chamber volume. If combustion chamber volume plus cylinder volume in A is 9 times as large as combustion chamber volume in B then the compression ratio is 9 to 1.

■ COMPRESSION RATIOS

The compression ratio of an engine is an important factor in determining its performance. It is the ratio of total cylinder volume (piston at bottom dead center) to combustion chamber volume (piston at top dead center) **(Figure I–17)**. In general, higher compression ratios increase power, reduce fuel consumption, increase the cranking load, and are more prone to engine pinging and knock caused by detonation. (See Chapter 2 for details about normal and abnormal combustion.)

Compression ratios generally range from around 8:1 to about 10:1. Turbocharged or supercharged engines normally have a lower compression ratio than most naturally aspirated engines in order to reduce the tendency to knock. (See Chapter 8 for turbocharger and supercharger details.)

Detonation and serious engine damage are the result of too high a compression ratio. Combustion chamber design and type of gasoline (octane or anti-knock rating) used also affect the point at which detonation will occur. Detonation is the ignition of the fuel due to the high temperature caused by the high pressure in the combustion chamber. Fuel may be ignited before the spark occurs at the spark plug, and burning is rapid and uncontrolled. This causes parts to be subjected to excessive heat and stress. See Chapter 1 for a detailed discussion of detonation and preignition.

Compression Ratio: Diesel Engines

The compression ratio of a diesel engine is much higher than that of a gasoline engine. This is possible since air only is compressed. Compressing air at diesel compression ratios causes air molecules to collide rapidly with each other. The friction caused by these collisions creates heat. Temperatures of 1000°F (540°C) or higher can be reached depending on the compression ratio. This is hot enough to ignite the fuel when it is injected near the top of the compression stroke. Diesel engine compression ratios range from around 15:1 to about 22:1.

■ PISTON AND CRANK PIN TRAVEL

The speed and distance traveled by the crank pin can be considered to be constant and in a uniform path at any given engine speed. This is not the case, however, with piston speed and travel **(see Figure I–18)**.

When crank pin speed is uniform, the speed and distance traveled by the piston connected to it varies due to crank pin and connecting rod angle. When the piston reaches the TDC position, its speed is zero. As it begins to move downward, its speed increases rapidly. At a point where the crank pin is about 63° ATDC, the piston has reached its maximum speed. This is the point at which the crank throw centerline and the connecting rod centerline form an angle of 90°. After this point, the piston speed decreases until it reaches zero at the BDC position. As the piston moves upward from this point, its speed increases until it reaches its maximum at about 63° BTDC. From this point on the piston slows down until it reaches TDC again, where it once more comes to a stop.

Piston speed is normally stated as an average speed in feet per minute (ft/min) and can be calculated as follows:

piston speed = stroke (in feet) × rpm ÷ 2

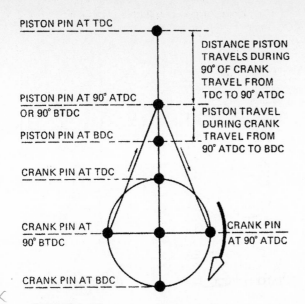

■ FIGURE I–18
*Piston and crankpin travel diagram. Note the
difference in distance travelled by the piston during
each 90 degrees of crankshaft rotation.*

You must divide by 2 because the piston travels the
stroke distance twice (up and down) during each revolution.

The distance traveled by the piston varies with
the crank angle. Starting with the TDC position of the
crank pin, the piston travels a greater distance during
the first 90° of crank rotation than it does during the
second 90°. As the crank pin continues past the BDC
position through the third 90° of rotation, the piston
travel is less than it is for the final 90° when it reaches
the TDC position.

The force of combustion pressure has no rotation
effect on the crankshaft when the piston is at the TDC
position. As the crank pin passes the TDC position on
the power stroke, the mechanical advantage through
the angle of the connecting rod increases until it
reaches its maximum at about 63° ATDC. This is the
point where the crank pin and connecting rod form a
90° angle. Thereafter, the force advantage decreases
rapidly while combustion pressure also decreases.

■ ENGINE CLASSIFICATIONS

Engines can be classified in a number of different
ways, depending on engine design.

1. *By cycles.* There are two-stroke- and four-
stroke-cycle engines.
2. *By cooling systems.* Liquid-cooled engines
and air-cooled engines are being used. Liquid-cooled
engines are the most common in the automotive
industry.
3. *By fuel system.* Gasoline, diesel, and propane
fuel systems are currently used in automobile engines.
4. *By ignition system.* Gas engines use the spark
(electrical) ignition system. The electrical ignition system causes a spark across the spark plug electrodes in
the cylinder at the end of the compression stroke
which ignites the vaporized fuel and air mixture.

Diesel (compression ignition) engines use the
heat from compressing the air to ignite the fuel when
it is injected into the cylinder at the end of the compression stroke. Since diesel engine compression
ratios (about 22:1) are much higher than gasoline
engine compression ratios, sufficient heat is generated by compressing the air to immediately ignite the
fuel upon injection.
5. *By valve arrangement.* Four types of valve
arrangements have been used, as shown in **Figure
I–19.** Of the four types (L, T, F, and I heads), the I head
is the most common on both in-block and overhead
camshaft designs.
6. *By the number of valves per cylinder.* There may
be two, three, or four valves.
7. *By cylinder arrangement.* Engine block
configuration or cylinder arrangement depends on
cylinder block design **(Figure I–14).** Cylinders may
be arranged in a straight line one behind the other in
the form of a V, or horizontally opposed or in the
form of a W.
8. *By displacement.* Engine displacement is the
amount of air displaced by the piston when it moves
from BDC to TDC; it varies with cylinder bore size,
length of piston stroke, and number of cylinders.

■   FIGURE I–19
*Different valve arrangements
used in engines past and
present. The most common is
the I head (valves in head)
shown second from the left.*

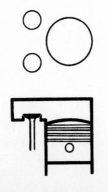

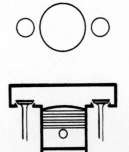
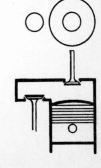

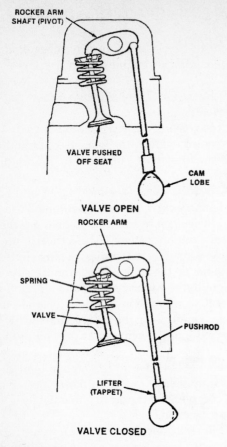

FIGURE I–20
In-block camshaft valve train operation. (Courtesy of Ford Motor Company.)

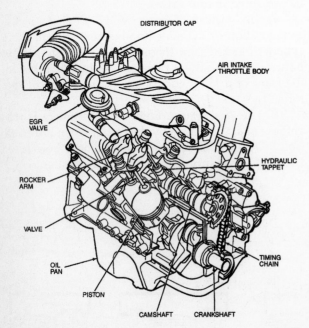

FIGURE I–21
This engine has the camshaft in the block. (Courtesy of Ford Motor Company.)

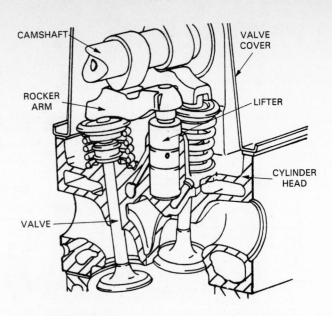

FIGURE I–22
Single overhead camshaft above the rocker arms. (Courtesy of Ford Motor Company.)

9. *By the number and location of camshafts.* In block, SOHC (single overhead camshaft) and DOHC (double overhead camshaft) **(Figures I–20 to I–26).**

■ ROTARY ENGINE

The Wankel rotary engine is unique in the way it operates. It has several advantages over the piston engine. It is light and compact and has high power output for its size. It can operate on low-octane gasoline since the rotating combustion chamber has a large surface/volume ratio to aid in cooling. The rotary engine runs very smoothly and quietly since it does not have reciprocating pistons or valves. The rotary engine's cooler combustion chamber results in its being less fuel efficient than the piston engine and it also produces more hydrocarbon emissions. At the same time it produces lower nitrogen oxide emissions.

The engine consists of a triangular rotor turning inside a housing **(Figure I–27).** The rotor has seals at each corner as well as on each side of the rotor to seal the combustion chambers. The rotor is mounted on a shaft in an eccentric manner, causing its apexes to follow the irregular surface of the housing. A set of phase gears with internal teeth on the rotor and external teeth on the housing keeps the rotor properly indexed (timed or phased) to the housing.

Combustion pressure forces the rotor to turn in the housing. Power is transmitted from the rotor to the eccentric shaft. Since the eccentric shaft turns three revolutions to each revolution of the rotor, the lobe on

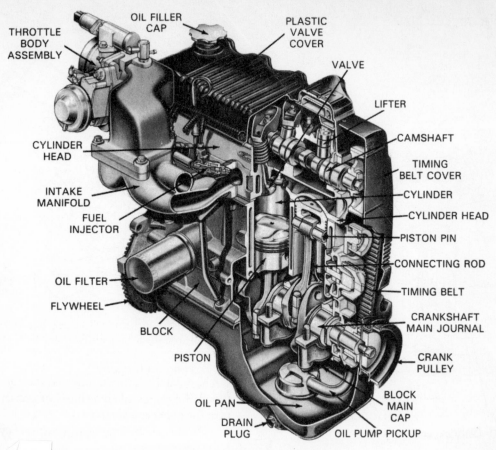

THROTTLE BODY ASSEMBLY

OIL FILLER CAP

PLASTIC VALVE COVER

VALVE

LIFTER

CAMSHAFT

TIMING BELT COVER

CYLINDER

CYLINDER HEAD

PISTON PIN

CONNECTING ROD

TIMING BELT

CRANKSHAFT MAIN JOURNAL

CRANK PULLEY

BLOCK MAIN CAP

OIL PUMP PICKUP

CYLINDER HEAD

INTAKE MANIFOLD

FUEL INJECTOR

OIL FILTER

FLYWHEEL

BLOCK

PISTON

OIL PAN

DRAIN PLUG

■ FIGURE I-

Cutaway view of four cylinder overhead camshaft engine. (Courtesy of Ford Motor Company.)

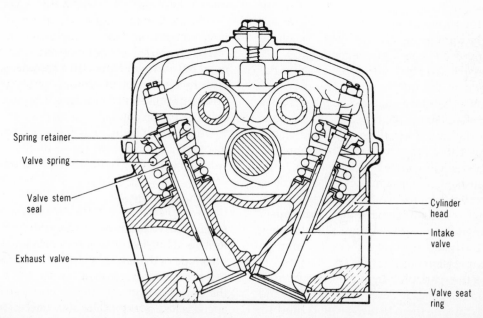

Spring retainer

Valve spring

Valve stem seal

Exhaust valve

Cylinder head

Intake valve

Valve seat ring

■ FIGURE I–24

Single overhead camshaft mounted below the rocker arms. (Courtesy of Chrysler Corporation.)

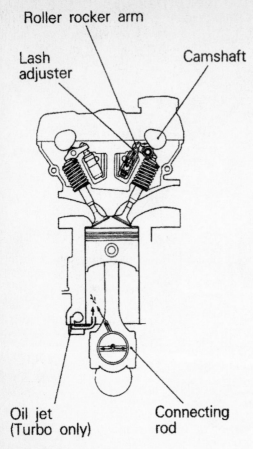

■ FIGURE I–25
Double overhead camshaft valve train with rocker arms. (Courtesy of Chrysler Corporation.)

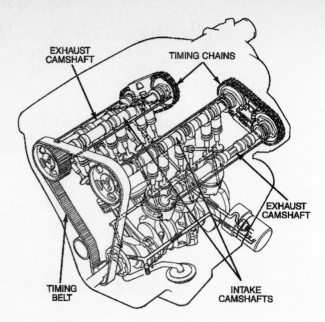

■ FIGURE I–26
Double overhead camshaft engine with direct acting bucket type cam followers (no rocker arms). (Courtesy of Ford Motor Company.)

the shaft is always in the right position for each power impulse. There are three power impulses for every revolution of the rotor. Engine power is transmitted directly from the rotor to the eccentric shaft. The phase gears are not involved in power transmission.

Intake and exhaust ports are located either in the rotor housing or in the side housing. The ports are both on the same side of the engine. The rotor creates three separate chambers in the housing. Depressions on the flats of the rotor form the combustion chambers. As the rotor turns the chambers change in volume. As can be seen in **Figure I–27** at number 1, the chamber is increasing in size at the next illustration to the right at number 2, then down to number 3 and left to number 4, where it is at its maximum. This causes the air–fuel mixture to be drawn into this chamber. This is called the intake phase. Further rotor rotation begins the compression phase in this chamber at 5, 6, 7, 8, and 9. At 9 the spark plugs ignite the compressed air–fuel mixture. Expanding gases push the rotor and eccentric shaft, causing them to turn at 10, 11, and 12. This is the power phase. As this chamber approaches the exhaust port at 13, the exhaust phase begins and continues through numbers 14, 15, 16, 17, and 18. As

the trailing apex of this chamber passes the exhaust port the cycle repeats itself.

As this chamber goes through its cycle the other two chambers are going through their cycles as well. In the cycle of events through 360° of rotor rotation each chamber is 120° away from the other two. Each chamber therefore completes all four phases (intake, compression, power, and exhaust) in one revolution of the rotor. This results in three power impulses per rotor revolution.

In a two-rotor engine the apexes of one rotor are indexed 60° from those of the second rotor. The lobes on the eccentric shaft are indexed at 180°. This results in an even-firing engine with six power impulses for each revolution of the rotors, as compared to three power impulses per crankshaft revolution in a six-cylinder piston engine.

The rotary engine has fuel, cooling, and lubricating systems similar to those of the piston engine. Additional cooling of the rotors with oil is required.

Electric Drive

Electric drive automobiles require large storage batteries and an electric motor to provide driving power. This type of drive has been used with limited success in automobiles because of the short trip limitations of the batteries and the higher cost per mile. Limited speed is also a factor. The most successful application of electric drive has been in golf carts and forklifts. However, with some state legislatures enacting laws that require a certain percentage of cars sold in the

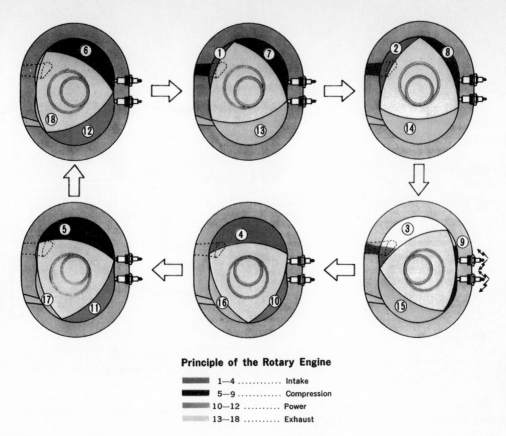

Principle of the Rotary Engine

1—4 .... Intake
5—9 .... Compression
10—12 .... Power
13—18 .... Exhaust

■ FIGURE I–27
Rotary engine operation. Follow the sequence of operation from number 1 through 18. (Courtesy of Toyo Kogyo Co. Ltd.)

state to have a zero emission level, the future of the electric car may have become brighter. All major automobile manufacturers have electric car programs, and some of them are producing electric cars in limited numbers.

Gas Turbine Engine

The gas turbine engine uses the expanding gases of burning fuel to spin a multivaned type of fan. The vanes are attached to a shaft for power output. The large gas turbine engine is highly efficient and reliable and can burn a variety of fuel types: oil, diesel fuel, gasoline, or kerosene. It is a very smooth-running engine since only rotating parts are involved in power transmission. The turbine engine also has a high power/weight ratio, making it very compact.

Although it was used experimentally to drive automobiles and trucks, the high cost of production and relatively poor fuel economy have kept it in the experimental stages. Current developments include a regenerative system to recover some of the waste energy from the turbine exhaust system. This requires the use of ceramic materials and special metals that add to the cost of the engine **(Figure I–28).**

■ ENGINE SYSTEMS

Several engine systems are needed to start the engine and keep it running. These systems must be in good condition in order to provide the expected level of performance and drivability. This includes the following.

1. *Engine Lubrication System*—provides lubrication to moving parts of the engine to reduce friction, reduce wear, help cool engine parts, help seal between moving engine parts, and help keep engine parts clean **(See Chapter 2).**

2. *Engine Cooling System*—speeds engine warmup, removes excess heat from the engine, maintains proper engine operating temperature, and provides heat for the passenger compartment **(See Chapter 10).**

3. *Starting and Charging Systems*—provide electrical energy for starting the engine, for the ignition system, and the computer control systems **(See Chapter 5).**

4. *Ignition System*—provides adequate spark at the spark plugs at exactly the correct time for starting and running the engine **(See Chapter 6).**

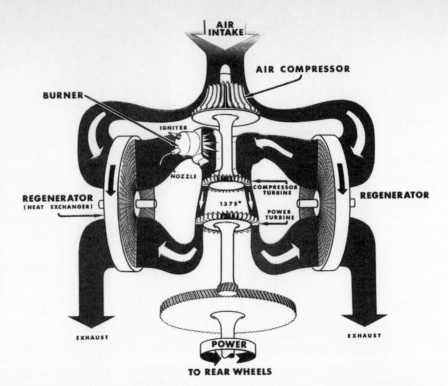

■ FIGURE I–28
Major components and layout of gas turbine engine. (Courtesy of Chrysler Corporation.)

5. *Fuel System* —provides the correct amount of atomized and vaporized fuel to all engine cylinders at exactly the correct time for all engine operating conditions **(See Chapter 7).**

6. *Intake and Exhaust Systems* —provides the correct amount of intake air to the engine for proper combustion, removes exhaust gases from the engine, treats exhaust gases to reduce harmful emissions to the atmosphere **(See Chapter 8).**

7. *Emission Control Systems*—reduce the amount of harmful emissions produced by the engine and emitted to the atmosphere **(See Chapter 9).**

■ PASSENGER COMFORT, CONVENIENCE, AND INFORMATION SYSTEMS

Passenger comfort requires the temperature and humidity to be controlled by the heating and air conditioning systems at the desired levels. Passenger convenience is provided by a variety of power assisted devices and accessories such as power windows, power seats, power door locks, and the like. Information systems provide data about engine operation, vehicle speed, fuel consumption, elapsed time and distance travelled, outside air temperature, fluid levels, and the like. These are displayed on the instrument panel and message centers both continuously and when the driver activates the system to provide specific information. See chapters 11 and 12 for

detailed problem diagnosis and service of these systems.

■ PERFORMANCE AND DRIVABILITY

The driver of a car or other vehicle expects the engine to start and perform in an acceptable and reliable manner over a long period of time. Good performance and drivability (and their absence) are readily recognized by the driver. The comfort of the driver and passengers is also a factor that must be provided by the vehicle. Good performance, drivability, and comfort must be provided whether the engine is hot or cold and regardless of weather conditions. Good performance, drivability, and comfort require the following conditions to be present.

1.   The engine must start quickly and easily.

2.   The engine must idle smoothly (no missing, backfire, stumble, or stalling).

3.   There must be good idle speed control (the proper idle speed must be maintained even when cooling fans or the A/C compressor cut in).

4.   Acceleration must be smooth and powerful (no hesitation, stumble, or stalling).

5.   There must be good fuel economy (fuel consumption must be low during all normal driving—heavy acceleration and frequent hard braking

increase fuel consumption as do low tire inflation pressures, dragging brakes, a faulty transmission, and poor wheel alignment).

6. Exhaust emissions must be low (harmful emissions must not exceed prescribed limits).

7. The temperature and humidity levels in the passenger compartment must be maintained at the desired setting.

For this kind of performance, drivability, and comfort to be present the following conditions must be present.

1. The engine must be in good mechanical condition (no excessive wear in cylinders, piston rings, valves, valve guides, valve seats, valve springs, camshafts, camshaft drives, engine bearings, bearing journals, lubrication system, and cooling system components).

2. The battery, starting, and charging systems must all be in good condition.

3. The ignition system must provide a good spark at each spark plug at exactly the right time every time.

4. The air intake system must provide an adequate volume of clean air to the engine under all operating conditions.

5. The exhaust system must remove all the engine's exhaust under all operating conditions without excessive exhaust backpressure, exhaust gas leakage, or noise.

6. The fuel system must deliver the correct amount of atomized fuel to each cylinder under all operating conditions.

7. The emission control systems must keep emissions within specifications under all operating conditions.

8. The computer control system must provide the control over engine systems that keeps them performing at their most efficient level at all times.

9. The heating and air conditioning systems must provide proper control of the temperature and humidity in the passenger compartment.

10. The instrument panel and message center must provide accurate information to the driver at all times.

11. Power accessories must provide the convenience they were designed to provide.

■ TEAMWORK

Many of the systems mentioned are designed to work together as a team and often share common sensors. A problem in one system may affect performance in another. For example the fuel injection sys-

tem and ignition system may share common sensors. A problem in the ignition system could therefore also affect the fuel injection system. An incorrect engine idle speed may cause automatic transmission/transaxle shift problems. A worn engine with low compression and low power may affect shift timing and quality. Excessive fuel consumption may be caused by a faulty ignition system, air intake problem, fuel system problem, or a worn engine. Low engine power may be caused by a worn engine, or a faulty ignition, fuel, air intake, or exhaust system. A restricted exhaust system may cause low power and excessive fuel consumption. Refer to specific chapters in this book for detailed information about performance, drivability, problem diagnosis, and problem correction procedures.

■ "RIGHT TO KNOW" LAWS

The U.S. right to know law originated with the Occupational Safety and Health Administration specifically for companies where hazardous materials were stored and handled. Most states extended these regulations to include the automotive service industry. Canadian workplace safety and health regulations are similar.

These laws require the employer to provide a safe working environment for their employees in three areas of responsibility.

1. Employers must provide training to their employees about their rights under the legislation, the nature of hazardous materials present in the workplace, the proper labeling of the hazardous materials, the posting of safety data sheets that provide precautionary information about the handling of these materials, protective equipment required, and procedures to follow in case of accidental spills and other safe handling procedures.

2. All hazardous materials must be labeled indicating their health, fire, and reactivity hazards. These labels must be clearly understood by users before product application or usage. A list of all hazardous materials used in the work area must be posted where the employees can read it.

3. Employers and shops must maintain documentation in the workplace on proof of training provided, records of accidents or spills involving hazardous materials.

Hazardous waste includes both solids and liquids and is categorized in four ways. Waste is hazardous if it is listed on the government's list of hazardous materials or falls into any of the following categories.

1. *Ignitability.* If the liquid flash point (temperature at which liquid will ignite) is below 140°F (45.8°C) or if the solid will spontaneously ignite (self-ignite due to heat generated by reaction of the materials).

2. *Corrosivity.* If it burns the skin or dissolves metals.

3. *Reactivity.* If it reacts violently with water or other substances, or releases dangerous gases when exposed to low pH acid solutions, or generates toxic vapors, fumes, mists, or flammable gases.

4. *EP Toxicity.* If it leaches any of eight listed heavy metals in concentrations greater than 100 times the concentration found in standard drinking water.

Every automotive shop should obtain all the current applicable information regarding workplace safety and health, and the handling and disposal of hazardous materials and waste. Failure to comply with regulations may result in heavy fines or imprisonment.

■ USED AND WASTE MATERIALS DISPOSAL SAFETY

The automotive service industry is concerned about energy conservation and the consequences of the indiscriminate disposal of used materials resulting from normal automotive service operations. Waste materials generated by the auto service industry must be recovered and recycled or disposed of in an environmentally friendly manner. The quality of the air we breathe, the purity of the water we use, and the condition of the land we live on are critical to the survival of all living creatures and plant life on earth.

Among the materials commonly handled in the automotive service industry, many can be recovered and recycled, while others must be disposed of in accordance with federal and local regulations. These include engine oil, gasoline, diesel fuel, solvents, transmission/transaxle and differential fluids, engine coolant (ethylene glycol), A/C refrigerants, batteries, sulphuric acid, tires, belts, cleaning fluids and chemicals, paints, brake fluid, and the like. Federal and local regulations governing the recovery, recycling, and safe disposal of these materials must be followed. As time goes on and more is learned about the harmful effects of improper handling and disposal of materials, these regulations become more and more stringent.

Review Questions

1. Engine power is needed to _____ the vehicle.
2. The air/fuel charge is forced into the engine's cylinders by _____ _____.
3. Combustion in the engine occurs at a _____ rate.
4. Combustion creates high _____ which forces the piston _____ in the cylinder.
5. What four events occur in the engine during each cycle?
6. The engine bore size is the _____ diameter.
7. In an oversquare engine the _____ is larger than the _____.
8. In general a higher compression ratio increases _____ and reduces _____ _____.
9. In a four cylinder four stroke cycle engine a power impulse occurs every _____ degrees of _____ rotation.
10. In a two rotor rotary engine the apexes of one rotor are indexed _____ degrees from those on the second rotor.
11. Diesel engines do not require spark plugs. True or False?
12. Engine systems are needed to _____ the engine and to keep it _____.
13. The driver of a car expects it to start _____ and _____ in an acceptable manner.
14. The passenger comfort level includes proper passenger compartment _____ and _____ levels.

Test Questions

1. Gasoline engines produce power by
   a) burning gasoline only
   b) pressure buildup in the cylinders
   c) throttle pressure
   d) crankshaft rotation
2. Combustion takes place in the engine in
   a) alternate cylinders at evenly spaced intervals
   b) all cylinders at the same time
   c) the crankcase
   d) the fuel injectors
3. In an oversquare engine
   a) the bore and stroke dimensions are the same
   b) the combustion chambers are square
   c) the bore dimension is larger than the stroke dimension
   d) the stroke dimension is larger than the bore dimension
4. Higher compression ratios generally
   a) produce less power
   b) produce more power
   c) increase oil consumption
   d) decrease oil consumption
5. The four strokes in a four stroke cycle engine occur in the following order
   a) exhaust, intake, power, compression
   b) compression, power, intake, exhaust

c) exhaust, intake, power, compression

d) intake, compression, power, exhaust

6. In a four cylinder two stroke cycle engine a power impulse occurs every _____ degrees of crankshaft rotation.

a) 720

b) 360

c) 180

d) 90

7. In a rotary engine each rotor creates how many separate chambers?

a) three

b) six

c) two

d) one

8. The air/fuel charge in a diesel engine is ignited by

a) high air temperature in the cylinder

b) high speed of fuel injection

c) a spark at the spark plug

d) a glow plug

9. Engines may be classified by

a) their operating cycles

b) the location of the camshaft

c) the cylinder arrangement

d) all of the above

10. The performance and drivability of a car depend on the

a) driver

b) size of the engine

c) ability of the engine to start quickly and run smoothly

d) experience of the operator

Engine Performance Factors

INTRODUCTION

A number of factors determine the ability of an engine to produce usable power. Some of these factors such as cylinder bore, stroke, displacement, and compression ratio are determined by the manufacturer and were described earlier. Other factors, such as pressure, vacuum, and atmospheric pressure, affect the power output of an engine. The power an engine is able to produce is measured in several ways, as is the efficiency of an engine. All of these factors, terms, and conditions must be properly understood to gain an understanding of their individual and combined effects on engine performance and how to diagnose and correct a performance problem.

LEARNING OBJECTIVES

After completing this chapter, you should be able to:
- Describe the relationship between altitude and atmospheric pressure.
- Describe intake manifold vacuum and absolute pressure.
- Describe normal and abnormal combustion.
- List the factors contributing to abnormal combustion.
- Define the octane rating of gasoline.
- List the possible alternate automotive fuels.
- Describe engine efficiency.
- Define engine power.
- Describe the difference between engine torque and horsepower.
- Describe the function of a dynamometer.

TERMS YOU SHOULD KNOW

Look for these terms as you study this chapter and learn what they mean.

atmospheric pressure	propane
altitude	LPG
vacuum	CNG
absolute pressure	diesel fuel
preignition	volumetric efficiency
detonation	thermal efficiency
spark knock	fuel efficiency
dieseling	mechanical efficiency
octane number	engine power
reformulated gasoline	brake horsepower
ethanol	engine torque
methanol	dynamometer

■ AIR AND ATMOSPHERIC PRESSURE

Automotive engines require a great deal of air to produce the power required. It is air pressure (atmospheric pressure) that forces air into the engine (and the turbocharger or supercharger). Atmospheric pressure and the relative humidity of the air are important factors in how well an engine performs and the power it is able to produce. The atmosphere is a layer of air surrounding the earth's surface. This layer of air exerts a force against the earth's surface because of the earth's force of gravity. This force or pressure of the atmosphere against the earth's surface is called atmospheric pressure.

Atmospheric pressure is greatest at sea level, since there is more atmosphere above a given point at sea level than there is at a given point on a high mountain. The air is, therefore, also less dense (air molecules not packed together as tightly) at higher altitudes.

A 1-in.^{2} column of atmosphere at sea level weighs 14.7 lb. Atmospheric pressure at sea level is, therefore, 14.7 psi. However, at the top of a 10,000-ft-high mountain, a 1-in.^{2} column of air weighs only 12.2 lb; therefore, atmospheric pressure is 12.2 psi at that altitude. It is important to recognize this fact since the air intake of an engine is affected adversely by increased altitude **(Figure 1–1).**

The temperature of air also has a bearing on an engine's ability to produce power. When air is heated, it expands and becomes less dense. The engine is not able to take in as much air on the intake stroke because of this and will, therefore, produce less power. Air density is stated as lb/ft.^{3} or as kg/m^3.

The humidity of the air is the percentage of moisture the air is able to keep in suspension at a given temperature. At 100% humidity, the air cannot support any additional moisture. At 50% humidity, there is half as much moisture in the air as it is able to support at that temperature. Moisture in the air improves engine performance since it has a cooling effect. Engines do not perform as well in hot, dry air.

Atmospheric pressure is measured with a barometer and is expressed in inches or millimeters of mercury. At sea level, 14.7 psi of atmospheric pressure results in 29.92 in. of mercury in the barometer. To convert inches of mercury to pounds per square inch of pressure, multiply the reading in inches of mercury (Hg) by 0.4912 (psi = in.Hg × 0.4912). In metric terms, barometric pressure at sea level is expressed as 101.35 kPa since 1 in. of mercury is equal to 3.38 kPa. Or to put it another way, atmospheric pressure at sea level is 14.7 psi (101.35 kPa). 1 psi of pressure is equal to 6.895 kPa. Another unit of pressure measurement is the bar. One bar is equal to 0.986923 atmosphere.

A kilopascal is 1000 pascal since the prefix *kilo* represents 1000. A pascal is equal to 1 newton of force applied over 1 square meter.

■ PRESSURE AND PRESSURE MEASUREMENT

Pressure can be defined as a force applied over a specific area. For example, 100 lb of metal resting on a 10-in.^{2} area exerts a pressure of 100 lb over the 10 in.^{2} of area. The pressure exerted on 1 in.^{2} is, therefore, 100 lb divided by 10 in.^{2} (100 ÷ 10), which is 10 psi of pressure.

Compression pressure in the engine's cylinder is measured in pounds per square inch. A typical example could be a compression pressure of 100 psi. In metric terms pressure is stated in kilopascal (kPa). For purposes of comparison, 1 psi is equal to 6.895 kPa. A typical compression pressure could be 700 kPa. A compression gauge set is shown in **Figure 1–2.**

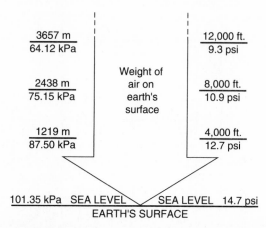

| 3657 m | 12,000 ft. |
| 64.12 kPa | 9.3 psi |

Weight of air on earth's surface

| 2438 m | 8,000 ft. |
| 75.15 kPa | 10.9 psi |

| 1219 m | 4,000 ft. |
| 87.50 kPa | 12.7 psi |

101.35 kPa   SEA LEVEL   SEA LEVEL   14.7 psi
EARTH'S SURFACE

■ FIGURE 1–1
Atmospheric pressure is greatest at sea level and diminishes with altitude.

■ FIGURE 1–2
Compression gauges and adapters. Both screw-in and push-in gauges are shown. (Courtesy of Ford Motor Company.)

To understand the metric term *kilopascal*, we know that the prefix *kilo* means 1000. Therefore, the term *kilopascal* means 1000 pascal. A pascal is a force of 1 newton over an area of 1 square meter (1 N/m^2).

Pressure testing gauges used in the automotive industry register zero at atmospheric pressure. All pressure measurements taken therefore actually measure pressures above atmospheric pressure, except for vacuum measurements.

■ INTAKE MANIFOLD VACUUM AND ATMOSPHERIC PRESSURE

The difference between atmospheric pressure and the absolute pressure in the engine's intake manifold and cylinders determines the amount of air each cylinder will be able to take in on the intake stroke. When this pressure difference is greater more air is taken in and more power is produced. A smaller pressure difference means less air is taken in and less power is produced. With the engine in good condition (rings and valves sealing tightly), its ability to produce low pressures in the cylinders is good. When the rings and valves do not seal properly they allow air to bypass them into the cylinders on the intake stroke thereby lowering the vacuum in the cylinders and intake manifold. Higher absolute pressure in the intake

manifold reduces the pressure difference and therefore the engine's ability to produce power.

Intake manifold vacuum is measured with a vacuum gauge in inches (or millimeters) of mercury (hg). This is based on the use of a U tube manometer to measure pressure difference. A U tube device partially filled with mercury with graduations in inches or millimeters is used. One end of the tube is open to atmosphere (and atmospheric pressure) while the other end is connected to the intake manifold. With the engine running the difference in the height of mercury in the two columns is the amount of vacuum present **(Figure 1–3)**. Modern automotive vacuum gauges are based on this system of measurement.

Normal intake manifold vacuum at engine idle is about 20 inches of hg **(Figure 1–4)**. At idle the throttle plates are nearly closed allowing very little air into the engine. Twenty inches of hg translates into about 10 psi of absolute pressure. At cruising speeds intake manifold vacuum drops due to increased throttle opening which allows more air into the engine. At higher altitudes and lower atmospheric pressure less dense air enters the engine and less power is produced. Vacuum is used in the automobile to operate a variety of devices such as the power brake booster, air flow control door actuators in the heating and air conditioning systems, EGR valve controls, cruise control, and the like. On some carbureted engines the EGR valve may be controlled

■   FIGURE 1–3
The difference in the height of the mercury in the two legs of the U tube indicates the engine's intake manifold vacuum.

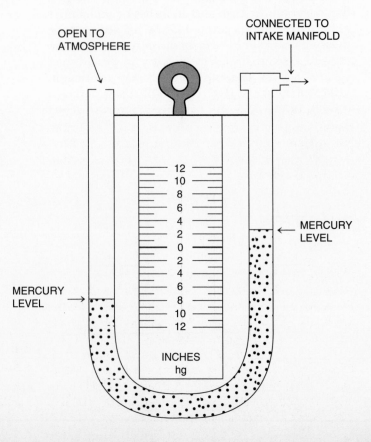

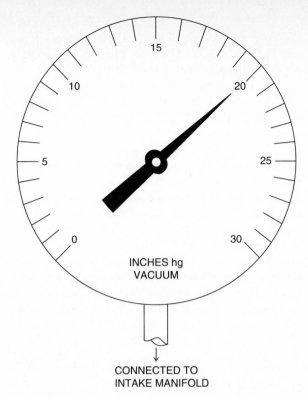

■ FIGURE 1–4
Vacuum gauge showing normal vacuum at engine idle.

by ported vacuum or venturi vacuum. Ported vacuum is taken from a point just above the closed throttle plate. As the throttle is opened ported vacuum increases. Venturi vacuum is taken from a point in the throat of the carburetor venturi. The venturi vacuum is a more accurate indicator of engine load and speed. Many carbureted cars have a vacuum reservoir to provide vacuum to vacuum actuators when engine intake manifold vacuum is low (as during heavy loads or high speeds). The reservoir is connected to intake manifold vacuum via a hose and one way check valve.

■ NORMAL AND ABNORMAL COMBUSTION

Normal combustion occurs in the engine's cylinders when the air/fuel mixture is ignited by the spark at the spark plug and the flame front progresses evenly across the combustion chamber without any sign of detonation. Abnormal combustion occurs when the air–fuel mixture ignites by some other means than by the spark across the spark plug electrodes, or the spark occurring too early. *Preignition, detonation, dieseling,* and *spark knock* are terms used to describe different kinds of abnormal combustion.

Preignition

As the term implies, preignition is the condition when the air–fuel mixture is ignited before the spark plug fires. It can occur as the result of overheated spark plug electrodes (using spark plugs with too low a heat range), by a tiny glowing bit of carbon, or a glowing sharp edge of metal in the combustion chamber **(Figure 1–5).** The result is a light pinging or knocking sound. Severe preignition causes excessive pinging and knocking and can result in detonation. If not corrected, this condition can cause severe engine damage.

Detonation

Detonation occurs after normal spark plug ignition. It is the self-ignition of end gases in the combustion chamber caused by very high pressures and temperatures. As the flame front advances, the unburned end gases are highly pressurized and overheated to the point of self-ignition. As combustion continues on two fronts, they collide with explosive force, creating a severe knock and vibration **(Figure 1–6).** This can cause severe engine damage, such as cracked or broken pistons, broken piston rings, cracked spark plug insulators, and cracked cylinder heads.

Spark Knock

Spark knock occurs when the spark plug fires too soon in relation to piston position: in other words, when ignition timing is too far advanced. Spark timing that is too far advanced results in com-

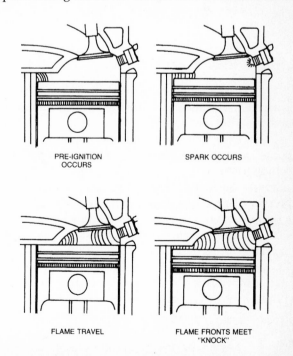

■ FIGURE 1–5
How preignition occurs. (Courtesy of Chrysler Corporation.)

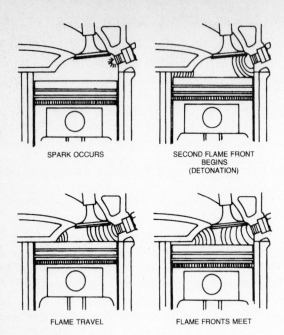

SPARK OCCURS

SECOND FLAME FRONT BEGINS (DETONATION)

FLAME TRAVEL

FLAME FRONTS MEET

■ FIGURE 1–6

How detonation occurs. (Courtesy of Chrysler Corporation.)

bustion taking place before the piston has reached TDC. The rising combustion pressures oppose the rising piston. Maximum combustion chamber pressures are reached before the piston reaches TDC instead of just after TDC. As a result, spark knock or pinging occurs under load or acceleration.

Factors that Contribute to Detonation and Knock

1. *Octane number of fuel.* Using gasoline with a lower than recommended octane number may result in detonation and knock.

2. *High compression ratio.* Compression ratios range from about 8:1 to 10:1 in today's cars. Higher compression ratios result in higher combustion chamber pressures and temperatures. High compression ratio engines require the use of high octane gasoline to avoid detonation and knock.

3. *Turbocharging.* Turbocharging or supercharging forces more air into the engine cylinders. This results in higher combustion chamber pressures and temperatures. Higher octane gasoline is required in turbocharged engines to avoid detonation and knock. A knock sensor helps adjust timing to control knock.

4. *Engine operating temperature.* Above normal engine operating temperatures or localized hot spots in an engine raise combustion chamber temperatures and promote detonation and knock.

5. *Carbon deposits.* Excessive carbon deposits in combustion chambers increase the compression ratio and the pressure and temperature in the cylinder, thereby promoting detonation and knock.

6. *High intake air temperature.* Higher intake air temperatures result in higher combustion chamber temperatures, thereby promoting detonation and knock.

7. *Combustion chamber design.* A hemispherical combustion chamber with a centrally located spark plug reduces the distance travelled by the flame front. This results in more even combustion and a lower tendency for detonation and knock.

8. *Ignition timing advanced too far.* When ignition occurs too early in relation to piston position, combustion chamber pressures and temperatures are increased, thereby promoting detonation and knock.

9. *Fuel mixture too lean.* Excessively lean air/fuel mixtures burn slower thereby creating more heat in the combustion chamber. This can cause detonation and knock.

■ DIESELING

Dieseling is a condition in which the engine continues to run after the ignition key is turned off. It occurs in carbureted gasoline engines and is sometimes referred to as after running. This can occur only when two conditions are present: fuel continues to enter the combustion chambers, and combustion chamber temperatures are hot enough for self-ignition to occur. Dieseling cannot occur if no fuel is allowed to enter the combustion chambers after the engine is shut off.

■ GASOLINE OCTANE NUMBER

The octane number of a gasoline **(Figure 1–7)** is a measure of its antiknock quality or ability to resist detonation during combustion. Detonation can be defined as an uncontrolled explosion of the last portion of the burning air–fuel mixture due to excessive temperature and pressure conditions in the combustion chamber. Since detonation creates shock pressure waves, and hence audible knock, rather than smooth combustion and expansion of the air–fuel mixture, it results in loss of power, excessive localized temperatures, and engine damage if sufficiently severe.

Increasing the pressure of the fuel mixture in the combustion chamber before ignition helps to increase the power of an engine. This is done by compressing the fuel mixture to a smaller volume. Higher compression ratios not only boost power but also

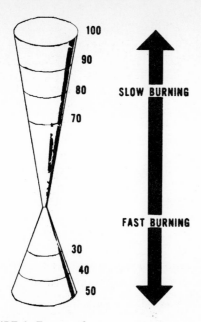

■ FIGURE 1–7
The octane rating of gasoline and the cetane rating of diesel fuel. Higher octane gasoline burns slower. Higher cetane diesel fuel burns faster than lower cetane fuel. (Courtesy of Ford Motor Company.)

give more efficient power. But as the compression ratio goes up, knocking tendency increases and the antiknock value of the fuel becomes critical. Higher octane gasoline is then required.

Determining the Octane Number of Gasoline

There are two commonly used methods of determining the octane number of motor gasoline: the motor method (ASTM D-2699) and the research method (ASTM D-2700). Both use the same type of laboratory single-cylinder engine, which is equipped with a variable head and a knock meter to indicate knock intensity. Using the test sample as fuel, the engine compression ratio and the air–fuel mixture are adjusted to develop a specified knock intensity. Two primary standard reference fuels, normal heptane and iso-octane, arbitrarily assigned 0 and 100 octane numbers, respectively, are then blended to produce the same knock intensity as the test sample. The percentage of iso-octane in the blend is considered the octane number of the test sample. Thus if the matching reference blend is made up of 15% n-heptane and 85% iso-octane, the test sample is rated 85 motor or research octane number, according to the test method used.

Road octane number is the rating of the gasoline, in terms of reference fuels, by a test car under full throttle acceleration from 10 to 50 mph (16 to 81 km). However, road octane tests are both inconvenient and expensive; they are usually avoided. An approximation may be made by calculation of the average of research and motor octane numbers: $(R + M)/2$. A number of factors besides the compression ratio affect the octane requirement. Some of these are listed with their degrees of effect in **Figure 1–8.**

Some high-octane gasolines are from 1 to 2% lower in density than regular grades and therefore provide less energy than regular grades. The value of higher octane gasoline is obtained only when an engine is designed and adjusted to take advantage of it. Most engines are satisfied by regular-grade gasoline and do not require high-octane premium grade; but those that are not satisfied (those that knock) will provide better fuel economy and performance (drivability) when converted to a higher octane gasoline.

Note: The American Society for Testing and Materials (ASTM), Committee D on petroleum products, is an organization of producers, users, and general-interest people who develop product standards and test methods that are widely used around the world.

Reformulated Gasoline

Reformulated gasolines help reduce air pollution through reduced exhaust emissions. In general, these gasolines contain less benzene, less aromatics and olefins, less sulfur, and have a lower Reid vapor pressure (RVP). A small percentage of oxygenate such as methyl tertiary butyl ether (MTBE) is added to the fuel. Reducing the benzene content has beneficial results since benzene is a toxic chemical. Reducing the aromatic and olefin content reduces smog formation. Reducing the sulfur content enhances catalytic converter operation, thereby reducing HC, CO, and NO_x emissions. Lowering the Reid vapor pressure lowers evaporative emissions. Adding an oxygenate compensates for the reduction in aromatics, boosts the octane rating, and also reduces HC and CO emissions.

■ ETHANOL AND METHANOL

There are two types of alcohol that have potential as an automotive fuel. Ethyl alcohol or ethanol is derived from such farm products as grains, potatoes, and soybeans. Methyl alcohol or methanol can be produced from wood products, garbage, and manure.

Alcohols have considerably lower heat values than gasoline but have a higher octane rating. Their heat of vaporization is more than double that of

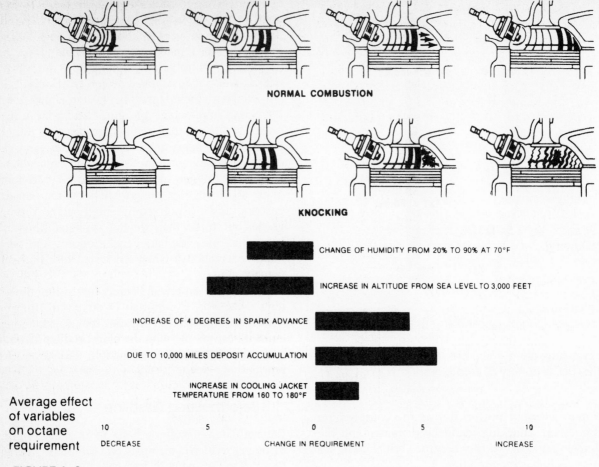

NORMAL COMBUSTION

KNOCKING

CHANGE OF HUMIDITY FROM 20% TO 90% AT 70°F

INCREASE IN ALTITUDE FROM SEA LEVEL TO 3,000 FEET

INCREASE OF 4 DEGREES IN SPARK ADVANCE

DUE TO 10,000 MILES DEPOSIT ACCUMULATION

INCREASE IN COOLING JACKET TEMPERATURE FROM 160 TO 180°F

Average effect of variables on octane requirement

10	5	0	5	10
DECREASE		CHANGE IN REQUIREMENT		INCREASE

■   FIGURE 1–8

Flame propagation in normal combustion is even and progressive, as shown at the top. Knocking or detonation occurs when end gases in the combustion chamber ignite spontaneously due to extremely high pressure and temperature. (Courtesy of General Motors Corporation.)

gasoline. The lower heat values mean that larger fuel tanks are required and fuel economy is lower. The higher octane rating reduces the tendency to knock. The higher heat of vaporization translates into harder starting. The exception is the use of gasohol, which is a mixture of gasoline and ethanol (up to 10% ethanol and 90% gasoline). The use of straight methanol as a fuel requires modifications to the fuel system to make it compatible. Cars with "flexible fuel" systems are being produced allowing the use of gasoline and methanol blends with up to 15% methanol.

Gasohol is a mixture of unleaded gasoline and grain alcohol (ethanol). Approximately 90% unleaded gasoline and 10% ethanol form the mixture. It may be used in many vehicles where unleaded gasoline is normally recommended. If drivability or performance problems are experienced as a result of using gasohol, its use should be discontinued and only 100% unleaded fuel should be used.

Hydrogen as a Fuel

Hydrogen is an excellent automotive fuel. Combustion is near perfect while leaving only carbon dioxide and water residues. Hydrogen is present in abundance in our world. Water is H_2O, which means that two-thirds of the makeup of water is hydrogen. Hydrogen gas can be produced by passing electric current through salt water (electrolysis). The process is still too expensive to be practical and the cost of storage is too high.

■ PROPANE (LIQUEFIED PETROLEUM GAS)

Propane is a by-product of natural gas production and the crude oil refining process in the production of gasoline and diesel fuels. LPG is primarily propane with up to 8% butane. It is a vapor above

−40°F (−40°C), but it is stored under pressure, which changes it into a liquid. As a liquid it is much easier to handle, store, and transport. It is stored in strong tanks able to withstand 200 psi (1380 kPa) and is converted to vapor before it enters the engine's cylinders. The effects of temperature on pressure of propane, butane, and propane–butane mixtures are illustrated in **Figure 1–9.** The heat energy of propane and butane is less than that of gasoline on the basis of volume. The octane rating of LP gas, however, is higher than that of gasoline but it burns more slowly. For this reason, engine compression ratios can be slightly higher in propane-fueled engines, and ignition timing may be advanced.

Some of the advantages of using LP gas include the following:

- Less engine wear
- Less oil consumption
- Fewer emissions
- Longer engine life
- Lower maintenance costs
- Lower fuel costs

These advantages are offset to some degree by some disadvantages of using LP gas, such as:

- Fewer refueling stations
- Harder to start in cold weather
- Higher cost of fuel system components
- Higher cost of fuel storage and handling equipment

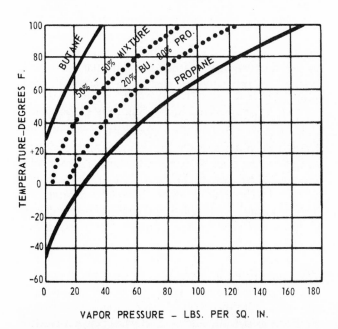

■ FIGURE 1–9

Effect of temperature on butane, propane, and butane–propane mixtures.

The advisability of using LP gas depends on the relative cost and availability of LP gas as compared to other fuels in any particular locality. The use and handling of LP gas is quite safe if all proper procedures are followed and only recommended equipment is used. Anyone using or servicing LP gas or LP gas vehicles should do so only if fully qualified regarding its use and the servicing of LP gas equipment. All local, state, or provincial and federal regulations regarding the use of LP gas and the servicing of LP gas vehicles must be followed. See NFPA 58 or CAN/CGA-B149.2-M91 for U.S. and Canadian propane codes.

■ COMPRESSED NATURAL GAS

The compressed natural gas (CNG) system is similar in many ways to the LPG system described above. A major difference is that fuel is stored under much higher pressure, 3000 psi (over 20,000 kPa), which requires much stronger fuel tanks. Aluminum alloy tanks of special construction allow sufficient fuel to be carried for automotive applications without the prohibitive weight problem of equivalent-capacity steel tanks. Aluminum's interior surfaces also prevent rust and corrosion from moisture sometimes found in natural gas.

■ DIESEL FUELS

Cetane Number

The cetane number is a measure of the autoignition quality of a diesel fuel. The shorter the interval between the time the fuel is injected and the time it begins to burn (called the ignition delay period), the higher the cetane number. It is a measure of the ease with which the fuel can be ignited and is most significant in low-temperature starting, warm-up, and smooth, even combustion **(Figure 1–10).**

Why Diesels Knock

All diesel engines normally have a slight knocking sound (similar to detonation in a gasoline engine) since diesel fuel ignites by detonation. In diesel engines, abnormal knock is due to the fuel igniting too slowly. It should start to burn almost as soon as it is injected. If there is much delay, a fuel buildup results, which burns with explosive force and causes knocking **(Figure 1–10).**

Why Diesels Smoke

White smoke is caused by tiny droplets of unburned fuel. It is usually caused by low engine temperatures and disappears when the engine warms

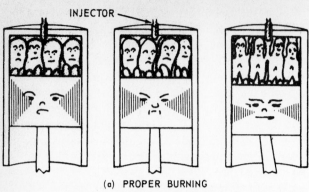

(a) PROPER BURNING

(Fuel Charge Ignites Early and Burns Evenly
To Overcome Knocking)

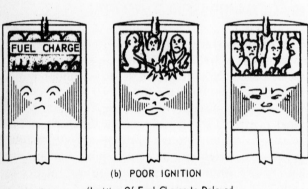

(b) POOR IGNITION

(Ignition Of Fuel Charge Is Delayed,
Followed By A Small Explosion)

■ FIGURE 1-10
Normal combustion in a diesel engine (top). Knock
occurs when ignition is delayed (bottom).

up. Black smoke is caused by a mechanical defect
such as a faulty injector, restricted air filter, or by
overloading and/or overfueling the engine. Blue-
gray smoke is the result of burning lube oil. It indicates a mechanical defect such as stuck or broken
piston rings. Diesel engines producing smoke also
tend to produce objectionable odors.

■ ENGINE EFFICIENCY

The degree of engine efficiency is expressed in percentage figures resulting from a comparison of the
theoretical power of an engine without any power
losses, to the actual power available from the engine.
Mechanical efficiency and thermal efficiency are two
ways used to express engine efficiency.

Volumetric Efficiency

The amount of air an engine is able to take into the
cylinder on the intake stroke, compared to filling the
cylinder completely with air at atmospheric pressure, is known as the volumetric efficiency of an en-

gine. Another way to describe it would be to say that
volumetric efficiency is the engine's ability to get rid
of exhaust gases and take in the air-fuel mixture, as
compared to the displacement of the engine.

The engine is not able to take in a 100% fill on
each intake stroke because of design limitations.
Such factors as valve and port diameters, manifold
runner configuration, valve timing, engine speed,
and atmospheric pressure all affect volumetric
efficiency.

An engine running at 3000 rpm will have only
half the time to fill the cylinder on each intake stroke
as it would have at 1500 rpm. Since this is the case,
volumetric efficiency drops as engine speed increases. As a result, engine torque also decreases (when
engine speed exceeds a certain range).

An engine operating in an area that is 5000 ft
above sea level will have less volumetric efficiency
than the same engine at sea level because atmospheric pressure is lower at 5000 ft above sea level
than at sea level. Since it is atmospheric pressure
that forces the air-fuel mixture into the cylinder, it is
easy to see that there will be a corresponding decrease in volumetric efficiency as the altitude (at
which an engine operates) increases.

Volumetric efficiency is increased by the use of
tuned intake and exhaust systems, multivalve engine design, two-stage air intake systems, turbochargers, and superchargers. These are described
later in this book.

Thermal Efficiency

The thermal efficiency of an engine is the degree to
which the engine is successful in converting the energy of the fuel into usable heat energy or power. It
is the heat energy in the cylinder that forces the
pistons to move, which results in crankshaft rotation.

The engine is not able to burn 100% of the fuel
delivered to the cylinders. Some of it remains unburned in colder areas of the cylinder and as a result
of not having enough oxygen to burn. Theoretically,
an air-fuel mixture of 14.7 parts air to 1 part fuel by
weight is capable of 100% complete combustion.
This is known as a stoichiometric mixture, a chemically correct mixture for complete combustion in a
gasoline engine.

Some of the heat energy produced by the fuel
that has burned in the cylinder is removed from the
engine by the exhaust system. Some heat energy is
removed from the engine by the cooling system. The
lubrication system and the effects of heat radiation
carry additional heat from the engine.

Approximately 35% of heat energy is lost
through the cooling system and another 35%

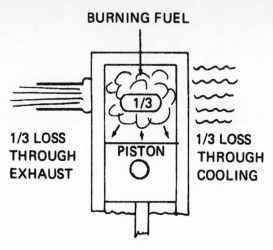

BURNING FUEL

1/3 LOSS THROUGH EXHAUST

1/3

PISTON

1/3 LOSS THROUGH COOLING

■ FIGURE 1–11
Of the available heat energy in gasoline, only about one-third is usable energy in the internal combustion engine.

through the exhaust system **(Figure 1–11).** This leaves only 30% of heat energy as usable power, from which another 5% is lost through engine friction.

Gasoline engine thermal efficiency ranges from about 20 to 30%. The thermal efficiency of a diesel engine can approach 40%. The diesel engine is able to operate on a leaner air/fuel mixture than a gasoline engine and has a higher thermal efficiency because it has a much higher compression ratio. Since most diesel engines do not have a throttle plate to restrict air intake, there is always an excess of air intake.

Fuel Efficiency

Fuel efficiency is actually the rate of fuel consumption over a distance traveled. It is expressed in miles traveled per gallon of fuel consumed or in liters of fuel consumed per 100 km traveled. Fuel efficiency is dependent on all the foregoing factors as well as vehicle weight, size, and load.

Federal legislation requires that car manufacturers achieve a specific corporate average fuel economy (CAFE) for all the models they produce. If too many large cars are produced, CAFE standards may not be met. The legislation is designed to reduce energy consumption. Fuel economy is measured in miles per gallon (mpg) in the U.S. system and in liters per 100 kilometers (L/100 km) in the metric system.

Mechanical Efficiency

Indicated power is the theoretical power an engine is able to produce, as discussed earlier. It is expressed as horsepower or as kilowatts. Brake power is the actual power delivered by an engine expressed in horsepower or kilowatts.

The formula for calculating the mechanical efficiency of an engine compares the brake power to the indicated power and is calculated by dividing IP into BP.

Other Efficiency Factors

Additional energy losses occur due to such factors as drive train friction, rolling resistance, air resistance, and vehicle speed. As much as 5% of the heat energy of the fuel may be lost through drive train friction.

Rolling resistance varies depending on tire type used, tire inflation pressures, and condition of road surfaces. Radial tires have less rolling resistance than bias ply tires. Underinflated tires increase rolling resistance, as do soft road surfaces.

Air resistance is directly related to vehicle speed, vehicle body design, and direction and speed of wind. Aerodynamically designed car bodies have less wind resistance than do square boxlike designs. Larger frontal body areas increase wind resistance. Increased wind velocity and driving into the wind cause greater air resistance. All of these factors have a bearing on how much heat energy (and therefore fuel) will be required to operate the vehicle. Driving habits such as frequent and rapid acceleration and braking increase the fuel consumption of any vehicle.

■ ENGINE POWER

To produce power an automotive engine must expend energy in the form of work. Work is said to be done when an applied force overcomes a resistance and moves through a distance. Work produces measurable results. When sufficient energy is expended through an application of force to overcome the resistance to motion, movement of the engine's pistons and crankshaft is the result.

Power is the rate at which work is being done. Engine power in the English system is stated in horsepower and in the metric system in kilowatts. Both systems are explained here. The formula for calculating power is

$$P = F \times D \div T$$

where F = force
D = distance
T = time

Engine Brake Horsepower

A man named Watt, observing the ability of a horse to do work in a mine, decided arbitrarily that this ability to do work was the equivalent of raising 33,000 lb of coal a distance of 1 ft in 1 minute. This became the standard measurement of a unit of power called horsepower (hp). This can be expressed as a formula:

$$1 \text{ hp} = 33,000 \text{ lb} \times 1 \text{ ft} \times 1 \text{ min}$$

This formula allows the horsepower of an engine to be calculated if certain factors are known. These factors are: the force produced by an engine and the distance through which that force moves in 1 minute.

A device known as the prony brake can be used to obtain these factors. Since the prony brake is a braking device, the output of an engine is stated in terms of brake power. To determine the brake horsepower of an engine, we need to calculate the engine's force times the distance through which that force travels in 1 minute, and divide Watt's formula for 1 horsepower into the result of that calculation.

A prony brake uses a drum attached to the engine flywheel. A contracting brake band surrounds the drum. The band can be tightened to increase the load on the engine. An arm is attached at one end to the band. The other end of the arm is connected to a scale through a knife-edge device. This assures accuracy of arm length from the center of crankshaft rotation to the scale **(Figure 1–12).**

With the engine running, the band is slowly tightened. This causes the arm to exert pressure on the scale. The brake horsepower output of an engine can be calculated using Watt's formula for 1 horsepower and the prony brake test results. Simply divide Watt's formula into the prony brake test results.

Let's calculate the brake horsepower of a theoretical engine, assuming the following conditions.

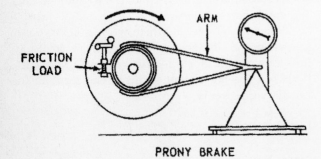

■   FIGURE 1–12
Prony brake.

- *Engine speed:* 2000 revolutions per minute (rpm)
- *Arm length:* 3 ft (radius of circle arm would make if allowed to turn)
- *Reading on scale:* 100 lb

Don't forget the formula: $F \times D \times T$ divided by 33,000 lb $\times$ 1 ft $\times$ 1 min = brake horsepower (bhp). And don't forget that to determine the circumference of a circle, we calculate $2\pi \times$ radius or $2\pi\, r$, and we know that π is $\frac{22}{7}$, or 3.1419265. Therefore,

$$F = 100 \text{ lb}$$
$$D = 3 \text{ ft} \times 2\pi \times 2000$$
$$T = 1 \text{ min}$$

Using this information produces this formula:

$$\frac{2\pi \times 3 \times 2000 \times 100 \times 1}{33,000 \times 1 \times 1} = \frac{3 \times 2000 \times 100 \times 1}{5252}$$

$$= \frac{600,000}{5252}$$

$$= 114.24 \text{ bhp}$$

Dividing 2π into 33,000 gives us the denominator of 5252. Multiplying the remaining numerator figures results in 600,000. One horsepower is equal to 0.746 kilowatt (kW). Therefore, 114.24 bhp = 85.22 kW.

Indicated Power

Indicated power (IP) is the theoretical power an engine is able to produce. It is calculated by using the following factors:

- P = mean effective pressure in the cylinder in pounds per square inch
- L = length of piston stroke in feet
- A = area of cylinder cross section in square inches
- N = number of power strokes per minute for one cylinder
- K = number of cylinders in the engine

The formula for calculating indicated horsepower IHP is, therefore,

$$\frac{\text{PLANK}}{33,000} = \text{IP}$$

Using this formula, it is possible to calculate the IP (IHP) of an engine if the number of cylinders in the engine, the engine's bore and stroke, the engine's speed, and the mean effective pressure in the cylinder are known.

Friction Power Losses

Some force (push or pull) is required to slide one object over the surface of another. This resistance to motion between two objects in contact with each other is called friction. Friction increases with pressure or load. It requires more effort to slide a heavy object across a surface than it does to slide a lighter object over the same surface.

The condition of the two surfaces in contact also affects the degree of friction. Smooth surfaces produce less friction than rough surfaces. Dry surfaces cause more friction than surfaces that are lubricated or wet.

Residual oil clinging to the cylinder walls, rings, and pistons of an engine that has been stopped for some time will produce a greasy friction when the engine is started. As soon as the engine starts, the lubrication system supplies increased lubrication, which results in viscous friction.

Friction power is the power required to overcome the friction of the various moving parts of the engine as it runs. Friction power increases as engine size and speed are increased. The friction power of an engine can be calculated (if the indicated power and brake power are known) by subtracting the BP from the IP (IP − BP = FP) or (IHP − BHP = FHP).

Inertia

Some power is required to overcome inertia. Inertia is the tendency of an object in motion to stay in motion or the tendency of an object at rest to stay at rest. The first can be called kinetic inertia and the latter static inertia. The moving parts of an engine are affected by kinetic inertia. A piston moving in one direction tries to keep moving in that direction because of kinetic inertia. The crankshaft and connecting rod must overcome this kinetic inertia by stopping the piston at its travel limit and reversing its direction. The static inertia of a car that is stopped must be overcome by engine power to cause the car to move.

SAE Power

SAE power is the power of an engine as determined by the Society of Automotive Engineers. Tests are performed under rigorously controlled conditions including the inlet air temperature, ambient temperature, humidity, and the like. A number of specific conditions, such as inlet air restriction and exhaust restriction are also stated, since these are determining factors. Other factors and conditions must also be met.

Aside from all these factors and conditions, SAE power is measured at the transmission output shaft, with all normal engine accessories mounted and operating. This includes the air cleaner and exhaust system. Since a particular engine model may be used by a vehicle manufacturer for several different applications and may be equipped differently on different models, the SAE power for a particular engine varies depending on how it is equipped.

Engine Power—Kilowatts (kW)

In the metric system engine power is stated in kilowatts.

The power output of an engine is calculated, as stated earlier, by using the formula

$$P = W \div T$$

Where P = power
W = work
T = time

Force in the metric system is measured in newtons (N). Distance is measured in meters (m). Therefore, work can be expressed in terms of newton meters (N · m).

Time is stated in minutes. To determine the power of an engine, we calculate force times distance divided by time $(F \times D \div T)$.

The watt is the unit of electrical power and is the equivalent of 1 joule per second. One kilowatt is 1000 watts.

To summarize:

$$1 \text{ N} \cdot \text{m} = 1 \text{ joule}$$
$$1 \text{ joule per second} = 1 \text{ watt (W)}$$
$$1000 \text{ watts} = 1 \text{ kilowatt (kW)}$$

Assuming an engine speed of 2000 rpm, we would obtain the engine speed per second by dividing 2000 by 60, since kilowatts is joules per second.

$$2000 \div 60 = 33.33$$

Assuming further that the applied force at the end of the torque arm is 1000 N and the length of the torque arm is 1 m, we calculate as follows:

$$2\pi \times 1 \times 33.33 = 209.4 \text{ kW}$$

or

$$\frac{2000}{60} \times 2\pi \times 1 = 209.4 \text{ kW}$$

or

$$2\pi \times 1 \times \frac{2000}{60} = 209.4 \text{ kW}$$

One kilowatt is 1.341 horsepower. Therefore, 209.4 kW is equal to 280.8 hp.

Engine Torque and Brake Power

As an engine runs, the crankshaft is forced to turn by the series of pushes or power impulses imposed on the crank pins by the pistons and rods. This twisting force is called *torque*.

Engine torque and engine horsepower are closely related. For instance, as we learned earlier, if we know the torque and speed of an engine, we can calculate its power.

Torque is equal to $F \times R$, where F is the force applied to the end of a lever and R is the length of the lever from the center of the turning shaft to the point on the lever at which force is being applied. R represents the radius of a circle through which the applied force would move if moved through a complete revolution. Therefore, $T = F \times R$.

Engine torque can also be calculated as follows: $T = \text{hp} \times 5252 \div \text{rpm}$. With 115 hp at 3000 rpm an engine would develop 201 ft-lb of torque; $115 \times 5252 \div 3000 = 201$. Engine torque is expressed in terms of pound-feet in the English system and in newton meters in the metric system.

Maximum torque is produced in an engine when there is maximum pressure in the cylinders. Peak torque is, therefore, reached when there is maximum air and fuel delivery to the engine. This normally occurs at a somewhat lower engine speed than that at which maximum brake power is produced.

Engine torque drops off as engine speed increases to the point where cylinders take in less air. At this point, engine brake power is still increasing due to the increased number of power impulses per minute. Engine brake power drops off when the effect of an increased number of power impulses is offset by the reduced air intake of the cylinders. As can be seen from this, engine torque and engine brake power are closely related to the volumetric efficiency of the engine.

■ DYNAMOMETERS

The dynamometer is a reliable tool of the trade used to measure all aspects of vehicle performance. This can be done by simulating road load and driving conditions without taking the vehicle being tested out of the service shop. Steep grades, level roads, stop-and-go city driving, acceleration and deceleration, and a wide range of load conditions all can be simulated in the shop. With the proper diagnostic equipment connected to the vehicle during these tests, engine condition and performance can be accurately determined in a very few minutes. This kind of diagnosis and testing cannot be done on the road nor can it be done in the shop without a dynamometer. In addition to the test results obtained from the auxiliary test equipment, the dynamometer indicates vehicle or engine speed and power.

Most dynamometers, whether of the engine type or the chassis type, convert the torque and speed factors automatically to a brake power or road power reading on a dial **(Figure 1–13)**.

The engine converts the heat energy of combustion to mechanical energy to drive a drive shaft or drive wheels. The drive shaft or drive wheels transfer this mechanical energy to the dynamometer by means of a shaft in the case of an engine dynamometer, and by means of rollers mounted in the shop floor in the case of a chassis dynamometer. This mechanical energy is transmitted to the dynamometer's power absorption unit, which converts the mechanical energy back to heat energy.

The power absorption unit, the torque bridge, and the connecting arm serve the same function as the prony brake. The torque bridge, however, converts the applied force to an electrical signal, which varies with the amount of force applied. This electrical signal provides a reading on the brake horsepower dial. The dynamometer also measures speed, which is indicated on a second dial.

Chassis and engine dynamometers used in service shops are generally of the hydraulic type. The power absorption unit consists basically of two units: a drive unit and a driven unit. The drive unit is a drum with vanes attached to it internally. The driven unit is also a drum with vanes attached to its interior. The drive unit has an arm attached to it. The other end of the arm is connected to the torque bridge. The drive unit and driven unit are enclosed

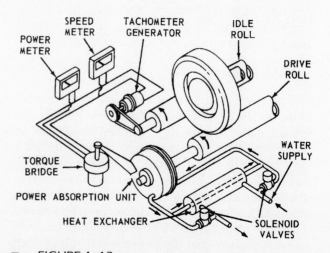

■ FIGURE 1–13
Major components of an in-floor dynamometer.

in a sealed housing, which can be filled and emptied of fluid.

The fluid used in some dynamometers is water; others may use oil. In either case, the amount of load applied is in direct proportion to the amount of fluid permitted to enter the power absorption unit. This is controlled by electrically operated solenoid valves. The solenoids are operated by a hand-held control device.

As fluid is allowed to enter the power absorption unit, the rotating drive member throws the fluid against the driven member, which is held by the connecting arm. As more fluid is allowed to enter the unit (more load applied), the force against the driven member is increased, causing the arm to move slightly. This arm movement is converted to an electrical signal by the torque bridge, which then is indicated on the dial in brake horsepower. In this manner any combination of vehicle or engine speed and load can be observed.

As a load is applied to the dynamometer, the fluid in the power absorption unit heats up. To prevent overheating, this heat must be dissipated. In the open water-type dynamometers, the absorption unit is connected to a cool-water pressure source that is constant (city main water) in order to keep the unit cool and dissipate the heat. The heated water is directed to the floor drain. In the closed hydraulic-type of absorption unit, the oil is circulated through a heat exchanger, which is water cooled. This type requires less water.

Many dynamometers are equipped with an inertia flywheel, usually belt-driven from the rollers in the floor. The inertia flywheel can be used to simulate vehicle inertia during acceleration, deceleration, and coasting modes. It is useful in diagnosing engine and drive train problems. The flywheel can be engaged or disengaged by a manually operated lever.

When doing any type of dynamometer testing, make sure that the engine or vehicle is in a safe condition to be tested. Serious damage to the engine or vehicle can result from improper testing methods. Be sure to follow all procedures recommended by the vehicle manufacturer and by the manufacturer of the equipment (dynamometer) being used. It must be remembered that all test results observed during dynamometer testing are valid only for the conditions that existed at the time of the test, including engine and vehicle condition.

Review Questions

1. Atmospheric pressure is approximately _____ at sea level.

2. Atmospheric pressure and the _____ and _____ of the air are factors that affect engine performance.

3. Intake manifold vacuum is measured in _____ or _____ of mercury.

4. Twenty _____ of vacuum is equal to about _____ psi of absolute pressure.

5. A vacuum _____ is used on some cars to store extra _____.

6. Preignition is a condition when the air/fuel charge is ignited _____ it is ignited by the _____.

7. Detonation occurs _____ spark plug ignition.

8. The octane number of a gasoline is a measure of its _____.

9. The amount of air entering the cylinder on the intake stroke compared to filling the cylinder completely is called _____ _____.

10. Indicated power is the _____ _____ an engine should be able to produce.

11. The dynamometer is a tool used to measure _____.

12. Engine _____ and engine _____ are closely related but are not the same.

Test Questions

1. Atmospheric pressure at sea level is about
   a. 14.2 psi
   b. 14.7 psi
   c. 17.4 psi
   d. 12.7 psi
2. Compression pressure in an engine's cylinder is measured in
   a. square inches
   b. square centimeters
   c. inch pounds
   d. pounds per square inch
3. The intake manifold vacuum of an engine is measured in
   a. inches of pressure
   b. inches of mercury
   c. inches of water
   d. inches of rhodium
4. The highest level of intake manifold vacuum occurs when
   a. the engine is running at high speed
   b. the engine is not running
   c. the throttle plates are nearly closed
   d. the throttle plates are wide open
5. Preignition occurs in an engine when
   a. the air/fuel mixture is ignited by the spark plug
   b. the air/fuel mixture is ignited before the spark occurs at the spark plug

c. the air/fuel mixture is not fully compressed

d. the air/fuel mixture enters the cylinder too soon

6. Spark knock relates to
   a. the air/fuel ratio
   b. spark intensity
   c. a broken spark plug
   d. spark timing

7. The octane number of a gasoline is a measure of its ability to
   a. mix with air
   b. delay combustion
   c. resist plug fouling
   d. resist detonation

8. Reformulated gasolines help reduce
   a. exhaust emissions
   b. detonation
   c. preignition
   d. fuel consumption

9. The amount of air an engine is able to take into a cylinder during the intake stroke compared to filling the cylinder completely with air is known as
   a. fuel efficiency
   b. thermal efficiency

c. volumetric efficiency

d. mechanical efficiency

10. How much of the gasoline's total heat energy is transferred into useful work by the engine?
    a. 25%
    b. 75%
    c. 50%
    d. 100%

11. The potential or ability to work is defined as
    a. work
    b. power
    c. horsepower
    d. energy

12. Technician A says a dynamometer is a device used to measure vehicle performance. Technician B says a dynamometer is a device used to simulate road and driving conditions. Who is correct?
    a. Technician A
    b. Technician B
    c. both are correct
    d. both are incorrect

2 Drivability, Performance Diagnosis, and Tune Up

INTRODUCTION

It is important to be accurate when diagnosing engine problems since inaccurate diagnosis results in wasted time, effort, money, replacement of parts that are not faulty, failure to correct the problem, poor shop productivity, dissatisfied customers, and comebacks. Engine diagnosis requires a keen sense of sight, sound, smell, and touch. The technician should look for leaks, cracks, part damage, contamination, and the like. He should listen for abnormal noises such as squeaks, rattles, knocks, and hissing and notice any abnormal smell. The smell of leaking fluid can help determine if it is coolant, oil, or some other fluid. Rubbing a fluid between thumb and forefinger can also help identify the fluid. A rough-running engine can be recognized by sight (shaking or vibration), sound (irregular exhaust noise), or feel (vibration or shaking). Engine diagnosis requires the ability to select and use the proper testing and diagnostic tools and interpret the test results correctly. The technician must know the function of each system and each component and how they operate before accurate diagnosis is possible. The ability to select and use the appropriate service manual is also required.

The drivability of a vehicle depends on the performance of the engine and its related systems. Performance problems affect its drivability and fuel economy. The performance and drivability of an engine that is in good mechanical condition can be restored by proper diagnosis and tune-up procedures. The technician must follow proven techniques and procedures to be a successful diagnostician. **Figure 2–1** illustrates the usual sequence. This chapter describes the equipment and procedures required.

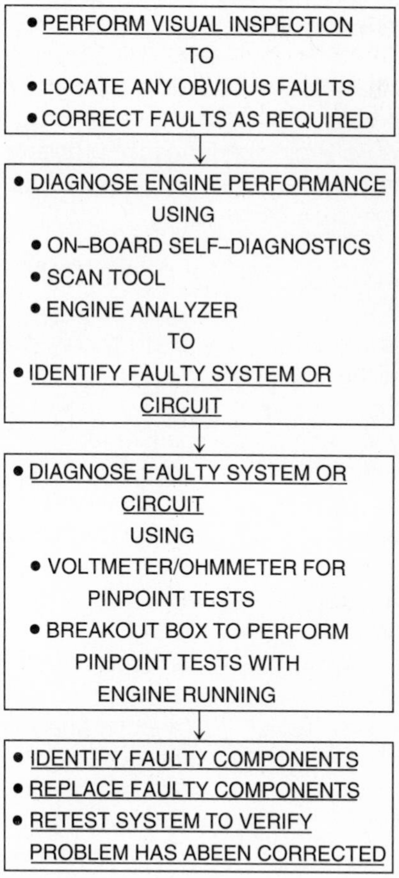

- PERFORM VISUAL INSPECTION
  TO
- LOCATE ANY OBVIOUS FAULTS
- CORRECT FAULTS AS REQUIRED

↓

- DIAGNOSE ENGINE PERFORMANCE
  USING
  - ON–BOARD SELF–DIAGNOSTICS
  - SCAN TOOL
  - ENGINE ANALYZER
  TO
- IDENTIFY FAULTY SYSTEM OR
  CIRCUIT

↓

- DIAGNOSE FAULTY SYSTEM OR
  CIRCUIT
  USING
  - VOLTMETER/OHMMETER FOR
    PINPOINT TESTS
  - BREAKOUT BOX TO PERFORM
    PINPOINT TESTS WITH
    ENGINE RUNNING

↓

- IDENTIFY FAULTY COMPONENTS
- REPLACE FAULTY COMPONENTS
- RETEST SYSTEM TO VERIFY
  PROBLEM HAS ABEEN CORRECTED

■   FIGURE 2–1
Typical diagnostic sequence. (Courtesy of F T Enterprises.)

LEARNING OBJECTIVES

After completing this chapter, you should be able to:

- Explain why accurate engine diagnosis is important.
- List common signs of engine problems.
- Identify and pinpoint abnormal engine noises.
- Diagnose worn valve guides.
- Diagnose valve timing problems.
- Diagnose a worn camshaft.
- Diagnose detonation and preignition problems.
- Analyze engine exhaust smoke.
- Perform a compression test and analyze the results.
- Perform a cylinder leakage test and analyze the results.
- Perform a vacuum leak test.
- Perform a combustion leakage test.
- Describe common engine performance problems.
- Describe the use of engine performance testing equipment.
- Diagnose engine performance problems.
- Perform normal engine tune-up procedures.

TERMS YOU SHOULD KNOW

Look for these terms as you study this chapter and learn what they mean.

bearing knock	exhaust smoke
piston slap	spark tester
piston pin knock	timing light
detonation	tach-dwell meter
preignition	electronic ignition tester
exhaust smoke	multimeter
compression test	VOM
wet compression test	DVOM
cylinder leakage test	fuel injection tester
vacuum leak test	scanner
combustion leak test	computer analyzer
poor cranking	breakout box
no-start condition	exhaust gas analyzer
hard to start	compression tester
misfiring	cylinder leakage tester
surging	engine analyzer
pinging	wave form display
backfire	digital display
low power	printer
poor fuel economy	tune-up
dieseling	

■ ENGINE OPERATING PROBLEMS

Engine performance depends on the efficient operation of all engine systems. An engine performance problem is any engine problem that adversely affects engine operation and drivability. A customer information sheet may be used to help identify the problem **(Figure 2–2).** Some of the more common engine performance problems include the following.

Engine Does Not Crank or Cranks Over Slowly

This indicates a problem in the starting system: low or dead battery, poor battery cable connections, faulty relay, faulty solenoid, or dragging starting motor. Perform diagnostic tests described in Chapter 5 to isolate the problem. If the starting system tests OK, the engine is seized.

Engine Cranks Normally but Won't Start

This condition is caused by total failure of the ignition system, fuel system, or engine component. Pull one plug wire and perform a spark intensity test. A bright, snapping spark should be evident. If not, the ignition system is at fault. Perform diagnostic tests described in Chapter 6 to identify the faulty component. If a good spark is present, check for fuel delivery. With throttle body injection, observe the injector spray. With a carbureted system operate the throttle linkage and observe the fuel spray from the accelerator pump discharge. With port injection remove one injector (if easily accessible) and observe fuel discharge, or check for the presence of fuel under pressure at the fuel rail test port. If both spark and fuel are present, the problem must be in an engine component such as a jumped timing chain or belt or other severe engine mechanical problem. Perform diagnostic tests described later in this chapter to identify the problem.

Engine Is Hard to Start

Hard starting is evidenced by long cranking periods required before the engine starts. This condition indicates partial failure of the fuel system, ignition

■ FIGURE 2–2
This kind of customer information sheet can be used to help identify the performance problem. (Courtesy of Ford Motor Company.)   →

Customer Information Worksheet

Repair Order No. _____

CUSTOMER NAME _____   DATE _____

<u>PLEASE HELP US HELP YOU</u> by checking off all the boxes below that describe the drive problem which brought you here today.

Engine Problem Description

Engine Starting Problems	Engine Quits Running Problems	Engine Idle Problems With The Vehicle Not Moving	Engine Problems While The Vehicle Is Moving
__ Will Not Start – Will Not Even Crank __ Cranks But Will Not Start __ Tries To Start, But Won't __ Starts, But Takes A Long Time	Engine Quits: __ Right After Starting __ While Idling __ When Put Into Gear __ On Acceleration __ During Steady Speed Driving __ On Deceleration __ Right After the Vehicle Is Brought To A Stop __ When Parking	__ Engine Speed Is Too Slow All The Time __ Engine Speed Is Too Slow When The A/C Is On __ Engine Speed Is Too Fast __ Engine Speed is Rough or Uneven	__ Runs Rough __ Bucks and Jerks __ Hesitates/Stumbles On Acceleration __ Misfires- Cuts Out __ Engine Knocks or Rattles __ Lack of Power __ Backfires __ Poor Fuel Economy

About how often does the problem happen?   __ All the time   __ Most of the time   __ Occasionally

When does the problem usually occur? In the: __ Morning   __ Later in the day   __ Anytime

About how long after starting the engine does the problem happen?
__ Within 2 minutes of starting the engine.
__ Between 2 and 10 minutes after the engine starts.
__ At least 10 minutes or longer after starting the engine.
__ It could happen any time after starting the engine.

About how long does the engine have to be off before the problem will happen again?
__ 4 hours or more.
__ More than 30 minutes but less than 4 hours.
__ Less than 30 minutes of being turned off.
__ It does not matter how long the engine was off.

Do weather conditions affect the problem?   __ No   __ Yes
 If yes, which ones?   __ Hot   __ Cold   __ Rain   __ Fog   __ Snow   __ Humid   __ Dry
Does outside temperature affect the problem?   __ No   __ Yes
 If yes, what temperature?   _____ °F

Please check any of these driving conditions that cause the problem.   __ Accelerating   __ Decelerating   __ Turning Right/Left

__ Steady Speed   (approximate vehicle speed _____ MPH)

What are the traffic conditions that cause the problem?   __ In / Around town (frequent stops)   __ Highways (expressways)   __ Offroad   __ Anytime

Was The Check Engine Light On?   __ Yes   __ No   __ Flashing

Were Other Warning Lights On?   __ Yes   __ No   Which Ones? _____

Additional Comments:
_____
_____
_____
_____
_____

Please use the back of this sheet if needed.

system or an engine in poor mechanical condition. Insufficient fuel, low-intensity spark at the spark plugs, or low compression are indicated. Check each system carefully to identify the faulty component.

Engine Starts but Stalls (Dies) as Soon as the Ignition Key Is Released

This is caused by a faulty ignition coil feed with the key in the RUN position. Check for a faulty resistor, poor connection or open in this circuit.

Engine Stalls (Dies)

Stalling may occur at idle, after a hot start, after a cold start, and during heavy acceleration or deceleration. Causes of stalling include a low idle speed, faulty cold-start enrichment device, faulty heated-air intake, vacuum leak, or inadequate fuel delivery.

Hesitation on Acceleration (Stumble)

Hesitation or stumble during acceleration is a delay between the time the accelerator is depressed and when the vehicle accelerates. The engine may actually "cut out" or die momentarily before acceleration is felt. This condition results from a momentarily lean air–fuel mixture. A faulty or maladjusted throttle position sensor may be the cause with fuel injection. With a carburetor it may be the accelerator pump or pump adjustment.

Engine Misfires

One or more cylinders fail to produce power at idle, cruise, or during acceleration. Missing may be caused by a problem with the injectors, spark plugs, plug wires, distributor cap, rotor, corroded terminals, carbon tracking, or a vacuum leak.

Surging at a Steady Speed

Surging is a fluctuation of engine speed and power at a steady throttle position. Power and speed increase and decrease without any throttle movement. Surging may be caused by fluctuating fuel delivery, faulty exhaust system, faulty fuel tank filler cap, or an ignition system or computer control problem. Check those items first that take the least time, then perform the necessary tests to identify the problem.

Pinging (Spark Knock)

Pinging is a light tapping noise that can sound like a rattle during acceleration under load. It is caused by preignition or detonation. Pinging may be caused by advanced ignition timing, use of low-octane fuel, carbon buildup in the combustion chambers, or no EGR. Abnormal combustion is described in Chapter 1.

Backfire is combustion taking place in the intake manifold or exhaust system. It usually produces a loud popping noise. Backfire may be caused by incorrect ignition timing, cracks or carbon tracking in the distributor cap, crossed spark plug wires, lack of fuel during acceleration, a faulty ignition advance system, or faulty air injection.

Lack of Power

Poor acceleration is the result of a lack of engine power. When the accelerator pedal is pressed down the vehicle gains speed at a much slower rate than it should. Problems that can cause a lack of power include the mechanical condition of the engine, a faulty fuel system, ignition system, computer control system, emission control system, restricted exhaust system, or restricted air intake.

Poor Fuel Economy

An engine that uses more fuel than it should over any distance driven has poor fuel economy. Fuel economy is measured by miles driven per gallon of fuel used or by the liters of fuel used per 100 k of driving. Poor fuel economy can be caused by a variety of problems or conditions. Some of the more common are poor driving habits, a rich air–fuel mixture, incorrect ignition timing, engine mechanical condition, fuel leakage, low tire pressures, incorrect wheel alignment, dragging brakes, faulty automatic transmission, heavily loaded vehicle, strong headwinds, and poor road surface.

Dieseling (Carbureted Engines)

Dieseling occurs when the engine continues to run after the ignition has been shut off. It is also called after-running or run-on. Dieseling results from spontaneous combustion caused by fuel still being delivered to an engine that is hot enough to ignite the fuel without any spark at the spark plugs. Dieseling may be caused by a high idle speed, faulty throttle positioner or antidieseling solenoid, overheated engine, vacuum break, glowing carbon particles in the combustion chamber, or low-octane fuel.

Gasoline Engine Exhaust Smoke

Exhaust smoke is most evident when accelerating or decelerating and is less evident at a constant engine speed. The color of the exhaust smoke can indicate the cause. Blue smoke is evidence of oil being burned in the combustion chambers. It may get there due to worn piston rings, worn cylinders, worn valve guides, or leaking valve stem seals. Black smoke indicates an excessively rich air–fuel mixture, which is a fuel system problem. White smoke (not to be confused with exhaust vapors on a cold day) indicates coolant leakage into the combustion chamber. This could be a leaking head gasket or a cracked head.

Engine Overheats

The first indication a driver has that the engine may be overheating is a high temperature gauge reading. Detonation and pinging may also occur. The high temperature gauge reading may be caused by either an engine that is actually running too hot or by a faulty temperature gauge that incorrectly indicates a reading that is higher than the actual engine temperature.

A quick check with a coolant testing thermometer to measure actual coolant temperature in the radiator will determine whether the car's temperature gauge is at fault. (*Caution:* See Chapter 10 for proper procedure.) If coolant temperature is normal in spite of an excessively high dash gauge reading the dash gauge unit, the engine temperature sensor (sending unit), or the connecting electrical wiring may be at fault. If the test thermometer indicates above normal coolant temperature the cooling system or the engine may be at fault. See Chapter 10 for cooling system diagnosis and service.

Engine Temperature Below Normal

Automotive engines are designed to operate most efficiently when they are at the normal specified operating temperature. If the engine does not reach the normal operating temperature combustion will be less efficient, fuel consumption and exhaust emissions will be greater. Overcooling is caused by a defective thermostat, a thermostat that is below the recommended temperature range for the engine, excessive heat loss through radiation (during very cold ambient temperatures), or a combination of these. See Chapter 10 for cooling system diagnosis and service.

■ ENGINE MECHANICAL PROBLEM DIAGNOSIS

SYMPTOMS OF ENGINE MECHANICAL PROBLEMS

Engine mechanical problems may occur after extended use (high odometer reading), lack of proper maintenance (infrequent oil and filter changes), overheating, overloading (lugging the engine), or abusive driving habits. Usually, there is some indication that all is not well with the engine before complete breakdown occurs. Some of these indicators are:

- Abnormal engine noises (knocks, rattles, hissing, squeals)
- Exhaust smoke (blue, black, or white)
- Excessive oil consumption (oil leaks or oil burning, worn rings, cylinders, or valve guides)
- Oil-fouled spark plugs (oil getting into combustion chambers)
- Blowby (combustion gases forced past the piston rings into the crankcase)
- Coolant in the engine oil (leaking head gasket or cracked head)
- Engine lacks power (worn rings or cylinders, burned valves)
- Engine idles rough, misses, and vibrates (burned valves)

■ ENGINE NOISE DIAGNOSIS

An important aspect of engine diagnosis is the interpretation of engine noises. An engine with a noise problem will usually develop additional problems if the noise problem is not corrected. The first step in diagnosing engine noise is to be able to distinguish between normal and abnormal noise. Not all engines sound the same. Different engines (size, make, model) have different noise characteristics. Loud, unusual engine noise usually indicates serious engine problems that require prompt attention. A stethoscope and/or a piece of rubber hose are valuable aids in locating engine noises.

Pinpointing Abnormal Engine Noises

Abnormal engine noises may occur at various engine speeds or loads, or during acceleration or deceleration. The technician must cycle the engine through these different operating modes to help identify the source of such noise. Noises such as clicks, rattles, knocks, tapping, clunks, rapping, popping, or hissing may be encountered.

To aid in identifying the source of internal noise, a technician's stethoscope should be used. It amplifies the sound, making it easier to locate. To use the stethoscope, place the head set in your ears and use the probe to touch the suspected area. The abnormal noise originates from the spot where it is loudest. A piece of flexible hose (heater hose works fine) may be used in the same manner. The hose can also be used to locate vacuum leaks. Place one end of the hose to your ear and use the other end to probe the suspected area. *Caution:* be careful to keep the probe away from spinning fans or belts. The following are examples of abnormal engine noises that may be encountered.

Main Bearing Noise

Main bearing noise due to excessive bearing clearance is evidenced by heavy metallic knocking, most noticeable during acceleration or under load. The knock may be more severe just after starting since little oil will be present in the bearing to soften the knock. Main bearings that knock due to excessive clearance may also cause low oil pressure.

Connecting Rod Bearing Noise

Similar to main bearing noise, but less severe, is connecting-rod bearing knock, which is heard as a light tapping noise when the engine is under light load. As engine speed and load are increased, the knocking becomes louder and increases in frequency in proportion to engine speed. Momentarily disconnecting the spark plug wire from each cylinder in turn will serve to identify the affected cylinder, since the noise will decrease noticeably when the plug wire is disconnected from the cylinder with the bad bearing. A convenient method is to short out each cylinder in turn as in a cylinder power balance test using an engine analyzer.

Piston Slap

Too much piston-to-cylinder wall clearance results in a noise known as piston slap. It appears as a metallic clicking or rattle at idle and under light loads. The noise is most noticeable when the engine is cold before the pistons have expanded due to heat. If the noise is not severe and disappears during warm-up, it is not considered to be a problem. If the noise continues after the engine reaches operating temperature, the piston may crack and the rings may break. The noise is not affected by disconnecting spark plug wires.

Piston Pin Noise

A loose piston pin will cause a regular, sharp, light metallic rapping sound. If several pins are affected, the noise will be a rattle at idle and low speeds. If the noise is not constant but rather appears in intervals, it is probably the result of a lock ring left out or broken. In this case cylinder damage will result.

Valve Train Noise

Noise from the valve train with excessive lash results in a clicking noise at one-half crankshaft speed. The most common valve train noise is caused by faulty hydraulic lifters. Mechanical lifter valve train noise usually results from excessive valve lash. Extensive engine damage can be caused by excessive lash.

Crankshaft End-Play Noise

Excessive crankshaft end play may cause a sharp metallic rap. On cars equipped with a manual transmission, the noise can be brought in when releasing or engaging the clutch. An easy check for crankshaft end play can be made by mounting a dial indicator at the front end of the crankshaft and prying the crankshaft back and forward to its travel limits. If end play is excessive, thrust bearing failure can occur.

Flywheel or Flexplate Noise

A loose flywheel will cause a definite knock, particularly evident when the engine is shut off and just before it comes to a stop. This is also true for a broken flexplate.

Detonation and Preignition Noise

Detonation causes a knocking or pinging sound and can cause damage to pistons, rings, valves, and head gaskets. Causes of detonation include:

1. *Octane number of fuel.* Using gasoline with a lower than recommended octane number may result in detonation and knock.
2. *High compression ratio.* Compression ratios range from about 8:1 to 10:1 in today's cars. Higher compression ratios result in higher combustion chamber pressures and temperatures. High compression ratio engines require the use of high octane gasoline to avoid detonation and knock.
3. *Turbocharging.* Turbocharging or supercharging forces more air into the engine cylinders. This results in higher combustion chamber pressures and temperatures. Higher octane gasoline is required in turbocharged engines to avoid detonation and knock.

Detonation may be caused by:

- Excessive combustion chamber temperatures
- Faulty EGR valve operation
- Preignition

- Lean fuel mixture
- Lugging the engine
- Excessive carbon deposits in combustion chambers
- Incorrect ignition timing
- Increased compression ratio due to head or block milling
- Fuel octane rating too low

Preignition can cause severe damage to pistons, rings, valves, and head gaskets. Causes of preignition include:

- Glowing particles of carbon in combustion chamber
- Sharp, glowing edges in combustion chamber
- Spark plug heat range too high
- Loose spark plugs
- Excessive combustion chamber temperature
- Ignition cross-firing
- Detonation

Other Engine Noises

A variety of other engine noises can develop which also indicate a problem that requires attention. Some of the more frequent noises are listed here.

1. Worn timing chain dragging on or hitting the timing cover
2. Broken motor mount, causing a knock when engine load is applied and released
3. Manifold heat control valve shaft and bushings worn, causing a rattling sound
4. Fuel pump knock due to broken rocker arm spring (mechanical fuel pumps)
5. Piston ring hitting ridge in cylinder, due to cylinder ridge not being removed when rings were replaced
6. Piston hitting carbon deposits in combustion chamber, causing a knock
7. Piston hitting head gasket, which extends past edge of cylinder
8. Mechanical fuel pump mounting bolts loose
9. Alternator, A/C compressor, power steering pump, or air pump mounting bracket loose or broken
10. Rocker arms striking valve cover as a result of dented cover or incorrect cover gasket thickness
11. Cracked fan blade
12. Worn water pump bearing.

Noises caused by belt-driven components such as the water pump, alternator, fan, power steering pump, air conditioning compressor, or air pump can easily be isolated by removing the drive belt and running the engine briefly. If the noise is gone with the belt removed, the belt-driven component is at fault. The stethoscope can also be used to detect noisy water pump bearings, power steering pumps, air pumps, alternator bearings, fuel pump knock, and the like, and can save valuable time. Experience is required, however, to be able to distinguish between normal and abnormal noises, since all components in operation make some noise.

■ ANALYZING EXHAUST SMOKE

Gasoline Engine

Exhaust smoke is most evident when accelerating or decelerating. It is less evident at a constant engine speed. The color of the exhaust smoke can indicate the cause. *Blue smoke* is evidence of oil being burned in the combustion chambers, due to worn piston rings, worn cylinders, worn valve guides, or leaking valve stem seals. *Black smoke* indicates an excessively rich air–fuel mixture, which is a fuel system problem. *White smoke* (not to be confused with exhaust vapors on a cold day) indicates coolant leaking into the combustion chamber caused by a leaking head gasket or a cracked head. (See Chapter 9 for analysis of exhaust emissions.)

Diesel Engine

Blue smoke from the exhaust is evidence of engine oil entering the combustion chamber in the same manner as in a gasoline engine. Black smoke indicates unburned fuel due to low compression, incorrect fuel usage, or fuel injection problems. White smoke indicates a cold engine or coolant leaking into the combustion chambers.

■ LUBRICATION SYSTEM PROBLEM DIAGNOSIS

Oil Consumption and Oil Leaks

A certain amount of oil consumption is normal. It is, therefore, also normal that oil may have to be added between oil changes. To determine whether a vehicle is using an excessive amount of oil, the method of checking the oil level must be applied consistently over a period of time and mileage.

Oil consumption may be the result of worn piston rings, worn valve guides, excessive bearing clearance, and oil leakage. If an oil consumption problem exists, any oil leakage must be corrected first before the condition of the engine is blamed. If no oil leakage exists, a thorough diagnosis of the engine's mechanical condition should be performed to determine the cause. A wet and dry compression test can help to decide whether the piston rings, valve guides, or seals may be at fault.

Oil Dilution

Oil dilution is the result of unburned fuel getting past the rings and into the oil in the oil pan. An overly rich air–fuel mixture, a poorly tuned engine, or an engine running at below normal temperature can cause unburned fuel to dilute the oil and seriously affect its ability to lubricate, seal, and reduce wear.

Oil Pressure Testing

If for any reason an oil pressure problem is suspected, a master test gauge with a range of 0 to 100 psi (0 to 689.5 kPa) should be used to verify actual oil pressure produced by the engine **(Figure 2–3).**

Generally, procedures include bringing the engine oil to operating temperature. The engine is then turned off and the test gauge installed at the point indicated in the service manual (usually, a plug in the main oil gallery). The engine is restarted and readings are taken at specified engine speeds. These readings are then compared to those provided in the shop manual.

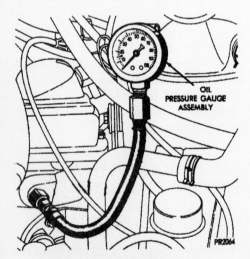

Oil Pressure Check:
Oil temperature —80°C (176°F)
Engine speed —2000 rpm
Min. pressure —193 KPa (28 psi)

■ FIGURE 2–3
Using a test pressure gauge to check engine oil pressure. Specifications shown are one example. Refer to the service manual for actual specifications. (Courtesy of Chrysler Corporation.)

If the oil pressure is too high, the problem is usually a stuck oil pump pressure relief valve. The relief valve should be removed and polished with crocus cloth to correct this condition. Relief valve spring pressure should also be checked at this time.

If the oil pressure is too low, the cause may be any of the following:

- Worn oil pump
- Excessive bearing clearances (camshaft or crankshaft)
- Weak or broken pressure relief valve spring
- Relief valve stuck in the open position
- Excessive oil dilution
- Plugged oil pickup screen
- Air leak into oil pump inlet

If the oil pump is worn, it is usually replaced. The oil pump must be removed and checked as outlined here to determine its condition. If the bearing clearances are excessive, they must be corrected to bring clearances to specified limits. This requires replacement of the bearings, and may require replacing the camshaft and crankshaft as well. If the relief valve or spring is at fault, it should be cleaned or replaced.

Excessive oil dilution requires changing the engine oil and filter and correcting the cause of oil dilution. This may require adjusting or replacing the automatic choke or correcting any fuel delivery system problems resulting in excessive fuel delivery to the cylinders. If the oil pickup tube or screen is faulty, it should be cleaned or replaced.

■ DIAGNOSING VALVE TRAIN PROBLEMS

Diagnosing Worn Valve Guides

Check for worn valve guides in any of the following ways.

1. With the transmission in neutral, run the engine at about 3000 rpm for a few seconds, then quickly close the throttle and allow the engine to return to idle speed. Note whether the engine tends to shake momentarily just when idle speed is reached. If so, worn valve guides are indicated, assuming that there are no other reasons for a rough idle.

2. Drive the vehicle on the road at about 50 mph (80 km/h). Then take your foot off the gas pedal and watch for blue-gray exhaust smoke. During deceleration the vacuum in the engine cylinders is high; therefore, the greatest amount of oil will get past the valve stems during this high-vacuum condition.

3. A vacuum gauge may be used to check for worn valve guides. Connect the gauge to the intake manifold and observe the gauge needle with the engine running at idle. A quivering needle indicates possible worn valve guides.

Diagnosing Valve Timing Problems

Incorrect valve timing can result from broken timing gear teeth, worn timing chain and sprockets, or worn timing belt. One of the symptoms of incorrect valve timing is "popping" through the carburetor or throttle body and the exhaust. This is usually accompanied by a considerable loss in engine power.

A quick check of valve timing problems on most engines can be made by removing the valve cover and observing rocker arm action while rotating the crankshaft forward and back several times. If there is a noticeable delay in rocker arm or camshaft movement when reversing crankshaft rotation, the timing chain or gears are worn. Other indications include low intake manifold vacuum, low compression on all cylinders, and a lack of power.

Badly worn gears can result in gear teeth breaking. Severe chain wear can result in chain breakage or the chain jumping one or more sprocket teeth. A badly worn timing belt can result in jumping a cog or two or in the belt breaking or jumping off. Severe damage may result from pistons striking open valves.

Diagnosing a Worn Camshaft

Camshaft lobe wear can be checked without camshaft removal on pushrod engines as follows.

1. Move the rocker arm and pushrod out of the way of the cam lobe to be measured.
2. Place an old pushrod that has been ground flat on the rocker arm end in place with the flat end up.
3. Mount a dial indicator so that the plunger contacts the flat end of the pushrod. Make sure that plunger travel is in line with pushrod movement and not at an angle.
4. Rotate the crankshaft and note the total dial indicator reading obtained from a full turn of the camshaft (two turns of the crankshaft). The total indicator reading is the amount of lobe lift. Compare the reading with specifications to determine lobe wear.

On OHC engines remove the valve cover to expose the camshaft. Measure cam lobe wear with an outside micrometer if cam lobes are accessible. If not use a dial indicator mounted to measure total cam lobe action and compare to specifications.

■ ENGINE TESTING SAFETY

1. Follow the operating instructions provided with the test equipment. Failure to follow proper procedures can result in injury and damage to test equipment and vehicle components.
2. Follow the procedures in the appropriate service manual to avoid injury or damage.
3. Wear eye and face protection whenever needed.
4. Do not look into a throttle body or carburetor air horn while cranking or running the engine. Backfire may occur and cause burns.
5. Keep all tester leads, extension cords, and hoses away from engine fans and belts and away from hot engine parts.
6. Observe static electrical discharge precautions when handling electronic parts. (See Chapter 4 for details.)
7. Observe all precautionary measures required by the service manual to avoid accidental deployment of air bags. (See Chapter 12 for details.)

■ TEST EQUIPMENT FUNCTIONS

Many different kinds of test equipment are needed to perform the various engine performance tests. A brief review of the major items and their functions follows.

1. *Spark tester:* **(Figure 2–4)** used to check spark intensity produced by the ignition system (see Chapter 6).
2. *Timing light:* **(Figure 2–5)** used to check ignition timing and ignition advance (see Chapter 6).

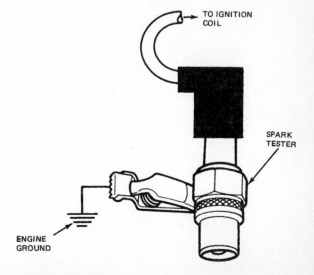

■ FIGURE 2–4
Spark intensity tester. (Courtesy of Ford Motor Company.)

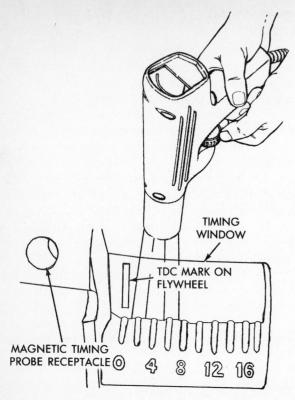

TIMING WINDOW

TDC MARK ON FLYWHEEL

MAGNETIC TIMING PROBE RECEPTACLE ⊙ 4 8 12 16

■ **FIGURE 2–5**
Checking vacuum and centrifugal advance with a timing light equipped with a degree meter. (Courtesy of Chrysler Corporation.)

3. *Tach-dwell meter:* measures engine speed and coil primary on time or dwell.

4. *Electronic ignition tester:* checks the operation of the electronic ignition system and its components (see Chapter 6).

5. *Multimeter (VOM):* voltmeter, ohmmeter, and milliameter combined in one test instrument; tests electrical current, voltage, and resistance.

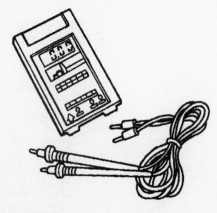

■ **FIGURE 2–6**
High-impedance digital volt/ohmmeter (DVOM) must be used to test many electronic components. (Courtesy of Ford Motor Company.)

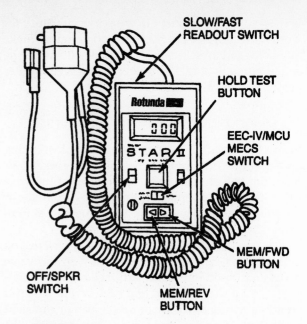

SLOW/FAST READOUT SWITCH

HOLD TEST BUTTON

EEC-IV/MCU MECS SWITCH

MEM/FWD BUTTON

MEM/REV BUTTON

OFF/SPKR SWITCH

■ **FIGURE 2–7**
Computer-controlled ignition system tester. This STAR (Self Test Diagnostic Readout) tester or scan tool is used on Ford vehicles. (Courtesy of Ford Motor Company.)

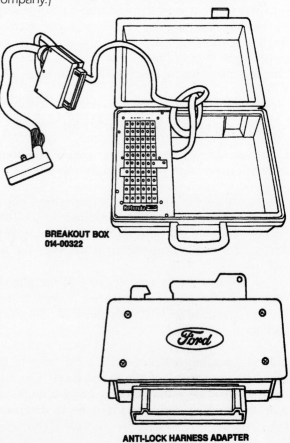

BREAKOUT BOX 014-00322

ANTI-LOCK HARNESS ADAPTER T90P-50-ALA

■ **FIGURE 2–8**
Breakout box type of tester allows testing of sensors and output devices while vehicle is in operation. (Courtesy of Ford Motor Company.)

■ FIGURE 2–9
Computer type of engine analyzer.
(Courtesy of Bear Automotive.)

6. *Digital volt-ohmmeter (DVOM):* **(Figure 2–6)** multimeter with digital display and 10,000-Ω impedance required for testing many electronic components, where very small voltages are involved and components are easily damaged with low-impedance meters.

7. *Electronic fuel injection tester:* tests electronic fuel injection systems and system components (see Chapter 7).

8. *Scanner:* **(Figure 2–7)** plugs into diagnostic connector in wiring harness. Displays fault codes and performs a number of tests on computer control systems and system components (see Chapter 4).

9. *Breakout box:* breakout box connectors are fitted between wiring harness connectors on the vehicle in a manner that keeps the sensors, output devices, and control module connected so that the

■   FIGURE 2–10
Four-gas analyzer with diagnostic features. Five-gas analyzers have the added capability of testing for NOx content.(Courtesy of OTC Division, SPX Corporation.)

system and its components can be tested while the vehicle is in operation. This allows pinpoint testing with a digital multimeter at the test points indicated in the service manual **(Figure 2–8).**

10. *Computer analyzer:* includes a hand-held scanner and a code storage unit that can be connected to the analyzer. The system connects to the vehicle diagnostic connector and can be used while driving the vehicle to store information about engine operation **(Figure 2–9).**

11. *Exhaust gas analyzer:* used to check the level of harmful exhaust emissions produced by the engine. The percentage of CO, CO_2, O_2, and the HC content in ppm are indicators of the performance of the fuel system, ignition system, emission control systems, and engine condition. Chapter 8 discusses exhaust analysis test procedures **(Figure 2–10).**

12. *Vacuum leak tester:* a hand-held self-powered unit with an indicator light or beeper signal.

13. *Combustion leak tester:* used to check for the presence of combustion gases in the engine cooling system.

14. *Cylinder leakage tester:* used to check for pressure leakage past piston rings or valves.

15. *Oil leak detector:* a dye additive which is added to the engine oil to help pinpoint the source of engine oil leaks.

Scan Tester

A scanner (scan tool) is used by plugging it into the wiring harness diagnostic connector. The vehicle's computer communicates a variety of information to the scanner which is displayed in digital form as fault codes or in word form. Some of this information is difficult or impossible to obtain without a scanner. Using a scanner saves diagnosis time and

can avoid the unnecessary replacement of good parts when other testing methods are used. The scanner is not able to pinpoint the exact location of a problem in a circuit but is able to identify the problem circuit. Pinpoint tests with a digital voltmeter or ohmmeter are performed to isolate the problem within the circuit.

A scanner can be used to detect intermittent problems related to the wiring harness and wiring connectors. The scanner is plugged into the diagnostic connector with the engine not running. The wiring harness, connectors, and terminals can then be manipulated and wiggled while observing the scanner display. Faulty wires and connectors can be detected in this way **(figures 2–7 and 2–9).**

The scanner can also be used to check operation while the vehicle is being driven under conditions that caused the check engine light to turn on, indicating a problem. The scanner should be observed in each test position while driving the vehicle. With the proper accessories the data can be recorded for later analysis in the shop. Follow the instructions supplied with the scanner and the procedures outlined in the service manual for test procedures and interpretation of test results.

The following 16 pages are typical of modern diagnostic procedures that also include the use of a scan tool (referred to here as a Tech 1 tool). The procedures are for a specific General Motors 3800 model engine as they appear in the service manual. They are presented here courtesy of General Motors Corporation as an example of a systematic step by step process that is both thorough and effective. Reference is made to other sections and charts in the service manual for further diagnosis. Always refer to the appropriate service manual for specific procedures and specifications for the vehicle being serviced.

IMPORTANT PRELIMINARY CHECKS

BEFORE USING THIS SECTION

Before using this section you should have performed the "Diagnostic Circuit Check" and determined that:
1. The PCM and "Service Engine Soon" light are operating correctly.
2. There are no diagnostic codes stored, or there is a diagnostic code but no "Service Engine Soon" light.

SYMPTOM

Verify the customer complaint, and locate the correct symptom in the table of contents. Check the items indicated under that symptom.

VISUAL/PHYSICAL CHECK

Several of the symptom procedures call for a Careful Visual/Physical Check. The importance of this step cannot be stressed too strongly - it can lead to correcting a problem without further checks and can save valuable time. This check should include:
● PCM grounds and sensors for being clean, tight and in their proper location.
● Vacuum hoses for splits, kinks, and proper connections, as shown on "Vehicle Emission Control Information" label. Check thoroughly for any type of leak or restriction.
● Air leaks at throttle body mounting area and intake manifold sealing surfaces.
● Ignition wires for cracking, hardness, proper routing and carbon tracking.
● Wiring for proper connections, pinches and cuts.

INTERMITTENTS

(Page 1 of 2)

Definition: Problem may or may not turn "ON" the "Service Engine Soon" light or store a code.

DO NOT use the diagnostic code charts in "Engine Components/Wiring Diagrams/Diagnostic Charts" Section "6E3-A" for intermittent problems. The fault must be present to locate the problem. If a fault is intermittent, use of diagnostic code charts may result in replacement of good parts.

- Most intermittent problems are caused by faulty electrical connections or wiring. Perform careful visual/physical check as described at start of "Symptoms" Section "6E3-B." Check for:
  - Poor mating of the connector halves. or terminal not fully seated in the connector body (backed out).
  - Improperly formed or damaged terminal. All connector terminals in the problem circuit should be carefully reformed or replaced to insure proper contact tension.
  - Poor terminal to wire connection. This requires removing the terminal from the connector body to check. Refer to "Introduction" in "Driveability and Emissions," Section "6E," "Wiring Harness Service."

- If a visual/physical check does not find the cause of the problem, the car can be driven with a voltmeter connected to a suspected circuit. A Tech 1 can also be used to help detect intermittent conditions. An abnormal voltage, or "Scan" reading, when the problem occurs, indicates the problem may be in that circuit. If the wiring and connectors check OK, and a diagnostic code was stored for a circuit having a sensor, except for Codes 43, 44 and 45, substitute a known good sensor and recheck.

- Loss of diagnostic code memory. To check, disconnect TPS and idle engine until "Service Engine Soon" light comes "ON." Code 22 should be stored, and kept in memory when ignition is turned "OFF." If not, the PCM is faulty.

- An intermittent "Service Engine Soon" light with no stored diagnostic code may be caused by:
  - Ignition coil shorted to ground and arcing at spark plug wires or plugs.
  - "Service Engine Soon" light wire to PCM shorted to ground (CKT 419).
  - Diagnostic "test" terminal wire to PCM, shorted to ground (CKT 451).
  - PCM grounds, refer to PCM wiring diagrams.

INTERMITTENTS

(Page 2 of 2)

Definition: Problem may or may not turn "ON" the "Service Engine Soon" light or store a code.

- Check for an electrical system interference caused by a defective relay, PCM driven solenoid, or switch. They can cause a sharp electrical surge. Normally, the problem will occur when the faulty component is operated.

- Check for improper installation of electrical options such as lights, 2 way radios, car phones, CB antenna lead near PCM harness causing false readings and codes, etc.

- EST wires should be routed away from spark plug wires, coil and generator.

- Check for open diode across A/C compressor clutch, located in the harness approximately 10 - 15 inches from the A/C compressor, and for other open diodes (refer to wiring diagrams).

- If problem has not been found, refer to "PCM Connector Symptom" charts at the end of Section "6E3-B."

HARD START

Definition: Engine Cranks OK, but does not start for a long time. Does eventually run, or may start but immediately dies.

PRELIMINARY CHECKS

- Perform the careful visual/physical checks as described at start of "Symptoms" Section "6E3-B."
- Make sure the driver is using the correct starting procedure.

SENSORS

- **CHECK:** Coolant Temperature Sensor (CTS) using a Tech 1, compare coolant temperature with ambient temperature on cold engine.
  - If coolant temperature readings is 5 degrees greater than or less than ambient air temperature on a cold engine, check resistance in coolant sensor circuit or sensor itself. Compare CTS resistance value to the "Diagnostic Aids" chart on Code 15 chart.
- **CHECK:** TPS for binding or a high TPS voltage with the throttle closed (should read between .33 volt and .46 volt and 0% throttle angle.)

FUEL SYSTEM

- **CHECK:** Fuel pump relay operation - pump should turn "ON" for 2 seconds when ignition is turned "ON." Use CHART A-5.
- **CHECK:** Fuel pressure, use CHART A-7.
- **CHECK:** For contaminated fuel and sufficient fuel quantity.
- **CHECK:** Both injector fuses (visual inspect).
- **NOTE:** A faulty in-tank fuel pump check valve will allow the fuel in the lines to drain back to the tank after engine is stopped. To check for this condition, perform fuel system diagnosis CHART A-7.

IGNITION SYSTEM

- **CHECK:** For proper ignition voltage output with spark tester J 26792 or equivalent (ST-125).
- **CHECK:** Spark plugs. Remove spark plugs, check for wet plugs, cracks, wear, improper gap, burned electrodes, or heavy deposits. Repair or replace as necessary.
- **CHECK:** Bare or shorted wires
- **CHECK:** Loose ignition module ground (mounting screws).

ADDITIONAL CHECKS

- **CHECK:** IAC Operation - use CHART C-2B.
- **CHECK:** Basic engine problem. Refer to ENGINE MECHANICAL DIAGNOSIS (SECTION 6A).
- **CHECK:** Service Bulletins for MEM-CAL updates.
- **CHECK:** PCV system for leaks.

SURGES AND/OR CHUGGLES

Definition: Engine power variation under steady throttle or cruise. feels like the car speeds up and slows down with no change in the acceleration pedal.

PRELIMINARY CHECKS

- Perform the careful visual checks as described at start of "Symptoms," Section "6E3-B."
- Be sure driver understands transmission torque converter clutch, and A/C compressor operation as explained in the owner's manual.

SENSORS

- **CHECK:** Oxygen (O_2) sensor. The Oxygen (O_2) sensor should respond quickly to different throttle position, if it does not, check the Oxygen (O_2) sensor for silicon or other contaminations from fuel, or use of improper RTV sealant. The sensor may have a white, powdery coating and result in a high but false signal voltage (rich exhaust indication). The PCM will then reduce the amount of fuel delivered to the engine, causing a severe driveability problem. Also, watch for green glychol contamination or cracking.

FUEL SYSTEM

- **NOTE:** To determine if the condition is caused by a rich or lean system, the car should be driven at the speed of the complaint. Monitoring block learn and fuel integrator will help identify a problem. Refer to typical "Scan" data definitions (6E3-A) for an explanation of block learn and integrator. A poor PCM ground at the ignition module mounting bracket causes the fuel integrator to read about 150.
- **CHECK:** Fuel pressure while condition exists. Use CHART A-7.
- **CHECK:** In-line fuel filter. Replace if dirty or plugged.

IGNITION SYSTEM

- **CHECK:** For proper ignition voltage output using spark tester (ST-125) J 26792 or equivalent.
- **CHECK:** Spark Plugs. Remove spark plugs, check for wet plugs, cracks, wear, improper gap, burned electrodes, or heavy deposits. Repair or replace as necessary. Also, check condition of spark plug wires.

ADDITIONAL CHECKS

- **CHECK:** PCM grounds for being clean, tight and in their proper location.
- **CHECK:** Vacuum lines for kinks or leaks.
- **CHECK:** Generator output voltage. Repair if less than 9 or more than 16 volts.
- **CHECK:** Speedometer reading, with the speed on a Tech 1, are equal.

LACK OF POWER, SLUGGISH OR SPONGY

Definition: Engine delivers less than expected power. Little or no increase in speed when accelerator pedal is pushed down part way.

PRELIMINARY CHECKS

- Perform the careful visual/physical checks as described at start of "Symptoms," Section "6E3-B."
- Compare customer's car to similar unit. Make sure the customer has an actual problem.
- Remove air filter and check air filter for dirt, or for being plugged. Replace as necessary.

FUEL SYSTEM

- **CHECK:** Restricted fuel filter.
- **CHECK:** Fuel pressure, use CHART A-7.
- **CHECK:** Contaminated fuel.

IGNITION SYSTEM

- **CHECK:** Secondary voltage using a spark tester J 26792 (ST-125), or equivalent, to check for a weak coil.
- **CHECK:** ESC system for false retard due to mechanical noise.

ADDITIONAL CHECKS

- **CHECK:** PCM grounds for being clean, tight and in their proper locations. See PCM wiring diagrams.
- **CHECK:** Generator output voltage. Repair if less than 9 or more than 17 volts.
- **CHECK:** Exhaust system for possible restriction. Refer to CHART B-1.
  - Inspect exhaust system for damaged or collapsed pipes.
  - Inspect muffler for heat distress or possible internal failure.
- **CHECK:** Torque Converter Clutch (TCC) for proper operation. Refer to AUTOMATIC TRANSMISSION (SECTION 7A).

ENGINE MECHANICAL

- **CHECK:** Engine valve timing and compression.
- **CHECK:** Engine for correct or worn camshaft. Refer to ENGINE MECHANICAL DIAGNOSIS (SECTION 6A).

DETONATION/SPARK KNOCK

Definition: A mild to severe ping, usually worse under acceleration. The engine makes sharp metallic knocks that change with throttle opening. Sounds like popcorn popping.

PRELIMINARY CHECKS

- Perform the careful visual/physical checks as described at start of "Symptoms," Section "6E3-B."
- PRNDL switch. Be sure "Scan" indicates drive with gear selector in drive or overdrive.
- **NOTE:** If "Scan" tool readings are normal (see facing page of "Diagnostic Circuit Check") and there are no engine mechanical faults, fill fuel tank with a premium gasoline that has a minimum octane reading of 92 and revaluate vehicle performance.
- **CHECK:** TCC operation, TCC applying too soon. Use CHART C-8.

COOLING SYSTEM

- Check for obvious overheating problems:
  - Low engine coolant
  - Loose water pump belt
  - Restricted air flow to radiator, or restricted water flow through radiator.
  - Inoperative electric cooling fan circuit, use CHART C-12.
  - Correct coolant solution should be a 50/50 mix of GM #1052753 anti-freeze coolant (or equivalent) and water.

FUEL SYSTEM

- **NOTE:** To determine if the condition is caused by a rich or lean system, the car should be driven at the speed of the complaint. Monitoring block learn will help identify problem.
- **CHECK:** Fuel pressure, use CHART A-7.

IGNITION SYSTEM

- **CHECK:** Spark plugs for proper heat cause. Refer to "Owner's Manual."
- **CHECK:** ESC system for proper operation, use CHART C-5.

ENGINE MECHANICAL

- **CHECK:** For excessive oil in the combustion chamber.
  Valve oil seals for leaking
- **CHECK:** Combustion chambers for excessive carbon build up. Remove carbon with top engine cleaner and follow instructions on can.
- **CHECK:** Combustion chamber pressure by performing a compression test. See ENGINE MECHANICAL DIAGNOSIS (SECTION 6A).
- **CHECK:** For incorrect basic engine parts such as cam, heads, pistons, etc.

ADDITIONAL CHECKS

- **CHECK:** TCC operation, TCC applying too soon. See CHART C-8.
- **CHECK:** For correct MEM-CAL. (See Service Bulletins.)

HESITATION, SAG, STUMBLE

Definition: Momentary lack of response as the accelerator is pushed down. Can occur at all car speeds. Usually most severe when first trying to make the car move, as from a stop sign. May cause engine to stall if severe enough.

PRELIMINARY CHECKS

- Perform the careful visual/physical checks as described at start of "Symptoms," Section "6E3-B."

SENSORS

- **CHECK:** TPS - Check TPS for binding or sticking. Voltage should increase at a steady rate as throttle is moved toward Wide Open Throttle (WOT).
- **CHECK:** Oxygen (O_2) sensor ground (caused by corroded threads in exhaust manifold).

FUEL SYSTEM

- **CHECK:** Fuel pressure, use CHART A-7.
- **CHECK:** Contaminated fuel.
- **CHECK:** Canister Purge System for proper operation. Use CHART C-3.
- **CHECK:** Fuel injectors. Perform injector balance test, use CHART C-2A.

IGNITION SYSTEM

- **CHECK:** Spark plugs for being fouled, or for there being faulty secondary wiring.
- **CHECK:** Ignition system ground (module mounting bolts).

ADDITIONAL CHECKS

- **CHECK:** For correct MEM-CAL. (See Service Bulletins.)
- **CHECK:** Engine thermostat functioning correctly and proper heat range.
- **CHECK:** Generator output voltage. Repair if less than 9 or more than 17 volts.
- **CHECK:** For air leaks between MAF sensor and the throttle body.

CUTS OUT, MISSES

(Page 1 of 2)

Definition: Steady pulsation or jerking that follows engine speed, usually more pronounced as engine load increases, not normally felt above 1500 rpm or 48 kph (30 mph). The exhaust has a steady spitting sound at idle or low speed.

PRELIMINARY CHECKS

- Perform the careful visual/physical checks as described at start of "Symptoms," Section "6E3-B."

IGNITION SYSTEM

- Check for cylinder miss by:
    1. Start engine, allow engine to stabilize then disconnect IAC motor. Remove one spark plug wire at a time, using insulated pliers. If Tech 1 is available, it may be used to short out the cylinders rather than disconnecting spark plug wires.

       CAUTION: Do Not perform this test for more than 2 minutes, as this test may cause damage to the catalytic converter.

    2. If there is an rpm drop on all cylinders (equal to within 50 rpm), go to "Rough, Unstable, or Incorrect Idle, Stalling" symptom. Reconnect IAC valve.
    3. If there is no rpm drop on one or more cylinders, or excessive variation is drop, check for spark on the suspected cylinder(s) using a J 26792 (ST-125) spark tester or equivalent. If no spark, refer to "Ignition System" Section "6E3-C4." If there is a spark, remove spark plug(s) in these cylinders and check for:
       - Insulator Cracks
       - Wear
       - Improper Gap
       - Burned Electrodes
       - Heavy Deposits
- **CHECK:** Spark plug wires by connecting ohmmeter to ends of each wire in question. If meter reads over 30,000 ohms, replace wire(s).
- **CHECK:** With engine running, spray coils and plug wires with fine water mist to check for shorts.

FUEL SYSTEM

- **CHECK:** Fuel system - Plugged fuel filter, low pressure. Use CHART A-7.
- **CHECK:** Contaminated fuel
- **CHECK:** Injector drivers. Disconnect all injector harness connectors. Connect J 34730-2 Injector Test Light or equivalent 6 volts test light between the harness terminal, of each injector connector and note light while cranking. If test light fails to blink at any connector, refer to CHART A-3 (Page 2 of 4).
- **CHECK:** Perform the Injector Balance Test. Refer to CHART C-2A.

CUTS OUT, MISSES

(Page 2 of 2)

Definition: Steady pulsation or jerking that follows engine speed, usually more pronounced as engine load increases, not normally felt above 1500 rpm or 48 kph (30 mph). The exhaust has a steady spitting sound at idle or low speed.

ENGINE MECHANICAL

- **CHECK:** Compression. Perform compression check on questionable cylinder(s) found above. If compression is low, repair as necessary. Refer to ENGINE MECHANICAL DIAGNOSIS (SECTION 6A).
- **CHECK:** Base engine. Remove rocker covers. Check for bent pushrods, worn rocker arms, broken valve springs, worn camshaft lobes and valve timing. Repair as necessary. See ENGINE MECHANICAL DIAGNOSIS (SECTION 6A).

ADDITIONAL CHECKS

- **CHECK:** For EMI interference. A missing condition can be caused by Electromagnetic Interference (EMI) on the reference circuit. EMI can usually be detected by monitoring engine rpm with a Tech 1. A sudden increase in rpm with little change in actual engine rpm change, indicates EMI is present. If the problem exists, check routing of secondary wires, check ignition module ground circuit.
- **CHECK:** Intake and exhaust manifold passage for casting flash.
- **CHECK:** For a misaligned crank sensor or a bent vane on the interrupter ring. Inspect for proper clearance at each vane using tool J 37089 or equivalent and the procedure in "Ignition System (DIS)/EST," Section "6E3-C4."

ROUGH, UNSTABLE, OR INCORRECT IDLE, STALLING

(Page 1 of 2)

Definition: Engine runs unevenly at idle. If severe, the engine or car may shake. Engine idle speed may vary in rpm. Either condition may be severe enough to stall engine.

PRELIMINARY CHECKS

- Perform the careful visual/physical checks as described at start of "Symptoms," Section "6E3-B."
- **CHECK:** For vacuum leaks
- **CHECK:** PCM grounds for being clean, tight and proper routing. See PCM wiring diagrams.

FUEL SYSTEM

- **NOTE:** Monitoring block learn and fuel integrator will help identify the cause of some problems. Refer to typical "Scan" data definitions for an explanation of the block learn and fuel integrator.
- **CHECK:** Injector balance. Refer to CHART C-2A.
- **CHECK:** Clean injectors.
- **CHECK:** For fuel in pressure regulator hose. If fuel is present, replace regulator assembly.
- **CHECK:** Evaporative Emission Control System (EECS), use CHART C-3.
- **CHECK:** The Oxygen (O_2) sensor should respond quickly to different throttle positions, if it does not, check the Oxygen (O_2) sensor for silicon contamination from fuel, or use of improper RTV sealant. The sensor will have a white, powdery coating, and will result in a high but false signal voltage (rich exhaust indication). The PCM will then reduce the amount of fuel delivered to the engine, causing a severe driveability problem.

IGNITION SYSTEM

- **CHECK:** Ignition system; wires, plugs, etc.

ENGINE MECHANICAL

- **CHECK:** Perform a cylinder compression check. See ENGINE MECHANICAL DIAGNOSIS (SECTION 6).
- **CHECK:** For correct camshaft or weak valve springs.

ROUGH, UNSTABLE, OR INCORRECT IDLE, STALLING

(Page 2 of 2)

Definition: Engine runs unevenly at idle. If severe, the engine or car may shake. Engine idle speed may vary in rpm. Either condition may be severe enough to stall engine.

ADDITIONAL CHECKS

- **CHECK:** Throttle linkage for sticking or binding.
- **CHECK:** P/N switch circuit. Use Tech 1 and be sure tool indicates vehicle is in drive with gear selector in drive or overdrive.
- **CHECK:** IAC operation, use CHART C-2B.
- **CHECK:** A/C signal to PCM, "Scan" tool should indicate A/C is being requested when ever A/C is selected. If problem exists with A/C "ON," check A/C system operation CHART C-10.
- **CHECK:** PCV valve for proper operation. See "Positive Crankcase Ventilation (PCV)," Section "6E3-C13."
- **CHECK:** Service Bulletins for MEM-CAL updates.
- **CHECK:** For broken motor mounts.
- **CHECK:** Generator output voltage. Repair if less than 9 or more than 17 volts.

POOR FUEL ECONOMY

Definition: Fuel economy, as measured by an actual road test, is noticeably lower than expected. Also, economy is noticeably lower than it was on this car at one time, as previously shown by an actual road test.

PRELIMINARY CHECKS

- Perform the careful visual checks as described at start of "Symptoms," Section "6E3-B."
- Visually (physically) check: Vacuum hoses for splits, kinks, and proper connections as shown on "Vehicle Emission Control Information" label.
- Check owner's driving habits.
  - Is A/C "ON" full time (Defroster mode "ON")?
  - Are tires at correct pressure?
  - Are excessively heavy loads being carried?
  - Is acceleration too much, too often?
- Check air cleaner element (filter) for dirty or being plugged.

IGNITION SYSTEM

- **CHECK:** Spark plugs. Check for wet plugs, cracks, wear, improper gap, burned electrodes, or heavy deposits. Repair or replace as necessary.

COOLING SYSTEM

- **CHECK:** Engine coolant level.
- **CHECK:** Engine thermostat for faulty part (always open) or for wrong heat range. Refer to ENGINE COOLING (SECTION 6B).

ENGINE MECHANICAL

- **CHECK:** Compression. See ENGINE MECHANICAL DIAGNOSIS (SECTION 6A).

ADDITIONAL CHECKS

- **CHECK:** TCC operation. Use CHART C-8. A Tech 1 should indicate an rpm drop, when the TCC is commanded "ON."
- **CHECK:** For exhaust system restriction. Use CHART B-1.
- **CHECK:** For proper calibration of speedometer.
- **CHECK:** Induction system and crankcase for air leaks.

EXCESSIVE EXHAUST EMISSIONS OR ODORS

Definition: Vehicle fails an emission test. Vehicle has excessive "rotten egg" smell. Excessive odors do not necessarily indicate excessive emissions.

PRELIMINARY CHECKS

- Perform "Diagnostic Circuit Check."
- **NOTE:** IF EMISSION TEST shows excessive CO and HC check items which cause car to run RICH. Refer to "Diagnostic Aids" on facing page of Code 45.
- **NOTE:** If EMISSION TEST shows excessive NOx, check items which cause car to run lean or too hot. Refer to "Diagnostic Aids" on the facing page of Code 44 chart.

COOLING SYSTEM

- If the "Scan" tool indicates a very high coolant temperature and the system is running lean:
  - CHECK: Engine coolant level
  - CHECK: Engine thermostat for faulty part (always open) or for wrong heat range. Refer to ENGINE COOLING (SECTION 6B).
  - CHECK: Cooling fan operation, use CHART C-12.

FUEL SYSTEM

- **NOTE:** If the system is running rich (block learn near 118 with canistor purge disconnected), refer to "Diagnostic Aids" on facing page of Code 45.
  If the system is running lean (block learn near 142) refer to "Diagnostic Aids" on facing page of Code 44.
- **CHECK:** For properly installed fuel cap.
- **CHECK:** Fuel pressure. Use CHART A-7.
- **CHECK:** Injector balance test. Use CHART C-2A.
- **CHECK:** Canister for fuel loading. Use CHART C-3.

IGNITION SYSTEM

- **CHECK:** Spark plugs, plug wires, and ignition components. Refer to ENGINE ELECTRICAL in the Electrical Systems Manual.

ADDITIONAL CHECKS

- **CHECK:** For vacuum leaks.
- **CHECK:** For lead contamination for catalytic converter (look for the removal of fuel filler neck restrictor).
- **CHECK:** Carbon build-up. Remove carbon with top engine cleaner. Follow instructions on can.
- **CHECK:** PCV valve for being plugged or stuck or fuel in the crankcase.
- **CHECK:** For correct MEM-CAL (see Service Bulletins).

DIESELING, RUN-ON

Definition: Engine continues to run after key is turned "OFF," but runs very roughly. If engine runs smoothly, check ignition switch and adjustment.

PRELIMINARY CHECKS

- Perform the careful visual/physical checks as described at start of "Symptoms," Section "6E3-B."

FUEL SYSTEM

- **CHECK:** Injectors for leaking. Refer to "Fuel System Diagnosis" CHART A-7.

BACKFIRE

Definition: Fuel ignites in intake manifold, or in exhaust system, making loud popping noise.

PRELIMINARY CHECKS

- Perform the careful visual/physical checks as described at start of "Symptoms," Section "6E3-B."

IGNITION SYSTEM

- **CHECK:** Proper ignition coil output voltage with spark tester J 26792 or equivalent (ST-125).
- **CHECK:** Spark plugs. Remove spark plugs, check for wet plugs, cracks, wear, improper gap, burned electrodes, or heavy deposits. Repair or replace as necessary.
- **CHECK:** Spark plug wires for crossfire, also inspect spark plug wires, and proper routing of plug wires.
- **NOTE:** If an intermittent condition exists in the ignition system, see "Ignition System/EST," Section "6E3-C4" or ENGINE ELECTRICAL in the Electrical Systems Manual.

ENGINE MECHANICAL

- **CHECK:** Compression - Look for sticking or leaking valves.
- **CHECK:** Valve timing, refer to ENGINE MECHANICAL DIAGNOSIS (SECTION 6A).
- **CHECK:** Intake and exhaust manifold passages for casting flash.
- **CHECK:** Balancer rings for bent or missing vanes.

FUEL SYSTEM

- **CHECK:** Perform fuel system diagnosis check, see CHART A-7.
- **CHECK:** Fuel Injectors. Perform injector balance test, refer to CHART C-2A.

ADDITIONAL CHECKS

- **CHECK:** Intake and exhaust manifold for casting flash.

Breakout Box

Some diagnostic procedures require testing of individual components such as sensors, output devices, and control modules with all the electrical connections in place. This normally requires the use of a breakout box and a number of test lead adapters **(Figure 2–8).** The breakout box connectors are fitted between wiring harness connectors on the vehicle in a manner that keeps the sensors, output devices, and control module connected so that the vehicle can be operated during testing. This allows the technician to perform a number of checks and tests under actual operating conditions. Refer to the wiring diagrams in the service manual to locate wiring connectors and circuits and the test procedures in each case. Each test is independent of the others. Within each test there are test sequences that can identify a condition or a problem without requiring the completion of the entire test procedure. The test strategy usually involves the following steps.

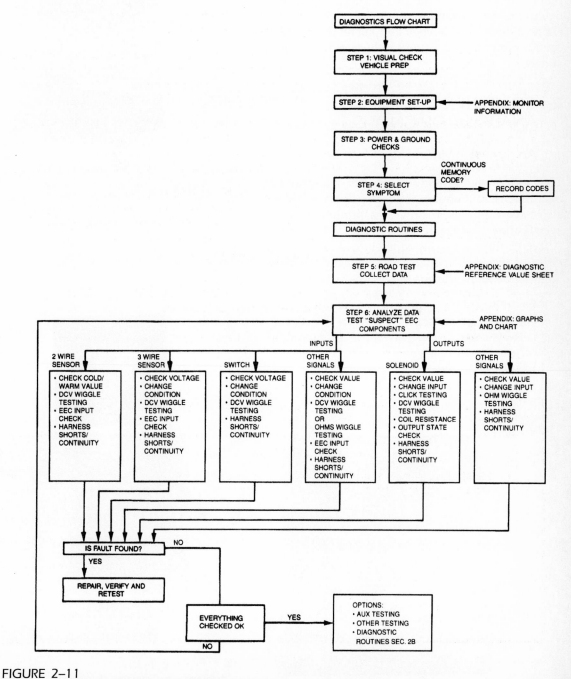

■ FIGURE 2–11
Diagnostic flow chart for Ford EEC-IV monitor box. Study the procedure carefully. (Courtesy of Ford Motor Company.)

1. Check the voltage or resistance value.
2. Change the input signal.
3. Perform a click test.
4. Perform a wiggle test.
5. Perform a coil resistance test.
6. Perform an output signal test.
7. Check for harness shorts.
8. Check for harness opens.

See **Figure 2–11** for an example of test strategies for solenoids, relays, computer output signals, and computer input signals. Consult the service manual to determine the meaning of devices identified by abbreviations. Terminology and abbreviations differ considerably among various vehicle manufacturers and service manuals.

■ COMPUTER ENGINE ANALYZER DIAGNOSIS

Analyzer Components

The modern engine analyzer consists of a set of test instruments, a computer, and a display screen. Many also have a printer to provide a printed record of specifications and test results **(Figures 2–12 to 2–14).** Although there are many different makes and models of analyzer, their function is basically the same. Some of the more obvious differences include:

- *Controls:* rotary switches, pushbuttons, keyboard, remote control
- *Display screen:* digital, waveform, color monitor
- *Meters:* digital, analog
- *Exhaust gas analyzer:* built in or separate

■ FIGURE 2–13
Diagnostic computer engine analyzer with printout capability. (Courtesy of Alltest.)

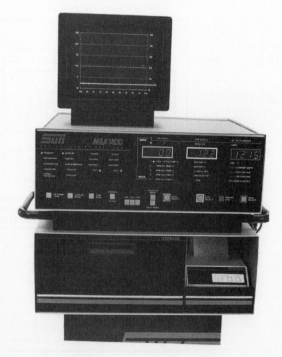

■ FIGURE 2–14
Modular computer engine analyzer allows user to choose from a number of available modules to custom design the analyzer. (Courtesy of Sun Electric Corporation.)

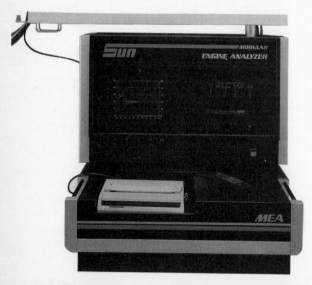

■ FIGURE 2–12
Modular computer engine analyzer with remote control and printer. (Courtesy of Sun Electric Corporation.)

- *Printer:* records test data
- *Data entry:* bar code and cards, compact disc
- *Modem:* access to mainframe computer data

Engine analyzers typically have the following kinds of test equipment:

1. Voltmeter, ammeter, ohmmeter
2. Tachometer
3. Dwellmeter
4. Timing light
5. Cylinder balance tester
6. Vacuum gauge
7. Vacuum pump
8. Exhaust gas analyzer
9. Display screens, oscilloscope, color monitor
10. Printer
11. Modem

Engine analyzers are normally used to check the following:

1. Battery
2. Charging system components
3. Starting system components
4. Ignition system components
5. Fuel system components
6. Emission control systems components
7. Exhaust emissions
8. Engine condition
9. Computer control systems

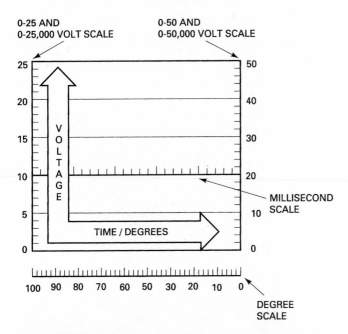

■ FIGURE 2–15
Height of display pattern on oscilloscope screen indicates voltage. Horizontal display indicates time (in milliseconds) and degrees of rotation. (Courtesy of F T Enterprises.)

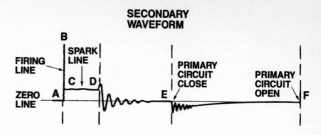

■ FIGURE 2–16
Typical secondary voltage display pattern. (Courtesy of Champion Spark Plug Company.)

Wave Form Displays

Wave forms have horizontal and vertical dimensions. The vertical dimensions represent positive and negative voltage values. Wave forms above the zero line are positive, while lines below the zero line are negative. Voltage values may be displayed on different scales, depending on the voltage scale selected. For example, a typical voltage scale on the left side of the screen may be used to display voltages from 0 to 25 V or 0 to 25,000 V. The scale on the right side can display values from 0 to 5 V or from 0 to 50,000 V. The term *kilovolts* (kV) is often used to express large voltage values. One kilovolt equals 1000 volts; therefore, 50 kV represents 50,000 V. Voltage values are useful in determining whether the ignition, starting, charging, and other electrical system voltage output is within specifications.

The horizontal dimensions of a wave form represent time in relation to degrees of crankshaft rotation or actual time in milliseconds. One millisecond is one thousandth of a second. Horizontal dimensions are important in determining whether the firing time, coil oscillation time, dwell time, fuel injection time, and alternator output are within acceptable limits **(Figures 2–15** and **2–16);** see **Figures 2–17** to **2–27** for explanation of typical wave forms.

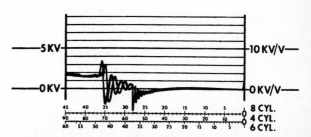

■ FIGURE 2–17
Superimposed pattern has all cylinders displayed on top of each other for comparison. (Courtesy of Sun Electric Corporation.)

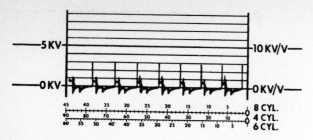

■ FIGURE 2–18
Parade pattern displays all cylinders individually across the screen. (Courtesy of Sun Electric Corporation.)

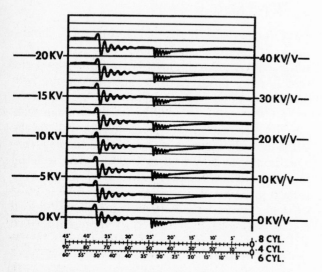

■ FIGURE 2–19
Raster (stacked) pattern shows all cylinders in vertical display for comparison. (Courtesy of Sun Electric Corporation.)

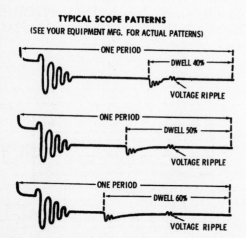

■ FIGURE 2–20
Variation in dwell time between cylinders on some GM HEI electronic ignitions is normal. (Courtesy of General Motors Corporation.)

■ FIGURE 2–21
Maximum coil voltage output using the secondary display pattern. Low-voltage spikes indicate normal required plug firing voltage. High-spike is the result of a disconnected plug wire. (Courtesy of Ford Motor Company.)

Digital Display

Most modern engine analyzers have a display feature. Engine electrical systems, fuel system, and emission control system performance values are displayed in easy-to-read lists **(Figure 2–27)**.

Analyzer Printer

A printer is often used with an engine analyzer to provide a printed record of test results that can be used to show actual before and after tune-up test results **(Figure 2–28)**. The printer may be integrated with the analyzer or it may be a free-standing unit.

Cylinder Balance Test (Typical)

A cylinder balance test is performed to determine whether all cylinders are producing equal power. It is also called a power balance test. In this test the

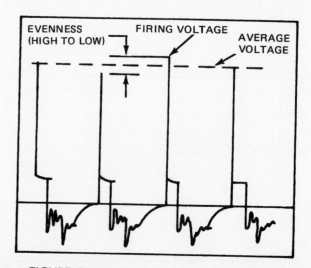

■ FIGURE 2–22
Variation between firing voltage spikes should not exceed 5KV. (Courtesy of Ford Motor Company.)

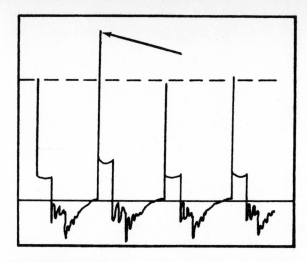

■ FIGURE 2–23
A consistently high-firing voltage spike in one or more cylinders may be caused by a wide spark plug gap, badly eroded spark plug electrode, disconnected spark plug wire, open spark plug wire, or excessive rotor gap (in distributor systems). (Courtesy of Ford Motor Company.)

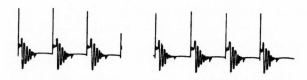

■ FIGURE 2–24
This pattern indicates a fouled spark plug at the low voltage spike. (Courtesy of Ford Motor Company.)

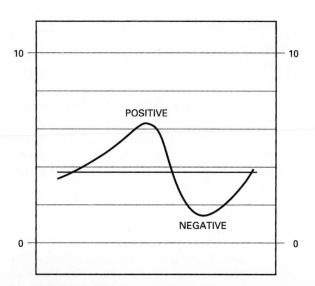

■ FIGURE 2–25
Electronic ignition pickup coil display shows normal peak positive and negative voltages on low voltage scale. (Courtesy of F T Enterprises.)

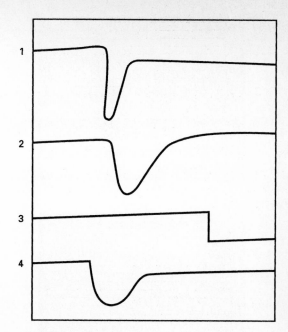

■ FIGURE 2–26
Electronic injector wave forms. 1) normal; 2) injector sticking; 3) open injector; 4) partially shorted injector solenoid. (Courtesy of F T Enterprises.)

power output of each cylinder is compared to that of all the other cylinders. As each cylinder is shorted, there should be a noticeable drop in engine speed. If one or more cylinders show little or no rpm drop, those cylinders have a problem. The problem could be leaking valves, worn cylinders and rings, a leaking head gasket, or a faulty ignition or fuel system.

PRO TIP:

Before proceeding with a power balance test, refer to the service manual for any special precautions or procedures that may be required. Due to the many variations in ignition, fuel, and emission control systems, special precautions or procedures may be necessary. Some of these are:

1. Disconnect the vacuum or electrical connection to disable the EGR valve. EGR valve cycling during the test can cause faulty readings.

2. On engines with an oxygen sensor disconnect and plug the air injection hose going to the catalytic converter or the hose going from the switching valve to the check valve. On engines without an oxygen sensor, disconnect and plug the air pump on the valve side. Air leakage in the system can upset test readings.

3. Bypass the electric cooling fan control with a jumper wire so that the fan runs continually. Cooling fan cycling affects rpm readings.

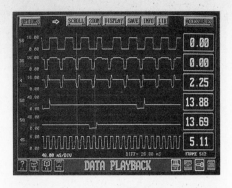

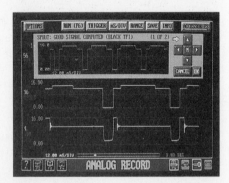

```
SERIAL STREAM DATA

1983 OLDSMOBILE 305 CID
ENGINE CODE = Y

PROM ID = 3303

NO FAULT CODES


COOLANT = + 85 DEG C +185 DEG F    282 OHMS
VACUUM + 61.9 KPA  .89 PSI 3.94 V
MPH                          0
RPM                          800
OXYGEN                       .83 V
AIR CONTROL SOLENOID         ON
AIR SWITCH SOLENOID          OFF
EGR SOLENOID                 OFF
TRANSMISSION CONVERTER
    CLUTCH SOLENOID          OFF
AIR/FUEL SOLENOID TEST       OFF
EGR ENABLED                  YES
THROTTLE WIDE OPEN           NO
3RD GEAR SWITCH              CLOSED
TPS                          10 %
                             .54 V
DUTY CYCLE                   72 %
                             3.74 V
CARBURETOR                   RICH
LOOP                         CLOSED
```

■ **FIGURE 2–28**

Engine analyzer printout provides permanent record of before and after tests. (Courtesy of Bear Automotive Equipment.)

4. To prevent unburned fuel from overloading and overheating the catalytic converter, short each cylinder no longer than 15 seconds. Let the engine run for at least 30 seconds before shorting another cylinder.

5. Disconnect the idle speed control or idle air control to prevent the computer from increasing the throttle opening to compensate for shorted cylinders.

Test Procedure

1. Connect the engine analyzer leads according to the instructions supplied with the equipment.

2. Start the engine and run it until it reaches operating temperature.

3. Turn off all accessories, such as air conditioning, that might interfere with test readings.

4. Stabilize engine speed at about 1000 rpm.

5. Short each cylinder in turn and note the drop in rpm for each cylinder.

If all the readings are nearly even, all cylinders are producing power equally and the engine can be assumed to be in good mechanical condition. If one or more cylinders shows little or no drop in rpm, a problem is indicated. Further tests are then required to determine whether the problem is mechanical (compression test), in the fuel system (Chapter 7), or in the ignition system (Chapter 6).

Engine Acceleration Test

An acceleration test may cause a problem to show up on the analyzer screen that is not evident at idle speeds. Higher voltage is required to fire the spark plugs during acceleration. This puts greater demands on the ignition system that may result in breakdown at higher speeds. To perform an acceler-

■ **FIGURE 2–27**

Various analyzer displays. Top, six different wave form displays at one time; second, graphic display of diagnostic information; third, automated sweep test of sensors, actuators, grounds and reference voltages; bottom, comparing wave form from test vehicle to known good wave form stored in analyzer software. (Courtesy of Sun Electric Corporation.)

ation test, set the scope on parade. While watching the firing lines on the scope, quickly snap the throttle valve open and then release it. The firing voltage should increase to about 20 kV on electronic ignition systems. If firing lines are too high or too low, a problem is indicated. Firing lines that are too high place excessive demands on the ignition system and indicate excessive secondary resistance. Firing lines that are too low may indicate low compression, shorting, or fouling of plugs.

Ignition Coil Output Test

An ignition coil output test can be performed on some engines with an engine analyzer.

CAUTION: On some engines this test is not allowed, due to possible damage to the ignition system. Check the service manual for information.

To perform a coil output test, set the analyzer on display or parade. Run the engine at about 1000 rpm. Using insulated pliers remove one spark plug wire and hold it away from ground. Read the voltage at the top of the firing line. Compare this voltage to specifications. Depending on the type of ignition system, coil output voltage should be from about 25 to 40 kV. If voltage is below specifications, check the secondary circuit condition before replacing the coil. Excessive secondary resistance reduces secondary output.

Sensor Testing with an Oscilloscope

The modern oscilloscope is capable of testing a variety of sensors and actuators: electrical circuit signals such as pickup coil output, O_2 sensor output, EGR sensor output, crankshaft position sensor output, fuel injector waveforms, and the like. Test capability includes AC, DC, and digital output (**figures 2–27** and **2–28**). The test sequence and test procedures are not the same among the different types of oscilloscopes. Follow the equipment manufacturer's procedures and test sequence for safety and accuracy.

■ COMPRESSION TESTING

Gasoline Engine

Cylinder compression tests are performed to determine cylinder compression pressures in comparison with each other and with specifications. Compression pressures may be lower than specified for the following reasons:

- Leakage past the valves (burned valves)
- Leakage past the rings (worn or broken rings)
- Leakage past a cylinder head gasket, particularly between adjacent cylinders (blown head gasket)
- Low cranking speed (low battery charge or high-current-draw starter)

Compression pressure considerably above specifications indicates carbon buildup in the combustion chamber and on the piston head. To perform a compression test, proceed as follows with a tester capable of 200 psi (1300 to 1400 kPa) (**Figure 2–29**).

1. The engine should be at operating temperature.
2. The battery and cranking system should be in good condition. Remove the air cleaner.
3. Carefully remove the spark plug wires from the spark plugs. Do not pull on the high-tension wire since this will damage the wires. Grasp the plug boot by hand or with the appropriate tool. Twist and pull the boot from the plug.
4. Loosen all spark plugs one full turn only. Blow any dirt or carbon from the spark plugs to prevent entry of dirt into the cylinders when the plugs are removed. Remove the spark plugs.

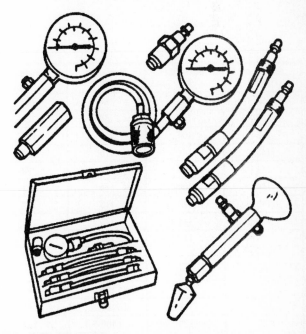

■ FIGURE 2–29
Compression gauges and adapters. Both screw-in and push-in gauges are shown. (Courtesy of Ford Motor Company.)

PRO TIP

Removing spark plugs from aluminum heads at operating temperature may damage threads. Cooldown may be required before plug removal.

5. Disable the ignition system usually by disconnecting the primary wire from the coil. Disable the fuel injection system to prevent fuel spray during the compression test. Consult the service manual for the proper procedure. Removing the appropriate fuse is common practice.

6. Remove all spark plugs, keeping them in order so that you know which plug came from each cylinder. This allows spark plugs to be analyzed to help determine cylinder condition.

7. Block the throttle body plates fully open during compression tests to prevent air intake restriction during testing.

8. Starting with the number 1 cylinder, install a screw-in or hold-in adapter into the spark plug hole in a manner that will prevent any pressure leakage through the spark plug hole. Crank the engine through at least five compression strokes; note the highest compression reading. Repeat the test on each of the remaining cylinders, cranking the engine the same number of strokes as were needed to obtain the highest reading on the number 1 cylinder.

9. Record the results of each cylinder tested.

Analyze the results of the compression test as follows:

1. *Normal.* Compression builds up quickly and evenly to specified pressure on each cylinder.

2. *Low readings.* Use one tablespoon of SAE 30 engine oil squirted into cylinders that have a low reading and repeat the compression test for that cylinder. If compression pressure increases considerably as a result, leakage past the piston rings is the cause. If compression pressure does not increase appreciably, leakage past the valve or head gasket is indicated.

3. *Very low readings on adjacent cylinders.* This would indicate a blown head gasket between the affected cylinders.

4. *Excessively high readings.* This would indicate a buildup of carbon deposits in the combustion chamber. This condition is usually also evidenced by pinging on acceleration and may also cause preignition and detonation. Carbon deposits should be removed only as specified by the vehicle manufacturer.

5. *Comparison between cylinders.* For cylinders to produce relatively even power output, compression pressures should be similar within certain limits. Some manufacturers allow a maximum difference in pressures between cylinders of 20 to 25%. A greater than 30% difference requires repair of the affected cylinder **(Figure 2–30).**

Maximum PSI	Minimum PSI	Maximum PSI	Minimum PSI	Maximum PSI	Minimum PSI	Maximum PSI	Minimum PSI
134	101	164	123	194	145	224	168
136	102	166	124	196	147	226	169
138	104	168	126	198	148	228	171
140	105	170	127	200	150	230	172
142	107	172	129	202	151	232	174
144	108	174	131	204	153	234	175
146	110	176	132	206	154	236	177
148	111	178	133	208	156	238	178
150	113	180	135	210	157	240	180
152	114	182	136	212	158	242	181
154	115	184	138	214	160	244	183
156	117	186	140	216	162	246	184
158	118	188	141	218	163	248	186
160	120	190	142	220	165	250	187
162	121	192	144	222	166		

■ FIGURE 2–30

Typical maximum and minimum compression pressures for gasoline engines. (Courtesy of Ford Motor Company.)

Diesel Engine

To perform a compression test on a diesel engine, proceed as follows with a tester capable of 500 psi (3450 kPa).

1.   The engine should be at operating temperature.
2.   The batteries and cranking system should be in good condition.
3.   Remove the air cleaner.
4.   Disable the fuel system and glow plug system. This may require disconnecting a fuel solenoid lead on some models, as well as glow plug connections. Refer to the service manual for the procedure to follow.
5.   Remove either the glow plugs or injectors to allow installation of the compression tester. Some engines are compression tested through the glow plug holes, while others are tested through the injector holes. Compression testers may be equipped with screw-in or clamp-in adapters, depending on application.
6.   Install the compression tester into the number 1 cylinder.
7.   Crank the engine through at least six compression strokes. Note the highest compression reading and the number of strokes required to obtain the reading. Repeat the test on each of the remaining cylinders, cranking the engine the same number of strokes as were required to obtain the highest reading for the number 1 cylinder.
8.   Record the results from all cylinders.

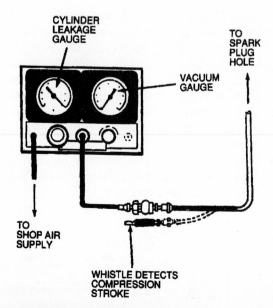

**CYLINDER
LEAKAGE
GAUGE**

**TO
SPARK
PLUG
HOLE**

**VACUUM
GAUGE**

**TO
SHOP AIR
SUPPLY**

**WHISTLE DETECTS
COMPRESSION
STROKE**

■   FIGURE 2–31

Cylinder leakage tester. (Courtesy of Ford Motor Company.)

Analyze the test results as follows:

1.   *Normal.* Compression builds up quickly and evenly to specified compression pressure on all cylinders.
2.   *Piston ring leakage.* Compression low on the first stroke but tends to build up on following strokes. Does not reach normal cylinder pressure.

PRO TIP

Due to the high compression ratio of diesel engines and the very small combustion chamber volume, do not add oil to any cylinder for compression testing. Extensive engine damage can result from this procedure.

■ CYLINDER LEAKAGE TESTING

A cylinder leakage test can be performed to determine whether compression pressures are able to leak past the rings into the crankcase, past the exhaust valves into the exhaust system, or past the head gasket into the engine coolant. Shop air pressure of 100 to 150 psi (700 to 1000 kPa) is required for this test. A leakage tester is shown in **Figure 2–31.**

To perform a cylinder leakage test proceed as follows:

1.   The engine should be at operating temperature.
2.   Carefully remove the spark plug wires from the spark plugs as outlined for the compression test for gasoline engines.
3.   Remove the air cleaner. Disconnect the battery ground cable at the battery.
4.   Perform steps 4, 6, and 7 as outlined under the compression test for gasoline engines.
5.   Install an air line adapter into the number 1 cylinder.
6.   Remove the crankcase oil dipstick, oil filter cap, and radiator cap.
7.   Turn the crankshaft to the position number 1 piston at TDC position on the compression stroke. Make sure that the piston is exactly at TDC on the upstroke of the compression stroke. This is important for three reasons. First, the piston will be forced down by shop air if not exactly at the TDC position. Second, the piston rings should be at the bottom of their grooves for this test. Moving the piston up will do this. Third, both valves are closed with the piston in this position.
8.   Now connect shop air to the adapter in the number 1 cylinder.
9.   Listen for air leakage into the exhaust system at the tailpipe. If present, this indicates exhaust

■ FIGURE 2–32
Ultrasonic vacuum leak detector. (Courtesy of Mac Tools, Inc.)

■ FIGURE 2–33
Oil leak detector kit. (Courtesy of Ford Motor Company.)

valve leakage. Listen for air leakage at the air intake. If present, this indicates intake valve leakage. Listen for air leakage at the oil filler cap or dipstick tube. If present, this indicates leakage past the rings. Listen for leakage at the spark plug holes of cylinders adjacent to the one being tested. If present, this indicates cylinder head gasket leakage to the cooling system.

10.   Disconnect the shop air line from the cylinder adapter and repeat the test procedure for all cylinders.

■ VACUUM LEAK TESTING

Vacuum leaks can cause engine problems such as too lean an air–fuel mixture and rough idle. Vacuum leaks are easily located with a leak detector **(Figure 2–32)**. It is a self-powered unit and will detect vacuum leaks in the engine intake system and in vacuum control systems. A quick check can be made by squirting some SAE 30 engine oil on the suspected area. If this corrects the malfunction (rough idle, hiss), the leak has been located.

■ OIL LEAK DETECTION

The use of a dye additive and a black light makes detection of oil leaks somewhat easier. The procedure is to add a special fluorescent dye to the engine oil, then operate the engine to disperse the dye thoroughly in the oil. The suspected leakage areas are thoroughly cleaned. Next, the engine is operated until leakage occurs. Inspection with the black light will determine if it is engine oil that is leaking since it will glow under the black light **(Figure 2–33)**.

■ COMBUSTION LEAK TESTING

Combustion gases can enter the cooling system through a defective head gasket or minute cracks in the cylinder head or block. There are several ways to detect whether combustion gases are present in the cooling system.

1.   Use an exhaust gas infrared tester to check the air space in the top of the radiator tank. Do not contact the coolant with the tester probe.

2.   Use a combustion leak tester. Draw the vapors from the top of the radiator tank through the chemical test solution. The test solution will turn from blue to yellow if combustion gases are present.

Combustion leaks into the coolant require engine disassembly to correct.

■ TUNE-UP PROCEDURE

An engine tune-up is performed to restore (as much as possible) an engine to its new car performance, reliability, and economy. To do this, any part that is defective must be overhauled or replaced as necessary to correct any problems diagnosed, at the same time reducing vehicle emissions to specified limits. If the engine is not mechanically sound, a tune-up will not restore its full potential. The principle of good tune-up is to determine whether the following four conditions are present in sufficient quantity and quality to ensure good performance and economy, and to meet emissions standards.

1.   *Adequate compression.* Poor compression indicates a mechanically unsound engine, which should be corrected before a tune-up can be performed properly.

2.   *Correct air/fuel ratio.* An air/fuel ratio that is too rich or too lean or of insufficient quantity will adversely affect performance, economy, and emissions.

3. *Adequate ignition at the spark plugs at the correct time.* The spark at the spark plug gaps must be of sufficient intensity and duration to promote good combustion of the air–fuel mixture. The spark must occur at each spark plug at the correct time every time the piston is in a position to be fired.

4. *Low exhaust emissions.* The tune-up must result in achieving exhaust emission levels that meet emission standards prescribed by law.

An orderly sequence of service operations to be performed is essential to systematic diagnosis and faulty correction in any tune-up. The following tune-up procedures can be used to achieve good results. Always use fender covers and abide by the general precautions given in each chapter. Refer to the appropriate chapter for inspection and service of the different engine systems. The order in which these operations are performed will vary with vehicle make and model and with test results.

1. Identify the customer's complaint **(See Figure 2–2).**
2. Activate self-diagnosis on computer-controlled engines to obtain fault codes or perform engine analysis with the engine analyzer. (See Chapter 4 for details about self-diagnosis procedures.)
3. Check and correct all fluid levels.
4. Check the fluid lines and hoses for condition, routing, and leaks.
5. Check the vacuum lines for condition, routing, and leaks.
6. Check the wiring and harness connectors for condition and routing.
7. Check the drive belts for condition and tension.
8. Clean and inspect the battery and cable connections.
9. Test the battery.
10. Test the cranking voltage and/or starter draw.
11. Test the alternator output, voltage, and current.
12. Test the ignition timing and timing advance (centrifugal, vacuum).
13. Test the ignition coil input and output.
14. Inspect the distributor cap and rotor.
15. Inspect and test the secondary wires.
16. Perform a cylinder balance test.
17. Perform a compression test.
18. Replace or service the spark plugs.
19. Test or replace the PCV valve.
20. Replace the fuel filter and air filter.
21. Inspect the exhaust system for leaks and restriction.
22. Test the heated intake air system.
23. Test the manifold heat control valve operation.
24. Test the EGR valve operation.
25. Test the secondary air injection system.
26. Adjust the valve lash (if required).

■ ADJUSTING THE VALVES

The objective in adjusting the solid lifter valve train is to provide sufficient valve lash (clearance) to allow for any thermal expansion of parts and still ensure that valves will be fully seated when closed. At the same time, there must not be excessive lash, which would retard valve timing and cause rapid wear of valve train parts. The objective in adjusting the automatic lash adjuster valve train is to center the plunger in the lash adjuster. This provides zero lash in operation and allows the lash adjusters to automatically compensate for wear or expansion and contraction of valve train parts.

A static valve adjustment is required after an engine overhaul to ensure proper engine starting and prevent damage to the valves from pistons striking the valves. Normally, if the static valves are adjusted accurately, no further valve adjustment is required unless the cylinder heads are tightened. Valve adjustment may be done as a routine service procedure when there is no engine overhaul involved. This is done with the engine stopped or running at a slow idle speed. In this case provision must be made to prevent oil from squirting and spraying over other engine parts. When adjusting a hydraulic lifter valve train, the adjusting screw or nut must be turned down slowly to allow for lifter leakdown and to prevent the valve from being held open when it should be closed. Care must be taken not to overadjust and cause the lifters to bottom out and damage valve train parts. Adjustment should only be made within the limits prescribed in the manufacturer's shop manual.

Adjusting Solid Lifter Valves (Tappet Clearance)

This may be done with the engine cold or hot. Clearance specifications are usually 0.002 in. (0.05 mm) greater for cold engines than for hot engines. Follow the recommendation for hot or cold engine adjustment and the clearance specifications in the appropriate service manual.

Select the feeler gauge thickness for the clearance specified. Clearance is usually greater for hotter running exhaust valves than intake valves. Turn the crankshaft until the number 1 piston is near the top of the compression stroke. You can feel air coming

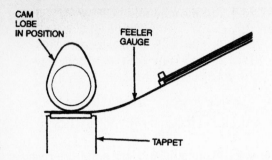

■ FIGURE 2–34
Valve lash is checked with the cam follower on the base circle of the cam lobe. (Courtesy of Ford Motor Company.)

out of the spark plug hole as the piston comes up on this stroke. Do not turn too far. The intake and exhaust valves are both closed with the piston in this position (lifters on base circle of cam lobes). Both valves can now be adjusted **(Figure 2–34).**

Slide the correct feeler gauge between the valve stem tip and the rocker arm. If it will not go in, back off the rocker arm adjusting screw until it does. If there is a locknut on the screw, it must be loosened first. Tighten the adjusting screw until you feel a slight drag as you slide the feeler gauge back and forth. Then tighten the locknut, making sure that the adjustment does not change. Adjust both valves in the same manner. Follow the same procedure on the remaining cylinders.

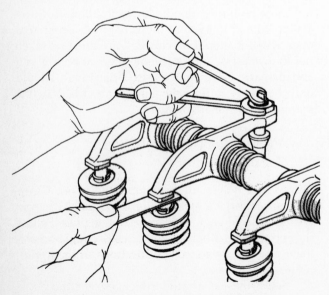

■ FIGURE 2–35
Adjusting valve lash on pushrod engine with solid lifter valve train. (Courtesy of Chrysler Corporation.)

When you adjust the number 1 cylinder first, you can proceed to do the other cylinders in the order of the engine's firing order. This allows you to turn the crankshaft only half a turn to place the next piston in the right position for adjustment and so on through the firing order on a four-cylinder engine. On a six-cylinder engine it would be one-third of a turn, and a quarter-turn on an eight-cylinder engine **(Figures 2–35** and **2–36).**

Nonadjustable Hydraulic Lifters

Some nonadjustable valve trains use selective-length pushrods to center the lifter plunger after valves and seats are ground. Special tools are used to determine the pushrod length required. Refer to the appropriate service manual for procedures **(Figure 2–37).** On other nonadjustable stud- or pedestal-mounted rocker arms, the nuts or bolts are simply tightened to the specified torque. Adjustment is achieved during the valve grinding procedure by correcting the valve stem length **(Figure 2–38).**

Adjusting Hydraulic Lifters (Adjustable Type)

Hydraulic lifters may be adjusted with the engine running or with the engine off. Many technicians prefer to adjust lifters with the engine running. To adjust hydraulic lifters with the engine running, first install oil spray stoppers or otherwise shield the oil spray from the rocker arms before starting the engine **(Figure 2–39).** With the engine running at operating temperature, tighten any noisy rockers just enough to stop all rocker clatter. Working from front to rear, adjust each rocker as follows.

1.   Loosen the adjustment until it clatters, then slowly tighten the adjuster just enough until it quiets down. This is the zero lash position. This position can also be established by turning the pushrod between the thumb and forefinger while slowly tightening the adjuster. Turning effort will increase at precisely the zero lash point **(Figure 2–40).**

2.   From the zero lash point, tighten the adjuster the additional specified amount. This is most often one additional turn of the adjuster. (Check in the service manual.) This will center the lifter plunger midway between its upper and lower travel limits in the lifter body. Be sure to tighten the adjuster slowly to prevent the engine from missing or stalling and to prevent the valve from being held open and struck by the piston.

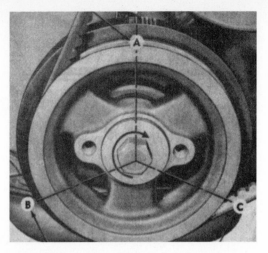
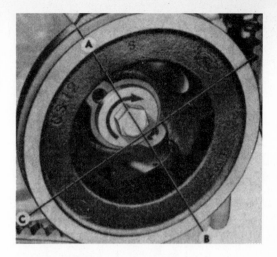

■ FIGURE 2–36

A static valve adjustment must be performed prior to starting an engine after a valve grind or overhaul to avoid pistons striking valves on startup. To adjust valves proceed as follows. 1) Put piston number one in firing position at TDC on the compression stroke; 2) adjust both valves for piston number one to specifications; 3) Turn crankshaft clockwise 120° for six cylinder engines, 90° for eight cylinder engines, and 180° for four cylinder engines. This places the next cylinder in the firing order sequence in position for valve adjustment; 4) adjust both valves for this cylinder; 5) repeat this procedure until all valves are adjusted. (Courtesy of Ford Motor Company.)

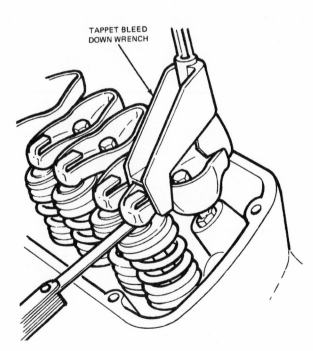

■ FIGURE 2–37

Checking tappet clearance while holding lifter in bled-down position. If clearance is incorrect, a different length pushrod must be used. (Courtesy of Ford Motor Company.)

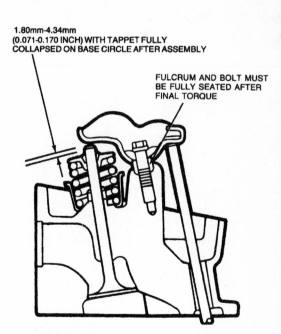

■ FIGURE 2–38

Nonadjustable valve train. Rocker arm bolt is tightened to specified torque during assembly. (Courtesy of Ford Motor Company.)

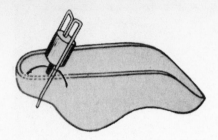

■ FIGURE 2–39
Rocker arm oil spray stopper. (Courtesy of Mac Tools, Inc.)

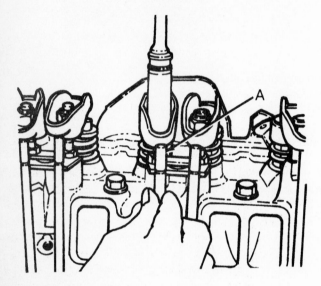

■ FIGURE 2–40
Establishing the zero lash point by turning the pushrod (A) while adjusting the rocker stud nut. (Courtesy of General Motors Corporation.)

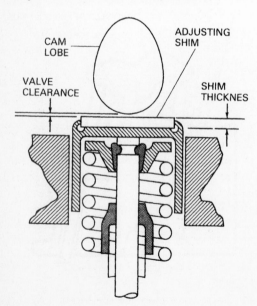

■ FIGURE 2–41
Close-up of adjusting shim location on OHC engine. (Courtesy of F T Enterprises.)

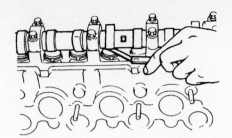

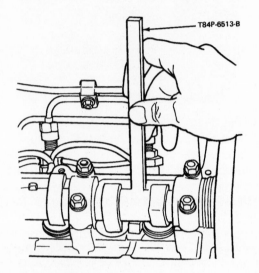

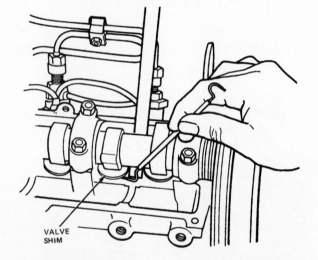

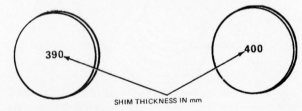

SHIM THICKNESS IN mm

■ FIGURE 2–42
Adjusting shimmed lash adjustment on OHC engine. Shim adjustment is used on several engine makes and models. Top, checking clearance; second from top, installing cam follower retaining tool; third from top, replacing adjusting shim; bottom, different shim sizes. (Courtesy of Ford Motor Co. of Canada Ltd.)

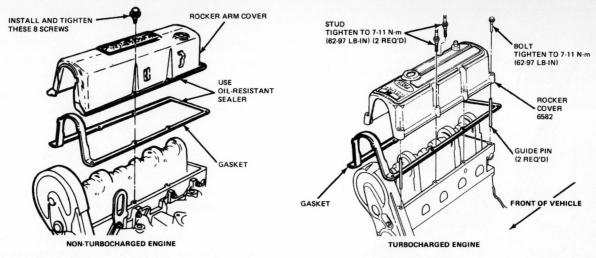

■ FIGURE 2–43

Valve cover installation instructions for Ford 2.3 liter engine. (Courtesy of Ford Motor Company.)

Adjusting the Overhead Cam Mechanical Valve Train

Solid valve train adjustment may be by an adjusting screw in the rocker arm or by selective thickness adjusting shims. Clearance is measured with a feeler gauge. The old shim is removed and measured with an outside micrometer to calculate the required thickness of the new shim and the new shim installed. The procedure for adjusting shim removal and installation varies. Refer to the appropriate service manual for procedure. One example of adjusting shim location is shown in **Figures 2–41** and **2–42.** A third method uses a screw adjustment which is part of the lifter.

Replacing the Valve Cover Gasket

Leaking valve covers are one of the more common locations of oil leakage. Valve covers are easily distorted, and if not straightened or replaced, may leak shortly after installation. Overtightening of screws or bolts is the most common problem. Valve covers are made of stamped steel, cast aluminum, or plastic. Valve covers use either silicone sealer or gaskets. Gaskets may be cork, rubberized cork, or synthetic rubber.

Make sure that the valve cover is clean and that there is no old sealer or gasket material left on the sealing surfaces. Check that the cover is not warped by placing it sealing surface down on a flat surface. The cover should make contact with the flat surface all the way around. Stamped steel covers can be straightened with a hammer. A pair of pliers can also be used. Be careful not to kink the metal. Warped plastic covers must be replaced. Cast aluminum covers can sometimes be trued by machining if not too severely warped.

On covers with gasket retaining clips or notches, position the gasket on the cover so that it will stay in position. On others apply a thin coat of adhesive on the contact surface around the cover. Allow it to become tacky, then stick the gasket in place on the cover (**Figure 2–43**). Do not use silicone sealer instead of a gasket on covers designed for use with a gasket. The gasket thickness provides clearance between the cover and the rocker arms in many cases. If silicone sealer is to be used, shimming between the cover and head at the screw holes is required in such instances. Use load spreading washers if so equipped (**Figure 2–44**).

On covers designed for use with silicone or RTV sealer, make sure that the sealing surfaces are clean and dry. Apply a continuous bead of sealer about $\frac{3}{32}$ in. (2.38 mm) to the sealing surface of the cover (**Figure 2–45**). Follow the instructions on the sealer package regarding time allowed to set. Install the valve covers and start the screws or bolts by hand. Tighten the screws in the specified sequence and to the specified torque. Over-tightening can crack the gasket or bend the cover, causing leakage. Covers with center-mount bolts are easily spread wider at the base by overtightening, allowing oil leakage.

■ FIGURE 2–44

Load-spreading washers are used on some engine valve covers. (Courtesy of F T Enterprises.)

■ FIGURE 2–45
Using RTV gasket maker on a valve cover. (Courtesy of Loctite Corporation.)

Diesel Engine Tune-up

A diesel engine tune-up differs somewhat from a tune-up on a gasoline engine. There are no spark plugs or an ignition system to service. Typical preventive maintenance procedures include the following.

1. Inspect and clean or replace the air filter element.
2. Drain water from water traps and filters.
3. Clean or replace fuel filters and bleed air from the fuel system.
4. Check and adjust the injection timing.
5. Check and adjust the engine idle speed.
6. Check operation of the throttle linkage.
7. Check operation of the emission control system.
8. Adjust valve lash as required.

Review Questions

1. Engine performance depends on the efficient operation of all _____ _____.
2. Fuel igniting ahead of the spark in the cylinder is called _____.
3. Main bearings that knock due to _____ _____ may also cause low oil pressure.
4. Piston slap is caused by too much _____ _____ _____.
5. Oil dilution is the result of _____ _____ getting past the _____ into the oil in the oil pan.
6. Camshaft wear can be checked without removing the camshaft. True or False.
7. Be sure to observe static electrical discharge precautions when handling electronic parts. True or False.
8. A cylinder balance test is performed to determine which _____ are producing equal _____.
9. Coil output voltage should be between _____ and _____.
10. When performing a compression test, should two adjacent cylinders have low compression this could be caused by _____, _____ and _____.
11. It is *not* possible to adjust hydraulic lifters without the engine running. True or False.
12. The PCV valve should always be checked when performing a tune up. True or False.

Test Questions

1. If an engine cranks normally but does not start,
    a. perform a spark intensity test
    b. observe the injector spray on throttle body injection systems while cranking the engine
    c. both of the above
    d. none of the above
2. If an engine starts but dies when the ignition key is released, the cause is a faulty
    a. injector feed
    b. ignition coil
    c. ignition coil feed
    d. computer feed
3. Misfiring may be caused by faulty
    a. spark plugs, wires, injectors, piston rings
    b. spark plugs, pistons, injectors
    c. injectors, spark plugs, wires
    d. wires, camshaft, spark plugs
4. Technician A says engine mechanical problems are the result of overloading the engine. Technician B says they are the result of overheating. Who is correct?
    a. Technician A
    b. Technician B
    c. both are correct
    d. both are wrong
5. Engine noise may be located with a stethoscope or
    a. a piece of rubber hose
    b. a piece of metal rod
    c. a vacuum gauge
    d. a compression gauge

6. Main bearing noise is most noticeable
   a. under no load at idle
   b. at no load at 3000 rpm
   c. under load or during acceleration
   d. under load or during deceleration

7. Piston slap is caused by too much
   a. piston to pin clearance
   b. piston to cylinder wall clearance
   c. oil on the rings
   d. or too little oil on the rings

8. When checking for worn valve guides during a road test
   a. while driving at 50 mph (80 km/h) take your foot off the gas pedal and watch for exhaust smoke
   b. while driving at 30 mph (50 km/h) accelerate rapidly to 50 mph (80 km/h) and watch for exhaust smoke
   c. have engine idle in neutral and watch for exhaust smoke
   d. run the engine at 3000 rpm and watch for exhaust smoke

9. Compression pressures that are too low are the result of
   a. carbon buildup
   b. excessive cranking speeds
   c. high compression ratios
   d. cylinder leakage

10. The scope pattern consists of the following three sections
    a. the primary, secondary, and intermediate
    b. the intermediate, secondary, and firing
    c. the firing, intermediate, and dwell
    d. the dwell, primary, and secondary

11. A very high firing spike on a scope pattern indicates
    a. low resistance in the primary circuit
    b. high resistance in the primary circuit
    c. low resistance in the secondary circuit
    d. high resistance in the secondary circuit

12. An oscilloscope primary circuit pattern does not show five distinct oscillations. Technician A says the pattern is similar to defective condenser pattern. Technician B says the coil primary winding may be defective. Who is correct?

    a. Technician A
    b. Technician B
    c. both are correct
    d. both are wrong

13. Basic ignition timing is important on engines with adjustable timing
    a. for more complete combustion and less emissions
    b. to make sure that all spark plugs will receive the same voltage
    c. to make sure the advance system is working
    d. to assure proper idle speed

14. A cylinder leakage test does *not* check for
    a. leakage past the rings
    b. leakage past the valves
    c. leakage past the gaskets
    d. leakage past the oil pump

15. If adding oil to a cylinder during a compression test increases pressure considerably, the problem with the cylinder is leakage past the
    a. intake valve
    b. piston rings
    c. exhaust valve
    d. head gasket

16. A cylinder balance test is performed to determine whether all cylinders
    a. are the same
    b. are the same weight
    c. produce equal power
    d. produce equal emissions

17. After shorting a cylinder during a cylinder balance test, how much time should be allowed before shorting the next cylinder?
    a. 60 seconds
    b. 6 seconds
    c. 3 seconds
    d. 30 seconds

18. To obtain maximum performance, minimum fuel consumption, and lowest emissions, there must be
    a. adequate cylinder compression
    b. correct air–fuel mixtures
    c. adequate spark at the correct time
    d. all of the above

3 Electrical Systems Diagnosis and Service Principles

■ ■ ■

INTRODUCTION

A remarkable electrical system is housed under the hood of an automobile. It produces electrical energy, stores it in chemical form, and delivers it on demand to any of the automobile's electrical systems—from low voltages, 0.5 V from some sensors, to as much as 40,000 V to the ignition system.

Many components are operated by electricity, the starting motor that cranks the engine, the ignition that keeps your car running after it has started, the lighting systems that light the road after dark and signal your intentions to other drivers, heating and air conditioning systems for passenger comfort, the instrument panel that tells the driver about vehicle operation, and the sound systems that entertain and inform the passengers. These are but a few of the many applications of electricity and electronics in the automobile.

A thorough understanding of how electricity acts is absolutely essential for the automotive technician to intelligently diagnose and service electrical and electronic systems and their components.

The automobile uses a variety of electrical and electronic devices. These range from a simple on/off switch to a computer capable of doing a multitude of jobs. The automotive technician should have a good understanding of how these devices operate in order to diagnose and correct electrical system problems successfully. The basic operation of these devices is described here, and examples of their use and repair are given as well. Chapter 4 deals with computers and computer control systems.

LEARNING OBJECTIVES

After completing this chapter, you should be able to:
- Describe electrical wiring, wiring harness, terminals, and connectors.
- Describe different types of manual and automatic electrical switches, solenoids, and relays.
- Describe permanent magnet motors and stepper motors.
- Describe different types of fuses, fusible links, circuit breakers, and voltage limiters.
- Describe different types of resistors and capacitors.
- Describe different types of transducers.
- Describe diodes and transistors.
- Identify, locate, and state the function of electrical and electronic devices on an automobile.
- Define volts, amperes, ohms, and Ohm's law.
- Define electrical power.
- Explain the operating characteristics of series, parallel, and series–parallel electrical circuits.
- Calculate resistance in a circuit.
- List common electrical problems.
- Use basic electrical test equipment to test electrical components.

TERMS YOU SHOULD KNOW

Look for these terms as you study this chapter and learn what they mean.

wires	insulation
conductors	wire size
solid wire	wire gauge
stranded wire	wire harness
primary wiring	clips
secondary wiring	retainers

boots
straps
tubing
terminals
connectors
crimping
soldering
locking device
wiring diagram
switch
manual switch
automatic switch
push-pull
rotary
toggle
slider
thermal switch
vacuum switch
pressure switch
relay
solenoid
fuse
fusible link
circuit breaker
voltage limiter
resistor
ballast resistor
potentiometer
rheostat
thermistor
capacitor
condenser
transducer
sensor

diode
zener diode
transistor
polarity
volts
electromotive force
potential difference
current
amperes
resistance
ohms
Ohm's law
electrical power
watts
circuit
series circuit
parallel circuit
series–parallel circuit
open
short
ground
feedback
jumper wire
test lamp
self-powered test light
circuit breaker
voltmeter
ohmmeter
ammeter
multimeter
VOM
digital multimeter
voltage drop

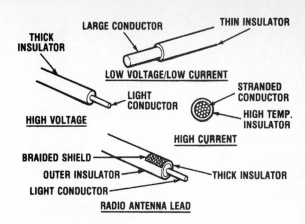

■ FIGURE 3–1
Different types of insulators and conductors are used in the automobile to carry the flow of electricity. Large-diameter conductors are required for high amperage. Heavily insulated smaller-diameter conductors are used for low amperage and high voltage. (Courtesy of Chrysler Corporation.)

Stranded wires are used throughout the automobile as electrical conductors for lights, accessories, and power-operated devices as well as for the charging and ignition systems. Soft-copper wire is used extensively for stranded wires because of its flexibility, low resistance, and low cost. Automotive wiring is further classified into primary and secondary wiring. All primary wiring carries low voltage and is used throughout the vehicle, with the exception of the ignition system secondary. Primary wiring is sufficiently insulated to prevent current loss with rubber, plastic, and other insulating materials. Secondary wiring is used in the ignition secondary system to conduct high-voltage current from the coil to the spark plugs. High-voltage secondary wiring has a heavy layer of synthetic material to prevent voltage loss and cross firing. Cross firing occurs when current jumps from one spark plug wire to the next due to deterioration of the insulating material.

■ ELECTRICAL WIRING

Electrical wires are used to conduct electricity to operate the electrical and electronic devices. There are two categories of automotive wiring: solid wires and stranded wires. Solid wires are single-strand conductors, while stranded wires are made up of a number of small solid wires twisted together to form a single conductor **(Figures 3–1** and **3–2).** The printed circuits used in instrument panels use solid conductors. They are flat strips of metal embedded on a flat insulating plate **(Figure 3–3).** Another example of solid wire is to be found in the stator windings of the alternator in the charging system.

■ FIGURE 3–2
Stranded wire is a group of wires twisted together and covered with insulation. Note that 12-gauge wire is larger than 16-gauge (not actual size). (Courtesy of Chrysler Corporation.)

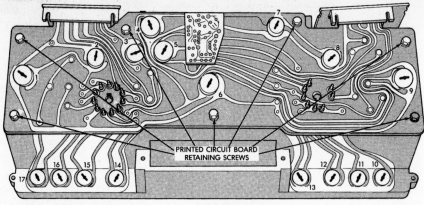

■ FIGURE 3–3
Printed instrument panel circuit
reduces the number of wires
required. (Courtesy of Chrysler
Corporation.)

1. Fuel and Voltmeter Illumination
2. Tachometer-Voltmeter Illumination
3. Airbag Warning
4. Tachometer Illumination
5. Check Gauges
6. Speedometer-Tachometer Illumination
7. Speedometer Illumination
8. Speedometer-Oil Gauge Illumination
9. Oil Pressure-Temperature Gauge Illumination
10. Fasten Seat Belt
11. Left Turn Signal
12. Brake System Warning
13. Low Fuel Warning
14. Oil Pressure Warning
15. High-beam Indicator
16. Right Turn Signal
17. Check Engine

Insulation

Low-voltage electrical wires are covered with a thermoplastic insulating material to prevent them from contacting other wires or metal parts. This contact must be prevented to avoid shorted circuits or unwanted grounding of the wires.

High-voltage electrical wires are covered with a flexible, high-temperature-resistant insulating material that will not break down under extreme conditions. Synthetic rubber and silicone are examples of this material.

Today's cars with several on-board computers use specially shielded twisted cable for protection from unwanted induced voltages that could interfere with computer operation **(Figure 3–4)**. Insulation also prevents deterioration by moisture, rust, and corrosion, all of which are detrimental to electrical system operation. Automotive wiring is color coded with solid colors, striping, or both to make tracing circuits easier.

Wire Sizes

The current-carrying capacity and the amount of voltage drop in an electrical wire are determined by the cross-sectional area or gauge of the wire and by its length and temperature. Doubling the length of a wire doubles its resistance, while doubling the cross-sectional area of a wire cuts its resistance in half. Large-diameter wires can carry higher current than can small-diameter wires.

Wire sizes are established by the Society of Automotive Engineers (SAE), which is the American Wire Gauge (AWG) system. Sizes are designated by a number system ranging from No. 0 to No. 20, with No. 0 being the largest and No. 20 the smallest in cross-sectional area. Most of the wiring in an automobile ranges from No. 10 to No. 18, with 12-V battery cables usually being No. 4 gauge. Interior and exterior lighting usually uses No. 16 or No. 18 gauge.

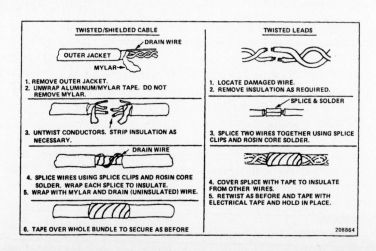

■ FIGURE 3–4
Typical wire repair procedure. (Courtesy of
General Motors Corporation.)

METRIC SIZE (mm²)	CURRENT GAUGE
0.5	20
0.8	18
1.0	16
2.0	14
3.0	12
5.0	10
8.0	8
13.0	6
19.0	4

■ FIGURE 3–5
Wire-size chart. (Courtesy of General Motors Corporation.)

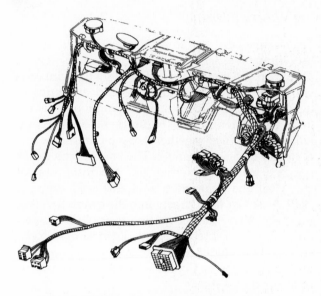

COMPLEX HARNESS

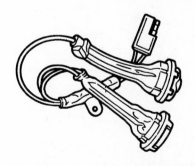

SIMPLE HARNESS

■ FIGURE 3–6
Typical wiring harnesses. (Courtesy of Chrysler Corporation.)

Metric wire sizes are designated in millimeters squared (mm²) of cross-sectional area. Metric and gauge sizes are compared in **Figure 3–5.**

Wire Harness

Wire harnesses are an assembled group of wires that branch out to the various electrical components of a vehicle. Groups of insulated wires are wrapped together with tape or inserted in insulating tubing to form a harness. There are several more complex wiring harnesses in an automobile as well as a number of simple harnesses. The engine compartment harness and the underdash harness are examples of a complex harness. Lighting and accessory circuits use a more simple harness **(Figure 3–6).**

The wiring harness makes for easier assembly and replacement and requires fewer supporting clips or clamps. A harness, however, makes it harder to locate a problem in the wires enclosed in it.

Supporting Clips and Devices

Proper routing and support of electrical wire is achieved with various types of insulated clips, retainers, boots, straps, and tubing. All of these are mounted to avoid any tension or stretching of the wiring. Without these devices wiring could chafe or come in contact with exhaust systems or moving parts **(Figure 3–7).**

Wire Terminals and Connectors

A variety of terminals and connectors is used to connect the wiring to the different electrical components in the automobile. This includes round connectors, spade or blade-type connectors, junction blocks, and bulkhead connectors **(Figure 3–8).** Connectors and terminals may be attached to the wiring by soldering or by crimping or both. Soldering fuses the solder to

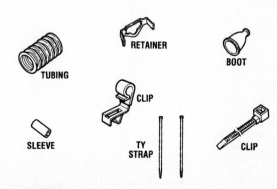

■ FIGURE 3–7
Wiring supports and clips. (Courtesy of Chrysler Corporation.)

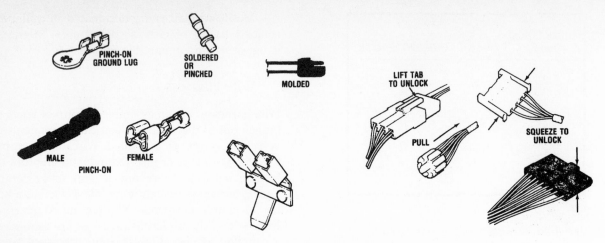

■ FIGURE 3–8

Common types of wiring terminals and connectors. (Courtesy of Chrysler Corporation.)

the wire and the terminal, making a good electrical connection as well as a good mechanical connection. Crimping squeezes the terminal tightly around the wire, actually partially biting into the wire. Crimping requires that both the terminal and the wire end be "electrically" clean to provide a good electrical connection. A good mechanical connection is not necessarily a good electrical connection.

Spade or blade terminals, junction blocks, and bulkhead connectors usually have locking devices or tabs to ensure that the connections do not come apart from vibration during vehicle operation. To disconnect these devices requires disengaging the locking device before pulling them apart. Pulling on the wires without unlocking the connection can cause the wires to be pulled out of their terminals. This would require repair or replacement of the harness.

Wiring Repairs

The fast and easy way to repair electrical wiring is to use crimp-style terminals and connectors. Remove about $\frac{3}{8}$ in. (10 mm) of insulation from the wire ends. Slip the terminal onto the wire end and crimp it tightly onto the wire with a crimping tool. This will form a good connection **(Figure 3–9).** Two pieces of wire can be joined together using a crimp-type connector in the same manner. The connections can be soldered using a soldering gun and rosin-core solder. Heat the connection with the soldering gun until the solder flows freely into the connection **(Figure 3–4).** Allow the connection to cool then tape it up with at least three layers of electrical tape. Never use acid-core solder for electrical repairs because of its corrosive effects. **Figure 3–10** shows another type of crimped wire repair.

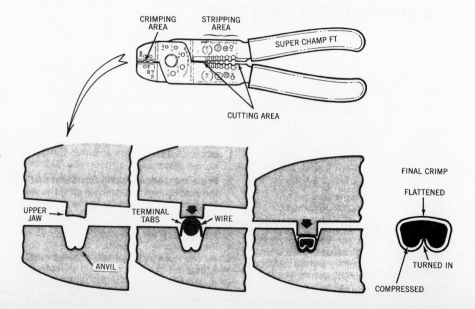

■ FIGURE 3–9

Using a wire cutting, stripping, and crimping tool. (Courtesy of Ford Motor Company.)

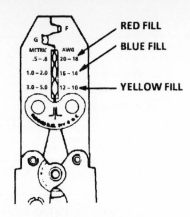

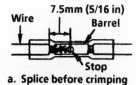

a. Splice before crimping

b. Splice after crimping

■ FIGURE 3–10

Crimping pliers (top) and insulated crimp connector wiring repair. Heating the crimp insulator shrinks and seals the insulation. (Courtesy of General Motors Corporation.)

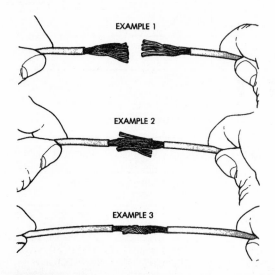

■ FIGURE 3–11

Braided wire repair. The braided ends are meshed, twisted, then soldered and taped. (Courtesy of Chrysler Corporation.)

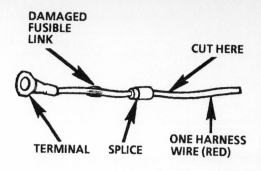

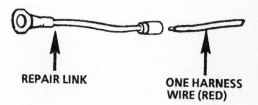

■ FIGURE 3–12

Typical fusible link repair. (Courtesy of General Motors Corporation.)

To join braided wires together without using a crimp connector, spread the exposed braided ends apart, then push them together and twist them tightly together. Heat the connection with a soldering gun until the solder flows freely into the connection. Allow the connection to cool, then tape it up **(Figure 3–11)**.

A burned-out fusible link is replaced with a new one using similar procedures **(Figure 3–12)**. Shielded twisted wiring used in computer control system wiring requires special procedures and special kinds of tape. Refer to the service manual for specific instructions.

■ WIRING DIAGRAMS

Wiring diagrams are provided in service manuals to show the electrical connections between the various electrical components and to show the routing of wires and wiring harness. Wiring diagrams use electrical symbols to identify electrical components. A symbol code chart is provided to help identify components correctly. Typical symbols are shown in **Figure 3–13**. Although a wiring diagram may appear complex at first glance, usually only one circuit at a time is dealt with making it relatively simple to follow. The insulated positive side is always shown in its entirety while the negative grounded side is often indicated only by a ground symbol.

LEGEND OF SYMBOLS USED ON WIRING DIAGRAMS			
+	POSITIVE	→»—	CONNECTOR
−	NEGATIVE	→—	MALE CONNECTOR
⏚	GROUND	>—	FEMALE CONNECTOR
FUSE symbol	FUSE	Y Y Y	MULTIPLE CONNECTOR
CIRCUIT BREAKER symbol	CIRCUIT BREAKER	⌐	DENOTES WIRE CONTINUES ELSEWHERE
CAPACITOR symbol	CAPACITOR	⋋	SPLICE
Ω	OHMS	◇J2◇2	SPLICE IDENTIFICATION
RESISTOR symbol	RESISTOR	◆◇	OPTIONAL WIRING WITH WIRING WITHOUT
VARIABLE RESISTOR symbol	VARIABLE RESISTOR	THERMAL symbol	THERMAL ELEMENT (BI-METAL STRIP)
SERIES RESISTOR symbol	SERIES RESISTOR	"Y" windings symbol	"Y" WINDINGS
COIL symbol	COIL	88:88	DIGITAL READOUT
STEP UP COIL symbol	STEP UP COIL	lamp symbol	SINGLE FILAMENT LAMP
OPEN CONTACT symbol	OPEN CONTACT	dual lamp symbol	DUAL FILAMENT LAMP
CLOSED CONTACT symbol	CLOSED CONTACT	LED symbol	L.E.D.-LIGHT EMITTING DIODE
CLOSED SWITCH symbol	CLOSED SWITCH	thermistor symbol	THERMISTOR
OPEN SWITCH symbol	OPEN SWITCH	gauge symbol	GAUGE
CLOSED GANGED SWITCH symbol	CLOSED GANGED SWITCH	TIMER	TIMER
OPEN GANGED SWITCH symbol	OPEN GANGED SWITCH	motor symbol	MOTOR
TWO POLE SINGLE THROW symbol	TWO POLE SINGLE THROW SWITCH	armature symbol	ARMATURE AND BRUSHES
PRESSURE SWITCH symbol	PRESSURE SWITCH	grommet symbol	DENOTES WIRE GOES THROUGH GROMMET
SOLENOID SWITCH symbol	SOLENOID SWITCH	□ #36	DENOTES WIRE GOES THROUGH 40 WAY DISCONNECT
MERCURY SWITCH symbol	MERCURY SWITCH	#19 STRG COLUMN	DENOTES WIRE GOES THROUGH 25 WAY STEERING COLUMN CONNECTOR
DIODE symbol	DIODE OR RECTIFIER	INST PANEL #14	DENOTES WIRE GOES THROUGH 25 WAY INSTRUMENT PANEL CONNECTOR
ZENER symbol	BY-DIRECTIONAL ZENER DIODE		RH983

Wiring diagrams normally provide the following information:

1. *Color coding of wiring:* different solid colors are used as well as colored wire with a striped tracer along the entire length of the wire.

2. *Wire and wiring harness connectors:* these indicate how wires are connected together and how they connect to the various electrical components.

3. *Drawings of electrical components:* line drawings of electrical components to make locating components on the wiring diagram easier.

4. *Electrical symbols:* used to identify smaller electrical components.

To use a wiring diagram locate the desired diagram in the appropriate service manual, verify that the color coding matches that of the vehicle being serviced, then follow the lines that are part of the affected circuit. Test the components in this circuit and make the necessary repairs.

■ SWITCHES, RELAYS, SOLENOIDS, AND MOTORS

Switches

Electrical switches are used to open and close electrical circuits. Some of these are operated manually; others operate automatically. Manually operated switches include the push-pull, toggle, rotary, and slider types. They are used to operate: headlamps, radios, tape players, speakers, heaters, air conditioners, rear window defoggers, windshield wipers, speed control, power seats, power door locks, power trunk locks, power gas fill locks, glow plugs, the ignition system, the starting system, trip and fuel calculators, and the like. Some are switched on manually but switch off automatically; others must be switched on and off manually.

Automatic switches include those controlled by heat, pressure, vacuum, solenoids, and relays. Heat-sensitive switches are used for coolant temperature indicators controlled by a thermal sending unit in contact with engine coolant. They may control cold engine temperature indicator lights as well as hot engine indicators. An example of a pressure-sensitive switch is the oil pressure indicator sending unit screwed into a main engine oil gallery. With the engine off, there is no oil pressure: the switch is closed. When the ignition switch is turned on, the oil pressure indicator light goes on. When the engine is

started and engine oil pressure rises above approximately 8 to 12 psi (55 to 82 kPa), the switch contacts separate, opening the circuit; then the dash indicator light goes out **(Figure 3–14).**

A vacuum-operated switch in the intake manifold sends an electrical signal to the engine control computer, which, in turn, adjusts the air/fuel ratio and ignition timing to suit engine speed and load. Intake manifold vacuum is an accurate indicator of engine load.

Relays

A relay is an electromagnetic switch in which a low current controls the operation of a higher current. Automobiles use relays to operate starters, horns, electric radiator fans, and convertible top circuits.

A relay consists of an electromagnetic coil winding, a stationary iron core, and a set of switch contacts. A control switch is used to control current to the relay coil circuit. Battery current is supplied to one of the relay contacts while the other contact is connected to the unit to be operated. When the control switch is closed, it supplies current to the electromagnet, which pulls the movable contact against the stationary contact, completing the circuit to the operating device. When the control switch is released (or opened), the relay contacts are pulled apart by spring tension since the electromagnetism

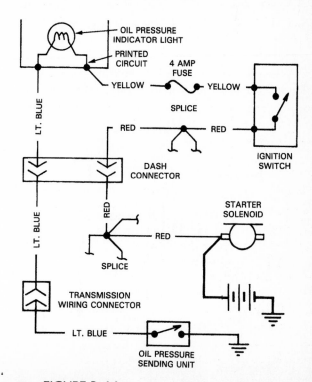

■ FIGURE 3–13 (Opposite)
Commonly used electrical wiring diagram symbols. (Courtesy of Chrysler Corporation.)

■ FIGURE 3–14
Oil pressure sending unit and dash indicator light wiring diagram. (Courtesy of Chrysler Corporation.)

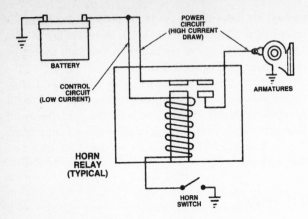

■ FIGURE 3–15
Horn relay schematic. Small amount of current from battery makes electromagnet out of coiled wire and core when horn switch completes circuit to ground. Magnetism pulls upper contact against lower contact to complete the circuit from battery to horns. (Courtesy of Chrysler Corporation.)

is no longer present **(Figure 3–15).** The use of a relay reduces the need for much long, heavy electrical wiring. Electronic control systems make extensive use of relays between the computer and the various output devices **(See Figure 3–19).**

Solenoids

A solenoid is an electromagnetic switch with a coil winding and a movable iron core. The movable iron core is connected to the device to be operated, such as a starting motor shift fork, power door lock, or deck lid release.

When the solenoid pull in winding (in a starter solenoid) is electrically energized, a magnetic field is

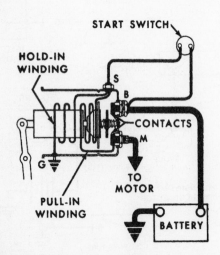

■ FIGURE 3–16
The starter solenoid is used to engage the starter pinion gear with the flywheel ring gear. (Courtesy of General Motors Company.)

created. This moves the core or plunger against the plunger spring. The plunger operates the shift fork or other device. When the solenoid is deenergized, spring pressure returns the plunger to its original position since the magnetic field is no longer present **(Figure 3–16).**

Solenoids are used in power door locks, power deck lids, automatic transmissions/transaxles, and the like.

Multifunction Switch

Many vehicles use a multifunction switch mounted on the steering column. This switch controls such items as windshield wipers and washers, signal lights, headlight dimmer, speed control, and hazard warning lights (see Chapter 12).

■ PERMANENT-MAGNET MOTORS

Many of the small motors used in automotive applications use permanent magnets, rather than electromagnets, to provide the stationary magnetic field. Since the field strength is constant, permanent-magnet motors provide constant-speed operation, and are used for such applications as windshield wipers, blower motors, window regulators, and seat positioners. Motor operation is very similar to starting motor operation described in Chapter 5.

The major differences are:

- Permanent-magnet fields are used on some starters as well.
- Motors carry much less current than starters since they carry much lighter loads.
- Motors are much smaller than starter motors.

Under normal operating conditions, motors are generally designed to last the life of the vehicle. Problems are usually the result of poor connections, poor ground, faulty switches or wiring, and the like. Faulty motors are normally replaced, not repaired.

■ STEPPER MOTORS

A stepper motor is an electric motor that turns in either direction on command from the computer. It turns only a small part of a turn at a time to adjust the controlled device with speed and precision. Stepper motors are used, for example, to control the idle air bypass on the throttle body of fuel injection systems. See Chapter 7 for details.

■ CIRCUIT PROTECTION DEVICES

Fuses

A chain is only as strong as its weakest link; when an overload is applied, the weakest link will break. In the same way, a fuse or a fusible link is the weakest point electrically in an electric circuit. It is needed to protect wiring and other components in the circuit from damage due to overloading of the circuit. Circuit overload can occur due to mechanical overload of the electrical device (i.e., windshield wiper motor, heater motor) or to shorts or grounds in the circuit.

Because of their lower current capacity, fuses and fusible links are designed to "blow" or "burn out" at a predetermined value, depending on the circuit capacity they are designed to protect. One type of fuse is the cylindrical glass type with the fusible link visible in the glass and connected at each end to a metal cap **(Figure 3–17)**. The metal capped ends snap into place between two spring clip connectors in the fuse holder. Another type is enclosed in transparent plastic and has two blade terminals that plug into corresponding connectors in the fuse holder **(Figure 3–18)**. Fuse capacity ranges anywhere from about 3 to 30 A. A failed fuse is easily identified by the gap in the wire visible in the fuse. The cause for fuse failure should be determined and corrected before fuse replacement. Replacement fuses should never exceed original fuse capacity. Fuses may be located in a fuse box in the instrument panel area or under the hood in a power distribution center or both **(Figure 3–19)**.

Fusible Links

A fusible link is a short piece of wire of smaller diameter than the wire in the circuit it is designed to protect. When the circuit is overloaded, it burns in two before damage can occur to the rest of the circuit. Fusible links are identifiable in the wiring harness by color code or by a tag attached to them. Fusible links are insulated in the same way as the rest of the circuit. A failed fusible link can often be identified by heat-damaged insulation or exposed wire. They are used in such circuits as charging and lighting systems **(Figures 3–20 and 3–21)**.

Circuit Breakers

Circuit breakers are designed for circuit protection, as are the fuse and the fusible link. The circuit breaker is more costly but has the advantage of opening and closing the circuit intermittently. In a headlight circuit, for example, the circuit breaker allows headlights to go on and off, which allows the driver to pull over to the side safely and stop. A fuse or fusible link failure in this circuit would cause the lights to go out completely, leaving the driver in the dark.

A circuit breaker has a pair of contact points, one of which is attached to a bimetal arm **(Figure 3–22)**. The arm and contacts are connected in series

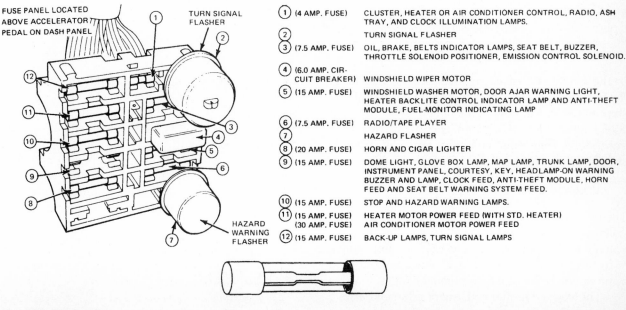

■ FIGURE 3–17

Individual circuit overload protection is provided by fuses or circuit breakers as shown in this fuse block. (Courtesy of Ford Motor Co. of Canada Ltd.)

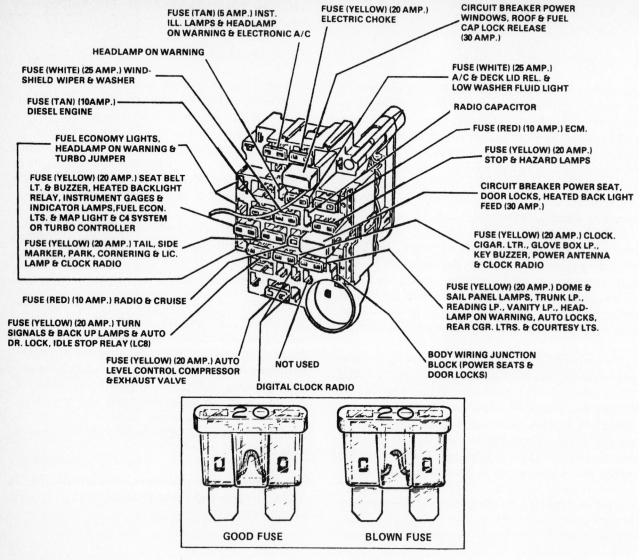

FUSE (TAN) (5 AMP.) INST. ILL. LAMPS & HEADLAMP ON WARNING & ELECTRONIC A/C

HEADLAMP ON WARNING

FUSE (WHITE) (25 AMP.) WIND-SHIELD WIPER & WASHER

FUSE (TAN) (10AMP.) DIESEL ENGINE

FUEL ECONOMY LIGHTS, HEADLAMP ON WARNING & TURBO JUMPER

FUSE (YELLOW) (20 AMP.) SEAT BELT LT. & BUZZER, HEATED BACKLIGHT RELAY, INSTRUMENT GAGES & INDICATOR LAMPS, FUEL ECON. LTS. & MAP LIGHT & C4 SYSTEM OR TURBO CONTROLLER

FUSE (YELLOW) (20 AMP.) TAIL, SIDE MARKER, PARK, CORNERING & LIC. LAMP & CLOCK RADIO

FUSE (RED) (10 AMP.) RADIO & CRUISE

FUSE (YELLOW) (20 AMP.) TURN SIGNALS & BACK UP LAMPS & AUTO DR. LOCK, IDLE STOP RELAY (LC8)

FUSE (YELLOW) (20 AMP.) AUTO LEVEL CONTROL COMPRESSOR & EXHAUST VALVE

NOT USED

DIGITAL CLOCK RADIO

FUSE (YELLOW) (20 AMP.) ELECTRIC CHOKE

CIRCUIT BREAKER POWER WINDOWS, ROOF & FUEL CAP LOCK RELEASE (30 AMP.)

FUSE (WHITE) (25 AMP.) A/C & DECK LID REL. & LOW WASHER FLUID LIGHT

RADIO CAPACITOR

FUSE (RED) (10 AMP.) ECM.

FUSE (YELLOW) (20 AMP.) STOP & HAZARD LAMPS

CIRCUIT BREAKER POWER SEAT, DOOR LOCKS, HEATED BACK LIGHT FEED (30 AMP.)

FUSE (YELLOW) (20 AMP.) CLOCK. CIGAR. LTR., GLOVE BOX LP., KEY BUZZER, POWER ANTENNA & CLOCK RADIO

FUSE (YELLOW) (20 AMP.) DOME & SAIL PANEL LAMPS, TRUNK LP., READING LP., VANITY LP., HEAD-LAMP ON WARNING, AUTO LOCKS, REAR CGR. LTRS. & COURTESY LTS.

BODY WIRING JUNCTION BLOCK (POWER SEATS & DOOR LOCKS)

GOOD FUSE   BLOWN FUSE

■   FIGURE 3–18

Typical mini-fuse panel. Note difference between good fuse and blown fuse. (Courtesy of General Motors Corporation.)

in the circuit. When circuit overload current heats the bimetal arm, the arm bends to open the contacts, stopping electrical flow in the circuit. When the arm cools, the contacts close again, energizing the circuit once more. This action continues until the circuit is switched off or repaired.

Voltage Limiter

The instrument voltage regulator is designed to limit voltage to the instrument panel gauges. Power to the voltage limiter is supplied when the ignition switch is in the ON or ACC. position. Voltage is limited to approximately 5 V at the instrument gauges.

The voltage limiter consists of a bimetal arm, a heating coil, and a set of contact points enclosed in a housing **(Figure 3–23)**. Two terminals provide connections in series into the circuit. When the ignition switch is turned on, the heating coil heats the bimetal arm causing it to bend and open the contacts. This disconnects the voltage supply from the heating coil as well as from the circuit. When the bimetal arm cools sufficiently, the contacts close and the cycle repeats itself. The rapid opening and closing of the contacts results in a pulsating voltage at the output terminal averaging approximately 5 V. The voltage limiter protects the instrument gauges against high-voltage surges and prevents erroneous gauge readings caused by voltage fluctuations.

■ RESISTORS

Resistors are devices used in electrical circuits to reduce current and voltage levels from those supplied by the power source. Resistors are usually

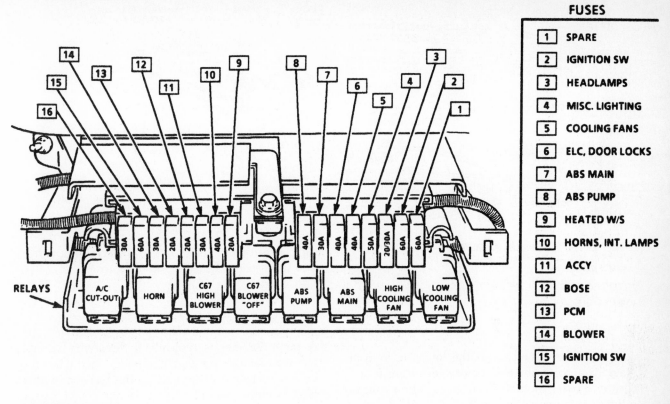

FUSES

1	SPARE
2	IGNITION SW
3	HEADLAMPS
4	MISC. LIGHTING
5	COOLING FANS
6	ELC. DOOR LOCKS
7	ABS MAIN
8	ABS PUMP
9	HEATED W/S
10	HORNS, INT. LAMPS
11	ACCY
12	BOSE
13	PCM
14	BLOWER
15	IGNITION SW
16	SPARE

■ FIGURE 3–19

Typical power distribution center showing fuses and relays. (Courtesy of General Motors Corporation.)

made from wire or carbon. They are used to protect devices or circuits designed to operate at a lower voltage level than that supplied by the battery or charging system. They are also used to control current and voltage levels produced by charging systems, to control light intensity and ignition systems **(Figure 3–24).**

Resistors provide opposition to electron flow. This opposition causes the electrons to work harder to try to get through. The increased electron activity generates heat. Since some of the electrical energy is used up to produce heat, the voltage through the resistor is at a reduced level. Several types of resistors are used in the automobile.

Fixed Resistors

Standard resistors are basically of fixed resistance values except for minor variations due to changes in their temperature. They include wire coil and carbon types. The resistance of a resistor is measured in ohms. The greater the ohm rating of the resistor,

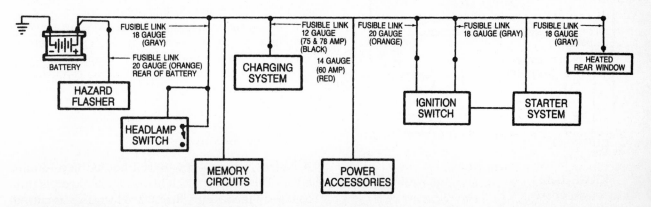

■ FIGURE 3–20

Typical application of fusible links. (Courtesy of Chrysler Corporation.)

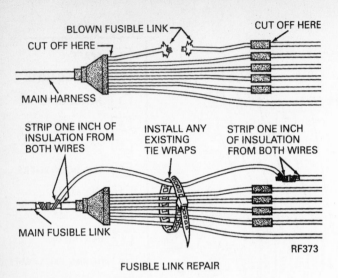

FUSIBLE LINK REPAIR

RF373

■   FIGURE 3–21
Typical fuse links and fuse link repair. (Courtesy of
Chrysler Corporation.)

the higher its resistance and the lower its output
voltage. Examples of this type of resistor are found
in heater blower motors, electronic ignition control
modules, resistor spark plugs, and spark plug
wires.

Variable Resistors
Rheostat

A rheostat is an adjustable resistor in which resistance varies according to setting. A rheostat consists
of a circular coil element with a sliding contact connected to a rotating knob. Two wires provide a voltage and ground to the rheostat. A sliding contact
inserts more or less resistance into the circuit,
depending on switch position. The rotary dash light
dimmer is an example of a rheostat **(Figure 3–24).**

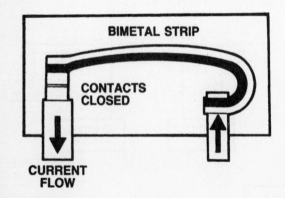

■   FIGURE 3–22
Circuit breaker design. (Courtesy of Chrysler
Corporation.)

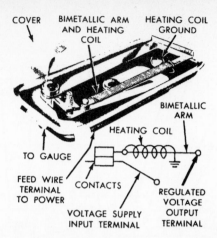

■   FIGURE 3–23
Typical instrument panel voltage limiter, components,
and schematic. (Courtesy of Ford Motor Co. of
Canada Ltd.)

Potentiometer

A potentiometer is typically a three-wire variable
resistor that acts as a voltage divider. Two wires provide a voltage and ground to the resistor. A third
wire is connected to a sliding contact called a wiper
that slides across the resistor between the voltage
supply source and ground. The position of the wiper
on the resistor inserts more or less resistance into the
circuit, depending on the position of the sliding contact **(Figure 3–25).** Output voltage varies proportion-
ately. The throttle position sensor and airflow sensor
are examples of potentiometer applications.

Thermal Resistors
Thermistor

A thermistor is a temperature-sensitive device used
to provide a voltage signal to the engine computer.
Voltage output increases with the temperature of
the semiconductor material in the sensing element.
This type of sensor (with minor variations) is used
as an engine coolant temperature sensor, ambient
air temperature sensor, and intake air temperature
sensor. **Figure 3–26** shows the relationship between
temperature and resistance in a typical coolant
sensor. This type of sensor has a negative temperature coefficient. This means that as the semiconductor material temperature increases its resistance
decreases.

Ballast Resistor

A ballast resistor is a wire coil housed in a ceramic
block. The ceramic block helps regulate temperature
change in the resistor. Resistance increases as current
is increased to the resistor. Increased current heats

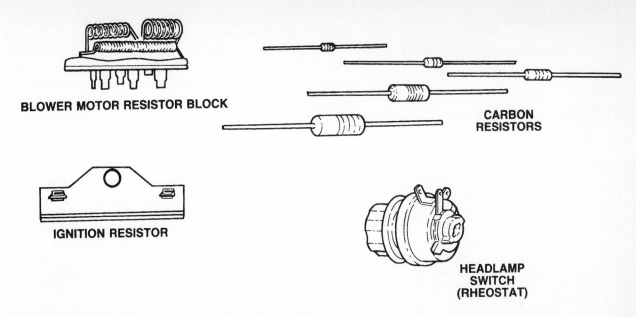

BLOWER MOTOR RESISTOR BLOCK

CARBON RESISTORS

IGNITION RESISTOR

HEADLAMP SWITCH (RHEOSTAT)

■ FIGURE 3–24
Common types and applications of resistors. (Courtesy of Chrysler Corporation.)

the resistor coil, which increases its resistance. Ballast resistors are used in some contact point and electronic ignition systems to limit supply voltage to the ignition coil, thereby protecting the coil. A bypass circuit allows full battery voltage to the coil during cranking to improve starting. **Figure 3–24** shows an ignition ballast resistor.

■ CAPACITORS (CONDENSERS)

A capacitor is a device that is used in an electrical circuit to store an electrical charge temporarily until it is needed to perform its job or until it can be safely dissipated if it is not to be used. The typical condenser consists of several thin layers of electrically conductive material, such as metal foil, separated by thin insulating material known as dielectric material. Alternate layers of foil are connected to one terminal of the condenser. The other layers of foil are connected to ground. The entire assembly is rolled up tightly and enclosed in a metal cylinder. The unit is completely sealed and moisture proof. The metal container is the ground connection, and a pigtail lead provides the other connection **(Figure 3–27).** In the older point ignition system, the condenser is connected in parallel with the ignition points. When the points open, the surge of current (excess electrons) enters the condenser and is stored on the condenser plates. The condenser prevents arcing of current across the points as they separate, thereby prolonging point life.

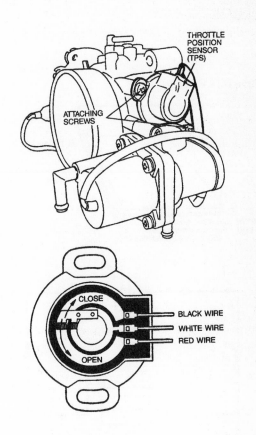

■ FIGURE 3–25
Throttle position sensor is a potentiometer with variable-voltage output. (Courtesy of Ford Motor Company.)

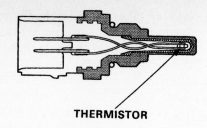

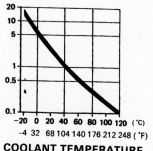

■ FIGURE 3-26

A thermistor is used in a coolant temperature sensor. As coolant temperature increases, thermistor resistance decreases. Resistance on left of chart is in kilohms (kΩ). (Courtesy of Robert Bosch Canada Ltd.)

In a capacitor discharge ignition system, electrical energy is stored in the capacitor and discharged at the precise instant when the plug should be fired. The capacitor is then recharged and discharged repeatedly and as rapidly as required, depending on engine speed.

Capacitors of various types and sizes are used in electrical circuits to collect and dissipate stray or unwanted current. This prevents the unwanted current from interfering with other electrical functions. A radio-suppressor type of capacitor is a typical example. The capacity or capacitance of a condenser is measured in units called *farads*. A farad is a charge of 1 ampere for 1 second, producing a 1 volt potential difference. A microfarad (μF) is 0.000001 ($\frac{1}{1,000,000}$ farad). Automotive point ignition condensers have an approximate capacitance of 0.15 to 0.28 μF.

■ TRANSDUCERS

A transducer is a device that changes a condition or action to an electrical signal. There are two kinds of transducers used in the automobile: active and passive. The active transducer generates its own voltage. Examples of active transducers are magnetic sensors, oxygen sensors, and knock sensors. A passive transducer relies on a voltage input to generate an output voltage signal. Examples include airflow sensors and throttle position sensors. Transducers or sensors are used in ignition, fuel injection, air conditioning, antilock brakes, automatic level control, active suspension, and automatic transmissions and transaxles. Refer to the appropriate chapters for more details.

■ DIODES

A diode (**Figure 3–28**) is a solid-state (completely static) device that allows current to pass through itself in one direction only (within its rated capacity).

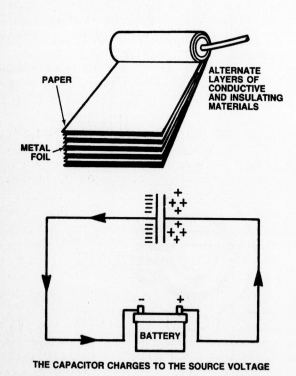

■ FIGURE 3-27

Construction and operation of a capacitor used in point ignition and for radio suppression. (Courtesy of Chrysler Corporation.)

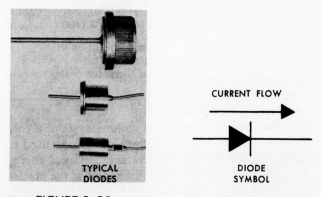

■ FIGURE 3-28

Typical diodes and diode symbol showing direction of current. (Courtesy of General Motors Corporation.)

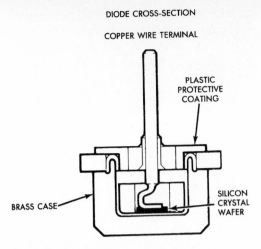

DIODE CROSS-SECTION

COPPER WIRE TERMINAL

PLASTIC PROTECTIVE COATING

BRASS CASE

SILICON CRYSTAL WAFER

■   FIGURE 3–29

Cross-sectional view of diode construction. Materials used vary somewhat in different diodes. (Courtesy of Chrysler Corporation.)

Acting as a one-way electrical check valve, it allows current to pass in one direction and blocks it in the other direction.

The silicon wafer is chemically treated to produce either a positive or a negative diode **(Figure 3–29)**. Diodes may be encased in noncorrosive heat-conductive metal with the case acting as one lead and a metal wire connected to the opposite side of the wafer as the other lead. The unit is hermetically sealed to prevent the entry of moisture. This type of diode is used in some ac charging system alternators. A minimum of six diodes is used—three positive diodes and three negative diodes to provide full-wave rectification (changing alternating current to direct current). Many charging systems use more than six diodes.

Other diodes used in electronic systems are much smaller and may be sealed in epoxy resins with two leads for connection into the circuit. Diodes in computers may be very tiny in comparison to the more visible charging system diode. Negative diodes are identified by a black paint mark, a part number in black, or a black negative sign. Positive diodes are similarly identified in red or with a red positive sign.

The manner in which the metallic disc is installed in the diode assembly determines whether the diode is negative or positive. (Inverting the disc in a positive diode would make it a negative assembly.) This disc is only 0.008 to 0.010 in. thick and approximately one-eighth of an inch square, depending on current rating. Some rectifier assemblies contain diodes that are exposed, while others have them built in. Those with built-in diodes contain only the wafer portion of the diode.

The silicon crystal material for diodes and transistors is processed or "doped" by adding other material to it. Phosphorus or antimony may be used to produce a negative or N-type material. These materials have five electrons in the outer ring of their atoms. This results in the atoms of the N material having one extra or free electron. The free electron can be easily made to move through the material when voltage is applied. Electrons are considered to be negative current carriers.

Boron or indium may be used to treat silicon crystal to produce a positive or P-type material. These elements have only three electrons in the outer ring of their atoms. This leaves a shortage of one electron in the atoms of P-type material. This shortage or vacancy is called a *hole*. Holes are considered to be positive current carriers.

A diode consists of a very thin slice of each material, P type and N type placed together. The area where the two materials meet is called the junction. When the N-material side of the diode is connected to a negative current supply, such as the battery negative terminal, and the P-material side is connected to the positive battery terminal, the diode will conduct current. This happens because the negative battery terminal has an excess of electrons that repel the electrons in the diode toward the positive side. At the same time, the positive holes in the P material move toward the N side. This interchange of electrons and holes occurs at the junction of the N and P material in the diode. Connecting a diode in this manner is called forward bias.

When a diode is connected in the opposite manner (reverse bias) it will not conduct current. It cannot do so since the N-material side of the diode is connected to the positive battery terminal and the P-material side to the negative battery terminal. The electrons in the N material are attracted to the positive battery terminal side away from the diode junction. At the same time, the holes in the positive diode material are attracted to the negative battery terminal side of the diode away from the junction area. This in effect creates an open circuit which cannot conduct current.

Of course, these conditions apply only if normal diode design voltage is not exceeded. When applied in reverse bias, excessive current will cause the bond structure to break down and allow reverse current, which causes the diode to be damaged. Diodes are designed with the necessary current and voltage capacity for the circuit in which they are to be used.

Excessive reverse current will destroy a diode due to excessive heat. A "blown" diode will not conduct current, resulting in an open circuit. Blown diodes must be replaced. A shorted diode will conduct current in both directions and must be

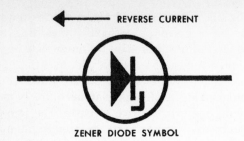

■ FIGURE 3–30
The zener diode will allow current in the reverse direction when specified voltage is imposed. (Courtesy of General Motors Corporation.)

replaced. Light-emitting diodes (LEDs) may be used for digital display of instrument panel gauges on some vehicles.

Zener Diode

The zener diode **(Figure 3–30)** is a specially designed diode that conducts current like a normal diode but will also safely conduct current in a reverse direction when reverse current reaches the specified design voltage. A zener diode can prevent reverse current if it is below design voltage, but when reverse current reaches and exceeds design voltage, the zener diode will conduct reverse current. This type of diode is used in control circuits such as in the field current in an alternator.

■ TRANSISTORS

A transistor **(Figure 3–31)** is a solid-state switching device used to control current in a circuit. It operates like a relay except that it has no moving parts. A relatively small current is used to control a larger current. The transistor either allows current to pass or stops it.

Transistors used in automotive applications are usually of the PNP type. This means that they are designed with a thin slice of N material sandwiched between two pieces of P material. The P material on one side is called the emitter, the N material in the middle is called the base, and the other P material is called the collector.

The very thin slice of N-type base material is attached to a surrounding metallic ring which provides the means for circuit connection. The emitter and collector material are also provided with circuit connections. The physical arrangement of the three pieces of material is such that the distance between the emitter and the collector is shorter than the distance between the emitter and the base. This feature results in the unique manner in which the transistor controls current.

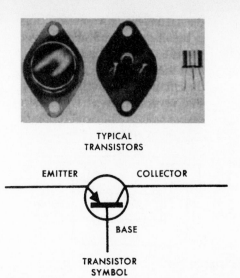

■ FIGURE 3–31
Typical transistor and transistor symbol. A small base current turns the transistor on, allowing a larger current from emitter to collector. (Courtesy of General Motors Corporation.)

A transistor is connected into a circuit in a manner that allows a low base–emitter current to control a larger collector–emitter current. A typical example of this is in the control module of an electronic ignition system.

When the base circuit is energized (by closing the ignition switch, for example), a small base current is applied to the transistor emitter–base. This causes the electrons and holes in the emitter–base to act in a similar manner as in a diode described earlier. However, since the emitter is closer to the collector than it is to the base, most of the current is conducted by the emitter–collector section of the transistor. This is caused by the fact that electricity normally follows the path of least resistance. The control current is called base current. The base circuit or current controls the emitter–collector current **(Figure 3–32).**

The same type of semiconductor material used in diodes is also used in transistors. The transistor, however, uses a second section of this material resulting in three terminals instead of two (as in the diode). If, for example, the base circuit of a transistor is energized with 5 A of current, the transistor divides this current into base current and emitter–collector current. This is known as the current gain factor. This factor varies with transistor design. The emitter–collector current may be 24 times that of the base current. In this example, therefore, base current would be 0.2 A and emitter–collector current would be 4.8 A.

Transistors are used in electronic voltage regulators to control charging system voltage, in electronic ignition systems to control ignition coil primary current, and in computers.

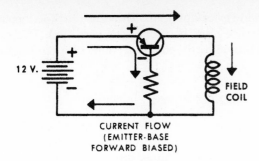

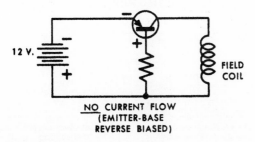

■ FIGURE 3–32
Diagrams showing transistor operation. (Courtesy of General Motors Corporation.)

■ ELECTRICAL MEASUREMENTS

Electricity is measured in volts and amperes. Resistance to electrical flow is measured in ohms. The electrical power required to operate a light or electric motor is stated in watts. These terms and their relationship to each other must be understood to be able to diagnose and service the automobile's electrical systems and their components.

Voltage (Volts)

Voltage is an electrical pressure or electromotive force. In the automobile this voltage is applied by the battery and alternator. Voltage can be described as a potential difference (in electrical pressure). The potential difference between the two posts on a 12–volt (V) battery is normally about 12.6 V. Voltage is measured with a voltmeter. The symbol for voltage is V. For electromotive force the symbol is EMF or E. They represent the same force. One volt is equal to 1 ampere (explained later) of current across 1 ohm (explained later) of resistance when 1 watt of power is being consumed **(Figure 3–33).**

Current (Amperes)

Current is the rate of electron flow. Electron flow (or current) increases as voltage increases provided that resistance remains constant. Electrical current is measured in amperes with an ammeter. One ampere (A) is equivalent to the current produced by 1 volt

■ FIGURE 3–33
(Courtesy of Chrysler Corporation.)

when applied across a resistance of one ohm. Another term for amperes is *intensity* of current. The symbol for current intensity is I.

Resistance (Ohms)

Electrical resistance is opposition to electron flow. It is measured in ohms with an ohmmeter. One ohm is the resistance that allows 1 ampere of current to flow when 1 volt is applied. The letter R is the symbol for resistance. The Greek capital letter omega (Ω) is the symbol for ohms. The resistance of an electrical wire increases as its length is increased and as its temperature is increased. The diameter or cross-sectional area of the wire is also a factor. Wires with a greater cross-sectional area have less resistance. This can be compared to the flow of water in a pipe or hose: the larger the inside diameter of the hose or pipe, the greater the flow of water. A smaller diameter hose or pipe has greater resistance to the flow of water; therefore, the flow is reduced. In the same way if the hose or pipe is flattened, the resistance to flow is increased, resulting in less flow.

Ohm's Law

When any two values in an electrical circuit are known, the third can be calculated by using Ohm's law. Ohm's law can be expressed in several ways, as shown here.

$$Ohm's\ Law$$
$$E = I \times R$$
$$I = E \div R$$
$$R = E \div I$$

where E is electromotive force, in volts
I is current, in amperes
R is resistance, in ohms

You already know that many automotive electrical circuits operate at battery voltage (12 volts). If you know that a circuit operates at 3 amps you can calculate the normal resistance in the circuit as follows:

$$12V \div 3A = 4 \text{ ohms.}$$

If resistance in the circuit is too high, 6 ohms for example, then there will be less current available to operate the electrical device in the circuit. The current available can be calculated as follows:

$$12V \div 6\,\Omega = 2 \text{ amps.}$$

This is a 33 percent reduction in current. Reduced current causes lights to dim and electric motors to run slower or not at all. The cause for the increased resistance must be found and corrected. This could be loose or corroded connections or a faulty electrical device.

Electrical Power

The rate of work done by electricity is called electrical power and is measured in watts (W). If the voltage and current values are known, the power in watts can be calculated simply by multiplying the

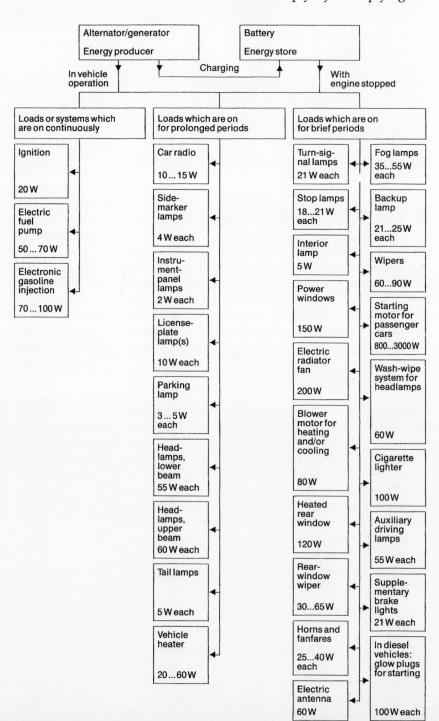

■ FIGURE 3–34
(Courtesy of Robert Bosch Canada Ltd.)

number of volts times the number of amperes: $V \times A = W$. For example, a 12-V starting system using 150 A would use 1800 W. The proper amount of power can only be delivered if voltage, current, and resistance values are as they should be. Typical power requirements for automotive electrical components are shown in **Figure 3–34**.

■ ELECTRICAL CIRCUIT RESISTANCE

Every electrical system requires a complete circuit to function. A complete circuit provides an uninterrupted path for electricity to flow from its source through all circuit components and back to the electrical source. Whenever the circuit is interrupted (broken), electricity will not flow. This interruption can be in the form of a switch or an open (broken) wire.

There are three basic types of automotive electrical circuits: series, parallel, and series–parallel. An electrical system may have one or more of these circuit types.

Series Circuit

A series circuit provides only one path for current to flow from the electrical source through each component and back to source. If any one component fails, the entire circuit will not function. Total resistance in a series circuit is simply the sum of all the resistances in the circuit. For example, a series circuit with a light and two switches would have a total resistance of 4 Ω if the light had a resistance of 2 Ω and each switch had a resistance of 1 Ω. Total resistance = 2 + 1 + 1 = 4 Ω. Another example is shown in **Figure 3–35.**

Parallel Circuit

A parallel circuit provides two or more paths for electricity to flow. Each path has several resistances (loads) and operates independently or in conjunction with the other paths in the circuit. If one path in the parallel circuit does not function, the other paths in the circuit are not affected. One example of this is the headlight circuit: If one headlight burns out, the other headlight will still function. To calculate the total resistance in a parallel circuit, the following method may be used:

$$R = \cfrac{1}{\cfrac{1}{R_1}+\cfrac{1}{R_2}+\cfrac{1}{R_3}} \quad \text{or} \quad \frac{1}{R}=\frac{1}{R_1}+\frac{1}{R_2}+\frac{1}{R_3}$$

depending on the number of resistances involved. If R_1, R_2, and R_3 are 4, 6 and 8 Ω, respectively, the total resistance can be calculated as follows:

$$R = \frac{1}{1/4+1/6+1/8}$$

$$= \frac{1}{6/24+4/24+3/24}$$

$$= \frac{1}{13/24} \quad \text{or} \quad 1 \div \frac{13}{24}$$

$$= 1 \times \frac{24}{13} \quad \text{or} \quad 1.85 \ \Omega$$

In a parallel circuit the total resistance is always less than the resistance in any single device in the circuit. This is because there is more than one path for electricity to follow. **Figure 3–36** is another example.

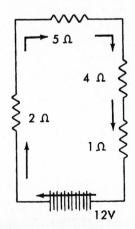

■ FIGURE 3–35
This series circuit has a total resistance of 12 Ω.
(Courtesy of General Motors Corporation.)

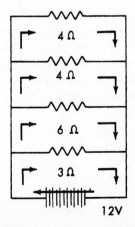

■ FIGURE 3–36
This parallel circuit has a total resistance of 1 Ω.
(Courtesy of General Motors Corporation.)

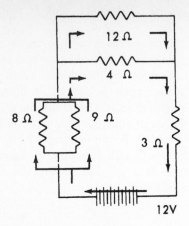

■   FIGURE 3–37
Example of a series/parallel circuit. (Courtesy of
General Motors Corporation.)

Series–Parallel Circuits

A series–parallel circuit combines the series and parallel circuits. A series–parallel circuit is shown in
Figure 3–37. In a headlight circuit the headlight and
dimmer switches are in series, while the headlights
are in parallel with each other. To calculate total
resistance in a series–parallel circuit, calculate the
series portion of the circuit as described earlier. Then
calculate the parallel portion of the circuit and add
to the series resistance.

Printed Circuit

A printed circuit is mounted on an insulating board
or panel. Flat strips of metal conductor material are
used instead of conventional wiring. Printed circuits
are used in instrument panels and computers
because of their compact design **(Figure 3–38).**

Integrated Circuit

Integrated circuits are used in complex electronic
and computer control systems. An integrated circuit
contains many very tiny diodes, transistors, resistors, and capacitors integrated on a tiny wafer such
as a silicone chip **(Figure 3–39).** Integrated circuits
are described more fully in Chapter 4.

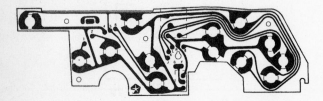

■   FIGURE 3–38
Printed circuit board. (Courtesy of Chrysler
Corporation.)

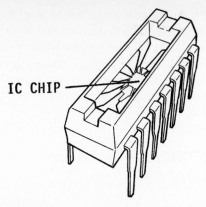

■   FIGURE 3–39
Integrated circuit chip is less than $\frac{1}{4}$ in. (6 mm) across
but has many diodes, transistors, resistors, and
capacitors. (Courtesy of Chrysler Corporation.)

■ COMMON GROUND PRINCIPLE

In many illustrations showing basic circuits in this
book, a return or ground wire is shown as the
method to connect the circuit or component to the
negative or ground terminal of the battery. However, this is not the case with most automotive electrical circuits and components. It is not necessary
and would require many more wires than are actually used. Instead manufacturers use the common
ground method, which uses the vehicle frame or
body as part of the return circuit. A starting motor,
for example, is bolted directly to the engine while
the engine is grounded by a ground strap. The
internal circuits of the starter are grounded to the
starter frame and through it to the engine and
ground. A separate ground wire for the starter
therefore is not needed. Other components may be
mounted in plastic and must have a short ground
wire to connect them to ground. With the increased
use of plastics throughout the vehicle some manufacturers have adopted a system of common
ground terminals at various points in the vehicle to
provide good grounds and keep ground wires to a
minimum.

■ COMMON ELECTRICAL PROBLEMS

Common electrical problems include incorrect resistance values, loose or corroded connections, electrical feedback, opens, shorts, and grounds **(Figure
3–40).** Many electrical problems are easily corrected
if these basic problems are recognized and understood.

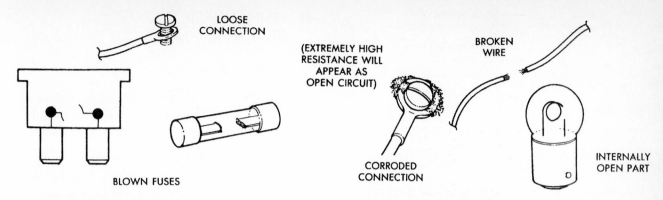

■ FIGURE 3–40
Common electrical problems. (Courtesy of Chrysler Corporation.)

Incorrect Resistance

All electrical wiring and components have some resistance. The effective operation of these components depends on their resistance values being correct or as specified in the service manual. If a wire or electrical component has excessive resistance, electric current and power are reduced. If an electrical component has no resistance, it is inoperative and acts as if it were switched off.

Corroded and Loose Connections

Connections that are loose or corroded cause high resistance. High resistance creates an extra load and causes a voltage drop. This causes electrical components to operate at reduced capacity or not at all. Heating due to arcing at a loose connection can cause corrosion of the terminal and high resistance. Water and road salt add to the corrosion. Loose or corroded connectors may be hard to spot; however, connections in a faulty circuit are easily cleaned and tightened to ensure a good electrical connection. If the locking tabs on an electrical connector are broken, vibration can cause electrical contact to be broken. Unplug, inspect, clean, and repair or replace any faulty connectors as required.

Electrical Feedback

Electrical feedback can cause lamps to light or accessories to operate when they are not supposed to. The most common cause of feedback is a blown or faulty fuse or fusible link. This can allow current to find a different electrical path since some circuits are fed from several sources. Inspect and test suspected fuses or fusible links with an ohmmeter. Make sure that there is no current in the component being tested since this would damage the ohmmeter. Make sure that all ground connections are clean and tight at all electrical components. A poor ground or an open bulb filament can cause other bulbs to light. Replace any faulty bulbs.

Voltage Drop Testing

As current passes through a resistance, circuit voltage across it will drop. Total voltage drop in an electrical circuit will always equal available voltage at the source of electrical pressure.

Circuit resistance, if excessive at any point, will result in excessive voltage drop across that portion of the circuit. The voltage drop method is commonly used to determine circuit resistance. The voltage drop across a battery cable, for example, should not exceed ²⁄₁₀ V per 100 A at 68°F (20°C).

The voltage drop method is the SAE recommended method for checking cable resistance. When checking voltage drop, the voltmeter is connected in parallel over the portion of the circuit being tested, and the results are compared to specifications.

Voltage drop can only be measured in a circuit when there is a flow of electricity present. With no electrical flow, the voltage (potential difference or pressure) remains the same anywhere in the circuit. Shop voltmeters are designed to indicate positive voltage potential on the upscale side of zero.

Opens, Shorts, and Grounds

Electrical systems may develop an open circuit, a shorted circuit, or a grounded circuit. Each of these conditions will render the circuit more or less ineffective.

Opens

An open circuit is a circuit in which there is a break in continuity. As stated earlier, for electricity to be able to flow there must be a complete and continuous path from the electrical source through the circuit back to the electrical source. If this path is bro-

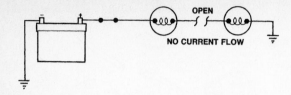

■ FIGURE 3–41

An open circuit (break in circuit) results in no current flow. (Courtesy of Chrysler Corporation.)

ken, the condition is referred to as an open circuit. An open circuit, therefore, is no longer operational and acts the same as if it were switched off **(Figure 3–41).**

Shorts

A shorted circuit is a circuit that allows current to bypass part of the normal path. An example of this would be a shorted coil, solenoid, or motor winding. Coil windings are normally insulated from each other; however, if this insulation breaks down and allows copper-to-copper contact between turns, part of the windings will be bypassed. In an ignition coil primary winding, this condition would reduce the number of windings through which electricity will flow. If the short caused 50 windings of approximately 200 windings to be bypassed, this would reduce coil capacity by 25%. Another example is shown in **Figure 3–42.**

Grounds

A grounded circuit is a condition that allows current to return to ground before it has reached its intended destination. An example of this would be a grounded taillight circuit. If the wire leading to the taillight has an insulation breakdown allowing the wire to touch the frame or body of the vehicle, electricity will flow to ground at this point and return directly to the battery without reaching the taillight.

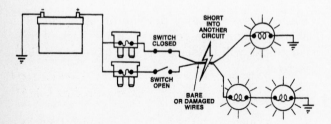

■ FIGURE 3–42

This short circuit causes lamps to light even though the switch controlling them is off. (Courtesy of Chrysler Corporation.)

■ USING BASIC TEST EQUIPMENT

Jumper Wire

The simplest electrical troubleshooting tool is also one of the most important—a jumper wire. Make it at least a meter in length and use alligator clips on the ends **(Figure 3–43).**

Connect one end to battery positive and you have an excellent 12-V power supply. Use it to check lamp bulbs, motors, or as a power feed to any 12-V component. But be careful and do not drop the other end; any place you touch on the engine or body is ground—battery negative—big sparks and high current will result, possible "cooking" the jumper wire!

Test Lamp

Sometimes you want to look for power, rather than supply it. That is when a test lamp **(Figure 3–44)** is perfect. Just ground one side and you can go to most "hot" 12-V points in the car and the lamp will light **(Figure 3–45).** But sometimes it will not light up fully with a hot circuit—for example, if you test the circuit after the voltage has "dropped" over a load. Try it at the ballast resistor. The battery side will light the lamp, but the lowered voltage after the resistor will only cause the lamp to glow dimly.

Self-Powered Test Light

The self-powered test light is used to check for continuity in a circuit or load device **(Figure 3–46).** The self-powered test light is connected and performs the same basic checks for continuity as an ohmmeter. It is also effective in checking for shorts to ground **(Figure 3–47).**

Circuit Breaker

A circuit breaker reacts to excess current by heating, opening up, and cutting off the excess current. With no current flowing, the heating stops, and the breaker closes again and restores the circuit. If the high-current cause is still in the circuit, the breaker will open again. This cycling on and off will continue as long as the circuit is overloaded.

You can use a cycling breaker fitted with alligator clips in place of a fuse that keeps blowing. The circuit breaker will keep the circuit "alive" while you check the circuit for the cause of high current draw—usually, a short **(Figure 3–48).**

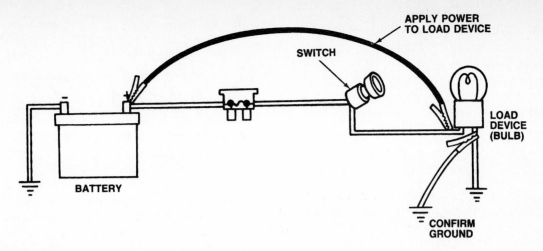

■   FIGURE 3–43

Using a jumper wire to bypass a switch that is suspected of being defective.
(Courtesy of Chrysler Corporation.)

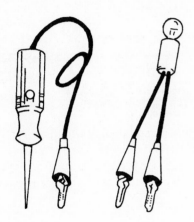

■   FIGURE 3–44

Two types of test light for checking electrical circuits.
(Courtesy of Chrysler Corporation.)

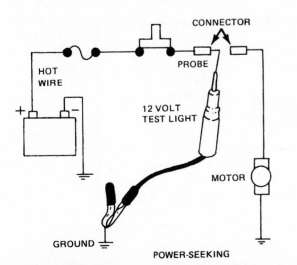

■   FIGURE 3–45

Isolating portions of a circuit to identify faulty section.
(Courtesy of Chrysler Corporation.)

Voltmeter

A voltmeter **(Figure 3–49)** is connected in parallel with a circuit—it reads directly in volts. In parallel the meter draws only a small current—just enough to sample the voltage. That is why you can "short" right across the battery terminals with a voltmeter without damaging it. However, never try to check voltage by putting the meter in series. The voltmeter hookup should always parallel the circuit being measured because you do not want the high-resistance meter disrupting the circuit in a series connection.

Closed-Circuit Voltage

In **Figure 3–50** the voltage at A is 12 V positive. There is a drop of 6 V over the 1.0-Ω resistor and the reading is 6 V positive at B. The remaining voltage drops in the fan load and the voltmeter reads zero (12 V negative) at C, indicating normal motor circuit operation.

Open-Circuit Voltage

Now we read the voltage in the same circuit as above but with no electricity flowing because there is an open circuit (broken wire or poor ground) at point X. The voltage at A, B, and C will be 12 V positive, indicating circuit continuity up to, but not through, point X. Remember, there is no voltage drop across a resistor or load if there is no electrical flow. Voltage drop checks are shown in **Figure 3–51.**

Ammeter

You measure current draw with an ammeter **(Figure 3–52).** But unlike the parallel voltmeter, you must put the ammeter in series with the load to read the

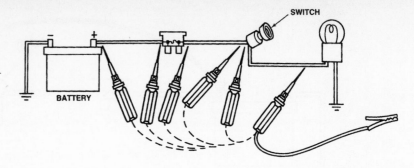

■ FIGURE 3–46
Checking for voltage in a circuit with a self-powered test light. (Courtesy of Chrysler Corporation.)

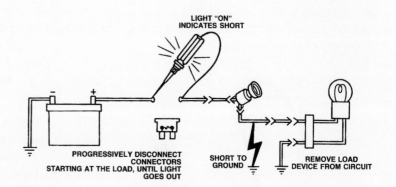

■ FIGURE 3–47
Using a 12V test light to locate a short to ground. (Courtesy of Chrysler Corporation.)

HIGH CURRENT DRAW OPENS CIRCUIT PROTECTION DEVICE

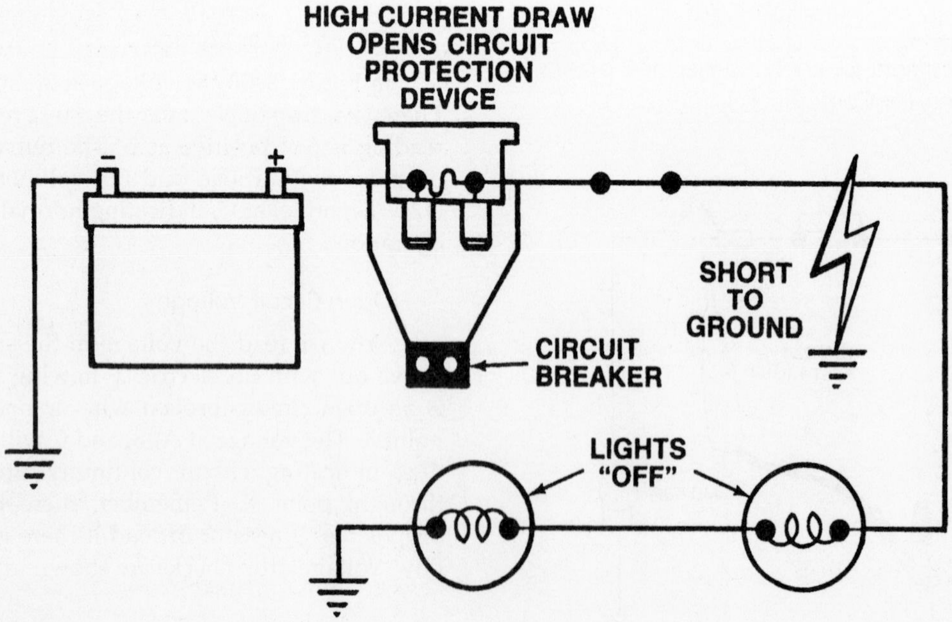

■ FIGURE 3–48
Using a circuit breaker type of tester across a suspected blown fuse allows the circuit being tested to remain live in order to locate faulty portion of circuit with other test equipment. (Courtesy of Chrysler Corporation.)

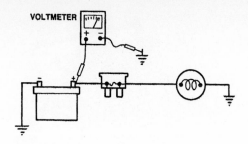

■   FIGURE 3–49
Voltmeter connected in parallel measures voltage at any point in circuit. (Courtesy of Chrysler Corporation.)

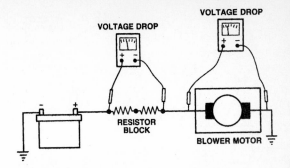

■   FIGURE 3–51
Voltmeter can be used to measure voltage drop across any component in the circuit. Excessive voltage drop indicates excessive resistance. (Courtesy of Chrysler Corporation.)

current draw. That means disconnecting the load and reconnecting with all the current going through the meter. Polarity must be followed—the red lead going to the positive side. Be sure to use only the induction type of ammeter with the clamp type of induction pickup on computer-equipped cars.

Always use an ammeter that can handle the expected current since excessive current can damage a meter. Also, never connect an ammeter across a circuit (parallel) or you may damage the meter or the circuit.

Ohmmeter

An ohmmeter is used to measure the resistance (in ohms) of a circuit or electrical component. The ohmmeter must never be connected to any circuit or component where voltage is present. The item being tested must be disconnected from the vehicle battery before being tested. The ohmmeter may be part of a

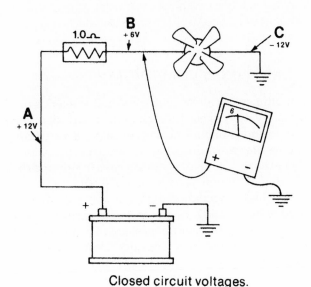

Closed circuit voltages.

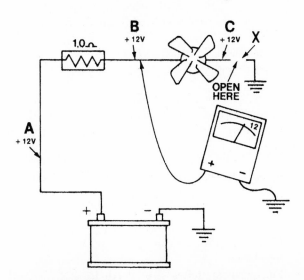

■   FIGURE 3–50
Using a voltmeter to isolate a problem in a motor circuit.

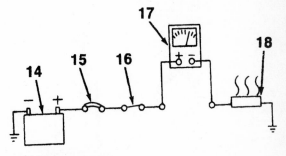

14. Power Source
15. Circuit Breaker
16. Switch (Closed)
17. Ammeter
18. Load

■   FIGURE 3–52
Ammeter connected in series to measure current draw. (Courtesy of General Motors Corporation.)

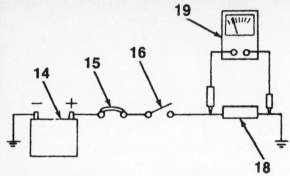

14. Power Source   18. Load
15. Circuit Breaker   19. Ohmmeter
16. Switch (Open)

■ FIGURE 3–53
Ohmmeter is used to measure resistance of electrical components. Component being tested must be isolated from any electrical current. (Courtesy of General Motors Corporation.)

multimeter that combines the ohmmeter, voltmeter, and ammeter in a single unit or it may be a separate tester.

To use an ohmmeter select the scale appropriate to the test being conducted: low reading scale for low resistance, high reading scale for high resistance. The ohmmeter leads are connected across the item being tested. The reading is taken and compared to specifications **(Figures 3–53** and **3–54).** If the reading is above or below specifications, the part is defective. The ohmmeter can be used to check continuity in a wire or wiring harness. Just clip the ohmmeter to each end of the wire and it will show very close to zero if the wire is good.

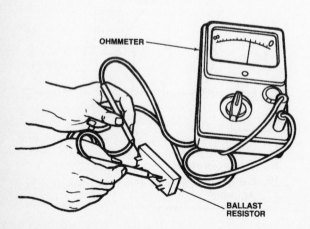

■ FIGURE 3–54
Measuring resistance with an analog ohmmeter. (Courtesy of Chrysler Corporation.)

■ FIGURE 3–55
Digital multimeter combines voltmeter, ammeter, and ohmmeter. (Courtesy of Hastings Manufacturing Company.)

Multimeter/VOM/DVOM

A multimeter or VOM (volt-ohm-milliameter) is used to test a variety of electrical components. It has several test positions that allow measuring voltage, current, and resistance. Multimeters are available in analog or digital form. The analog version has a needle and dial. The digital version has a numerical display.

A high-impedance digital multimeter must be used when testing many of the electrical components of computer control systems. The high impedance protects the very sensitive electronic components from excessive current. Many specifications require the use of a digital multimeter since analog scales do not provide the accuracy required when fractions of a volt are involved **(Figure 3–55).**

Scan Tool, Breakout Box, and Oscilloscope

The scan tool, breakout box, and oscilloscope are more sophisticated test instruments than those described here. The use of these items is described in Chapter 2.

Review Questions

1. Electrical wires are used to conduct electricity to operate the _____ and _____ _____.
2. Doubling the length of a wire _____ its resistance.
3. Electrical switches are used to _____ and _____ electrical circuits.
4. A solenoid is an electromagnetic switch. True or False.

5. Solenoids may be used on automatic transmissions. True or False.
6. An electric motor that turns in either direction on command from the computer is a _____ _____.
7. A fuse is used to protect an _____ _____.
8. Circuit breakers are designed for circuit protection. True or False.
9. Resistors are usually made from _____ or _____.
10. Two kinds of transducers used in the automobile are _____ or _____.
11. Current is the rate of _____ _____.
12. EMF is the symbol for _____.
13. The rate of work done by electricity is called electrical power and it is measured in _____.
14. High resistance can be caused by loose or corroded connections. True or False.
15. A break in the continuity of an electrical circuit is called an _____.
16. You measure current draw with an _____.

Test Questions

1. When a material has many bound electrons it is called
   a. conductor
   b. insulator
   c. semiconductor
   d. insulator-conductor
2. Current flow is the movement of
   a. bound electrons
   b. free electrons
   c. valence rings
   d. free neutrons
3. The unit for measuring the amount of electrical force is
   a. volt
   b. ohm
   c. ampere
   d. watt
4. The unit for measuring the rate of current flow is
   a. volt
   b. ohm
   c. ampere
   d. watt
5. The unit for measuring electrical resistance is
   a. volt
   b. ohm
   c. ampere
   d. watt
6. Electrical power can be calculated as follows
   a. amperes multiplied by ohms
   b. ohms multiplied by volts
   c. volts multiplied by amperes
   d. amperes divided by ohms
7. Current in a circuit can be calculated by
   a. multiplying amperes by ohms
   b. multiplying volts by watts
   c. dividing volts by ohms
   d. dividing ohms by volts
8. Circuit resistance can be calculated by
   a. dividing amperes into volts
   b. dividing volts into amperes
   c. multiplying volts by amperes
   d. multiplying watts by ohms
9. Some cars have a flat piece of insulating material for the instrument panel connections which has a series of conduction strips. This is called
   a. a wiring diagram
   b. a printed circuit
   c. an insulation strip
   d. a wiring harness
10. An integrated circuit is one that
    a. integrates all electrical components in one circuit
    b. has very tiny diodes, transistors, resistors, and capacitors
    c. does not need any transistors
    d. does not need any diodes
11. A break in an electrical circuit creates
    a. infinite resistance
    b. free current flow
    c. positive current
    d. bound electrons
12. Current has only one path to follow in a
    a. series circuit
    b. parallel circuit
    c. series–parallel circuit
    d. open circuit
13. Total resistance in a circuit with parallel resistances of 3 ohms, 4 ohms, and 6 ohms each is
    a. 7.5 ohms
    b. 0.75 ohms
    c. 1.33 ohms
    d. 1.67 ohms
14. Electrical feedback
    a. is one side of the alternating current
    b. is a harmless phenomenon
    c. can cause lamps to light when they are not supposed to
    d. can reverse charge a battery
15. The voltage drop method can be used to check system
    a. voltage
    b. current
    c. feedback
    d. resistance

Computer Control System Diagnosis and Service Principles

4

INTRODUCTION

Almost every system on today's automobile is now computer controlled. Computer control of an automotive system makes it act and react with more precision and speed. Although earlier computer systems acted independently now most major systems share common input sensors. To understand the operation of these systems and to have the confidence to service them is essential in this age of the "smart car." This chapter provides an overview of computers, input sensors, and output devices; how they operate and how to service them. The appropriate service manual should always be consulted for specific procedures and specifications.

LEARNING OBJECTIVES

After completing this chapter, you should be able to:
- Describe computer types and locations.
- Describe the input, processing, and output functions of a computer control system.
- Describe the basic operation of a computer.
- List the major automotive computer systems, their input sensors, and output devices.
- Describe the function of the most common automobile computer, input sensors, and output devices.
- Access computer fault codes and interpret fault code charts in service manual.
- Test the computer, its input sensors, and output devices.

TERMS YOU SHOULD KNOW

Look for these terms as you study this chapter and learn what they mean.

ECM	processing	CTS
PCM	output	TPS
ECA	millisecond	O$_2$S
ECU	integrated	ESS
MPA	circuit	CPS
CPU	IC	CS
SBEC	digital	VSS
EEC	binary	TS
CCC	voltage	KS
processor	regulator	BS
logic module	clock	GS
engine	buffer	PSS
controller	analog	WSS
engine control	memory	ACCS
computer	RAM	IATS
body control	ROM	actuator
computer	PROM	self-diagnosis
automatic	KAM	fault code
temperature	KAPWR	fault code
control	sensor	chart
computer	potentiometer	scanner
antilock brake	pulse	analyzer
computer	generator	static
suspension	relay	electricity
system	solenoid	protection
computer	servomotor	reference
automatic	control	voltage
transmission/	module	voltmeter
transaxle	lighted display	digital
computer	AFS	voltmeter
instrumentation	MAP	ohmmeter
computer	ATS	multimeter
input	BPS	

■ AUTOMOTIVE COMPUTER TERMINOLOGY, TYPES, AND LOCATION

Computer Terminology

A variety of names has been used to identify what is generally known as a computer. Different service manuals refer to it in different ways. To aid in understanding the terminology, here are some of the more common terms used.

- Electronic control module (ECM)
- Powertrain control module (PCM)
- Electronic control assembly (ECA)
- Processor
- Microprocessor assembly (MPA)
- Central processing unit (CPU)
- Engine controller
- Single-board engine controller (SBEC)
- Engine control unit (ECU)
- Electronic engine control (EEC)
- Computer command control (CCC)

Remember that these terms all refer to what is essentially a computer. In this chapter and in the rest of the book the terms *computer, control module,* or *electronic control unit* are used. (For SAE STANDARD J1930 ABBREVIATIONS see the Appendix in this book.)

Computer Types

Many of today's cars have a number of computers, each controlling one or more systems. Some of the more common types are:

1. *Engine control computer:* controls the ignition system and the fuel injection system in response to a variety of sensors; may also control the EGR valve, alternator output, radiator fan relay, fuel pump relay, A/C clutch relay, self-diagnosis, and theft alarm.

2. *Body control computer:* monitors as many as 25 or more functions and conditions about lights, doors, fuel consumption, radios, theft security, fluid levels, and the like, and provides visual and audible outputs to inform the driver.

3. *Automatic temperature control computer:* monitors outside air temperature, inside air temperature, and engine coolant temperature, and controls the in-vehicle temperature, airflow, and fan speed of the ATC system.

4. *Antilock brake computer:* controls rapid application and release of brakes (when traction conditions warrant) in response to wheel speed and steering sensors.

5. *Suspension system computer:* may control vehicle ride height, shock absorber action, or air suspension system in response to vehicle speed sensors, height sensors, *g*-force sensors, and steering sensors.

6. *Automatic transmission/transaxle computer:* controls transmission shifting and torque converter clutch in response to engine sensors, vehicle speed, and shift lever sensors.

7. *Instrumentation computer:* monitors a variety of vehicle operating information sensors and displays these conditions on the instrument panel.

A computer consists of two major sections: the logic module and the power module. The logic module controls the power module. In most computers

■ FIGURE 4–1
Computer with the top removed exposes many tiny components. (Courtesy of Robert Bosch Canada Ltd.)

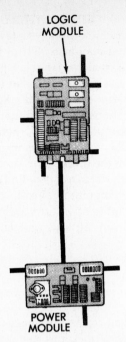

■ FIGURE 4–2
Two-piece computer control with separate logic module and power module. (Courtesy of Chrysler Corporation.)

the logic module and power module are combined in a single unit **(Figure 4–1)**. In other designs they are separate **(Figure 4–2)**.

Computer Locations

Computers may be located behind the dash, behind a kick panel under the dash, on the firewall or side panel in the engine compartment, under the seat, or in the trunk. Computers are usually located where they are well protected and close to the sensors and outputs to keep wiring to a minimum **(Figure 4–3)**.

■ COMPUTER OPERATION

The computer is designed to operate in three steps: input, processing, and output **(Figure 4–4)**.

- *Input:* switches and sensors monitor conditions which they convert to electrical signals and send to the computer
- *Processing:* computer uses input data from sensors and computer memory to decide what actuators should do
- *Output:* computer produces output voltage to operate actuators

Speed of Computer Operation

Computer systems are extremely fast. How long does it take for the following sequence of events to occur?

- Sensor notes a change in condition.
- Sensor sends signal to computer.
- Computer decides what to do about it.
- Computer activates output device to compensate for change in condition.

All of this happens in a few milliseconds (thousandths of a second). Try counting as fast as you can for 1 second. How far did you get? This will help you realize how short a second really is. A millisecond is much shorter and is faster than the blink of an eye. Computers are constantly working at this speed to keep the systems they control at their most efficient and practical operating level.

Integrated Circuit (Computer Chip)

A computer chip is an integrated circuit (IC) on a tiny piece of silicon. To integrate means to form or unite. An integrated circuit is the formation and interconnection of a number of semiconductor mate-

■ FIGURE 4–3
Typical computer locations. (Courtesy of F T Enterprises.)

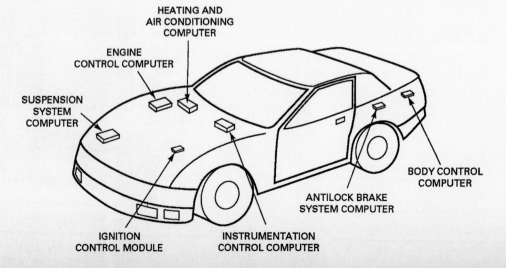

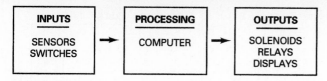

■ FIGURE 4–4

Basic computer operating steps. (Courtesy of F T Enterprises.)

rials deposited on a silicon chip. These semiconductor deposits form the diodes, transistors, and resistors of the chip. All of these components are microscopic in size and are produced under a microscope. Very fine high-quality metal conductors connect the components to each other and to the multipin input and output connectors **(Figure 4–5).**

Digital System

Automotive computers are digital computers except for a few older analog models. That is, they use digits—zero (0) and one (1)—to distinguish between different data **(Figure 4–6).** The computer can turn transistors on or off using digital data, where zero (0) represents *off* and one (1) represents *on*. Since only two numbers (or digits) are used, the system is called a binary system. This binary system can use a combination of several zeros and ones to represent other data **(Figure 4–7).** A zero (0) or a one (1) is called a bit. Eight bits constitute a byte. One kilobyte is 1024 bits or 128 bytes. Computer memory is measured in kilobytes.

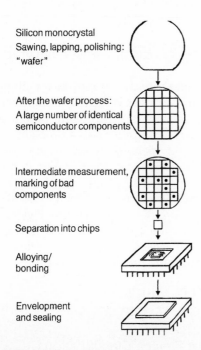

■ FIGURE 4–5

Steps in the production of a computer chip. (Courtesy of Robert Bosch Canada Ltd.)

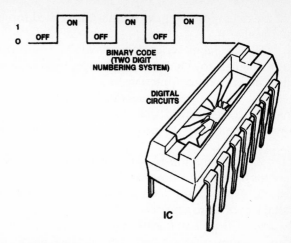

■ FIGURE 4–6

Digital integrated circuit with binary numbering system. (Courtesy of Chrysler Corporation.)

■ COMPUTER FUNCTIONS AND COMPONENTS

The computer has a number of jobs it must perform. Each section of a computer is responsible for part of the action taking place. These are the major components of a computer and their function.

1. *Voltage regulator:* reduces input voltage to the computer and maintains it at a precise level. Voltage fluctuations in computer operating voltage cannot be tolerated.

2. *Clock:* pulse generator that produces steady pulses one bit in length. This constant pulse serves as a reference signal to which other signals are compared. This allows the computer to distinguish between different digital binary signals.

3. *Buffer:* serves as temporary storage space when data entry is too fast, then releases it as required.

4. *Analog converter:* converts analog voltage signals from sensors and switches to digital form

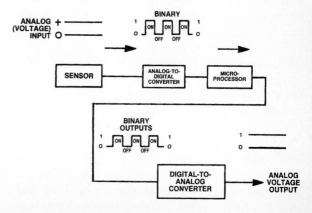

■ FIGURE 4–7

Analog and digital converters in computer. (Courtesy of Chrysler Corporation.)

that the microprocessor can handle (also called input interface).

5. *Digital converter:* converts digital computer output signals to analog voltage to operate actuators (also called an output interface).

6. *Microprocessor:* integrated circuit chip that analyzes data received from sensors, switches, and computer memory to produce output signals to operate actuators.

7. *Memory:* integrated circuit chip that stores data for use by microprocessor.

8. *Power transistors:* step up computer output voltage to operate actuators.

9. *Circuit board:* fiber panel with printed electrical circuitry that connects components mounted on board.

10. *Housing:* box that contains and protects computer components from damage and from outside electrical interference.

11. *Multiple connector:* multipin electrical connector that connects computer to wiring harness.

■ COMPUTER MEMORY

The computer stores information or data in memory chips in the digital form just described. It uses this information and the information from switches and sensors to decide what the output devices should do. There are several kinds of memory in automotive computers: RAM, ROM, PROM, KAM, and KAPWR **(Figure 4–8).**

1. *Random access memory (RAM).* This system stores information or data on a temporary basis. This data comes from input sensors and switches.

2. *Read-only memory (ROM).* This information is permanent and is programmed into the computer at the factory based on the make and model of the vehicle.

3. *Programmed read-only memory (PROM).* This information is also permanent and is programmed into the computer at the factory. The data are specific to engine size, transmission type, fuel system, ignition system, turbo or nonturbo, gear ratios, and a variety of other options. Although the PROM (or calibration unit) rarely fails, it can be replaced on many computers. Should the computer require replacing, the PROM is removed from the old computer and installed in the new computer. Data stored in the PROM remain during computer replacement.

4. *Keep alive memory (KAM).* A number of battery-powered locations in the computer allow it to store input failures during normal operation. These can be accessed in the self-diagnostic mode or with a scan tool by the technician for diagnosis. KAM is also the system that adapts calibration data to compensate for changes in the vehicle system due to normal wear and deterioration.

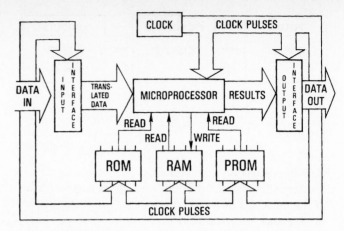

■   FIGURE 4–8
Computer memory functions. (Courtesy of General Motors Corporation.)

5. *Keep alive power (KAPWR).* The battery supplies the computer with keep alive power. This allows the computer to retain service information in memory even after the ignition key is turned off.

■ REFERENCE VOLTAGE

The computer puts out a reference voltage to some sensors. This voltage is fixed at 5 volts or 9 volts, depending on the make and model of vehicle. Reference voltage sent to the sensor is modified by the sensor based on the conditions being sensed such as changes in pressure, temperature, speed, and the like. This modified voltage signal is sent back to the computer for processing.

■ COMPUTER LIMP-IN MODE

The computer control system has a limp-in mode designed to take over vehicle operation when any of its critical sensors fail to provide proper input signals. When the computer sees a problem with one of these signals it operates on fixed values stored in the computer's permanent memory or it generates a replacement value by computing input from other input signals. For example if there is no MAP sensor signal the computer generates a new value based on signals from the throttle position sensor and the engine speed sensor. This allows engine operation to continue until the problem is corrected.

■ INPUT AND OUTPUT DEVICES

Input Device Classifications

Input devices include switches and sensors **(Figure 4–9).**

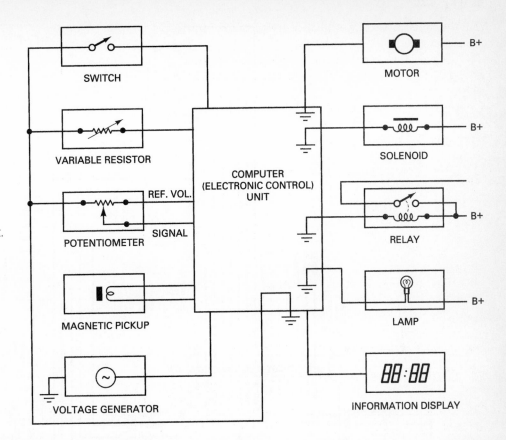

Computer control system with input devices at left and output devices at right. B+ represents battery positive connections.

1. *Switch:* indicates on or off condition.

2. *Variable resistance sensor:* internal resistance of sensor changes with a change in temperature or pressure. Sensor output voltage signals change accordingly.

3. *Potentiometer:* variable resistor with a sliding contact actuated by movement of a part like the airflow vane or throttle.

4. *Voltage-generating sensor:* generates its own voltage signal (e.g., oxygen sensor, knock sensor).

5. *Magnetic pulse generator:* uses a magnetic field and part movement to generate a voltage signal (e.g., camshaft sensor, crankshaft sensor).

Output Device Classifications

Output device or actuator types include the following **(Figure 4–9).**

1. *Relay.* Computer activates relay to control greater current.

2. *Solenoid.* Computer activates solenoid by energizing the solenoid windings. Solenoid acts on another device.

3. *Switching transistor.* Computer energizes base current of transistor to control greater current: in effect, an electronic relay.

4. *Servomotor.* Computer sends current to motor to cause rotation.

5. *Lighted display.* Computer sends current to activate liquid crystal or fluorescent display.

6. *Control module (power module).* Computer sends voltage signal to control module. Control module amplifies current to operate output device.

Active and Passive Sensors

Input devices or sensors are classified as active or passive. An active sensor generates its own voltage signal and does not require an external voltage source. Active sensors include magnetic pickup sensors, knock sensors, and oxygen sensors. Passive sensors rely on an external voltage supply. The sensor's internal resistance changes with a change in sensed conditions to produce a variable-voltage output signal to the computer. Passive sensors include throttle position sensors, temperature sensors, magnetic sensors, and switching sensors. (See **Figures 4–10** to **4–22.**)

■ VEHICLE SENSORS AND THEIR FUNCTION

Today's automobiles use a variety of sensors to monitor engine and vehicle operating systems **(Figures 4–10** and **4–11).** The computer adjusts the operation of these systems based on information provided by these sensors. Since engine and vehicle operation vary, sensor signals to the computer also vary. The computer constantly makes adjustments accordingly. Many of these sensors are shared by different systems.

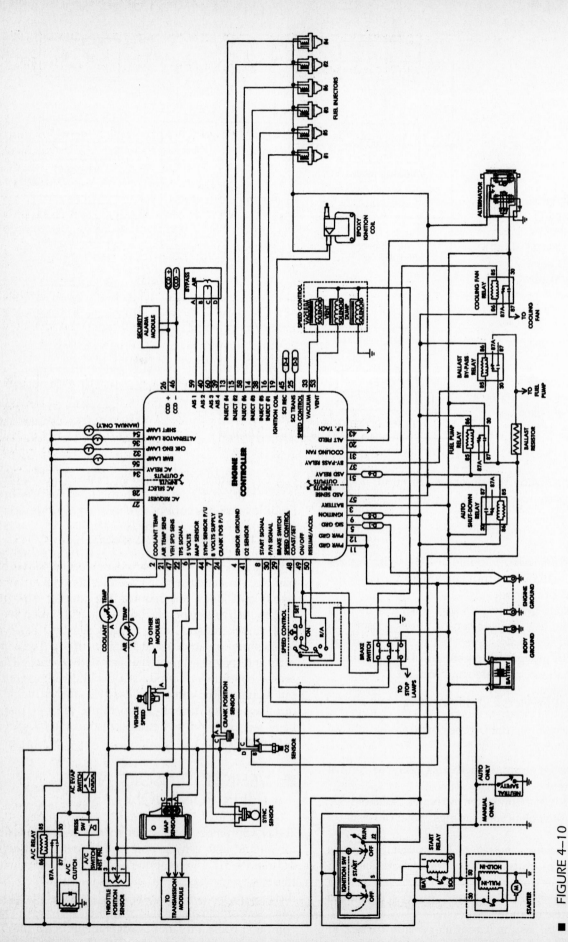

■ FIGURE 4–10

Engine computer control system input and output devices. Study this diagram carefully and locate all the components. (Courtesy of Chrysler Corporation.)

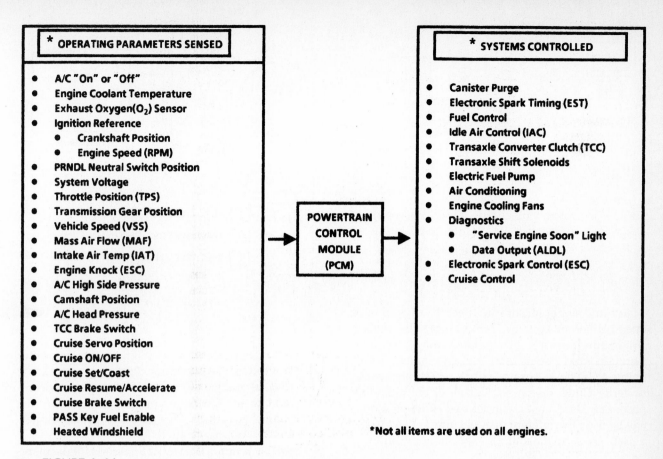

FIGURE 4–11
This computer control system has 25 inputs and 14 outputs. (Courtesy of General Motors Corporation.)

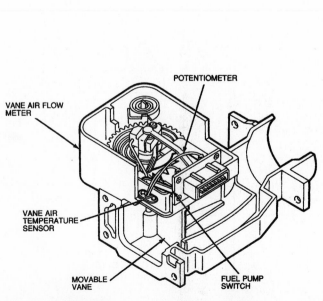

FIGURE 4–12
Passive vane airflow meter is a potentiometer with a variable-voltage output signal in proportion to vane position. (Courtesy of Ford Motor Company.)

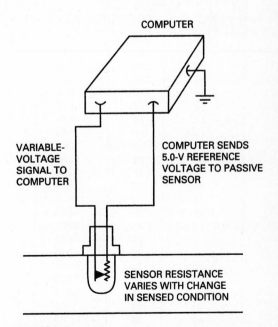

FIGURE 4–13
Passive intake air temperature sensor receives reference voltage from computer and puts out a variable-voltage signal based on intake air temperature. (Courtesy of F T Enterprises.)

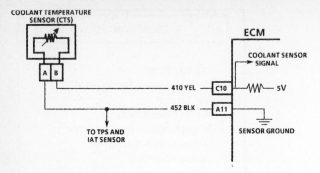

■ FIGURE 4–14

Passive-type coolant temperature sensor receives input voltage from computer (ECM). Sensor internal resistance varies with coolant temperature change producing a variable-voltage output signal to the computer. (Courtesy of General Motors Corporation.)

A fault in a single sensor can affect the operation of several different systems. For example the coolant temperature sensor controls open and closed loop operation, cold engine start fuel enrichment, spark timing, EGR flow, canister purge, and transmission converter clutch operation. Not all of the following sensors are used on all vehicles and different names may be used by different manufacturers. Refer to the appropriate service manual for specific applications.

COOLANT SENSOR		
TEMPERATURE VS. RESISTANCE VALUES (APPROXIMATE)		
°C	°F	OHMS
100	212	177
90	194	241
80	176	332
70	158	467
60	140	667
50	122	973
45	113	1188
40	104	1459
35	95	1802
30	86	2238
25	77	2796
20	68	3520
15	59	4450
10	50	5670
5	41	7280
0	32	9420
-5	23	12300
-10	14	16180
-15	5	21450
-20	-4	28680
-30	-22	52700
-40	-40	100700

■ FIGURE 4–15

Coolant temperature sensor resistance at various coolant temperatures. (Courtesy of General Motors Corporation.)

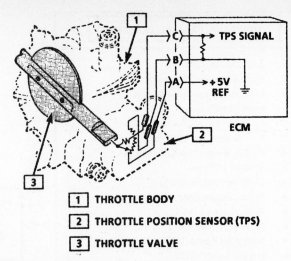

1	THROTTLE BODY
2	THROTTLE POSITION SENSOR (TPS)
3	THROTTLE VALVE

■ FIGURE 4–16

Throttle position sensor schematic. (Courtesy of General Motors Corporation.)

• *A/C Compressor Sensor.* Signals the computer that the A/C compressor clutch is on or off. The computer adjusts engine idle speed to accommodate the variations in load imposed on the engine as a result. This may be a pressure-operated or electrical switch.

• *Air Temperature Sensor (ATS).* Senses intake manifold air temperature. The computer uses this information to adjust fuel delivery to the engine. An ambient air temperature sensor is used by the computer to help control the automatic tempera-

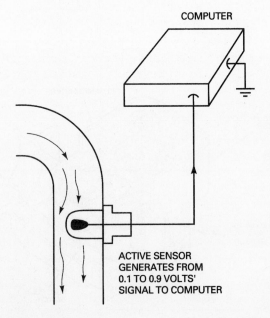

■ FIGURE 4–17

Oxygen sensor generates its own voltage signal to send to the computer based on oxygen content of exhaust gases. (Courtesy of F T Enterprises.)

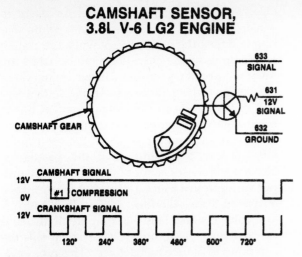

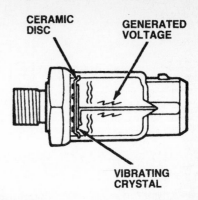

CERAMIC DISC   GENERATED VOLTAGE

VIBRATING CRYSTAL

■ FIGURE 4–20
Knock sensor construction. (Courtesy of Ford Motor Company.)

■ FIGURE 4–18
(Courtesy of General Motors Corporation.)

ture control system to provide maximum passenger comfort. As the air temperature increases sensor resistance decreases. As the air temperature decreases sensor resistance increases.

- *Battery Voltage Sensor.* Senses battery voltage to help the computer and the charging system maintain proper system voltage.
- *Brake Sensor (BS).* Signals the computer to disengage the torque converter clutch when the brakes are applied. On some applications it lowers engine speed to idle as well.
- *Barometric Pressure Sensor (BARO).* Senses atmospheric pressure that changes with altitude and weather conditions. The computer adjusts fuel delivery and ignition timing accordingly.
- *Coolant Temperature Sensor (CTS).* Senses engine coolant temperature. The computer uses this information to regulate fuel delivery during open loop operation, provide startup fuel enrichment, regulate ignition timing, control EGR flow, control canister purge, idle speed, and transmission converter clutch operation.
- *Crankshaft Position Sensor (CPS).* Provides information about engine speed and when each piston is at the TDC position. The computer uses this information to adjust fuel delivery and ignition timing. A Hall-effect device or pulse genera-

tor may be used for this purpose. Some engines use a camshaft position sensor to tell the computer when each piston is at the TDC position.
- *EGR Valve Position Sensor (EGRS).* Tells the computer when the EGR valve is open or closed. The computer adjusts the fuel delivery accordingly.
- *EGR Back Pressure Sensor.* Senses exhaust pressure in the backpressure chamber of the EGR valve. This variable voltage signal tells the computer when the EGR valve is closed, when it is open, and how far it is open. The computer adjusts the fuel delivery and ignition timing accordingly.
- *Heated Windshield Sensor (HWS).* Tells the computer when the electric heater system is on or off. The computer adjusts the idle speed in accordance with the resulting engine load changes.
- *Knock Sensor (KS).* Senses when the engine is pinging. The computer then retards the ignition timing to reduce pinging. There may be one knock sensor on each bank of cylinders on V engines. On some engines with distributorless ignition systems each cylinder may have a knock sensor.
- *Idle Switch (IS).* Senses closed throttle position. Switch is open at closed throttle position and closed at any other throttle position. The computer uses this information to help control the engine idle speed motor.
- *Manifold Absolute Pressure Sensor (MAP).* Senses intake manifold air pressure (absolute pressure)

■ FIGURE 4–19
Vehicle speed sensor schematic. (Courtesy of General Motors Corporation.)

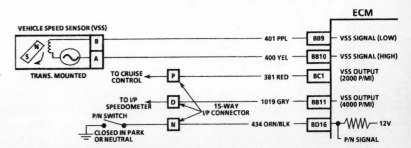

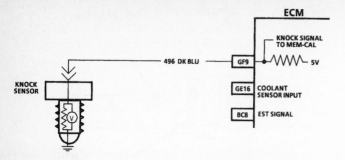

■ FIGURE 4–21
Knock sensor generates its own voltage signal to send to computer. (Courtesy of General Motors Corporation.)

or vacuum. This signal is directly related to engine load. The computer uses this information to adjust fuel delivery and ignition timing according to changes in pressure. Since this sensor measures intake manifold air absolute pressure it compensates for changes in atmospheric pressure resulting from different altitudes and weather conditions.

- *Mass Air-Flow Sensor (MAF).* Measures the mass or volume of airflow entering the engine. It is an indicator of throttle opening and engine load. The computer uses this information to adjust fuel delivery and ignition timing. Different types of airflow sensors include the vane, plate, hot wire, and film element types.
- *Neutral, Drive, Reverse Switch.* Used with automatic transmissions and transaxles. The computer uses this information to adjust the idle speed in accordance with the load changes on the engine resulting from selector lever position changes.

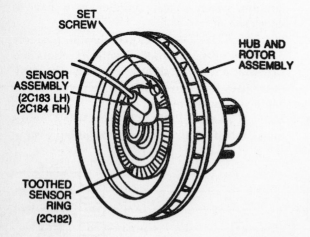

■ FIGURE 4–22
Magnetic pulse-type wheel speed sensor generates its own voltage signal to send to antilock brake system computer. (Courtesy of Ford Motor Company.)

- *Oxygen Sensor (O$_2$S).* Senses oxygen content in exhaust gases. The computer uses this information to adjust the fuel delivery when the system is operating in the closedloop mode. There are several types of O$_2$ sensors. The zirconium dioxide element type generates a varying voltage signal in proportion to the oxygen content in the exhaust gases as compared to the oxygen content of outside air. An air passage in the sensor provides access to outside air. If this passage is blocked the sensor cannot function. Voltage output varies from a lean 0.1 v to a rich 0.9 v. A 0.5 V output indicates the ideal 14.7 air/fuel ratio. A low voltage signal tells the computer to increase fuel delivery and a high voltage signal tells the computer to reduce fuel delivery. This type of O$_2$ sensor must be very hot in order to function. Later types are provided with a heating element to reduce the warmup period and to maintain sensor operating temperatures during engine idle or low load operation. Another type that does not generate any voltage acts like a variable resistor. Its resistance is low when the air/fuel ratio is rich. As the air/fuel mixture becomes leaner sensor resistance increases. A reference voltage provided by the computer is modified by the sensor in relation to sensor resistance to produce an output voltage signal to the computer.
- *Power Steering Sensor (PSS).* Senses power steering fluid pressure. The computer uses this information to regulate power steering fluid pressure in electronic variable power steering systems.
- *Power Steering Switch.* Tells the computer when the steering is turned to extreme right or left. The computer adjusts the idle speed in response to the increased load imposed on the engine under these conditions.
- *Throttle Position Sensor (TPS).* Tells the computer how fast the throttle is being opened and the relative position of the throttle. The TPS is a variable resistor (potentiometer). Resistance varies with throttle opening. The computer uses this information to adjust fuel delivery to the engine.
- *Inside Air Temperature Sensor (IATS).* Senses air temperature in the passenger compartment. The computer uses this information to help maintain the desired inside air temperature.
- *Wheel Speed Sensors (WSS).* Measure the rotating speed of the wheels. The computer uses this information to determine when to activate the antilock brakes and traction control.
- *Height Sensors (HS).* Measure vehicle suspension height on automatic height control suspension systems. The computer uses this information to help maintain the proper suspension height with varying load conditions.

- *Impact Sensors (IS).* Detect severe collision impacts and deploy the air bags when the impact is severe enough.
- *G Force Sensors (GS).* Detect acceleration, deceleration, and lateral G forces. The computer uses this information to help control suspension height, antilock braking, and traction control.
- *Information Sensors.* A variety of different sensors designed to inform the driver about special conditions that may exist. This includes engine oil level, brake fluid level, windshield washer fluid level, fuel level, door ajar, deck lid unlatched, lamp out, and the like. Many of these inform the driver that service is required.

Computer-Controlled Actuators

Actuators are designed to do what the computer tells them to do. Power transistors in the computer provide the voltage to operate the actuators when the computer energizes the transistor base circuit by grounding it. Actuators include solenoids, relays, servomotors, and lighting displays. An electronic transmission shift solenoid is an example. Engine speed, vehicle speed, and throttle position sensors provide input to the computer. When conditions are right for an upshift, the computer energizes the power transistor to provide voltage to the transmission shift valve solenoid. The solenoid is energized and moves the valve to the upshifted position.

An example of a computer-controlled relay is the electric radiator fan relay. When the engine temperature reaches a certain value, the coolant temperature sensor sends a signal to the computer. The computer grounds the fan drive motor relay to energize the fan motor. An example of a computer-controlled electric motor is the idle speed control motor of a fuel injection system. (See **Figure 4–10** for other examples.)

■ ACCESSING COMPUTER FAULT CODES

Computers are designed to monitor the performance of input sensors, switches, output devices, themselves, and related wiring harness. When a problem occurs often enough, a fault code is stored in computer memory. A malfunction indicator lamp on the dash goes on to alert the driver to take the vehicle in for repair. The technician can activate the computer memory to generate fault codes. These will appear as a flashing light, a number code, or a message on the dash. They can also appear as a fluctuating needle when an analog voltmeter is used to generate the code.

A diagnostic connector (self-test connector or assembly line diagnostic link, ALDL) in the wiring harness provides the means for activating fault codes. The diagnostic connector may be located in the engine compartment, under the dash, behind the side panel below the dash, behind the glove compartment, or in some other location. To activate the self-diagnostic mode and generate the fault codes, different methods are used on different vehicle makes and models. Some typical methods are described here.

1. Use a paper clip or jumper wire to connect the two specified terminals together in the diagnostic connector to activate the dash light. Light flashes are converted to fault code numbers **(Figure 4–23)**.

2. Use a jumper wire to connect the specified terminal in the diagnostic connector to ground to activate the dash light. Light flashes are converted to fault code number.

3. Connect an analog voltmeter to the battery positive terminal and the designated terminal in the diagnostic connector. Use a jumper wire to connect the pigtail wire (near the diagnostic connector) to the specified terminal in the diagnostic connector. Voltmeter needle fluctuations are converted to a fault code number **(Figures 4–24** and **4–25)**.

4. Turn the ignition key on and off in the specified sequence and time to activate the dash light. Light flashes are converted to fault code number.

5. Connect a test light to specified terminals in the diagnostic connector. Light flashes are converted to fault code number.

6. Press two specified climate control buttons in at the same time. Light flashes, fault code numbers, or word messages are generated depending on the vehicle make and model **(Figure 4–26)**.

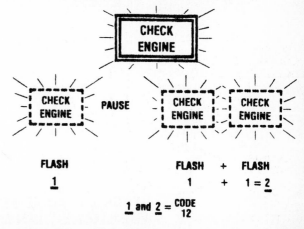

■ FIGURE 4–23
Flashing "check engine" light fault code interpretation. (Courtesy of General Motors Corporation.)

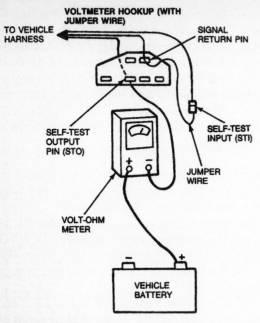

■ FIGURE 4–24
Jumper wire and voltmeter hookup used on some vehicles to access fault codes. (Courtesy of Ford Motor Company.)

7. Connect a scanner into the diagnostic connector and note the display on the scanner. The display may be a fault code number, a flashing light, or a bar graph depending on the type of scanner being used **(Figures 4–27 to 4–30).**

Follow the procedures given in the appropriate service manual to generate fault codes and how to use them.

Fault Code Charts

Fault code charts are provided in service manuals. They list all the possible fault code numbers and what each fault code number means. Fault codes direct the technician to the malfunctioning circuit. However, the circuit itself may not be causing the trouble. Trouble in a related component can cause the fault code to be triggered. It is therefore important to understand which vehicle systems are interrelated and may have common sensors.

■ COMPUTER CONTROL SYSTEM TESTING

Scan Testers

A scanner (scan tool) is used by plugging it into the wiring harness diagnostic connector **(Figures 4–27 and 4–28).** The vehicle's computer communicates a variety of information to the scanner, which is displayed in digital form as fault codes or in word form. Some of this information is difficult or impossible to obtain without a scanner. Using a scanner saves diagnosis time and can avoid the unnecessary replacement of good parts when other testing methods are used. The scanner is not able to pinpoint

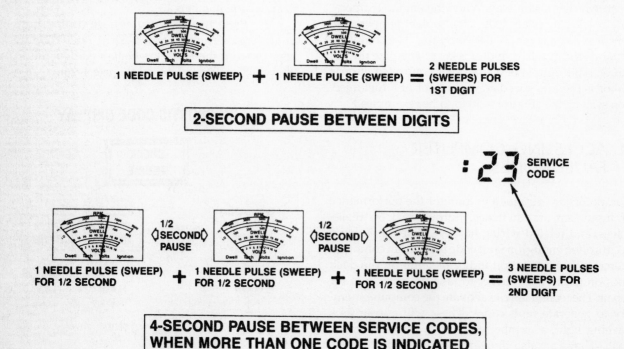

■ FIGURE 4–25
Interpreting voltmeter needle fluctuations to determine fault codes. (Courtesy of Ford Motor Company.)

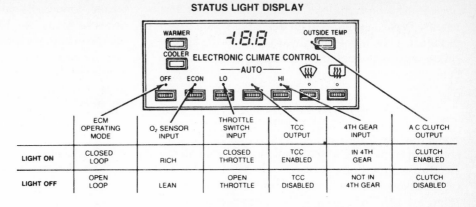

STATUS LIGHT DISPLAY

	ECM OPERATING MODE	O₂ SENSOR INPUT	THROTTLE SWITCH INPUT	TCC OUTPUT	4TH GEAR INPUT	A C CLUTCH OUTPUT
LIGHT ON	CLOSED LOOP	RICH	CLOSED THROTTLE	TCC ENABLED	IN 4TH GEAR	CLUTCH ENABLED
LIGHT OFF	OPEN LOOP	LEAN	OPEN THROTTLE	TCC DISABLED	NOT IN 4TH GEAR	CLUTCH DISABLED

■ FIGURE 4–26
This on-board self-diagnostic system displays trouble codes on the A/C control panel. (Courtesy of General Motors Corporation.)

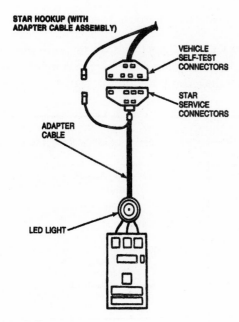

■ FIGURE 4–27
This STAR (self test diagnostic readout) tester is used on Ford vehicles. (Courtesy of Ford Motor Company.)

the exact location of a problem in a circuit but is able to identify the problem circuit. Pinpoint tests with a digital voltmeter or ohmmeter are performed to isolate the problem within the circuit. Substituting suspected components with known good components is another method of pinpointing faulty components.

A scanner can be used to detect intermittent problems related to the wiring harness and wiring connectors. The scanner is plugged into the diagnostic connector with the engine not running. The wiring harness, connectors, and terminals can then be manipulated and wiggled while observing the scanner display. Faulty wires and connectors can be detected in this way.

The scanner can also be used to check operation while the vehicle is being driven under conditions that caused the check engine light to turn on, indicating a problem. The scanner should be observed in each test position while driving the vehicle.

Different names are used by different manufacturers for their scan tools. Among these are Tech 1 (GM), DRB II (Chrysler), STAR (Ford), Monitor 4000E (OTC), MT2500 (Snap-On), Pro Link (MPSI), and others.

Follow the instructions supplied with the scanner and the procedures outlined in the service man-

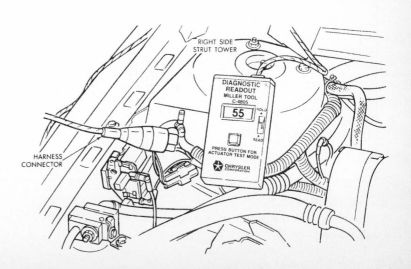

■ FIGURE 4–28
Diagnostic readout tool connected to diagnostic connector in wiring harness. (Courtesy of Chrysler Corporation.)

ual for test procedures and interpretation of test results. Typical scan tool data descriptions are given in **Figure 4–29** and **4–30**. Always refer to the appropriate service manual for specific data for the vehicle being serviced.

Breakout Box

Some diagnostic procedures require testing the sensors, output devices, and control module with all the electrical connections in place. This requires the use of a breakout box and a number of test lead adapters **(Figure 4–31)**. The breakout box connectors are fitted between wiring harness connectors on the vehicle in a manner that keeps the sensors, output devices, and control module connected so that the vehicle can be operated during testing. This allows the technician to perform a number of pinpoint checks and tests under actual operating conditions. Refer to the wiring diagrams in the service manual to locate

wiring connectors and circuits and the test procedures in each case. Each test is independent of the others. Within each test there are test sequences that can identify a condition or a problem without requiring the completion of the entire test procedure. The test strategy usually involves the following steps.

1. Check the voltage or resistance value.
2. Change the input signal.
3. Perform a click test.
4. Perform a wiggle test.
5. Perform a coil resistance test.
6. Perform an output signal test.
7. Check for harness shorts.
8. Check for harness opens.

(See **Figures 4–34** to **4–46** for examples of test strategies for solenoids, relays, computer output signals, and computer input signals. Consult the

Diagnosis item	Diagnosis code			Check item (Remedy)
	Output signal pattern	No.	Memory	
Engine control unit	H ⎍ L 12A0104	–	–	(Replace engine control unit)
Oxygen sensor	 H ⎍ L 12A0104	11	Retained	• Harness and connector • Oxygen sensor • Fuel pressure • Injectors (Replace if defective) • Intake air leaks
Air flow sensor	 H ⎍ L 12A0104	12	Retained	• Harness and connector (If harness and connector are normal, replace air flow sensor assembly.)
Intake air temperature sensor	 H ⎍ L 12A0104	13	Retained	• Harness and connector • Intake air temperature sensor
Throttle position sensor	 H ⎍ L 12A0104	14	Retained	• Harness and connector • Throttle position sensor • Idle position switch
Engine coolant temperature sensor	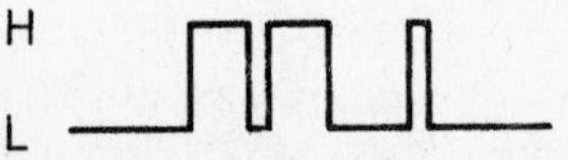 H ⎍ L 12A0107	21	Retained	• Harness and connector • Engine coolant temperature sensor

■ FIGURE 4–29
Typical bar graph diagnostic code information. (Courtesy of Chrysler Corporation.)

TYPICAL TECH 1 DATA DEFINITIONS

PCM DATA DESCRIPTION

A list of explanations for each data message displayed on the Tech 1 "Scan" tool begins below.

This information will assist in tracking down emission or driveability problems, since the displays can be viewed while the vehicle is being driven. See the "Diagnostic Circuit Check" for additional information.

ENGINE SPEED - RANGE 0-9999 RPM
Engine speed is computed by the PCM from the fuel control reference input. It should remain close to desired idle under various engine loads with engine idling.

DESIRED IDLE - RANGE 0-3175 RPM
The idle speed that is commanded by the PCM. The PCM will compensate for various engine loads to keep the engine at the desired idle speed.

COOLANT TEMP - RANGE -40° TO 199°C, -40° TO 389°F.
The Coolant Temperature Sensor (CTS) is mounted in the intake manifold and sends engine temperature information to the PCM. The PCM supplies 5 volts to the coolant temperature sensor circuit. The sensor is a thermistor which changes internal resistance as temperature changes. When the sensor is cold (internal resistance high), the PCM monitors a high signal voltage which it interprets as a cold engine. As the sensor warms (internal resistance decreases), the voltage signal will decrease and the PCM will interpret the lower voltage as a warm engine.

INTAKE AIR TEMPERATURE SENSOR - RANGE -40° TO 199°C, -40° TO 389°F.
An Intake Air Temperature (IAT) Sensor (Previously MAT) measures the air temperature in the air cleaner box and relays this information to the PCM. The PCM supplies 5 volts to the sensor.

The sensor, a thermistor, changes its internal resistance as temperature changes similar to the coolant temperature sensor. When the sensor is cold (internal resistance high), the PCM will monitor a high signal voltage which it interprets as cold air. As the sensor warms (internal resistance decreases), the voltage signal will decrease and the PCM will interpret the lower voltage as warm air.

THROTTLE POS - RANGE 0-5.10 VOLTS
Used by the PCM to determine the amount of throttle demanded by the driver. Should read .33-46 volt at idle to near 4.2 volts at wide open throttle.

THROTTLE ANGLE - RANGE 0-100%
Computed by the PCM from TPS voltage (Throttle pos) should read 0% at idle, 100% at wide open throttle.

MASS AIR FLOW - RANGE 0-255.9 GM/SEC.
The PCM converts the mass air flow sensor input signal into grams/seconds, indicating the amount of airflow entering the engine.

LV8 - RANGE 0-255
LV8, or engine load, is calculated by the PCM by engine speed and mass airflow. Should increase with an increase in rpm or airflow.

OXYGEN SENSOR - RANGE 0-1800 mv
Represents the exhaust oxygen sensor output voltage. Should fluctuate constantly within a range between 100 mv (lean exhaust) and 1000 mv (Rich exhaust) when operating in "Closed Loop."

RICH/LEAN FLAG - TECH 1 DISPLAYS RICH OR LEAN
Indicates whether exhaust oxygen sensor voltage is above (rich) or below (lean) the 450 mv oxygen sensor threshold voltage. Should change constantly indicating that the PCM is controlling the air/fuel mixture properly.

O_2 CROSS COUNTS - RANGE 0-255
The number of times the oxygen sensor voltage crosses over the rich/lean threshold during a one second interval.

AIR FUEL RATIO - RANGE 0.00-99.99
The reading reflects the commanded value. This should be at or near 14.7.

A lower number indicates a richer commanded air fuel mixture while a higher number indicates a leaner mixture.

SPARK ADVANCE - RANGE -90° TO 90°
This is a display of the spark advance (EST) calculation which the PCM is commanding to the ignition system. It computes the desired spark advance using data such as; engine temperature, rpm, load, vehicle speed, and operating mode.

FUEL INTEGRATOR - RANGE 0-255
Fuel integrator represents a short-term correction to fuel delivery by the PCM in response to the amount of time the oxygen sensor voltage spends above or below the 450 mv threshold. If the oxygen sensor voltage has mainly been below 450 mv, indicating a lean air/fuel mixture, fuel integrator will increase to tell the PCM to add fuel. If the oxygen sensor voltage stays mainly above the threshold, the PCM will reduce fuel delivery to compensate or the indicated rich condition. Under certain conditions such as extended idle and a high ambient temperature, canister purge may cause fuel integrator to read less than 100 counts.

■   FIGURE 4–30
(Courtesy of General Motors Corporation.)

TYPICAL TECH 1 DATA DEFINITIONS

BLOCK LEARN - RANGE 0-255
Block learn is derived from the fuel integrator value and is used for long-term correction of fuel delivery. A value of 128 counts indicates that fuel delivery requires no compensation to maintain a 14.7:1 air/fuel ratio. A value below 128 counts means that the fuel system is too rich and fuel delivery is being reduced (decreased injector pulse width). A value above 128 counts indicates that a lean condition exists and the PCM is compensating by adding fuel (increased injector pulse width). Block learn tends to follow fuel integrator, a value of less than 100 counts due to canister purge at idle should not be considered unusual.

OPEN/CLOSED LOOP - TECH 1 DISPLAYS OPEN OR CLOSED
"Closed Loop" displayed indicates that the PCM is controlling fuel delivery according to oxygen sensor voltage. In "Open Loop," the PCM ignores the oxygen sensor voltage and bases the amount of fuel to be delivered on TPS, coolant, and MAF sensor inputs only. "Closed Loop" operation should begin when the O_2 sensor becomes active, coolant temperature exceeds 50°C (122°F) for more than 30 seconds and the PCM has seen a RPM of 1200 or greater for 10 seconds.
At extremely high ambient temperatures or towing a trailer, it is possible for the PCM to remain in "Open Loop" operation to control converter temperatures.

BLOCK LEARN CELL - RANGE 0-15
Block learn cell is dependent upon engine speed and mass air flow readings. A plot of rpm vs MAF is broken into 16 cells. BLM cell indicates which cell is currently active.

KNOCK RETARD - RANGE 0°-90°
Indicates the amount of spark advance the PCM is removing from EST in response to the knock sensor (ESC) signal. Should read 0° at idle.
KNOCK SIGNAL - TECH 1 DISPLAYS YES OR NO
Indicates whether or not a knock signal is being detected by the PCM. Should read "NO" at idle.

IDLE AIR CONTROL - RANGE 0-255
Displays the commanded position of the idle air control pintle in counts. The higher the number of counts, the greater the commanded idle speed. Idle air control should respond fairly quickly to changes in engine load to maintain desired idle rpm.

VEHICLE SPEED - RANGE 0-255 KPH, 0-159 MPH
The vehicle speed sensor signal is converted into kph and mph for display. Should closely match speedometer reading.

TCC Mode - The three modes of operation are "OFF," "APPLY" and "ON." The "APPLY" mode will be active for approximately 1 to 5 seconds.

TCC Duty Cycle - This is the relative position of the PWM solenoid that controls TCC apply pressure. 100% is low pressure, 0% is high pressure.

TCC Slip - The amount of slip between engine speed and transmission speed. When TCC is "ON" there should only be a small amount of slip.

CURRENT WEAK CYL - TECH 1 DISPLAYS CYLINDER NUMBER OR NONE
The PCM monitors all 6 cylinders, and when one cylinder is out of balance for more than 25 consecutive crankshaft revolutions that cylinder number is displayed.

PURGE DUTY CYCLE - RANGE 0-100%
A proportional signal used to control canister purge function. 0% implies the valve is commanded fully closed while 100% implies that the valve is fully open.

BATTERY VOLTAGE - RANGE 0-25.5 VOLTS
This represents the battery voltage measured by the PCM at the ignition 1 feed to the PCM.

A/C REQUESTED - TECH 1 DISPLAYS YES OR NO
Represents the state of the A/C request input from the control head.

A/C CLUTCH - TECH 1 DISPLAYS "ON" OR "OFF"
Represents the commanded state of the A/C clutch control relay. Clutch should be engaged when "YES" is displayed.

A/C HEAD PRESSURE - TECH 1 DISPLAYS OK OR HIGH PRESS
Represents the state of the A/C head pressure switch. When the A/C refrigerant pressure rises above 1448 kPa (210 psi) the switch should close, informing the PCM to turn "ON" the high speed coolant fans.

C/C Brake Switch - When the brake pedal is depressed, the Brake Switch sends a signal to the PCM and disengages cruise control. Tech 1 displays YES when the pedal is depressed.

TCC Brake Switch - When the brake pedal is depressed, the switch sends a signal to the PCM to disengage the TCC.
DISPLAY: YES/NO (Yes with the pedal depressed).

■   FIGURE 4–30
Continued

TYPICAL TECH 1 DATA DEFINITIONS

C/C Set Speed - The speed that the cruise control system is trying to maintain.
DISPLAY: Range 0 - 255

Desired Cruise (Desired Servo Position) - A value given in percent calculated from the cruise set speed. It is the reference point for the PCM as to where the Servo Position Sensor (SPS) should be at a given speed.

Cruise Feedback (Actual Servo Position) - The actual position of the Servo Position Sensor (SPS) given in percent.

Cruise Mode - There are seven different modes in which cruise control may be operating in, they are: "OFF," "DISABLED," "STAND-BY," "CRUISE," "RESUME," "ACCEL" and "COAST."

C/C Servo Position - When the servo is at rest, the Tech 1 should display a value of 15 to 85 counts and be holding steady.

C/C "ON"/"OFF" Switch -
C/C RES/ACCEL Switch -
C/C SET/COAST Switch -
These parameters are the Cruise Control (C/C) switches. The Tech 1 may be used to determine if the cruise control switches are functioning properly.
When the "ON"/"OFF" switch is "ON" and the brake is not depressed, the display on the Tech 1 will switch from "OFF" to "ON" as the corresponding switch is pushed.

C/C Vac Solenoid -
C/C Vent Solenoid -
The cruise control Vac and Vent solenoid are PCM controlled outputs that control the amount of vacuum applied to the servo. The throttle will increase when the Vac solenoid is "ON" and the Vent solenoid is "ON." The throttle will decrease when the Vac solenoid is "OFF" and the Vent solenoid is "OFF."

PRNDL P,A,B,C - A transaxle mounted switch used as an input to the PCM to let the PCM know what position the gear select lever is in. Tech 1 status will switch from "HI" to "LOW" as different combinations are met. In "PARK" PRNDL, P and A will be "LO" and B and C will "HI."

PRNDL Position - The actual position of the gear select lever.

Desired Gear - The gear that the PCM is commanding the 4T60E transaxle to be in. In "PARK," the Tech 1 will display "First."

Park/Neutral - A PCM input to let the PCM know when the gear select lever is out of "PARK" and in "REVERSE" or a "DRIVE" gear. Tech 1 display "YES/NO."

2nd, 3rd, 4th Gear - The PCM looks at "PRNDL" position and "desired gear." The actual forward gear that the transaxle is in will be the lower of the two because the manual shaft can override the PCM commanded gear. Tech 1 will display "YES."

Fan 1 (Lo) - When the PCM is commanding the fans to be "ON" in low speed, the Tech 1 display will switch from "OFF" to "ON."

Fan 2 (Hi) - When the PCM is commanding the fans to be "ON" in high speed, the Tech 1 display will switch from "OFF" to "ON."

QDM 1, 2, (A, B) - Quad driver modules are used to power various systems. The Tech 1 will display "LO" and switch to "HIGH" if there is a circuit problem. Some QDMs may normally switch to "HIGH" and not have a circuit problem, such as QDM 1 (A) will switch to "HIGH" when the brake pedal is depressed.

Heated Windshield Req. - A PCM input signaling when the heated W/S is requested to command the desired idle speed to 1200 rpm to provide extra power for the heavy load on the alternator.

PASS Key (VATS) (Fuel Enable) - A PCM input that controls the fuel to the engine for the PASS key. The Tech 1 will normally display "OK (YES)." If the PASS key test has been failed, the display will switch to "NOT OK (NO)" and the fuel system may be disabled.

MEM-CAL ID - The MEM-CAL identification describes the particular MEM-CAL being used in the PCM. The Tech 1 display number is not the service part number.

Time From Start - A measure of how long the engine has been running. When the engine stops, it is reset to zero.

■   FIGURE 4–30
Continued

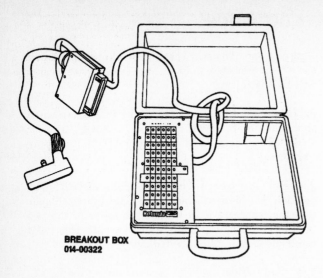

BREAKOUT BOX
014-00322

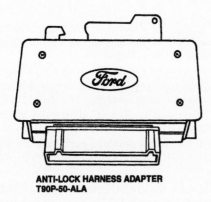

ANTI-LOCK HARNESS ADAPTER
T90P-50-ALA

■   FIGURE 4–31
Breakout box type of tester allows testing of sensors
and output devices while vehicle is in operation.
(Courtesy of Ford Motor Corporation.)

service manual to determine the meaning of devices
identified by abbreviations. Terminology and abbreviations differ considerably among various vehicle
manufacturers and service manuals. See the SAE
J1930 standard in the Appendix.)

Pinpoint Testing

Pinpoint testing is normally done after completing
self-diagnosis. Pinpoint tests involve testing individual components of the system identified as having a
fault. This includes testing switches, sensors, actuators, wiring harness, and connectors. Service manual
procedures must be followed precisely for pinpoint
tests, including test equipment connections and test
terminal identification. Making the wrong connections can cause damage to testers and system components. Component testing is described later in this
chapter as well as in other chapters where computer
controls are involved.

Computer Analyzer

A computer analyzer is a hand-held analyzer that
plugs into the car's diagnostic connector, and a code
storage unit that can be connected to the analyzer. It
can be used while testing in the shop or in the car
while driving. The stored information can be taken
back to the shop, where it is connected to a computer monitor for analysis. The system also provides
a telephone hot-line service to help with problem
diagnosis **(Figure 4–32).** Small software packages
make the system adaptable to different makes of
vehicles and provide for updating to new models.

Some computer analyzer systems provide a
modem service that allows the computer analyzer in
the shop to communicate with a mainframe computer by telephone. The mainframe computer provides large amounts of diagnostic information that
help solve difficult to diagnose troubles. Most vehicle manufacturers make this system available to
their dealers **(Figure 4–33).**

PRO TIP

HANDLING ELECTRONIC COMPONENTS *Many solid-
state electronic components can be damaged by a
discharge of static electricity from the human body.
Among these are: radios, control modules, engine
controllers, computers, programmers, transceivers,
amplifiers, automatic day/night mirrors, and others.
Some display a warning label while others do not.*

■   FIGURE 4–32
After test driving the car with a scanner and data
recorder connected to the vehicle, the technician
feeds the data into the computer for diagnosis.
(Courtesy of OTC Division, Sealed Power Corporation.)

■ FIGURE 4–33

This diagnostic system is connected to the car's computer control system and to a remote mainframe computer with a very large data bank. A modem allows communication to take place in both directions between the diagnostic tester and the mainframe computer to speed the diagnostic process. (Courtesy of General Motors Corporation.)

Damage to electronic parts can occur when the part is touched and the static electricity from the human body is discharged into the part (**Figures 4–34** and **4–35**). To avoid possible damage, either of two methods may be used as follows:

1. Use a static protection kit to ground out static electricity when working with solid-state components **(Figure 4–36).**

Activity	Relative Humidity	
	Low (10-20%)	High (65-90%)
	Volts	Volts
Walking Across a Carpet	35,000	1,500
Walking Over a Vinyl Floor	12,000	250
Working at a Bench	6,000	100
Sliding Across a Vehicle Seat	25,000	1,000

■ FIGURE 4–35

Static electricity voltages that are generated under various conditions. (Courtesy of Ford Motor Company.)

2. Discharge personal static electricity by touching a good metal ground point on the car. This should be done frequently, especially after sitting down or getting up, after walking, and after any movement across the car seat.

Other critical precautions that must be observed when handling solid-state components include the following.

1. Do not touch electric terminals on components or connectors with your finger or any tools.

2. When using a screwdriver or similar tool to disconnect a connector, never let the tool come in contact with or come between the exposed terminals.

3. Never jump ground or use test equipment probes on any components or connectors unless specified in diagnosis. When using test equipment, always connect the ground lead first.

NOTICE

CONTENTS SENSITIVE TO STATIC ELECTRICITY

■   FIGURE 4–34

Static electricity caution notice placed on many electronics parts packages. (Courtesy of General Motors Corporation.)

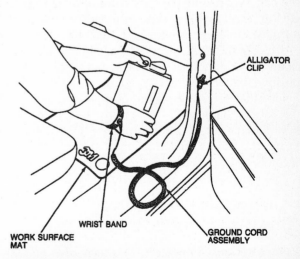

■   FIGURE 4–36

Static electricity protection equipment. (Courtesy of Ford Motor Company.)

4. Do not open the solid-state component's package until you are ready to install the part.

5. Always touch the solid-state component's package to a ground before opening.

6. Never bump or drop a solid-state component.

7. Do not lay solid-state components on any metal surfaces that operate electrically, such as a workbench, radio, TV set, or oscilloscope.

Preliminary Inspection

Before getting involved in testing system components, a preliminary inspection should be made. Look for likely causes of trouble such as loose or corroded wire terminals and connectors, disconnected or leaking vacuum hoses, or obvious damage to parts. The problem may be as simple as a partially disconnected wire harness connector or corroded connector terminals. Some manufacturers recommend a wiggle test of wiring connections. This involves grasping the connector with one hand on each side and wiggling it back and forth. This may restore a poor connection. If it does, the connector should be inspected and replaced if necessary. If the locking tabs have been damaged, vehicle vibration may loosen a plug-in connector. A careful visual inspection takes only a few minutes but could save a lot of time later.

Clearing Keep Alive Memory

When a faulty component is replaced (e.g., emission control or electronic system component) the keep alive memory (KAM) should be cleared to remove information stored by the processor from the original component. To clear KAM, disconnect the negative battery cable for at least 5 minutes. Reconnect the battery cable. Drive the car for at least 10 miles (16 km) to allow the processor to relearn new values for maximum performance and drivability.

Other methods are used on other models, for example, to disconnect the ECM power feed at the positive battery terminal pigtail, the in-line fuse holder that originates at the positive connection at the battery, or the ECM fuse in the fuse block. The key must be off in order to prevent ECM damage. Leave the power feed disconnected for at least 30 seconds and then reconnect the power feed. Refer to the service manual for specific instructions.

Testing Reference Voltage to Passive Sensors

Passive sensors do not generate their own voltage. They require a reference voltage fed to them by the computer. This reference voltage can be checked as follows:

1. Disconnect the electrical leads from the sensor.

2. Turn the ignition key on.

3. Connect a digital voltmeter to the leads disconnected from the sensor.

4. Read the voltage and compare to specifications.

5. If reference voltage is low, check the wiring and connections for looseness, corrosion, or opens **(Figures 4–37 and 4–38).**

Testing Passive Sensors

To test a passive sensor, disconnect it from the reference voltage supply. Test it with an ohmmeter to measure its internal resistance and compare to specifications **(Figure 4–39).** In the case of a temperature sensor the sensor must be heated to the specified temperature and the temperature checked with a thermometer. The resistance is then measured at the specified temperature and compared to specifications **(Figures 4–40 and 4–41).** A second method is to measure the voltage drop across the sensor with the wires connected and the ignition key on. Compare the voltage drop to specifications. A potentiometer can be tested in different positions for output voltage **(Figure 4–42).** A switching sensor can be tested with an ohmmeter as shown in **Figure 4–43.**

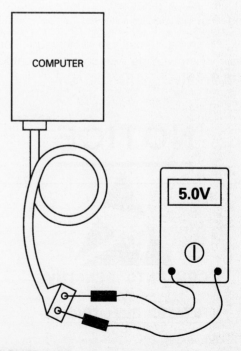

■ FIGURE 4–37

Testing computer reference voltage output at sensor harness plug.

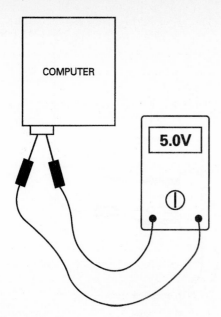

■ FIGURE 4–38
Testing computer reference voltage output at the computer.

Testing Active Sensors

Active sensors produce their own voltage signals for input to the computer. Several methods are used to test active sensors, depending on the type of sensor being tested and the vehicle make. For example, a voltmeter is used to check sensor operating voltage with the sensor in operation. This requires a high-impedance digital voltmeter. Another method is to measure the resistance in a magnetic sensor coil with an ohmmeter. If test results indicate a good sensor, check the wiring and connections to ensure continuity and no excessive resistance **(Figures 4-44 to 4–46).**

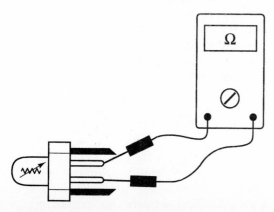

■ FIGURE 4–39
Testing a passive sensor with an ohmmeter.

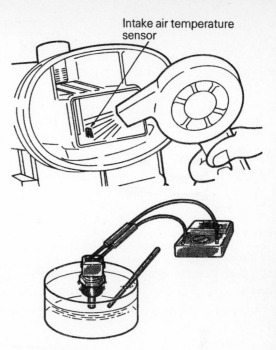

■ FIGURE 4–40
Heating an intake air temperature sensor with a heat gun prior to testing with an ohmmeter (top). Heating a coolant temperature sensor in hot water during resistance testing with an ohmmeter. (Courtesy of Chrysler Corporation.)

Additional Information

More information on computer control systems service is provided in other chapters of this book. Refer to them for additional information. Always refer to the appropriate service manual for the vehicle being serviced for specific procedures and specifications.

Testing Actuators

Actuators include relays, servomotors, solenoids, instrumentation displays, and similar devices. All actuators that have coil windings can be tested

Temperature °C (°F)	Resistance kΩ
0 (32)	5.9
20 (68)	2.5
40 (104)	2.7
80 (176)	0.3

■ FIGURE 4–41
Typical temperature and resistance values for a coolant temperature sensor. Refer to service manual for actual specifications. (Courtesy of Chrysler Corporation.)

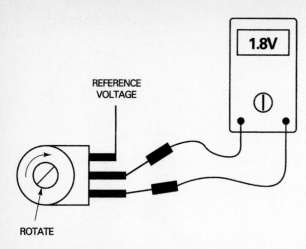

■   FIGURE 4–42
Testing potentiometer output voltage in different positions.

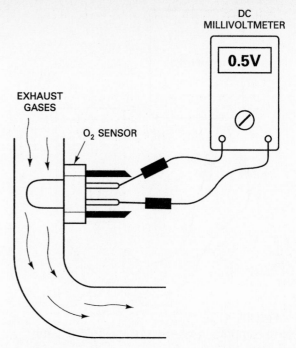

■   FIGURE 4–45
Testing an exhaust oxygen sensor for voltage output while the engine is running and sensor plug disconnected. (Courtesy of F T Enterprises.)

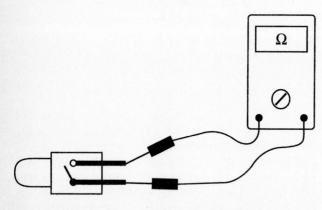

■   FIGURE 4–43
Testing a thermal switch with an ohmmeter. Switch is tested cold and hot. (Courtesy of F T Enterprises.)

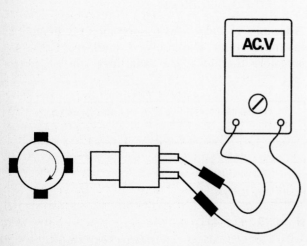

■   FIGURE 4–44
Pulse generator test hookup with voltmeter. (Courtesy of F T Enterprises.)

with an ohmmeter for resistance and the test results compared to specifications. Remember that items to be tested with an ohmmeter must first be disconnected from any voltage supply **(Figures 4–47** and **4–48)**. In many cases a solenoid or servo-motor can be checked simply by using a jumper wire to provide power directly from the battery. If the unit tests good, the wiring and connectors should be checked for looseness, corrosion, and continuity.

To test a relay for operation and output voltage, use a jumper wire to feed the relay from the battery. Connect a test lamp to the output side of the relay. If the test lamp lights when the jumper wire supplies power to the relay, it is not at fault. Check the wiring and connectors for looseness, corrosion, and continuity. Refer to the appropriate service manual for specific testing procedures.

■   COMPUTER SERVICE

The computer is usually the last item to be suspected and tested when servicing a computer control system. The usual procedure is to test the suspected input switches and sensors, the output actuators, and the related wiring. If the problem still exists after eliminating all possible input, output, and

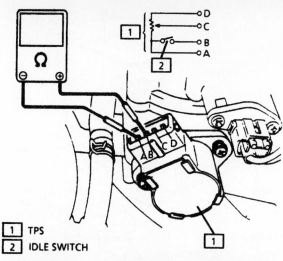

1 TPS
2 IDLE SWITCH

TERMINALS	CONDITION	RESISTANCE
Between A and B terminals (Idle Switch)	Throttle valve is at idle position.	Continuity
	When throttle lever-to-stop screw clearance is 0.3 mm (0.012 in.)	Continuity
	When throttle lever-to-stop screw clearance is 0.9 mm (0.035 in.)	No Continuity
Between A and D terminals	Throttle valve is at idle position	4.37 - 8.13 kΩ
Between A and C terminals	Throttle valve is at idle position	240 - 1140 Ω
	Throttle valve is fully opened	3.17 - 6.6 kΩ

■ FIGURE 4–46

Typical throttle position sensor tests and data. Refer to service manual for actual specifications. (Courtesy of General Motors Corporation.)

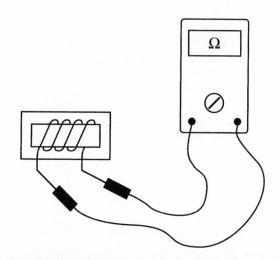

■ FIGURE 4–47

Testing a solenoid or relay winding with an ohmmeter. (Courtesy of F T Enterprises.)

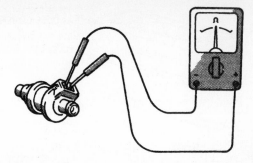

■ FIGURE 4–48

Testing a fuel injector solenoid with an ohmmeter. (Courtesy of Chrysler Corporation.)

wiring-related problems, the computer is tested, and if faulty, it or the calibration unit is replaced.

Computer Testing

Computer testing involves testing output voltage. This can be a small voltage to a sensor, a dwell signal to an injector, supply voltage to operate an actuator, and the like. Tests are made with a digital voltmeter. Follow service manual instructions for specific procedures. Typical reference voltage is 5.0 or 9.0 V **(Figure 4–38)**. Always consult the service manual for computer output specifications and test connections. Never make any connections that are not specified in the service manual. Serious damage can result from even an accidental error in connections. If computer output signals are incorrect, the calibration unit—Mem-Cal or PROM—or the computer may have to be replaced.

Calibration Unit (PROM) Service (GM)

The calibration unit, PROM or Mem-Cal, can be replaced on many engine control computers **(Figures 4–49 and 4–50)**. On others it is part of the computer and cannot be removed. Since calibration units seldom fail, they are usually removed from the old computer and installed in the new one when replacing the computer. To remove the PROM, first remove the cover. Use the PROM removing tool to grasp the PROM carrier and PROM. Pull it straight out of the computer, being careful not to bend the pins.

To install the PROM carrier and PROM, first make sure that the IC chip is fully flush with the top of the carrier. Use a small, blunt-end wooden dowel and push gently on all four corners until the chip is flush with the top of the carrier. Position the PROM into the computer with the reference mark aligned. Push the PROM down until it is fully seated. Install the cover plate.

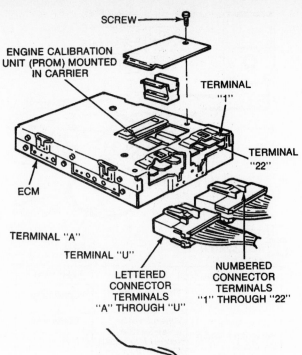

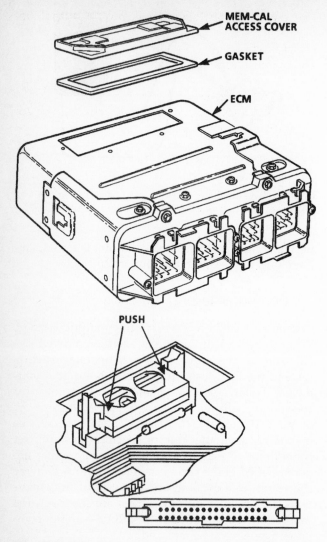

■   FIGURE 4–49
Replacing a Mem-Cal unit in a computer. (Courtesy of General Motors Corporation.)

■   FIGURE 4–50
Removing a PROM unit with a special tool. (Courtesy of General Motors Corporation.)

| 3 | PROM CARRIER |
| 9 | PROM REMOVAL TOOL |

PRO TIP

Do not press too hard or you may crack the circuit board. An improved PROM is available to replace the original unit for some vehicles. The updated PROM provides improved performance.

Review Questions

1. There are a variety of names used for what is generally known as the computer. True or False.
2. The engine control computer controls the _____ and the _____ _____ system.
3. The antilock brake computer controls rapid _____ and _____ of brakes (when traction conditions warrant).

4. The computer is designed to operate in three steps _____, _____, and _____.
5. RAM refers to _____ _____ _____.
6. ROM refers to _____ _____ _____.
7. Potentiometer is a _____ _____ with a sliding contact actuated by movement.
8. MAP sensor measures _____ or _____ in the intake manifold.
9. Oxygen sensor measures the amount of oxygen in the _____ _____.
10. Fault code charts are found in service manuals. True or False.
11. Fault codes direct the technician to the _____ _____.
12. A scanner tool is used by plugging it into the wiring harness _____ _____.
13. Discharge personal static electricity by touching a good _____ _____.

14. Passive sensors do not _____ their own voltage.
15. Active sensors produce their _____ _____ for input to the computer.
16. Computer testing involves testing _____.

Test Questions

1. Which of the following is not a computer?
   a. Hall-effect unit
   b. electronic control unit
   c. central processing unit
   d. electronic control assembly
2. The computer operates in the following three steps
   a. sensing, memory, output
   b. input, processing, computing
   c. input, processing, output
   d. sensing, memory, computing
3. A computer chip is
   a. an integrated circuit
   b. a tiny piece of silver
   c. a fast operating transistor
   d. a semiconductor
4. Automotive computers are
   a. alphanumeric
   b. digital
   c. analog
   d. basal
5. Computer memory that is temporary is called
   a. RAM
   b. ROM
   c. PROM
   d. PRAM
6. An active sensor
   a. receives battery voltage
   b. generates its own voltage
   c. cannot generate voltage
   d. receives battery voltage intermittently
7. A passive sensor
   a. receives reference voltage
   b. generates its own voltage
   c. bypasses the computer
   d. passes battery voltage on to another sensor

8. Which of the following is not an output device?
   a. relay
   b. servomotor
   c. solenoid
   d. circuit breaker
9. Power transistors in the computer or control module actuate the
   a. sensors
   b. integrated circuit
   c. control module
   d. output devices
10. Fault codes stored in the computer can be accessed by
   a. using a scan tool
   b. disconnecting the computer
   c. triggering the sensors
   d. turning the ignition key off
11. Pinpoint testing is normally done
   a. after completing the self diagnosis
   b. before performing the self diagnosis
   c. after using the breakout box
   d. with a scan tool
12. To test a passive sensor use
   a. a voltmeter
   b. an ammeter
   c. a dwell meter
   d. an ohmmeter
13. All actuators that have coil windings can be tested with
   a. a voltmeter
   b. an ammeter
   c. a dwell meter
   d. an ohmmeter
14. On some computers the following unit is replaceable
   a. PROM
   b. PRAM
   c. ROM
   d. RAM

Battery, Starting, and Charging Systems Diagnosis and Service

5

INTRODUCTION

Chapter 3 discussed electrical principles and service. Voltage, current, resistance, and electrical power were also discussed. The battery is a source of voltage, current, and electrical power. This chapter discusses the function and service of batteries, starting systems, and charging systems.

The modern starting system makes it easy to start the car or truck. It is very reliable and has a long service life. Over extended use, however, wear and deterioration can cause problems. To properly diagnose and service the starting system a good understanding of electrical principles and the starting system is required. This chapter explains the kind of problems that may be encountered, and how to diagnose and service the system.

The charging system is an important component of the vehicle electrical system. If it fails to function properly, the battery will soon be discharged and none of the electrical systems will be able to function. The design and operation of the charging system must be thoroughly understood in order to maintain and service it properly. This chapter deals with the function and service of the charging system and its components.

LEARNING OBJECTIVES

After completing this chapter, you should be able to:
- Describe the function of the battery.
- Diagnose battery problems.
- Inspect, clean, test, and replace a battery.
- Charge a battery using a shop charger.
- Replace a battery.
- State the function of the starting system.
- List the major components of the starting system.

- List common starting system problems.
- Perform starting system operational checks and tests.
- Perform a current draw test.
- Perform voltage drop tests.
- Remove, disassemble, clean, repair, and install a starting motor.
- Describe the function of the charging system.
- List the major components of the charging system and state their function.
- List common charging system problems.
- Perform a preliminary inspection of a charging system.
- Perform charging system tests as required.
- Test and replace alternator components.
- Remove and replace an alternator.

TERMS YOU SHOULD KNOW

Look for these terms as you study this chapter and learn what they mean.

cell	dead battery	starter drive
electrolyte	hydrometer	starting motor
specific gravity	state of charge	neutral switch
battery	voltage test	clutch interlock
terminal	cell test	switch
battery voltage	drain test	armature
maintenance-	battery charger	field
free battery	fast charger	brushes
cold-cranking	slow charger	commutator
rating	load test	drive pinion
reserve	quick-charge	permanent
capacity	test	magnet
battery stand	sulfated battery	starter
battery hold-	ignition switch	brushes
down	starter relay	brush holders
battery cable	starter solenoid	drive housing

field frame
shift lever
reduction drive
solenoid pull-in
  winding
solenoid hold-
  in winding
solenoid
  switch
relay switch
overrunning
  clutch drive
noise
clicking
buzzing
humming
whirring
grinding
current draw
volt/ampere
  tester
starter draw
  tester
load control
voltage drop
  tests
armature tester
growler
armature open
  test
armature
  ground test
armature short
  test
field coil test
solenoid test

relay test
brush holder
  test
starter drive
  test
free-running
  test
charging
  system
ac
dc
alternator
drive belt
regulator
wiring harness
rotor
stator
rectifier
diode
brush holder
brushes
slip rings
drive end
  frame
rectifier end
  frame
fan
pulley
integral
  regulator
diode trio
single phase
three phase
capacitor
Y stator
delta stator

field current
charge
  indicator
computer-
  controlled
  charging
  system
alternator
  noise
overcharging
undercharging
voltmeter test
surface charge
base voltage
no-load test
load test
current
  output test
voltage
  output test
regulator
  bypass test
full field
  current
circuit
  resistance
  test
rotor winding
  resistance
continuity
stator
  winding
  resistance
diode test

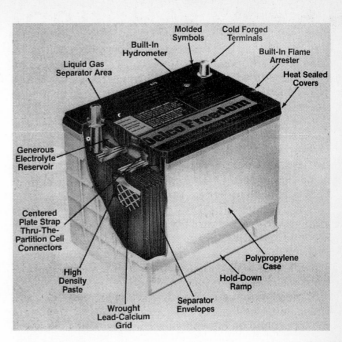

■ FIGURE 5–1
Battery with post terminals on top. (Courtesy of General Motors Corporation.)

The battery, starting system, and charging system work together as a team to provide electrical energy to the vehicle for starting, ignition, fuel injection, instrumentation, heating, air conditioning, lighting, and power accessories **(Figure 5–1).**

■ BATTERY FUNCTION

The battery performs the following tasks.

1. Provides all the electrical energy to the vehicle whenever the engine is not running

2. Operates the cranking motor, ignition system, fuel injection system, instrumentation, and other electrical devices during starting

3. Provides extra electrical power whenever power requirements exceed the output of the charging system

4. Stores energy over long periods of time

5. Acts as an electric shock absorber or capacitor to absorb stray voltages from the vehicle's electrical systems

Charging and Discharging

In operation, the battery is normally being partially discharged and recharged. There is a constant reversing of the chemical action taking place in the battery. The cycling of the charge and discharge modes slowly wears away the active materials on the battery cell plates. This eventually causes the battery positive plates to oxidize. When this oxidizing has reached the point of insufficient active plate area to charge the battery, the battery is worn out and must be replaced **(Figures 5–2 and 5–3).**

Battery Ratings

Battery capacity ratings are established by the Battery Council International (BCI) and the Society of Automotive Engineers. Commonly used ratings are as follows:

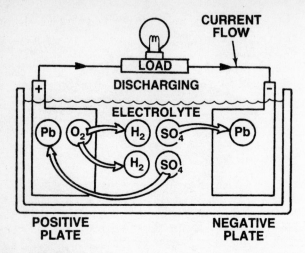

- **FIGURE 5–2**
Chemical action inside battery as current is being used and battery is discharging. Pb is sponge lead, O_2 is oxygen, therefore PbO_2 is lead oxide. H_2 is hydrogen, SO_4 is sulfate, therefore H_2SO_4 is sulfuric acid. (Courtesy of Chrysler Corporation.)

1. *Cold-cranking amperes.* The load in amperes a battery is able to deliver for 30 seconds at 0°F (−17.7°C) without falling below 7.2 V for a 12-V battery.
2. *Reserve capacity.* The time it takes to reduce a fully charged battery terminal voltage to 10.2 volts, or 1.7 volts per cell at a continuous discharge rate of 25 amperes at 80°F (26.7°C). The reserve capacity is stated on the battery in minutes. A reserve capacity of 90 minutes means that the driver has about 90 minutes of driving time (with a fully charged battery and the charging system not functioning) before the

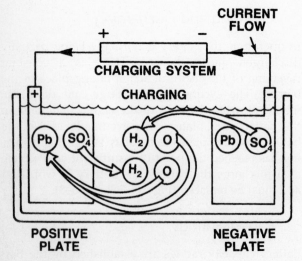

- **FIGURE 5–3**
During the charging cycle, chemical action inside the battery is the reverse of that shown in Figure 5–2. (Courtesy of Chrysler Corporation.)

battery goes dead. This allows enough time to get to a service facility to have the charging system repaired.

Factors that determine the battery rating required for a vehicle include engine size and type and climatic conditions under which it must operate. Battery power drops drastically as temperatures drop below freezing. As the temperature drops much below freezing, the engine is harder to crank, owing to increased friction resulting from oil thickening.

Maintenance-Free Battery

Maintenance-free batteries have several design features not always found on other batteries (**Figure 5–1**). This includes a larger electrolyte reserve capacity. Since all lead-acid batteries are subject to some vapor loss, water must be added periodically unless the reserve capacity for electrolyte is adequate for years of operation. Another feature is the use of calcium instead of antimony to strengthen the grid plates. The use of calcium reduces normal gassing. Instead of using separator plates between the positive and negative plates, each plate is encased in a porous fiberglass envelope. The envelopes prevent any material that may shed from the plates from causing a short between the plates and sediment collected in the bottom of the battery. Also provided is an expansion chamber to allow for internal expansion and contraction to occur. The top of the battery is sealed except for tiny indirect vapor vents. This reduces surface discharge and corrosion caused by electrolyte on the battery surface. A built-in hydrometer indicates the battery state of charge.

Battery Electrolyte (Acid)

Battery acid or electrolyte is a mixture of 36% sulfuric acid and 64% water. The specific gravity of water is 1.000. Sulfuric acid has a specific gravity of 1.835. The sulfuric acid and water solution in a battery has a specific gravity of 1.265. This makes it 1.265 times heavier than plain water. When the specific gravity of battery acid is too low, it may freeze in colder climates. When the specific gravity is too high, the plate grids in the battery will be damaged. The specific gravity of a maintenance-free battery is checked through the built-in hydrometer visible at the top of the battery (**Figures 5–4** and **5–5**). A squeeze bulb and float type of hydrometer is used on other batteries.

Battery acid is extremely corrosive and will cause skin burns if contacted. It will also burn holes in many kinds of clothing and damage metal and painted surfaces if allowed to come in contact with them.

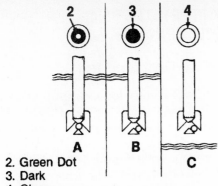

2. Green Dot
3. Dark
4. Clear
A. 65% or Above State of Charge
B. Below 65% State of Charge
C. Low Level Electrolyte

■ FIGURE 5–4

Built-in hydrometer operation. Note location of float ball in cases A, B, and C. (Courtesy of General Motors Corporation.)

■ BATTERY SERVICE PRECAUTIONS

1. Battery acid is extremely corrosive. Avoid contact with skin, eyes, and clothing. If battery acid should accidentally get into your eyes, rinse thoroughly with clean water and see your doctor. Contacted skin should be washed thoroughly with clean water; some baking soda with the wash will neutralize the action of the acid. Painted surfaces and metal parts are also easily attacked by acid, and contact should be avoided.

2. When making connections to a battery in or out of the vehicle, always observe proper battery polarity: positive to positive and negative to negative.

3. Avoid any arcing (sparks) or open flame near a battery. The battery produces highly explosive vapors that can cause serious damage if ignited.

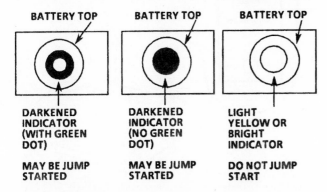

BATTERY TOP

DARKENED INDICATOR (WITH GREEN DOT)

MAY BE JUMP STARTED

BATTERY TOP

DARKENED INDICATOR (NO GREEN DOT)

MAY BE JUMP STARTED

BATTERY TOP

LIGHT YELLOW OR BRIGHT INDICATOR

DO NOT JUMP START

■ FIGURE 5–5

Check battery state of charge as shown here before jump starting. (Courtesy of General Motors Corporation.)

4. When disconnecting battery cables always remove ground cable first; and when connecting cables, always connect the ground cable last. This helps to avoid accidental arcing.

5. Observe equipment manufacturer's instructions when charging batteries. Never allow battery temperature to exceed 125°F (51.6°C).

6. Some battery manufacturers place restrictions on the use of a booster battery to jump start. Follow battery manufacturer's recommendations. One manufacturer says: "Do not charge, test, or jump start this battery when the built-in hydrometer is clear or yellow: battery must be replaced."

7. Use the proper battery carrier to handle the battery; this avoids injury and possible battery damage.

8. Use the proper protective clothing (apron, gloves, and face shield) when handling batteries to ensure safety.

9. Do not weld or smoke near a battery charging or storage area.

Jump Starting

PRO TIP

Do not push or tow the vehicle to start. Damage to the emission system and/or other parts of the vehicle may result. Do not jump start the vehicle unless the manufacturer of the battery or the vehicle with a dead battery allows this procedure.

CAUTION: Both the booster and discharged battery should be treated carefully when using jumper cables. Follow the procedure outlined below, being careful not to cause sparks. (See **Figure 5–6.**)

1. Set the parking brake and place automatic transmission in PARK (NEUTRAL for manual transmission). Turn off the ignition, lights, and all other electrical loads.

2. Check the built-in hydrometer. If it is clear or light yellow, replace the battery.

3. Only 12-V batteries can be used to start the engine. For systems other than 12-V, or other than negative ground, consult the appropriate service manual.

PRO TIP

When jump starting a vehicle with special high-rate charging equipment, be sure that charging equipment is 12-V negative ground. DO NOT USE 24-V charging equipment. Using such equipment can cause serious damage to the electrical system.

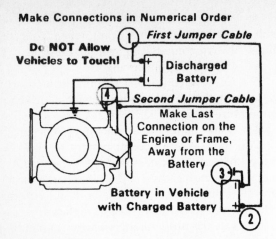

Make Connections in Numerical Order

Do NOT Allow Vehicles to Touch!

① **First Jumper Cable**

Discharged Battery

④ **Second Jumper Cable**

Make Last Connection on the Engine or Frame, Away from the Battery

Battery in Vehicle with Charged Battery

③

②

■ FIGURE 5–6

Jumper cable connections must be made in proper sequence as shown here. (Courtesy of General Motors Corporation.)

4. Attach the end of one jumper cable to the positive terminal of the booster battery and the other end of the cable to the positive terminal of the discharged battery. Do not permit vehicles to touch each other because this could cause a ground connection and counteract the benefits of the procedure.

5. Attach one end of the remaining negative cable to the negative terminal of the booster battery, and the other end to a solid engine ground (such as an AC compressor bracket or generator mounting bracket) at least 18 in. from the battery of the vehicle started. **(DO NOT CONNECT DIRECTLY TO THE NEGATIVE TERMINAL OF THE DEAD BATTERY SINCE THIS COULD IGNITE FUMES.)**

6. Start the engine of the vehicle that is providing the jump start and turn off electrical accessories. Then start the engine in the car with the discharged battery.

7. Reverse these directions exactly when removing the jumper cables. The negative cable must be disconnected from the engine that was jump started first.

■ BATTERY INSPECTION

Inspect the battery for dirt on top of the battery. Look for corroded battery cable connections, evidence of gassing (battery top wet with acid), case damage, and a damaged or dirty battery tray and hold-down. These problems must be corrected for good battery operation. On batteries with cell caps, check the electrolyte level. Add distilled water if the level is below the fill ring. Never overfill.

■ BATTERY TESTING AND SERVICE

Surface Discharge Test

A dirty or wet battery top can result in current loss and self-discharge across the top. This condition may result in low battery power and poor starting. To check for surface discharge, use a digital voltmeter on the low-voltage scale **(Figure 5–7)**. Connect the negative voltmeter lead to the battery negative post. Touch the surface area near the positive post with the positive voltmeter lead. If a voltage reading appears, battery current is being lost. The battery must be cleaned.

Cable Connection Test

To check for a poor connection between the battery cable and battery post, use a digital voltmeter to measure the voltage drop between the post and cable. Connect the negative lead to the cable end. With the ignition disabled (so the engine will not start), crank the engine while touching the positive lead to the battery terminal **(Figure 5–8)**. If the voltage drop exceeds 0.5 V, clean and tighten the cable connection.

Removing Battery Cable Connections

There are three kinds of battery cable connections: the flat ends bolted to side terminals, spring clamps, and clamps with bolts. To remove the side terminal type, simply remove the bolt with a wrench. Use pliers to spread and loosen the spring clamp cable end. To

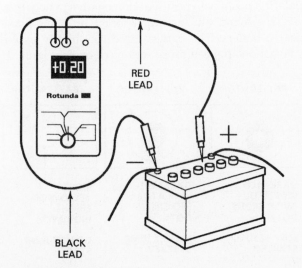

+0.20

Rotunda ■

RED LEAD

BLACK LEAD

– +

■ FIGURE 5–7

Surface discharge test. (Courtesy of Ford Motor Company.)

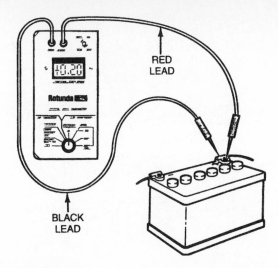

■ FIGURE 5–8
Cable connection resistance test. (Courtesy of Ford Motor Company.)

loosen the clamp bolt, use two wrenches, one to hold the bolt and the other to loosen the nut. With the nut loosened a few turns, use a battery cable puller to remove the clamp from the post **(Figure 5–9).**

Cleaning the Battery and Battery Terminals

After removing the battery use a baking soda and water solution to clean the battery, battery stand, and cable ends. Use a soft bristle brush with the solution. Be careful on non-maintenance-free batteries, not to allow any of the solution to enter the battery. After cleaning, rinse with clear water **(Figure 5–10).**

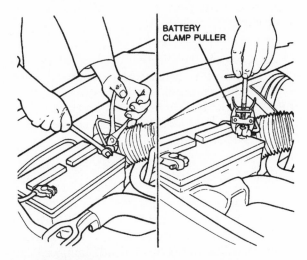

■ FIGURE 5–9
Removing a battery cable clamp. Loosen the clamp bolt first then remove the clamp with the proper puller. (Courtesy of Ford Motor Company.)

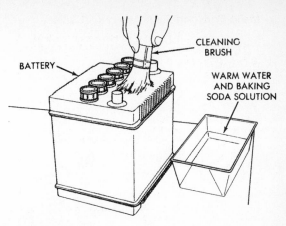

■ FIGURE 5–10
Cleaning the battery with a water and baking soda solution neutralizes the acid. The solution should not be allowed to enter the battery since it will do the same to the electrolyte. (Courtesy of Chrysler Corporation.)

Use a battery post and cable cleaner to clean the posts and cable ends **(Figures 5–11 and 5–12).** The wire bristles will remove any corrosion. Use a small wire brush to clean side terminals. After cleaning apply a thin coat of petroleum jelly to the terminals, then install them and tighten just enough for a good connection. Petroleum jelly prevents corrosion.

Checking the State of Charge

The specific gravity of the battery electrolyte indicates its state of charge. This is measured with a battery hydrometer. Maintenance-free batteries have a built-in hydrometer with a sight glass. When the

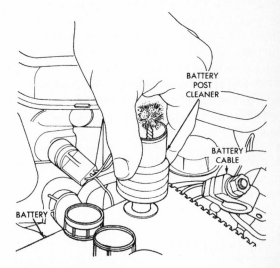

■ FIGURE 5–11
Battery post cleaner has internal wire brush. (Courtesy of Chrysler Corporation.)

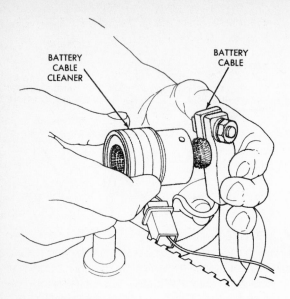

■ FIGURE 5–12
Cleaning a battery cable clamp. (Courtesy of Chrysler Corporation.)

green dot is visible, the battery is fully charged. When the sight glass shows dark with no green dot, the battery is discharged. When the sight glass shows a light yellow color, the battery should be replaced **(Figure 5–5)**. On batteries with cell caps a glass float hydrometer is used to check the specific gravity of the electrolyte. A fully charged battery in excellent condition has a specific gravity reading of 1.275 (±0.010). To use the hydrometer, squeeze the air out of the rubber bulb and insert the tube into the battery electrolyte. Slowly release the bulb to allow electrolyte to be drawn into the hydrometer. When the float has risen but does not touch the top, stop releasing the rubber bulb and note the reading on the float at the electrolyte level. Note the temperature of the electrolyte as well. Calculate the temperature corrected reading as shown in **Figure 5–13.** Test each cell in the same manner.

A ball-type hydrometer can be used in a a similar manner. Simply note the number of balls floating in the electrolyte and compare to tester instructions.

SAFETY CAUTION   Never allow battery acid to drip on your skin or the car finish. It will burn your skin and damage paint.

Battery Voltage and State of Charge Test

1. With the ignition off and no electrical loads on, connect the negative (–) lead of a voltmeter to the negative battery cable clamp. *Note:* The range setting on the voltmeter should be at least 0 to 15.

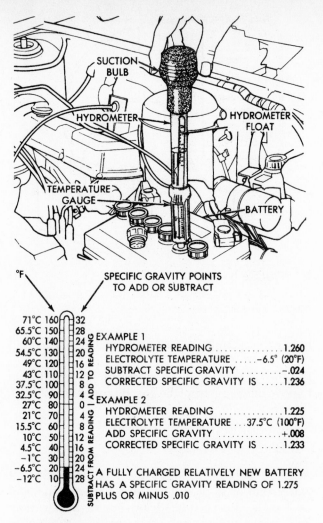

■ FIGURE 5–13
To accurately determine the battery state of charge with a hydrometer the reading must be temperature corrected as shown here. (Courtesy of Chrysler Corporation.)

2. Connect the positive (+) lead of the voltmeter to the positive battery cable clamp.

3. If the voltmeter reading is over 12.4 V at 70°F (21°C), the battery voltage is acceptable. If the reading is 12.4 V or less, the battery needs charging **(Figures 5–14 and 5–15).**

Cell Voltage Test

A cell voltage test determines whether the battery is defective or just discharged. It can only be performed on batteries with individual cell caps. To perform the test, insert the cadmium tips into adjoining cell pairs, one tip in each cell. Start at one end of the battery and test each cell this way. Note the voltage of each cell as it is tested. If cell voltage varies more than 0.10 V between cells, the battery should be replaced. If cell voltage is even, recharge the battery and test it again.

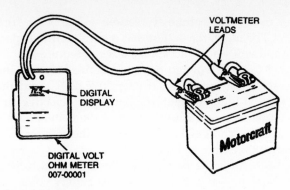

■   FIGURE 5–14
Testing battery open-circuit voltage to determine the state of charge. (Courtesy of Ford Motor Company.)

Quick-Charge Test

A quick-charge test can be performed to determine if the battery is sulfated. Charge the battery for 3 minutes at 30 to 40 A. Connect a voltmeter across the battery terminals and observe battery voltage during charging. If battery voltage exceeds 15.5 V on a 12-V battery, the battery is sulfated and must be replaced.

Charging the Battery

PRO TIP

Disconnect the negative battery cable before making charger connections. Failing to do so may result in a high-voltage surge and damage to electronic parts.

Batteries below 40°F (5°C) do not readily accept a charge. It may take 4 to 8 hours for a battery to warm up enough to take a charge. A completely discharged battery may also be slow to accept a charge. In this case the dead battery switch on the charger is used. However, the initial charge rate accepted is so low that it may not register on the charger ammeter. Follow the charger manufacturer's instructions on how to operate the charger.

OPEN-CIRCUIT VOLTS	PERCENT CHARGE
11.7 or less	0
12.0	25
12.2	50
12.4	75
12.6 or more	100

■   FIGURE 5–15
Battery open-circuit voltages and percent of charge.

There are two methods by which a battery may be charged: the automatic setting on chargers so equipped and the manual or constant-current setting. The automatic setting maintains a safe charging rate by automatically controlling the current and voltage to prevent spewing of electrolyte. It may take from 2 to 4 hours to charge a battery to a serviceable state. Several additional hours at 3 to 5 A are required to bring it to a fully charged state (**Figure 5–16**).

The manual or constant-current setting is initially set at 30 to 40 A for approximately 30 minutes or as long as there is no major gassing or spewing of electrolyte. If gassing is excessive, the rate must be reduced.

Battery Capacity Test (Load Test)

For this test the battery must be at or very near the fully charged state. Check the state of charge as outlined earlier. If necessary charge the battery to bring it up to a full charge. Remove the surface charge by applying the specified load for the battery being tested for 10 to 15 seconds only, then allow the battery to recover for two minutes. Battery electrolyte temperature should be at 70°F (21°C). Never load test a battery with electrolyte temperature below 60°F (17°C). If the tester has an adjustment for temperature correction be sure to set it at the proper setting. A high-rate-discharge battery starter tester combined with a voltmeter is used for this test (**Figure 5–17**).

1.   Turn the control knob on the tester to the OFF position.
2.   Turn the voltmeter selector switch to the 10- or 20-V position.
3.   Connect both positive test leads to the positive battery post and both negative test leads to the negative battery post. The voltmeter clips must contact the battery posts and not the high-rate-discharge

State of Charge	Specific Gravity	Charge Rate	Charging Time
Fully Charged	1.280		
75% Charged	1.225	20	50 min
50% Charged	1.190	20	70 min
25% Charged	1.155	20	90 min
Discharged	1.120	5	12 hrs

■   FIGURE 5–16
Charging rate and charging time required depend on the battery state of charge. (Courtesy of Chrysler Corporation.)

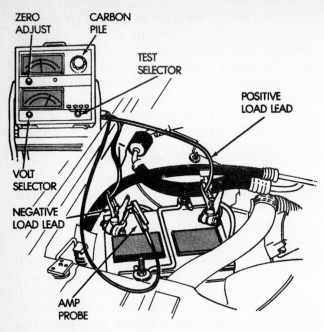

FIGURE 5–17
Battery load test connections. The ampere lead has an inductive pickup clamp. (Courtesy of Chrysler Corporation.)

tester clips. Unless this is done, the actual battery terminal voltage will not be indicated.

4. Turn the load control knob in a clockwise direction until the ammeter reads approximately one-half the cold-cranking ampere rating of the battery. A battery with a 400-cold-cranking ampere rating should be tested at 200 A (one-half the cold-cranking rating; see **Figure 5–18**).

5. With the ammeter reading the required load for 15 seconds, note the voltmeter reading. Avoid leaving the high discharge load on the battery for periods longer than 15 seconds. (Allow about 30 seconds for battery voltage to stabilize before proceeding.)

COLD-CRANKING AMPERES	AMPERE-HOUR RATING (APPROX.)	WATT RATING	LOAD TEST AMPERES
200	35–40	1800	100
250	41–48	2100	125
300	49–62	2500	150
350	63–70	2900	175
400	71–76	3250	200
450	77–86	3600	225
500	87–92	3900	250
550	93–110	4200	275

FIGURE 5–18
Load test figures for various battery ratings.

6. If the voltmeter reading is 9.6 V at 70°F (21°C) or more, the battery has a good output capacity and will readily accept a charge, if required.

7. If the voltage reading obtained during the capacity test is below 9.6 V at 70°F (21°C) and the battery is fully charged, the battery is defective and must be replaced. If unsure about the battery's state of charge, charge the battery. See the temperature and voltage chart in **Figure 5–19**.

8. After the battery has been charged, repeat the capacity test. If the capacity test battery voltage is still less than 9.6 V, replace the battery. If the voltage is 9.6V or more, the battery is satisfactory for service.

Battery Drain Test

The battery drain test will show whether battery current is being used with the ignition key off. Most computer-controlled cars have a small current drain to maintain computer memory, which must be taken into consideration. Vehicles with air suspension or load-leveling systems may have key-off temporary current drains ranging from 0.1 up to 20 A when the compressor is cycling. This can occur any time up to 70 minutes after the key is turned off. Make sure that all battery loads are off before proceeding with the test. Compare test results with specifications.

Drain Test with Clamp-On Ammeter

1. Turn the ignition to the OFF position and ensure that there are no electrical loads.

2. Clamp the meter clip securely around positive battery cable (all cables if two or more lead to post). *Note:* Do not start vehicle with clip on cable.

The current reading (current drain) should be less than 0.05 A. If it exceeds 0.05 A, it indicates a constant current drain that could cause a discharged battery. Possible sources of current drain problems are vehicle lamps (under hood, glove compartment, luggage compartment, etc.) that do not shut off properly.

ESTIMATED TEMPERATURE	MINIMUM VOLTAGE
70° F. (21° C.)	9.6
50° F. (10° C.)	9.4
30° F. (0° C.)	9.1
15° F. (−10° C.)	8.8
0° F. (−18° C.)	8.5
0° F. (BELOW: −18° C.)	8.0

FIGURE 5–19
Battery load test temperature and voltage chart. (Courtesy of General Motors Corporation.)

If the drain is not caused by a vehicle lamp, remove fuses one at a time until the cause of the drain is located. If drain is still undetermined, disconnect leads at starter relay one at a time to find the problem circuit.

Drain Test with Digital Voltmeter

The meter must read within 0.01 millivolt (mV). Also required is a shunt assembly similar to that shown in **Figure 5–20.**

1. Turn ignition to the OFF position and ensure that there are no electrical loads.
2. Check the battery voltage. If the voltage is under 11.5 V, charge the battery.
3. Disconnect the negative battery cable.
4. Connect the shunt assembly as shown.

PRO TIP

Do not crank the engine. It could destroy the shunt. Also, do not use the shunt to measure starting currents.

---

5. Set the volt/ohmmeter to the 200 or 300 mV scale for an accurate reading (must be within 0.01 mV).
6. Connect meter leads to shunt as shown. With this size shunt (50 mv = 50 amps) and meter, a direct current drain measurement can be made.

The current reading (current drain) should be less than 0.05 A. If the reading is between 0.2 and 0.9, a possible source is a vehicle lamp (glove compartment, under hood, luggage compartment, etc.) that does not turn off. If the problem is not a lamp, remove the fuses one at a time until the cause of the drain is located. If the drain is still undetermined, disconnect the leads at the starter relay one at a time to find the problem circuit.

■ BATTERY SELECTION AND INSTALLATION

The correct shape, physical size, post location, and battery rating requirements must all be considered when replacing a battery. Use only the type size and rating that are equal to original specifications. Install the new battery in a clean tray. Make sure that the tray has no protrusions that could damage the battery case. Place the hold-down in position and bolt it in place. Lightly coat the terminals and cable ends with petroleum jelly, place them in position, and tighten the bolts **(Figure 5–21).**

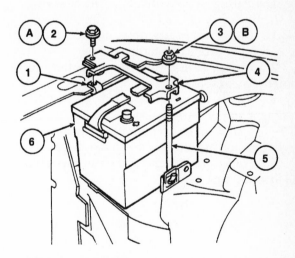

Part Number	Description
1. N623333-S2	U-Nut
2. N606690-S2	Screw (1 Req'd)
3. N801521-S2	Nut (1 Req'd)
4. 10755	Bracket
5. 10K700	J-Bolt
6. 10655	Battery Assy
A	Tighten to 7.0-10.0 N-m (62-88 Lb-in)
B	Tighten to 3.0-5.0 N-m (26-44 Lb-in)

■ FIGURE 5–21

Typical Battery Installation detail. (Courtesy of Ford Motor Company.)

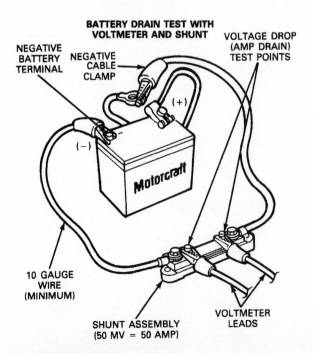

■ FIGURE 5–20

(Courtesy of Chrysler Corporation.)

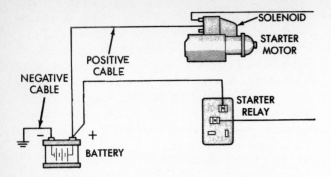

■ FIGURE 5–22

Major components of a starting system. (Courtesy of Chrysler Corporation.)

■ STARTING SYSTEM FUNCTION AND COMPONENTS

The starting system is designed to change the electrical energy of the battery to mechanical energy through the use of the starting motor. The system must crank the engine over at sufficient speed to allow the engine to run when the cylinders begin to fire. Basic starting system components are shown in **Figure 5–22.**

The starting system consists of the following.

1. *Battery and battery cables:* provide the electrical power to operate the starting motor
2. *Ignition switch:* connects the battery to the starter relay or solenoid
3. *Starter relay:* connects the battery to the starting motor or starter solenoid
4. *Starter solenoid:* connects the battery to the starting motor and engages the starter drive
5. *Starter drive:* connects the starting motor to the flywheel ring gear

6. *Starting motor:* cranks the engine over for starting
7. *Neutral switch:* prevents starting when transmission is in gear
8. *Clutch interlock switch:* prevents starting when clutch pedal is not depressed

Starting Motor Types

There are several types of starting motors used on cars today. They include the following.

1. *Electromagnetic field type.* Starter fields are electromagnets **(Figure 5–23).**
2. *Permanent-magnet type.* Starter fields are permanent magnets **(Figure 5–24).**
3. *Solenoid type.* Drive pinion is shifted by a solenoid **(Figures 5–23 to 5–25).**
4. *Movable-pole-shoe type.* Drive pinion is shifted by a movable pole shoe **(Figure 5–26).**
5. *Direct-drive type.* Drive pinion is mounted on armature shaft (with no gear reduction) to provide direct drive **(Figures 5–23 and 5–26).**
6. *Gear reduction type.* A gear reduction is provided between the armature shaft and the drive pinion **(Figures 5–24 and 5–25).**

Starter Control Circuit

The starting system actually consists of two separate but related circuits: the starter control circuit and the motor feed or power supply circuit. The control circuit includes the starting portion of the ignition switch, the neutral start switch, and the wire that connects these components to the relay or solenoid. The motor feed circuit consists of heavy-gauge cable from the battery to relay, to the solenoid, or directly from the battery to the solenoid. The heavy cable

■ FIGURE 5–23

Cutaway view of starter with electromagnetic fields and solenoid shift. (Courtesy of Chrysler Corporation.)

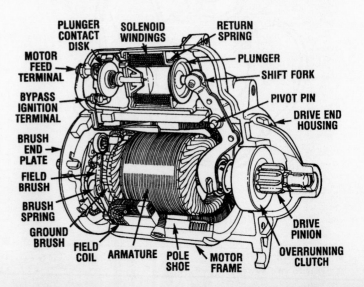

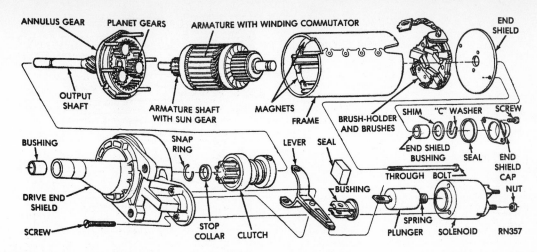

■ FIGURE 5–24
Exploded view of starter with permanent magnet fields, solenoid shift, and
planetary gear reduction. (Courtesy of Chrysler Corporation.)

■ FIGURE 5–25
Solenoid shift gear reduction starter.
(Courtesy of Chrysler Corporation.)

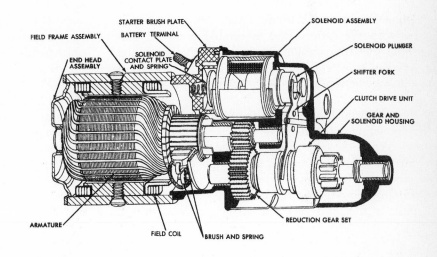

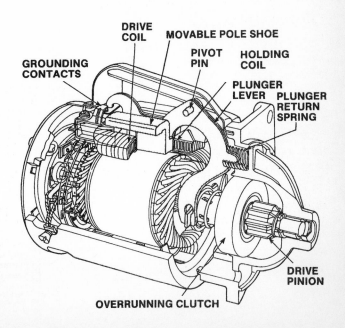

■ FIGURE 5–26
Movable-pole shoe direct-drive starter. (Courtesy of
Ford Motor Company.)

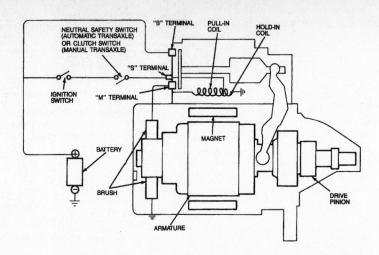

■ FIGURE 5–27
Typical electrical circuit for permanent magnet, solenoid type starter. (Courtesy of Ford Motor Company.)

carries the high current required to operate the starter motor **(Figures 5–27 and 5–28).**

Solenoid Operation

The solenoid on a cranking motor closes the circuit between the battery and the cranking motor, and shifts the drive pinion into mesh with the engine flywheel ring gear. This is accomplished by means of a linkage between the solenoid plunger and the shift lever on the cranking motor. Solenoids are energized directly from the battery through the switch or in conjunction with a relay.

When the circuit is completed to the solenoid, current from the battery is through two separate windings, the pull-in and hold-in windings. These windings produce a combined magnetic field that pulls in the plunger, so the drive pinion is shifted

into mesh and the main contacts in the solenoid switch are closed, completing the cranking motor circuit **(Figures 5–29 and 5–30).**

Closing the main contacts in the solenoid switch at the same time shorts out the pull-in winding, since it is connected across the main contacts. The heavy current through the pull-in winding occurs only during the movement of the plunger.

When the control circuit is broken after the engine is started, current no longer reaches the hold-in winding. Tension of the return spring then causes the plunger to return to the at-rest position. Low system voltage or an open circuit in the hold-in winding will cause clicking due to an oscillating action of the plunger. The pull-in winding has sufficient magnetic strength to close the main contacts, but when they are closed the pull-in winding is shorted out, and there is no magnetic force to keep the contacts closed.

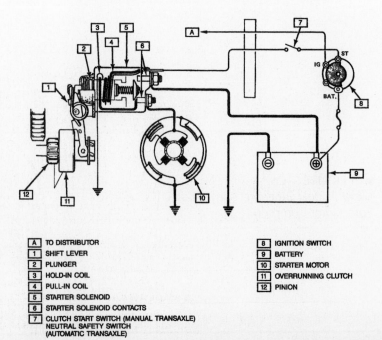

■ FIGURE 5–28
Electrical circuit for starter with electromagnetic fields and solenoid shift. (Courtesy of General Motors Corporation.)

A	TO DISTRIBUTOR
1	SHIFT LEVER
2	PLUNGER
3	HOLD-IN COIL
4	PULL-IN COIL
5	STARTER SOLENOID
6	STARTER SOLENOID CONTACTS
7	CLUTCH START SWITCH (MANUAL TRANSAXLE) NEUTRAL SAFETY SWITCH (AUTOMATIC TRANSAXLE)

8	IGNITION SWITCH
9	BATTERY
10	STARTER MOTOR
11	OVERRUNNING CLUTCH
12	PINION

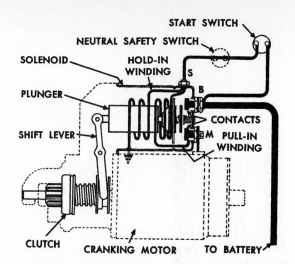

- FIGURE 5–29
Starter solenoid electrical schematic. (Courtesy of General Motors Corporation.)

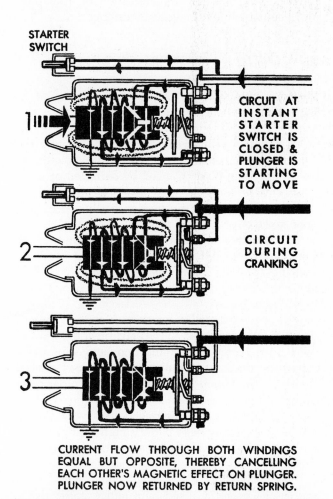

CIRCUIT AT INSTANT STARTER SWITCH IS CLOSED & PLUNGER IS STARTING TO MOVE

CIRCUIT DURING CRANKING

CURRENT FLOW THROUGH BOTH WINDINGS EQUAL BUT OPPOSITE, THEREBY CANCELLING EACH OTHER'S MAGNETIC EFFECT ON PLUNGER. PLUNGER NOW RETURNED BY RETURN SPRING.

- FIGURE 5–30
Starter solenoid operation. (Courtesy of General Motors Corporation.)

Relay Operation

The starter relay is a magnetic switch that connects the starter to the battery through the heavy battery cables for the brief period that the engine is being cranked. The relay is mounted near the battery or the starter to keep the cables as short as possible.

When the relay coil is activated by the ignition switch, the movable core or plunger is drawn into contact with the internal contacts of the battery and starter terminals. This provides full battery current to the starting motor. A secondary relay function is to initiate the alternate electrical path to the ignition coil, bypassing the resistance wire (or ballast resistor). This is accomplished by an internal connection that is energized by the relay plunger disc when it completes the circuit between the battery and starter internal contacts **(Figure 5–31).**

Both relays and solenoid switches are electromagnets used to control the switching of circuits. The relay opens and closes circuits by means of a pivoted contact arm, while the solenoid switch uses the movable core principle.

Neutral Start Switch Operation

Vehicles require a means of preventing the engine from being started in gear. If not, when the engine starts, the car would tend to lunge forward (or backward), possibly causing an accident. Automobile manufacturers include a switch in the starting circuit that is opened by the shift lever when moved to any position other than NEUTRAL or PARK. The neutral switch may be located at the transmission/transaxle or in the steering column. (For the wiring schematic, see **Figures 5–27** and **5–28**.)

Clutch Interlock Switch

Many cars equipped with a clutch and manual transmission have a clutch interlock switch. The car cannot be started until the clutch pedal is depressed

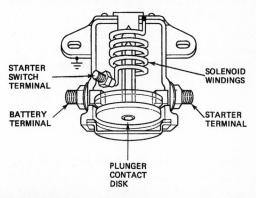

- FIGURE 5–31
Starter relay cross section. (Courtesy of General Motors Corporation.)

closing the circuit to the starter through the clutch switch. (For the wiring schematic, see **Figures 5–27** and **5–28**.)

Starter Drive Mechanism Functions

The drive mechanism has two functions. The first is to transmit the cranking torque to the engine flywheel when the cranking motor is operated and to disconnect the cranking motor from the flywheel after the engine has started. The second is to provide a gear reduction between the cranking motor and the engine so that there will be sufficient torque to turn the engine over at cranking speed. There are approximately 15 teeth on the flywheel for every tooth on the drive pinion. This means that the cranking motor armature will rotate about 15 times for every engine revolution on a direct-drive starter.

If the cranking motor drive pinion remained meshed with the flywheel ring gear at engine speeds above 1000 rpm, and the pinion transmitted its rotation to the cranking motor armature, the armature would be spun at high speeds. Such speeds, approaching 15,000 rpm, would cause the armature windings to be thrown from the armature slots and the segments to be thrown from the commutator. To avoid this, the drive mechanism must disengage the pinion from the flywheel ring gear as soon as the engine begins to operate.

Overrunning Clutch Drive

The overrunning clutch is the device that has made the solenoid-actuated type of starter feasible. It is a roller-type clutch that transmits torque in only one direction, turning freely in the other. In this way, torque can be transmitted from the starting motor to the flywheel, but not from the flywheel to the starting motor.

A typical overrunning clutch is shown in **Figure 5–32**. The clutch housing is internally splined to the starting motor armature shaft. The drive pinion turns freely on the armature shaft within the clutch housing. When the clutch housing is driven by the armature, the spring-loaded rollers are forced into the small ends of their tapered slots and wedge tightly against the roller race. This locks the pinion and clutch housing solidly together, permitting the pinion to turn the flywheel and thus crank the engine.

When the engine starts, the ring gear begins to drive the pinion faster than the starter motor because of the pinion-to-ring gear reduction ratio. This action unloads and releases the clutch rollers, permitting the pinion to rotate freely around the armature shaft without stressing the starter motor.

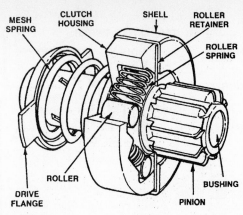

■   FIGURE 5–32
Cutaway view of overrunning clutch drive. (Courtesy of Ford Motor Company.)

The operator should always be careful not to reengage the cranking motor drive too soon after a false start. It is advisable to wait at least 5 seconds between attempts to crank. Burred teeth on the flywheel ring gear are an indication of attempted engagement while the engine is running.

■ STARTING SYSTEM PROBLEMS

The following are some of the more common starting system problems **(Figure 5–33)**.

1. *Single click sound.* The click is usually the sound of the solenoid contacts closing with no cranking taking place. Caused by corroded or loose battery cable connections, a nearly dead battery, a faulty starting motor, burned or badly worn solenoid contacts, or a seized engine.

2. *Clicking or buzzing sound.* The sound results from rapid solenoid plunger movement in and out with no cranking taking place. May be caused by loose or corroded battery cable connections or a nearly dead battery.

3. *No sound and no cranking.* Nothing happens when the key is turned to the start position. Caused by a dead battery, no connection between battery cables and terminals, a faulty relay, solenoid, neutral safety switch, clutch interlock switch, or other component **(Figure 5–34)**.

4. *Slow cranking.* Engine cranks very slowly. Caused by a nearly dead battery, high starting motor current draw, or poor electrical connections **(Figure 5–35)**.

5. *Humming or whirring sound after initial starter engagement.* Caused by a faulty starter drive, overrunning clutch, or badly worn pinion gear teeth. In either case the starter motor is running but is not cranking the engine.

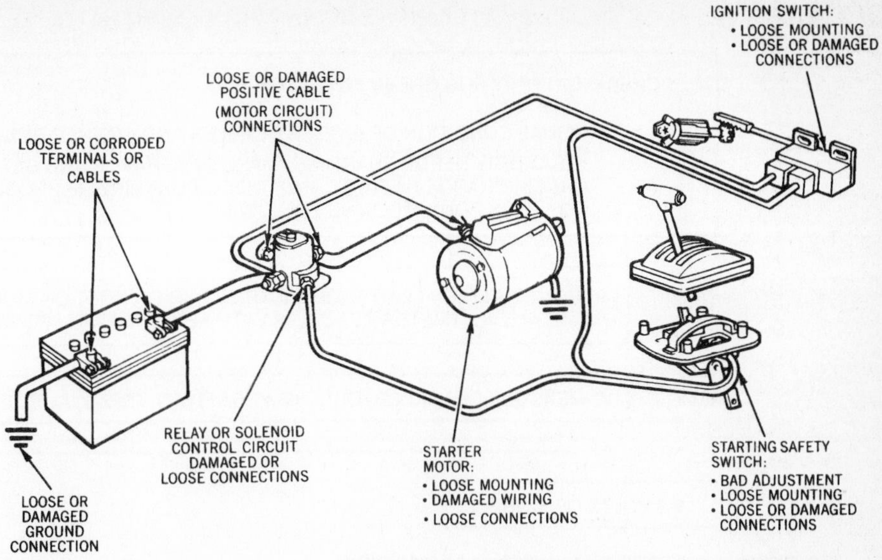

IGNITION SWITCH:
• LOOSE MOUNTING
• LOOSE OR DAMAGED
  CONNECTIONS

LOOSE OR DAMAGED
POSITIVE CABLE
(MOTOR CIRCUIT)
CONNECTIONS

LOOSE OR CORRODED
TERMINALS OR
CABLES

■ FIGURE 5–33
Typical starting system
problems. (Courtesy of Ford
Motor Company.)

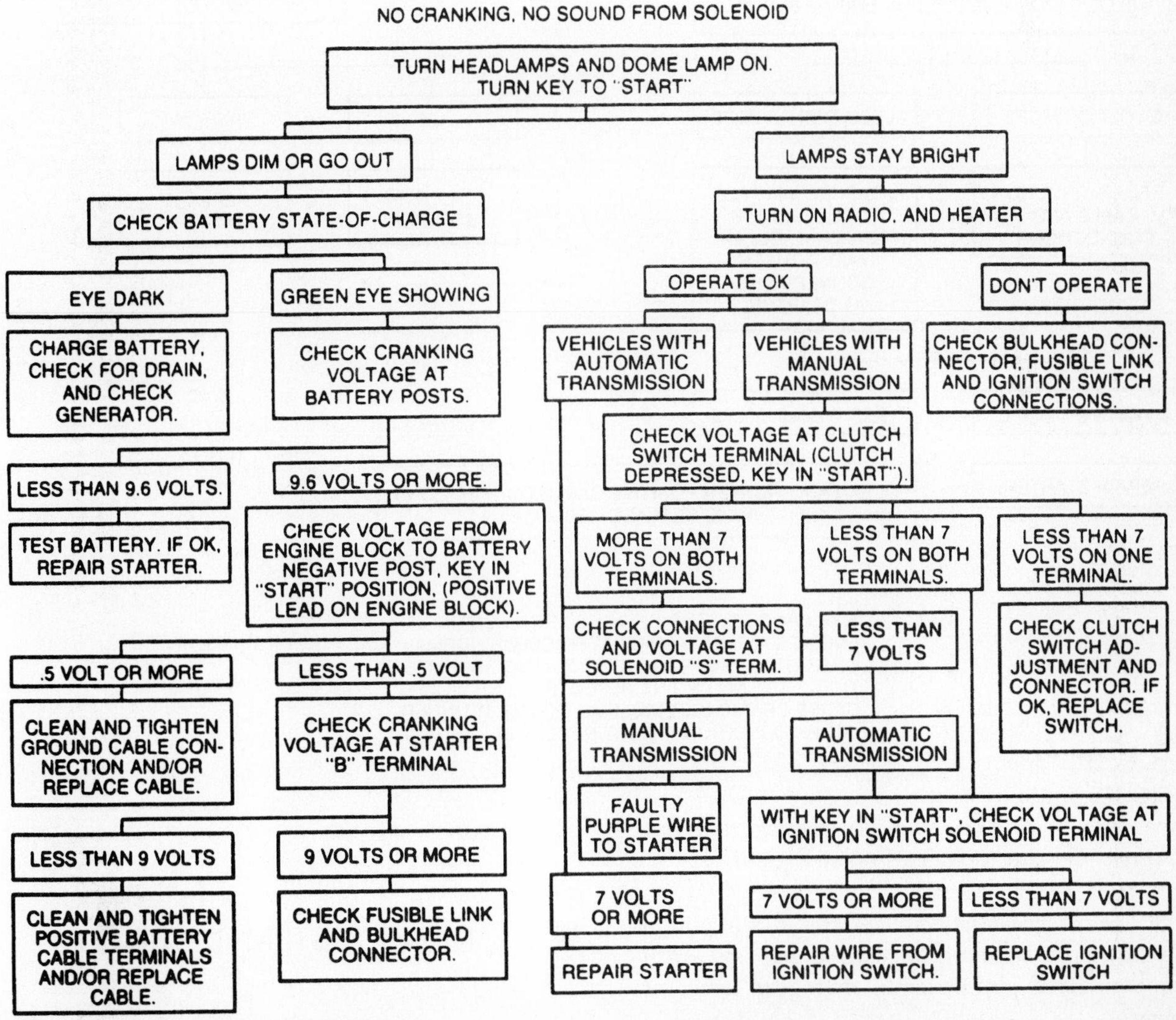

RELAY OR SOLENOID
CONTROL CIRCUIT
DAMAGED OR
LOOSE CONNECTIONS

LOOSE OR
DAMAGED
GROUND
CONNECTION

STARTER
MOTOR:
• LOOSE MOUNTING
• DAMAGED WIRING
• LOOSE CONNECTIONS

STARTING SAFETY
SWITCH:
• BAD ADJUSTMENT
• LOOSE MOUNTING
• LOOSE OR DAMAGED
  CONNECTIONS

NO CRANKING, NO SOUND FROM SOLENOID

TURN HEADLAMPS AND DOME LAMP ON.
TURN KEY TO "START"

LAMPS DIM OR GO OUT

CHECK BATTERY STATE-OF-CHARGE

EYE DARK

CHARGE BATTERY,
CHECK FOR DRAIN,
AND CHECK
GENERATOR.

LESS THAN 9.6 VOLTS.

TEST BATTERY. IF OK,
REPAIR STARTER.

.5 VOLT OR MORE

CLEAN AND TIGHTEN
GROUND CABLE CON-
NECTION AND/OR
REPLACE CABLE.

LESS THAN 9 VOLTS

CLEAN AND TIGHTEN
POSITIVE BATTERY
CABLE TERMINALS
AND/OR REPLACE
CABLE.

GREEN EYE SHOWING

CHECK CRANKING
VOLTAGE AT
BATTERY POSTS.

9.6 VOLTS OR MORE.

CHECK VOLTAGE FROM
ENGINE BLOCK TO BATTERY
NEGATIVE POST, KEY IN
"START" POSITION, (POSITIVE
LEAD ON ENGINE BLOCK).

LESS THAN .5 VOLT

CHECK CRANKING
VOLTAGE AT STARTER
"B" TERMINAL

9 VOLTS OR MORE

CHECK FUSIBLE LINK
AND BULKHEAD
CONNECTOR.

LAMPS STAY BRIGHT

TURN ON RADIO, AND HEATER

OPERATE OK

VEHICLES WITH
AUTOMATIC
TRANSMISSION

VEHICLES WITH
MANUAL
TRANSMISSION

CHECK VOLTAGE AT CLUTCH
SWITCH TERMINAL (CLUTCH
DEPRESSED, KEY IN "START").

MORE THAN 7
VOLTS ON BOTH
TERMINALS.

CHECK CONNECTIONS
AND VOLTAGE AT
SOLENOID "S" TERM.

MANUAL
TRANSMISSION

FAULTY
PURPLE WIRE
TO STARTER

7 VOLTS
OR MORE

REPAIR STARTER

LESS THAN 7
VOLTS ON BOTH
TERMINALS.

LESS THAN
7 VOLTS

AUTOMATIC
TRANSMISSION

WITH KEY IN "START", CHECK VOLTAGE AT
IGNITION SWITCH SOLENOID TERMINAL

7 VOLTS OR MORE

REPAIR WIRE FROM
IGNITION SWITCH.

LESS THAN 7
VOLTS ON ONE
TERMINAL.

CHECK CLUTCH
SWITCH AD-
JUSTMENT AND
CONNECTOR. IF
OK, REPLACE
SWITCH.

LESS THAN 7 VOLTS

REPLACE IGNITION
SWITCH

DON'T OPERATE

CHECK BULKHEAD CON-
NECTOR, FUSIBLE LINK
AND IGNITION SWITCH
CONNECTIONS.

■ FIGURE 5–34
Typical diagnostic chart for a "nocranking, no sound from solenoid" condition.
(Courtesy of General Motors Corporation.)

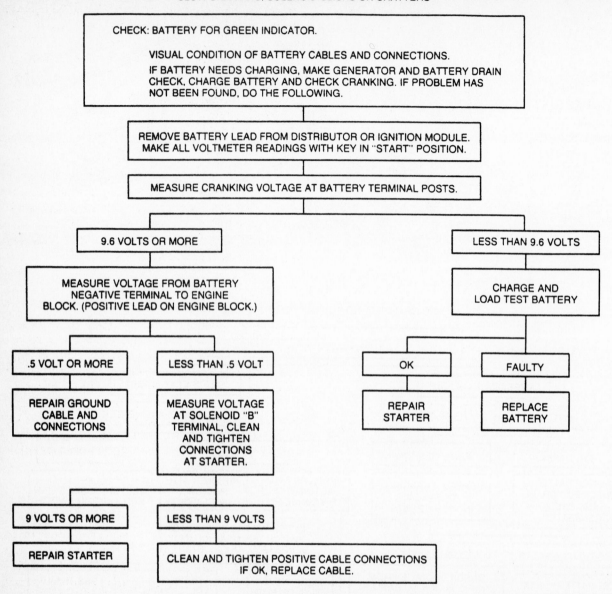

■ FIGURE 5–35
Diagnostic chart for "slow cranking, solenoid clicks or chatters" condition.
(Courtesy of General Motors Corporation.)

6. *Harsh grinding noise.* Starter drive pinion teeth clash against ring gear teeth. Caused by worn or broken drive pinion teeth, ring gear teeth, or both.

7. *Engine starts, then dies as soon as the ignition key is released.* Caused by an open in the circuit from the starter solenoid to the coil primary.

■ STARTING SYSTEM TESTING

Precautions

1. Always disconnect the battery ground cable before disconnecting the wiring from the starting motor or removing the starting motor.

2. For any cranking tests, make sure that the transmission is in neutral or park with the parking brake applied. Follow directions to disconnect the ignition system to prevent engine starting.

3. Be sure that all tester leads are free and clear of rotating engine parts.

4. Do not wash or immerse electrical components in solvent; clean with compressed air only.

Preliminary Inspection

Begin with a visual check of the supply circuit parts to note any trouble sources, such as corroded or loose connections. The supply circuit consists of the battery, battery cables, clamps, and connectors. Many slow-turning starters have been corrected simply by cleaning the battery terminal posts and cable clamps. Inspect starter and ground cables for corrosion or damage. Test the battery to make sure that it is in good condition and is fully charged. Test the battery if necessary as described earlier.

Starting Test with Headlights On

A quick check of the starting system can be made to help identify the problem. With the headlights on, try to start the engine. Note any change in the brightness of the headlights. No headlights and no cranking indicate a dead battery, poor battery connections, or a blown fusible link. If the lights stay on bright without cranking, the problem could be in the ignition switch, starter solenoid, relay, cable connections, or wiring. If the lights go out (or nearly out), the battery may not be charged, the starting motor may be dragging, or the engine may be very hard to crank.

Neutral Safety Switch Check

The neutral safety switch may prevent starting if it is out of adjustment or is faulty. To check if it is out of adjustment, try starting the engine while holding the brake pedal down and shifting through all the selec-

tor lever positions. If starting occurs in any lever position other than PARK or NEUTRAL, the switch needs adjustment. If starting does not occur through the entire range of lever positions, the switch should be replaced or the wiring to the switch may be defective.

Starter/Clutch Interlock Switch Check

The starter clutch interlock switch is normally open when the clutch pedal is up. With the clutch pedal depressed the switch contacts close, completing the starter circuit from the ignition start switch to the starter relay. If the switch is defective, it may result in a no-start condition. An ohmmeter or self-powered test light can be used to check switch continuity with the clutch pedal depressed.

Ignition Switch Test

To check the ignition switch start position, use a test light to check for current at the start terminal on the solenoid or starter relay. The test light should light with the ignition key in the start position and go off when the key is released. If the test light did not go on, the problem is in the wiring between the ignition switch and relay or solenoid or in the ignition switch itself. The test light check can be made on the start terminal of the ignition switch to determine whether the switch or the wire is at fault.

Current Draw Test

The starter current draw test reveals the condition of the starting motor. If current draw is too high or too low, further tests are required. Connect a volt/ampere tester to the positive and negative battery posts **(Figure 5–36).** Set the selector knob on the 20-V scale. Connect a remote starter switch to the starter relay. Ground the ignition coil output terminal. Crank the engine and note the exact reading on the

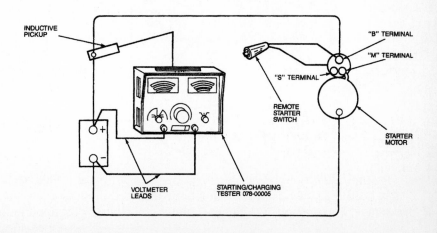

■ FIGURE 5–36
Starter tester and remote start switch hookup on solenoid type starter. (Courtesy of Ford Motor Company.)

voltmeter. Turn the test load control clockwise until the voltmeter reads the same voltage as during the cranking test. Switch the test selector to the amperage position and read the ampere scale. This reading is the starter current draw.

If the current draw was higher than specifications, the starter will require further testing on the bench. If the current draw was low but the starter turns slowly, recheck all circuit connections before removing the starter for bench testing. High current draw indicates a short in the starter armature or an engine that is hard to turn over. Low current draw indicates an undercharged or defective battery, or excessive resistance in the starting circuit.

Voltage Drop Tests

Battery-to-Solenoid Terminal Test

This test will help to isolate corroded connections, defective cables, or a defective solenoid. Set the voltmeter control to the 3- or 4-V scale. Connect the positive lead to the battery positive post and the negative lead to the field coil terminal of the starter solenoid. The meter will read off scale to the right until the starter is engaged. With the coil output terminal grounded, crank the engine and observe the voltmeter reading. If the voltmeter shows 0.3 V or less, the cable, solenoid, and their connections are good. If the voltmeter reads above 0.3 V, there is high resistance in the insulated circuit **(Figure 5–37)**.

Battery-to-Starter Field Coil Test

Connect the negative lead to the post of the field coil and repeat the test. During this test, if the voltmeter reading changes by more than 0.1 V between the solenoid field terminal and the solenoid battery terminal, replace the solenoid.

Battery-to-Starter Case Test

A ground test should be performed to locate any faulty connections in the ground circuit. Connect the voltmeter positive lead to one of the starter through-bolts, and the negative lead to the negative battery post. With the coil output terminal grounded, crank the engine and observe the voltmeter. If the voltmeter shows more than 0.2 V, there is excessive resistance in the ground circuit **(Figure 5–38)**.

Starter Solenoid Test

Ground the coil output terminal to prevent the engine from starting. Connect a heavy jumper wire to the battery terminal and the solenoid terminal of the starter relay. This bypasses the starter control circuit. If the engine cranks, the solenoid is good **(Figure 5–39)**.

Starter Relay Test

Check for battery voltage at the starter relay with a voltmeter. Connect a jumper wire between the relay battery terminal and the ignition switch terminal. If the engine cranks, the relay is good; however, either the neutral switch, or the circuit to it, could be defective **(Figure 5–40)**.

■ STARTER SERVICE

Starter Removal

1. Disconnect the negative cable at the battery.
2. Disconnect the cable and wires at the starting motor.

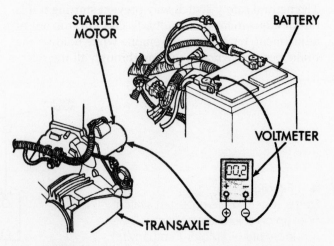

■ FIGURE 5–37
Battery positive to solenoid terminal resistance using the voltage drop method. (Courtesy of Chrysler Corporation.)

■ FIGURE 5–38
Testing voltage drop between the battery negative post and the starter case to determine ground circuit resistance. (Courtesy of Chrysler Corporation.)

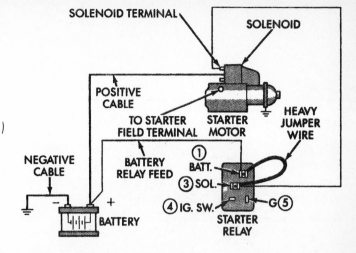

■   FIGURE 5–39
Starter solenoid test. (Courtesy of Chrysler Corporation.)

3.   Remove the starter mounting bolts and the starter.

Starter Disassembly

Procedures vary considerably depending on design (i.e., positive engagement, gear reduction, planetary gear reduction, inertia drive, solenoid type, etc.). Refer to the appropriate service manual for specific procedures. The general procedure is to remove the through-bolts and separate the drive end housing, field frame, armature, brush holder assembly, or end plate. The solenoid or positive engagement assembly is also removed. Typical starter problems to look for are shown in **Figure 5–41.**

Cleaning

Do not wash the starter drive because this will destroy the lubricant and cause the drive to slip. Use a soft bristle brush and compressed air to clean the drive, armature, field frame, drive housing, brush holder, solenoid, and end plate.

CAUTION: Always wear eye protection.

Armature Short Test

To perform these tests, a growler will be needed. Place the armature in a growler and hold a thin steel blade parallel to the core. Slowly rotate the armature and observe the steel blade. If the blade begins to vibrate, or pull toward the core, it is shorted and must be replaced **(Figure 5–42).**

Armature Ground Test

Place the armature in a growler. Use a continuity tester. If there is continuity between the armature core and any bar of the commutator, the armature is grounded, and it must be replaced **(Figure 5–43).**

Armature Open Test

This can be done on a growler equipped with a continuity tester or by using an ohmmeter. Touch the commutator segments with the meter prods to determine if continuity exists between segments. If there is infinite resistance on any segment, that segment is open and the armature must be replaced. A burned segment indicates an open in the armature **(Figure 5–44).**

■   FIGURE 5–40
Starter relay test. (Courtesy of Chrysler Corporation.)

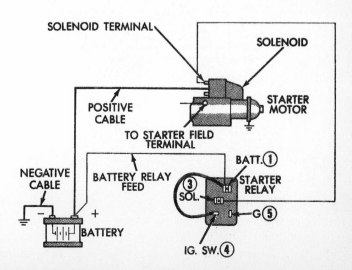

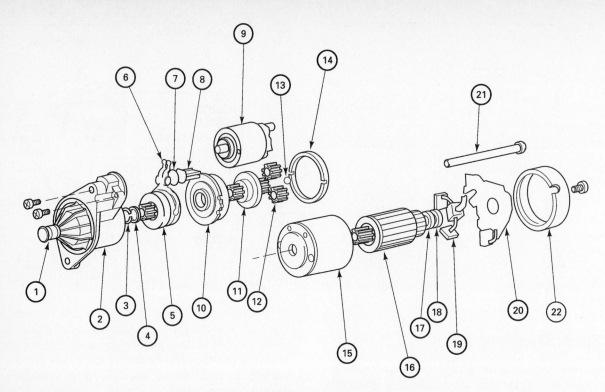

■ FIGURE 5–41

Typical starter problems include: 1) bushing worn or loose; 2) drive end housing cracked; 3) snap ring out of groove; 4) stop ring broken; 5) starter drive teeth worn; 6) clutch yoke worn or bent; 7) yoke washer worn; 8) retainer broken; 9) solenoid defective; 10) planetary ring gear worn; 11) planet carrier and shaft worn; 12) planet pinions worn; 13) armature shaft ball worn; 14) seal ring cracked; 15) housing defective; 16) armature defective; 17) bearing worn; 18) washer worn; 19) brushes worn; 20) brush holder defective; 21) through bolt threads stripped; 22) end cover damaged. (Courtesy of Chrysler Corporation.)

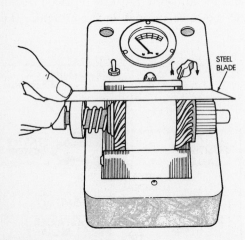

■ FIGURE 5–42

Armature short test. (Courtesy of Chrysler Corporation.)

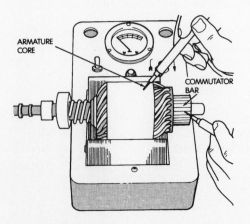

■ FIGURE 5–43

Armature ground test. (Courtesy of Chrysler Corporation.)

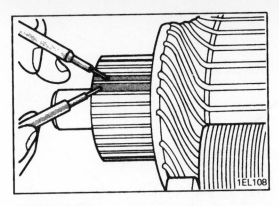

■ FIGURE 5–44
Armature open test. (Courtesy of Chrysler Corporation.)

Armature Commutator Inspection

Inspect the commutator for runout, wear, or damage **(Figure 5–45).** Minor imperfections can be lightly sanded with very fine sandpaper. Do not use emery cloth since some of the abrasives are electrical conductors. If the commutator is badly worn or the shaft is bent, it should be replaced.

Field Coil Test

Inspect the field coils for any evidence of burnt insulation. Replace if burnt. To test for a grounded field coil, attach one lead of a continuity tester to a field brush and touch the other lead to the field housing. If continuity exists, replace the field coil assembly.

Brush Holder Test

To test the brush holder, attach one lead of the continuity tester to the brush holder frame and the other to each of the field brush holders. If either shows

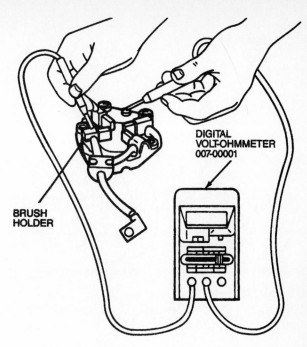

■ FIGURE 5–46
Brush holder test. (Courtesy of Ford Motor Company.)

continuity, replace the assembly. The ground brushes and holders should show continuity to the frame. Replace worn brushes or weak brush holder springs **(Figures 5–46 and 5–47).**

Drive Gear and Ring Gear Teeth Inspection

Inspect the teeth on the drive gear and ring gear for excessive wear or damage **(Figure 5–48).** A normal wear pattern indicates full tooth engagement on the drive side of both gears. A small wear pattern on

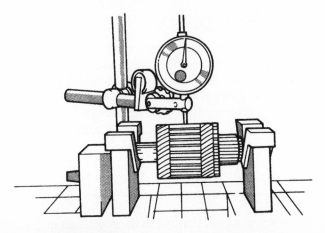

■ FIGURE 5–45
Checking for a bent armature. (Courtesy of Chrysler Corporation.)

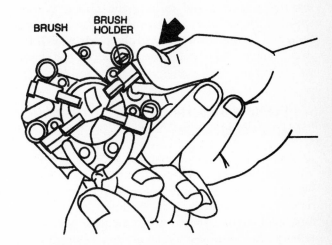

■ FIGURE 5–47
Checking brush spring tension and free movement of brushes in brush holder. (Courtesy of Ford Motor Company.)

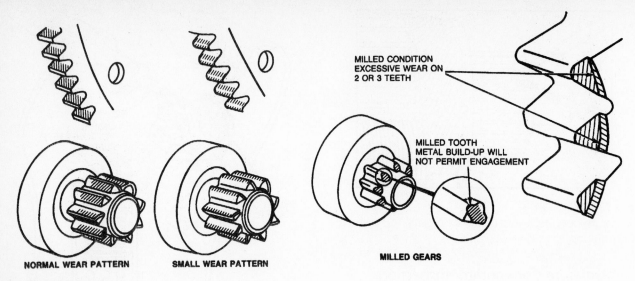

■   FIGURE 5–48
Typical gear tooth wear patterns and tooth damage on drive pinion and
starter ring gear. (Courtesy of Ford Motor Company.)

only the outer area of the teeth indicates insufficient engagement due to improper starter mounting alignment. Excessive wear and damage on the leading edge of the drive pinion and ring gear teeth is the result of gear clashing during starter engagement. This is usually the result of a faulty starter drive and requires drive pinion and ring gear replacement to correct.

Starter Clutch Drive Unit Test

The clutch drive unit should be inspected carefully for worn or broken teeth on the drive pinion. If damage is found, inspect the ring teeth on the flywheel and repair if needed. Test the drive clutch by holding the assembly and turning the pinion gear. It should turn smoothly with some effort in one direction, and lock up when turned the other way. If the drive clutch feels rough, or can be turned backwards, replace the assembly.

Bushing Inspection and Replacement

Check to see if the armature has made contact with the field pole shoes. If contact is evident the bushings are worn and must be replaced. Insert the armature shaft into the bushings to check for looseness. If the shaft can be wiggled excessively replace the bushings. Press or drive out the old bushings and replace with new ones. Some bushings are made of porous bronze and must be pre-lubricated before installation. Place the new bush-

ing on your forefinger, closing off that end. Fill the bushing with engine oil and squeeze the oil in the bushing lightly between thumb and forefinger until the oil "sweats" through to the outside of the bushing.

Starter Assembly and No Load Test

Reassemble the starter in the reverse order of disassembly. Lubricate with recommended lubricant only, and only in areas specified in the manual. Make sure that all parts are properly aligned and operate freely before and during tightening of fasteners and through bolts. Check to see that bushes make full contact with the commutator and operate freely. Make sure that starter drive end clearance is as specified (**Figure 5–49**).

Free-Running Bench Test (No Load)

Before installing the starter, a bench test will verify that the starter has been properly repaired and assembled. To perform the test, mount the starter securely in a vise with soft jaws. Connect a 12-V battery and proceed with a current draw test.

PRO TIP

Do not overspeed. Armature damage may result.

Compare your reading to the specification in the shop manual. If the reading is okay, install the starter on the engine (**Figure 5–50**).

CHECKING PINION CLEARANCE

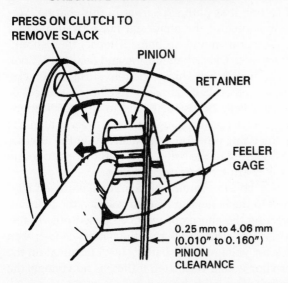

PRESS ON CLUTCH TO
REMOVE SLACK

PINION

RETAINER

FEELER
GAGE

0.25 mm to 4.06 mm
(0.010" to 0.160")
PINION
CLEARANCE

When the starter motor has been disassembled or the solenoid has been replaced, it is necessary to check the pinion clearance. Pinion clearance must be correct to prevent the buttons on the shift lever yoke from rubbing on the clutch collar during cranking.
1. Disconnect the motor field coil connector from the solenoid motor terminal and insulate it carefully.
2. Connect one 12 volt battery lead to the solenoid switch terminal and the other to the starter frame.
3. Flash a jumper lead momentarily from the solenoid motor terminal to the starter frame. This will shift the pinion into cranking position and it will remain so until the battery is disconnected.
4. Push the pinion back as far as possible to take up any movement, and check the clearance with a feeler gage. The clearance should be 0.25 mm to 4.06 mm (0.010" to 0.160").
Means for adjusting pinion clearance is not provided on the starter motor. If the clearance does not fall within limits, check for improper installation and replace all worn parts.

■ FIGURE 5–49
(Courtesy of General Motors Corporation.)

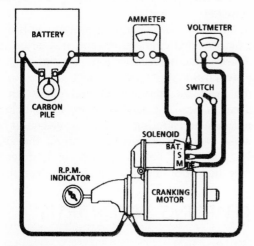

■ FIGURE 5–50
Starter free running, no load, bench test. (Courtesy of General Motors Corporation.)

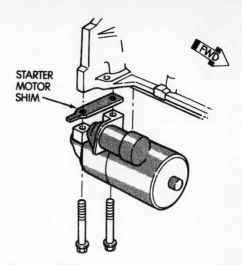

■ FIGURE 5–51
Starter alignment shim is used on some starters. (Courtesy of Chrysler Corporation.)

Starter Installation

Place the starter in position on the engine. Make sure any alignment shims are replaced between the starter and engine **(Figure 5–51)**. Start the mounting bolts by hand, then tighten them while keeping the starter in alignment. Tighten the mounting bolts to specifications. Reconnect all electrical connections. Make sure that terminals do not turn while tightening the terminal nuts. Reconnect the battery ground cable. Start the engine several times to ensure proper operation.

■ CHARGING SYSTEM FUNCTION AND COMPONENTS

While the engine is running, the charging system provides the power needed to operate all of the vehicle's electrical systems and to charge the battery whenever needed. It does this by converting mechanical energy into electrical energy.

The major components of the ac charging system are:

1. *Alternator:* converts engine mechanical power to electrical power
2. *Alternator drive belt:* connects the crankshaft pulley to the alternator pulley to drive the alternator
3. *Voltage regulator:* controls the output voltage of the alternator
4. *Charge indicator:* dash-mounted ammeter, voltmeter, or indicator light informs the driver of charging system operation

5. *Battery:* provides current to energize the alternator initially; also acts as a voltage stabilizer

6. *Wiring harness:* connects charging system components to each other

■ CHARGING SYSTEM TESTING AND SERVICE PRECAUTIONS

Remember the following precautions when servicing charging systems.

1. Cars equipped with a heated windshield require from 30- to 110-V alternator output for operation during heating. Follow service manual instructions to avoid potentially severe electrical shock and possible electrocution.

2. Always disconnect the negative battery cable from the battery before connecting a battery charger and before removing any charging system components.

3. Always observe battery polarity when making connections. Reversing polarity can damage electronic components.

4. Do not accidentally ground any electrical system components. Grounding an electrical terminal can cause damage. Never ground or short an electrical terminal unless instructed to do so by the service manual.

5. Do not operate the alternator on open circuit (disconnected output). Uncontrolled output may cause alternator damage.

6. Follow the service manual and equipment manufacturer's instructions to perform charging system tests.

7. Never remove either battery cable with the engine running. Serious electrical system damage could result.

■ CHARGING SYSTEM PROBLEMS

Charging system problems result in one or more of the following symptoms.

1. *Dead battery:* will not crank the engine.

2. *Abnormal noise:* belt squeal, noisy alternator bearing, loose mounting bolts, buzzing contacts in regulator.

3. *Overcharged battery:* top of battery moist from gassing, corroded battery terminals. Premature light burnout and possible electronic system damage may result.

4. *Charge indicator reading is abnormal:* indicator light stays on or gauge reading is always low.

Verify whether the battery is dead by inspecting and testing it as outlined earlier in this chapter. Verify the source of the abnormal noise by inspecting the alternator mounting bolts; if loose, they should be tightened. Check belt tension and condition. Look for glazing (hard shiny friction surface), cracks, tears, or other belt damage. Replace a glazed or damaged belt. Adjust belt tension to specifications using a belt tension gauge. Do not overtighten the belt since this puts too great a strain on the alternator bearings and the belt. Use a stethoscope to locate a noisy bearing or buzzing regulator.

If a booster battery or charger have been connected to the battery in reverse polarity, the fuse link protecting the alternator may be burned out. To test the fuse link, first check that the battery is OK, then check for voltage at the battery (BAT) terminal on the alternator with a voltmeter. If there is no voltage, the fuse link is probably burned out.

■ CHARGING SYSTEM INSPECTION

Look for obvious signs of trouble—abnormal conditions that you can see or detect with your hands.

CAUTION: Be careful not to come in contact with rotating or hot engine parts.

1. Check the alternator drive belt for proper tension, glazing, cracks, or other damage. Adjust the belt tension to specifications or replace the belt if necessary.

2. Inspect the battery and battery cables for loose connections, corroded terminals, or other damage. Check the battery state of charge at the built-in hydrometer.

3. Inspect the charging system wiring for loose or corroded connections and insulation damage. Check whether connections are tight by wiggling the wires.

4. With the engine running, check for any abnormal noises. A glazed or loose drive belt may squeal when accelerating. Check for alternator bearing noise with a stethoscope. Running the engine briefly with the belt removed will determine whether the belt or alternator is causing the noise.

■ CHARGING SYSTEM TESTS

Battery Test

Although a dead battery is often the reason for suspecting charging system problems, the battery may be at fault. Always test the condition of the battery as outlined earlier in this chapter before proceeding with other tests.

Computer-Controlled Charging System Tests

A computer-controlled charging system will alert the driver that a problem exists by a dash warning light or message. If the problem has occurred, often enough a fault code will be stored in computer memory. To access the fault code, the technician must activate the self-diagnosis mode by following a specific procedure. (See Chapter 4 for different ways of accessing fault codes and their interpretation.) The fault code is then displayed on the dash. A scan tool is used to plug into the wiring harness diagnostic connector to access fault codes and to perform a series of charging system tests **(Figures 5–52** and **5–53).** Follow service manual instructions for test procedures. After performing the scan tool tests, additional charging system checks and tests may have to be performed, depending on the scan tool test results. These checks and tests are the same as

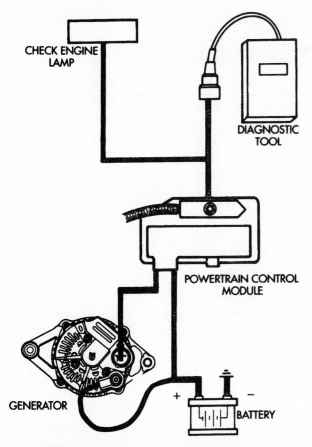

CHECK ENGINE LAMP

DIAGNOSTIC TOOL

POWERTRAIN CONTROL MODULE

GENERATOR

BATTERY

■ **FIGURE 5–52**
Using a scan tool to access fault codes in a computer-controlled charging system. (Courtesy of Chrysler Corporation.)

those for other charging systems and are described here.

Voltmeter Tests

Voltmeter testing of the charging system can be used to indicate voltage and current output. These tests are easily done and require only a voltmeter.

1. Turn the headlights on for 15 seconds to remove any surface charge from the battery.
2. Turn the voltmeter knob to the 20-V scale, or nearest thereto.
3. With the engine and all accessories off, connect the positive voltmeter lead to the positive battery post and the negative lead to the negative post and note the voltmeter reading. It should be about 12.6 V with a fully charged battery in good condition. This is the base or open circuit voltage reading.
4. Start the engine and turn off all accessories. Run the engine at 1500 to 2000 rpm and note the voltmeter reading. This is the no-load test. The voltmeter reading should be a minimum of 0.5 V higher than base voltage. If voltage increase is more than 3 V, the charging rate is probably too high. The regulator or wiring are faulty. If the voltage does not increase, the alternator, regulator, or wiring is faulty.
5. If the no-load test results are normal, a full load test should be performed. Start the engine, turn all electrical accessories, lights, heater, and air conditioning blowers on high, and turn headlights on high beam, to apply a full load to the charging system. Run the engine at 2000 rpm and note the voltmeter reading. It should be 0.5 V higher than base voltage. This indicates that the charging system produces enough current to operate all the electrical devices and is able to charge the battery as well. If the load test voltage is not 0.5 V above base voltage, perform a regulator bypass test.

Alternator Output Tests

An alternator output test checks alternator current and voltage output. The same type of tester is used as when performing a starter current draw test **(Figure 5–54).** It includes a voltmeter, ohmmeter, and load application function. Typical test procedures are performed as follows:

Current Output Test

1. Make sure that the battery is in good condition and is fully charged and that the alternator drive belt is in good condition and adjusted to proper tension.

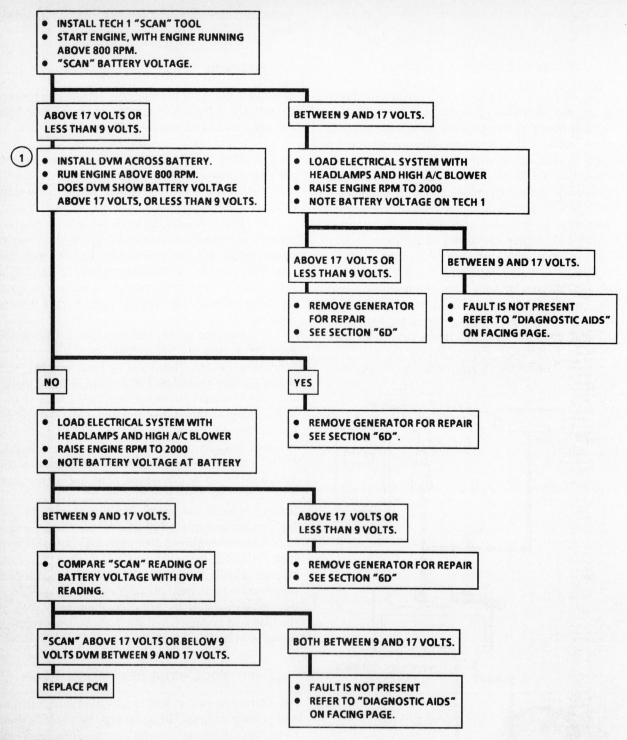

■ FIGURE 5-53
Example of diagnostic flow chart for scan tool diagnosis of charging system.
(Courtesy of General Motors Corporation.)

2. Obtain the proper alternator current and voltage output specifications from the service manual. (Output may range from about 14.0 to 15.0 volts.)

3. Connect the tester according to the test equipment instructions.

4. Start the engine and turn off all accessories.

5. Increase engine speed and hold it at 2000 rpm.

6. Turn the load control knob to increase the load until the highest possible reading is obtained on the ammeter while maintaining a voltmeter reading of 12 V or slightly above 12 V.

7. Amperage reading should be within range of rated output. Add 10 to 15 A to the reading to compen-

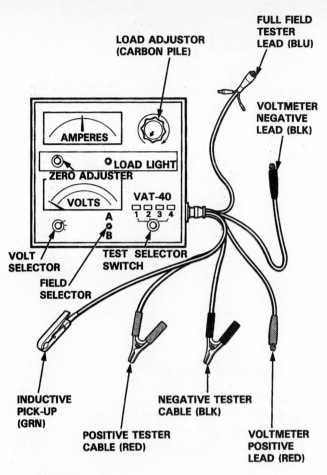

■ FIGURE 5–54
Charging system tester. (Courtesy of Sun Test Equipment.)

sate for engine operation. Turn the load control knob off as soon as you have taken the ammeter reading.

Voltage Output Test

The voltage output test checks the regulator calibration and whether voltage output is too high or too low. With the tester connected as in the current output test and with the load control off, run the engine at 2000 rpm and note the voltage reading. Compare the reading to specifications. If the reading is steady but is too high or too low, the regulator is at fault. Normal charging system voltage usually ranges between 13.5 and 14.7 V. If the reading is not steady, there may be loose or corroded wiring connections, or a faulty alternator or regulator.

Regulator Bypass Test

When the charging system fails the current and voltage output tests, a regulator bypass test should be done. The general procedure is the same as for the current output test except that full field current is applied to the alternator. This bypasses the regulator

and determines whether the alternator or regulator is at fault. The procedure is also known as *full fielding* an alternator. Full fielding makes the alternator produce maximum output.

Several methods are used to apply full field current to an alternator, depending on charging system design. One method is to ground the field with a screwdriver through an access hole at the back of the alternator. This method is used on many GM alternators with an internal regulator (**Figure 5–55**). Another method uses a jumper wire to connect the battery terminal to the field terminal at the back of the alternator. This method is used on some alternators with an external regulator. A third method used on Ford alternators with an external regulator is to unplug the connector from the voltage regulator and use a jumper wire between the A and F terminals of the connector (**Figure 5–56**). Always follow service manual procedures for full fielding an alternator. Never ground or connect any two terminals to each other unless instructed to do so by the service manual. Making the wrong connections can cause serious damage to the system.

Circuit Resistance Tests

Circuit resistance tests are used to pinpoint excessive resistance in the charging circuit. Too much resistance on the insulted side of the circuit or the

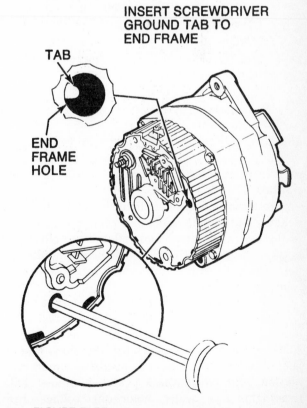

■ FIGURE 5–55
Grounding the field with a screwdriver on a GM Delco alternator. (Courtesy of General Motors Corporation.)

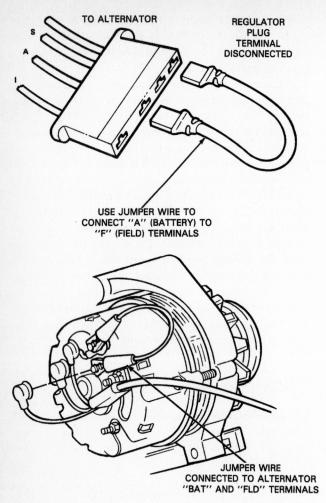

TO ALTERNATOR

S

A

I

REGULATOR
PLUG
TERMINAL
DISCONNECTED

USE JUMPER WIRE TO
CONNECT "A" (BATTERY) TO
"F" (FIELD) TERMINALS

JUMPER WIRE
CONNECTED TO ALTERNATOR
"BAT" AND "FLD" TERMINALS

■   FIGURE 5–56
Grounding the field on a system with an external
regulator (top), and with an integrated regulator
(bottom). (Courtesy of Ford Motor Company.)

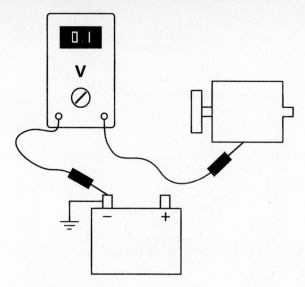

■   FIGURE 5–57
Ground circuit resistance test. (Courtesy of F T
Enterprises.)

Regulator Service

When charging system tests determine that the
regulator is at fault, it must be replaced. On some,
an adjusting screw is turned to increase or
decrease the voltage setting. To replace an externally mounted regulator, disconnect the negative
battery cable, disconnect the wiring from the regulator, and remove the mounting screws. To install
the new regulator, reverse this procedure. On alternators with an integral regulator the alternator
must be removed and disassembled to replace the
regulator.

■ ALTERNATOR SERVICE

Alternator Removal

1.   Disconnect the negative battery cable at the
battery.

SAFETY CAUTION   Failure to observe this step may
result in injury from the hot battery lead at the alternator.

2.   Disconnect the wiring leads from the alternator (Figure 5–58).
3.   Loosen the adjusting bolts and move the
alternator to provide slack in the belt.
4.   Remove the alternator drive belt.
5.   Remove the bolts that retain the alternator
(Figure 5–59).
6.   Remove the alternator from the car.
7.   Replace or test and repair the alternator.

grounded side results in reduced output. Corroded
or loose terminals or plug-in connectors and poor
wire insulation are common causes of too much
resistance.

To perform a ground circuit resistance test, full
field or load the alternator and connect a voltmeter
to the negative battery terminal and the alternator
housing (Figure 5–57). The voltmeter should not
read above 0.1 V. If it does, check for loose or corroded connections.

To perform an insulated circuit test, connect
the tester as outlined in the service manual. Insulated circuit tests are not recommended on some
charging systems. The general procedure is to connect a voltmeter across each insulated circuit connection with the charging system under load
(headlights and heater motor on). Voltage drop
across all connections should not exceed 0.5 V
(Figure 5–58).

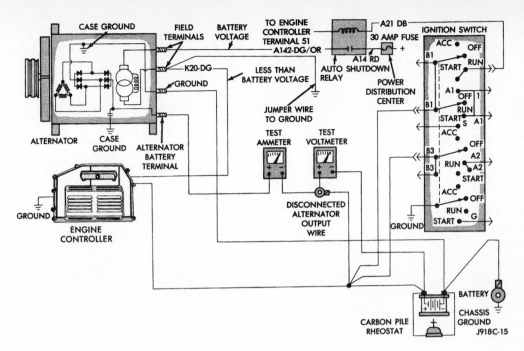

FIGURE 5–58

Alternator output wire resistance. (Courtesy of Chrysler Corporation.)

Alternator Disassembly

Some alternators can be repaired, while others must be replaced as a unit. Check the service manual to determine whether repair is recommended. Usually, the pulley and fan are removed from the old alternator and installed on the new one. This involves removing the pulley nut (if so equipped) and then removing the pulley. On others, the pulley is a press fit on the rotor shaft and is removed with a puller. Refer to the appropriate service manual for specific

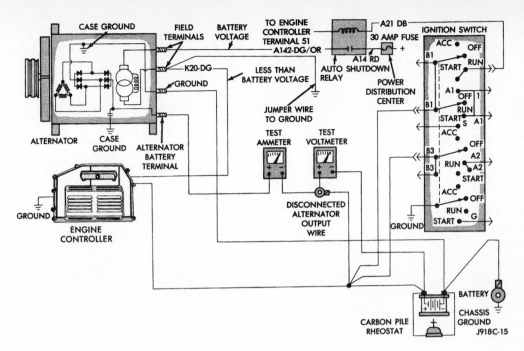

■ FIGURE 5–59

Typical alternator wiring connections. Disconnect before alternator removal. (Courtesy of Chrysler Corporation.)

disassembly procedures, which vary depending on alternator design.

Stator Testing

The stator windings must be tested for open circuits or shorts to ground. To perform this test the stator leads must be removed from the rectifier for accurate results. If the leads are soldered, hold the lead with long-nose pliers and unsolder the connection. Do not blow away molten solder with compressed air. This could cause a short in the rectifier.

Touch each of the three leads with a continuity tester, ohmmeter, or tester light. If there is no continuity, replace the stator coil assembly. To check for a grounded stator, touch the test probes to one stator lead and the stator frame. If continuity is shown, the stator is grounded and must be replaced (**Figure 5–60**).

Rotor Testing

The rotor field coil should be tested for continuity. Touch the tester probes to the slip rings. If there is no continuity, the field windings are open and the rotor must be replaced. Examine the slip rings for dirt or roughness. If the slip rings cannot be smoothed with light sanding, replace the rotor assembly. The rotor must also be tested for ground. Touch one test probe to a slip ring and the other to the rotor core. If there is continuity, the coil is shorted to ground and the rotor must be replaced (**Figure 5–61**).

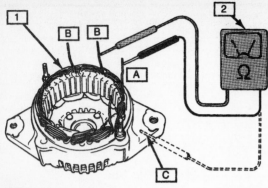

[A] NEUTRAL POINT
[B] PHASE LEAD
[C] GROUND
[1] STATOR COIL
[2] OHMMETER

■ FIGURE 5-60
Testing the stator for opens or shorts. (Courtesy of General Motors Corporation.)

Field Brush Testing

The field brushes should be inspected for excessive wear or damage, and replaced if needed. If visual inspection reveals no problem, test the brushes for continuity. If no continuity is observed, replace the brushes **(Figure 5-62).**

Diode Testing

If a diode malfunctions, it can allow ac current to leave the alternator and possible damage to the vehicle's electrical system. There are two methods of

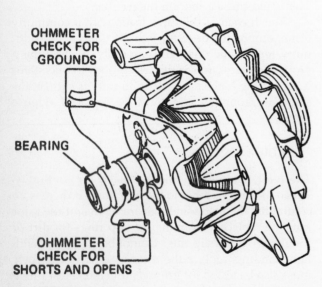

■ FIGURE 5-61
Testing the rotor field coil for grounds or opens. (Courtesy of General Motors Corporation.)

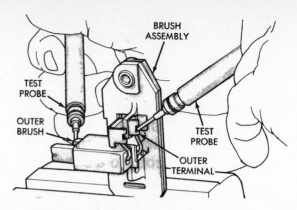

■ FIGURE 5-62
Brush continuity test. (Courtesy of Chrysler Corporation.)

testing diodes. If a special diode tester is being used, it is not necessary to disconnect the stator leads from the rectifier. If an ohmmeter or other continuity tester is being used, unsolder or unbolt the stator leads prior to testing.

Place one test probe on the diode heat sink and the other on the diode pin. Reverse the probes and note the reaction. If the tester shows continuity one way but not the other, the diode is good. If there is no continuity, the diode is open. If there is continuity both ways, the diode is shorted. Repeat this procedure on all pins in the positive and negative diodes **(Figures 5-63** and **5-64).** Test the diode trio as shown in **Figure 5-65.** Diode problems may also be checked with an oscilloscope. Typical patterns are shown in **Figure 5-66.**

Alternator Bearing Service

The bearings in an alternator will usually be sealed ball bearings or needle bearings. During alternator service, examine the bearings carefully for signs of wear or roughness when turning. If a needle bearing assembly is replaced, do not add any lubricant to the

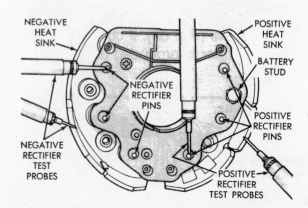

■ FIGURE 5-63
Testing the diodes in the rectifier assembly. (Courtesy of Chrysler Corporation.)

COMPONENT	TEST CONNECTION	NORMAL READING	IF READING WAS:	TROUBLE IS:
Rotor	Ohmmeter from slip ring to rotor shaft	Infinite resistance	Very low	Grounded
	Test lamp from slip ring to shaft	No light	Lamp lights	Grounded
	Test lamp across slip rings	Lamp lights	No light	Open
Stator	Ohmmeter from any stator lead to frame	Infinite resistance	Very low	Grounded
	Test lamp from lead to frame	No light	Lamp lights	Grounded
	Ohmmeter across any pair of leads	Less than $\frac{1}{2}\,\Omega$	Any very high reading	Open
Diodes	Ohmmeter across diode, then reverse leads	Low reading one way; high reading other way	Both readings low Both readings high	Shorted Open
	12-V test lamp across diode, then reverse leads	Lamp lights one way, but not other way	No light either way Lamp lights both ways	Open Shorted

■ FIGURE 5–64

bearing. The bearing assembly will come pre-lubricated. Handle the assembly carefully so that dirt won't get into the needle bearing unit before installation **(Figures 5–67 and 5–68).**

Alternator Assembly

Alternator assembly procedures vary with alternator design. Typically, the procedure is as follows.

    1.   Install front and rear bearings.
    2.   Install all the components in the slip ring end frame.

    3.   Assemble the slip ring end frame, stator, and drive end frame. Make sure that the aligning marks or pins are aligned. On some alternators the brushes must be held back against spring pressure with a small pin or hex wrench. Push the brushes back far enough to allow the pin to be inserted through the holes **(Figure 5–69).** This keeps the

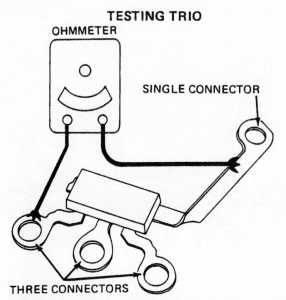

To check diode trio, connect ohmmeter as shown. then reverse lead connections. Should read high and low. If not, replace diode trio.

■ FIGURE 5–65
(Courtesy of General Motors Corporation.)

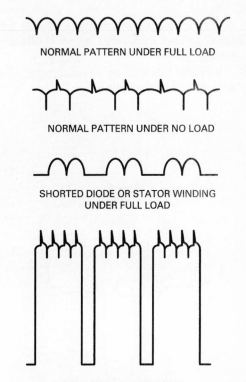

■ FIGURE 5–66
Typical alternator oscilloscope patterns. (Courtesy of F T Enterprises.)

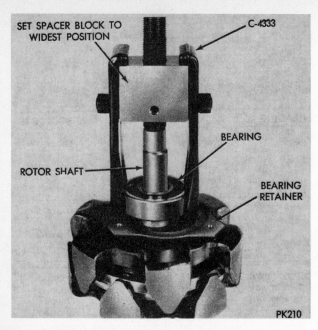

SET SPACER BLOCK TO WIDEST POSITION

C-4333

BEARING

ROTOR SHAFT

BEARING RETAINER

PK210

■ FIGURE 5–67
Removing the drive end bearing from the rotor shaft with a puller. (Courtesy of Chrysler Corporation.)

brushes out of the way while the rotor is inserted into the end frame. On others the brushes may be installed from the outside after alternator assembly.

4.   Install the through bolts, making sure that the three major components remain aligned and are fully seated against each other before tightening the through bolts.

5.   Remove the wire or Allen wrench to allow the brushes to contact the slip rings.

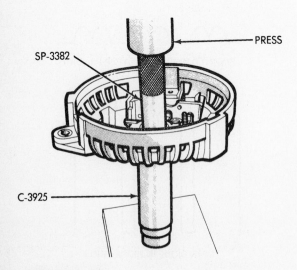

PRESS

SP-3382

C-3925

■ FIGURE 5–68
Removing the bearing from the rectifier end frame with special adapters and a press. (Courtesy of Chrysler Corporation.)

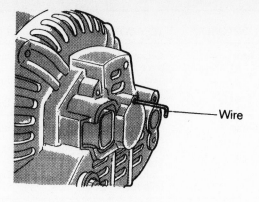

Wire

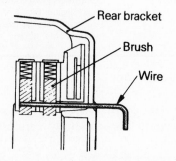

Rear bracket

Brush

Wire

■ FIGURE 5–69
Wire pin holds brushes back against spring pressure during alternator assembly. (Courtesy of Chrysler Corporation.)

6.   Check to make sure that the rotor turns freely without any unusual noise.

7.   Install any spacer, the fan, pulley, lock washer, and nut on the front of the shaft. Tighten the nut to specifications (**Figures 5–70** and **5–71**).

8.   Test alternator output on a bench tester if available.

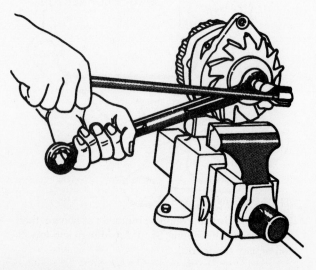

■ FIGURE 5–70
Installing the pulley and pulley retainer nut. (Courtesy of Chrysler Corporation.)

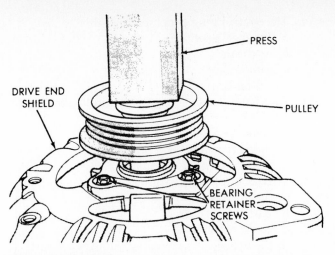

FIGURE 5–71
Press-fit pulley installation. (Courtesy of Ford Motor Company.)

Alternator Installation

1. Install the alternator to the mounting bracket with bolts, washers, and nuts. Do not tighten.
2. Install the drive belt.
3. Tighten the belt to the specified belt tension. See the engine cooling section (Chapter 10) for proper belt tensioning procedures.
4. Tighten the bolts.
5. Install the alternator terminal and battery leads to the alternator.
6. Connect the negative battery cable.

Review Questions

1. The battery provides electrical energy to the vehicle whenever the engine is *not* running. True or False.
2. Battery acid or electrolyte is a mixture of 36% _____ and 64% _____.
3. When charging a battery never allow the electrolyte temperature to exceed _____.
4. Add _____ _____ if the electrolyte level is below the fill ring.
5. A starting system is designed to change _____ to _____ energy.
6. A starter solenoid connects the battery to the _____ _____ and engages the _____.
7. On a vehicle with an automatic transmission the _____ _____ avoids starting in any shift position except _____ _____.
8. Always disconnect the battery _____ _____ before you begin to remove the starter.
9. You may wash all electrical components in solvents then blow them dry. True or False.
10. The neutral safety switch may require position adjustment. True or False.

11. A _____ _____ test of the starting motor circuit will indicate whether further tests are required.
12. Do not wash the starter drive, use a soft brush and air to clean it. True or False.
13. Using a continuity tester, continuity between any commutator bar and the armature core indicates the _____ _____ _____.
14. The alternator converts _____ _____ to _____ _____.
15. Always observe battery _____ when making battery connections.
16. Check the alternator for bearing noise with a stethoscope. True or False.
17. Voltmeter testing of the charging system can be used to indicate _____ and _____ output.
18. Field brushes should be inspected for excessive _____ or _____ and replaced as needed.

Test Questions

1. The water in a battery, properly called electrolyte, is a solution of
   a. sulfuric acid diluted with water
   b. lead peroxide and hydrogen peroxide
   c. sulfuric acid and lead peroxide
   d. water and lead
2. Each cell of an automotive battery can produce about
   a. 1.2 volts
   b. 2.1 volts
   c. 4.2 volts
   d. 6 volts
3. While a battery is being charged, the gas which is given off by the electrolyte is
   a. explosive
   b. non-poisonous
   c. green in color
   d. likely to burn slowly if ignited
4. A fully charged battery has a specific gravity reading of
   a. 1.260
   b. 1.225
   c. 1.55
   d. 1.20
5. The top of the storage battery should be cleaned off with a solution of
   a. table salt and water
   b. baking soda and water
   c. soap and water
   d. solvent
6. To check the state of charge in a maintenance-free battery
   a. use a squeeze bulb hydrometer
   b. check the sight glass on the battery top
   c. use a battery charger
   d. use an ammeter

7. To perform a battery drain test use
   a. an ammeter or voltmeter
   b. a voltmeter or ohmmeter
   c. an ohmmeter or ammeter
   d. a battery charger
8. A large displacement engine may require a starting current of
   a. 50 amps
   b. 100 amps
   c. 200 amps
   d. 300 amps
9. The starting system includes
   a. the starter circuit
   b. the control circuit
   c. both a and b
   d. neither a nor b
10. The neutral start switch is connected between the
    a. battery and ignition switch
    b. solenoid and ignition switch
    c. battery and solenoid
    d. coil and ignition switch
11. When diagnosing starting system problems the procedure is to first test the
    a field current draw
    b. battery and battery cables
    c. starting motor current flow
    d. solenoid hold-in winding
12. Technician A says some starters use permanent magnets instead of field windings. Technician B says all starters use field windings. Who is right?
    a. Technician A
    b. Technician B
    c. both are right
    d. both are wrong
13. When armatures are tested on a growler, a vibrating blade indicates the armature is
    a. polarized
    b. shorted
    c. opened
    d. grounded

14. The overrunning clutch protects the
    a. flywheel gear teeth
    b. armature
    c. pinion gear
    d. starter brushes
15. Alternator current output is controlled by the
    a. battery current
    b. stator resistance
    c. diode type and size
    d. field current
16. What controls the charging system voltage?
    a. the voltage regulator
    b. partial field current
    c. stator resistance
    d. the battery
17. Alternator output current is
    a. DC
    b. AC
    c. three phase
    d. single phase
18. The magnetic field of an alternator is carried by the
    a. stator
    b. rotor
    c. housing
    d. slip rings
19. The output of an alternator is created in the
    a. stator
    b. rotor
    c. housing
    d. brushes
20. An alternator cannot start operation independently because
    a. it has an externally grounded field circuit
    b. there is not enough residual magnetism in the rotor poles to induce voltage when the engine first begins to turn
    c. it does not have an excitation circuit
    d. the diodes won't rectify field current

6

Ignition System Diagnosis and Service

INTRODUCTION

Ignition systems have undergone many design changes, especially since the electronic revolution. The model T Ford of the early 1900s had four "buzz" coils, one for each cylinder and an ignition timer. Contact-point ignition with a single coil and ignition distributor came next, still in the early 1900s. In the early 1970s electronic ignition did away with the need for contact points. Then came computer-controlled ignition timing and more recently computer-controlled distributorless ignition.

All ignition systems operate on the same basic principle of changing low-voltage primary current to high-voltage secondary current to fire the spark plugs. The difference is in how the primary current is switched on and off and in how ignition timing is regulated.

To determine whether there is a problem in the ignition system requires a systematic step by step process of checks and tests. A thorough knowledge of the different kinds of ignition systems and how they work is also required. This chapter deals with the inspection, testing, diagnosis, and service of ignition systems.

LEARNING OBJECTIVES

After completing this chapter, you should be able to:
- Describe the function of the ignition system.
- Perform preliminary diagnostic procedures.
- Use ignition system testers to diagnose problems.
- Access self-diagnosis fault codes on computer ignition.
- Test ignition sensors with a DVOM.
- Test coil input voltage.
- Test ignition resistors with an ohmmeter.

- Test ignition coil resistance.
- Replace an ignition coil.
- Test the ignition switch.
- Replace the ignition switch.
- Test centrifugal and vacuum advance.
- Set initial timing.
- Service the secondary wires.
- Service the spark plugs.
- Service the distributor components.
- Service the ignition control unit and the computer.

TERMS YOU SHOULD KNOW

Look for these terms as you study this chapter and learn what they mean.

electronic ignition
distributorless ignition
computer-controlled
   ignition
primary voltage
secondary voltage
spark timing
switching transistor
coil primary
   energization
magnetic field
dwell period
magnetic field collapse
induced voltage
reserve capacity
distributor cam
resistor
condenser
pulse generator
vacuum advance
centrifugal advance

coil pack
Hall effect
optical sensor
high-tension wires
spark plug
heat range
thread diameter
reach
self-diagnosis
fault codes
sensor failure
harness failure
bad connection
computer failure
scanner
analyzer
electronic ignition tester
high-impedance DVOM
spark tests
coil voltage test
resistor test

coil resistance test
ignition switch tests
centrifugal advance test
vacuum advance test
vacuum supply test
initial timing
timing light
timing meter
secondary wire
    insulation test

secondary wire
    resistance test
spark plug gap
cap and rotor inspection
pickup coil test
control module service
dwell meter
distributor timing

is fired and continues as long as the engine is running. When the ignition key is turned off, current to the coil is shut off. This prevents any high voltage from being produced and prevents the spark plugs from firing, thereby shutting off the engine.

■ IGNITION SYSTEM FUNCTION AND COMPONENTS

The ignition system must perform several important tasks as follows.

1. Provide the means to turn the ignition on and off.
2. Convert low primary voltage to high secondary voltage to fire the spark plugs.
3. Time the spark to occur when the piston nears TDC on the compression stroke.
4. Fire the spark plug at each cylinder in the sequence of the engine's firing order.
5. Vary the spark timing to suit the changes in the engine speed and load.

The major components of the ignition system and their function are (Figures 6–1 to 6–6):

1. *Battery (and charging system):* battery provides initial power to the ignition system during

■ IGNITION SYSTEM OPERATING PRINCIPLES

When the ignition switch is turned on and the switching device is closed, current flows through the coil, energizing its primary winding. As the piston nears TDC the switching device opens, stopping current to the primary coil winding and causing the coil secondary winding to produce the high voltage necessary to jump the spark plug gap from 7000 to 9000 V at engine idle (may reach 40,000 V or more with high secondary resistance). The opening and closing of the switching device is repeated every time a spark plug

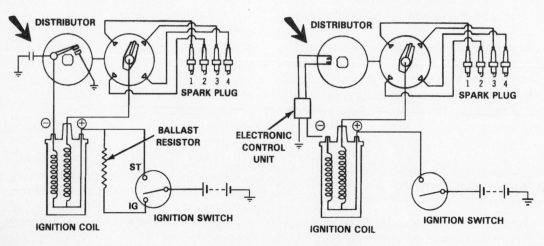

■ FIGURE 6–1
In the ignition system at the left, contact points close and open to switch the coil primary on and off. The period during which the coil primary is energized is called the dwell period. In the electronic ignition system on the right, coil primary voltage is switched on and off by a switching transistor in the electronic control unit in response to signals from the pickup coil in the distributor. (Courtesy of Chrysler Corporation.)

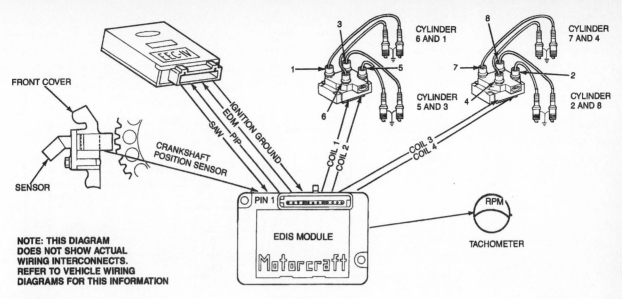

■ FIGURE 6–2

Direct ignition system (distributorless) components for a V8 engine. (Courtesy of Ford Motor Company.)

starting after which the charging system provides the power with the engine running.

2. *Ignition switch:* provides the means to start and stop the engine.

3. *Ignition coil:* converts low primary (battery) voltage to high secondary voltage.

4. *Switching device (switching transistor or contact points):* switches primary voltage to the coil on and off.

5. *Spark plugs:* provide gap between two electrodes in the combustion chamber across which spark jumps to ignite the air–fuel mixture.

6. *Electrical wiring:* connects ignition system components to each other.

■ PRIMARY AND SECONDARY CIRCUITS

All ignition systems have a low voltage primary circuit and a high voltage secondary circuit. The components differ depending on system design. The primary circuit consists of the following: battery, ignition switch, resistor (some systems), starter

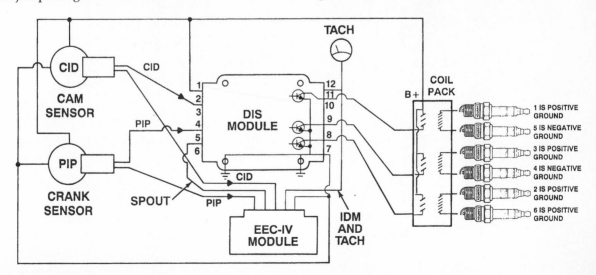

■ FIGURE 6–3

Spark plug pairs are connected in series to coil secondary. This results in opposite plug polarity for each plug in each pair. The high voltage output capacity of this system overcomes the high resistance of positive plug polarity of one of the plugs. (Courtesy of Champion Spark Plug Company.)

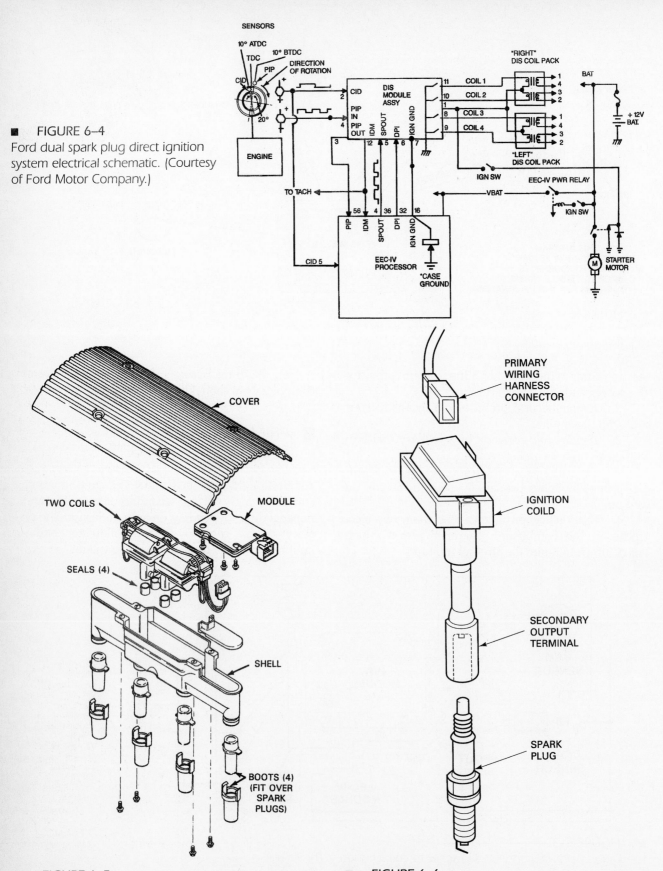

■ FIGURE 6–4
Ford dual spark plug direct ignition system electrical schematic. (Courtesy of Ford Motor Company.)

■ FIGURE 6–5
Integrated direct ignition system. (Courtesy of General Motors Corporation.)

■ FIGURE 6–6
This integrated direct ignition system has one of these units for each cylinder.

bypass (some systems), coil primary winding, switching device and connecting wiring. The secondary circuit consists of the following: ignition coil secondary winding, distributor cap and rotor (some systems), spark plug wires (some systems), coil wire (some systems), spark plugs.

■ IGNITION SYSTEM PROBLEMS

Engine Cranks Normally but Does Not Start

If the engine cranks normally but does not start, proceed as follows.

1. Visually inspect the ignition system. Look for loose primary circuit connections; check that plug-in connectors are fully engaged; check to make sure that all plug and coil secondary wires are connected; on distributor ignition systems check for a broken rotor or poor rotor-to-cap connection.

2. Perform a spark intensity test. Connect a tester spark plug to one of the plug wires and to ground. With the ignition switch on crank the engine and observe the spark (**Figures 6–7** and **6–8).** If no spark is present, perform the same test with the spark tester connected to the coil secondary wire. This test may also be performed without the tester as shown in **Figure 6–9.**

3. Interpret the test results. A bright, snapping spark indicates that the ignition system output voltage is good. The no-start condition may be due to a no-fuel condition, a fuel-flooded engine, or fouled spark plugs. If the spark is weak or there is no spark, further tests are required as described in this chapter.

Engine Starts and Runs but Has a Drivability Problem

If the engine starts and runs but does not perform normally, the problem may be in the ignition system or it may be in any of several other systems. Poor

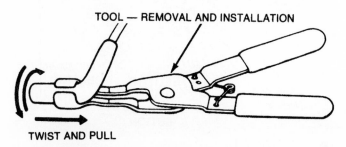

TOOL — REMOVAL AND INSTALLATION

TWIST AND PULL

■ FIGURE 6–7
Proper method of removing a spark plug wire. (Courtesy of Ford Motor Company.)

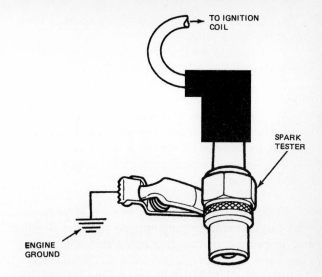

TO IGNITION COIL

SPARK TESTER

ENGINE GROUND

■ FIGURE 6–8
Spark intensity tester. (Courtesy of Ford Motor Company.)

drivability may be due to problems in the fuel system, air intake system, valve timing, engine condition, or the transmission. Refer to the appropriate chapters in this book for diagnosis of these systems. To determine whether the ignition system is at fault, on-board self-diagnostics, engine analyzer diagnosis, or portable testers may be used to test the entire system and its individual components.

■ IGNITION SYSTEM TESTING AND DIAGNOSIS PROCEDURE

The following steps are typical of the procedure used in preliminary diagnosis of the ignition system.

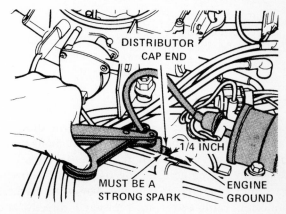

DISTRIBUTOR CAP END

1/4 INCH

MUST BE A STRONG SPARK   ENGINE GROUND

■ FIGURE 6–9
Checking coil secondary output. (Courtesy of Ford Motor Company.)

1.   Check to see if a good strong spark is available at the spark plugs.

2.   Check to see if a good strong spark is available at the coil secondary output.

3.   Check for adequate input voltage at the coil primary (BAT +) terminal.

4.   Check to see if the primary circuit control system is working; input sensors on computerized ignition, pickup coil on electronic ignition.

5.   Access the fault codes in a computer-controlled ignition.

Depending on the results of each step, further tests can be made to pinpoint the problem. Testing and inspection of the distributor cap, rotor, spark plug wires, spark plugs, ignition coils, input sensors, control module, pickup coil, and timing may have to be made.

On-Board Self-Diagnosis

Computer-controlled ignition systems have self-diagnosis capability. The engine control computer is programmed to monitor the ignition system components as well as other engine control functions. If the computer senses a fault often enough to indicate a problem, a fault code is stored in the computer for later recall by the technician. Fault codes are accessed in different ways on different makes and models of cars. They may be displayed through an indicator light on the dash, through a message center, or on a diagnostic tester or analyzer. The fault code is then compared to a fault code chart in the service manual to identify the problem.

Rather than pinpointing the problem, the fault code tells you that there is a problem in a certain part of the system. A fault code can be caused by any of the following:

- Sensor failure
- Harness failure
- Bad connection
- Output device failure
- Computer failure

Accessing Fault Codes

Fault codes are accessed and cleared in different ways on different vehicles. Follow instructions in the appropriate service manual in each case. Ford's EEC IV system can be accessed by using Ford's special tester and plugging it into the diagnostic harness connector. Fault codes are registered directly and compared to the fault code chart in the service manual. Another method is to use an analog voltmeter connected to the appropriate test connector pin.

Voltmeter needle fluctuations are then interpreted according to service manual instructions and compared to the fault code chart. With General Motor's Computer Command Control (CCC) system, just turn the ignition switch on and observe the light flashes on the dash. These must be interpreted and compared to service manual fault codes. With Chrysler's computerized ignition system, cycle the ignition switch ON, OFF, ON, OFF, ON within 5 seconds, but do not start the engine. The light flashes are interpreted and compared to service manual codes. Clearing the fault codes may only require disconnecting and reconnecting the quick disconnect at the battery on some models. Other procedures may be required on other systems. Refer to the service manual for proper procedures. See Chapter 4 for detailed information on how to access fault codes and how to clear the keep alive memory.

■ USING A SCAN TOOL

A scanner (scan tool) is used by plugging it into the wiring harness diagnostic connector, **Figure 6–10** and as described in Chapters 2 and 4. The vehicle's computer communicates a variety of information to the scanner, which is displayed in digital form, as fault codes, or in word form. Some of this information is difficult or impossible to obtain without a scanner. Using a scanner saves diagnosis time and can avoid the unnecessary replacement of good

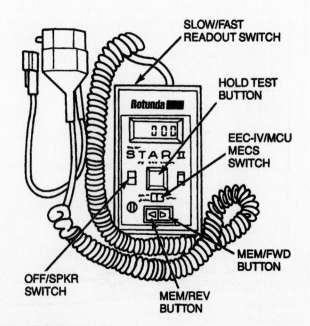

■   FIGURE 6–10

Computer-controlled ignition system tester. This STAR (self test diagnostic readout) tester is used on Ford vehicles. (Courtesy of Ford Motor Company.)

parts when other testing methods are used. The scanner is not able to pinpoint the exact location of a problem in a circuit but is able to identify the problem circuit. Pinpoint tests with a digital voltmeter or ohmmeter are performed to isolate the problem within the circuit. Substituting suspected components with known good components is another method of pinpointing faulty components.

A scanner can be used to detect intermittent problems related to the wiring harness and wiring connectors. The scanner is plugged into the diagnostic connector with the engine not running. The wiring harness, connectors, and terminals can then be manipulated and wiggled while observing the scanner display. Faulty wires and connectors can be detected in this way.

The scanner can also be used to check operation while the vehicle is being driven under conditions that caused the check engine light to turn on, indicating a problem. The scanner should be observed in each test position while driving the vehicle.

Follow the instructions supplied with the scanner and the procedures outlined in the service manual for test procedures and interpretation of test results. Typical scan tool data descriptions are given in Chapters 2 and 4.

Fault Code Charts

Fault code charts are provided in service manuals. They list all the possible fault code numbers and what each fault code number means. Fault codes direct the technician to the malfunctioning circuit. However, the circuit itself may not be causing the trouble. Trouble in a related component can cause the fault code to be triggered. It is therefore important to understand which vehicle systems are interrelated and may have common sensors.

Breakout Box Tests

Some diagnostic procedures require testing the sensors, output devices, and control module with all the electrical connections in place. This requires the use of a breakout box and a number of test lead adapters **(Figure 2–18)** in Chapter 2. The breakout box connectors are fitted between wiring harness connectors on the vehicle in a manner that keeps the sensors, output devices, and control module connected so that the vehicle can be operated during testing. This allows the technician to perform a number of checks and tests under actual operating conditions. Refer to the wiring diagrams in the service manual to locate wiring connectors and circuits and the test procedures in each case. Each test is independent of the others. Within each test there are test sequences that

can identify a condition or a problem without requiring the completion of the entire test procedure. The test strategy usually involves the following steps.

1. Check the voltage or resistance value.
2. Change the input signal.
3. Perform a click test.
4. Perform a wiggle test.
5. Perform a coil resistance test.
6. Perform an output signal test.
7. Check for harness shorts.
8. Check for harness opens.

See Chapters 2 and 4 for examples of test strategies for solenoids, relays, computer output signals, and computer input signals. Consult the service manual to determine the meaning of devices identified by abbreviations. Terminology and abbreviations differ considerably among various vehicle manufacturers and service manuals.

Pinpoint Testing

Pinpoint testing is normally done after completing self-diagnosis. Pinpoint tests involve testing individual components of the system identified as having a fault. This includes testing switches, sensors, actuators, wiring harness, and connectors. Pinpoint tests are made under different conditions as specified in the service manual. Examples are KOEO-key on, engine off, ER-engine running, etc. **(Figures 6–11 and 6–12)**. Service manual procedures must be followed precisely for pinpoint tests, including test equipment connections and test terminal identification. Making the wrong connections can cause damage to testers and system components. Component testing is described in Chapter 4 as well as in other chapters where computer controls are involved.

Engine Analyzers

Modern engine analyzers are capable of a wide variety of tests on all types of ignition systems. The analyzer displays the test results on a screen in wave form or a digital display. Analyzers equipped with a printer can generate a printout of test results. See Chapter 2 for more on engine analyzers and display patterns.

Direct Ignition System Testing

Computer-controlled direct ignition system testing involves testing the input sensors, output devices, and the computer. Modern engine analyzers have

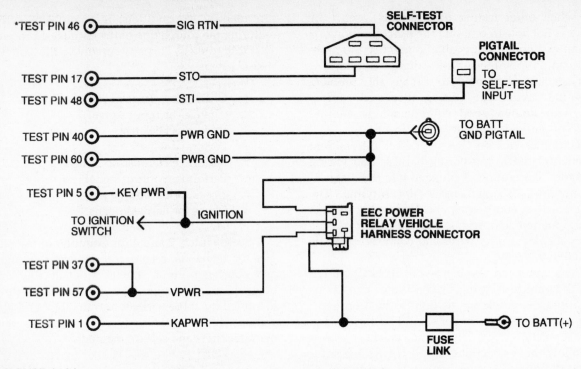

■ FIGURE 6–11
Example of test pin identification given in service manual for pinpoint testing.
(Courtesy of Ford Motor Company.)

DIS testing capability. Portable testers may also be used. One method uses a diagnostic wiring harness that interconnects all sensors, control modules, and coils. The harness functions with either an EECIV monitor or a breakout box to access fault codes. Another method uses two testers, a module tester, and a coil/sensor tester **(Figure 6–13).** The module tester has an interface harness connector and can monitor all input and output signals. If this tester indicates that a problem exists, the coil/sensor tester is used to determine if the wiring harness or other component has failed. Always follow service manual and test equipment instructions for all tests.

■ SENSOR TESTING WITH A DVOM

To test input sensors for computer-controlled ignition systems, a high-impedance digital volt/ohmmeter (DVOM) must be used **(Figure 6–14).** It must have at least 10,000 Ω (10 KΩ) of input impedance. Otherwise, the sensors will be damaged. Specifications for many sensors are given in tenths of a volt, which is impossible to read on an analog voltmeter. A narrow operating range may also be given which cannot be read on an analog voltmeter. Follow service manual procedures for spe-

cific tests and specifications. Some sensors are tested for resistance values under specified conditions, while others are tested for voltage output. Ignition system sensors include the crankshaft sensor, camshaft sensor, coolant temperature sensor, manifold absolute pressure sensor, and detonation sensor. See Chapter 4 for details on how to test sensors.

■ COIL TESTING AND REPLACEMENT

Coil Input Voltage Test

This test will determine whether the primary circuit voltage supply system to the coil has excessive resistance **(Figure 6–15).**

1. Connect the voltmeter positive lead to the positive primary terminal of the coil and attach the other lead to a good ground.
2. Set the voltmeter to the proper scale.
3. Disconnect and ground the coil high-tension lead from the distributor cap to prevent the engine from starting.
4. Turn the ignition switch to the starting position and observe the voltage while cranking. The voltage should not be below specifications.

SENSORS/ INPUTS	Signal Pin #	KOEO	Units	HOT IDLE	30 MPH	55 MPH	Units
TP	47	.9-1.0	DCV	.9-1.0	1.2-1.4	1.4-1.7	DCV
EVP	27	.3-.4	DCV	.3-.4	.3-.4	1.8-4.4	DCV
ECT	7	.5-.7	DCV	.5-.7	.5-.7	.5-.7	DCV
ACT	25	.7-2.8	DCV	.7-2.8	.7-2.8	.7-2.8	DCV
MAP	45	157	Hz	103-106	106-118	118-136	Hz
IDM	4	0-12	RPM	650-750	1520-1710	2080-2380	RPM
PIP	56	0-12	RPM	650-750	1520-1710	2080-2380	RPM
HEGO	29	0	DCV	switching (4)	switching (4)	switching (4)	DCV
FPM - red	8	0	DCV	VBAT	VBAT	VBAT	DCV
ACCS	10	0	DCV	VBAT (1)	0	0	DCV
NGS/CES	30	5.0/VBAT	DCV	0 (2)	5.0/VBAT	5.0/VBAT	DCV
STI	48	5.0	DCV	5.0	5.0	5.0	DCV
ACTUATORS/ OUTPUTS							
INJ BANK 2	59	VBAT (3)	DCV	5.0-5.8	6.6-8.2	8.2-10.6	mS
INJ BANK 1	58	VBAT (3)	DCV	5.0-5.8	6.6-8.2	8.2-10.6	mS
EVR	33	VBAT (3)	DCV	0	0	50-75	%
STO/MIL	17	.1-.9	DCV	VBAT	VBAT	VBAT	DCV
CANP	31	VBAT	DCV	VBAT	.1-.2	.1-.2	DCV
ISC	21	VBAT	DCV	9.4-10.0	8.0-9.5	6.0-8.2	DCV
FP	22	VBAT	DCV	.1-.9	.1-.9	.1-.9	DCV
SPOUT	36	0-12	RPM	650-750	1520-1710	2080-2380	RPM
AM1	51	VBAT	DCV	.1-.2	.1-.2	.1-.2	DCV
OTHER							
IGN TIMING	TIMING	N/A	DEG	20-24	38-42	42-48	DEG

NOTES:

(1) — A/C on.

(2) — Clutch pedal depressed.

(3) — Monitor in DCV Manual Mode, Reference Pin to PWR GND (40/60).

(4) — HEGO should switch from rich (red LED) to lean (green LED), or lean to rich, at least once every 3 seconds. HEGO voltage should toggle above and below .450 DCV and should never be a negative value.

Reference values shown may vary ± 20% depending on operating conditions and other factors. RPM values are axle and tire dependent.

■   FIGURE 6–12
Typical pinpoint test data from service manual. Always refer to the service manual for proper specifications and procedures. (Courtesy of Ford Motor Company.)

DIS Harness
(Rotunda #07-0044)

DIS 600A Module Tester   DIS 601A Coil/Sensor Tester
(Rotunda #07-0070)

■ FIGURE 6–13

Direct ignition system test equipment (typical). (Courtesy of Ford Motor Company.)

5. If the voltage is too low, the reason could be one or more of the following:
   (a) Battery condition
   (b) Excessive starter current draw
   (c) Excessive resistance in ignition resistor bypass circuit

6. With the voltmeter connected as in step 1 and with the ignition switch in the run position (engine off), the voltmeter should read the specified voltage (usually approximately 7.5 V).

7. If the voltage is below specifications, the reason could be one or more of the following:
   (a) Battery condition
   (b) Ignition switch resistance
   (c) Excessive resistance in ignition ballast resistor or resistor wire

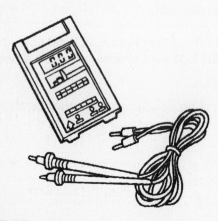

■ FIGURE 6–14

High-impedance digital volt/ohmmeter (DVOM) must be used to test electronic sensors. (Courtesy of Ford Motor Company.)

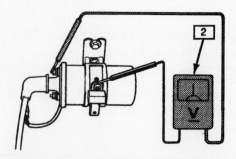

■ FIGURE 6–15

Testing coil input voltage. (Courtesy of Chrysler Corporation.)

Ballast Resistor and Resistor Wire Test

Some older ignition systems have a ballast resistor in the coil primary feed circuit. Others may have a resistance wire. In either case, if coil input voltage is above or below specifications, the ballast resistor or resistor wire should be tested with an ohmmeter. Connect an ohmmeter across the resistance and note the meter reading. Compare the reading with specifications. If above or below requirements, replace the resistor or resistance wire.

Coil Resistance Tests

Coil output and the entire secondary system can be tested with an oscilloscope. If an oscilloscope is not available, test the coil with an ohmmeter **(Figures 6–16 to 6–18).**

    1.   Connect the ohmmeter leads to the primary terminals on the coil.
    2.   Read the ohmmeter scale.
    (a) An infinite reading indicates an open primary winding; replace coil.
    (b) The ohmmeter reading should meet specifications.

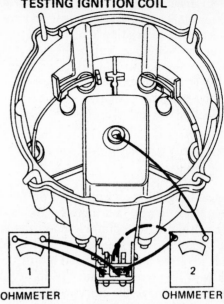

■   FIGURE 6–17
Testing an integrated coil in an HEI distributor. (Courtesy of General Motors Corporation.)

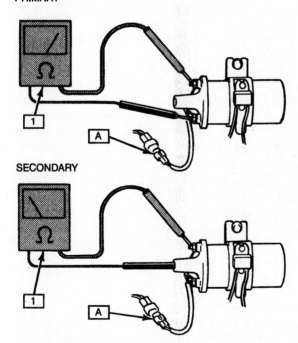

PRIMARY

SECONDARY

| A | CONNECTOR DISCONNECTED |
| 1 | OHMMETER |

■   FIGURE 6–16
Testing coil primary resistance (top) and secondary resistance (bottom). (Courtesy of Chrysler Corporation.)

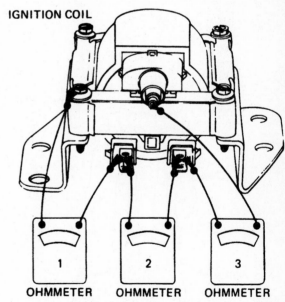

IGNITION COIL

    2. **Check ignition coil with ohmmeter for opens and grounds:**
        Step 1. — Use high scale. Should read very high (infinite). If not, replace coil.
        Step 2. — Use low scale. Should read very low or zero. If not, replace coil.
        Step 3. — Use high scale. Should not read infinite. If it does, replace coil.

■   FIGURE 6–18
Testing a coil removed from an HEI distributor. (Courtesy of General Motors Corporation.)

3. Connect the ohmmeter to the coil primary positive terminal and to the high-tension terminal.

(a) An infinite reading indicates an open secondary winding (replace the coil).

(b) The ohmmeter resistance reading should meet specifications. (A reading that is too low indicates a shorted secondary winding; replace the coil.)

Replacing the Ignition Coil or Coil Pack

To replace an ignition coil mounted on the engine, disconnect the wires and remove the mounting bolts. Install the new coil and connect the wires to the coil. Make sure that you do not reverse the wires, since this reverses coil polarity and reduces coil output. To replace a coil mounted in the distributor **(Figure 6–19)**, remove the coil cover and disconnect

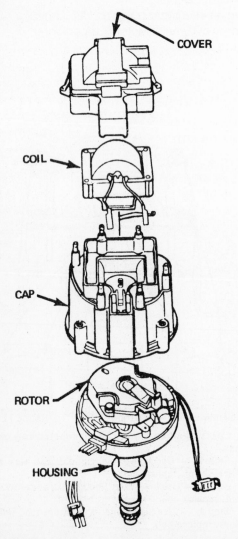

■ FIGURE 6–19
Removing the coil from an integrated HEI distributor. (Courtesy of General Motors Corporation.)

the coil leads. Remove the coil attaching screws and lift the coil from the cap. Install the new coil in reverse order of disassembly. To replace a direct ignition coil pack mounted on the engine may require special procedures and the use of a special heat transfer grease applied to the mounting base. To replace integrated direct ignition coil assemblies, follow the procedures in the service manual.

■ IGNITION SWITCH SERVICE

A faulty ignition switch may cause a no-cranking or no-start condition, it may not be possible to shut off the engine, or the starter will not disengage. To check ignition switch operation, use a test light **(Figure 6–19).** With the switch held in the start position, touch the test light to the start terminal—it should light. Next touch it to the run terminal and it should not light. With the ignition switch in the run position, touch the test light to the run position—it should light. Touch it to the start position and it should not light. With the key in the off position, the test light should not light when touching the start or run terminals. A switch that does not pass these tests must be replaced.

To test ignition switch resistance, disconnect the current supply to the switch and test the start and run positions with an ohmmeter. If resistance is excessive, replace the switch.

Replacing the Ignition Switch

The ignition switch may be mounted in the dash or on the steering column. The dash-mounted unit usually combines the lock cylinder and switch in a single assembly. The column-mounted switch is separate from the lock cylinder. It is usually mounted farther down on the steering column and connected by linkage to the cylinder. The dash-mounted switch is usually removed by inserting a pin in a small hole or removing a retaining screw in the front of the switch and turning the key. This releases the lock cylinder for removal. The procedure is reversed for installation. With a column-mounted switch the steering column mounting bolts holding it to the dash may have to be removed to lower the column **(Figures 6–20 to 6–22).** This provides access to the switch for removal and installation. Refer to the service manual for specific procedures.

■ SETTING INITIAL TIMING (DISTRIBUTOR IGNITION)

On distributor ignition, base or initial timing must be set any time the distributor has been removed and reinstalled. Initial timing is set without any vac-

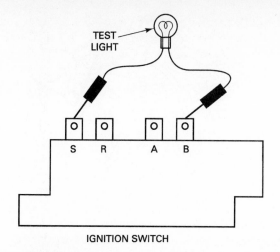

■ FIGURE 6–20
Testing an ignition switch with a test light. (Courtesy of F T Enterprises.)

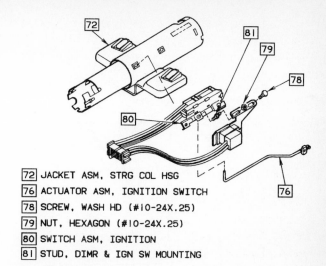

72 JACKET ASM, STRG COL HSG
76 ACTUATOR ASM, IGNITION SWITCH
78 SCREW, WASH HD (#10-24X.25)
79 NUT, HEXAGON (#10-24X.25)
80 SWITCH ASM, IGNITION
81 STUD, DIMR & IGN SW MOUNTING

■ FIGURE 6–22
Ignition switch removal from steering column. (Courtesy of General Motors Corporation.)

uum, centrifugal, or electronic advance. Timing is adjusted by slightly turning the distributor in the engine. Turning the distributor housing in the direction of shaft rotation retards ignition timing. Turning it opposite to shaft rotation advances ignition timing. Timing that is too far advanced will cause spark knock or pinging during acceleration or under load. Timing that is too late (retarded too much) causes poor performance, poor fuel economy, and poor acceleration. The direction of shaft rotation is easily established by checking the position of the vacuum-advance unit on the distributor. The vacuum-advance unit is offset on the distributor housing. A line through the center of the vacuum-advance unit points in the direction of shaft rotation. Ignition timing is normally checked and adjusted with the use of a timing light.

To connect a timing light, connect the two small leads to the battery terminals. Connect the third lead to the number 1 spark plug lead. Some timing lights have a clip-on inductive lead. Others clip to a short

metal lead placed between the spark plug and the spark plug wire. Before starting the engine, locate the timing marks **(Figure 6–23)**. They may be on the timing cover and harmonic balancer or they may be on the flywheel. Clean the area if necessary to help make the marks more visible. Chalk may be used to highlight the marks. Next loosen the distributor hold-down bolt just enough to allow the distributor housing to be turned. Disconnect the vacuum line from the distributor and plug the line. With the timing light connected and the leads and light away from any rotating fan or belts, start the engine and let it idle. Holding the timing light, aim the flashing light at the timing marks **(Figure 6–24)**. They will appear to stand still. Note the degree marking that aligns with the reference line. Note whether timing is early or late according to specifications. If it is late, turn the distributor slightly against shaft rotation

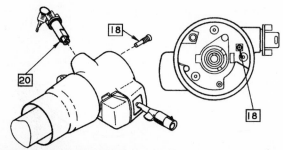

18 SCREW, LOCK RETAINING
20 LOCK CYLINDER SET, STRG COL

■ FIGURE 6–21
Ignition switch lock cylinder removal. (Courtesy of General Motors Corporation.)

■ FIGURE 6–23
Ignition timing degree markings at crankshaft pulley. (Courtesy of Chrysler Corporation.)

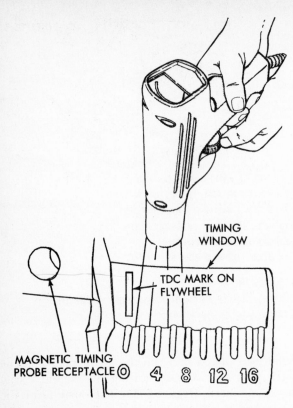

FIGURE 6–24
Checking vacuum and centrifugal advance with a timing light equipped with a degree meter. (Courtesy of Chrysler Corporation.)

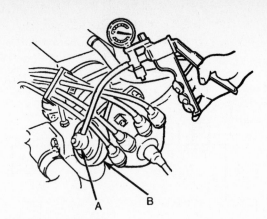

FIGURE 6–25
Using a hand vacuum pump to apply vacuum to advance unit to check vacuum advance unit operation. (Courtesy of Chrysler Corporation.)

Vacuum-Advance Test

The vacuum-advance unit can be checked by applying a vacuum to the diaphragm and observing pickup assembly movement. Another method is to disconnect the distributor vacuum hoses and connect a hand vacuum pump to the advance unit (**Figure 6–25**). With the engine idling the specified amount of vacuum can be applied and the timing checked for the proper advance based on the vacuum applied. A faulty vacuum-advance unit must be replaced. To test the vacuum supply to the vacuum advance, disconnect the vacuum hose from the vacuum-advance unit. Connect a vacuum gauge to

until timing is as specified; if it is early, turn the distributor slightly in the same direction as shaft rotation until timing is as specified. Tighten the distributor hold-down bolt and recheck the timing. If the timing has a built-in degree meter, it can be used to measure distributor centrifugal and vacuum advance with the engine running. Follow the instructions provided with the timing light. Reconnect the vacuum line.

Centrifugal-Advance Test

The centrifugal and vacuum advance can be checked without distributor removal. The operation of the centrifugal advance mechanism can be checked by disconnecting and plugging the vacuum advance hose. With a timing light connected, the timing mark should advance as the engine speed is increased. If it does not, check the governor weights and springs for binding. An adjustable timing light or magnetic timing equipment can be used to measure the amount of timing advance at a specified rpm, which can be compared to specifications. If the centrifugal advance weights or pins or springs are worn or damaged, they must be replaced.

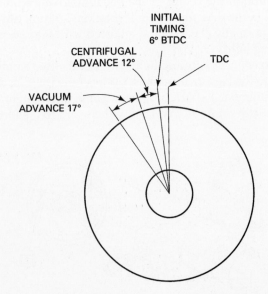

TOTAL CENTRIFUGAL AND VACUUM ADVANCE 29°

FIGURE 6–26
Total ignition advance includes initial timing, vacuum advance, and centrifugal advance.

the vacuum line. Start the engine and run it a specified speed. Compare the vacuum reading to specifications. If correct, inspect the vacuum line for leaks, and test the thermal vacuum switch and vacuum delay valve or its possible reverse installation. Replace any faulty parts. Total centrifugal and vacuum advance can be checked at specified engine speeds and compared to specifications **(Figure 6–26).**

■ SECONDARY WIRE TESTING AND SERVICE

Secondary Wire Insulation Test

Secondary wire insulation must be in good condition to prevent arcing to ground or cross firing between closely positioned wires. Secondary wire insulation can be tested by running the engine at idle with the hood up. The engine compartment must be darkened by draping finder covers over the sides of the hood. A secondary wire test light or grounded screwdriver can be used to check the entire length of each wire. If there are any sparks or the tester lights up, leakage of secondary voltage is occurring. Replace any wires that do not pass this test. If there is no insulation breakdown, remove the wires and test the wires for resistance.

Secondary Wire Removal

Most spark plug wires have a resistance-type conductor that is easily damaged if not handled properly. If the wires are stretched or kinked during handling, the conductor will separate and no voltage can reach the spark plug. Never pull on the wires to remove them from the spark plugs. Grasp the insulator boot with the proper tool, twist the boot slightly to loosen it from the plug, then use the tool to pull the boot and wire away from the plug.

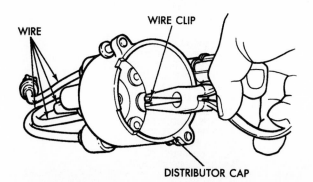

■ FIGURE 6–27
Unlocking high tension wires from inside the distributor cap. (Courtesy of Chrysler Corporation.)

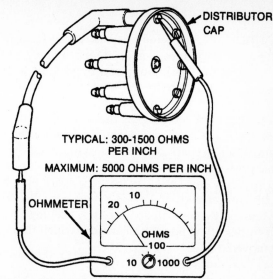

Measuring Wire Resistance Through Distributor Cap

■ FIGURE 6–28
(Courtesy of Ford Motor Company.)

Use the same method, where possible, at the distributor cap. On some distributor caps the wire must be released inside the cap **(Figure 6–27).** On others a retainer plate must be removed to expose the wires.

Secondary Wire Resistance Test

Spark plug and coil wires can be tested with an ohmmeter to determine their resistance. Set the ohmmeter to the proper scale for the test. Check the service manual for resistance values. Connect the ohmmeter, one lead to each end of the wire, and read the result **(Figure 6–28).** Compare the result to specifications. Resistance values of secondary wires vary with application and wire length. Replace wires that fail the test.

■ SPARK PLUG DIAGNOSIS AND SERVICE

Spark Plug Problems

Spark plug problems can cause misfiring, hard starting, poor fuel economy, and power loss. Spark plug electrodes eventually erode, widening the gap. Carbon and other combustion by-products or oil may be deposited on the spark plug electrodes. These conditions may make it impossible for a spark to be produced across the electrodes. Spark plugs can be tested using an oscilloscope, or they can be removed and their condition inspected.

Spark Plug Removal

CAUTION   Never remove spark plugs from a hot engine because threads in cylinder head may strip.

Grasp the spark plug boot (by hand or with the proper tool) and twist the boot back and forth to loosen it from the plug, pulling on the boot at the same time. Never pull on the wire since this can break the electrical resistance conductor inside the wire. Using a spark plug socket (with a rubber insert that grips the insulator), loosen each plug one or two turns. Blow any dirt away from the spark plug holes with compressed air so that it will not fall into the cylinders. Remove all spark plugs, keeping them in the order of cylinder number from which they were removed.

Spark Plug Inspection

See **Figure 6-29** and compare the condition of the spark plugs with the illustrations. Note any oil fouling, gap bridging, preignition damage, carbon fouling, and the like. Note the cause of these conditions.

Cleaning Spark Plugs

Spark plugs can be cleaned in an air-powered sand-blasting device that removes deposits by abrasion. Care must be taken not to abrade the insulator by overcleaning, since this can cause deposit buildup and fouling. All abrasive material must be removed from the plugs to avoid any sand from falling into the cylinder, with consequent cylinder scoring and damage. Spark plugs are usually replaced instead of cleaning and gapping them. The time required for cleaning and gapping offsets the cost of new plugs. Replacement spark plugs must be of the correct type, heat range, thread type, reach, and sealing method as specified by the vehicle manufacturer. Using the wrong plug can result in poor performance, shorter plug life, and even engine damage.

Gapping Spark Plugs

All spark plugs, whether new or used, should be properly gapped just before installation. Use a wire-type spark plug gauge to measure the gap **(Figure**

IDENTIFIED BY LIGHT TAN OR GRAY DEPOSITS ON THE FIRING TIP.

IDENTIFIED BY MELTED OR SPOTTY DEPOSITS RESEMBLING BUBBLES OR BLISTERS.
CAUSED BY SUDDEN ACCELERATION.

IDENTIFIED BY DEPOSIT BUILDUP CLOSING GAP BETWEEN ELECTRODES.
CAUSED BY OIL OR CARBON FOULING.

IDENTIFIED BY MELTED ELECTRODES AND POSSIBLY BLISTERED INSULATOR; COULD INDICATE ENGINE DAMAGE.
CAUSED BY WRONG TYPE OF FUEL, INCORRECT IGNITION TIMING OR ADVANCE, TOO HOT A PLUG, BURNT VALVES OR ENGINE OVERHEATING.

OIL FOULED

IDENTIFIED BY WET, BLACK DEPOSITS ON THE INSULATOR SHELL BORE ELECTRODES.
CAUSED BY EXCESSIVE OIL ENTERING COMBUSTION CHAMBER THROUGH WORN RINGS AND PISTONS, EXCESSIVE CLEARANCE BETWEEN VALVE GUIDES AND STEMS, OR WORN OR LOOSE BEARINGS.

CARBON FOULED

IDENTIFIED BY BLACK, DRY, FLUFFY CARBON DEPOSITS ON INSULATOR TIPS, EXPOSED SHELL SURFACES AND ELECTRODES.
CAUSED BY TOO COLD A PLUG, WEAK IGNITION, DIRTY AIR CLEANER, DEFECTIVE FUEL PUMP, TOO RICH A FUEL MIXTURE, IMPROPERLY OPERATING HEAT RISER OR EXCESSIVE IDLING.

OVERHEATING

IDENTIFIED BY A WHITE OR LIGHT-GRAY INSULATOR WITH SMALL BLACK OR GRAY-BROWN SPOTS AND BLUISH BURNT APPEARANCE ON ELECTRODES.
CAUSED BY ENGINE OVERHEATING, WRONG TYPE OF FUEL, LOOSE SPARK PLUGS, TOO HOT A PLUG, LOW FUEL PUMP PRESSURE OR INCORRECT IGNITION TIMING.

■   FIGURE 6-29
Spark plug analysis. (Courtesy of Ford Motor Company.)

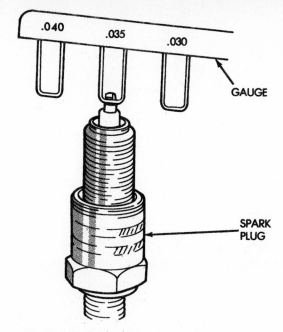

■ FIGURE 6–30
Use only a round wire gauge to check spark plug gap. (Courtesy of Chrysler Corporation.)

6–30). The gauge should fit snugly between the two electrodes when properly set. Adjustment to the gap is made by bending the side electrode with the proper tool (usually part of the gapping gauge). Set the gap to specifications obtained from the service manual.

Installing the Plugs

Spark plugs should be started by hand to avoid cross threading. A spark plug socket and extension or a short piece of hose may be used to grip the plug. Start the threads at least two turns before using the wrench to tighten them. Recommendations for tightening spark plugs vary. Some service manuals recommend tightening to specifications with a torque wrench. Others recommend seating the plug, then tightening an additional one-half turn. Follow the tightening specifications given in the appropriate service manual.

Spark Plug Hole Thread Repair

If the threads in a spark plug hole in the cylinder head are badly damaged, they can be repaired with a thread repair insert. The cylinder head must be removed from the engine before installing a Tapersert. Performing this procedure while the cylinder head is on the engine will cause metal chips to fall into the cylinder. Once in the cylinder, these chips can damage the cylinder wall when the engine is started. A Tapersert kit is shown in **Figure 6–31.**

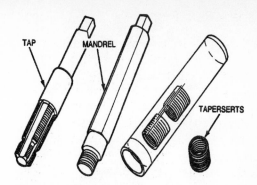

■ FIGURE 6–31
(Courtesy of Ford Motor Company.)

1. Thoroughly clean the spark plug counterbore, seat, and threads of all dirt or other foreign material.

2. Start the tap into the spark plug hole, being careful to keep it properly aligned. As the tap begins cutting new threads, apply aluminum cutting oil to the tap. Continue cutting threads and applying oil until the stop ring bottoms against the spark plug seat.

3. Remove the tap. Remove all metal chips using compressed air.

4. Coat the threads of the mandrel with cutting oil. Thread Tapersert onto the mandrel until one thread of the mandrel extends beyond the Tapersert.

5. Thread the Tapersert into the tapped spark plug hole using a torque wrench. Continue tightening the mandrel until the torque wrench indicates 61 N · m (45 lb-ft).

6. To loosen the mandrel for removal, hold the mandrel stationary and turn the mandrel body approximately one-half turn. Remove the mandrel.

■ DISTRIBUTOR CAP AND ROTOR SERVICE

Removing the Cap and Rotor

The distributor cap may be held in place by spring clips or screws **(Figure 6–32).** Screws are removed by turning them counterclockwise. Spring clips must be carefully pried away from the cap. Be careful not to crack the cap. Pull and wiggle the cap free from the distributor **(Figure 6–33).** Press-fit rotors are normally easily pulled from the distributor shaft. Pry under the rotor with a flat-blade screwdriver if necessary. Rotors secured with screws require screw removal before rotor removal.

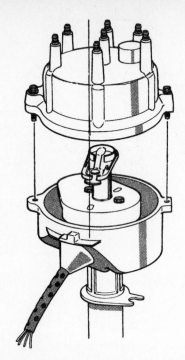

■ FIGURE 6–32
To remove this distributor cap, the retaining screws must first be removed. (Courtesy of Chrysler Corporation.)

Inspecting the Cap and Rotor

PRO TIP

It may be more cost effective to simply replace the cap and rotor instead of spending much time on inspection.

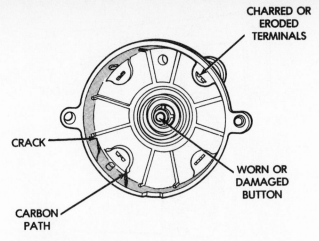

■ FIGURE 6–34
Distributor cap inspection. (Courtesy of Chrysler Corporation.)

Inspect the distributor cap for cracks, carbon tracking, burned or eroded inside terminals, and burned or corroded plug wire sockets (**Figures 6–34 and 6–35**). These problems can cause the engine to misfire, cross fire, or backfire. Cracks or carbon trace formation can cause coil output voltage to go to ground or to the wrong distributor terminal. Replace a faulty distributor cap. Inspect the rotor for cracks, carbon tracking, burned or eroded tip or center contact, and for fit on the distributor shaft. The rotor should fit snugly on the shaft. If it is loose or otherwise faulty, it should be replaced.

Replacing the Rotor and Cap

To install a press-fit rotor, align the flats or the tab and slot and press the rotor onto the shaft until fully seated. On screw-secured rotors, align the square or

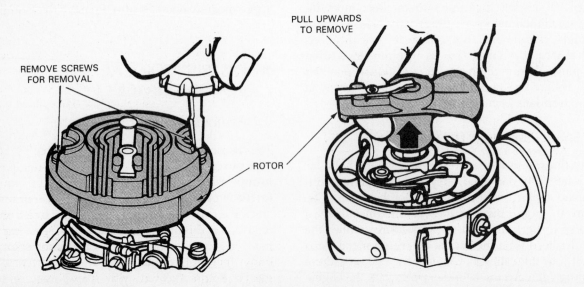

■ FIGURE 6–33
Typical rotor removal methods. (Courtesy of Chrysler Corporation.)

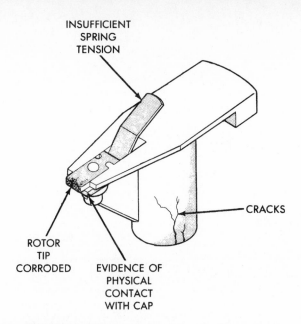

FIGURE 6–35
Rotor inspection. (Courtesy of Chrysler Corporation.)

round dowel with the hole in the distributor and install the retaining screws. To install the distributor cap, align the notch or tab with the corresponding tab or notch in the distributor housing. Push the cap down until it is fully seated and does not wobble on the distributor. Install the retaining clips or screws. If the cap or rotor are not installed properly, the cap or rotor can break as soon as the engine is started.

■ PICKUP COIL AND CONTROL MODULE SERVICE

Pickup Coil Service

The pickup coil windings or leads can break, causing no-start, missing, stalling, and power-loss problems. The pickup coil output may be tested with a low reading or digital AC voltmeter while cranking the engine. A small AC voltage will be produced while cranking the engine if the pickup coil is functioning properly. Refer to the service manual for specifications and procedures.

The pickup coil can also be tested with an ohmmeter. Connect the ohmmeter to the disconnected leads from the pickup module **(Figures 6–36 to 6–38).** The resistance through the pickup coil windings should be as specified in the shop manual for the unit being serviced. On some Chrysler systems the resistance should be between 150 and 900 Ω. On some Ford Dura Spark systems the resistance should be between 400 and 1000 Ω. Some HEI systems have a resistance between 500 and 1500 Ω. On some systems the air gap between the pickup and the relutor or armature is adjustable. This clearance must be

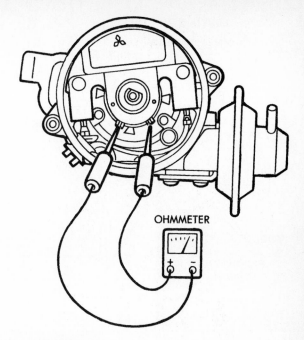

FIGURE 6–36
Testing pickup coil resistance with an ohmmeter. (Courtesy of Chrysler Corporation.)

measured with a nonmagnetic-type feeler gauge and adjusted to specifications **(Figure 6–39).** On systems where this clearance is not adjustable but the original clearance has been altered, the pickup coil or armature must be replaced since it has been damaged.

Control Module Service

If a problem still exists after checking and correcting all other ignition system components, the control module may be at fault. If the module is mounted in the engine compartment the usual procedure is to replace it with a known good unit. If the problem is corrected, the module was at fault. If the module is mounted in the distributor, it can be tested with a module tester before replacement. In some designs the module is mounted under the coil pack or on the intake manifold.

To replace an electronic ignition control unit mounted in the engine compartment or under the dash, simply disconnect the wiring connector and remove the attaching screws and control unit. To install the new unit, proceed in the reverse order.

To replace a control module mounted inside a unitized distributor, remove the distributor cap and coil, remove the rotor and disconnect the pickup coil leads, and remove the magnetic shield, retaining ring, pickup coil, magnet, and pole piece. Remove the module attaching screws and module. Reassemble in the reverse order **(Figure 6–40).** Apply silicone

TESTING PICKUP COIL

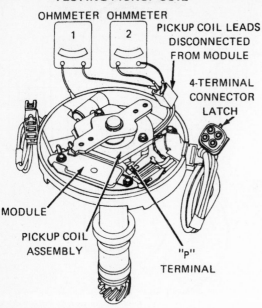

■ FIGURE 6–37

Remove rotor and pickup coil leads from module. Connect ohmmeter test 1 and then test 2. If vacuum unit is used, connect vacuum source to vacuum unit. Replace unit if inoperative. Observe ohmmeter throughout range; flex leads by hand without vacuum to check for intermittent opens. Test 1 should read infinite at all times. Test 2 should read steady at one value within 500 to 1500 range. Note: ohmmeter may indicate reading change if operating the vacuum unit causes the teeth to align. This is not a defect. If pickup coil is defective, replace. (Courtesy of General Motors Corporation.)

TESTING HALL EFFECT SWITCH

14. Connect 12-volt battery and voltmeter to switch; carefully note polarity markings.

15. Without knife blade, voltmeter should read less than 0.5 volts. If not, switch is defective.

16. With knife blade, voltmeter should read within 0.5 volts of battery voltage. If not, switch is defective.

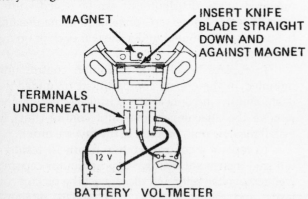

■ FIGURE 6–38

(Courtesy of General Motors Corporation.)

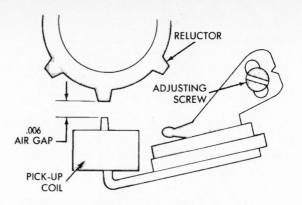

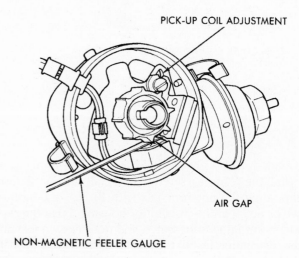

■ FIGURE 6–39

Adjusting the air gap in a Chrysler electronic distributor. (Courtesy of Chrysler Corporation.)

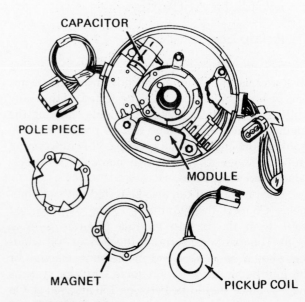

■ FIGURE 6–40

Access to this HEI control module requires the removal of the pickup coil, pole piece, and magnet. (Courtesy of General Motors Corporation.)

between the module and base to ensure good heat dissipation.

■ COMPUTER SERVICE

There are basically two kinds of computers that control the ignition system: one controls only the ignition system, the other (an engine control computer) controls the ignition system and fuel injection system and may control several other systems as well. The computer is usually the last item to check when servicing the ignition system since it does not often cause a problem. The computer can be activated to display a fault code on the dash or through a scanner-type tester that is plugged into the wiring harness. The fault code is compared to a fault code chart in the service manual, where the problem area is identified and further testing procedures are explained. For more information on computer service and replacement, see Chapter 4.

■ DISTRIBUTOR SERVICE

Distributor Removal

1. Disconnect all high-tension wires at the distributor. The procedure varies and requires removal of the distributor cap in some cases to unlock the high-tension wires.
2. Disconnect the remaining electrical and vacuum connections at the distributor.
3. Remove the distributor hold-down clamp.
4. Lift out the distributor. The distributor may be a little tight and may require twisting and pulling at the same time to aid in removal.

Distributor Rebuilding

Electronic ignition distributors usually last the entire life of the car. Rebuilding the distributor includes disassembly, cleaning, inspection, replacement of faulty or worn parts, reassembly, and testing. Procedures vary considerably with design differences. Refer to the service manual for specific instructions and specifications. Distributor problems include a worn cam, worn base plate, bent or weak advance springs, a worn shaft or bushings, and a worn drive connection or gear. After rebuilding, the distributor should be tested to ensure that proper advance characteristics are achieved and that it performs to specifications. **Figures 6–41** and **6–42** show disassembled distributors.

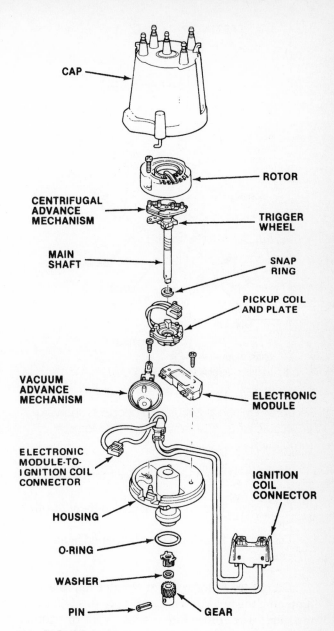

■ FIGURE 6–41
Typical HEI electronic ignition distributor components, non-integral coil type. (Courtesy of General Motors Corporation.)

Distributor Installation

1. Position the engine crankshaft so that the number 1 piston is at the TDC position on the compression stroke and the ignition timing indicator is at zero degrees.
2. Position the distributor shaft prior to installation to achieve the following results when the distributor is in place:

- Armature tooth and pickup pole piece properly aligned

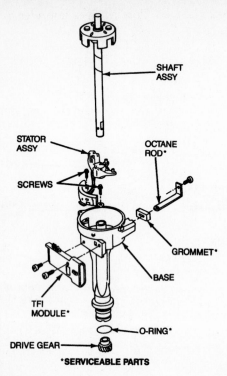

■   FIGURE 6–42
Electronic ignition distributor components showing serviceable parts. (Courtesy of General Motors Corporation.)

- Rotor tip aligned with number 1 terminal in distributor cap
- Oil pump drive fully engaged (where applicable)
- Distributor housing flange bottomed against the engine

Do not try to force the distributor into place by tightening the hold-down clamp since this will cause breakage. The procedure varies with distributor drive design and location. Timing should be adjusted further as described earlier.

Review Questions

1. All ignition systems operate on the same basic principle of changing _____ _____ primary current to _____ _____ secondary current.
2. Ignition coil secondary output could go as high as _____ volts with high resistance.
3. Secondary coil circuit is energized by the collapse of the _____ _____.
4. The purpose of the distributor cap and rotor is to _____ _____ at the proper _____ to each cylinder.
5. Many engines today do *not* have a distributor, they have a _____ on each spark plug operated by the computer system.
6. If an oscilloscope is not available test the coil with an _____.
7. Most distributors have two basic advance mechanisms. They are _____.
8. On a distributor type ignition system timing is adjusted by _____ the _____ forwards or reverse.
9. Timing is set by using a _____ _____.
10. Secondary wires are checked for _____ with an _____.
11. Never remove spark plugs from a _____ engine as it could _____ _____ in the cylinder head.
12. Use a _____ _____ spark plug gauge to properly gap spark plugs.
13. The pickup coil can be tested with an _____.
14. If your tests suggest the control module is at fault, it is often _____ _____ _____ _____ _____ to verify your diagnosis.
15. A fault code is compared to a _____ _____ chart to diagnose your problem.

Test Questions

1. To test the secondary output of an ignition system use
   a. an ammeter
   b. a spark intensity tester
   c. an ohmmeter
   d. a voltmeter
2. Computer controlled ignition input sensors should be tested with
   a. a high impedance digital volt/ohmmeter
   b. a low impedance analog volt/ohmmeter
   c. a spark intensity tester
   d. a dwell meter
3. Which of the following is not a cause of low coil input voltage?
   a. ignition switch resistance
   b. secondary wire resistance
   c. battery condition
   d. high resistance in the ballast resistor
4. When testing coil primary resistance an infinite reading on the ohmmeter indicates
   a. a short
   b. a ground
   c. an open
   d. low resistance
5. To check ignition switch operation use a test light and touch the test light lead to the different terminals with the switch
   a. in the off position
   b. in the run position
   c. in different positions
   d. in the start position

6. To advance initial timing on distributor ignition
   a. turn the distributor in the same direction as distributor shaft rotation
   b. turn the distributor against distributor shaft rotation
   c. turn the crankshaft ahead
   d. turn the crankshaft back

7. Light-emitting diodes are used in
   a. a magnetic pulse generator
   b. a metal detector
   c. an optical detector
   d. a breaker point assembly

8. In solid-state ignition, there is usually no means to adjust
   a. dwell
   b. timing
   c. advance
   d. condenser capacity

9. A secondary wire insulation test is performed to
   a. determine continuity
   b. check insulation thickness
   c. check for resistance
   d. check for insulation breakdown

10. Which of the following is not caused by faulty spark plugs?
    a. cross firing
    b. misfiring
    c. poor fuel economy
    d. loss of power

11. Which of the following does not refer to setting the spark plug gap?
    a. bending the side electrode
    b. bending the center electrode
    c. wire gauge tool
    d. distance between electrodes

12. Which of the following does not refer to distributor cap inspection?
    a. carbon tracking
    b. cracks
    c. eroded terminals
    d. distance between terminals

13. To test the pickup coil in electronic ignition use
    a. an ohmmeter
    b. a spark intensity tester
    c. a dwell meter
    d. an ammeter

14. When installing an ignition distributor
    a. number one piston must be at TDC and the rotor must point to number one terminal
    b. number one piston must be at BDC and the rotor must point to number one terminal
    c. rotor position does not matter
    d. piston position does not matter

7 Fuel Supply and Fuel Injection System Diagnosis and Service

INTRODUCTION

The gasoline fuel injection system has almost universally replaced the carburetor. With electronic sensors and computer control, fuel delivery to the engine has become very precise. This chapter discusses the function, components, and service of throttle body and port fuel injection systems. A good background in fuel injection systems is essential to being able to diagnose and service these systems. This chapter discusses how to diagnose, test, and repair fuel injection systems. In addition, the appropriate service manual should be used for specific procedures and testing methods.

LEARNING OBJECTIVES

After completing this chapter, you should be able to:
- Describe the function of the fuel injection system.
- Explain the classification of fuel injection systems.
- Diagnose and service the fuel supply system and its components.
- Visually inspect the fuel injection system to locate problems.
- Relieve injection system fuel pressure.
- Use on-board self-diagnosis to access fault codes.
- Use a fuel injection system tester.
- Use a high-impedance digital volt/ohmmeter to test system sensors.

- Identify fuel injection system problems.
- Service the throttle body.
- Replace fuel injection system components.
- Service electronic and CIS injectors.
- Test and replace the ECU, computer, and PROM.

TERMS YOU SHOULD KNOW

Look for these terms as you study this chapter and learn what they mean.

fuel tank	current test
fuel lines	on-board self-diagnosis
fuel hoses	fault codes
fuel tank cap	check engine light
vapor return line	injection system tester
mechanical fuel pump	engine analyzer
electric fuel pump	high-impedance digital
in-tank fuel pump	volt/ohmmeter
fuel gauge sending unit	VOM
fuel filter	fuel pressure relief
relieving fuel system	infinite resistance
pressure	graduated container
fuel pump pressure test	injection leakage
fuel volume test	injector opening
pump vacuum test	pressure
electric fuel pump tests	ECU
volume test	computer
leakdown test	PROM

■ FUEL SUPPLY SYSTEM FUNCTION

The fuel supply system is designed to provide a continuous and adequate supply of fuel under sufficient pressure for all operating conditions. The evaporative emission control system prevents the escape of raw fuel vapors from the fuel system to the atmosphere. **Figures 7–1** and **7–2** show the fuel supply system.

■ FUEL SUPPLY SYSTEM PROBLEMS

If a fuel supply system problem is suspected, the fuel lines, filters, fuel pump, pressure regulator, and electrical connections should be inspected and tested as required **(Figure 7–1).**

Performance, economy, and emissions problems can result from fuel supply system problems. However, it must be remembered that similar symptoms may be caused by other systems, such as air cleaners, carburetors, fuel injection equipment, electrical, exhaust, cooling, lubrication, and engine mechanical problems. A complete understanding of all systems must be acquired to diagnose problems in a manner that will identify the problem system and isolate the problem component in the system.

■ FUEL SYSTEM SERVICE PRECAUTIONS

SAFETY CAUTION Servicing fuel systems requires fully recognizing all the potential hazards of handling highly volatile and explosive fuels and dangerously poisonous carbon monoxide exhaust gases. Serious personal injury and property damage may result from a careless attitude toward safe service procedures. Unless required for testing, disconnect the negative battery cable for safety during fuel system service.

Fuel Supply System Inspection

Carefully inspect the fuel tank, fuel filler cap, fuel lines, fittings, and filter for leakage, looseness (support brackets), damage from road debris, and kinked, flattened, deteriorated, swollen, or brittle rubber lines **(Figure 7–2).** Inspect the fuel pump (if externally mounted) for leaks. Make sure the pump is mounted securely. Check for any damage or loose connections in the electrical wiring that operates the fuel pump **(Figure 7–3).** Make sure the fuse is not burned out. Replace or repair any faulty components as described later in this chapter.

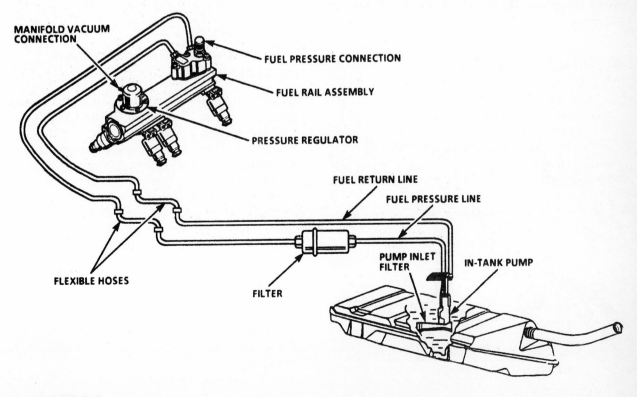

■   FIGURE 7–1
Fuel supply system check points. (Courtesy of General Motors Corporation.)

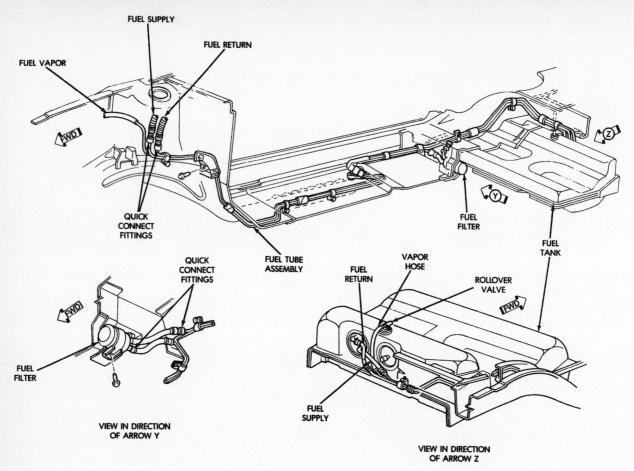

■ FIGURE 7–2
Details of fuel line, vapor line, and fuel filter locations. (Courtesy of Chrysler Corporation.)

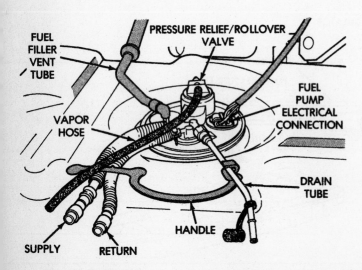

■ FIGURE 7–3
Fuel line and electrical connections at in-tank electric fuel pump. (Courtesy of Chrysler Corporation.)

Relieving Gasoline Fuel Injection System Pressure

Gasoline fuel injection systems are under constant pressure of from 25 to 80 psi (172 to 550 kPa). This pressure remains in the system even with the engine being shut off for several days. Pressure in the system must be relieved before disconnecting any fuel system components. Consult the service manual to determine the proper method to use.

Any of several different methods are used depending on system design and accessibility. The following four methods are typical.

SAFETY CAUTION   Use eye protection.

1. Remove the fuel pump fuse, start and run the engine until it dies from lack of fuel, then crank the engine over several times to eliminate any remaining pressure.

2. Remove the fuel tank filler cap. Disconnect the vacuum line (not the fuel line) from the fuel pressure regulator. Connect a hand-operated vacuum pump to the vacuum fitting on the fuel pres-

sure regulator. Operate the hand pump until there is 20 in. (500 mm) of vacuum applied to the regulator. This opens the valve to the fuel return line, thereby relieving fuel pressure in the system. Install the filler cap.

SAFETY CAUTION   Do not allow any fuel to spray anywhere on the engine. Use a small screwdriver or pin punch to push the test port valve in (while absorbing all the fuel being released with shop towels) until all pressure has been relieved. Dispose of the shop towels in the approved manner. Replace the test port cap and install the fuel tank filler cap.

■ ELECTRIC FUEL PUMP TESTING

Electric fuel pumps are tested for pressure, volume, and leak-down. The following procedure is typical.

Pressure Test

1.   Release fuel system pressure.
2.   Locate the pressure test port and connect a 0 to 100 psi (0 to 690 kPa) pressure gauge to the port.
3.   Start the engine and run at specified speed.
4.   Note the gauge reading and compare to specifications **(Figure 7–4)**.
5.   Shut off the engine.

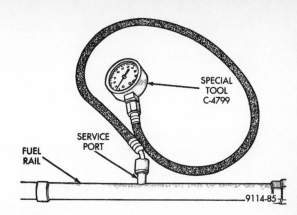

■   FIGURE 7–4
Electric fuel pump pressure test with test gauge connected to service port on fuel rail. (Courtesy of Chrysler Corporation.)

If fuel pressure is too high, the fuel return line is restricted or the pressure regulator is at fault. If fuel pressure drops off or is too low, there may be a leaky fuel injector, leaking fuel hose, faulty accumulator, leaking check valve, restricted fuel filter, or faulty pump.

Volume Test

1.   Release fuel system pressure.
2.   Connect a fuel line to the pressure test port and secure the free end into an approved graduated gasoline container **(Figure 7–5)**.

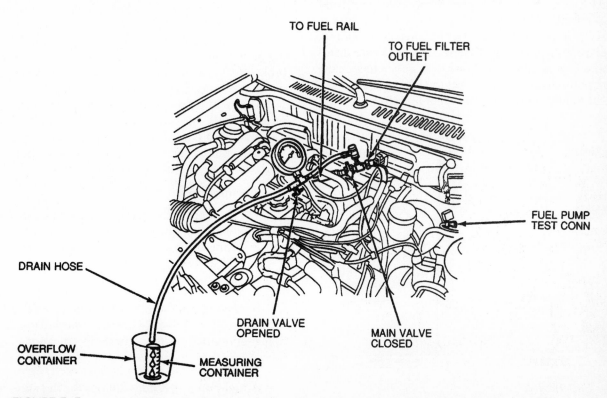

■   FIGURE 7–5
Electric fuel pump volume test. (Courtesy of Ford Motor Company.)

3.   Start the engine and run at the specified speed and time.

4.   Shut off the engine.

A good fuel pump should deliver a pint of fuel (½ liter) in 30 seconds.

Leakdown Test

1.   Perform steps 1 to 5 under "Pressure Test."

2.   Leave the gauge connected for 30 minutes with the engine off, then note the gauge reading. Compare the pressure drop to specifications.

Electric Circuit Test

If the pump fails to run at all, electric circuit tests should be performed. Broken wires, blown fuses, faulty relays, and computer problems can result in no current reaching the pump. Follow the circuit testing procedure in the manual to locate the faulty component.

■ ELECTRIC FUEL PUMP REPLACEMENT

To replace an in-tank electric fuel pump, first disconnect the electrical and fuel line connections. In some cases the fuel tank must be removed to allow pump removal. Use the special tool or a hammer and brass drift punch carefully to tap the lock ring counterclockwise to release the pump. Remove the pump and seal ring (**Figures 7–6** and **7–7**). To install the pump, place a new seal ring in position, install the pump, and carefully install the lock ring in a clockwise direction with a hammer and brass drift punch to lock the fuel pump in place. Reconnect the fuel lines and electrical connections. To replace an in-line electric pump,

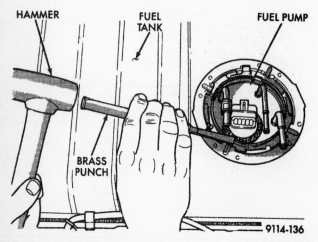

■ FIGURE 7–6

Removing fuel pump retaining ring. (Courtesy of Chrysler Corporation.)

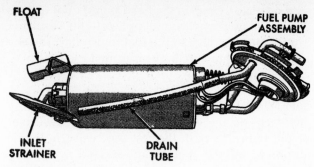

■ FIGURE 7–7

Electric fuel pump removed from fuel tank. (Courtesy of Chrysler Corporation.)

disconnect the fuel lines and electrical connections. Disconnect the pump from the mounting bracket. Reverse the procedure to install the new pump.

■ MECHANICAL FUEL PUMP TESTING (CARBURETED ENGINES)

Mechanical fuel pump problems include leaks, low fuel pressure, low fuel delivery, and abnormal noise. Fuel leakage may be external or internal. External leakage usually occurs through the small vent hole in the pump body. This indicates a ruptured pump diaphragm. The pump must be replaced. A ruptured diaphragm may also allow fuel to leak into the engine crankcase, where it dilutes the oil. In this case the oil usually has a gasoline odor. Fuel pump noise (a knocking or clicking sound) is usually caused by a weak or broken rocker arm return spring. Use a stethoscope to verify that the noise comes from the pump.

When low fuel delivery is suspected, the fuel pump should be tested for pressure, volume, and vacuum. Before testing the pump, the fuel lines and filters should be checked for possible restriction, and of course there should be fuel in the tank.

Pressure Test

1.   Connect a fuel pump pressure gauge to the outlet side of the pump.

2.   Run the engine at the specified idle speed.

3.   Observe the reading on the gauge and compare to specifications.

Fuel pump pressure for a carburetor fuel system should range from about 4 to 8 psi (28 to 55 kPa). Refer to the service manual for accurate specifications.

Volume Test

A fuel pump that does not deliver the necessary volume of fuel starves the engine of fuel at cruising speeds. To check for volume of fuel delivered, use a graduated container. Connect a hose to the output side of the fuel pump and into the container. The hose should have a shutoff device to control fuel flow safely **(Figure 7–8)**. With the engine running at specified idle speed the pump should deliver the specified amount of fuel in a specified time, usually about 1 pint (0.5 liter) in 30 seconds. Refer to the service manual for these specifications.

Vacuum Test

A fuel pump that fails the pressure and volume tests should be tested for vacuum. The vacuum test results indicate the ability of the pump to draw fuel from the fuel tank. If the fuel lines or filters are restricted the pump could fail the pressure and volume tests but still not be at fault. If the pump fails the pressure and volume tests but passes the vacuum test, the lines and filters should be inspected for restrictions. To measure fuel pump vacuum, connect a vacuum gauge to the inlet side of the fuel pump. (Most fuel pump test gauges are designed to test both pressure and vacuum.) With the output fuel hose still in the graduated container, start the engine and take the vacuum gauge reading. Compare the reading with specifications. Fuel pump vacuum is normally around 6 to 10 in.Hg (150 to 250 mm).

■ MECHANICAL FUEL PUMP REPLACEMENT

To remove a mechanical fuel pump, disconnect all lines from the pump, then remove the bolts holding the pump in place. If the pump is stuck, a plastic hammer may be used to tap the pump to free it. If pushrod-actuated, measure the pushrod for wear and check for straightness. Replace if worn or bent **(Figure 7–9)**.

To install a new pump, first clean the gasket surface on the engine. Use a new gasket and a good gasket sealer. Position the eccentric on the camshaft away from the pump to make installation easier. If a pump actuating plunger is used, make sure that it is in place before installing the pump. Align the pump and start the cap screws by hand. Keeping the pump aligned, tighten the cap screws alternately to specifications and reconnect the lines.

■ FUEL LINE SERVICE

SAFETY CAUTION   Do not loosen or disconnect any fuel lines before releasing fuel pressure in the fuel supply system as described earlier.

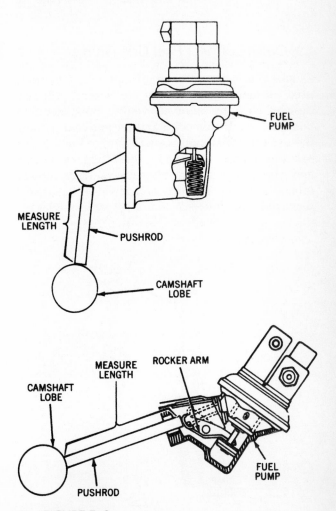

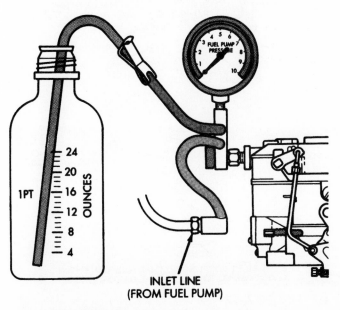

■ FIGURE 7–8
Volume and pressure test setup for mechanical fuel pump. Note fuel shut-off clamp on hose. (Courtesy of Chrysler Corporation.)

■ FIGURE 7–9
When replacing a pushrod actuated pump replace the pushrod if it is bent or worn shorter. (Courtesy of Ford Motor Company.)

1. Use tubing wrenches to disconnect and remove the fuel lines and fittings. Use the proper method to disconnect quick-connect fittings. A special tool is required on some quick-connect fittings.

2. Prefabricated replacement lines can be used or the lines can be fabricated. Use approved tubing and fittings only. Use a tubing bender to form the tubing. Use a tubing cutter and flaring tool to form the tubing ends. Form double lap flares only—single flaring is not adequate for fuel lines. Use the old tubing as a guide for forming.

3. Route the new line exactly where the original line was routed. Reinstall all support brackets and clips.

4. Use synthetic rubber hoses only where they were used originally. Use approved synthetic rubber fuel line only. Make sure that the hose is not twisted when it is installed. Make sure that the hose ends cover their fittings fully before tightening the clamps.

5. Make sure that all fittings and clamps are tight. Start the engine and inspect the repair for leaks.

Quick-Connect Fuel Line Fittings

Quick-connected fuel line fittings are commonly used on most cars. There are several different designs used by different vehicle manufacturers. Some can be disconnected and reconnected without the use of special tools. Others require the use of a specified tool to disconnect the fitting. Seal rings and garter springs are replaceable on some fittings; others cannot be repaired and must be replaced if damaged. See **Figures 7–10** to **7–12** for examples.

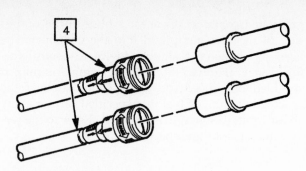

■ FIGURE 7–11
Twist-type quick-connect fuel line fittings. (Courtesy of General Motors Corporation.)

Cutting and Flaring Tubing

There are three kinds of tubing flares: the single flare, the double-lap flare, and the ISO flare (**Figures 7–13** and **7–14**). The type of flare used is determined by the type of fittings used with the tubing. Single flares are not recommended. The double-lap flare has greater strength and resistance to cracking due to vibration.

Never use a hacksaw to cut tubing. It does not cut squarely and leaves a ragged edge. Steel and copper tubing should be cut with a tubing cutter (**Figure 7–15**). Avoid applying too much pressure during cutting. This can collapse the tube. Low-pressure lines need only a single flare, whereas brake lines require double-lap flaring or ISO flaring.

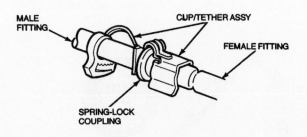

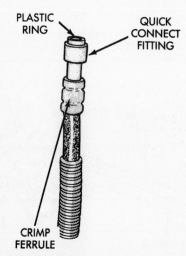

■ FIGURE 7–10
Quick-connect fuel line fitting with plastic ring. (Courtesy of Chrysler Corporation.)

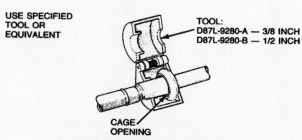

■ FIGURE 7–12
Quick-connect fuel line coupling with spring lock (top). Special tool is needed to disconnect this type of coupling. (Courtesy of Ford Motor Company.)

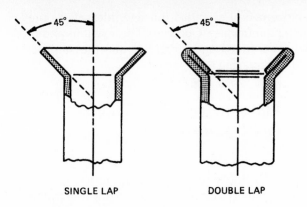

SINGLE LAP   **DOUBLE LAP**

■ FIGURE 7–13
Completed single lap flare for low-pressure lines and
double-lap flare for high pressure lines.

Flaring Procedure (Conventional Flare)

1. Obtain tubing of the correct diameter.
2. Obtain tubing fittings of the correct size and type, either the ones from the tubing being replaced or new ones.
3. Cut the tubing to the required length with a tubing cutter. Do not use a hacksaw, since it does not cut squarely and leaves ragged edges. Allow an additional ⅛ in. (3.2 mm) for each double flare. The required length is the length of the old tubing plus an allowance for flared ends. Ream the inside of the tubing ends to remove any burrs that could prevent making a good flare. Be sure to remove all metal chips from the tubing.

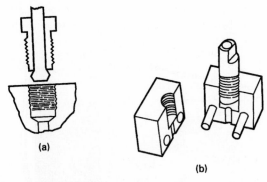

(a)

(b)

■ FIGURE 7–14
(a) completed ISO flare; (b) ISO flare forming tool.
(Courtesy of General Motors Corporation.)

■ FIGURE 7–15
Tubing cutter with reamer attached. (Courtesy of
Proto Canada Div., Ingersoll-Rand Canada, Inc.)

■ FIGURE 7–16
Flaring tool kit required to flare metal tubing. (Courtesy
of Proto Canada Div., Ingersoll-Rand Canada, Inc.)

4. Clamp one end of the tubing tightly in the flaring bar with the tubing end exposed above the bar **(Figure 7–16).** Use the gauging device that comes with the flaring tool to measure the amount of tubing protruding above the flaring bar.
5. Install the double-lap-flare adapter into the exposed end of the tubing and compress it firmly with the flaring cone. Remove the adapter **(Figure 7–17).**
6. Finish the flare by forcing the flaring cone down against the exposed tubing until it bottoms firmly. Remove the tubing from the tool.
7. Install both tubing fittings on the tubing with the threaded ends facing opposite ends of the tubing.
8. Repeat steps 4 through 7 on the other end of the tubing.
9. Use a tubing bender to bend the tubing to match the tubing being replaced, using the tubing bender shown in **Figure 7–18.**

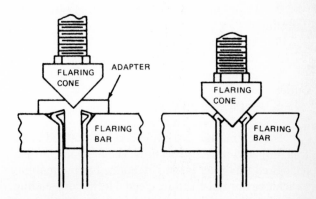

■ FIGURE 7–17
Example of double-lap flaring procedure required for
high pressure lines.

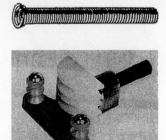

■ FIGURE 7–18

Two types of tubing benders. (Courtesy of Proto Canada Div., Ingersoll-Rand Canada, Inc.)

10.   Install the tubing, maintaining the required clearance and using the necessary support clips.

ISO Flare

1.   Perform steps 1 through 3 just given.
2.   Install tubing in the ISO flaring tool with tubing protruding the measured amount through the tool. Clamp the tubing firmly in position.
3.   Install the forming screw and bottom it firmly against the tubing to form the flare (see **Figure 7–13**).
4.   Install the appropriate tubing fittings on the tubing with the threaded ends facing opposite ends of the tubing.
5.   Repeat the flaring procedure on the other end of the tubing.
6.   Bend the tubing and install it as in steps 9 and 10 just outlined.

■ FUEL FILTER SERVICE

Fuel filters may be found in the following locations depending on design.

1.   In the fuel line fitting in the carburetor
2.   In the fuel line between the fuel pump and carburetor
3.   In the fuel pump
4.   In the fuel tank on the fuel pickup tube
5.   In the fuel line near the electric fuel pump outlet
6.   In the fuel injectors

Foreign matter in the fuel becomes lodged in the fuel filter and restricts fuel flow. The first indication of a clogged fuel filter is usually noticed as the inability to achieve normal cruising speed. Hesitation, stalling, and power loss occur at cruising speeds. Sintered bronze fuel filters can be removed and cleaned. Other filters must be replaced. Fuel filter service is usually

performed at specified mileage intervals as preventive maintenance. Observe all precautions and procedures outlined under fuel line and fuel tank service when replacing fuel filters.

■ FUEL GAUGE SENDING UNIT SERVICE

An inaccurate fuel gauge reading may be caused by the gauge, the wiring circuit, or the sending unit in the tank. Connect a fuel gauge tester to the fuel gauge feed wire disconnected from the sending unit **(Figure 7–19)**. Set the tester at the full, half, and empty positions in turn. If the gauge readings do not correspond to the tester settings, the gauge or the electrical circuit is at fault. If the gauge readings match the tester settings the sending unit in the tank may be at fault.

To test the sending unit, remove it from the fuel tank. Remove the lock ring and lift the unit out of the tank **(Figure 7–20)**. Measure the resistance of the unit at specified positions with an ohmmeter **(Figure 7–21)**. If test results do not meet specifications, the sending unit must be replaced. Use a new seal or gasket and make sure that the lock ring is fully seated. Wiring continuity can be tested with an ohmmeter.

■ GASOLINE FUEL TANK SERVICE

Fuel tank problems include leaks, dents, collapse, and contamination by rust, dirt, or water. Leaks can be caused by physical damage, flying stones, and vibra-

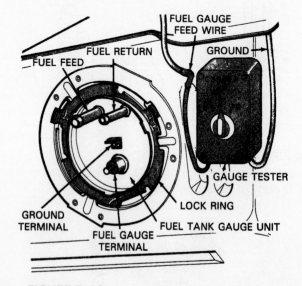

■ FIGURE 7–19

Fuel gauge tester connected to wires leading from the sending unit to the fuel gauge. (Courtesy of Chrysler Corporation.)

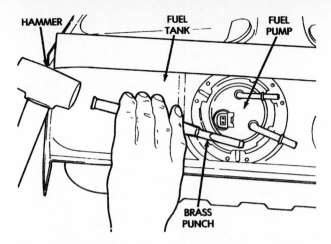

■ FIGURE 7–20
Removing the sending unit lock ring with a hammer and brass punch. (Courtesy of Chrysler Corporation.)

tion. Foreign material may enter the tank when refueling or the interior of the tank may be deteriorated.

SAFETY CAUTION   Never weld, solder, or use an open flame on or near the fuel tank, even when empty; it too can explode. A faulty fuel tank should

be removed and sent to a specialist for service or it should be replaced.

Fuel Tank Removal and Installation

Before doing anything else remove all the fuel from the tank. This should be done with approved equipment such as an approved storage tank equipped with a hand pump and hose **(Figure 7–22).** After the tank is empty, disconnect all fuel and return lines, electrical connections, and filler pipe connection at the tank. Loosen and remove the support straps or bolts and remove the tank.

SAFETY CAUTION   Wipe up any fuel spills immediately with a shop rag to reduce the fire hazard. To install the tank, make sure that all insulators are in place and in good condition. Install the mounting straps or bolts loosely, then check the positioning of the tank and insulators. Next tighten mounting straps or bolts and reconnect the lines, filler pipe, and electrical connections.

■ FUEL INJECTION SYSTEM FUNCTION

The fuel injection system is designed to provide the proper amount of fuel to the engine for all operating conditions and driver demands. In addition, the fuel

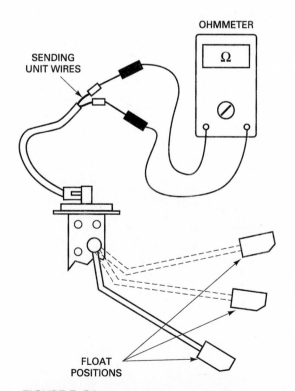

■ FIGURE 7–21
Testing the sending unit with an ohmmeter. Resistance must be within specifications at each float position.

■ FIGURE 7–22
Removing fuel from tank before tank removal. Note electrical ground wire for safety. (Courtesy of Chrysler Corporation.)

must be atomized and vaporized to allow proper mixing with intake air. Advantages of fuel injection over carburetion include more equal fuel delivery to each cylinder, no choke or heated manifold required, better fuel economy, better performance, and lower exhaust emissions.

FUEL INJECTION SYSTEM CLASSIFICATION

Gasoline fuel injection systems are classified in several ways: by where the fuel is injected, the type of control system used, and whether injection is continuous or timed. Terms used to identify fuel injection system types include the following.

1. *Single-point, central, or throttle body fuel injection.* Fuel is injected into the throttle body only **(Figures 7–23 to 7–27).**

2. *Multipoint or port fuel injection.* Fuel is injected into each intake port at the intake valve **(Figures 7–28 to 7–31).**

3. *Continuous fuel injection.* Fuel is sprayed continuously from the injectors.

4. *Pulse-timed fuel injection.* Fuel injectors are pulsed on and off in relation to valve timing.

5. *Simultaneous fuel injection.* All injectors inject fuel at the same time.

6. *Group fuel injection.* Injectors are pulsed on and off in groups of two or more at the same time but never all at the same time.

7. *Sequential fuel injection.* Injectors are pulsed on and off, one at a time, in the same order as the engine firing order.

8. *Mechanical fuel injection.* Fuel injection controlled by mechanical means only.

9. *Electronic fuel injection.* Fuel injection is controlled electronically by an electronic control unit or assembly (ECU or ECA) or by computer.

10. *Two-stage fuel injection.* Primary and secondary injection systems controlled by computer **(Figures 7–32 and 7–33).**

Multifuel Injection System

Some cars are equipped with specially designed fuel injection systems that can operate on any of several types of fuel. These include gasoline, gasoline with 10% ethanol, and gasoline with 10 to 15% methanol. A special sensor detects the type of fuel being used and sends this information to the engine control computer. The computer then makes the necessary adjustments to the ignition timing and the injector pulse width (fuel metering) to provide the best operating characteristics for the type of fuel being used.

FUEL INJECTION SYSTEM PROBLEMS

If the cause of the problem is not found during the visual inspection, a more detailed diagnosis using special testers or fuel injection system analyzers must be used to locate the problem. If the engine and all other systems are working properly, some of the problems that may occur are:

- Cranks but will not start
- Hard starting
- Stalls after starting
- Rough idle
- No fast idle

FIGURE 7–23
Single-point (central or throttle body) fuel injection. 1. Fuel pressure regulator 2. Air temperature sensor 3. Fuel injector coil 4. Throttle body 5. Throttle plate. (Courtesy of Robert Bosch Canada Ltd.)

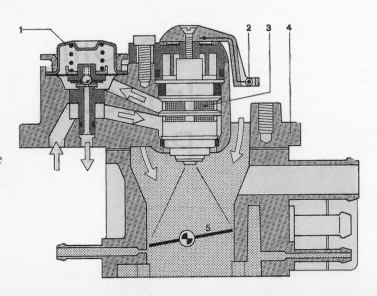

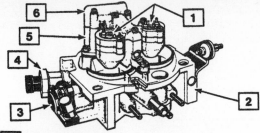

1 FUEL INJECTORS
2 THROTTLE BODY ASSEMBLY
3 THROTTLE POSITION SENSOR (TPS)
4 IDLE AIR CONTROL (IAC) VALVE ASSEMBLY
5 FUEL METER BODY ASSEMBLY
6 FUEL METER COVER ASSEMBLY

■ FIGURE 7–24
(Courtesy of General Motors Corporation.)

- Prolonged fast idle
- Hesitation on acceleration
- Poor fuel economy
- Poor high-speed performance

■ FUEL INJECTION SYSTEM TESTING

Carefully inspect all the fuel injection system components and related systems in the engine compartment. Check for loose electrical connections; disconnected or misconnected vacuum lines; vacuum leaks; fuel leaks; kinked, pinched, or damaged vacuum or fuel lines; linkage interference or damage, and the like. Sometimes, connections that look good

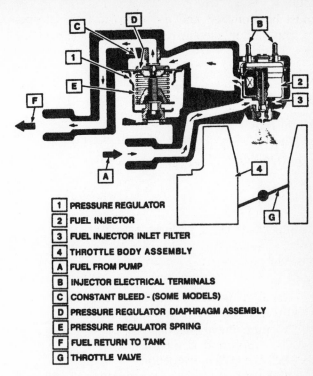

1 PRESSURE REGULATOR
2 FUEL INJECTOR
3 FUEL INJECTOR INLET FILTER
4 THROTTLE BODY ASSEMBLY
A FUEL FROM PUMP
B INJECTOR ELECTRICAL TERMINALS
C CONSTANT BLEED - (SOME MODELS)
D PRESSURE REGULATOR DIAPHRAGM ASSEMBLY
E PRESSURE REGULATOR SPRING
F FUEL RETURN TO TANK
G THROTTLE VALVE

■ FIGURE 7–25
(Courtesy of General Motors Corporation.)

may not be good. Plug-type electrical connectors may be corroded, impeding current flow. Simply unplugging and reconnecting an electrical connector can sometimes restore electrical flow. Make sure that all ignition system wiring is properly connected and free of corrosion.

Inspect the following (as they apply) to ensure that wires and lines are not kinked, damaged, or restricted, and electrical connections are clean and tight **(Figure 7–34).**

■ FIGURE 7–26
(Courtesy of Robert Bosch Canada Ltd.)

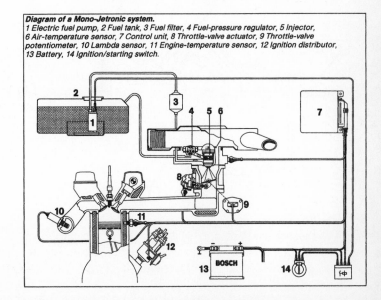

Diagram of a Mono-Jetronic system.
1 Electric fuel pump, 2 Fuel tank, 3 Fuel filter, 4 Fuel-pressure regulator, 5 Injector, 6 Air-temperature sensor, 7 Control unit, 8 Throttle-valve actuator, 9 Throttle-valve potentiometer, 10 Lambda sensor, 11 Engine-temperature sensor, 12 Ignition distributor, 13 Battery, 14 Ignition/starting switch.

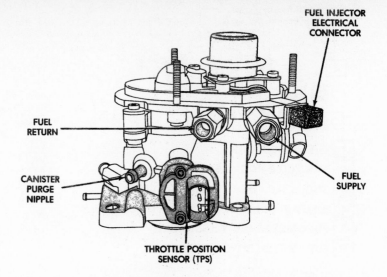

■ FIGURE 7–27
Throttle body fuel injection assembly. (Courtesy of Chrysler Corporation.)

- Vacuum line to the fuel pressure regulator
- Oxygen sensor wire to the O_2 sensor
- Vacuum line to the brake booster
- Air supply and air filter restriction
- Exhaust system restriction
- Temperature sensor wire connection
- Transmission switch wire connection
- Wiring harness to fuel injectors
- MAP sensor connection
- BP sensor connection
- MAT sensor connection
- Throttle position sensor connection
- Automatic idle-speed motor connection
- Cold-start injector connection
- Thermo-time switch connection

- Air conditioning clutch switch connection
- Brake on/off switch connection
- Power steering sensor connection
- Radiator fan switch connection
- Speed control switch connection
- Vacuum line to speed control motor
- Engine speed sensor connection
- Vehicle speed sensor connection
- EGR valve position sensor connection
- Throttle body temperature sensor

Tools and Equipment Needed

Make sure that you have the following equipment to perform the necessary tests.

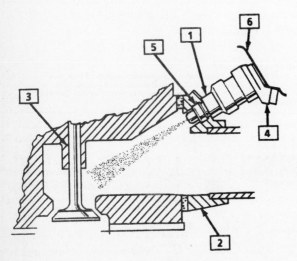

■ FIGURE 7–28
Port fuel injection cross section. 1) injector; 2) intake manifold; 3) intake valve; 4) electrical connector; 5) O-ring seal; 6) fuel rail. (Courtesy of General Motors Corporation.)

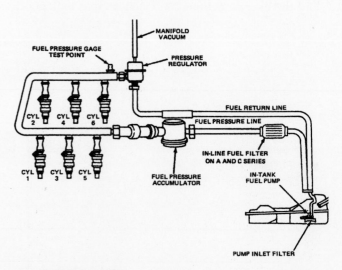

■ FIGURE 7–29
Fuel supply system for multipoint port fuel injection. (Courtesy of Chrysler Corporation.)

28) Motronic system overview.
1 Fuel tank, 2 Electric fuel pump, 3 Fuel filter, 4 Pressure regulator, 5 Control unit, 6 Ignition coil, 7 High-voltage distributor, 8 Spark plug, 9 Injection valve, 10 Throttle valve, 11 Throttle-valve switch, 12 Air-flow sensor, 13 Air-temperature sensor, 14 Lambda sensor, 15 Engine-temperature sensor, 16 Rotary idle actuator, 17 Engine-speed and reference-mark sensor, 18 Battery, 19 Ignition and starting switch, 20 A/C switch.

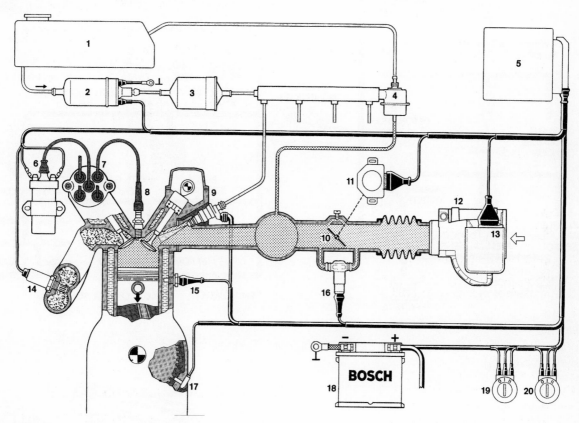

■ FIGURE 7–30
Multipoint fuel injection system with electronic controls. (Courtesy of Robert Bosch Canada Ltd.)

- Volt/ohmmeter (digital and analog)
- Ohmmeter
- Jumper wires
- Auxiliary vacuum supply (hand-held vacuum pump)
- Vacuum gauge
- Tachometer
- Oscilloscope
- High-pressure gauge
- Computer scanner

Engine Analyzer

Modern engine analyzers are capable of a wide variety of performance tests, including the fuel injection system. The analyzer provides test results on a screen in wave form or digital readouts. Testers equipped with a printer can provide a printout of test results. See Chapter 2 for engine analyzer information.

On-Board Self-Diagnosis

Many electronic fuel injection systems have self-diagnosis capability. The engine control computer is programmed to monitor fuel injection system components as well as other engine control functions. If the computer senses a fault often enough to indicate a problem, a fault code is stored in the computer for later recall by the service technician. Fault codes can be called up by the technician through the check engine light on the instrument panel or through the use of a diagnostic scanner which must be connected to the diagnostic connector in the wiring harness. The fault code is then compared to a fault code chart in the service manual to identify the problem.

The fault codes displayed by the logic module are excellent for diagnosis of an EFI-equipped vehicle. However, they must be used properly; they

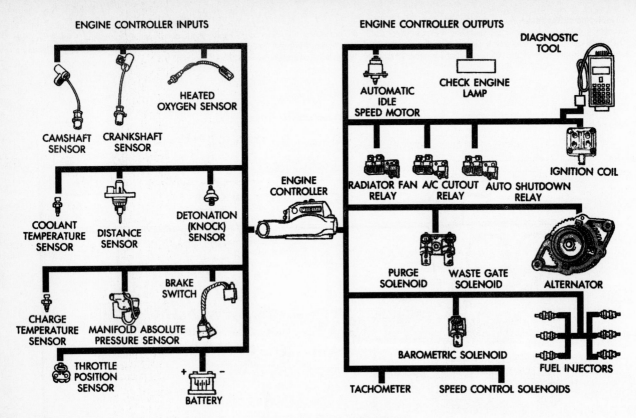

■ FIGURE 7–31
Computer-controlled fuel injection system inputs and outputs. (Courtesy of Chrysler Corporation.)

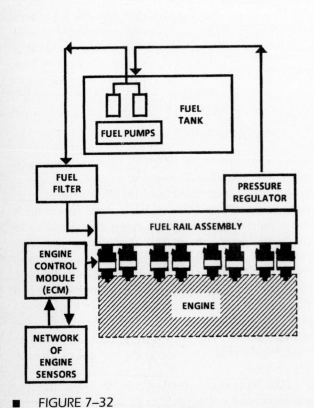

■ FIGURE 7–32
Two-stage fuel injection system schematic. (Courtesy of General Motors Corporation.)

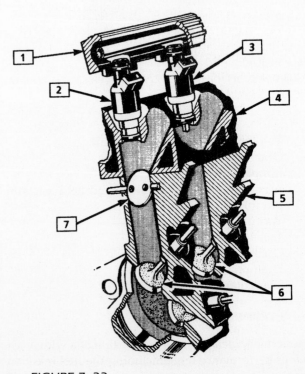

■ FIGURE 7–33
Primary and secondary injectors. 1) fuel rail; 2) secondary injector; 3) primary injector; 4) injector housing; 5) cylinder head; 6) intake valves; 7) secondary port throttle. (Courtesy of General Motors Corporation.)

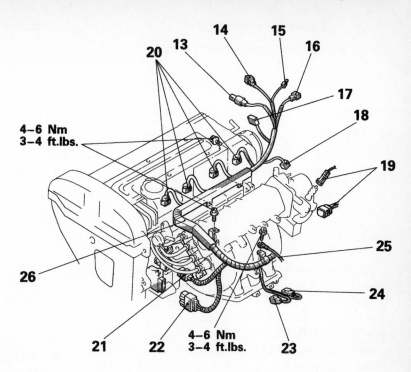

■ FIGURE 7–34
Electronic fuel injection system electrical inspection points. Wiring connections are as follows: 13. Oxygen sensor 14. Coolant temperature sensor 15. Coolant temperature gauge 16. Coolant temperature A/C switch 17. Crank angle sensor 18. TPS 19. ISC 20. Fuel injector 21. Ignition coil 22. Power transistor 23. Knock sensor 24. EGR temperature sensor 25. Ground (Courtesy of Chrysler Corporation.)

only give you part of the information you need for an accurate test. Rather than telling what the problem is, a fault code only tells the technician that there is a problem. To determine the actual problem, the technician should refer to the diagnostic procedures in the appropriate service manual. Remember that a fault code can be caused by any of the following:

- Sensor failure
- Harness failure
- Bad connection
- Logic module failure
- Power module failure
- Output device failure

Fuel Injection System Scanner

Most electronic fuel injection systems have a diagnostic connector in the wiring harness to which a fuel injection scan tester, or diagnostic readout box, can be connected **(Figures 7–35 and 7–36).** The scanner can then be used to identify problems in the system. The tester has a number of control buttons and switches to allow selection of various test modes. The display panel readings (numbers, lights, or messages) are compared to fault code charts to determine where the fault may be. A variety of testers are offered by test equipment manufacturers and vehicle manufacturers for different applications. Follow the equipment manufacturer's instructions. See Chapters 2 and 4 for examples of scan tool test procedures and their interpretation.

Accessing Fault Codes

Fault codes are accessed and cleared in different ways on different vehicles. Follow instructions in the appropriate service manual in each case. Ford's EEC IV system can be accessed by using Ford's special tester and plugging it into the diagnostic harness connector. Fault codes are registered directly and compared to the fault code chart. Another method is to use an analog voltmeter connected to the appropriate test connector pin. Voltmeter needle fluctuations are then interpreted according to service manual instructions and then compared to the fault code chart **(Figure 7–37).**

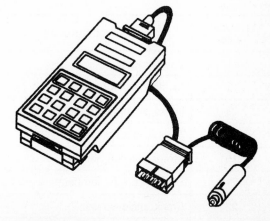

■ FIGURE 7–35
Scan tool plugs into diagnostic connector in wiring harness to diagnose fuel injection system problems. (Courtesy of General Motors Corporation.)

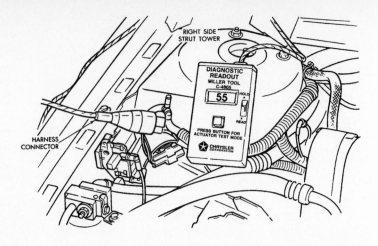

■ FIGURE 7–36
Scan tool connected to wiring harness. (Courtesy of Chrysler Corporation.)

With General Motor's Computer Command Control (CCC) system, just turn the ignition switch on and observe the light flashes in the dash. These must be interpreted and compared to service manual fault codes. With Chrysler's computerized injection system cycle the ignition switch ON, OFF, ON, OFF, ON within 5 seconds but do not start the engine. The light flashes are interpreted and compared to service manual fault codes.

Clearing the fault codes may only require disconnecting and reconnecting the quick disconnect at the battery on some models. Other procedures may be required on other systems. Refer to the service manual for proper procedures. See Chapter 4 for detailed information on how to access and clear fault codes.

■ RELIEVING INJECTION SYSTEM PRESSURE

Fuel injection systems are under constant pressure of from 35 to 80 psi (207 to 550 kPa). This pressure remains in the system even with the engine being shut off for several days. Pressure in the system must be relieved as described earlier in this chapter before disconnecting any fuel system components **(Figures 7–38 and 7–39).**

■ FUEL INJECTOR PROBLEMS

A faulty fuel injector can cause hard starting, rough idle, poor fuel economy, poor performance, and excessive exhaust emissions. Fuel injectors may leak when they should be closed, they may not have the proper spray pattern, they may not deliver enough fuel, or they may not operate at all.

Injectors that leak when they are closed enrich the fuel mixture excessively. Leakage may be caused by a worn nozzle valve and seat, deposit buildup, or a weak or broken return spring. Improper spray patterns may be caused by deposit buildups, wear, or a weak return spring. A dirty injector may restrict fuel flow, causing the air–fuel mixture to be too lean. An injector that does not operate at all has open or shorted solenoid coil windings, or electrical current

Malfunction code	Diagnosis item	Malfunction code	Diagnosis item
11	Oxygen sensor	24	Vehicle speed sensor (reed switch)
12	Air flow sensor	25	Barometric pressure sensor
13	Intake air temperature sensor	36	Ignition timing adjustment signal
14	Throttle position sensor	41	Injector
15	Motor position sensor	42	Fuel pump
21	Engine coolant temperature sensor	43	EGR <California>
22	Crank angle sensor	–	–
23	No.1 cylinder TDC sensor		

■ FIGURE 7–37
Typical fault code chart for fuel injection system. (Courtesy of Chrysler Corporation.)

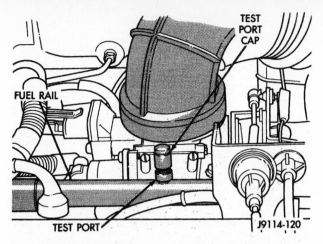

■   FIGURE 7–38

Pressure test port location. (Courtesy of Chrysler Corporation.)

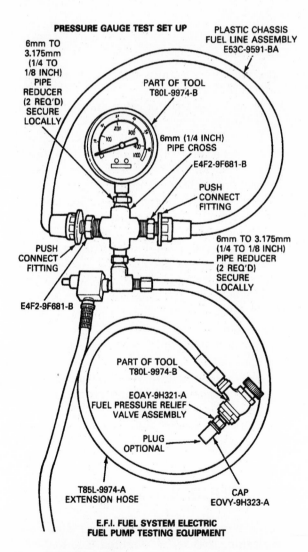

■   FIGURE 7–39

This test hookup can be used to relieve fuel system pressure and for testing fuel pressure in the fuel rail. (Courtesy of Ford Motor Company.)

is not reaching the injector. Nonelectronic continuous injectors are subject to the same problems except for electrical problems.

Fuel Injector Cleaner

Fuel injector cleaning equipment is designed to clean clogged and restricted fuel injectors without removing them from the vehicle. The equipment consists of a portable tank equipped with a 60 psi (413.7 kPa) pressure gauge, a hose with a control valve, an in-line filter, and a pressure relief valve. The hose has a fitting that connects to the fuel pressure test port on the vehicle (Figure 7–40). A mixture of ½ gallon of unleaded gasoline and 5% specified engine cleaner is used in the tank. The following procedure is typical. The procedure is not recommended on some vehicles. Consult the service manual for specific instructions.

1.   Disable the fuel pump on the vehicle and close off the fuel return line.

2.   Connect the cleaner hose to the pressure test port.

3.   Close the in-line control valve on the hose.

4.   Pressurize the cleaner tank to 25 psi (172 kPa) using the hand pump in the tank.

5.   Open the in-line control valve ¼ turn, start the engine, and run it at 2000 rpm for 10 minutes.

6.   Shut off the engine, close the in-line control valve, and disconnect the cleaner hose from the test port. Install the cap, and reconnect the fuel pump.

■   FIGURE 7–40

Fuel injector cleaning equipment hand-operated and electric-operated pressurizing pumps. (Courtesy of Kent Moore.)

■ THROTTLE BODY INJECTOR SERVICE

To check whether TBI injectors are working, remove the intake air connection from the throttle body. With the engine cranking, observe whether fuel is spraying from the injector. A rapidly pulsing fuel spray should be visible. If no spray is evident, the power supply to the injector must be checked. To check voltage to the injector use a digital voltmeter to probe the wiring harness connectors. If there is no voltage, there may be a problem with the wiring harness or the computer. If voltage supply is normal, the injector is faulty and should be replaced. To replace a TBI injector, the following procedure is typical. Consult the service manual for specific procedures.

1. Relieve the fuel system pressure as outlined earlier.
2. Disconnect the negative battery cable.
3. Disconnect the wiring harness from the injector.

SAFETY CAUTION Do not remove the fuel meter cover retaining screws on models so equipped. It contains a powerful spring under heavy compres-

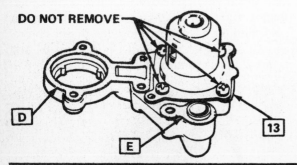

13 FUEL METER COVER

D FUEL METER COVER GASKET (INSTALL ON FUEL METER BODY)

E FUEL RETURN PASSAGE GASKET (INSTALL ON FUEL METER COVER)

CAUTION: Do not remove the four screws securing the pressure regulator to the fuel meter cover. The fuel pressure regulator includes a large spring under heavy compression which, if accidentally released, could cause personal injury. Disassembly might also cause a fuel leak between the diaphram and the regulator container.

■ FIGURE 7–41
(Courtesy of General Motors Corporation.)

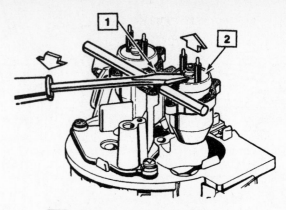

1 FUEL METER COVER GASKET
2 FUEL INJECTOR ASSEMBLY

■   FIGURE 7–42
Prying out the fuel injector with a screwdriver. (Courtesy of General Motors Corporation.)

sion and could cause serious injury if accidentally released **(Figure 7–41)**.

4. Remove the injector cover and the injector retaining screws.
5. Carefully pull or pry out the injector, making sure not to damage the throttle body **(Figure 7–42)**.
6. Make sure that all the required washers and seals are in place to install the new injector. Use approved lubricant to aid in installation.
7. Place the new injector in position in the throttle body **(Figure 7–43)**. Make sure that it is properly indexed in the throttle body, then push it into place by hand **(Figure 7–44)**. Do not use any tools to force the injector into place. If properly aligned and lubricated, it can be pushed into place until fully seated.
8. Install the injector retaining screws and tighten to specifications.
9. Install the injector cover if so equipped.
10. Reconnect the wiring harness and battery cable **(Figure 7–45)**.
11. Start the engine and check for proper operations.

■ THROTTLE BODY SERVICE

The throttle body can be removed and disassembled for cleaning and repair **(Figures 7–46 to 7–50)**. The metal parts are cleaned in cold-soak cleaner, rinsed, and blown dry. Worn or damaged parts are replaced using new seals and gaskets during reassembly.

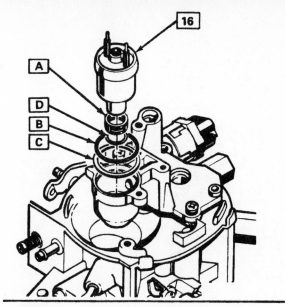

16 FUEL INJECTOR

A FILTER **C** STEEL BACK-UP WASHER

B LARGE "O" RING **D** SMALL "O" RING

■ FIGURE 7–43

Fuel injector installation. (Courtesy of General Motors Corporation.)

PRO TIP

Some throttle body assemblies are coated with a special sealant and therefore must not be cleaned. In some cases the throttle body is not serviceable and must be replaced if faulty. Refer to the appropriate service manual for instructions.

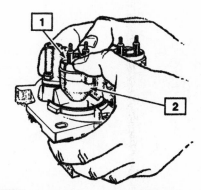

1 FUEL INJECTOR ASSEMBLY

2 FUEL METER BODY ASSEMBLY

■ FIGURE 7–44

Pushing the new fuel injector into place. (Courtesy of General Motors Corporation.)

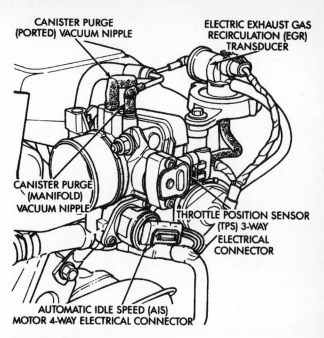

■ FIGURE 7–45

Throttle body electrical and vacuum connections (typical). (Courtesy of Chrysler Corporation.)

■ INJECTOR BALANCE TEST (MULTIPOINT ELECTRONIC INJECTION)

The injector balance test turns on one injector for a precise amount of time. The resulting drop in fuel supply pressure is recorded and compared to that of all the other injectors. The drop in fuel pressure should be the same (±1.5 psi) (±10 kPa) for all injectors. Any injector with a greater pressure drop is considered faulty **(Figure 7–51)**. The following procedure is typical. Refer to the service manual for specific procedures and specifications.

1. Shut off the engine for at least 10 minutes to allow it to cool down.

2. With the engine stopped, connect the fuel pressure test gauge to the pressure test port.

3. Disconnect the harness from all the injectors.

4. Connect the injector tester to one injector.

5. Turn the ignition switch on for 10 seconds to ensure maximum fuel pressure is present.

6. Energize the injector with the tester and note the pressure drop at its lowest point. Record that figure. Subtract that figure from the maximum pressure recorded earlier. The result is the pressure drop for that injector.

7. Repeat the procedure for all the injectors and record the results.

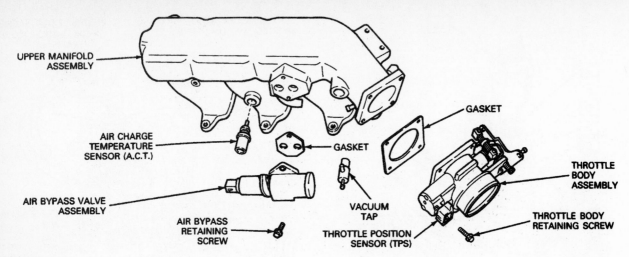

FIGURE 7–46
Removing the throttle body from the intake manifold. (Courtesy of Ford Motor Company.)

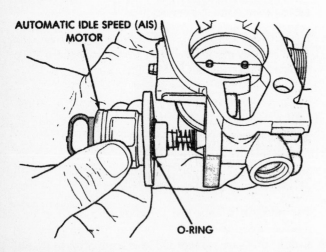

■ **FIGURE 7–47**
Automatic idle-speed motor removal/installation. (Courtesy of Chrysler Corporation.)

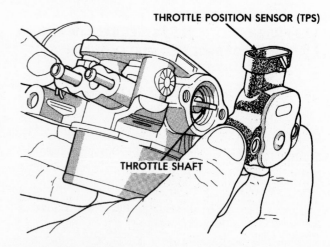

■ **FIGURE 7–49**
Throttle position sensor removal/installation. (Courtesy of General Motors Corporation.)

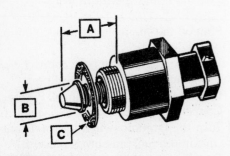

A DISTANCE OF PINTLE EXTENSION
B DIAMETER AND SHAPE OF PINTLE
C IAC VALVE GASKET

■ **FIGURE 7–48**
Idle air control (IAC) valve check points prior to installation. (Courtesy of General Motors Corporation.)

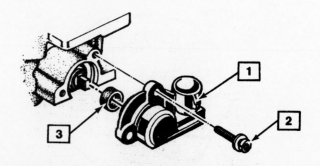

1 SENSOR - THROTTLE POSITION (TPS)
2 SCREW ASSEMBLY - TPS ATTACHING
3 SEAL - THROTTLE POSITION SENSOR

■ **FIGURE 7–50**
Throttle position sensor assembly. (Courtesy of General Motors Corporation.)

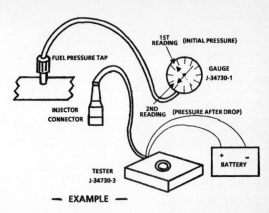

— EXAMPLE —

CYLINDER	1	2	3	4	5	6
1ST READING	225	225	225	225	225	225
2ND READING	100	100	100	90	100	115
AMOUNT OF DROP	125	125	125	135	125	110
	OK	OK	OK	FAULTY, RICH (TOO MUCH) (FUEL DROP)	OK	FAULTY, LEAN (TOO LITTLE) (FUEL DROP)

■ FIGURE 7–51

Injector balance test hookup and sample test results. (Courtesy of General Motors Corporation.)

8. Retest any injector that fails the test. If the injector fails the retest, replace the injector.

■ MULTIPOINT ELECTRONIC FUEL INJECTOR SERVICE

Electronic fuel injectors make a clicking sound as they are pulsed on and off during engine operation. This clicking sound is easily detected with a stethoscope by placing the pickup against each injector with the engine running at idle **(Figure 7–52).** If no clicking sound is detected, the injector is not operating. The injector coil may be open or shorted or current is not reaching the injector. The inoperative injector can be tested without removal. With the engine shut off, disconnect the electrical plug from the injector. With an ohmmeter measure the solenoid coil resistance. If the ohmmeter registers infinite resistance the coil winding is open. If there is no resistance the coil is shorted to ground. If the injector test results are normal, the supply voltage to the injector must be checked. Some injection systems supply full battery voltage to the injectors, while others use resistors to lower injector supply voltage. Always consult the service manual for the proper procedure for checking supply voltage and testing wiring circuits **(Figures 7–53 to 7–55).** See **Figure 7–56** for typical fuel injector diagnostic procedures.

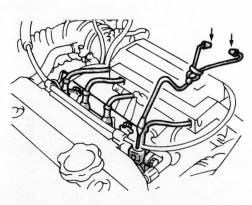

■ FIGURE 7–52

Stethoscope can be used to check injector solenoid operation. (Courtesy of Chrysler Corporation.)

■ FIGURE 7–53

Electronic fuel injector tester. (Courtesy of OTC Division, SPX Corporation.)

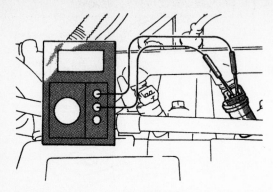

■ FIGURE 7–54

Testing for voltage supply to the fuel injector at the harness connector. (Courtesy of Chrysler Corporation.)

PRO TIP

Do not repeat the test more than once (including any retest on faulty injectors) without running the engine to prevent flooding.

Replacing Multipoint Electronic Injectors

On some engines the fuel injectors are easy to access, while on other engines they are hidden behind intake manifold plenums and other engine parts. These parts must be removed to gain access to the injectors. Once they are exposed, they are easy to replace. The following procedure is typical.

1.   Relieve fuel system pressure completely.

2.   Remove and tag the injector harness connectors with cylinder numbers.

3.   Disconnect the vacuum line from the fuel pressure regulator if it is part of the fuel rail assembly.

4.   Disconnect the fuel supply hose from the fuel rail.

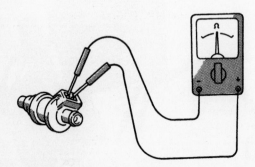

■ FIGURE 7–55

Testing fuel injector solenoid resistance. (Courtesy of Chrysler Corporation.)

5.   Remove the fuel rail mounting bolts.

6.   Remove the fuel rail and injectors by pulling with a slight rocking movement until all injectors are out of the manifold (**Figure 7–57**).

7.   Remove the injector retaining clips that hold the injector in place in the fuel rail (**Figures 7–58** and **7–59**).

8.   Install the new injectors (with new O-ring seals; **Figures 7–60** and **7–61**).

9.   Position the fuel rail so that the injectors enter the manifold. Push the assembly into place so that all injectors are fully seated.

10.   Install the fuel rail retaining bolts and tighten to specifications and install remaining parts removed for access (**Figure 7–62**).

■ CIS INJECTOR SERVICE

Access to the injectors varies with vehicle make and engine type; however, removal procedures are similar once access has been gained. The following removal testing and installation procedures are typical.

1.   Remove the fuel injectors, leaving the fuel lines attached.

2.   Place each injector into an individual graduated container making sure that the containers and injectors are secured and will remain in place during testing.

SAFETY CAUTION   Uncontrolled or uncontained gasoline spray is an extreme fire hazard.

On models with rigid steel fuel lines, disconnect the fuel line from the injector using two wrenches to avoid line twisting. Attach a piece of fuel hose between the fuel line and injector to allow positioning the injector in the graduated container. Make sure that all lines are properly positioned and secured.

3.   Use a jumper wire to bypass the fuel pump safety circuit (see service manual). Disconnect the electrical plugs at the pressure regulator and auxiliary air regulator. On some models the electrical plug to the cold-start valve must also be disconnected (refer to the service manual).

4.   Turn the ignition switch on and move the airflow sensor plate open. Hold the sensor plate open and observe the spray patterns until one graduated container has filled to 3.5 oz (100 ml). Check the fuel level in all the graduated containers. It should not vary more than 10 to 20% between containers.

5.   If one injector does not deliver fuel within these limits or has an unacceptable spray pattern, switch the injector to another fuel line and repeat the

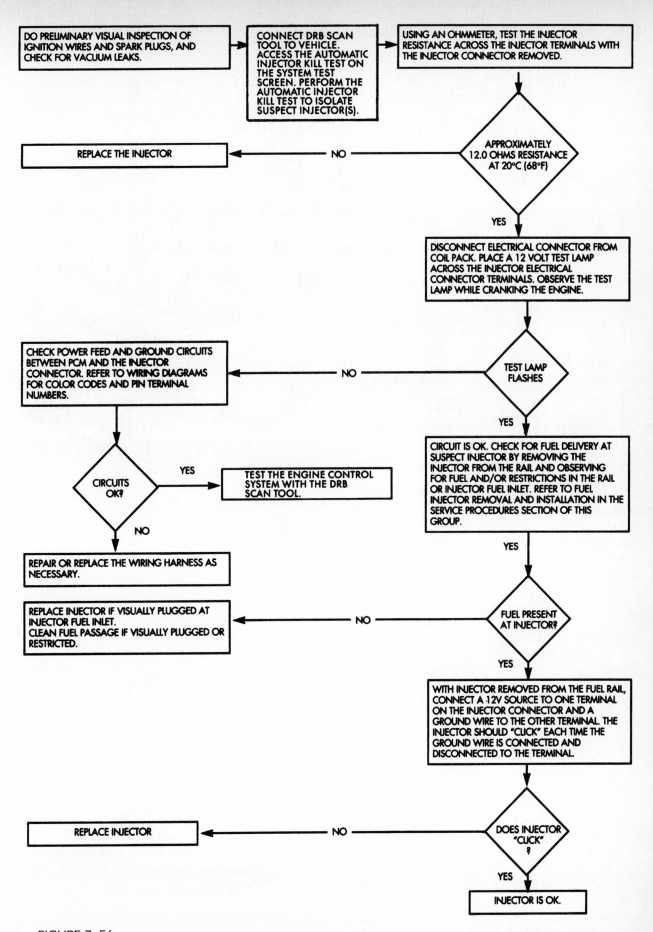

DO PRELIMINARY VISUAL INSPECTION OF IGNITION WIRES AND SPARK PLUGS, AND CHECK FOR VACUUM LEAKS.

CONNECT DRB SCAN TOOL TO VEHICLE. ACCESS THE AUTOMATIC INJECTOR KILL TEST ON THE SYSTEM TEST SCREEN. PERFORM THE AUTOMATIC INJECTOR KILL TEST TO ISOLATE SUSPECT INJECTOR(S).

USING AN OHMMETER, TEST THE INJECTOR RESISTANCE ACROSS THE INJECTOR TERMINALS WITH THE INJECTOR CONNECTOR REMOVED.

APPROXIMATELY 12.0 OHMS RESISTANCE AT 20°C (68°F)

NO → REPLACE THE INJECTOR

YES

DISCONNECT ELECTRICAL CONNECTOR FROM COIL PACK. PLACE A 12 VOLT TEST LAMP ACROSS THE INJECTOR ELECTRICAL CONNECTOR TERMINALS. OBSERVE THE TEST LAMP WHILE CRANKING THE ENGINE.

TEST LAMP FLASHES

NO → CHECK POWER FEED AND GROUND CIRCUITS BETWEEN PCM AND THE INJECTOR CONNECTOR. REFER TO WIRING DIAGRAMS FOR COLOR CODES AND PIN TERMINAL NUMBERS.

YES

CIRCUITS OK?

YES → TEST THE ENGINE CONTROL SYSTEM WITH THE DRB SCAN TOOL.

NO

REPAIR OR REPLACE THE WIRING HARNESS AS NECESSARY.

CIRCUIT IS OK. CHECK FOR FUEL DELIVERY AT SUSPECT INJECTOR BY REMOVING THE INJECTOR FROM THE RAIL AND OBSERVING FOR FUEL AND/OR RESTRICTIONS IN THE RAIL OR INJECTOR FUEL INLET. REFER TO FUEL INJECTOR REMOVAL AND INSTALLATION IN THE SERVICE PROCEDURES SECTION OF THIS GROUP.

YES

REPLACE INJECTOR IF VISUALLY PLUGGED AT INJECTOR FUEL INLET.
CLEAN FUEL PASSAGE IF VISUALLY PLUGGED OR RESTRICTED.

NO ← FUEL PRESENT AT INJECTOR?

YES

WITH INJECTOR REMOVED FROM THE FUEL RAIL, CONNECT A 12V SOURCE TO ONE TERMINAL ON THE INJECTOR CONNECTOR AND A GROUND WIRE TO THE OTHER TERMINAL. THE INJECTOR SHOULD "CLICK" EACH TIME THE GROUND WIRE IS CONNECTED AND DISCONNECTED TO THE TERMINAL.

REPLACE INJECTOR ← NO — DOES INJECTOR "CLICK" ?

YES

INJECTOR IS OK.

■ FIGURE 7–56
Typical fuel injector diagnostic chart. (Courtesy of Chrysler Corporation.)

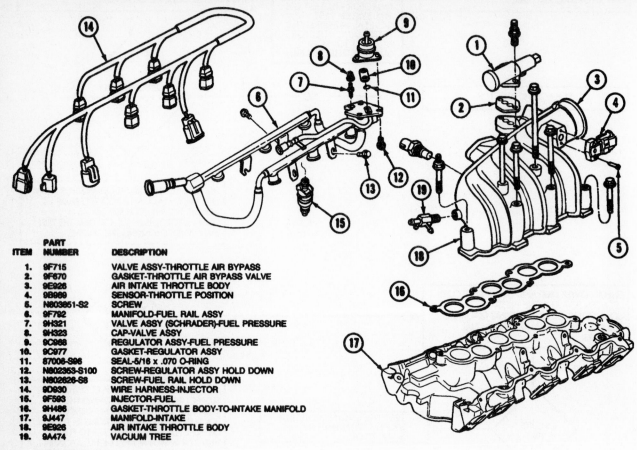

ITEM	PART NUMBER	DESCRIPTION
1.	9F715	VALVE ASSY-THROTTLE AIR BYPASS
2.	9F670	GASKET-THROTTLE AIR BYPASS VALVE
3.	9E926	AIR INTAKE THROTTLE BODY
4.	9B989	SENSOR-THROTTLE POSITION
5.	N803851-S2	SCREW
6.	9F792	MANIFOLD-FUEL RAIL ASSY
7.	9H321	VALVE ASSY (SCHRADER)-FUEL PRESSURE
8.	9H323	CAP-VALVE ASSY
9.	9C968	REGULATOR ASSY-FUEL PRESSURE
10.	9C977	GASKET-REGULATOR ASSY
11.	87006-S96	SEAL-5/16 x .070 O-RING
12.	N802353-S100	SCREW-REGULATOR ASSY HOLD DOWN
13.	N802626-S8	SCREW-FUEL RAIL HOLD DOWN
14.	9D930	WIRE HARNESS-INJECTOR
15.	9F593	INJECTOR-FUEL
16.	9H486	GASKET-THROTTLE BODY-TO-INTAKE MANIFOLD
17.	9J447	MANIFOLD-INTAKE
18.	9E926	AIR INTAKE THROTTLE BODY
19.	9A474	VACUUM TREE

■ FIGURE 7–57

Fuel injection system components disassembled. (Courtesy of Ford Motor Corporation.)

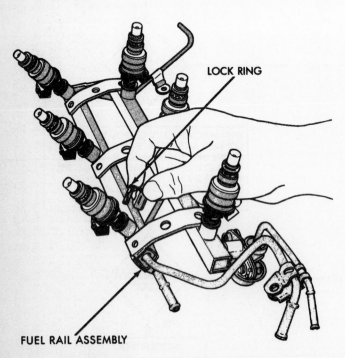

■ FIGURE 7–58

Assembling the fuel injectors to the fuel rail. (Courtesy of Chrysler Corporation.)

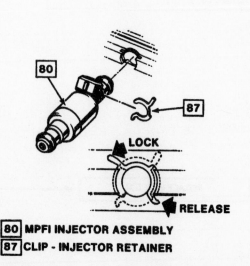

80 MPFI INJECTOR ASSEMBLY
87 CLIP - INJECTOR RETAINER

■ FIGURE 7–59

How to lock and unlock a fuel injector retainer clip. (Courtesy of General Motors Corporation.)

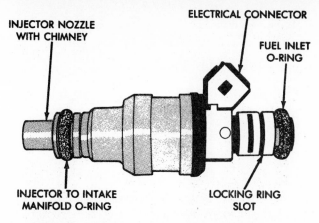

■ FIGURE 7–60
Fuel injector with new O-rings in place ready for installation. (Courtesy of Chrysler Corporation.)

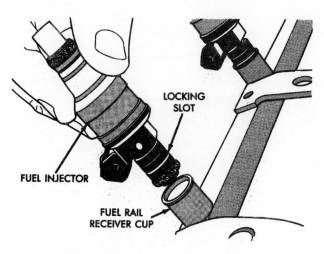

■ FIGURE 7–61
Installing an injector into the fuel rail. (Courtesy of Chrysler Corporation.)

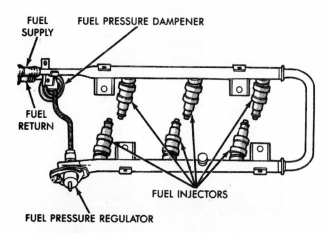

■ FIGURE 7–62
Fuel rail and injector assembly ready for installation. (Courtesy of Chrysler Corporation.)

test. If it now operates normally, the fuel distributor is faulty. If its output or spray pattern did not improve, the injector is faulty.

Injector Leakage and Opening Pressure Test

Faulty injectors can be removed, leak tested, and tested for valve opening pressure using an injector test stand equipped with a pump, fluid supply container, control valve, pressure gauge, and injector connector **(Figure 7–63)**. This tester can also be used to clean dirty injectors using special cleaning fluid. Follow the tester manufacturer's procedures to test the injectors.

CIS Fuel Distributor Service

If testing fuel injector output has indicated a faulty fuel distributor, it must be repaired or replaced. It is a precision fuel metering device which requires carefully following service manual procedures and specifications to ensure proper fuel delivery. Follow service manual procedures for service and replacement.

CIS Cold-Start Injector Service

To test the operation of the CIS cold-start injector, remove it from the engine, leaving the fuel line attached to the injector. Position the injector securely into a container to catch the fuel spray. Crank the engine over and observe the fuel spray pattern. It should be even and cone shaped. If the injector does not function, the thermo-time switch may be above the set temperature. If the thermo-time switch is at cold-start operating temperature and the cold-start injector does not operate, the thermo-time switch, wiring circuit, or injector may be faulty. Test the

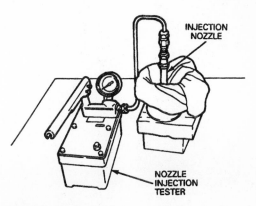

■ FIGURE 7–63
Fuel injector tester used for testing CIS injectors. (Courtesy of Ford Motor Company.)

available voltage at the injector electrical connector. If not present, test the thermo-time switch and wiring for continuity.

■ TESTING EFI SENSORS

EFI sensors can be checked using the on-board diagnostics and a digital readout tester or scanner as described earlier; sensors can also be checked independently using a digital VOM (volt-ohm-millimeter) tester when required (**Figures 7–64** to **7–70;** see also **Figures 7–71** and **7–72).** Follow the service manual procedures for specific tests and specifications. Some sensors are tested for resistance values under specified conditions, while others are tested for voltage output. If test specifications are not met, the sensor is replaced. See Chapter 4 for more detailed information on sensor testing.

To test input sensors for electronic fuel injection and computer-controlled ignition systems, a high-impedance digital volt/ohmmeter must be used. It must have at least 10,000 Ω (10 KΩ) of input impedance (see **Figure 7–73).** Otherwise, the sensors will be damaged. Specifications for many sensors are given in tenths of a volt, which is impossible to read on an analog voltmeter. A narrow operating range may also be given which cannot be read on an analog voltmeter. The following procedures are typical for sensor testing.

Oxygen Sensor Testing

A faulty O$_2$ sensor signal can cause the air–fuel mixture to be too rich or too lean. If a trouble code is indicated in the oxygen sensor circuit the sensor and sensor harness may require testing. Inspect the sensor wiring connection at the sensor for corrosion or damage. Make sure there is a good electrical connection between the harness and the sensor.

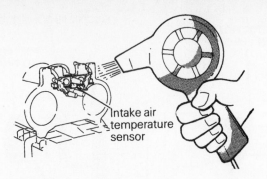

■ FIGURE 7–65
Heating an intake air temperature sensor for resistance tests. A digital thermometer is used to check sensor temperature. (Courtesy of Chrysler Corporation.)

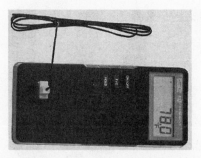

■ FIGURE 7–66
Digital thermometer. (Courtesy of Mac Tools, Inc.)

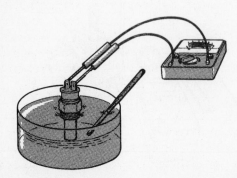

■ FIGURE 7–64
Coolant temperature sensor resistance test at specified temperatures. (Courtesy of Chrysler Corporation.)

MAT SENSOR		
TEMPERATURE VS. RESISTANCE VALUES (APPROXIMATE)		
°F	°C	OHMS
210	100	185
160	70	450
100	38	1,800
70	20	3,400
40	4	7,500
20	-7	13,500
0	-18	25,000
-40	-40	100,700

■ FIGURE 7–67
Manifold air temperature sensor resistance specifications (typical). (Courtesy of General Motors Corporation.)

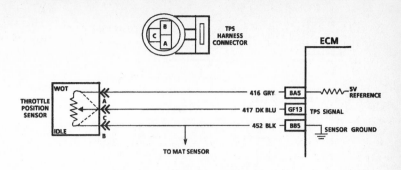

■ FIGURE 7–68

Throttle position sensor schematic. (Courtesy of General Motors Corporation.)

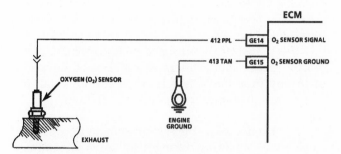

■ FIGURE 7–69

Oxygen sensor electrical connections. (Courtesy of General Motors Corporation.)

■ FIGURE 7–70

Oxygen sensor tester. (Courtesy of OTC DIVISION, SPX Corporation.)

COOLANT SENSOR		
TEMPERATURE VS. RESISTANCE VALUES (APPROXIMATE)		
°C	°F	OHMS
100	212	177
90	194	241
80	176	332
70	158	467
60	140	667
50	122	973
45	113	1188
40	104	1459
35	95	1802
30	86	2238
25	77	2796
20	68	3520
15	59	4450
10	50	5670
5	41	7280
0	32	9420
-5	23	12300
-10	14	16180
-15	5	21450
-20	-4	28680
-30	-22	52700
-40	-40	100700

■ FIGURE 7–71

Coolant temperature sensor resistance specifications at various coolant temperatures (typical). (Courtesy of General Motors Corporation.)

There are two types of O_2 sensors, the voltage generating type and the resistor type. The resistor type can be tested with an ohmmeter. Compare the test results with specifications. If the sensor does not meet specifications replace the sensor.

To test the voltage generating type check its output voltage with a high-impedance digital voltmeter. Do not use a low-impedance meter since it can damage the sensor. First bring the engine up to full operat-ing temperature and make sure it is operating in the closed-loop mode. Some systems revert to open-loop at engine idle. Unplug the sensor leads and connect the voltmeter leads to the sensor output terminal specified in the service manual. (Some O_2 sensors have only two leads. Heated O_2 sensors have three leads.) With the engine operating in closed-loop the O_2 sensor should put out a voltage signal that cycles from around 0.4V (400mV) to about 0.7V (700mV). An incorrect reading does not always indicate a faulty sensor. A defective fuel injector could cause a high or low reading. A vacuum leak could cause a low reading.

To check whether the sensor reacts to changes in the air–fuel ratio snap the throttle open and closed.

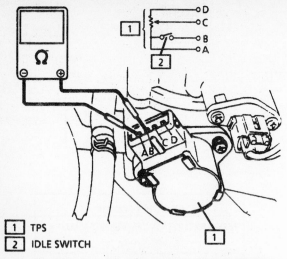

1 TPS
2 IDLE SWITCH

TERMINALS	CONDITION	RESISTANCE
Between A and B terminals (Idle Switch)	Throttle valve is at idle position.	Continuity
	When throttle lever-to-stop screw clearance is 0.3 mm (0.012 in.)	Continuity
	When throttle lever-to-stop screw clearance is 0.9 mm (0.035 in.)	No Continuity
Between A and D terminals	Throttle valve is at idle position	4.37 - 8.13 kΩ
Between A and C terminals	Throttle valve is at idle position	240 - 1140 Ω
	Throttle valve is fully opened	3.17 - 6.6 kΩ

■   FIGURE 7–72

Typical throttle position sensor tests and data. Refer to the service manual for actual specifications. (Courtesy of General Motors Corporation.)

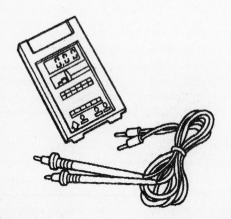

■   FIGURE 7–73

High impedance digital volt/ohmmeter used to test electronic sensors. (Courtesy of Ford Motor Company.)

This should cause the voltage reading to cycle up and down. A faulty sensor usually does not cycle up and down or the voltage reading may be too low. If the sensor checks out properly test the wiring harness for continuity. Repair or replace the harness if defective.

O_2 Sensor Replacement

Disconnect the negative battery cable and unplug the wiring harness connector from the O_2 sensor. Make sure to release the locks on the connector and do not pull on the wires. Some O_2 sensors have a short wire lead permanently attached, do not try to remove it.

Use a special O_2 sensor wrench to remove the sensor. Most manufacturers require sensor replacement any time the sensor is removed. To install a new sensor the typical procedure is as follows.

1.   Do not allow the sensor element to come in contact with anything during installation. Moisture, oil, grease, or carbon will affect sensor operation.

2.   Apply the recommended antiseize compound to the sensor threads to prevent thread seizure and damage. Do not allow any compound to come into contact with the sensor element.

3.   Start the sensor into the threads by hand to prevent crossthreading.

4.   Use the O_2 sensor wrench and tighten the sensor to specified torque. Do not overtighten.

5.   Make sure the external venting on the sensor is free of obstruction to ensure proper air circulation.

6.   Plug the wiring harness into the sensor connector. Make sure the connections are secure.

7.   Check sensor operation as outlined earlier to verify proper operation.

Throttle Position Sensor Testing

The throttle position sensor can be tested with an ohmmeter. Unplug the wiring connector from the sensor. Use an ohmmeter to connect it to the specified terminals. Check the continuity and the resistance at throttle opening positions specified in the service manual. Compare the test results to specifications. Replace a faulty sensor. A faulty throttle position sensor can cause incorrect fuel delivery and poor engine performance.

To replace a throttle position sensor it usually requires removing the staking that locks the mounting screws. Use a file to remove the staking, and remove the sensor. Install the new sensor and perform the required adjustment. This adjustment is critical and must be performed with precision to exact specifications. Refer to the service manual for specifications. Lock the adjustment in place.

Airflow Sensor Testing

A faulty airflow sensor can cause excessive fuel consumption and poor performance. There are several types of airflow sensors, as described earlier, each requiring different test procedures. Some have a vane or plate-operated variable resistor while others sense airflow electronically with a hot wire or film element. Variable resistor types can be tested with an ohmmeter at several specified vane positions. Resistance should be within specifications at each vane position. Others are tested with a digital high impedance voltmeter or with an ohmmeter under specified conditions. Always refer to the appropriate service manual for specific procedures and specifications. If the sensor element is faulty it must be replaced as outlined in the service manual.

Manifold Pressure Sensor Testing

A faulty manifold pressure sensor can affect the air–fuel ratio particularly during acceleration and deceleration. If the computer diagnostics indicate a faulty manifold pressure sensor, the sensor may have to be tested. Different types of sensors are used that may require different methods to be used. Refer to the service manual to ensure using the proper method. Usual methods include the following:

1. Use a hand vacuum pump to apply specified vacuum to the sensor while measuring output voltage with a digital voltmeter.
2. Measure sensor output voltage at the specified sensor terminal while the engine is running at specified speeds.
3. Disconnect the wire connector from the sensor and measure sensor resistance with an ohmmeter.

Compare test results with service manual specifications. Replace a faulty sensor. Use the specified sealing compound and tighten to specifications.

Intake Air Temperature Sensor Testing

A faulty intake air temperature sensor can affect fuel economy and engine performance. If the computer diagnostics indicate an intake air temperature trouble code the sensor and wiring may have to be tested. First make sure the problem is not just a poor connection at the sensor. To test the sensor use an ohmmeter and check sensor resistance at the different sensor temperatures specified in the service manual. A digital thermometer and blower type heater are required. Sensor resistance should be within specifications at each test temperature. Replace a sensor that does not meet specifications. Sensor wiring can be tested with an ohmmeter.

Idle Air Control Motor (Solenoid) Testing

A faulty idle air control motor (solenoid) does not maintain the proper engine idle speed. This may result in stalling and harsh transmission engagement. The idle air control motor or solenoid can be tested with an ohmmeter for winding continuity and resistance. Test results should be compared with specifications and the faulty unit replaced. Follow service manual procedures for replacement.

Inertia Switch

An inertia switch is used to prevent the electric fuel pump from continuing to operate after a severe collision. This reduces the possibility of serious fire from occurring. The switch interrupts electrical current to the fuel pump to prevent fuel operation. The switch may be located near the fuel pump or in the trunk. A button on the switch must be pressed to reset the switch and restore fuel pump operation.

■ TESTING THE ECU OR COMPUTER

Electronic control units and computers are tested using the on-board diagnostic system and diagnostic readout tester. If these tests indicate a faulty ECU, ECM, or computer, it is replaced with a new one. They are usually located under the dash or in the engine compartment. In some cases the PROM unit is removed from the old computer and installed in the new computer. The PROM (programmable read-only memory) is a computer chip programmed for use in a particular engine application. See Chapter 4 for details on computer testing and PROM replacement on GM vehicles.

■ FUEL INJECTION SYSTEM ADJUSTMENTS

Most fuel injection systems do not require periodic adjustments. Adjustments may not be recommended in many cases unless a specific problem has been identified. In this case more than an external adjustment is usually required. The usual procedure is to diagnose the system, note any faulty codes, consult the fault code chart in the service manual, and then test repair and adjust the faulty component as outlined earlier. On some models an idle-speed adjustment may be required. To adjust the idle speed, connect a tachometer to the engine and set the idle speed to the specifications on the emissions specifications label in the under-hood area of the vehicle.

Replacing a Carburetor with a Throttle Body Injection Conversion Kit

Retrofit throttle body fuel injection kits are available for some cars originally equipped with a carburetor fuel system. The kit provides all necessary parts to adapt the throttle body injection unit to the engine. This includes fuel pressure regulation, an electronic control unit, and all the required wiring. Complete instructions are also included for each step of the procedure. Advantages include better fuel economy, better performance, and lower exhaust emissions. The improved overall performance stems from the more closely controlled air–fuel mixture. Check for conversion kit availability before proceeding. Follow the conversion kit manufacturer's instructions carefully to ensure success.

Review Questions

1. The gasoline fuel injection system replaces the _____.
2. Two types of fuel injection systems are _____ _____ and _____.
3. _____ _____ and _____ can result from fuel system problems.
4. Gasoline fuel injection systems are under constant pressure from _____ _____.
5. Fuel injection system pressure remains in the system even with the engine shutoff. True or False.
6. Electric fuel pumps are tested for _____, _____ and _____ _____.
7. Mechanical fuel pumps are tested for _____, _____ and _____.
8. Fuel pumps can be disassembled and repaired. True or False.
9. Many electronic fuel injector systems have a self-diagnosis capability. True or False.
10. A fault code is stored in the _____ for later recall by the service technician.
11. Fault codes are compared to a _____ _____ _____ in the service manual to identify the problem.
12. Fuel injectors that leak when they are closed _____ the fuel mixture.
13. Fuel injector equipment is designed to clean injectors without removing them from the engine. True or False.
14. All throttle body injectors may be removed, cleaned, and repaired. True or False.
15. On a multipoint electronic fuel injector, the solenoid coil resistance can be measured with a _____.

16. Before removal of any fuel injector system parts, relieve the fuel system _____ completely.

Test Questions

1. Technician A says fuel pumps should be tested for output pressure only. Technician B says fuel pumps should be tested for fuel output volume only. Who is right?
   a. technician A
   b. technician B
   c. both are right
   d. both are wrong
2. The rollover valve is required to
   a. control vapors to the canister
   b. control EGR operation
   c. control fuel return to the tank
   d. prevent fuel spill in case of vehicle upset
3. Technician A says fresh air enters the vapor canister through a canister filter. Technician B says fresh air for the vapor canister comes from the air cleaner. Who is right?
   a. technician A
   b. technician B
   c. both are right
   d. both are wrong
4. Gasoline fuel tank caps contain two valves. They are
   a. pressure relief valve and vacuum valve
   b. pressure valve and an air valve
   c. atmosphere valve and vacuum valve
   d. vacuum valve and a separator valve
5. If the gas tank cap vent was to become plugged
   a. the engine would flood
   b. the fuel pump diaphragm would stop moving
   c. atmospheric pressure would collapse the tank as gasoline was pumped out
   d. the fuel supply system would become pressurized
6. Many modern electric fuel pumps are
   a. submerged in the fuel tank
   b. of the roller type
   c. shut off by an inertia switch in a collision
   d. all of the above
7. Which of the following does not cause an inaccurate fuel gauge reading?
   a. an empty fuel tank
   b. faulty wiring
   c. the tank sending unit
   d. the dash gauge unit
8. When an electric fuel pump fails to run, perform
   a. a pressure test
   b. a volume test

c. an electrical test

d. a vacuum test

9. Fuel injection system problems include
   a. hard starting, poor fuel economy, and rough idle
   b. rough idle, stalling, and low fuel consumption
   c. no fast idle, poor high speed performance, and excessive oil consumption
   d. excessive oil consumption, excessive fuel consumption, and hard starting

10. A fuel injection system fault code may be caused by any of the following:
    a. sensor failure and logic module failure
    b. harness failure and low fuel
    c. bad connection and low engine oil
    d. low engine oil and sensor failure

11. To access the self-diagnostic system use a
    a. tachometer
    b. ammeter
    c. test light
    d. scan tool

12. Before disconnecting any fuel injection fuel lines
    a. pressurize the system
    b. remove the battery
    c. relieve system pressure
    d. charge the battery

13. A faulty fuel injector can cause
    a. excessive exhaust emissions
    b. rough idle
    c. poor fuel economy
    d. all of the above

14. An injector balance test
    a. determines injector weight
    b. determines the pressure drop as each injector is pulsed
    c. compares a used injector with a new one
    d. none of the above

15. The solenoid winding in electronic fuel injectors can be tested with
    a. a dwell meter
    b. an ammeter
    c. an ohmmeter
    d. a pressure gauge

16. A stethoscope may be used to check
    a. pressure regulator operation
    b. electronic fuel injector operation
    c. step-up transformer operation
    d. voltage booster operation

17. Injectors for a continuous injection system are tested for
    a. resistance and voltage
    b. continuity and resistance
    c. voltage and fuel delivery
    d. fuel delivery and leakage

18. Electronic fuel injection system sensors are tested with
    a. a dwell meter
    b. a pressure tester
    c. a leakage tester
    d. an ohmmeter

8 Intake, Exhaust, and Turbocharger System Diagnosis and Service

INTRODUCTION

The air supply system provides air to the intake manifold and to each of the engine's cylinders for proper combustion during all phases of engine operation. The air supply includes all the components of the air cleaner assembly and the intake manifold on naturally aspirated engines **(Figure 8–1).** On turbocharged engines, it includes the turbocharger, its control system, and the intercooler. Engine efficiency, low emissions, and good performance depend on the supply of air to the engine. The exhaust system is an important part of the engine's "breathing" system and it also helps to reduce exhaust emissions. This chapter explains the function of the intake and exhaust systems and the diagnosis and service of these systems.

LEARNING OBJECTIVES

After completing this chapter, you should be able to:
- Describe the function of the air supply system.
- Explain the function of the exhaust system.
- List the components of the exhaust system.
- Diagnose air supply system faults and make the necessary repairs to correct the faults.
- Diagnose and correct turbocharger faults.
- Diagnose exhaust system problems.
- Replace faulty exhaust system parts.

TERMS YOU SHOULD KNOW

Look for these terms as you study this chapter and learn what they mean.

air cleaner	heat shields
resonator	crossover pipe
air filter element	back pressure
heated-air intake	heat riser valve
vacuum motor	single exhaust
airflow sensor	dual exhaust
intake manifold	two-way catalyst
variable volume intake	three-way catalyst
turbocharger wastegate	platinum
supercharger	palladium
intercooler	rhodium
exhaust manifold	HC
exhaust pipe	CO
muffler	NO_x
clamps	H_2O
hangers	CO_2
catalytic converter	leakage
intermediate pipe	restriction
resonator	noise
tailpipe	

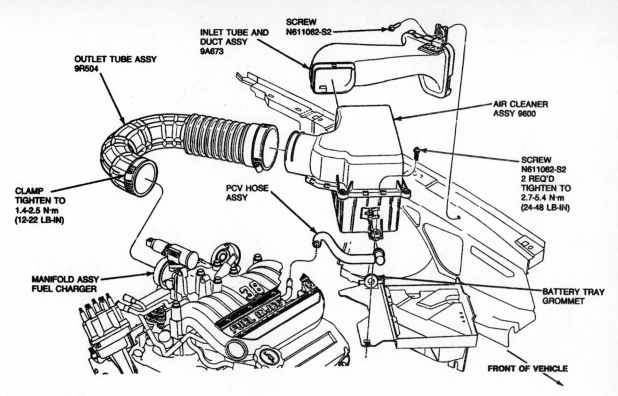

■ FIGURE 8–1

Air intake system components. (Courtesy of Ford Motor Company.)

■ AIR CLEANER FUNCTION

The air cleaner is needed to protect the engine from the harmful effects of dirt and abrasives present in air **(Figure 8–2)**. The air cleaner is not only an air filter, it may also have an intake air temperature control system and an air silencer. In some systems one or two separate resonance chambers are connected in parallel to the intake duct to reduce noise and improve midrange torque characteristics with a reserve supply of air **(Figure 8–3)**. The air cleaner may be mounted directly to a flange on the throttle body or the intake manifold (on diesel engines). It

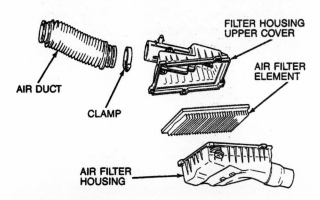

■ FIGURE 8–2

Air cleaner components. (Courtesy of Ford Motor Company.)

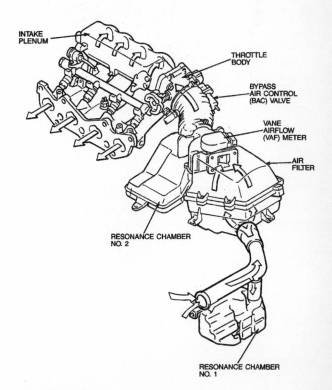

■ FIGURE 8–3

Air intake system with resonance chambers. (Courtesy of Ford Motor Company.)

may be mounted in a remote location in the engine compartment to reduce overall height. In this design, the air cleaner is connected to the intake system by air transfer ducts or tubing.

All incoming air must pass through the filter element before entering the engine. The air inlet system is sealed to prevent unfiltered air (possibly containing abrasives) from bypassing the filter and entering the engine. The air cleaner also provides filtered air to the PCV system. Under heavy acceleration or heavy engine loads crankcase vapors may reverse flow into the air intake system.

■ AIR CLEANER SERVICE

The air cleaner should be serviced or replaced at recommended service intervals. In dusty operating conditions it must be replaced more often. The air filter element (if not too dirty) can be cleaned in some cases by carefully tapping the element on a flat surface or by using compressed air **(Figure 8–4).** If the element is too dirty to be cleaned or is contaminated by oil or moisture, it should be replaced. If the air cleaner has a PCV filter, it too should be cleaned or replaced. Make sure that all connections are clean and airtight.

■ HEATED AIR INTAKE SERVICE

The intake air temperature control system provides heated intake air to the engine during engine warmup to improve engine performance, and allow leaner air–fuel mixtures to reduce hydrocarbon emissions. This system is not needed on most fuel injected cars since fuel metering is far more precise for all different operating conditions. The system supplies (A) all heated air, (B) a mixture of heated air and ambient (outside) air, or (C) all ambient air. During high under-hood temperature conditions or when ambient temperatures are high, no heated air is provided. The following is typical of heated intake air system service.

1. Inspect the system to be sure that all hoses and ducts are connected.

2. If the thermal vacuum switch is too warm (above room temperature), cool it down to room temperature with a cool, wet rag.

3. Start the engine. Watch the damper valve. When the engine is first started, the valve should be closed. As the thermal vacuum switch warms up, the valve should slowly open.

4. If the valve does not close when the engine is started, check for vacuum at the vacuum motor.

5. If vacuum is present, check for binding in the valve and operating link. If the valve moves freely, replace the vacuum motor. (Failure of the valve to close is more likely to result from mechanical bind due to a damaged or corroded assembly than from a failed diaphragm. This should be checked first, before replacing the vacuum motor.)

6. If no vacuum is present, check the hoses for disconnects, cracks, or pinches. Repair or replace as necessary.

7. If the hoses are OK, replace the thermal vacuum switch.

Vacuum Motor Test (Air Flow Control Valve)

The vacuum motor should move the valve from the full-cold-air position to the full-hot-air position when 5 to 7in. Hg (34.5 to 48 kPa) vacuum is applied to the motor nipple **(Figure 8–5).** Disconnect the vacuum hose that runs between the motor and the sensor at the motor nipple. Apply vacuum to the motor with a hand vacuum pump. The door should close. Pinch the hose while the vacuum is still applied and remove the vacuum source. The door should remain closed. If it does not, it indicates a leak in the motor, and the motor assembly should be replaced.

Thermal Sensor Quick Check

1. Start the test with the engine cold and the thermal sensor at a temperature below 77°F (25°C). If the engine has been in recent use, cool the sensor as described earlier. Momentarily disconnect the vacuum hose at the vacuum motor before proceeding with the test.

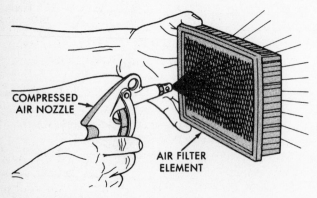

COMPRESSED AIR NOZZLE

AIR FILTER ELEMENT

■   FIGURE 8–4

Cleaning an air filter element with compressed air. Always refer to the service manual for proper procedure. CAUTION: Some air filter elements must not be cleaned this way. (Courtesy of Chrysler Corporation.)

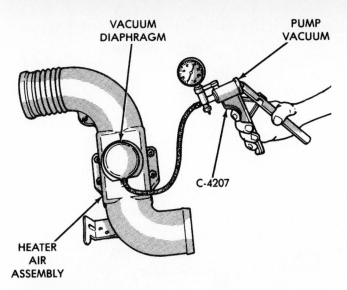

■ FIGURE 8–5
Using a hand-operated vacuum pump to check operation of the vacuum diaphragm in a heated air intake system. (Courtesy of Chrysler Corporation.)

2.   Observe the damper valve before starting the engine. It should be in the open position.

3.   Start the engine and allow it to idle. Immediately after starting the engine, the damper valve should be in the closed position.

4.   As the engine warms up, the damper valve should start to allow outside air and heated air to enter.

■ TWO-STAGE AIR INTAKE SYSTEM

Variable-volume, dual-stage, and *two-stage* are terms used to identify air intake systems that provide high-velocity, low-volume air intake at low engine speeds and high-volume, high-velocity air intake at high engine speeds. At low speed, engines use less air, which tends to reduce intake air velocity and swirl. By using a two-stage intake system, low-speed air velocity and swirl can be increased, for better mixing of the air and fuel.

A long, narrow runner curves from the central intake plenum to each intake valve, for increased velocity and swirl during low-speed operation. Above about 3500 to 4000 rpm the vacuum-actuated, computer-controlled throttle plates open in the intake plenum to provide a shorter intake path with less restricted, higher-volume air intake and increased power **(Figure 8–6).** Another arrangement for a four-cylinder engine is shown in **Figure 8–7** with a long runner tuned for low speed and a short runner tuned for high speed. The high-speed runner has a throttle

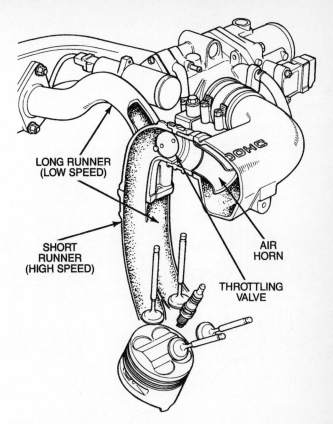

■ FIGURE 8–6
Two-stage air intake system. (Courtesy of Ford Motor Company.)

plate that stays closed until about 4000 rpm. It then opens to increase airflow and power at higher speeds. The low-speed runner provides the velocity and swirl for good air–fuel mixing at low speeds.

■ TURBOCHARGER COMPONENTS

The turbocharger is an exhaust-driven air pump designed to force extra air into the engine. It is usually located on one side of the engine **(Figure 8–8).** It consists of the following major components.

1.   *Turbine:* finned wheel driven by exhaust gases

2.   *Turbo shaft:* connects turbine and compressor wheels so they turn as an assembly

3.   *Compressor:* finned wheel forces air into intake system

4.   *Turbine housing:* encloses turbine and routes exhaust gases over turbine

5.   *Compressor housing:* encloses compressor and routes intake air over compressor wheel

6.   *Bearing housing:* supports turbo shaft assembly

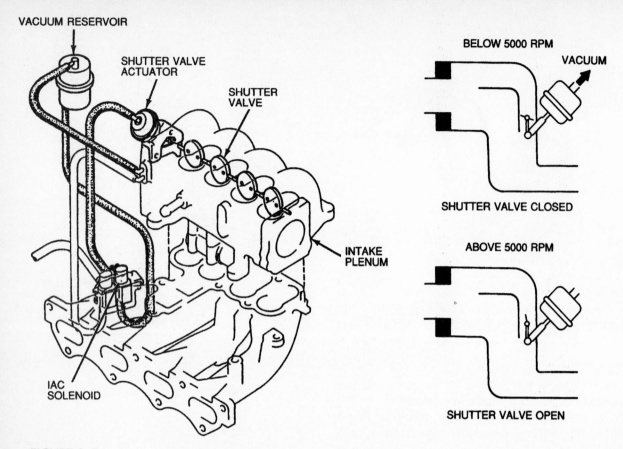

VACUUM RESERVOIR

SHUTTER VALVE
ACTUATOR

SHUTTER
VALVE

INTAKE
PLENUM

IAC
SOLENOID

BELOW 5000 RPM

VACUUM

SHUTTER VALVE CLOSED

ABOVE 5000 RPM

SHUTTER VALVE OPEN

■ FIGURE 8–7
Two-stage air intake for a four-cylinder engine. (Courtesy of Ford Motor
Company.)

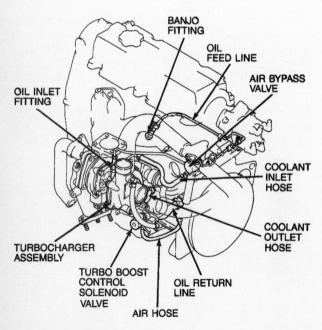

BANJO
FITTING

OIL
FEED LINE

AIR BYPASS
VALVE

OIL INLET
FITTING

COOLANT
INLET
HOSE

COOLANT
OUTLET
HOSE

TURBOCHARGER
ASSEMBLY

TURBO BOOST
CONTROL
SOLENOID
VALVE

OIL RETURN
LINE

AIR HOSE

■ FIGURE 8–8
Typical turbocharger system. (Courtesy of Ford Motor
Company.)

7. *Wastegate assembly:* controls boost pressure
by bypassing some exhaust gases when maximum
boost pressure is reached

■ TURBOCHARGER FUNCTION

The turbocharger provides pressurized air to the air
supply system to increase engine power output.
Engine exhaust gases are used to drive a small turbine and air compressor assembly at speeds up to
180,000 rpm. During acceleration there is a slight
delay in boost buildup known as turbo lag. This is
normal since it takes a few seconds for exhaust gases
to bring the turbine up to speed. The compressor
receives air from the air cleaner and pumps it
through an intercooler to the intake plenum. Boost
pressure ranges from about 4 to 9 psi (27.5 to 62.0
kPa). A bypass valve reacts to high intake vacuum
during deceleration, which opens to relieve high
compressor pressure and reduce noise. During acceleration or heavy load, boost pressure is controlled
by a wastegate. A solenoid-operated valve (controlled by the engine control computer) controls the

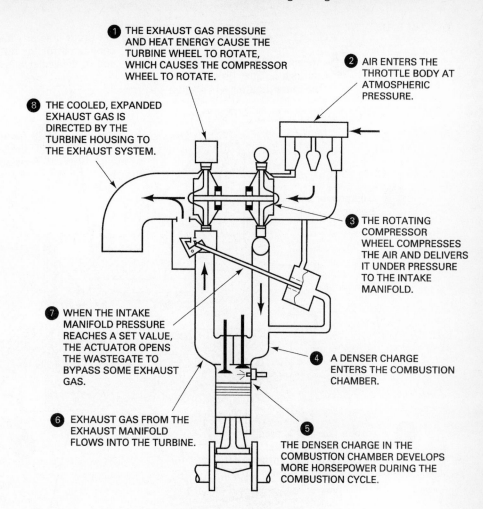

① THE EXHAUST GAS PRESSURE AND HEAT ENERGY CAUSE THE TURBINE WHEEL TO ROTATE, WHICH CAUSES THE COMPRESSOR WHEEL TO ROTATE.

② AIR ENTERS THE THROTTLE BODY AT ATMOSPHERIC PRESSURE.

⑧ THE COOLED, EXPANDED EXHAUST GAS IS DIRECTED BY THE TURBINE HOUSING TO THE EXHAUST SYSTEM.

③ THE ROTATING COMPRESSOR WHEEL COMPRESSES THE AIR AND DELIVERS IT UNDER PRESSURE TO THE INTAKE MANIFOLD.

⑦ WHEN THE INTAKE MANIFOLD PRESSURE REACHES A SET VALUE, THE ACTUATOR OPENS THE WASTEGATE TO BYPASS SOME EXHAUST GAS.

④ A DENSER CHARGE ENTERS THE COMBUSTION CHAMBER.

⑥ EXHAUST GAS FROM THE EXHAUST MANIFOLD FLOWS INTO THE TURBINE.

⑤ THE DENSER CHARGE IN THE COMBUSTION CHAMBER DEVELOPS MORE HORSEPOWER DURING THE COMBUSTION CYCLE.

■ FIGURE 8–9
Basic turbocharger operation. (Courtesy of Ford Motor Company.)

boost pressure directed at the wastegate. A knock sensor located on the engine (V engines may have one on each bank) signals the engine control computer to retard the spark timing when overboost occurs. Some systems are equipped with a warning chime that sounds when a fault develops in the system **(Figures 8–9 to 8–11).**

■ SUPERCHARGER FUNCTION AND OPERATION

A supercharger is an air compressor, belt driven from the engine crankshaft. It uses two counter-rotating lobed rotors to force air into the intake system. It turns at nearly three times crankshaft speed and creates a maximum boost pressure of about 12 psi. The rotors have a slight spiral position or twist to reduce pulsation and noise. Pulsation chambers are used to reduce noise from air backflowing from the compressor **(Figure 8–12).** Since the supercharger is engine driven, some engine power is lost. However, the slower running supercharger is easier to cool and lubricate than a turbocharger. One advan-

tage of superchargers over turbochargers is in their quicker response time. Turbochargers have some lag time since they are exhaust gas driven and must run at higher speeds. Supercharger output is controlled by a vacuum controlled bypass actuator and bypass valve. Excess blower output is redirected to the blower inlet.

■ TURBOCHARGER DIAGNOSIS AND SERVICE

PRO TIP

Before shutting off a turbocharged engine, let it run at idle for a few minutes. This allows the turbocharger to slow down and cool down to avoid possible turbocharger bearing seizure. If the engine is shut off while the turbocharger is running at high speed it will continue running for some time after engine shutdown. This may be long enough for it to run dry of lubrication and seize.

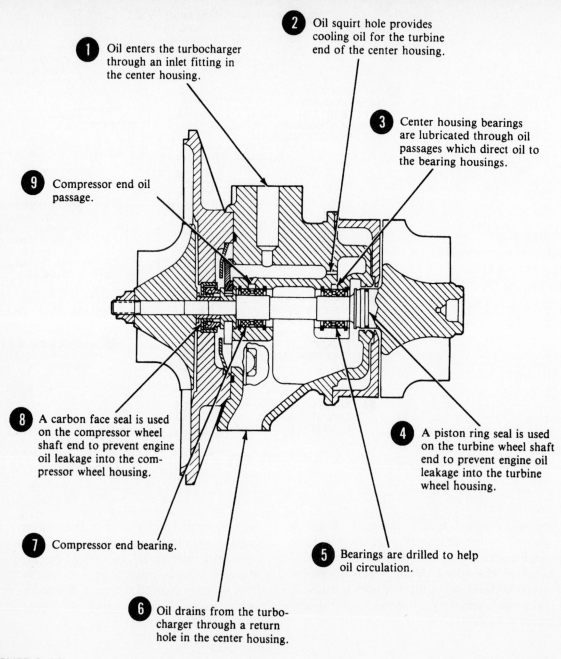

1 Oil enters the turbocharger through an inlet fitting in the center housing.

2 Oil squirt hole provides cooling oil for the turbine end of the center housing.

3 Center housing bearings are lubricated through oil passages which direct oil to the bearing housings.

9 Compressor end oil passage.

8 A carbon face seal is used on the compressor wheel shaft end to prevent engine oil leakage into the compressor wheel housing.

4 A piston ring seal is used on the turbine wheel shaft end to prevent engine oil leakage into the turbine wheel housing.

7 Compressor end bearing.

5 Bearings are drilled to help oil circulation.

6 Oil drains from the turbocharger through a return hole in the center housing.

■ FIGURE 8–10
Cross-sectional view of turbocharger lubrication. (Courtesy of Ford Motor Company.)

Turbocharger Problems

Turbocharger problems include:

1. *Boost pressure too low:* engine power is reduced
2. *Detonation:* too much boost, engine knocks
3. *Engine oil consumption:* leaking turbocharger seals
4. *Noise and vibration:* damaged compressor or turbine wheel

5. *Seized shaft:* failed compressor shaft bearings or lack of shaft lubrication

Turbocharger Visual Inspection

Inspect the air cleaner filter for restriction. Check the air ducts and hoses, the vacuum hoses, electrical connections, and other components for damage, looseness, pinching, binding, or restriction. Inspect the center housing of the turbocharger for signs of oil or coolant leakage, cracks, or a damaged seal or gasket.

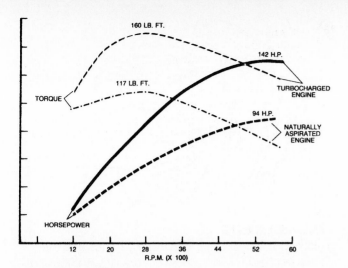

■   FIGURE 8–11
Comparison of naturally aspirated and turbocharged
2.2L engines. (Courtesy of Chrysler Corporation.)

Checking Boost Pressure

The usual procedure is to connect a fuel system vacuum/pressure gauge to a boost pressure output connection when the engine is cold **(Figure 8–13).** Warm the engine to normal operating temperature, increase the speed to specified rpm (around 3500 to 4500), note the boost pressure on the gauge, and compare to specifications. If boost pressure is below specifications and the turbocharger is in good condition, the turbocharger controls, compressor bypass control, or wastegate are at fault. Test the bypass control solenoid and bypass as outlined in the service manual.

Checking Wastegate Operation

Remove the air hose connected to the wastegate actuator and connect a pressure diagnostic gauge as shown in **Figure 8–14.** Apply 8.5 psi of air pressure and verify that the actuator rod moves.

PRO TIP

Do not apply more than specified air pressure to prevent actuator damage. If the actuator rod does not move, replace the actuator.

Checking Turbocharger Lubrication

With the engine off and cool, remove the oil lines at the turbocharger. Inspect to see if there is any blockage in any of the oil passages. If they are blocked, replace the turbocharger or oil line as required.

Turbocharger Shaft and Rotor Check

On a cool engine, remove the turbo air inlet and exhaust pipes to expose the rotor assembly at both ends. Apply axial pressure by hand in a back-and-forth motion to check for end play. Apply radial pressure up and down while turning the rotor to determine whether the rotor blades scrape or rub against the housing. Check to determine whether the rotor turns freely and smoothly by spinning it by hand **(Figure 8–15).** Visually inspect the turbine wheel and impeller wheel for wear or damage due to erosion, foreign objects, oil leakage, or overheating. Inspect the interior of the inlet and outlet pipes for the presence of oil. If any of these problems exist, replace the turbocharger.

■   FIGURE 8–12
Cross section of supercharger. The
bypass actuator and bypass valve
control boost pressure by
redirecting boost air to the blower
inlet. (Courtesy of General Motors
Corporation.)

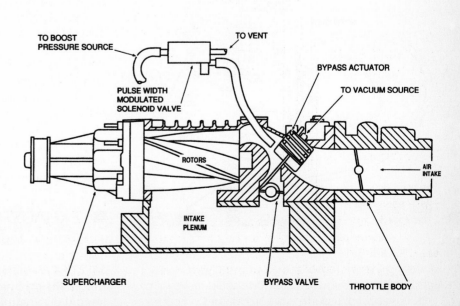

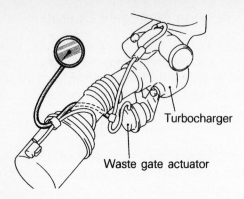

■ FIGURE 8-13
Checking turbocharger boost pressure. Boost pressure
may range between 5 and 11 psi (35 and 80 kPa) on
different models. (Courtesy of Chrysler Corporation.)

■ Exhaust System Function and Components

The exhaust system collects exhaust gases from the
engine, quiets exhaust noise, and carries the gas to
the rear of the vehicle. It reduces exhaust emissions
when equipped with a catalytic converter. In many
cases it also provides heat to preheat the intake air
for the induction system during engine warm-up.

Exhaust system components may be made from
steel or stainless steel. Stainless steel increases
exhaust system life. Exhaust system components
(see **Figure 8–16**) include the following:

1. *Exhaust manifold:* connects exhaust ports in
the cylinder head to the exhaust pipe. Exhaust manifolds are usually made from cast iron or steel.

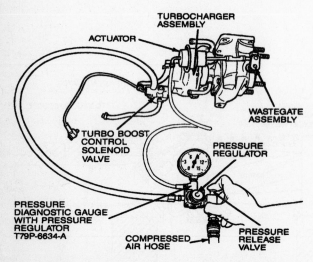

■ FIGURE 8-14
Checking the wastegate actuator by applying
specified air pressure. Actuator rod should move with
pressure applied. (Courtesy of Ford Motor Company.)

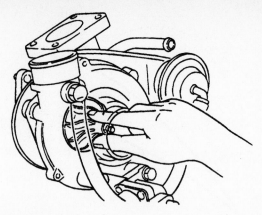

■ FIGURE 8-15
Checking turbocharger bearings by hand. Spin the
rotor to check for roughness or contact with housing.
Try to move the rotor radially and axially to detect any
looseness. (Courtesy of Ford Motor Company.)

2. *Exhaust pipe:* connects the exhaust manifold
to the muffler or catalytic converter.

3. *Muffler:* dampens exhaust pulsations and
noise. Consists of chambers and tubes enclosed in a
housing.

4. *Catalytic converter:* reduces harmful exhaust
emissions through the use of platinum, palladium,
and rhodium catalysts which are contained in a
metal housing.

5. *Intermediate pipe:* sometimes used between
the exhaust pipe and muffler or between the muffler
and catalytic converter.

6. *Resonator:* secondary muffler sometimes
used near the rear of the tailpipe to further dampen
noise.

7. *Tailpipe:* carries exhaust to the rear of the
vehicle.

8. *Hangers:* bracketlike devices used to attach
the exhaust system to the underside of the vehicle.

9. *Muffler clamps:* U-bolt clamps used to secure
exhaust system parts to each other.

10. *Heat shields:* shield the underbody from
the heat of the exhaust system, particularly from the
catalytic converter.

11. *Crossover pipe:* connects right and left
exhaust pipes together on V engines.

12. *Heat riser valve:* usually located near the
exhaust manifold outlet, it directs hot exhaust gases
to the intake manifold during engine warm-up
when the valve is closed.

■ EXHAUST SYSTEM SERVICE PRECAUTIONS

SAFETY CAUTION The normal operating temperature of the exhaust system is very high. Never work
around or attempt to service any part of the exhaust

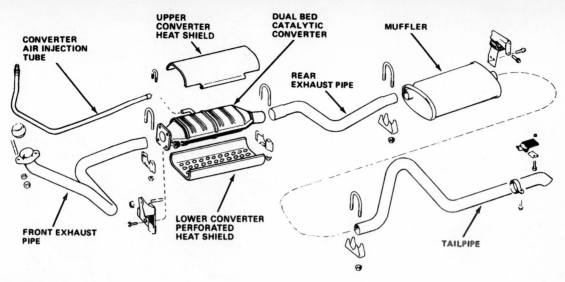

■ FIGURE 8–16

Exhaust system components. (Courtesy of Chrysler Corporation.)

system until it is cooled. Use special care when working around the catalytic converter. These units heat to a high temperature after only a short period of engine operation.

1. Do not park the vehicle over combustible material such as tall grass or piles of leaves.

2. Do not apply body undercoating to heat shields or exhaust components. It will reduce heat shielding and cause odors.

3. Do not short out or disconnect spark plug wires for diagnosis unless directed to do so by the service manual.

■ EXHAUST SYSTEM INSPECTION

To inspect the exhaust system raise the vehicle on a hoist and inspect all items from the exhaust manifold to the tailpipe. Look for problems such as leaks, rust, loose connections, discolored and overheated converter, faulty hangers, kinks, and dents severe enough to restrict exhaust flow, any possible contact between the exhaust system and the vehicle, condition of heat shielding, and the like **(Figure 8–17).**

Exhaust Gas Analysis

An exhaust gas analyzer is used to check the level of harmful exhaust emissions produced by the engine. The percentage of CO, CO_2, and O_2, and the HC content in parts per million (ppm), are checked. See Chapter 9 for procedures.

■ EXHAUST SYSTEM PROBLEMS

Exhaust system service is required if any of the following occurs:

- The heat riser valve is not functioning properly.
- There is exhaust leakage.
- There is an exhaust restriction.
- There is abnormal exhaust noise.

Heat Riser Valve Service

To function properly, the heat riser valve must operate freely without sticking. If it is stuck or sticky, use penetrating oil and work it back and forth until it operates freely or replace it. The heat riser valve control (bimetal spring or vacuum motor) must close the heat riser valve when the engine is cold and open it when the engine is at specified operating temperature. If it does not do this, it should be replaced or, in the case of the vacuum motor type, the source and supply lines of vacuum should be checked and corrected if required **(Figure 8–18).** The temperature control sensor and vacuum motor should be tested for proper operation. Make sure that vacuum and temperature specifications for these units are met. If faulty, they should be replaced. For proper inlet-air temperature control, the entire induction system should be free of leaks.

Exhaust Leakage

The entire exhaust system, exhaust manifolds, pipes, mufflers, resonators, and catalytic converters should be free of leaks. In most cases component replace-

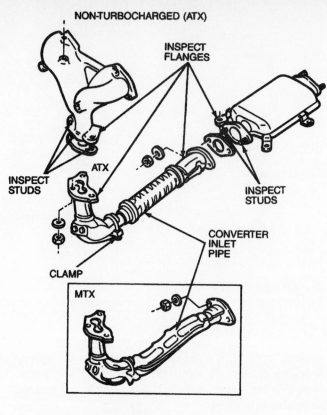

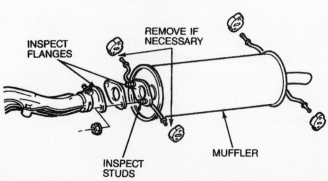

■ FIGURE 8–17
Exhaust system inspection points. Hanger brackets
and supports should also be inspected. (Courtesy of
Ford Motor Company.)

ment is required. Deterioration due to rust and corrosion requires replacement of the faulty unit.
Clamped connections may allow leakage if installed
incorrectly. Where this is the case, the connections
and clamps should be checked for correct size and
positioning and any errors corrected. Many tailpipes
and mufflers have small moisture drain holes, which
should not be considered as exhaust leaks requiring
repairs. An infrared exhaust gas analyzer may be
used to probe suspected exhaust gas leakage areas.

Exhaust Restriction

A restricted exhaust system usually results in
backfire, reduced engine power, and loss of speed.
Restriction may be the result of external damage
such as dents or the restriction may be internal in the
catalytic converter or muffler. A visual inspection of

the exhaust system will determine the extent of
external damage. Damaged parts should be
replaced. Internal restrictions are not as easily
detected. A muffler or resonator that is rusted or corroded internally may restrict the flow of exhaust
gases. A catalytic converter that has been overheated
(1600° F or more) may have resulted in a "melt
down" of the catalyst and substrate creating blocks
of solid material that do not allow the exhaust gases
to flow freely. A damaged catalytic converter must
be replaced to allow exhaust gases to flow freely and
to reduce exhaust gas emissions. If backfire and
reduced power are present verify that the condition
is not caused by the ignition or fuel system, then
perform a visual inspection to locate any external
damage. A restricted exhaust results in higher
exhaust backpressure and lower intake manifold
vacuum. This fact can be used to check for internal

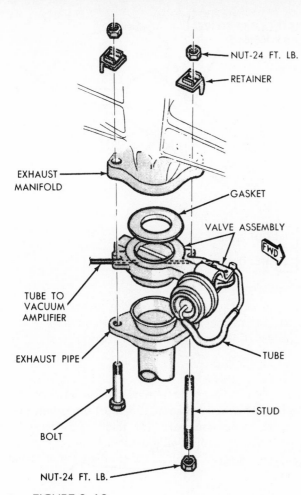

NUT-24 FT. LB.

RETAINER

EXHAUST
MANIFOLD

GASKET

VALVE ASSEMBLY

FWD

TUBE TO
VACUUM
AMPLIFIER

EXHAUST PIPE

TUBE

BOLT

STUD

NUT-24 FT. LB.

■   FIGURE 8–18
Some vehicles use a vacuum-controlled heat riser valve. Vacuum control ensures positive valve closing when the engine is cold. A thermal coolant switch cuts off the vacuum supply when the engine reaches specified temperature. (Courtesy of Chrysler Corporation.)

blockage in the catalytic converter and the muffler. Exhaust gas backpressure can be checked as follows:

1.   Remove the oxygen sensor and install a low reading pressure gauge in the opening.
2.   Take a pressure reading at between 1500 and 2500 rpm.
3.   Compare the reading with specifications. A 3 psi reading is usually considered to be excessive.

The following procedure may be used to check for internal restrictions in the exhaust:

1.   Attach a vacuum gauge to the intake manifold.
2.   Connect a tachometer.

3.   Start the engine and observe the vacuum gauge. The gauge should indicate a vacuum of 16 to 21 in.Hg (53.88 to 70.73 kPa).

Increase the engine speed to 2000 rpm and observe the vacuum gauge. The vacuum will decrease when speed is increased rapidly, but it should stabilize at 16 to 21 in.Hg (53.88 to 70.73 kPa) and remain constant. If the vacuum remains below 16 in.Hg (53.88 kPa), the exhaust system is restricted or blocked.

Exhaust Noise (Abnormal)

Exhaust noise may be the result of exhaust leakage, misalignment of the system (causing a rattle), or the muffler or resonator may have a loose internal baffle that causes a rattle. The faulty units should be replaced and the entire system aligned properly to provide adequate clearance at all suspension heights and when accelerating or decelerating.

PRO TIP

Overrich mixtures and malfunctions can overheat the converter and cause heat damage to vehicle components. This mixture can result in hotter reaction in the catalyst. Repair all engine malfunctions promptly. Avoid running an engine that misfires or has overrich mixtures. If engine misfiring occurs, avoid prolonged engine idling (hot or cold). Do not disconnect or short-plug wires during diagnosis. Any of these events can cause converter overheating and possible damage.

Overheating and Blockage

Overheating from overrich mixtures, late timing, or misfiring can melt the catalyst element. This will reduce the effectiveness of the converter by cutting off exhaust exposure to the catalyst. Extreme melting will produce a "lump" that blocks the exhaust flow out of the system. This will produce major engine problems such as backfire, low power, and overheating.

Lead Fouling

Catalytic converters require engine fuel without lead additives. Lead deposits will coat the catalyst and stop reaction—called lead fouling. The fuel filter neck restriction prevents entry of leaded fuel to a vehicle marked UNLEADED FUEL ONLY. A federal law also prohibits putting leaded fuel in a no-lead vehicle. If a vehicle fails an emissions inspection as a result of lead fouling, a new catalytic converter(s) must be installed. The lead cannot be removed.

■ EXHAUST SYSTEM COMPONENT REPLACEMENT

See **Figures 8–19** to **8–22.**

Removal

1. Raise the vehicle on a hoist and apply penetrating oil to the clamp bolts and nuts of the component being removed. Use a hacksaw or exhaust pipe cutter to cut the exhaust pipe at any welded connection for the component being replaced.

2. Remove the clamps and supports where necessary to permit alignment of parts during assembly.

3. Clean the ends of pipes and/or muffler to ensure mating of all parts. Discard broken or worn insulators, rusted clamps, supports, and attaching parts.

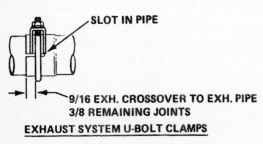

SLOT IN PIPE

**9/16 EXH. CROSSOVER TO EXH. PIPE
3/8 REMAINING JOINTS**

EXHAUST SYSTEM U-BOLT CLAMPS

**POSITION CLAMP AS SHOWN IN RELATION
TO SLOT TO PREVENT GAS LEAKS**

■ FIGURE 8–19
Clamp positioning is an important factor in preventing exhaust leaks. (Courtesy of General Motors Corporation.)

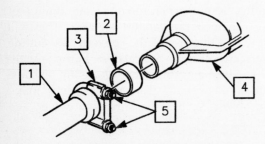

SLEEVE IS USED WHEN REPLACING CONVERTER
AND ONE PIPE, OR WHEN REPLACING COMPLETE
EXHAUST.

1	EXISTING MANIFOLD OR INTERMEDIATE PIPE	4	REPLACEMENT CONVERTER
2	INNER SLEEVE	5	35 N·m (26 LB. FT.)
3	GUILLOTINE TYPE CLAMP		

■ FIGURE 8–20
A sleeve may be required for some pipe connections. (Courtesy of General Motors Corporation.)

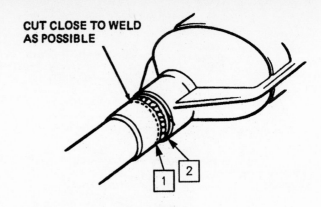

CUT CLOSE TO WELD
AS POSSIBLE

| 1 | CUT LINE |
| 2 | WELD |

■ FIGURE 8–21
Some exhaust system pipes must be cut and rewelded for muffler or converter replacement. (Courtesy of General Motors Corporation.)

When replacement is required on any component of the exhaust system, it is most important that original equipment parts (or their equivalent) be used to ensure proper alignment with other parts in the system and to provide acceptable exhaust noise levels.

Installation

1. Assemble pipes, muffler, converter shields, supports, and clamps loosely to permit proper alignment of all parts.

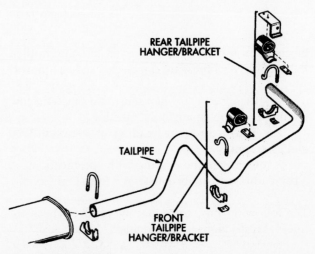

REAR TAILPIPE
HANGER/BRACKET

TAILPIPE

FRONT
TAILPIPE
HANGER/BRACKET

■ FIGURE 8–22
Typical tail-pipe mounting detail. (Courtesy Chrysler Corporation.)

2. Be sure that pipes are positioned to proper depth in muffler, converter, or resonator while tightening clamps.

3. Beginning at the front of the system, align and clamp each component to maintain position and proper clearance with underbody parts.

4. On models using ball-type connections, alternately tighten bolts to ensure that flanges are even and parallel.

5. Tighten all clamps and supports to the proper torques.

Review Questions

1. The air supply system provides air to each cylinder for _____ _____.
2. All incoming air must pass through the _____ _____ before entering the engine.
3. P.C.V. is an abbreviation for _____ _____ _____ system.
4. The turbocharger is an _____ _____ air pump.
5. A turbine is a finned wheel driven by exhaust gases. True or False.
6. The turbochargers provide pressurized air to the air supply system to increase _____ _____ _____.
7. During acceleration or heavy load, boost pressure is controlled by _____.
8. A supercharger is a belt driven _____.
9. Detonation in a turbocharged engine may be caused by too much _____.
10. If boost pressure is too low engine power will be _____.
11. The exhaust system equipped with a _____ _____ helps to reduce exhaust emissions.
12. The exhaust heat riser valve directs hot gases through the _____ _____ for quicker engine warmup.
13. Excessive exhaust restriction will cause low engine power. True or False.
14. Overrich air–fuel mixture will cause the catalytic converter to overheat. True or False.
15. Gasoline with lead added will cause the catalytic converter to become _____.

Test Questions

1. An engine which is supercharged, turbocharged, or equipped with ram air will have
   a. reduced volumetric efficiency
   b. no change in volumetric efficiency
   c. increased volumetric efficiency
   d. decreased volumetric efficiency

2. A leaking intake manifold gasket on a gasoline engine would usually result in
   a. engine running lean and rough at idle
   b. engine running smooth at idle only
   c. engine will not start when hot
   d. high idle speed

3. Technician A says that the thermal sensor in the carburetor air cleaner determines the position of the inlet air control valve. Technician B says that this job is done by the vacuum motor. Who is right?
   a. technician A
   b. technician B
   c. both are right
   d. both are wrong

4. The amount of exhaust gas bypassed through the wastegate is controlled by a
   a. throttle charger assembly
   b. spring loaded actuator
   c. turbine wheel
   d. exhaust heat

5. Technician A says that the air cleaner vacuum motor should be tested with a hand-operated vacuum source. Technician B says that the air valve should retain its position if the vacuum line is pinched shut while vacuum is applied and the vacuum source removed. Who is right?
   a. technician A
   b. technician B
   c. both are right
   d. both are wrong

6. Technician A says a turbocharger is driven by exhaust gas. Technician B says a supercharger is driven by exhaust gas. Who is right?
   a. technician A
   b. technician B
   c. both are right
   d. both are wrong

7. Boost pressure in a turbocharger is controlled by
   a. air density
   b. altitude
   c. wastegate
   d. engine vacuum

8. A blocked exhaust crossover passage in the intake manifold of a V-type engine causes
   a. faster engine warmup
   b. less fuel to be used
   c. poor fuel vaporization during warmup
   d. excessive fuel vaporization during warmup

9. The catalytic converter
   a. promotes oxidation of exhaust gases to reduce emissions
   b. provides quieter operation of exhaust only
   c. removes condensation and particulates
   d. reduces exhaust back pressure

10. A ball joint type exhaust manifold connection is used mainly on
    a. in-line 6-cylinder engines
    b. V8 engines
    c. all North American cars
    d. transverse mount engines
11. Heat riser operation is controlled by
    a. a mechanical link from the throttle
    b. a thermostatic spring or a temperature-sensitive vacuum switch
    c. a cable from the gas pedal
    d. a time delay switch
12. Air is injected into the converter assembly to
    a. cool the system
    b. improve fuel economy
    c. improve the chemical reaction
    d. slow the chemical reaction
13. In a catalytic converter an overrich mixture may
    a. overheat the system
    b. have no effect on the system
    c. cause the chemical reaction to stop
    d. cool the system
14. High exhaust backpressure
    a. increases exhaust gas recirculation
    b. decreases exhaust gas recirculation
    c. decreases engine power
    d. increases engine power

9

Emission Control Systems Diagnosis and Service

INTRODUCTION

Emission control systems on automobiles are designed to reduce the amount of harmful chemicals released into the atmosphere. The health and well-being of people are affected by the amount of harmful pollutants present in the atmosphere. A yellow-gray appearance of the atmosphere that limits visibility and irritates the eyes and breathing of people is called smog. The term is a contraction of the words smoke and fog. Smog occurs in major centers across North America and around the world. Automobile exhaust has been a major factor in air pollution. Emission control systems have been developed and improved to greatly reduce automotive emissions. This chapter deals with these systems.

Emission control system service involves inspection, testing, and repair of emission control systems and their components. When emission control systems malfunction, air pollution increases and vehicle performance may be adversely affected. It is important that the technician know how each system works in order to diagnose and repair them effectively. This chapter describes these procedures.

LEARNING OBJECTIVES

After completing this chapter, you should be able to:
- Describe the major vehicle emissions and name their sources.
- Describe the formation of smog and its effects on humans.
- Describe the major engine design modifications used to reduce emissions.
- List six emission control systems, their major components, and the emissions they control.
- Describe the function of a four-gas exhaust gas analyzer.
- Describe the five exhaust gases measured by an exhaust analyzer.
- Use an exhaust gas analyzer to analyze vehicle exhaust and interpret the test results.
- State the methods used to describe the amount of each of the four gases present in the exhaust.
- Inspect emission control systems and identify and correct faulty components.
- Test emission control system components to locate and correct faulty components.

TERMS YOU SHOULD KNOW

Look for these terms as you study this chapter and learn what they mean.

hydrocarbons	heated air intake
HC	exhaust gas
carbon monoxide	recirculation
CO	catalytic converter
oxides of nitrogen	air injection
O_2	rich mixture
particulates	lean mixture
smog	exhaust gas analyzer
thermal inversion	HC parts per million
high swirl	percentage of CO
hemispherical	content
peak combustion	percentage of CO_2
temperature	content
evaporative emission	percentage of O_2
control	content
positive crankcase	percentage of NO_X
ventilation	

■ VEHICLE EMISSIONS

The automobile produces four basic kinds of emissions:

1. *Hydrocarbons (HC).* Hydrocarbons are simply unburned fuel. Hydrocarbon emissions are caused by incomplete combustion and by fuel evaporization. Hydrocarbons are emitted into the atmosphere through a vehicle's exhaust system when the engine is not properly tuned. They are also emitted as vapors during refueling or by escaping from the fuel system.

2. *Carbon monoxide (CO).* Carbon monoxide is an odorless deadly toxic gas resulting from incomplete combustion. This can be caused by an overly rich air–fuel mixture or combustion chamber temperatures being too low.

3. *Oxides of nitrogen (NO_x).* When combustion chamber temperatures exceed approximately 2500° F (1370° C) nitrogen oxides are formed. Air is approximately 80% nitrogen and 20% oxygen. When combustion chamber temperatures are hot enough they combine to form NO_x. NO_x emissions create an unpleasant odor and contribute to the brownish color of smog. Any engine condition that results in excessive combustion chamber temperatures increases NO_x emissions.

4. *Particulates.* Particulates are small particles of carbon, soot, and fuel additive residues that result from combustion. The use of leaded fuel results in lead particulates being emitted. Engines that smoke release large quantities of particulates into the air.

Sources of Emissions

Vehicle emissions come from three sources.

1. Engine crankcase vapors resulting from combustion pressure blowby past the rings and from hot engine oil (20% of total emissions)
2. Fuel evaporization (20% of total emissions)
3. Exhaust emissions (60% of total emissions)

Air Pollution and Smog Formation

Ingredients necessary to form photochemical smog are hydrocarbons (HC) and nitrogen oxides (NO_x) in the presence of continued sunlight. Both of these gases exist in many forms and come from a variety of sources. One major source of NO_x and hydrocarbons is automobiles. The requirements for smog formation are sunshine and relatively still air. When the concentration of HC in the atmosphere becomes sufficiently high and NO_x is present in the correct ratio, the action of sunshine causes them to react chemically, forming photochemical smog. With a thermal inversion (where warmer air above prevents upward movement of cooler air near the ground), smog can accumulate under this lid all the way down to the ground within a few hours. The first effect of a smog buildup is reduced visibility and the blotting out of scenery in the distance; then as the buildup of smog approaches ground level, its irritating effects on eyes, nose, and throat are sensed.

■ ENGINE DESIGN MODIFICATIONS

A variety of engine design modifications and emissions control methods are used to minimize air pollution from the automobile **(Figure 9–1).**

Combustion Chamber Design

Engine manufacturers have improved engine design to promote the combustion of all the fuel in the combustion chamber and to keep combustion chamber temperatures at a level where NO_x production is minimized. The shape of the combustion chamber has been improved to eliminate close clearance spaces that tend to quench the flame before all the fuel is burned. A substantial reduction in HC and CO emissions has been achieved as a result. Compression ratios (compressed pressures) have been lowered to reduce peak combustion chamber temperatures and NO_x emissions. Relocation of the spark plug closer to the center of the combustion chamber has allowed the use of leaner air–fuel mixtures to reduce HC and CO emissions.

High swirl turbulence has been achieved due to combustion chamber design changes. This improves the mixing of the fuel with air to improve combustion and reduce HC emissions **(Figure 9–2).** The combustion chamber surface area-to-volume ratio has been reduced. This results in less heat being absorbed by the cylinder head and better combustion. The hemispherical combustion chamber is the best example of this feature.

Reducing Peak Combustion Temperatures

As emission control legislation in the 1970's became more restrictive with respect to NO_x emissions engines were designed with increased valve overlap. This left more exhaust gases in the combustion chamber, thereby reducing peak combustion temperatures and the formation of NO_x. During the early

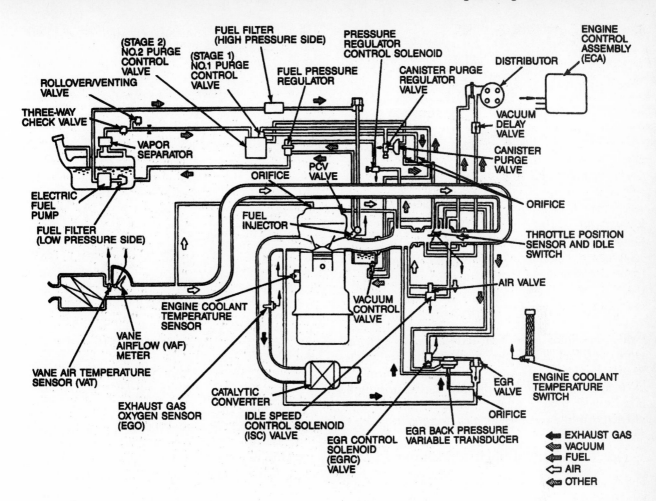

■ FIGURE 9–1
Emission control systems work together with fuel and ignition systems to control exhaust emissions. This diagram shows that relationship. (Courtesy of Ford Motor Company.)

1970s valve overlap was increased to the point where a smooth engine idle was no longer possible. With the application of exhaust gas recirculation (EGR) systems, there was no longer any need for large valve overlap.

Unleaded Gasoline and Hardened Valve Seats

The use of unleaded fuel requires harder valve seats and valves. The lead additive used to increase the octane rating of the fuel also provided a cushion between the valve face and seat, thereby reducing wear. Unfortunately, leaded gasoline use resulted in emitting harmful lead into the atmosphere. Leaded gasoline cannot be used with catalytic converters since lead contamination renders the catalysts ineffective. Unleaded fuels do not provide this cushioning, requiring induction-hardened valve seats and hardened valves to keep valve and seat wear at a minimum **(Figure 9–3).**

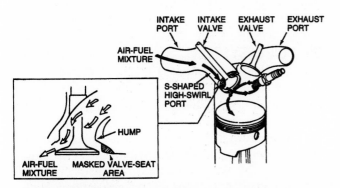

■ FIGURE 9–2
Intake port and combustion chamber design promote swirling action of air–fuel mixture, resulting in more complete combustion. (Courtesy of Chrysler Corporation.)

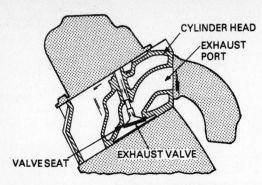

■ FIGURE 9–3
Better quality valves and induction-hardened valve seats are used to improve valve and seat life with the use of unleaded fuel.

Intake Manifold Design

Intake manifolds have been redesigned to provide more even fuel distribution to each cylinder. Equal-length runners and more rapid engine warm-up have improved fuel vaporization and distribution **(Figure 9–4)**. Plastic intake manifolds provide less restriction and more even flow characteristics.

Vacuum-Operated Heat Riser Valve

The vacuum-operated heat riser valve improves intake manifold preheating on carbureted engines for better fuel vaporization during engine warm-up **(Figure 9–5)**. A coolant vacuum control switch controls vacuum to the vacuum actuator. Below specified coolant temperature, manifold vacuum act-

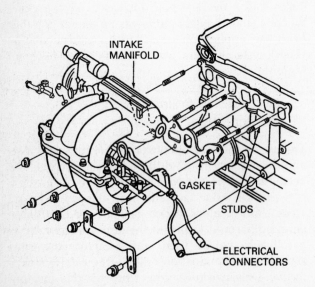

■ FIGURE 9–4
Typical tuned intake manifold. (Courtesy of Ford Motor Company.)

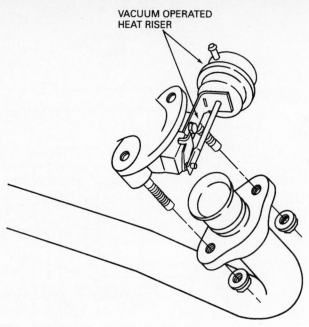

■ FIGURE 9–5
(Courtesy of General Motors Corporation.)

ing on the diaphragm closes the heat riser valve against spring pressure. When the coolant temperature rises above the specified level, vacuum to the actuator is cut off by the coolant control switch, allowing the heat riser valve to open.

Higher Engine Operating Temperatures

Higher temperature thermostats are used to raise normal engine operating temperatures slightly. This reduces HC and CO emissions. Engine parts around the combustion chamber are hotter, resulting in less combustion heat being absorbed by surrounding metal. This leaves more heat for improved combustion.

■ FUEL SYSTEM DESIGN CHANGES

Fuel system design changes have resulted in much more precise control over fuel metering and the air–fuel mixture. This results in more complete combustion, better fuel economy, and lower exhaust emissions. The exhaust gas oxygen sensor provides information about exhaust gas oxygen content. High oxygen content indicates a lean mixture. Low oxygen content indicates a rich mixture. This principle was applied to carburetors to operate a mixture control solenoid. On fuel injection systems the oxygen sensor provides the information to the computer.

The computer uses this information to control injector pulse width and the amount of fuel injected into the engine.

IGNITION SYSTEM DESIGN CHANGES

Design changes in ignition systems have resulted in producing a hotter spark at the spark plug to aid in burning the leaner air–fuel mixtures. More precise control of ignition timing results in better combustion and performance. Electronic ignition and computer-controlled timing have achieved these benefits.

TWO-STAGE AIR INTAKE SYSTEM

Variable-volume, dual-stage, and *two-stage* are terms used to identify air intake systems that provide high-velocity, low-volume air intake at low engine speeds and high-volume, high-velocity air intake at high engine speeds. At low speed, engines use less air, which tends to reduce intake air velocity and swirl. By using a two-stage intake system, low-speed air velocity and swirl can be increased, for better mixing of the air and fuel.

A long, narrow runner curves from the central intake plenum to each intake valve, for increased velocity and swirl during low-speed operation. Above about 3500 to 4000 rpm the vacuum-actuated, computer-controlled throttle plates open in the intake plenum to provide a shorter intake path with less restricted, higher-volume air intake and increased power **(Figure 9–6).** Another arrangement for a four-cylinder engine is shown in **Figure 9–7** with a long runner tuned for low speed and a short runner tuned for high speed. The high-speed runner has a throttle plate that stays closed until about 4000 rpm. It then opens to increase airflow and power at higher speeds. The low-speed runner provides the velocity and swirl for good air–fuel mixing at low speeds.

EMISSION CONTROL SYSTEMS AND THEIR FUNCTION

There are six major emission control systems used to reduce harmful vehicle emissions. The number and type of systems used on each model will vary. Consult the service manual for specific applications.

1. *Evaporative emission control system* **(Figure 9–8):** closed fuel system with no external venting of

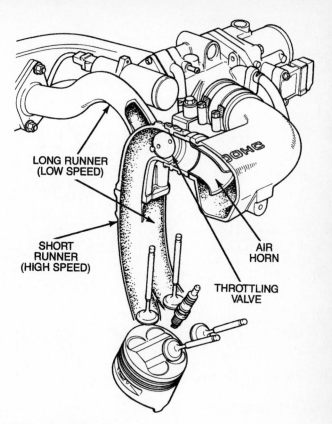

■   FIGURE 9–6

Two-stage air intake system. (Courtesy of Ford Motor Company.)

fuel vapors. Reduces HC emissions. The evaporative emission control system is part of the fuel supply system.

2. *Positive crankcase ventilation (PCV) system* **(Figure 9–9):** routes crankcase vapors (produced by combustion blowby and hot engine oil) into the engine where they are burned. Reduces HC and CO emissions. The PCV system is part of the engine lubrication system.

3. *Heated air intake system* (see **Figure 9–10):** intake air temperature is controlled at the desired temperature by a thermostatically controlled vacuum-operated valve to improve combustion and reduce HC and CO emissions. The heated air intake system is part of the air supply system.

4. *Catalytic converter* **(Figure 9–11):** muffler-like device in exhaust system uses precious metals as a catalyst to promote a heat-producing chemical reaction to reduce CO, NO_x, and HC emissions. The catalytic converter is part of the exhaust system.

5. *Exhaust gas recirculation (EGR) system:* adds burned exhaust gases to engine air intake to lower combustion temperatures **(Figure 9–12).** Reduces the formation of NO_x. The EGR system is discussed in this chapter.

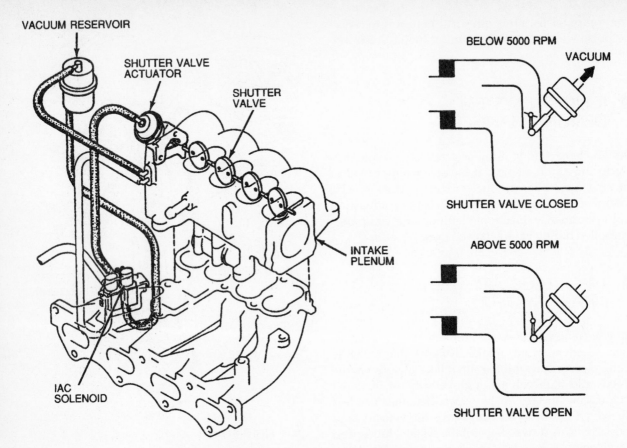

■ FIGURE 9–7

Four cylinder engine two-stage air intake system. (Courtesy of Ford Motor Company.)

6. *Air injection system* **(Figure 9–13):** adds fresh air to the exhaust to help burn any unburned fuel in the exhaust. Reduces HC and CO emissions.

■ EMISSION CONTROL SYSTEMS CERTIFICATION

The state of California and the California Air Resources Board (CARB) have led the way in requiring lower exhaust emissions than the rest of the federal United States or Canada. The emission control label in the engine compartment provides information stating whether the vehicle emission control system is certified for the state of California or for the other federal United States and Canada **(Figure 9–14).** Emissions control legislation for California has required more precise control of EGR systems, oxygen sensors, and secondary air injection. Computer control of these systems with the appropriate input sensors and computer programming is able to satisfy these requirements. Many of today's cars satisfy California emission standards as well as those of the federal United States and Canada. A number of other states and jurisdictions have also adopted the higher standards of the California emissions control legislation. When servicing the emission control system, check the under-hood

■ FIGURE 9–8

Evaporative emission control schematic. (Courtesy of Chrysler Corporation.)

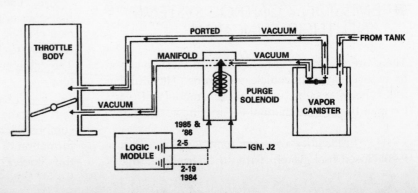

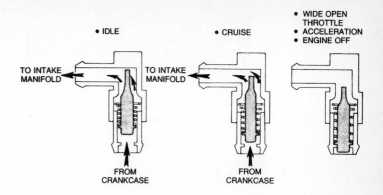

■ FIGURE 9–9
PCV valve operation. (Courtesy of Chrysler Corporation.)

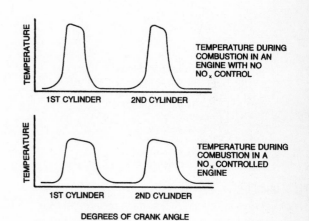

■ FIGURE 9–12
Comparing combustion temperatures with and without NO_x control. (Courtesy of Chrysler Corporation.)

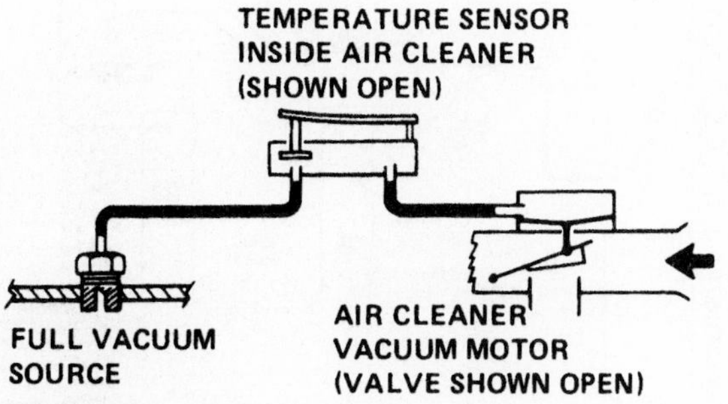

■ FIGURE 9–10
Bimetal switch senses intake air temperature and controls vacuum supply to the vacuum motor. (Courtesy of Ford Motor Company.)

information label to determine the area of certification, vacuum hose routing, adjustment procedures, and specifications.

■ EMISSION CONTROL SYSTEMS INSPECTION

If the exhaust gas analysis indicates a problem in any of the emission control systems, they must be inspected. The following inspection points are typical (see **Figure 9–1**):

1. Inspect the vacuum hose routing and compare to the vacuum hose diagram in engine compartment or service manual.
2. Check for vacuum leaks. Use a stethoscope or piece of hose to listen for a hissing sound with the engine running.
3. Check for pinched or damaged vacuum hoses.
4. Check for loose or disconnected electrical wiring.
5. Check the air filter in the air cleaner for restriction.
6. Check the PCV valve and hoses. Hoses must be in good condition and properly connected.
7. Check the canister purge control hoses for leaks and proper connections. Check the electrical connections for the purge control solenoid.
8. Check the EGR valve hoses for condition and proper connections.
9. Check the AIR (secondary air) system hoses and tubing for condition and proper connections.
10. Check the heated intake air system. Check vacuum motor and valve operation. Inspect heat shroud and duct for damage or cracks.

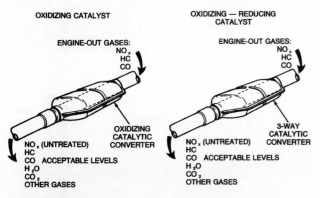

■ FIGURE 9–11
Catalytic converter operation. (Courtesy of Chrysler Corporation.)

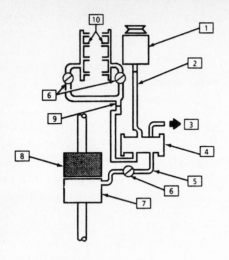

1	AIR PUMP
2	AIR TO AIR CONTROL VALVE
3	RELIEF PLUS DIVERT AIR TO ATMOSPHERE
4	AIR CONTROL VALVE (PEDES)
5	AIR TO OXIDIZING CATALYST
6	CHECK VALVE
7	OXIDIZING CATALYST
8	REDUCING CATALYST
9	AIR TO EXHAUST PORTS
10	AIR INJECTION PIPES

■   FIGURE 9–13

Air injection reaction (AIR) system schematic. Also called secondary air system. (Courtesy of General Motors Corporation.)

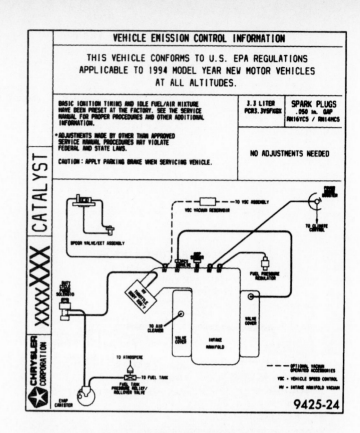

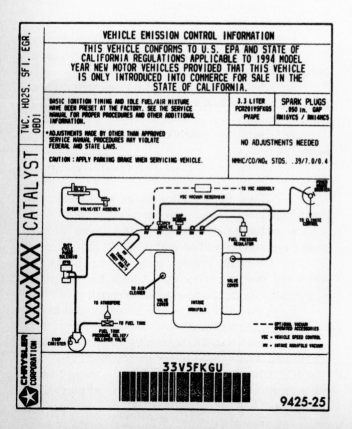

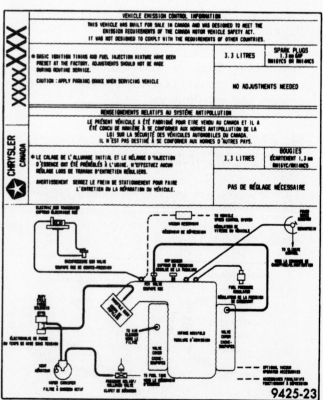

■   Figure 9–14

Emission control label located in engine compartment states area of emission certification of vehicle and provides information on engine adjustments and vacuum hose routing. (Courtesy of Chrysler Corporation.)

11.   Check the exhaust system for restriction, including the catalytic converter. See Chapter 8 for details on how to check for a restricted exhaust system and for exhaust system service.

12.   Check the fuel filler cap vacuum valve. A vacuum valve stuck in the closed position can cause the fuel tank to collapse and can reduce fuel delivery to the engine. Replace the vapor canister filter if dirty.

Any problems encountered must be corrected and the system retested to ensure proper operation.

■ COMPUTER-CONTROLLED EMISSION CONTROL SYSTEM SERVICE

The engine control computer controls several emission control systems. This includes exhaust gas recirculation, air injection, and canister purge systems. The EGR valve position sensor, EGR vacuum valve control solenoid, canister purge control solenoid, air injection air bypass solenoid, and diverter valve solenoid are examples of emission control input and output devices. Many other sensors and output devices in the ignition and fuel injection systems also affect the level of exhaust emissions.

When a malfunction occurs often enough in any of the computer control system devices, a fault code is stored in the computer. The driver is alerted

that a problem exists by the check engine light (malfunction indicator lamp) on the dash or by a fault code number appearing on the dash. The technician activates the on-board self-diagnosis feature of the computer, which then displays a fault code number or a flashing light fault code. The fault code is compared to a fault code chart in the service manual to identify the problem (see example below). The self-diagnosis mode is activated in different ways on different vehicles. A scan tool plugged into the wiring harness diagnostic connector may be used to diagnose the system **(Figure 9–15)**. See Chapter 4 for details. Once the problem area has been identified, further tests of sensor output devices and wiring are required to isolate the problem.

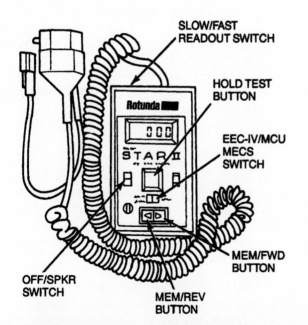

■ FIGURE 9–15
Scan tool is used to diagnose engine control systems. Tool plugs into diagnostic connector in wiring harness. (Courtesy of Ford Motor Company.)

Fault Code Chart (Typical)

Code	Definition
13	Left Oxygen Sensor (Open)
14	Coolant Sensor (High Temp)
15	Coolant Sensor (Low Temp)
16	DIS Fault Line Malfunction
21	TPS (Voltage High)
22	TPS (Voltage Low)
23	IAT Sensor (Temp Low)
24	Vehicle Speed Sensor
25	IAT Sensor (Temp High)
31	Cam Sensor Signal Problem
33	MAP Sensor (Voltage High)
34	MAP Sensor (Voltage Low)
36	DIS Fault Line/Missing or Extra EST Signal
41	Cylinder Select Error
42	EST System Malfunction
43	ESC System Malfunction
44	Left Oxygen Sensor (Lean)
45	Left Oxygen Sensor (Rich)
46	PASS-Key® Circuit
51	MEM-CAL Problem
52	Engine Oil Temp Sensor (Low Temp)
53	System Voltage Error
54	Fuel Pump Voltage Low
55	Fuel Lean Monitor
56	Vacuum Sensor Voltage Problem
61	Secondary Port Throttle System Malfunction
62	Engine Oil Temp Sensor High
63	Right Oxygen Sensor Circuit (Open)
64	Right Oxygen Sensor (Lean)
65	Right Oxygen Sensor (Rich)
66	Engine Power Switch Voltage (High or Low)

■ EXHAUST GAS ANALYSIS

Exhaust Gas Analyzers

An exhaust gas analyzer measures the harmful pollutants emitted by the vehicle exhaust. A probe is placed in the tail pipe to sense exhaust gases. The technician uses exhaust gas analysis information to determine the condition of the engine and the emission control systems **(Figure 9–16)**. Exhaust gas analyzers are also used by government-designated vehicle emission inspection stations to test the emission levels of cars and trucks in daily use.

There are several kinds of exhaust gas analyzers: two-, four-, and five-gas analyzers. The two-gas analyzer measures only HC and CO content of exhaust gases. The four-gas analyzer measures the HC, CO, CO_2, and O_2 content of exhaust gases **(Figure 9–17)**. The five-gas analyzer also measures NO_X content. Hydrocarbons (HC) and carbon monoxide (CO) are toxic pollutants. Carbon dioxide (CO_2) and oxygen (O_2) are nontoxic. All five gases provide information about engine operation, combustion efficiency, and emission control systems effectiveness. Exhaust gas analyzers measure HC in parts per million. CO, CO_2, O_2 and NO_X are measured as a percentage of exhaust gas volume. Always follow the test equipment manufacturer's instruction for analyzer setup and vehicle manufacturers' specifications from the service manual when analyzing vehicle exhaust. The emission levels allowed vary between different vehicle makes and models. Refer to the emission control sticker in the engine compartment for additional information.

■ FIGURE 9–16

Four gas analyzer with diagnostic features. (Courtesy of OTC Division, SPX Corporation.)

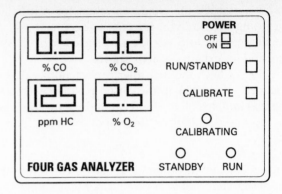

■ FIGURE 9–17

A four-gas analyzer has scales showing HC in parts per million (ppm), and CO, CO_2, and O_2 as a percentage of exhaust gas volume.

Using an Exhaust Gas Analyzer

The following procedure is typical for using an exhaust gas analyzer; however, the instructions supplied with the equipment should always be followed.

1. Plug in the analyzer.
2. Allow the analyzer and the engine to warm up as specified in equipment instructions.
3. Calibrate the meters.
4. Use shop exhaust to remove vehicle exhaust fumes.
5. Insert the analyzer pick up probe into the vehicle exhaust where specified.
6. Take readings only after meter readings have stabilized.
7. Readings are usually taken at idle and at about 2500 rpm.
8. A dynamometer is required to take readings under engine load conditions.
9. Compare readings with specifications.
10. Analyze results and make adjustments or repairs to vehicle as needed.
11. Retest to determine success of repairs.

Hydrocarbon (HC) Readings

Hydrocarbon readings are measured in parts per million (ppm). A reading of 100 ppm means that there are 100 parts of HC for every million parts of exhaust gas. A higher than normal HC reading is the result of too much unburned fuel in the exhaust. This may be caused by:

1. *Rich air–fuel mixture:* engine getting too much fuel; fuel injector, restricted air cleaner, computer, or sensor problem
2. *Ignition system problem:* faulty spark plugs, plug wires, distributor cap or rotor, preventing some cylinders from firing at times

3. *Incorrect ignition timing:* computer, sensor, or distributor problem or incorrect timing adjustment

4. *Emission control system problem:* PCV valve, catalytic converter, or canister purge control

5. *Engine mechanical problem:* worn rings, worn cylinder—too much blowby, leaking head gasket, burned valves, worn valve guides, faulty valve stem seals

Carbon Monoxide (CO) Readings

Carbon monoxide content is measured as a percentage of exhaust gas volume. A 2% reading means that 2% of the exhaust gas is carbon monoxide. A higher than normal CO reading is caused by an overly rich air–fuel ratio. A lower than normal CO reading results from an air–fuel mixture that is too lean. A high CO reading may be caused by:

1. *Leaking fuel injector:* allows fuel to enter engine when injector is supposed to be closed

2. *Computer or input sensor problem:* resulting in too much fuel being injected

3. *Emission control system problem:* PCV, catalytic converter, purge control

4. *Incorrect ignition timing:* computer, input sensor or distributor problem, or incorrect ignition timing setting

5. *Idle air control system problem*

Carbon Dioxide (CO₂) Readings

Carbon dioxide content is measured as a percentage of exhaust gas volume. A carbon dioxide reading of 10% means that 10% of total exhaust gas volume consists of carbon dioxide. CO_2 readings should normally be above about 8%. Carbon dioxide is formed during combustion by combining one carbon molecule with two oxygen molecules. Carbon dioxide content is normally compared with oxygen content to aid in diagnosing combustion efficiency. When the CO_2 content is greater than the O_2 content, the air–fuel ratio is on the lean side of stoichiometric. A stoichiometric ratio is the theoretically perfect ratio for complete combustion. A stoichiometric ratio is about 14.7:1.

Oxygen (O₂) and NOx Readings

Oxygen content is measured as a percentage of exhaust gas volume. O_2 readings should normally be between 1 and 2%. Oxygen is needed in exhaust gases to aid in burning HC and CO in the exhaust system catalytic converter. Since air is added to the exhaust by the air injection or pulse air system, the O_2 readings are an indicator of air injection system operation. The O_2 content in the exhaust also indicates whether the air–fuel mixture is rich or lean. A lean air–fuel mixture results in a higher O_2 reading. An excessively lean mixture can cause lean misfiring, an excessively high O_2 reading, and a high NOx reading. Excessive combustion chamber temperatures can cause high NOx readings.

■ EVAPORATIVE EMISSION CONTROL SYSTEM FUNCTION

The evaporative emission control system prevents the escape of raw fuel vapors into the atmosphere. Components of the system include the following **(Figure 9–18):**

1. *Sealed fuel tank cap:* fuel tank caps on older cars were vented to atmosphere. The sealed fuel tank filler cap prevents the escape of fuel vapors from the tank. It usually has a vacuum valve to allow air to enter the tank as fuel is consumed and a pressure relief valve in the event of extreme pressure buildup in the tank **(Figure 9–19).**

2. *Expansion chamber:* a domed section on top of the tank that provides room for fuel as it expands due to temperature increase.

3. *Vapor vent line:* carries fuel tank vapors to the charcoal canister.

■ FIGURE 9–18

Evaporative emission control system schematic. (Courtesy of General Motors Corporation.)

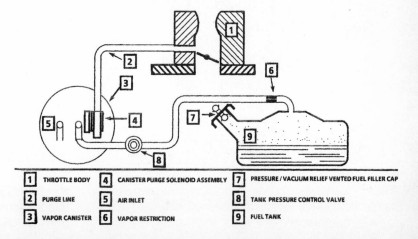

1	THROTTLE BODY	4	CANISTER PURGE SOLENOID ASSEMBLY	7	PRESSURE / VACUUM RELIEF VENTED FUEL FILLER CAP
2	PURGE LINE	5	AIR INLET	8	TANK PRESSURE CONTROL VALVE
3	VAPOR CANISTER	6	VAPOR RESTRICTION	9	FUEL TANK

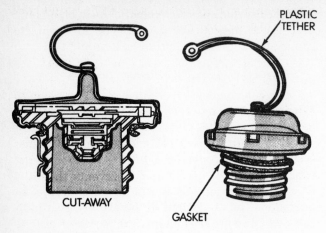

■ FIGURE 9–19
Fuel tank filler cap has a vacuum valve and pressure relief valve. (Courtesy of Chrysler Corporation.)

4. *Roll-over valve:* prevents the escape of raw fuel through the vapor line in case of vehicle upset. A check valve closes the line when the vehicle is upside down **(Figure 9–20).**

5. *Charcoal canister:* stores fuel vapors when the engine is not running. It contains activated charcoal granules that adsorb fuel vapors. The top of the canister has fittings to connect it to the fuel tank vapor vent line, the carburetor vent line, and the purge line. A vent valve is located at the top of the canister (carbureted system) that is open to allow bowl venting when the engine is off. Manifold vacuum closes the valve when the engine is running. Intake manifold vacuum draws fuel vapors from the canister to the induction system when the engine is running.

A filter at the bottom of the canister allows filtered air to enter the canister during purging. Dual canisters

are used in some applications to provide added capacity. A purge control solenoid valve is used on engines with computer controls **(Figure 9–21).**

- When the solenoid is electrically energized, it will not allow purge.
- When the solenoid is not electrically energized, it allows purge.
- Purge is enabled approximately 10 seconds after engine coolant temperature reaches 120°F (49°C).

At this time, fuel vapors move from the vapor canister through the purge solenoid to the throttle body. At closed throttle, the vapors enter the intake manifold through a small hole below the throttle valves. During off-idle, full canister purge is allowed through additional ports uncovered by the throttle valves.

6. *Purge line:* connects the canister to the intake manifold to allow fuel vapors to be drawn into the engine to purge (empty) the canister of fuel vapors.

Computer Controlled Canister Purge

In the typical computer controlled canister purge system the purge control solenoid is not energized during cold start warmup periods, hot start time delay, or open loop operation. During closed loop operation

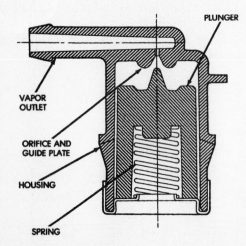

■ FIGURE 9–20
Rollover valve cross section. Weighted plunger shuts off fuel flow when vehicle rolls over. (Courtesy of Chrysler Corporation.)

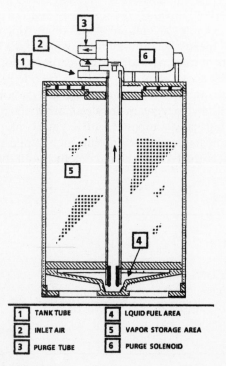

1	TANK TUBE	4	LIQUID FUEL AREA
2	INLET AIR	5	VAPOR STORAGE AREA
3	PURGE TUBE	6	PURGE SOLENOID

■ FIGURE 9–21
Vapor canister detail. (Courtesy of General Motors Corporation.)

the solenoid is energized and de-energized several times per second by the computer based on preprogrammed information and sensor signal inputs. Vapor flow is regulated by solenoid on-time (pulse width) based on fuel requirements. The purge control solenoid is located in the purge line between the vapor canister and the engine **(Figure 9–22)**.

■ EVAPORATIVE EMISSION CONTROL SYSTEM DIAGNOSIS

The escape of raw fuel vapors from faulty components of the evaporative emission control system emits harmful hydrocarbons into the atmosphere. A careful visual inspection will reveal any damaged components that could allow vapors to escape **(Figure 9–23)**. Damaged components should be replaced. If there are no damaged parts the system can be tested further with an exhaust gas analyzer for the presence of any hydrocarbons. Pass the probe slowly over any suspect areas such as the fuel tank cap, the vapor canister, and the vapor and fuel lines and connections. Repair or replace any components

where vapors escape. Make sure all lines and connections are leakproof after assembly.

Checking the Canister Purge Control Solenoid Valve

The purge control solenoid valve controls the flow of raw fuel vapors from the canister to the engine. When the engine is cold, is in the open loop operation, or is in the time delay period after a hot start the solenoid should not be energized and the valve should be closed. To check system operation disconnect the vacuum purge line at the purge control valve or at the canister. Check that vacuum is present at the line at specified engine speeds. Test the canister purge control solenoid. There should be no vacuum at the canister side of the purge control valve at engine idle. There should be vacuum at specified engine speeds. If not, check the supply voltage to the purge control solenoid. With the system in closed loop operation check for voltage at the solenoid electrical connection. If voltage is present the solenoid or valve is at fault and should be replaced. If there is no voltage determine the cause by checking electrical continuity in the circuit and

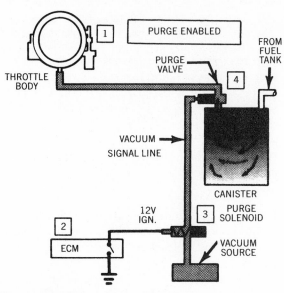
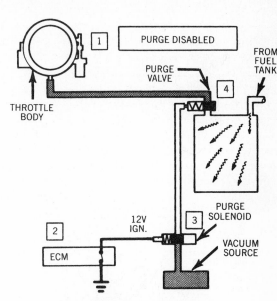

■ FIGURE 9–22

Computer-controlled canister purge operation. (Courtesy of General Motors Corporation).

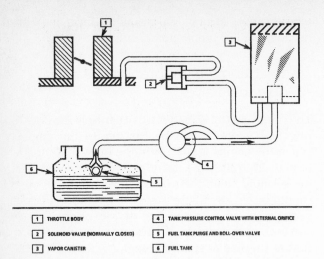

1	THROTTLE BODY	4	TANK PRESSURE CONTROL VALVE WITH INTERNAL ORIFICE
2	SOLENOID VALVE (NORMALLY CLOSED)	5	FUEL TANK PURGE AND ROLL-OVER VALVE
3	VAPOR CANISTER	6	FUEL TANK

■ FIGURE 9–23

Evaporative emission control system inspection points. (Courtesy of General Motors Corporation.)

correct the problem. The valve may be tested for opening and closing operation by using a hand vacuum pump to apply vacuum to the valve **(Figure 9–24).** Another method is shown in **Figure 9–25.** The solenoid can be tested with an ohmmeter. Replace faulty items.

■ POSITIVE CRANKCASE VENTILATION SYSTEM FUNCTION AND SERVICE

Positive crankcase ventilation (PCV) systems **(Figure 9–26)** are required to (1) prevent pressure buildup in the crankcase due to combustion pressure blowby; (2) remove harmful crankcase vapors and remove condensation; (3) prevent crankcase vapors from

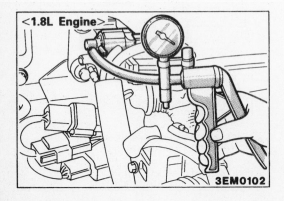

■ FIGURE 9–24

Using a hand vacuum pump to check purge control valve operation. (Courtesy of Chrysler Corporation.)

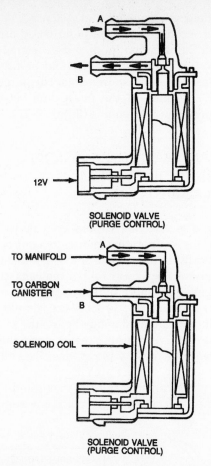

■ FIGURE 9–25

To check this canister purge solenoid, disconnect vacuum hoses at A and B and the solenoid valve electrical connection. Blow air into port A and confirm that no air exits from port B. Apply 12 volts to the solenoid connector pin and ground the other. Blow air into port A and confirm that air exits from port B. This confirms proper solenoid valve operation. (Courtesy of Ford Motor Company.)

being emitted into the atmosphere, where they would contribute to atmospheric pollution harmful to health; and (4) prevent backfire gases from entering the crankcase.

Crankcase vapors are directed to the intake manifold through the PCV valve **(Figure 9–27).** These vapors are then burned in the normal process of combustion. This creates a low-pressure area in the crankcase and causes fresh, clean air to flow from the air cleaner into the crankcase.

A PCV valve stuck in the closed position causes crankcase pressures to build up and the flow of vapors to reverse. A similar condition can develop under heavy acceleration and load. A malfunctioning PCV valve can affect the engine's ability to idle properly, since some of the air for engine idle is supplied through the PCV system.

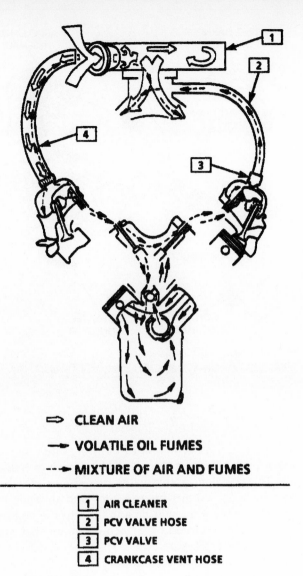

⇨ **CLEAN AIR**

➤ **VOLATILE OIL FUMES**

--➤ **MIXTURE OF AIR AND FUMES**

1	**AIR CLEANER**
2	**PCV VALVE HOSE**
3	**PCV VALVE**
4	**CRANKCASE VENT HOSE**

■ FIGURE 9–26
Positive crankcase ventilation system showing airflow and flow of crankcase fumes. (Courtesy of General Motors Corporation.)

PCV Valve Diagnosis and Service

1. With engine idling inspect as follows:
   (a) Remove the PCV valve from the engine. If the valve is not plugged, a hissing noise will be heard as air passes through the valve, and a strong vacuum should be felt when a finger is placed over the valve inlet (**Figures 9–28** and **9–29**).
   (b) Reinstall the PCV valve, and then remove the crankcase inlet air cleaner. Loosely hold a piece of stiff paper, such as a parts tag, over the opening. After allowing about a minute for the crankcase pressure to decrease, the paper should be sucked against the opening with noticeable force.
2. With engine stopped, remove the PCV valve from the engine and shake. A clicking noise should be heard to indicate that the valve is free.
3. If the ventilation system meets the tests in steps 1 and 2, no further service is required; if not, the PCV valve should be replaced and the system rechecked. Install a new PCV valve. *Do not attempt to clean the old PCV valve.*
4. With a new PCV valve installed (and the engine running), if the paper is not sucked against the crankcase inlet air cleaner opening in the rocker cover, it will be necessary to clean the PCV valve hose and passage in the throttle body.

Special PCV system testers are available. These should be used according to the tester manufacturer's instructions.

■ INTAKE AIR TEMPERATURE CONTROL SYSTEM FUNCTION AND SERVICE

The intake air temperature control system provides heated intake air to the engine during engine warmup to improve engine performance, and allow

■ FIGURE 9–27
PCV valve operation. (Courtesy of Chrysler Corporation.)

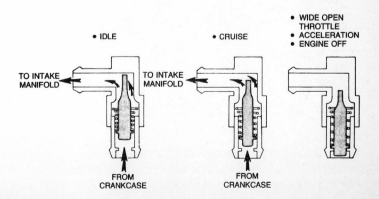

■ FIGURE 9–28
Checking PCV valve operation. With valve disconnected from engine and the engine running, there should be vacuum at the open end of the valve. (Courtesy of Chrysler Corporation.)

leaner air–fuel mixtures to reduce hydrocarbon emissions **(Figure 9–30).** This system is not needed on most fuel injected cars since fuel metering is far more precise for all different operating conditions. The system supplies (A) all heated air, (B) a mixture of heated air and ambient (outside) air, or (C) all ambient air **(Figure 9–31).** During high under-hood temperature conditions or when ambient temperatures are high, no heated air is provided. This prevents excessively high-temperature inlet air from entering the engine. Excessively high intake air temperatures adversely affect engine operation.

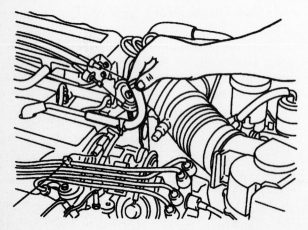

■ FIGURE 9–29
Check for presence of vacuum at PCV valve hose connection. Vacuum should be present with engine running. (Courtesy of Ford Motor Company.)

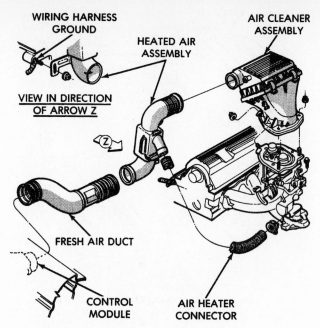

■ FIGURE 9–30
Heated air intake system. (Courtesy of Chrysler Corporation.)

A typical air temperature control system uses a valve in the air inlet to control the source of intake air. The position of this valve determines whether only heated air, a mixture of heated and ambient air, or only ambient air will be admitted to the engine. The valve is operated by a vacuum motor that acts against spring pressure.

A metal shroud surrounding the exhaust manifold collects manifold heat and directs it to the air cleaner through a connecting duct. Outside air is delivered through connecting ducts. The control valve is positioned between these connections in the air inlet in a position that allows closing of either passage or any position in between.

Vacuum to the vacuum diaphragm is controlled by a thermal vacuum switch. Intake temperature acting on the thermal vacuum determines the degree of vacuum allowed to reach the vacuum diaphragm **(Figure 9–32).** When the engine is cold, only heated air is allowed to reach the engine. As the engine warms up, an increasing amount of outside air mixes with the heated air. When intake air temperature is slightly above 100°F (38°C), the valve modulates heated and ambient air to maintain air temperature at about the 100°F (38°C) range. The result is a closely controlled intake air temperature which improves engine performance and reduces emissions.

When the engine is shut off, vacuum to the vacuum motor is no longer present. The spring in the

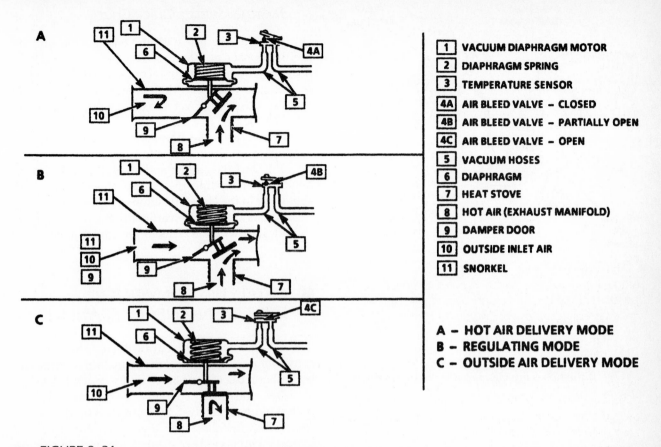

1	VACUUM DIAPHRAGM MOTOR
2	DIAPHRAGM SPRING
3	TEMPERATURE SENSOR
4A	AIR BLEED VALVE – CLOSED
4B	AIR BLEED VALVE – PARTIALLY OPEN
4C	AIR BLEED VALVE – OPEN
5	VACUUM HOSES
6	DIAPHRAGM
7	HEAT STOVE
8	HOT AIR (EXHAUST MANIFOLD)
9	DAMPER DOOR
10	OUTSIDE INLET AIR
11	SNORKEL

A – HOT AIR DELIVERY MODE
B – REGULATING MODE
C – OUTSIDE AIR DELIVERY MODE

■ FIGURE 9–31
Heated air intake operating modes. (Courtesy of General Motors Corporation.)

vacuum motor causes the valve to close the heated air opening and open the fresh air passage. As soon as the cold engine is started, the fresh air passage closes, and the heated air passage opens. Under heavy acceleration (engine cold), intake manifold vacuum will drop, which allows spring pressure to open the temperature control valve and allow denser cold air in to prevent hesitation.

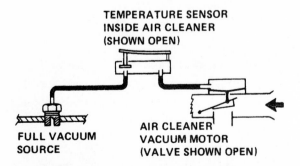

TEMPERATURE SENSOR
INSIDE AIR CLEANER
(SHOWN OPEN)

FULL VACUUM
SOURCE

AIR CLEANER
VACUUM MOTOR
(VALVE SHOWN OPEN)

■ FIGURE 9–32
Bimetal switch senses underhood air cleaner temperatures and controls vacuum supply to vacuum motor. (Courtesy of Ford Motor Co. of Canada Ltd.)

■ HEATED AIR INTAKE DIAGNOSIS AND SERVICE

1.   Inspect the system to be sure that all hoses and ducts are connected.

2.   If the thermal vacuum switch is too warm (above room temperature), cool it down to room temperature with a cool, wet rag.

3.   Start the engine. Watch the damper valve. When the engine is first started, the valve should be closed. As the thermal vacuum switch warms up, the valve should slowly open.

4.   If the valve does not close when the engine is started, check for vacuum at the vacuum motor.

5.   If vacuum is present, check for binding in the valve and operating link. If the valve moves freely, replace the vacuum motor. (Failure of the valve to close is more likely to result from mechanical bind due to a damaged or corroded assembly than from a failed diaphragm. This should be checked first, before replacing the vacuum motor.)

6.   If no vacuum is present, check the hoses for disconnects, cracks, or pinches. Repair or replace as necessary.

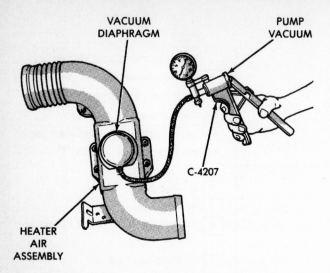

■ FIGURE 9–33
Using a hand-operated vacuum pump to check operation of the vacuum diaphragm in a heated air intake system. (Courtesy of Chrysler Corporation.)

7. If the hoses are OK, replace the thermal vacuum switch.

Vacuum Motor Test

The vacuum motor should move the valve from the full-cold-air position to the full-hot-air position when 5 to 7 in. Hg (34.5 to 48 kPa) vacuum is applied to the motor nipple **(Figure 9–33)**. Disconnect the vacuum hose that runs between the motor and the sensor at the motor nipple. Apply vacuum to the motor with a hand vacuum pump. The door should close. Pinch the hose while the vacuum is still applied and remove the vacuum source. The door should remain closed. If it does not, it indicates a leak in the motor, and the motor assembly should be replaced.

Thermal Sensor Quick Check

1. Start the test with the engine cold and the thermal sensor at a temperature below 77°F (25°C). If the engine has been in recent use, cool the sensor as described earlier. Momentarily disconnect the vacuum hose at the vacuum motor before proceeding with the test.

2. Observe the damper valve before starting the engine. It should be in the open position.

3. Start the engine and allow it to idle. Immediately after starting the engine, the damper valve should be in the closed position.

4. As the engine warms up, the damper valve should start to allow outside air and heated air to enter.

■ CATALYTIC CONVERTER FUNCTION AND OPERATION

Unlike other emission control devices the catalytic converter does not control the formation of emissions but rather reduces emissions to an acceptable level.

The converter contains a ceramic element coated with a catalyst **(Figure 9–34)**. A catalyst causes a chemical reaction that otherwise would not happen. Three kinds of catalyst are used in the catalytic converter: platinum, palladium, and rhodium. The elements (biscuit or pellets) are coated with catalyst material. A stainless steel mesh protects the elements from shock. The entire assembly is contained in a stainless steel shell.

The presence of platinum or palladium with heat and unburned fuel (HC, CO) adds oxygen to the reaction. This is called oxidizing. The oxidation of HC and CO produces H_2O and CO_2. In a combination oxidizing–reducing catalyst, the oxidizing portion uses platinum or palladium and the reduc-

■ FIGURE 9–34
Three-way closed coupled and two-way underfloor converter arrangement with air injection between the two. (Courtesy of Chrysler Corporation.)

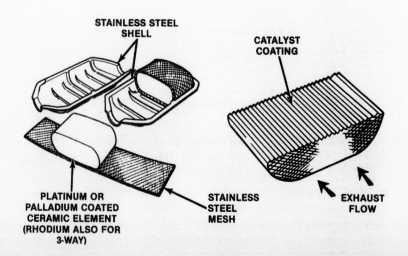

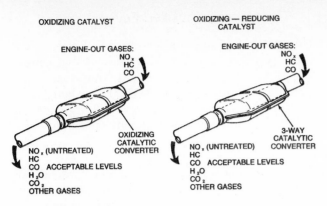

■ FIGURE 9–35

Effects of two-way oxidizing catalyst (left) and three-way oxidizing reducing catalyst (right) on exhaust gases. (Courtesy of Chrysler Corporation.)

ing portion uses rhodium as a catalyst. Rhodium in the presence of heat and NO_x removes oxygen from the compounds. This removal is called "reducing" because it reduces the amount of oxygen remaining in the compound. The complete converter assembly lowers HC, CO, and NO_x and is called a three-way catalyst. This type of converter requires very precise electronic engine control. **(Figure 9–35).**

Two types of three-way converters are used. The smaller type contains a mixture of oxidizing catalyst with reducing catalyst. The larger type contains two elements: an oxidizing catalyst and a three-way catalyst. On the latter type, air from the air injection system is supplied between the two elements. The additional air is used to improve the efficiency of the oxidizing catalyst by adding oxygen in the presence of very high heat and unburned fuel. In some cases, additional air forms NO_x. (It adds oxygen, whereas the reducing catalyst is trying to remove oxygen.) The switching of air is controlled by the air injection system.

On engines without electronic air switching, air is injected into the exhaust ports when the engine starts. The combination of combustion heat, unburned vapors due to rich mixtures, and fresh air begins the oxidation process in the exhaust port or manifold. When this hot, oxidizing mixture enters the converter, the gases flow through the honeycomb openings. The catalyst increases the reaction; much of the HC and CO converts to H_2O and CO_2 (water and carbon dioxide). In the three-way converter, the rhodium catalyst also reacts: It removes oxygen from the various oxides of nitrogen (NO_x) compounds formed during combustion.

On engines with air injection switching, the switch valve is calibrated to redirect air at specified engine temperature. When this occurs, air is injected into the converter assembly. This heightens the

chemical reaction because the converter is very hot. The additional oxygen improves the oxidizing efficiency of the converter. The AIR system is described later in this chapter.

Catalytic Converter Diagnosis and Service

Inspect the catalytic converters (and the entire exhaust system) for leakage or damage that may restrict the flow of exhaust gases. Large dents in the converter can cause flow restriction, converter overheating, and damage to the catalyst. Badly damaged or leaking components must be replaced. Inspect the heat shields for looseness or damage. See Chapter 8 for detailed exhaust system diagnosis and repair and the section on exhaust gas analysis in this chapter to determine catalyst effectiveness.

■ EXHAUST GAS RECIRCULATION SYSTEM FUNCTION AND SERVICE

The purpose of an exhaust gas recirculation system is to reduce oxides of nitrogen in the vehicle exhaust. This system recirculates a portion of the engine exhaust gas back into the induction system **(Figure 9–36).** This reduces combustion temperatures to reduce NO_x emissions since exhaust gases are inert and do not burn. Control of the exhaust gas recirculation rate is accomplished by several different methods as follows.

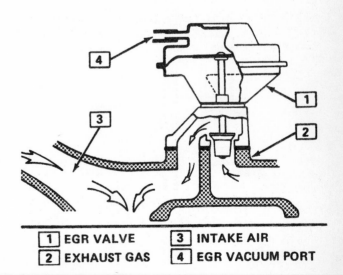

| 1 | EGR VALVE | 3 | INTAKE AIR |
| 2 | EXHAUST GAS | 4 | EGR VACUUM PORT |

■ FIGURE 9–36

Basic EGR valve operation. (Courtesy of General Motors Corporation.)

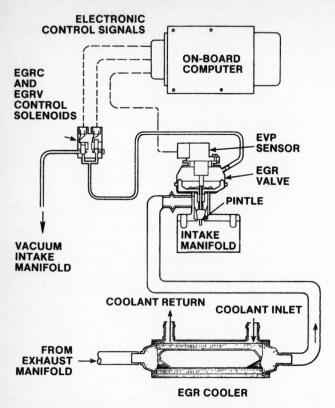

■ FIGURE 9–37
Example of electrically controlled EGR system.
(Courtesy of Ford Motor Company.)

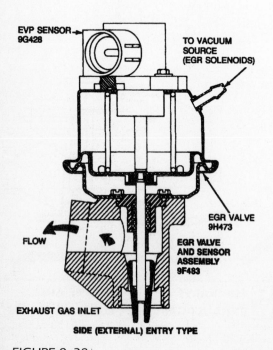

■ FIGURE 9–38
Electronic EGR valve with position sensor. (Courtesy of
Ford Motor Company.)

Computer-Controlled EGR

This system typically consists of the EGR valve, EGR valve position sensor, EGR vacuum valve control solenoid, exhaust back pressure transducer, and computer (**Figures 9–37 to 9–39**). The exhaust back pressure transducer generates a voltage signal that is sent to the computer. The EGR valve position sensor also sends a signal to the computer. The computer controls the EGR vacuum valve control solenoid to regulate the vacuum applied to the EGR valve. This controls how far the EGR valve will open and how much exhaust gas is allowed to enter the engine.

Pressure Feedback Electronic EGR System

This system controls the flow rate of exhaust gases into the intake by monitoring the pressure drop across a metering orifice connected to the engine exhaust. A pressure transducer sends a voltage signal to the electronic control unit in proportion to the pressure drop. The electronic control unit generates a duty-cycle output signal to control the EGR valve. An exhaust back pressure signal may also send a signal to the pressure transducer (**Figure 9–40**).

Ported Vacuum Control System

The ported vacuum control system utilizes a port in the throttle body, which is progressively exposed to an increasing percentage of manifold vacuum as the throttle plates open. This throttle body port is connected to the EGR valve by means of a hose. The flow rate is dependent on manifold vacuum, throttle position, and exhaust gas back pressure.

Venturi Vacuum Control System (Carbureted Engines)

The venturi vacuum control system uses a vacuum tap at the throat of the carburetor venturi to provide a control signal. Because of the low value of this signal, it is necessary to use a vacuum control unit (amplifier) to increase the signal strength to the level required to operate the valve. The amplifier uses manifold vacuum to provide the source of amplification. Elimination of EGR at wide-open throttle operation (WOT) is accomplished by a dump diaphragm that compares venturi and manifold vacuum to determine when WOT is achieved. At WOT, vacuum is dumped, limiting output to the EGR valve to manifold vacuum, which is at or near zero. As in the ported control system, the valve opening is set above the manifold vacuum available at WOT, permitting the valve to be closed at WOT. This system is dependent on engine intake airflow as

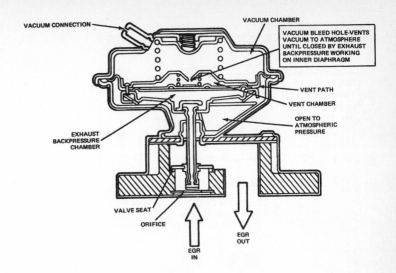

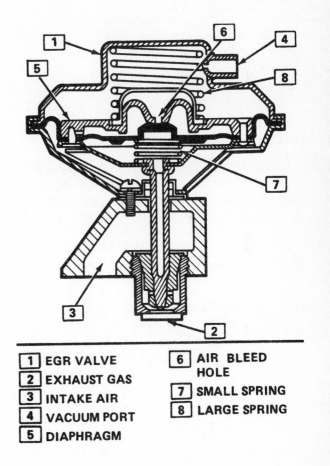

■ FIGURE 9–39
Integrated EGR valve and positive exhaust backpressure transducer (top). (Courtesy of Ford Motor Company.)
Negative back pressure EGR valve (bottom). This valve has the small spring on the opposite side of the diagram from the positive back pressure valve. (Courtesy of General Motors Corporation.)

1 EGR VALVE	**6** AIR BLEED HOLE
2 EXHAUST GAS	
3 INTAKE AIR	**7** SMALL SPRING
4 VACUUM PORT	**8** LARGE SPRING
5 DIAPHRAGM	

indicated by the venturi signal, and is also affected by intake vacuum and exhaust gas back pressure.

On some engines, an external vacuum reservoir tank is mounted on a bracket that is attached to the vacuum amplifier. The purpose of this external reservoir is to provide additional manifold vacuum as the source for amplification, if the vacuum in the amplifier has been dumped. The reservoir will provide manifold vacuum for EGR until the amplifier vacuum supply can be replenished.

Coolant Control Valve

Both the ported vacuum and venturi vacuum EGR control systems utilize an engine temperature-controlled exhaust gas recirculation control feature. The coolant temperature control valve opens so that vacuum is applied to the EGR valve, allowing exhaust gas to recirculate in the normal manner when specified coolant temperature is reached but not before.

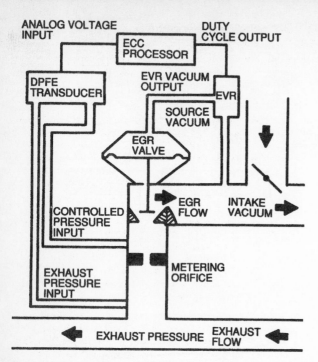

■   FIGURE 9–40
Pressure feedback electronic EGR system. (Courtesy of Chrysler Corporation.)

EGR Delay System

Some vehicles are equipped with an EGR delay system having an electrical timer mounted in the engine compartment, which controls an engine-mounted solenoid. The solenoid is connected by "tees" between the manifold vacuum source and the vacuum amplifier. The purpose of this system is to prevent exhaust gas recirculation for approximately 35 seconds after the ignition is turned on.

EGR System Diagnosis and Service

EGR System Inspection

A failed or malfunctioning EGR system could cause engine spark knock, hesitation, rough idle, and engine stalling. To ensure proper operation of the EGR system, all passages and moving parts must be free of deposits that could cause plugging or sticking. Ensure that the system hoses do not leak. Replace leaking components.

Inspect hose connections between intake manifold, EGR solenoid and transducer, and the EGR valve. Replace hardened, cracked, or damaged hoses. Replace faulty hoses.

EGR Valve and Control System Test

WARNING: APPLY PARKING BRAKE AND/OR BLOCK WHEELS BEFORE PERFORMING EGR SYSTEM TEST.

Check the EGR control system and EGR valve with the engine fully warmed up and running (engine coolant temperature over 170°F). With the transmission in neutral and the throttle closed, allow the engine to idle for 70 seconds. Abruptly accelerate the engine to approximately 2000 rpm, but not over 3000 rpm. The EGR valve stem should move when accelerating the engine. Repeat the test several times to confirm movement. If the EGR valve stem moves, the control system is operating normally. If the control system is not operating normally, refer to the appropriate diagnosis chart in the service manual to determine the cause. A typical EGR diagnosis chart is shown in **Figure 9–41.**

EGR Gas Flow Test

To determine if exhaust gas is flowing through the EGR system, connect a hand vacuum pump to the EGR valve vacuum motor **(Figure 9–42).** With engine running at idle speed, slowly apply vacuum. Engine speed should begin to drop when applied vacuum reaches 2.0 to 3.5 inches. Engine speed may drop quickly or engine may even stall. This indicates that EGR gas is flowing through the system.

If engine speed does not drop off when performing the test, remove both the EGR valve and EGR tube and check for plugged passages. Check and if necessary, clean these components for restoration of proper flow. Replace as necessary. Backpressure EGR valves may be tested as shown in **Figure 9–43.**

■   AIR INJECTION SYSTEM FUNCTION AND SERVICE

An air injection system is used to reduce carbon monoxide and hydrocarbons. The system adds a controlled amount of air to exhaust gases, causing oxidation of the gases and reduction of carbon monoxide and hydrocarbons in the exhaust stream **(Figure 9–44).**

Depending on system design and the make, year, and model of vehicle, air may be injected into one or more of the following locations:

- Exhaust ports in the cylinder head
- Exhaust manifold ports
- Exhaust pipe
- Catalytic converter
- Pipe between two converters

Air from the air injection system is used to pressure purge the charcoal canister in some systems. Air may be diverted from being injected into the exhaust gases by diverting it to one of the following:

ALL TESTS MUST BE MADE WITH FULLY WARM ENGINE RUNNING CONTINUOUSLY FOR AT LEAST TWO MINUTES.

WARNING: APPLY PARKING BRAKE AND/OR BLOCK WHEELS BEFORE PERFORMING TESTS.

Condition	Possible Cause	Correction
EGR VALVE STEM DOES NOT MOVE ON SYSTEM TEST.	(a) Cracked, leaking, disconnected or plugged hoses.	(a) Verify correct hose connections and leak check and confirm that all hoses are open. If defective hoses are found, replace hose harness.
		(b) Disconnect hose harness from EGR vacuum transducer and connect auxiliary vacuum supply. Raise engine rpm to 2000 rpm and hold. Apply 10" Hg vacuum while checking valve movement. If no valve movement occurs, replace valve/transducer assy. If valve opens (approx. 3 mm or 1/8" travel), hold supply vacuum to check for diaphragm leakage. Valve should remain open 30 seconds or longer. If leakage occurs, replace valve/transducer assy. If valve is satisfactory, check control system.
EGR VALVE STEM DOES NOT MOVE ON SYSTEM TEST. OPERATES NORMALLY ON EXTERNAL VACUUM SOURCE.	(a) Defective control system— plugged passages.	(a) Inspect and clean vacuum supply and back pressure passages. Use suitable solvent to remove deposits and check for flow with light air pressure. Normal operation should be restored to EGR system.
	(b) Defective control system— solenoid or solenoid control circuit.	(b) Refer to the DRB scan tool and the appropriate Powertrain Diagnostic Manual.
ENGINE WILL NOT IDLE. DIES OUT ON RETURN TO IDLE OR IDLE IS VERY ROUGH OR SLOW.	(a) High EGR valve leakage in closed position.	(a) If removal of vacuum hose from EGR valve does not correct rough idle,
		(a1) Turn engine off. Remove the air cleaner exposing the inlet to the throttle body.
		(a2) Disconnect the backpressure hose from the EGR valve.
		(a3) Using a nozzle with a rubber grommet connection, direct compressed air (50 to 60 psi) down through the steel backpressure tube on the EGR valve while opening and closing the throttle blade.
		(a4) If the sound from the compressed air changes distinctly in step a3, the poppet is leaking and air is entering the intake manifold. Replace the EGR valve.
	(b) EGR tube to intake manifold leak.	(b) Remove tube and visually inspect tube seal on gasket. Tube end should be uniformly indented on gasket with no signs of leak. If signs of exhaust gas leakage are present, replace gaskets and tighten flange nuts to 23 N·m (200 in. lbs.). If an intake plenum leak persists, replace EGR tube and gaskets, following installation instructions.
	(c) Solenoid or control signal to solenoid failure.	(c) Verify correct hose connections and leak check and confirm that all hoses are open. If defective hoses are found, replace hose harness.
		(c1) Refer to the DRB scan tool and the appropriate Powertrain Diagnostic Manual.

NOTE: DO NOT ATTEMPT TO CLEAN BACKPRESSURE EGR VALVE, REPLACE ENTIRE VALVE/TRANSDUCER ASSEMBLY IF NECESSARY.

■   FIGURE 9–41

Typical EGR diagnosis chart. Refer to the appropriate service manual for specific procedures for the vehicle being serviced. (Courtesy of Chrysler Corporation.)

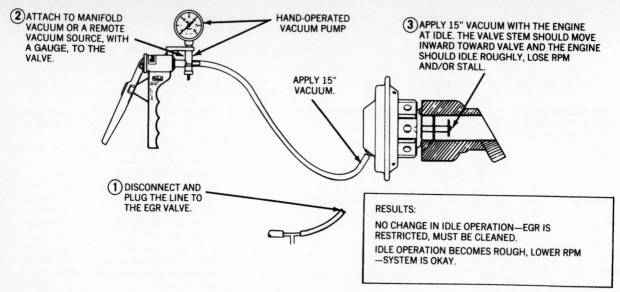

② ATTACH TO MANIFOLD VACUUM OR A REMOTE VACUUM SOURCE, WITH A GAUGE, TO THE VALVE.

HAND-OPERATED VACUUM PUMP

③ APPLY 15" VACUUM WITH THE ENGINE AT IDLE. THE VALVE STEM SHOULD MOVE INWARD TOWARD VALVE AND THE ENGINE SHOULD IDLE ROUGHLY, LOSE RPM AND/OR STALL.

APPLY 15" VACUUM.

① DISCONNECT AND PLUG THE LINE TO THE EGR VALVE.

RESULTS:

NO CHANGE IN IDLE OPERATION—EGR IS RESTRICTED, MUST BE CLEANED.

IDLE OPERATION BECOMES ROUGH, LOWER RPM —SYSTEM IS OKAY.

■ FIGURE 9–42

Typical EGR valve functional test. (Courtesy of Ford Motor Company.)

- The atmosphere
- The intake manifold
- The air cleaner

The air injection system consists of a belt-driven air pump, a combination diverter-pressure relief valve, rubber hoses, a check valve to protect the hoses and other components from hot gases, and an injection tube.

Air Injection Pump

The belt-driven air pump is mounted on the front of the engine **(Figure 9–45)**. This vane-type pump is driven from the crankshaft pulley and supplies a high volume of air at low pressure to the exhaust system. Air enters through a centrifugal filter fan at the front of the pump.

Diverter Valve

The purpose of the diverter valve is to prevent backfire in the exhaust system during sudden deceleration. Sudden throttle closure at the beginning of deceleration temporarily creates an air–fuel mixture too rich to burn. This mixture becomes burnable when it reaches the exhaust area and combines with injector air. The next firing of the engine will ignite this air–fuel mixture. The diverter valve senses the sudden increase in intake manifold vacuum, causing the valve to open and allowing air from the air pump to divert through the valve **(Figures 9–46 and 9–47)**.

A pressure relief valve, incorporated in the same housing as the diverter valve, controls pressure within the system by diverting excessive pump output at higher engine speeds to the

■ FIGURE 9–43

Testing GM backpressure EGR valves. (Courtesy of General Motors Corporation.)

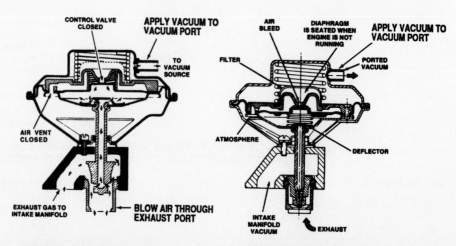

CONTROL VALVE CLOSED

APPLY VACUUM TO VACUUM PORT

TO VACUUM SOURCE

AIR VENT CLOSED

EXHAUST GAS TO INTAKE MANIFOLD

BLOW AIR THROUGH EXHAUST PORT

POSITIVE BACKPRESSURE

AIR BLEED

DIAPHRAGM IS SEATED WHEN ENGINE IS NOT RUNNING

APPLY VACUUM TO VACUUM PORT

FILTER

PORTED VACUUM

ATMOSPHERE

DEFLECTOR

INTAKE MANIFOLD VACUUM

EXHAUST

NEGATIVE BACKPRESSURE

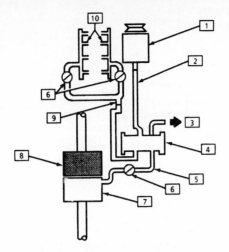

1 AIR PUMP
2 AIR TO AIR CONTROL VALVE
3 RELIEF PLUS DIVERT AIR TO ATMOSPHERE
4 AIR CONTROL VALVE (PEDES)
5 AIR TO OXIDIZING CATALYST
6 CHECK VALVE
7 OXIDIZING CATALYST
8 REDUCING CATALYST
9 AIR TO EXHAUST PORTS
10 AIR INJECTION PIPES

■ FIGURE 9–44
Air injection reaction (AIR) system schematic. Also called secondary air system. (Courtesy of General Motors Corporation.)

atmosphere through the silencer. A one-way check valve is located in the injection tube assembly. This valve prevents hot exhaust gases from backing up into the hose and pump. This valve will protect the system in the event of pump belt failure, abnormally high exhaust system pressure, or air hose ruptures.

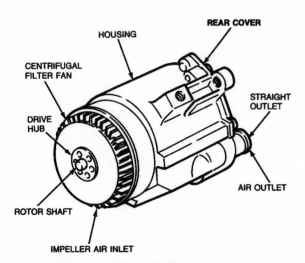

■ FIGURE 9–45
Air injection pump. (Courtesy of Ford Motor Company.)

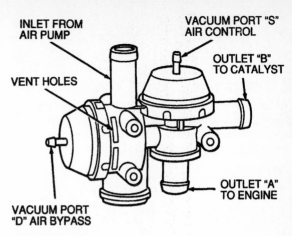

■ FIGURE 9–46
Combination air bypass and air control valve. (Courtesy of Ford Motor Company.)

Computer-Controlled Air Injection System

The computer system is used to inject air into the exhaust port of the cylinder head, exhaust manifold, or the catalytic converter. The system operates at all times and will bypass air during high speeds and loads on ECM command. The air management valve performs the bypass or divert function, and the check valve protects the air pump from damage by preventing a backflow of exhaust gas.

The AIR system helps reduce hydrocarbons (HC) and carbon monoxide (CO) contained in the exhaust gases by injecting air into the exhaust manifold during cold engine operation **(Figure 9–48).** This air injection helps the catalytic converter

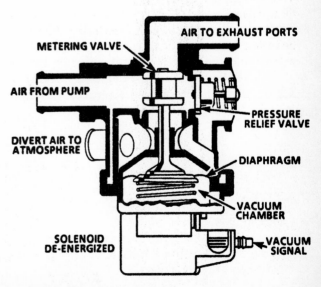

■ FIGURE 9–47
Electronically controlled AIR valve. (Courtesy of General Motors Corporation.)

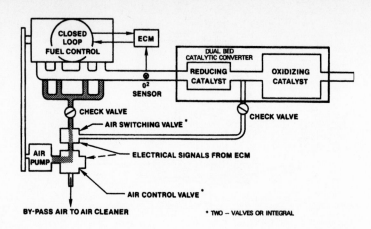

■ FIGURE 9–48
Typical air injection system in open-loop operation. Shaded areas show airflow. (Courtesy of General Motors Corporation.)

quickly reach proper operating temperature during warm-up. When the engine is warm or is in closed-loop mode **(Figure 9–49)**, the AIR system injects air between the beds of a dual-bed catalytic converter and diverts air on three-way converter to lower the HC and CO in the exhaust. The system utilizes the following components:

- Engine-driven AIR pump
- AIR management valves (air control, air switching, three-way air divert)
- AIR flow and control hoses
- Check valves
- Dual-bed catalytic converter
- Single-bed catalytic converter

When the engine is cold, the ECM energizes an AIR control solenoid. This allows air to flow to an AIR switching valve. The AIR switching valve is energized to direct air to the exhaust ports **(Figure 9–50)**.

Pulse Air System

Some engines have a pulse air system **(Figure 9–51)**. This valve utilizes exhaust pressure pulsation to draw air into the exhaust system, reducing carbon monoxide (CO) and, to a lesser degree, hydrocarbon (HC) emissions. It draws fresh air from the "clean" side of the air cleaner past a one-way valve.

The valve opens to allow fresh air to mix with the exhaust gases during negative pressure (vacuum) pulses that occur in the exhaust ports and manifold passages. If the pressure is positive, the valve closes, and no exhaust gas is allowed to flow past the valve and into the clean side of the air cleaner. The aspirator valve works most efficiently at idle and slightly off idle, where the negative pulses are maximum. At higher engine speeds, the aspirator valve remains closed.

Air Injection System Problems and Diagnosis

No Air Injection

If no air is being injected into the manifold or catalytic converter HC and CO exhaust emissions will be too high. No air injection may be caused by: 1) a broken air pump drive belt, 2) a damaged or seized air pump, or 3) the air bypass valve stuck in the bypass mode.

Continuous Air Injection

Air injected continuously into the exhaust system can cause the catalytic converter to overheat and cause damage to the catalyst. The cause may be a diverter valve stuck in the injection mode.

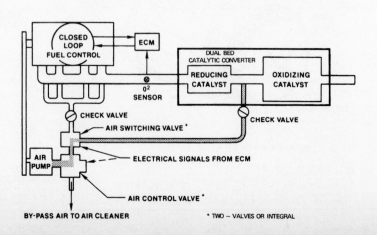

■ FIGURE 9–49
Air injection system in closed-loop operation. Note airflow directed between catalysts. (Courtesy of General Motors Corporation.)

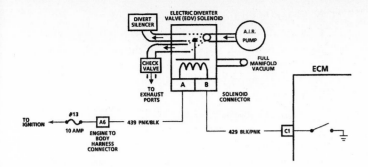

■ FIGURE 9–50
Electronically controlled air diverter valve schematic. (Courtesy of General Motors Corporation.)

Testing the Air Injection System

A four gas exhaust gas analyzer may be used to perform a system operational test. Run the engine at idle speed with the air injection system in the operating mode. Measure the oxygen (O_2) content in the exhaust and record the result. Disable the air injection system by removing the air pump drive belt or by pinching the air distribution hose shut. Measure the oxygen content again (with the AIR system disabled) and compare the two readings. With the system disabled the O_2 content should be between 2 to 5% lower than with air injection. If the two readings are the same the air injection system is not functioning and component testing may be required.

Check to see if the air pump pulley turns freely. If the air pump drive belt is missing or damaged it should be replaced. To test air pump output disconnect the pump output line and check output pressure with the engine running **(Figure 9–52)**. There should be about 2 to 3 psi (14 to 21 kPa) pressure. Replace the pump if it is seized or if there is no output pressure. Since there are many air switching valve designs refer to the service manual for test procedures.

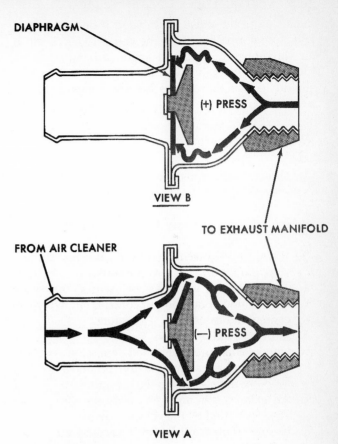

■ FIGURE 9–51
Aspirator valve operates to positive and negative exhaust pressures. (Courtesy of Chrysler Corporation.)

Pulse Air System Check

Inspect all hoses, lines, and connections for leaks or damage. Use a four gas analyzer to measure O_2 content with the system operational and again with the system disabled just as with the air injection system described earlier. If the readings are the same check

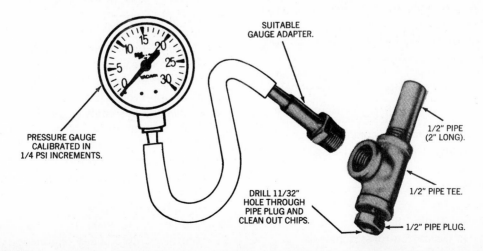

■ FIGURE 9–52
Gauge and adapter for testing air pump output. (Courtesy of Ford Motor Company.)

the action of the pulse air valve. If it does not open and close normally replace the valve. To check pulse air valve operation place a finger or hand over the inlet side of the valve with the engine running. You should feel suction pulses but there should be no pressure pulses.

Review Questions

1. Vehicle emissions come from three major sources, they are (1) _____ (2) _____ and (3) _____.
2. Ingredients necessary to form smog are _____ _____ and _____.
3. When lead was removed from gasoline, engines were built with _____ valve seats.
4. The exhaust gas oxygen sensor provides information about oxygen content. High oxygen content indicates a _____ mixture.
5. The abbreviation EGR is _____ _____ _____.
6. On a computer-controlled emission control system, when a malfunction occurs a _____ _____ will be stored in the computer.
7. An exhaust gas analyzer measures the _____ _____ emitted by the vehicle exhaust.
8. Hydrocarbon readings are measured in _____ _____ _____.
9. Carbon monoxide readings are measured in _____.
10. The escape of raw gas vapors into the air emits harmful _____ into the atmosphere.
11. Some PCV testers are available to test the system. True or False.
12. When testing the P.C.V. system, if the P.C.V. valve is faulty it should be _____.
13. When servicing the heated air intake system when the engine is first started the valve should be _____.
14. A three-way catalytic converter lowers _____, _____, and _____.
15. An over rich fuel air mixture will cause the catalytic converter to _____.
16. The purpose of the E.G.R. valve is to lower combustion chamber temperature. True or False.
17. The air injection pump supplies a _____ _____ of air at _____ _____ to the exhaust system.
18. An overheated catalytic converter may be caused by a faulty A.I.R. system. True or False.

Test Questions

1. The function of the charcoal canister in the evaporative emission control system is to
   a. evaporate overflow fuel and vent it to atmosphere
   b. separate liquid from vapor
   c. provide constant ventilation of the fuel bowl
   d. store raw fuel vapors when the engine is not running
2. Hydrocarbon emission results from
   a. lean mixture
   b. high combustion temperature
   c. engine misfiring
   d. using the wrong fuel
3. The four-gas infrared analyzer measures the exhaust gases for content of
   a. HC, CO, CO_2, O_2
   b. HC, CO_2, NO_2, O
   c. O, NO_x, CO_2, O_2
   d. O_2, HC_2, NO_x, CO
4. To diagnose computer-controlled emission control systems faults
   a. a scan tool may be used
   b. access the fault codes stored in the computer
   c. use an exhaust gas analyzer
   d. all of the above
5. When using an exhaust gas analyzer take readings only after
   a. calibrating the meters
   b. meter reading becomes stabilized
   c. allowing the engine and analyzer to reach operating temperature
   d. all of the above
6. Hydrocarbon content of exhaust gases is measured in
   a. ppm
   b. percentage
   c. cubic centimeters
   d. cubic inches
7. A lower than normal content of CO in the exhaust results from
   a. too lean an air–fuel mixture
   b. too rich an air–fuel mixture
   c. a cold engine
   d. a hot engine
8. If carbon dioxide content in the exhaust exceeds the oxygen content,
   a. the air–fuel ratio is too rich
   b. the air–fuel ratio is too lean
   c. the EGR system is inoperative
   d. the canister purge valve is stuck closed
9. To test EGR valve operation
   a. use a hand vacuum pump
   b. run the engine only at idle
   c. use a stethoscope
   d. none of the above
10. If there is no vacuum at the canister purge control solenoid at any engine operating mode,
    a. check supply voltage to the solenoid
    b. check the vacuum lines to the solenoid

c. check solenoid operation

d. all of the above

11. To check the heated air intake system for operation, use

a. a vacuum gauge in the line

b. a temperature gauge

c. an air velocity gauge

d. a pressure gauge

12. The main purpose for adding air-preheat to engines is to

a. reduce the level of harmful emissions

b. reduce carburetor icing to the minimum

c. improve engine starting

d. prevent engine from freezing up during below-zero temperatures

13. What effect does engine misfiring have on a catalytic converter?

a. no effect

b. temperature of the converter climbs

c. temperature of the converter goes down

d. temperature stays the same but the ceramic core is destroyed

14. The condition created by the catalytic converter that is the most dangerous is

a. high exhaust backpressure

b. high exhaust system temperatures

c. excessive weight

d. excessive cost to vehicle

15. The position of the PCV plunger is controlled by

a. intake manifold vacuum and spring pressure

b. exhaust manifold pressure

c. temperature

d. atmospheric pressure

10

Cooling System Diagnosis and Service

INTRODUCTION

Only a small part of the heat produced by an automotive engine is used to produce power. Some of it is discharged through the exhaust and some is dissipated into the atmosphere by radiation. A large percentage must be removed from the engine by the cooling system. This chapter discusses the function, design, operation, and service of the cooling system and its components. A thorough understanding of cooling system principles is needed to be able to diagnose and service cooling system problems.

LEARNING OBJECTIVES

After completing this chapter, you should be able to:
- Describe the functions of the cooling system.
- List the components of the liquid cooling system.
- Describe the operation of the liquid cooling system and its components.
- Describe the kinds of problems that cooling systems may develop.
- Diagnose and test a cooling system and its components to identify faults.
- Repair or replace faulty components to restore normal cooling system operation.

TERMS YOU SHOULD KNOW

Look for these terms as you study this chapter and learn what they mean.

air cooled	pressure relief valve
liquid cooled	vacuum valve
water pump	screw clamp
radiator	spring clamp
shroud	ethylene glycol
reservoir	antifreeze
fan	variable pitch
electric fan	fluid fan clutch
thermostat	electric drive fan
bypass	temperature indicator
hoses	fins
clamps	blower
block heater	air ducts
heater core	pressure test
impeller	combustion leak
cross flow	electrolysis
vertical flow	glazed belt
radiator cap	belt tension

■ COOLING SYSTEM FUNCTION

The automotive engine cooling system performs the following functions:

1. Helps warm up a cold engine as quickly as possible after starting
2. Removes excess heat from the engine
3. Maintains the engine at its most efficient operating temperature
4. Provides heat for the passenger compartment when needed

There are two kinds of cooling systems: air and liquid. The majority of automobiles use the liquid cooling system.

■ LIQUID COOLING SYSTEM COMPONENTS

The major components of a liquid cooling system include the following (see **Figures 10–1** and **10–2**).

1. *Water pump:* pumps coolant through engine and radiator
2. *Water jackets:* contain coolant surrounding engine cylinders and combustion chambers
3. *Radiator:* transfers heat from coolant in radiator to air flowing through radiator fins
4. *Coolant recovery reservoir:* stores coolant expelled from radiator as coolant expands due to increased temperature
5. *Fan:* causes airflow through radiator
6. *Thermostat:* controls engine operating temperature by controlling coolant circulation through engine and radiator
7. *Bypass:* allows water pump to circulate coolant through engine when thermostat is closed
8. *Heater core:* transfers heat from engine coolant to passenger compartment by coolant and air flowing through heater core
9. *Hoses:* connect cooling system components to each other to provide coolant circulation
10. *Engine block heater:* provides electrical heat to engine coolant to warm up engine and aid starting in cool weather

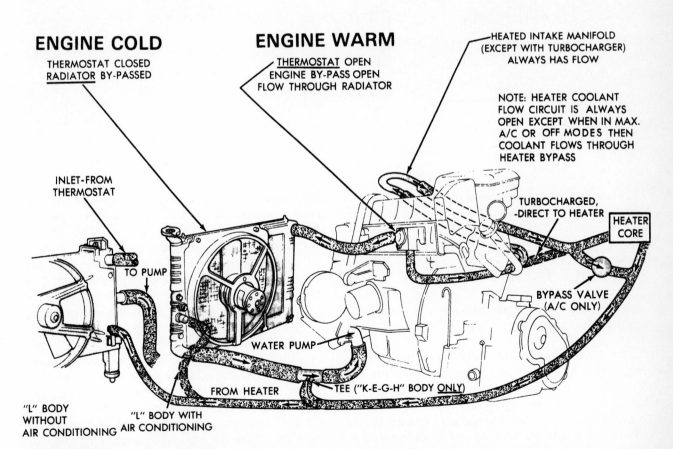

■ FIGURE 10–1

Cooling system components (typical) for electric drive fan cooling system. (Courtesy of Chrysler Corporation.)

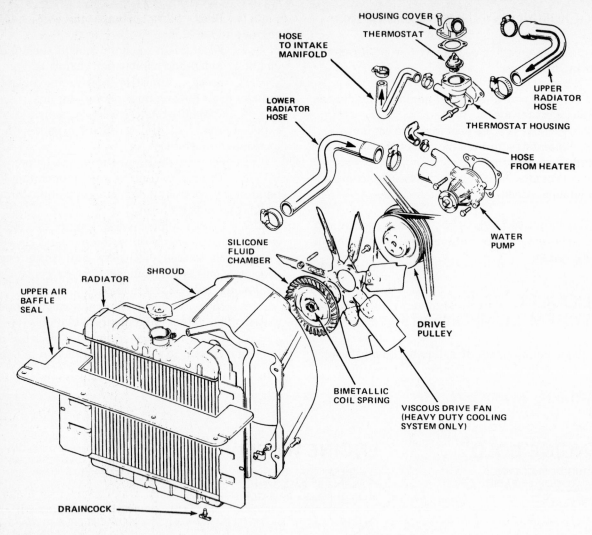

■   FIGURE 10–2
Cooling system with engine-driven fan. (Courtesy of Chrysler Corporation.)

11.   *Transmission oil cooler:* removes heat from automatic transmission fluid

■ COOLING SYSTEM SERVICE PRECAUTIONS

Some special precautions should be observed, including the following:

1.   Never remove the radiator cap under any conditions while the engine is operating. Failure to follow these instructions could result in damage to the cooling system or engine and in personal injury. To avoid having scalding hot coolant or steam blow out of the radiator, use extreme care when removing the cap from a hot radiator. If possible, wait until the engine has cooled, then wrap a thick cloth around the radiator cap and turn it slowly to the first stop.

Step back while the pressure is released from the cooling system. When you are sure all the pressure has been released, press down on the cap (still with the cloth), turn, and remove it.

2.   Always be careful not to make contact with rotating parts such as fans, pulleys, and belts. Contact can easily be made if careful attention is not given to staying clear of these items with hands, tools, or clothing.

3.   Never stand in the plane of a fast-turning fan. Fan blades have been known to separate from a turning fan, flying off in any direction at a very high speed. This could cause injury, death, or damage to vehicles. The fan should always be closely examined for any cracks (sometimes barely visible) before running the engine during underhood testing and diagnosis.

4.   Always be aware of the danger of burns and scalding from hot engine parts and hot coolant.

Never remove any parts from the cooling system that will release hot coolant unexpectedly.

5. Be careful of electric-drive cooling fans. Many of them will start turning at any time after the engine has been shut down due to heat soak.

6. **CAUTION:** Do not dump antifreeze or harmful chemicals down the drain. Obtain a proper drain pan large enough and of sufficient capacity to contain all the engine's antifreeze including any that drips from surrounding parts during the draining procedure. Recover and reclaim the antifreeze or dispose of it in the manner prescribed by law.

■ COOLING SYSTEM PROBLEM DIAGNOSIS

Cooling system diagnostic procedures are outlined in **Figure 10–3.** Study these charts carefully.

■ COOLING SYSTEM INSPECTION AND TESTING

Airflow Obstruction

Obstructions restricting air circulation through the radiator can cause overheating. Obstruction can be caused by insects, leaves, or even mud plugging the radiator. Thorough cleaning with compressed air or water will correct this problem. A net type of bug screen mounted on the radiator or air conditioning condenser can sufficiently reduce airflow to cause overheating in hot weather.

Coolant Inspection

Inspect coolant level and condition. Coolant should be of the correct type and at the proper level. Antifreeze should be tested for proper strength and corrected if necessary. Several different types of testers are available for this purpose. Coolant should also be clean. Rust or contamination can reduce flow and the ability to absorb heat.

If the coolant is contaminated, it should be drained and the entire cooling system thoroughly flushed to remove as much of the contamination as possible. Used coolant must be disposed of in a manner that meets environmental regulations or be saved for recycling.

Specific Gravity of Coolant (Freeze Protection)

To test the freeze protection of the coolant use a cooling system hydrometer. The hydrometer has a built in thermometer. The specific gravity of coolant should preferably be tested when the coolant is at operating temperature. To perform the test proceed as follows.

1. With the engine at operating temperature first release cooling system pressure then carefully remove the radiator cap. **CAUTION:** Use shop towels to protect hands from hot vapors and coolant.

2. Insert the hydrometer tube into the coolant and draw a sample of coolant into the hydrometer. Return the sample into the radiator. Repeat this 4 or 5 times to stabilize the temperature of the hydrometer. Follow the hydrometer manufacturer's instructions to adjust the temperature index of the hydrometer.

3. Draw enough coolant into the hydrometer to raise the float off the bottom. Hold the hydrometer in a vertical position to prevent the float from sticking to the sides of the glass tube **(Figure 10–4).**

4. Read the level on the float (holding the hydrometer at eye level) at which the coolant level contacts the float. Return the coolant sample to the radiator.

5. Compare the reading to the manufacturer's specific gravity and freeze protection chart to determine the degree of freeze protection provided by the coolant.

If freeze protection is too low the preferred method of correction is to replace the coolant with the required mix of ethylene glycol coolant and water to provide the desired level of freeze protection. Modern cars usually have a 50/50 mix. This provides good freeze protection as well as the required high boiling point needed.

Electrolysis of the Coolant

Electrolysis of the coolant (the coolant becoming an electrolyte) may occur as the result of poor electrical ground connections between the engine and the chassis. Electrolysis may cause silicone separation and jelling of the coolant, thereby clogging coolant passages and causing overheating. The coolant sensor may become coated and cause improper signals to be sent to the engine control computer. The result may be costly engine damage.

Electrolysis may be detected by using a digital voltmeter to check the coolant. Connect the positive probe to the radiator and the negative probe in the coolant and observe the voltage reading. A reading of 0.2 V is acceptable, 0.3 to 0.6 V is borderline, and 0.7 V or over requires system draining, flushing, and new coolant installed.

COOLING SYSTEM DIAGNOSIS

TO AVOID NEEDLESS TIME AND COST IN DIAGNOSING COOLING SYSTEM COMPLAINTS, THE CUSTOMER SHOULD BE QUESTIONED ABOUT DRIVING CONDITIONS THAT PLACE ABNORMAL LOADS ON THE COOLING SYSTEMS.

1. DOES OVERHEATING OCCUR WHILE PULLING A TRAILER?

If answer is "Yes"—how heavy is the trailer? If trailer weight is greater than 1,000 lbs. and the car is equipped with normal duty cooling system, a heavy duty cooling system is required (per trailer hauling specs.). Further diagnostic checks should not be required.

2. IS OVERHEATING OCCURRING AFTER PROLONGED IDLE IN GEAR, A/C SYSTEM OPERATING?

If answer is "Yes"—instruct owner on driving techniques that would avoid overheating, such as:
a. Idle in Neutral as much as possible-increase engine RPM to get coolant flow through radiator.
b. Turn A/C system off during extended idles if overheating is indicated by hot light or temperature gage. Further diagnostic checks should not be required.

3. IS OVERHEATING OCCURRING AFTER PROLONGED DRIVING IN SLOW CITY TRAFFIC, TRAFFIC JAMS, PARADES, ETC?

If answer is "Yes"—instruct owner on driving techniques that would avoid overheating—same as for prolonged idles—If answer is "No"—Further diagnostic checks should not be required.

IF NONE OF THE ABOVE APPLY, REFER TO CHARTS

CONDITION	POSSIBLE CAUSE	CORRECTION
Engine overheats (Engine Temp. light comes on and stays on. or Temp. Gage shows hot, or coolant overflows from reservoir onto ground while engine is running.)	Loss of coolant.	See "Loss of Coolant" condition below.
	Loss of system pressure.	Pressure check with BT-7002-3 or J-24460-01 with J-23699. Correct as necessary.
	Low coolant protection (should be -35°.)	Test solution.
	Belt tension too low.	Check with BT-7825—Adjust belt, or replace tensioner.
	Ignition timing retarded.	Set timing to specifications. Check neutral/park switch adj.
	Timing retarded by malfunctioning Computer Command Control System.	Check and correct. See Section 6E.
	Radiator fins obstructed.	Remove or relocate added-on parts that block air to radiator, clean away bugs, leaves, etc.
	Cooling system passages blocked by rust of scale.	Flush system—add fresh coolant.
	Reservoir hose pinched or kinked (especially at radiator filler neck.)	Relieve kinks by re-routing. Replace hose if necessary.
	Cooling fan inoperative (or does not operate on higher speed—two speed models.)	See "Electrical Diagnosis".

■ FIGURE 10–3
(Courtesy of General Motors Corporation.)

CONDITION	POSSIBLE CAUSE	CORRECTION
	Loose, damaged and/or missing air seals or deflector.	Repair or replace as required.
	Thermostat stuck in closed position.	Replace Thermostat.
	Malfunctioning water pump (eroded or broken impeller blades).	Replace water pump.
	Incorrect radiator	Check usage chart and if needed, replace radiator
Loss of Coolant.	Leaking radiator	Inspect radiator
	Cooling system pressure cap faulty, or filler neck distorted	Inspect cooling system and pressure check with BT-7002-3 or J-24460-01 with J-23669.
	Leaking coolant reservoir or hose.	Replace reservoir or hose.
	Loose or damaged hoses or connections.	Reseat or replace hoses or clamps.
	Water pump seal leaking.	Replace water pump.
	Water pump gasket leaking.	Replace gasket.
	Improper cylinder head bolt torque.	Torque bolts or replace cylinder head gasket(s) if required.
	Leaking intake manifold or cylinder head or gaskets, cylinder head or block core plug, heater core (or heater water valve where used).	Repair or replace as neccessary to correct leak.
Engine fails to reach normal operating temperature. (Cool air from heater.)	Thermostat stuck open or wrong type thermostat.	Install new thermostat of correct type and heat range.
	Coolant below add mark.	Add coolant. (Coolant/water solution see section OB for requirements.)
Hot Light "On" or High Temp Gage Reading, no loss of coolant.	Faulty engine temperature switch or circuit.	See "Electrical Diagnosis."

■ FIGURE 10–3 (cont.)

Checking for Combustion Leaks

The coolant can become contaminated and forced out of the system by a combustion leak into the cooling system. The most accurate method of checking for this type of leak uses a chemical that changes color when it comes in contact with combustion gases during the test. Leakage of this type is not visible externally and may be hard to detect without the proper test equipment. The causes could include head gasket leakage or small cracks in the block or cylinder head. Both of these require fairly extensive engine disassembly to correct.

Pressure Testing the System

Pressure testing the entire cooling system will help in locating external leaks. Internal leaks will show up on the tester if the system is left pressurized (with the tester in place) by a drop in pressure on the test gauge. Inspect all cooling system components for external leaks while the system is pressurized. Do not pressurize the system above rated capacity. Leaks should be corrected as required (Figure 10–5).

The radiator cap should also be pressure tested to assure that the cap will hold system design pressure and open at the specified pressure.

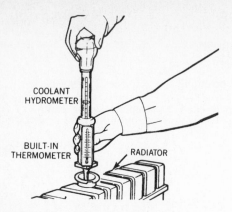

■ FIGURE 10–4
Testing freeze protection of coolant with a hydrometer. (Courtesy of Chrysler Corporation.)

A radiator cap that does not meet specifications must be replaced. A cap that does not hold the pressure it was designed to hold lowers the boiling point of the coolant and can cause boiling and overheating.

Fan Belt Service

Fan belts should be checked to be sure they are in good condition (not glazed, cracked, or worn) and adjusted to the proper tension. Glazed belts or belts not adjusted to the correct tension may slip and cause overheating. Replace belts that are damaged **(Figure 10–6)** and adjust to specifications **(Figure 10–7)** with a belt tension gauge. Some engines have automatic belt tensioners. Make sure that pulleys

and belts are in proper alignment. Correct any misalignment. Pay particular attention to ribbed belt alignment since it is easy to position the belt one groove out at any one pulley **(Figure 10–8)**.

Electric Cooling Fan Service

To check fan operation, note whether the fan operates when the engine is at operating temperature. If the fan does not run, check for a burned fuse, faulty relay, faulty temperature switch, faulty motor ground connection, faulty wiring connectors, or faulty wiring. To check fan motor operation, disconnect the fan motor electrical connector. Apply 12 V to the fan motor **(Figure 10–9)**. If it runs at proper speed, the problem is in the electrical supply circuit items mentioned above. Replace the fuse if it is burned. Clean and tighten the motor ground connection. Check the temperature switch with an ohmmeter. There should be near zero resistance when it is at operating temperature and infinite resistance when it is cold. To check relay operation, disconnect the wiring from the relay and bypass it by using a jumper wire. If the fan operates with the jumper connected, the relay is at fault.

If the fan runs continually, the temperature switch may be at fault. Check it with an ohmmeter **(Figure 10–10)**. If it has no resistance when cold, it should be replaced. If the relay is stuck in the *on* position, it can cause the fan to run continually as long as the temperature switch is closed. In this case it should be replaced.

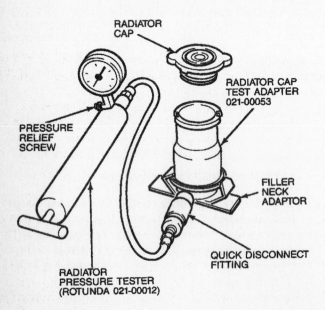

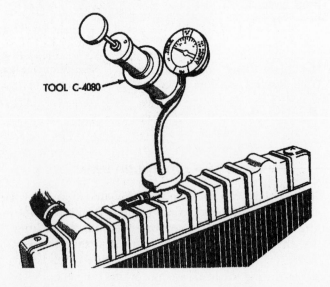

■ FIGURE 10–5
Cooling system pressure tester with radiator cap test adapter (left). (Courtesy of Ford Motor Company.) Pressure testing the cooling system (right). (Courtesy of Chrysler Corporation.)

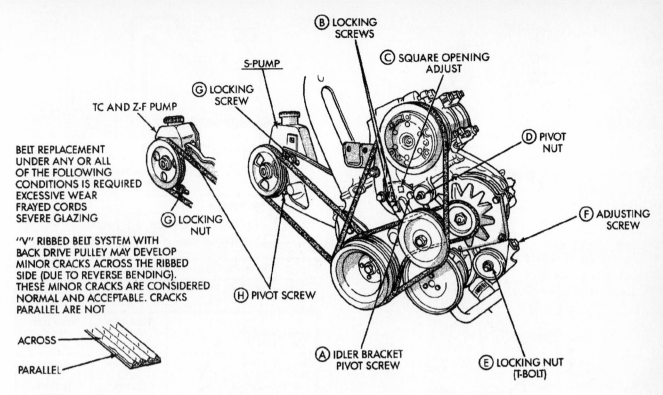

BELT REPLACEMENT UNDER ANY OR ALL OF THE FOLLOWING CONDITIONS IS REQUIRED
EXCESSIVE WEAR
FRAYED CORDS
SEVERE GLAZING

"V" RIBBED BELT SYSTEM WITH BACK DRIVE PULLEY MAY DEVELOP MINOR CRACKS ACROSS THE RIBBED SIDE (DUE TO REVERSE BENDING). THESE MINOR CRACKS ARE CONSIDERED NORMAL AND ACCEPTABLE. CRACKS PARALLEL ARE NOT

ACROSS
PARALLEL

■ FIGURE 10–6
Belt replacement guidelines (typical). (Courtesy of Chrysler Corporation.)

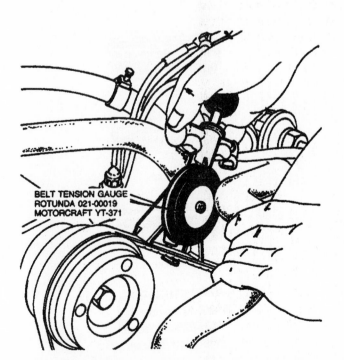

■ FIGURE 10–7
Checking drive belt tension with a belt tension gauge. (Courtesy of Ford Motor Company.)

Hose and Clamp Service

Hoses and clamps should be inspected to assure that there is neither leakage of coolant out of the system nor leakage of air into the system. Swollen hoses or internal hose deterioration can cause restricted coolant circulation and overheating **(Figure 10–11)**. Such hoses should be replaced and installed with properly tightened hose clamps.

If hose clamps are not tight, air may be drawn into the cooling system by the water pump thereby reducing the effectiveness of the cooling system. This may happen even when there is no apparent coolant leak at the problem point. Air in the cooling system will contribute to rust and oxidation, contaminating the coolant. Particular attention should be paid to the inlet hose of the water pump to avoid this problem.

Water Pump Inspection

The water pump should be checked for leakage and for a loose or noisy bearing. This can be done by relieving the belt tension and then grasping the fan or pulley to see if there is any radial movement of the water pump shaft and pulley **(Figure 10–12)**. Feel for any roughness by rotating the fan and pump shaft with a radially applied load. A water pump that leaks or has a rough or loose bearing should be replaced.

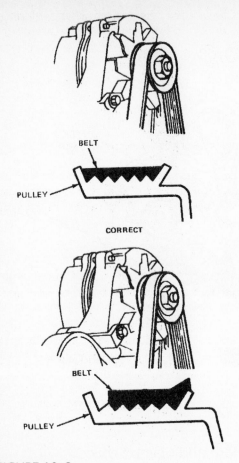

■ FIGURE 10–8
Correct and incorrect ribbed belt alignment. (Courtesy of Ford Motor Company.)

Thermostat Service

To diagnose thermostat operation see **Figure 10–13.** The thermostat, if suspected, should be removed and tested **(Figure 10–14).** The thermostat should remain closed until heated to the rated temperature, and it should be wide open at approximately 10 to 15°F above the temperature stamped on it. If the thermostat does not meet the required specifications, it should be replaced, using a new gasket.

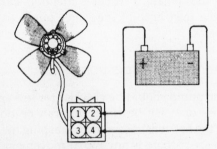

■ FIGURE 10–9
Checking electric drive fan motor operation by applying battery voltage. (Courtesy of Chrysler Corporation.)

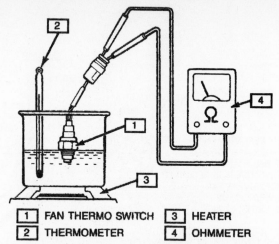

| 1 | FAN THERMO SWITCH | 3 | HEATER |
| 2 | THERMOMETER | 4 | OHMMETER |

Fan thermo switch functional spec. ± 5°C (9°F)		
Switch for thermostat	"A"	"B"
Temp. at switch "ON" (Continuity)	More than 98°C (208°F)	More than 102°C (215°F)
Temp. at switch "OFF" (No continuity)	Less than 93°C (199°F)	Less than 97°C (206°F)

■ FIGURE 10–10
Electric fan thermo switch testing. (Courtesy of General Motors Corporation.)

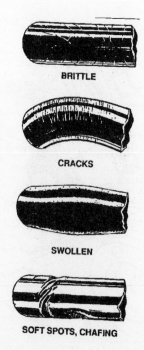

BRITTLE

CRACKS

SWOLLEN

SOFT SPOTS, CHAFING

■ FIGURE 10–11
Radiator hose problems that require hose replacement. (Courtesy of Ford Motor Company.)

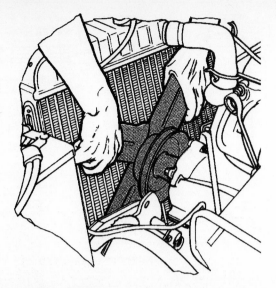

■ FIGURE 10–12
Checking for looseness in the water pump. Grasp the
fan blades and try to move them up and down.
(Courtesy of Chrysler Corporation.)

Care should be exercised when replacing a thermostat not to clamp it between the thermostat housing flange and the cylinder head. If this happens, the thermostat housing will crack when the bolts are tightened. Be sure the thermostat is installed with the temperature-sensitive element toward the engine.

Flushing the Cooling System

The cooling system should be flushed when rust or scale is found in the system. Reverse flushing is most effective. However, there are several other methods that may be used.

Quick Flush

A quick flush can be performed when only minor contamination is present. The coolant is drained and a water hose is connected to the engine heater hose connection. With the block drain open the water is turned on and the engine is flushed. Sometimes sludge accumulation at the block drain will prevent draining. This must be probed with a piece of wire to open it up. Then turn on the water and flush the engine until clean water emerges from the drain. The radiator can also be quick flushed.

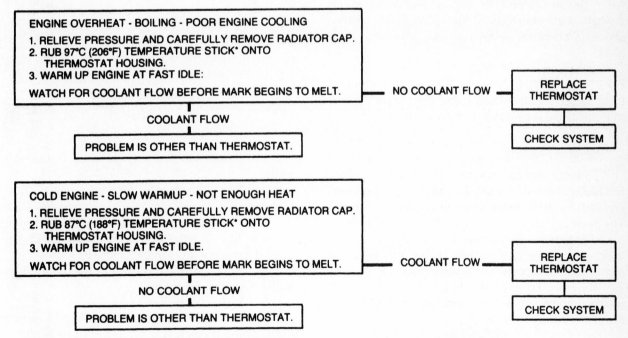

■ FIGURE 10–13
Thermostat diagnosis chart. (Courtesy of General Motors Corporation.)

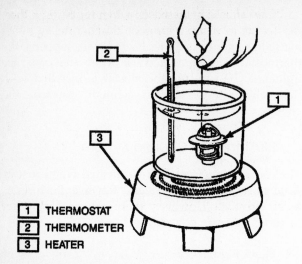

1 THERMOSTAT
2 THERMOMETER
3 HEATER

■ FIGURE 10–14
Testing thermostat operation. (Courtesy of General Motors Corporation.)

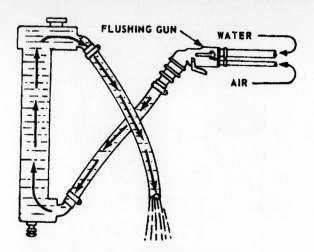

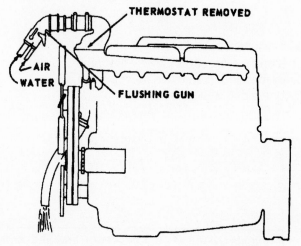

■ FIGURE 10–15
Reverse flushing the radiator with shop air and water with a special flushing gun (top). Reverse flushing head and block (bottom). (Courtesy of Chrysler Corporation.)

Chemical Flush

This method can be used when scale and rust are more severe. A chemical is added to the coolant and the engine is operated for a specified time to allow the chemical to act on the rust and scale. After this treatment the engine and radiator are flushed with water as in the quick-flush method above. A chemical neutralizer may also have to be used.

SAFETY CAUTION: Always follow the manufacturer's instructions when using chemicals. Chemicals can cause severe skin and eye damage.

Reverse Flushing

Both the engine and the radiator can be reverse flushed. A special flushing gun that dispenses water and air for turbulence is required (Figure 10–15). The flushing gun is attached to the lower radiator hose for radiator flushing and to the upper radiator to engine connection on the engine for head and block flushing. Hoses are disconnected for flushing as shown. Follow equipment manufacturer's instructions for air and water pressures required and for procedures.

Filling the System with Coolant

After all necessary flushing and cooling system repairs are made, the system should be filled with the recommended coolant as follows:

1. Close the drain cocks and install drain plugs.
2. Turn the heater temperature control to high.
3. Add coolant to the system until the radiator remains full. If equipped with an air bleed valve open it to let out any air, then close it.
4. Add additional coolant to the required level in the coolant reserve tank.
5. Install the radiator cap.
6. Start the engine and run until operating temperature is reached.
7. Switch the heater blower fan on; if the heater produces heat, the heater core is full; if not, accelerate the engine several times to remove the air lock from the heater until heat is produced.
8. Switch the engine off.

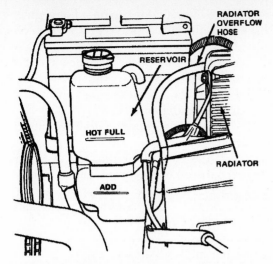

■ FIGURE 10–16
Coolant must be maintained at proper level between "hot full" and "add" lines on reservoir. (Courtesy of Ford Motor Company.)

9. Correct the coolant level in the reserve tank **(Figure 10–16).**
10. Make sure that there are no coolant leaks.

Review Questions

1. The cooling system maintains the engine at its most _____ _____ _____.
2. Two kinds of cooling systems are _____ and _____.
3. The purpose of the thermostat is to control exhaust temperature. True or False.
4. Engine cooling fans are driven by _____ or _____ _____.
5. The cooling system is pressurized to raise the _____.
6. Ethylene glycol mixed with water provides the required _____ protection and _____ _____.
7. To test freeze protection in the coolant a _____ is used.
8. Electrolysis may be detected in the coolant with the use of a _____.
9. Pressure testing the cooling system will help locate any external leaks. True or False.
10. A radiator cap should always be _____ _____.
11. If an electric fan runs continually the _____ _____ may be at fault.
12. A water pump that leaks or has a rough or loose bearing should be repaired. True or False.
13. Chemicals used for flushing cooling systems could cause skin or eye damage. True or False.

14. When checking the cooling system be sure the coolant is to the required level in the _____ _____ _____.

Test Questions

1. A hydrometer is used for checking
    a. speed
    b. distance
    c. hydro
    d. freezing protection
2. Pressurizing a cooling system
    a. raises the boiling point
    b. lowers the boiling point
    c. does not affect the boiling point
    d. is to keep the coolant from evaporating
3. A 50% solution of water and antifreeze will give protection to
    a. −90 degree F.
    b. −40 degree F.
    c. −34 degree F.
    d. 0 degree F.
4. The cooling system removes heat from the engine by the following methods
    a. conduction, convection, radiation
    b. radiation, evacuation, precipitation
    c. evacuation, conduction, convection
    d. convection, precipitation, evacuation
5. Technician A says antifreeze is used to provide freeze protection. Technician B says antifreeze is used to provide a higher boiling point. Who is right?
    a. technician A
    b. technician B
    c. both are right
    d. both are wrong
6. The primary purpose of the pressure cap is to
    a. prevent coolant leaks
    b. prevent air leaks
    c. reduce the cooling system pressure
    d. increase the coolant boiling point
7. Technician A says the cooling system should be pressure tested to determine engine internal leakage. Technician B says the cooling system should be pressure tested to determine external leakage. Who is right?
    a. technician A
    b. technician B
    c. both are right
    d. both are wrong
8. By placing a cooling system under one pound pressure, the boiling point is
    a. decreased by 3.25 degrees
    b. decreased by 7 degrees

    c. increased by 7.5 degrees

    d. increased by 3.25 degrees

9. When the cooling system thermostat is closed, water circulates mainly through

    a. the radiator

    b. the engine

    c. both engine and radiator

    d. the bypass and the engine

10. Technician A says the thermostat should be installed with the thermal element toward the radiator. Technician B says the thermostat should be pressure tested to determine whether it operates properly. Who is right?

    a. technician A

    b. technician B

    c. both are right

    d. both are wrong

11. Removing the radiator cap on a hot engine will usually result in a loss of coolant. This occurs because

    a. coolant pressure pushes the coolant out

    b. reduced pressure allows the coolant to boil

    c. the hot coolant has expanded and will push out of the radiator neck

    d. the pump has caused rapid coolant circulation

12. Technician A says air is directed over the hot engine parts of an air cooled engine by shrouds and ducts. Technician B says a belt driven blower provides flow for an air cooled engine. Who is right?

    a. technician A

    b. technician B

    c. both are right

    d. both are wrong

11 Heating and Air Conditioning System Diagnosis and Service

INTRODUCTION

The quality and temperature of the air in the vehicle passenger compartment are determined by the heating, ventilating, and air conditioning systems. The heating system uses hot engine coolant to heat incoming air. The ventilation system takes in fresh outside air and expels used inside air. The air conditioning system cools incoming air when necessary. The three systems work together to provide fresh outside air at a comfortable temperature to the passenger compartment. These systems may be controlled by the driver or by automatic controls.

A thorough understanding of the design and operation of heating and air conditioning systems and components is essential to be able to diagnose and correct heating and air conditioning problems.

LEARNING OBJECTIVES

After completing this chapter, you should be able to:
- Describe the principles of heat transfer.
- Describe the principles of refrigeration.
- List the major components of the heating, ventilating, and air conditioning systems.
- Describe the basic function of the major components of the heating, ventilating, and air conditioning systems.
- Visually inspect the heating and air conditioning systems to locate problems.
- Diagnose heating and air conditioning problems.
- Test the operation of the heating and air conditioning systems to locate problems.
- Leak test the heating and air conditioning systems.
- Discharge the air conditioning system and recover the refrigerant.
- Evacuate and charge the air conditioning system.

TERMS YOU SHOULD KNOW

Look for these terms as you study this chapter and learn what they mean.

heat transfer
conduction
convection
radiation
air-ventilating system
heating system
blend air
blower fan
heater core
temperature valve
mode valve
heat temperature
British thermal unit
Btu
state of matter
evaporation
condensation
latent heat
sensible heat
humidity
refrigerant
blower motor tests
heater problems
airflow control door problems

computer-controlled self-diagnosis
A/C performance tests
manifold (pressure) gauge set
R12
chlorofluoro-carbon
CFC
R134A
pressure-temperature relationship
low side
high side
compressor
magnetic clutch
compressor types
crankshaft
axial
radial
variable displacement
refrigerant oil
hoses
lines

receiver-drier
accumulator
service valves
Schraeder valves
three-position valves
refrigerant recovery and recycling
static pressure
high-side pressure
low-side pressure
leak detectors
discharging
condenser
evaporator
freeze control
expansion tube
orifice
cycling clutch
CCOT
expansion valve
STV
POA
relief valve

281

cutout switch	service valves	inputs
superheat	manual	outputs
switch	controls	evacuating
WOT switch	electronic	charging
A/C pressure	controls	refrigerant oil
transducer		

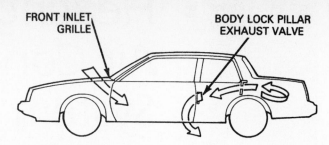

■ FIGURE 11–1
Ventilating airflow schematic. (Courtesy of General Motors Corporation.)

■ HEATING AND VENTILATING SYSTEM COMPONENTS AND FUNCTION

The heating system uses heat from the engine's coolant to provide heat for the passenger compartment. The system includes the following components **(Figures 11–1 to 11–5).**

1. *Heater hoses.* One hose carries hot engine coolant to the heater core inlet and the other hose returns it to the engine (usually to the inlet side of the water pump). Some systems use a vacuum-operated control valve to control coolant flow into the heater core.

2. *Heater core.* The heater core is a small tube-and-fin radiator-like unit. Hot engine coolant circulates through the heater core tubes. Air flowing through the heater core transfers heat to the passenger compartment.

3. *Blower (fan).* An electric motor-driven blower forces air through the heater core fins and

tubes (and through the evaporator core in the air conditioning system).

4. *Housing.* The housing surrounds the heater core, evaporator (on A/C-equipped cars) blower, and airflow control doors. Outside air may be brought in or inside air may be recirculated as desired.

The driver operates the heating system controls through levers and switches. Controls may be manual or automatic. With manual controls the driver selects the desired temperature, blower speed, and air outlets (floor, dash, defrost, or a combination of these). Manual controls include the following:

1. *Electric switch:* usually, a four-position switch with OFF, LOW, MEDIUM, and HIGH positions; used with a relay to control blower motor speed.

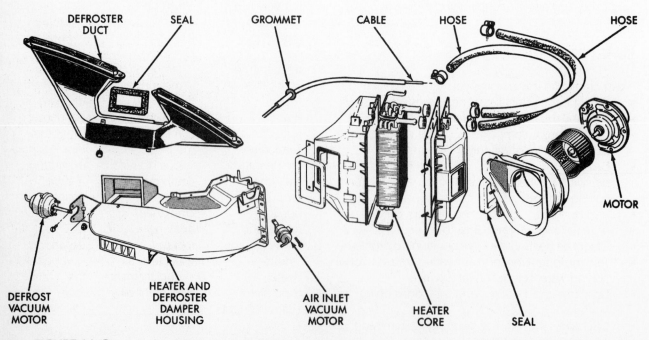

■ FIGURE 11–2
Heater core, housing, and components. (Courtesy of Chrysler Corporation.)

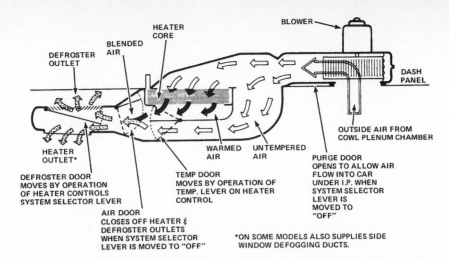

HEATER
CORE

BLOWER

DEFROSTER
OUTLET

BLENDED
AIR

DASH
PANEL

OUTSIDE AIR FROM
COWL PLENUM CHAMBER

HEATER
OUTLET*

WARMED
AIR

UNTEMPERED
AIR

PURGE DOOR
OPENS TO ALLOW AIR
FLOW INTO CAR
UNDER I.P. WHEN
SYSTEM SELECTOR
LEVER IS
MOVED TO
"OFF"

DEFROSTER DOOR
MOVES BY OPERATION
OF HEATER CONTROLS
SYSTEM SELECTOR LEVER

TEMP DOOR
MOVES BY OPERATION OF
TEMP. LEVER ON HEATER
CONTROL

AIR DOOR
CLOSES OFF HEATER &
DEFROSTER OUTLETS
WHEN SYSTEM SELECTOR
LEVER IS MOVED TO "OFF"

*ON SOME MODELS ALSO SUPPLIES SIDE
WINDOW DEFOGGING DUCTS.

■ FIGURE 11–3
Typical heating system airflow. (Courtesy of General Motors Corporation.)

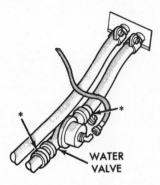

WATER
VALVE

■ FIGURE 11–4
Flow control valve in heater hose. (Courtesy of
Chrysler Corporation.)

2. *Levers and cables:* dash-mounted lever is connected to steel wire cable and housing. Used to operate airflow control doors inside the heater housing.

3. *Vacuum switch:* used to control engine manifold vacuum to vacuum motors that operate airflow control doors or a coolant flow control valve. Automatic temperature controls are described later in this chapter.

■ AIR CONDITIONING SYSTEM COMPONENTS AND FUNCTION

The automotive air conditioning system cools, dehumidifies, cleans, and circulates the air in the vehicle **(Figure 11–6).** The automotive air conditioning system consists of the refrigeration system, the air circulation system, and the temperature control system. Temperature control may be manual, semi-automatic, or fully automatic. Computer-controlled air conditioning systems are fully automatic.

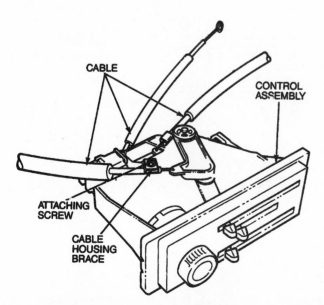

CABLE

CONTROL
ASSEMBLY

ATTACHING
SCREW

CABLE
HOUSING
BRACE

■ FIGURE 11–5
Control cable connections at manual control assembly.
(Courtesy of Ford Motor Company.)

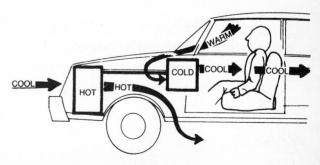

WARM

COOL

HOT

HOT

COLD

COOL

COOL

■ FIGURE 11–6
How A/C system cools passenger compartment.
(Courtesy of Chrysler Corporation.)

Refrigeration System

The refrigeration system consists of the refrigerant, compressor, condenser, flow control device, evaporator, receiver–drier or accumulator, and the tubing and hoses used to connect these items to each other **(Figure 11–7).**

Refrigerant

The refrigerant is the medium used to transfer heat from the car's interior to the outside. The refrigerant in the air conditioning system goes through four basic phases: compression, condensation, expansion, and vaporization. Heat transfer takes place during the condensation and vaporization phases.

Refrigerant Types

For many years a substance known as R12 has been used in air conditioning systems. R12 has a vaporization or boiling point of -21.7° F $(-29.8^\circ$ C) at sea level. It requires 79 Btu of latent heat to change 1 lb of R12 from a liquid at -21.7° F $(-29.8^\circ$ C) to a vapor or from a vapor to a liquid. R12 is compatible with all the materials used in systems designed for it. However, R12 is a chlorofluorocarbon (CFC) compound con-

taining chlorine and fluorine, which are harmful to the earth's ozone layer. It has also been used extensively in aerosol cans as a propellant. The emission of chlorofluorocarbons into the atmosphere has become a matter of serious concern to scientists and environmentalists because of its damaging effects. Many countries have passed legislation banning the use of these materials by a certain date. This has resulted in the development of new refrigerants that do not pose a threat to the environment. Among these is a substance called R134A which vaporizes at -15.08° F. The newer refrigerants require changes in the air conditioning system during manufacture to make them compatible: Hoses, fittings, and seals are different. Operation of the system remains essentially the same. Refrigerant 134A is a hydrofluorocarbon, does not contain any chlorine, but meets the required vaporization temperatures and other refrigerant requirements. The lower efficiency of R134A requires the use of larger condensers and evaporators.

■ LOW SIDE AND HIGH SIDE

The compressor pumps the refrigerant through the system. It draws low-pressure vapor from the evaporator, compresses it, and discharges it to the con-

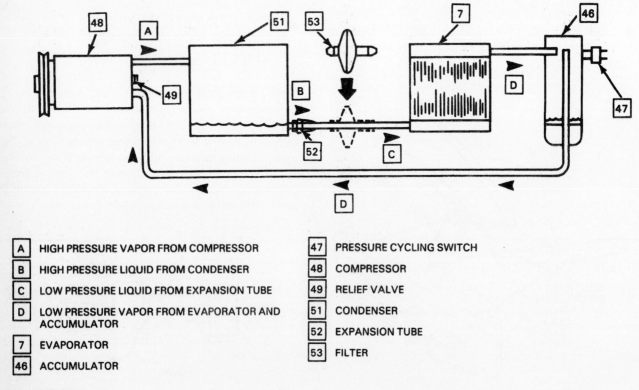

A	HIGH PRESSURE VAPOR FROM COMPRESSOR	**47**	PRESSURE CYCLING SWITCH
B	HIGH PRESSURE LIQUID FROM CONDENSER	**48**	COMPRESSOR
C	LOW PRESSURE LIQUID FROM EXPANSION TUBE	**49**	RELIEF VALVE
D	LOW PRESSURE VAPOR FROM EVAPORATOR AND ACCUMULATOR	**51**	CONDENSER
7	EVAPORATOR	**52**	EXPANSION TUBE
46	ACCUMULATOR	**53**	FILTER

■   FIGURE 11–7

Refrigeration system schematic. Arrows indicate refrigerant flow. (Courtesy of General Motors Corporation.)

denser. The compressor separates the low-pressure side from the high-pressure side. The high-pressure or discharge side consists of the parts between the compressor outlet and the flow control device. The low-pressure or suction side consists of the parts between the flow control device and the compressor inlet **(Figures 11–8** and **11–9).**

■ PRESSURE–TEMPERATURE RELATIONSHIP

When a vapor is placed under pressure (pressurized), its temperature rises, it gives off heat and is changed to a liquid. When the pressure is removed, its temperature drops, it absorbs heat and is changed to a vapor. This principle is used in the air conditioning system as the pressure on the refrigerant is changed from high to low to high in a repeating cycle **(Figure 11–10).** An increase in pressure on a liquid will raise its boiling point while a drop in pressure lowers its boiling point. The ability of the refrigerant to change its state easily and repeatedly makes it well suited to use in an air conditioning system. By changing the pressure on the refrigerant, its temperature can be controlled. This determines its ability to absorb heat and its ability to give off heat. The objective is to keep the refrigerant temperature in the evaporator as low

as possible without causing it to ice up with frozen condensation on its fins and tubes.

■ COMPRESSOR TYPES AND OPERATION

There are basically four types of A/C compressors: the crankshaft and piston type (in line or V), the multipiston axial type (fixed and variable displacement), the multipiston radial type, and the rotary vane type. With the crankshaft type (usually two-cylinder in line or V) the pistons move up and down to create the pumping action. As the piston moves down on the intake stroke, refrigerant is drawn into the cylinder through a one-way inlet valve. As the piston moves up on the compression stroke, the refrigerant is pressurized and forced out through a one-way exhaust valve. These valves, known as reed valves, are thin, flat pieces of metal that are normally in the closed position and allow refrigerant to flow in only one direction **(Figure 11–11).**

Magnetic Clutch Operation

A magnetic clutch is used to engage and disengage the compressor drive pulley and compressor. With the clutch disengaged the pulley freewheels and the

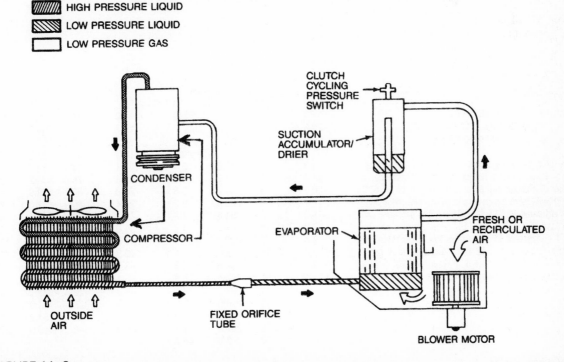

■ FIGURE 11–8

Refrigeration cycle. Note component locations, refrigerant flow, high and low pressure, and liquid and vapor sections. (Courtesy of Ford Motor Company.)

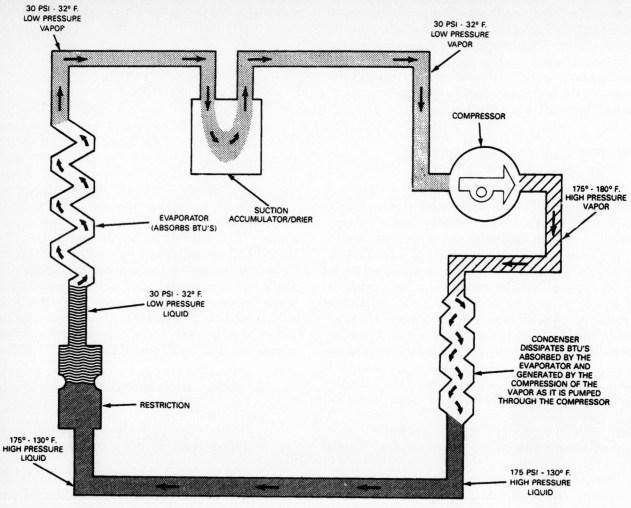

■ FIGURE 11–9

Typical refrigeration system schematic. (Courtesy of Ford Motor Company.)

REFRIGERANT – 12 PRESSURE – TEMPERATURE RELATIONSHIP			°C	°F	kPa	PSIG	°C	°F	kPa	PSIG
			-29.8	21.7	0	Atmos-	12.7	55	358.5	52.0
						pheric	15.5	60	397.8	57.7
						Pressure	18.3	65	439.2	63.7
The table below indicates the pressure of Refriger-			-28.8	-20	16.5	2.4	21.1	70	482.7	70.1
ant – 12 at various temperatures. For instance, a			-23.3	-10	31.0	4.5	23.8	75	530.2	76.9
drum of Refrigerant at a temperature of 26.6°C			-20.5	-5	46.9	6.8	26.6	80	579.9	84.1
(80°F) will have a pressure of 579.9 kPa (84.1 psi)			-17.7	0	63.4	9.2	29.4	85	632.3	91.7
If it is heated to 51.6°C (125°F), the pressure will			-15.0	5	81.4	11.8	32.2	90	686.7	99.6
increase to 1 154.9 kPa (167.5 psi). It also can be			-12.2	10	101.4	14.7	35.0	95	745.3	108.1
used conversely to determine the temperature at			- 9.4	15	122.0	17.7	37.7	100	806.0	116.9
which Refrigerant – 12 boils under various pres-			- 6.6	20	145.5	21.1	40.5	105	870.2	126.2
sures. For example, at a pressure of 207.5 kPa			- 3.8	25	169.6	24.6	43.3	110	937.7	136.0
(30.1 psi), Refrigerant – 12 boils at 0°C (32°F).			- 1.1	30	196.5	28.5	46.1	115	1010.1	146.5
			0	32	207.5	30.1	48.8	120	1083.2	157.1
			1.6	35	224.8	32.6	51.6	125	1154.9	167.5
			4.4	40	255.1	37.0	54.4	130	1234.2	179.0
			7.2	45	287.5	41.7	60.0	140	1410.0	204.5
			10.0	50	322.0	46.7				

■ FIGURE 11–10

Pressure/temperature relationship of R12. (Courtesy of General Motors Corporation.)

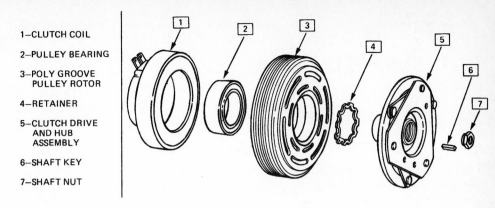

■ FIGURE 11–11
Magnetic clutch components. (Courtesy of General Motors Corporation.)

1—CLUTCH COIL

2—PULLEY BEARING

3—POLY GROOVE PULLEY ROTOR

4—RETAINER

5—CLUTCH DRIVE AND HUB ASSEMBLY

6—SHAFT KEY

7—SHAFT NUT

compressor is not driven. With the magnetic clutch engaged the compressor is driven through the clutch. The magnetic clutch consists of an electric coil, clutch plate, pulley, and bearing. These components are mounted on the front of the compressor shaft. When current is applied to the coil, a strong electromagnet is created that pulls the clutch plate toward the pulley and locks them together to drive the compressor. When current to the coil is shut off, the clutch plate returns to the released position, allowing the drive pulley to freewheel. The magnetic clutch is cycled on and off to meet the demands of the air conditioning system **(Figure 11–12)**.

Radial Compressor

The radial compressor has an eccentric mounted on the shaft that moves the pistons back and forth in the cylinder assembly. The pistons are arranged radially around the shaft and move toward and away from the shaft as they reciprocate. The entire assembly is enclosed in a shell or housing **(Figure 11–13)**.

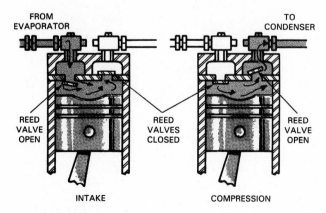

■ FIGURE 11–12
Basic compressor operation. Refrigerant vapor is drawn into compressor on intake stroke (inlet valve open, outlet valve closed). On compression stroke the inlet valve closes and forces refrigerant out past the outlet valve. (Courtesy of Ford Motor Company.)

Fixed Displacement Axial Compressor

The axial compressor has pistons moving back and forth parallel to the compressor shaft. The pistons are positioned around the shaft in a stationary ring assembly. The shaft and fixed wobble plate rotate to actuate the pistons **(Figure 11–14)**.

Variable-Displacement Compressor

The variable-displacement axial compressor uses a variable-angle wobble plate to control compressor displacement **(Figure 11–15)**. As the wobble plate angle is increased, displacement is increased. Displacement is varied to match air conditioning system demands. Higher cooling demands require greater displacement. As cooling demand decreases, the wobble plate angle decreases. The angle of the wobble plate is controlled by a bellows-actuated control valve located in the rear compressor head. Suction pressure acting on the diaphragm determines the required wobble plate angle. With this system there is no cycling of the compressor clutch. A differential pressure cutoff switch cuts off voltage to the compressor clutch when liquid refrigerant pressure drops to levels that could damage the compressor.

Rotary Vane Compressor

The rotary vane compressor has a slotted rotor mounted on the compressor shaft. A sliding vane is positioned in each rotor slot. The rotor and vanes spin inside an eccentric housing to create pumping action **(Figure 11–16)**.

Muffler

The muffler is a metal canister located in the compressor discharge line or internally in the compressor. It dampens the noise and pulsations produced by the compressor.

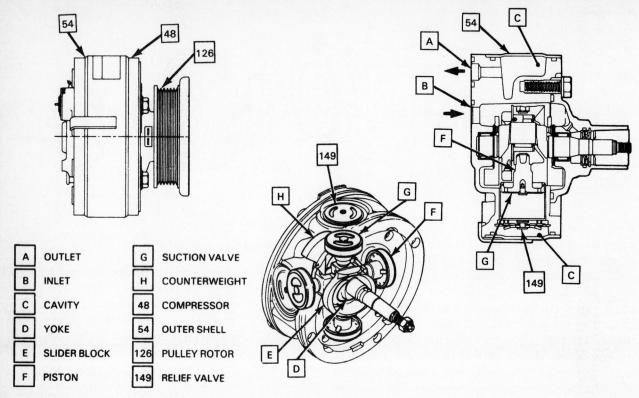

A	OUTLET	G	SUCTION VALVE
B	INLET	H	COUNTERWEIGHT
C	CAVITY	48	COMPRESSOR
D	YOKE	54	OUTER SHELL
E	SLIDER BLOCK	126	PULLEY ROTOR
F	PISTON	149	RELIEF VALVE

■   FIGURE 11–13

Radial compressor components. A shaft-mounted eccentric (slider block)
actuates the pistons. Pistons move in and out at 90° to the shaft. (Courtesy of
General Motors Corporation.)

■   FIGURE 11–14

Axial compressor cross section. Pistons
are actuated by the shaft and plate
assembly and move parallel to the
shaft. (Courtesy of General Motors
Corporation.)

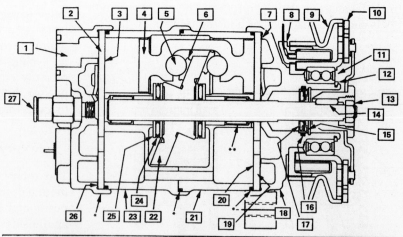

1—SUCTION PORT	13—SHAFT NUT	25—THRUST RACE
2—REAR VALVE PLATE	14—SHAFT KEY	26—HEAD GASKET
3—SUCTION REED PLATE	15—SEAL RETAINER	27—PRESSURE RELIEF
4—PISTON & RING ASSY.	16—SEAL O- RING	VALVE
5—PISTON BALL	17—SHAFT SEAL	28—REAR HEAD
6—SHOE DISC	18—FRONT HEAD	
7—HEAD GASKET	19—FRONT VALVE PLATE	
8—CLUTCH COIL ASSY.	20—SUCTION REED PLATE	* CYLINDER O-RING
9—PULLEY ROTOR	21—FRONT CYLINDER	SEALS
10—CLUTCH DRIVER	22—SHAFT & AXIAL	
11—PULLEY BEARING	PLAT ASSY.	** SHAFT BEARING
12—BEARING RETAINER	23—REAR CYLINDER	
RINGS	24—THRUST BEARING	

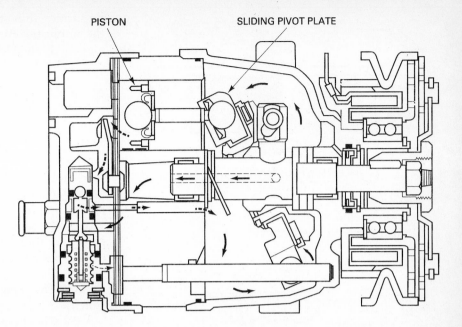

PISTON   SLIDING PIVOT PLATE

■ FIGURE 11–15
Variable-displacement compressor
cross section. Valve at lower left
controls angle of swash plate.

Refrigerant Oil

Refrigerant oil is of very high viscosity, in the 500 range. Refrigerant oil viscosity numbers are not the same as those for engine oil. Very fine droplets of refrigerant oil are suspended in the refrigerant to lubricate the entire system. The oil and refrigerant are splashed around in the compressor by the rotating and reciprocating parts and keep all the compressor parts lubricated. Air conditioning systems have a very specific amount and type of refrigerant

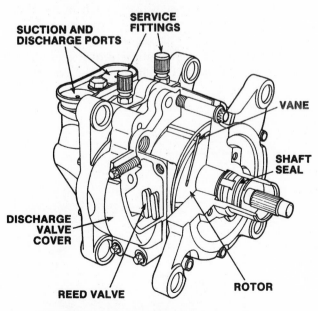

SUCTION AND
DISCHARGE PORTS

SERVICE
FITTINGS

VANE

SHAFT
SEAL

DISCHARGE
VALVE
COVER

REED VALVE   ROTOR

■ FIGURE 11–16
Rotary vane compressor. Vanes slide in and out in rotor slots as rotor and vanes spin inside eccentric housing. (Courtesy of Ford Motor Company.)

oil added to the system. Over- or underlubrication must be avoided.

Refrigerant oil for R134a systems is a polyalkaline glycol synthetic oil called PAG. It is the only lubricant to be used in R134a systems, and is not compatible with R12 refrigerant. Never use R12 system lubricant in R134a systems and never use R134a system lubricant in R12 systems. Failure to observe this rule will result in compressor failure.

■ A/C CONDENSER

The condenser consists of a long tube curved back and forth to fit in front near the car's radiator. Fins attached to the tubes aid in the dissipation of heat from the high-pressure refrigerant in the condenser. Air flowing across the fins absorbs the heat from the refrigerant and dissipates it to the atmosphere. Air is caused to flow across the condenser by ram air while driving and by the action of the engine fan or electric fan **(Figure 11–17).**

■ A/C EVAPORATOR

The evaporator **(Figures 11–18 and 11–19)** is similar in construction to the condenser and is located in the A/C housing, either in the passenger compartment or just outside the firewall under the hood. Evaporator pressure and temperature are controlled at approximately 28 psi (193.06 kPa) (30° F, –1° C). This allows the refrigerant to change to a vapor and absorb heat. Air is forced to flow over the evaporator coils, which remove the heat, moisture, and

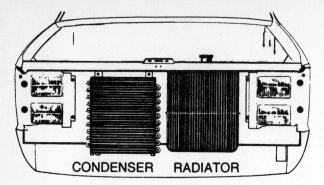

■ FIGURE 11-17
A/C condenser-mounted beside-engine radiator.
(Courtesy of Chrysler Corporation.)

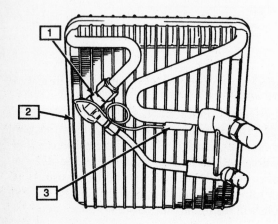

1	EXPANSION VALVE
2	EVAPORATOR CORE
3	REMOTE BULB

■ FIGURE 11-18
Evaporator core, expansion valve, and sensing bulb.
(Courtesy of General Motors Corporation.)

impurities from the air. Condensed moisture with the impurities from the evaporator drip into a tray and are drained to the outside of the vehicle.

■ EVAPORATOR FREEZE CONTROL METHODS

Moisture from the air of the car's interior condenses on the cooler evaporator surface. If evaporator pressure and temperature drop below a certain value [approximately 28 psi (193.06 kPa)], this moisture freezes and builds up to restrict airflow through the evaporator coils. This results in little cooling taking place. The three most common methods used to control evaporator pressure and temperature are:

1. The expansion tube and cycling compressor clutch
2. The thermostatic expansion valve
3. The variable displacement compressor (described earlier)

Expansion Tube and Cycling Clutch

This system is also called the cycling clutch and orifice tube (CCOT) system by some manufacturers. The expansion tube (orifice tube) has a precisely sized opening that meters the flow of refrigerant into the evaporator. The tube made of metal or plastic is located in or near the evaporator inlet (**Figures 11-20 to 11-22**). The restricted opening in the tube causes pressure to be lower on the evaporator side. A temperature- or pressure-sensitive switch in the outlet line of the evaporator regulates evaporator temperature at around 32° F (0° C) and 28 psi (193 kPa). When evaporator temperature drops enough, the cycling switch opens the circuit to the compressor

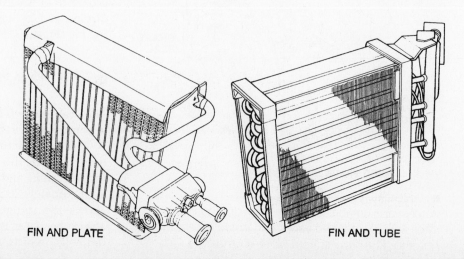

■ FIGURE 11-19
A/C evaporator designs. (Courtesy of Chrysler Corporation.)

FIN AND PLATE   FIN AND TUBE

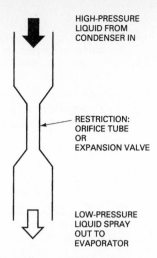

HIGH-PRESSURE
LIQUID FROM
CONDENSER IN

RESTRICTION:
ORIFICE TUBE
OR
EXPANSION VALVE

LOW-PRESSURE
LIQUID SPRAY
OUT TO
EVAPORATOR

■   FIGURE 11–20

Operating principle of orifice tube or expansion valve
is based on a pressure drop occurring through a
restriction. (Courtesy of F T Enterprises.)

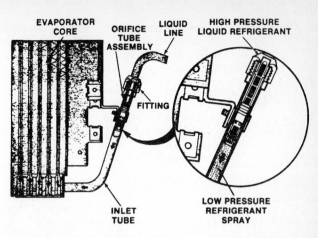

EVAPORATOR
CORE

ORIFICE
TUBE
ASSEMBLY

LIQUID
LINE

HIGH PRESSURE
LIQUID REFRIGERANT

FITTING

INLET
TUBE

LOW PRESSURE
REFRIGERANT
SPRAY

■   FIGURE 11–22

Details of orifice tube type of evaporator expansion
control. (Courtesy of Ford Motor Co. of Canada Ltd.)

clutch and the compressor stops. When evaporator
temperature rises sufficiently, the cycling switch
closes and completes the circuit to the compressor
clutch to drive the compressor. Cycling the compressor clutch on and off controls the pressure and temperature of the evaporator.

Expansion Valve

The expansion valve (also known as an H valve,
some applications) is a metering device that controls the flow of refrigerant into the evaporator. This
controls the pressure and temperature of the evaporator and thereby the amount of cooling. A thermal
bulb senses evaporator temperature. Gas in the

thermal bulb expands as its temperature rises.
Expansion and contraction of the gas in the sensing
bulb acts on a diaphragm in the expansion valve.
An actuating pin connected to the diaphragm acts
on the valve against spring pressure to vary the
flow of refrigerant through the valve opening. The
sensing bulb is connected to the diaphragm chamber in the expansion valve by a capillary (very
small diameter) tube. The sensing bulb is located at
the evaporator outlet. The expansion valve is
located in the line going to the evaporator inlet
(Figures 11–23 to 11–26).

One or two evaporator outlet control valves
may be used in addition to the expansion valve at
the evaporator inlet. These valves provide more pre-

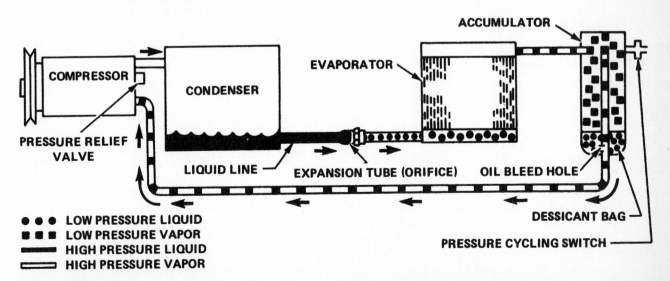

ACCUMULATOR

COMPRESSOR

CONDENSER

EVAPORATOR

PRESSURE RELIEF
VALVE

LIQUID LINE   EXPANSION TUBE (ORIFICE)   OIL BLEED HOLE

DESSICANT BAG

●●● LOW PRESSURE LIQUID
■■■ LOW PRESSURE VAPOR
━━━ HIGH PRESSURE LIQUID
▭▭▭ HIGH PRESSURE VAPOR

PRESSURE CYCLING SWITCH

■   FIGURE 11–21

Orifice tube A/C system schematic. (Courtesy of General Motors Corporation.)

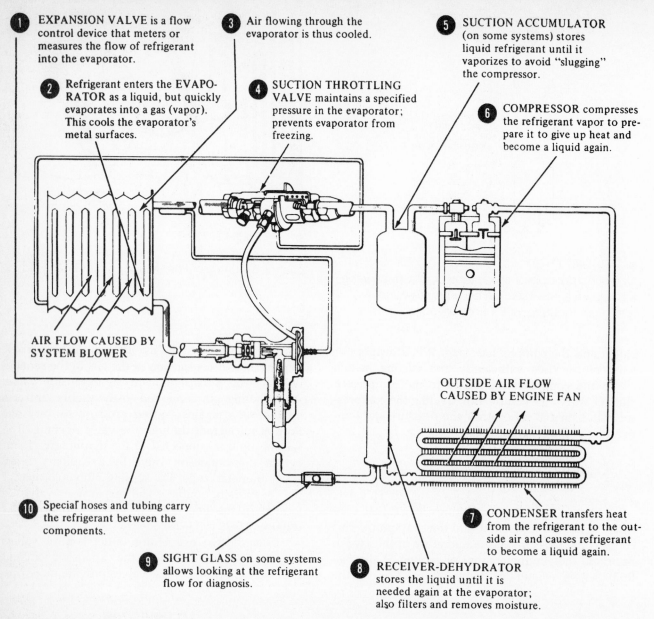

1 EXPANSION VALVE is a flow control device that meters or measures the flow of refrigerant into the evaporator.

2 Refrigerant enters the EVAPO-RATOR as a liquid, but quickly evaporates into a gas (vapor). This cools the evaporator's metal surfaces.

3 Air flowing through the evaporator is thus cooled.

4 SUCTION THROTTLING VALVE maintains a specified pressure in the evaporator; prevents evaporator from freezing.

5 SUCTION ACCUMULATOR (on some systems) stores liquid refrigerant until it vaporizes to avoid "slugging" the compressor.

6 COMPRESSOR compresses the refrigerant vapor to prepare it to give up heat and become a liquid again.

AIR FLOW CAUSED BY SYSTEM BLOWER

OUTSIDE AIR FLOW CAUSED BY ENGINE FAN

10 Special hoses and tubing carry the refrigerant between the components.

7 CONDENSER transfers heat from the refrigerant to the outside air and causes refrigerant to become a liquid again.

9 SIGHT GLASS on some systems allows looking at the refrigerant flow for diagnosis.

8 RECEIVER-DEHYDRATOR stores the liquid until it is needed again at the evaporator; also filters and removes moisture.

■   FIGURE 11–23
Refrigeration system with expansion valve and suction throttling valve type of evaporator freeze protection. (Courtesy of Ford Motor Company.)

cise control of evaporator pressure and temperature. This includes a suction throttling valve (STV) or pilot-operated absolute (POA) valve. Suction throttling valve outlet pressure is routed to the expansion valve through an equalizer line and acts on the opposite side of the expansion valve diaphragm from capillary tube pressure. A combination valve is used on some systems. The combination valve combines the STV and expansion valves in one unit. The term *valves in receiver* is used to identify a system that combines the expansion valve, suction throttling valve, and receiver–drier in a single assembly **(Figure 11–27)**.

■ **REFRIGERATION SYSTEM CONTROLS**

1. The A/C control switch on the dash allows the driver to switch the air conditioning system on or off.

2. A high-pressure relief valve may be used to protect the system from exceeding safe operating pressures. Usually located in the compressor discharge.

3. A high-pressure cutout switch may be used to shut off the compressor when discharge pressure reaches a preset maximum.

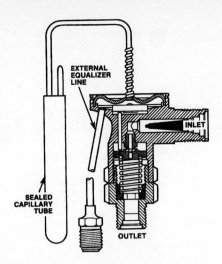

■ FIGURE 11–24

Thermostatic expansion valve with external equalizing. Equalizer senses evaporator outlet pressure. Capillary tube senses evaporator outlet temperature. Increased evaporator outlet pressure decreases valve opening and refrigerant flow. Decreased evaporator outlet pressure increases valve opening and refrigerant flow. As evaporator outlet temperature rises, valve opening and refrigerant flow increase. As outlet temperature decreases, valve opening and refrigerant flow decrease. (Courtesy of Ford Motor Company.)

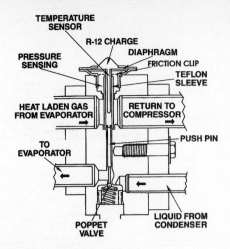

■ FIGURE 11–25

Expansion valve cross section. Poppet valve position regulates refrigerant flow from condenser to evaporator. Poppet valve position is controlled by expansion and contraction of refrigerant above diaphragm. Diaphragm acts on poppet valve through a push pin against spring pressure. This type of valve is used with a variable-displacement compressor. Temperature sensor senses refrigerant vapor heat coming from evaporator and acts on refrigerant charge above diaphragm. (Courtesy of Chrysler Corporation.)

4.   A low-pressure cutout switch may be used to shut off the compressor when system pressure drops too low due to a refrigerant leak. This prevents compressor damage.

5.   A superheat switch may be used to shut off the compressor when compressor temperature exceeds maximum limits. The switch senses compressor temperature and sends current to melt a fusible link in the thermal limiter, thereby cutting off current to the compressor.

6.   A wide-open throttle (WOT) cutout switch is used on cars with small engines to shut off the compressor and boost power during heavy acceleration. An electronic control module controls compressor clutch operation and turns the electric cooling fan at the condenser on before turning on the compressor.

■ RECEIVER–DRYER (ACCUMULATOR)

The receiver–dryer or accumulator stores liquid refrigerant from the condenser. It contains a desiccant (moisture-absorbing material) like silica gel or silica alumina. A filter is located at the bottom. As the refrigerant flows through the receiver–dryer, the desiccant removes any moisture and the filter removes any other contaminants that could damage

the compressor or valves. The dessicant is not the same for R134A as that for R12 systems. Therefore always make sure to use the type specified for the system. There may be a sight glass at the top to allow visual inspection of the refrigerant while the system is in operation (**Figure 11–28**).

A valves-in-receiver (VIR) unit combines the POA or STV valve, the thermostatic expansion valve and the receiver–dryer (see **Figure 11–27**). The receiver–dryer (or accumulator) should be replaced any time the system has lost its charge, has been open to atmosphere for any length of time, or a component has been replaced. This protects the compressor and the valves from contamination and damage.

■ REFRIGERATION HOSES, LINES, AND FILTERS

Special high-pressure hoses, tubing, and fittings are used to carry refrigerant to each component in the refrigeration system. Pressures as high as 300 psi (2068 kPa) must be contained over years of service. Special flared or ring-type fittings and hose clamps are used to prevent leakage (**Figure 11–29**). Hoses, lines, and fittings are not the same for R134A as those for R12 systems. They must therefore not be interchanged. The smaller molecules of R134a refrigerant permeate the walls of hoses designed for R12.

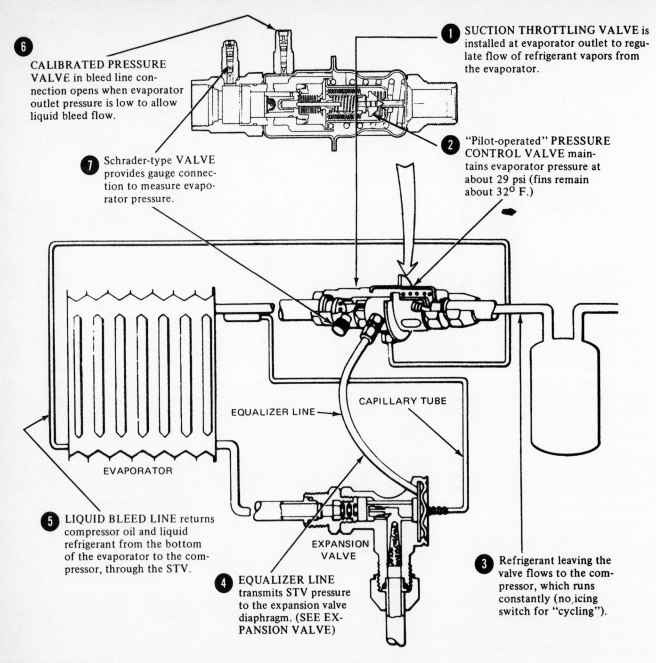

6 **CALIBRATED PRESSURE VALVE** in bleed line connection opens when evaporator outlet pressure is low to allow liquid bleed flow.

1 **SUCTION THROTTLING VALVE** is installed at evaporator outlet to regulate flow of refrigerant vapors from the evaporator.

7 Schrader-type **VALVE** provides gauge connection to measure evaporator pressure.

2 "Pilot-operated" **PRESSURE CONTROL VALVE** maintains evaporator pressure at about 29 psi (fins remain about 32° F.)

CAPILLARY TUBE

EQUALIZER LINE

EVAPORATOR

5 **LIQUID BLEED LINE** returns compressor oil and liquid refrigerant from the bottom of the evaporator to the compressor, through the STV.

EXPANSION VALVE

4 **EQUALIZER LINE** transmits STV pressure to the expansion valve diaphragm. (SEE EXPANSION VALVE)

3 Refrigerant leaving the valve flows to the compressor, which runs constantly (no icing switch for "cycling").

■ FIGURE 11–26
Refrigeration system with expansion valve, STV, and POA valve. (Courtesy of Ford Motor Company.)

An in-line filter in the liquid refrigerant line provides added filtering capacity to the system (**Figure 11–30**). Over time, contaminants tend to accumulate in various parts of the system. Compressor failure can result in tiny particles of metal and plastic entering the system. Flushing the system does not always remove all of these contaminants due to small internal passages and baffles. Contaminants left in the system can enter the compressor and cause compressor damage. An in-line filter protects the compressor from such damage. In-line filters may also contain a desiccant to supplement the drying capacity of the receiver–drier. Installing or changing the in-line filter after compressor failure and repair is good insurance against premature system failure.

■ SERVICE VALVES

Service valves are provided in the refrigeration system to allow test gauges to be connected to test A/C system performance. There are three kinds of service

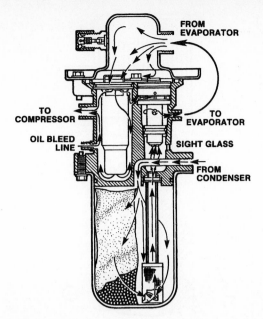

■ FIGURE 11–27
Valves in receiver (VIR) has expansion valve (top right) and POA valve (top left) inside receiver/drier assembly. Note refrigerant flow. (Courtesy of General Motors Corporation.)

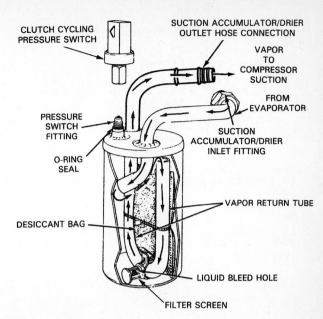

■ FIGURE 11–28
Receiver/drier cross section showing refrigerant flow. (Courtesy of Ford Motor Company.)

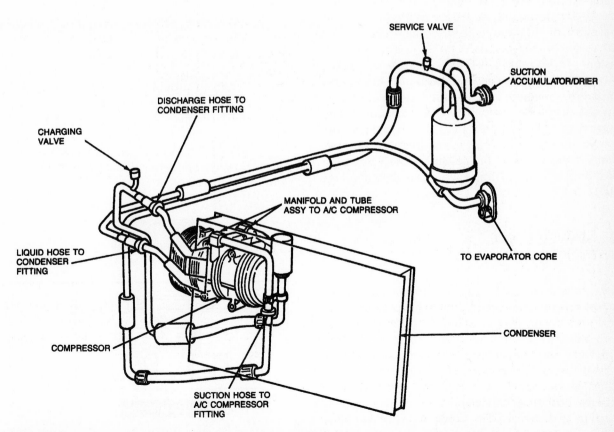

■ FIGURE 11–29
Refrigeration system hose connections. Note location of service valve and charge valve. (Courtesy of Ford Motor Company.)

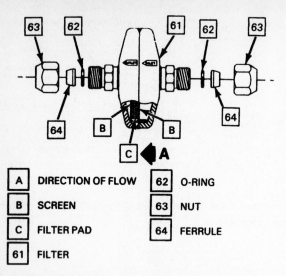

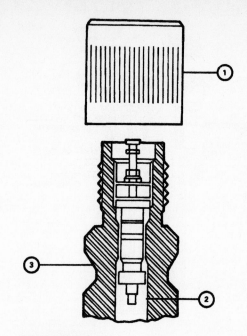

A	DIRECTION OF FLOW
B	SCREEN
C	FILTER PAD
61	FILTER
62	O-RING
63	NUT
64	FERRULE

■ FIGURE 11–30
In-line liquid refrigerant filter. (Courtesy of General Motors Corporation.)

ITEM DESCRIPTION
1. PROTECTIVE CAP (PRIMARY SEAL CAP MUST BE TIGHT)
2. VALVE CORE
3. VALVE BODY

■ FIGURE 11–31
Service valve cross section, Schraeder type. (Courtesy of Ford Motor Company.)

valves: the Schraeder type, the stem type, and the type used on R134a systems. Schraeder valves are most commonly used on both high- and low-pressure sides of the A/C system. Although they resemble ordinary tire valves, they are made from special materials compatible with the A/C refrigerant **(Figure 11–31)**. Schraeder valves are capped to prevent the entry of dirt and moisture. Stem-type service valves are sometimes used on A/C systems with piston- and crankshaft-type compressors. These valves can be backseated or frontseated. During performance testing a middle position is also used. The normal operating position is the backseated one (turned counterclockwise until seated against the rear valve seat). Stem-type valves are capped to prevent the entry of dirt or moisture. (The valve type used on R134a refrigeration systems is shown in **Figure 11–56).**

1. *Maximum:* provides maximum cooling and recirculates some inside air for faster cooling. Blower speed can be varied. Air is discharged from dash outlets.

2. *Normal:* provides normal air conditioning by cooling air drawn in from the outside. Blower speed can be varied. Air is discharged from dash outlets.

3. *Bi-level:* outside air is drawn in and cooled. The airflow is split between dash panel outlets and floor level outlets.

■ MANUAL A/C CONTROL SYSTEM

The manual A/C controls normally include an on/off switch, a fan speed switch, temperature control, and mode selector **(Figure 11–32)**. The fan switch usually has four positions: off, low, medium, and high. The temperature lever controls the position of the air blend door to regulate the heated, unheated, or cooled air mix. There are usually two extreme positions, warm and cool, as well as any position in between. The mode selector regulates airflow to the various outlets and may contain the A/C on/off switch. With this arrangement the typical mode selections possible are:

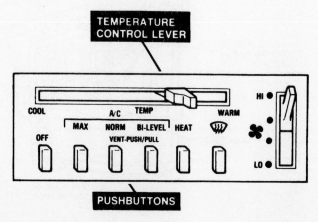

■ FIGURE 11–32
Control panel for manually controlled heating and air conditioning. (Courtesy of Chrysler Corporation.)

4. *Vent:* the air conditioning system is switched off. Outside air is drawn in and discharged from the dash outlets. Blower speed can be varied. The temperature control lever can be positioned to provide heater air. The mode lever directs vacuum to different vacuum motors that operate the flow control doors.

See **Figures 11–33** to **11–39** for components.

■ ELECTRONIC CONTROL SYSTEM

With an electronic climate control system the driver selects the desired temperature, which is then maintained automatically. The system regulates the blower speed and the airflow between dash panel outlets, floor outlets, windshield defroster outlets, and side window demister outlets. Manual override of the blower speed and airflow direction is possible if desired. The mode control panel typically contains the automatic on switch, off switch, temperature select switches, override switches for blower speed, maximum A/C, vent, panel-floor air, floor air, floor-defrost air, and defrost air. A temperature display window is also provided **(Figure 11–40)**.

Electronic Control Module

The electronic control module or computer receives input signals from the driver and several sensors. When the automatic mode is selected, the computer controls the blower speed and the direction of airflow. Electric or vacuum motors operate the airflow control doors based on output signals from the computer **(Figures 11–41 and 11–42)**.

Input Signals

1. *In-car temperature sensor:* usually located somewhere inside the dash panel; senses in-car temperature **(Figure 11–43)**.
2. *Ambient temperature sensor:* located in front of the condenser; senses outside air temperature **(Figure 11–44)**.
3. *Solar sensor:* located somewhere in the top of the instrument panel; senses solar heat **(Figure 11–45)**.
4. *Engine temperature sensor:* senses engine temperature to operate cold engine lockout.
5. *A/C pressure sensor:* senses refrigerant pressure; determines A/C compressor clutch cycling.
6. *Blend door position sensor*
7. *Mode selection by operator:* automatic or manual override.

Output Devices

1. *Blower speed controller:* controls blower speed **(Figure 11–46)**.
2. *Blend door actuator:* operates blend air door **(Figures 11–47 and 11–48)**.
3. *Floor-panel door actuator:* operates air door between floor and panel outlets.
4. *Panel-defrost door actuator:* operates air door between panel and defrost outlets.
5. *Inside–outside air door actuator:* operates door between inside and outside air intakes.

■ FIGURE 11–33

Blower motor and housing. (Courtesy of Ford Motor Company.)

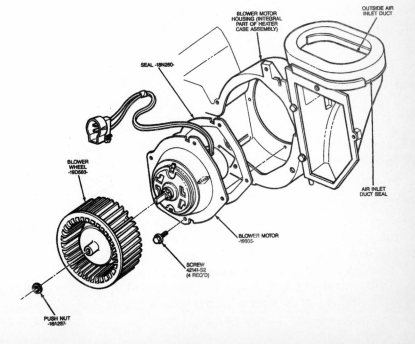

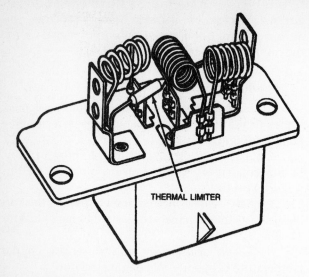

■ FIGURE 11–34
Resistor and thermal limiter assembly. Blower switch position determines which series resistance is added or bypassed to control blower speed. Thermal limiter serves as a temperature protection fuse. It has a set of contacts embedded in wax. At 250°F (121°C) the wax melts and the points open. Once the points are opened, the resistor assembly must be replaced. (Courtesy of Ford Motor Company.)

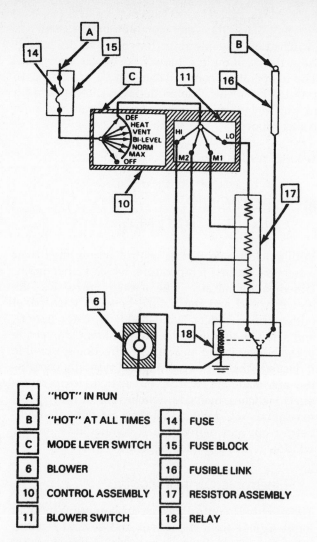

A	"HOT" IN RUN		
B	"HOT" AT ALL TIMES	14	FUSE
C	MODE LEVER SWITCH	15	FUSE BLOCK
6	BLOWER	16	FUSIBLE LINK
10	CONTROL ASSEMBLY	17	RESISTOR ASSEMBLY
11	BLOWER SWITCH	18	RELAY

■ FIGURE 11–35
Blower motor circuit. (Courtesy of General Motors Corporation.)

■ FIGURE 11–36
Stacked core reheat method of air temperature control. (Courtesy of F T Enterprises.)

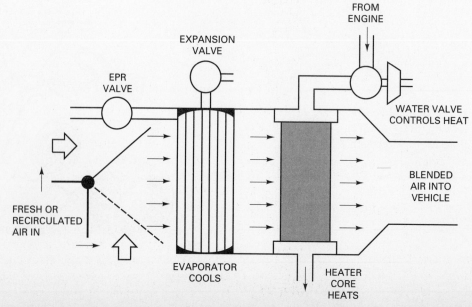

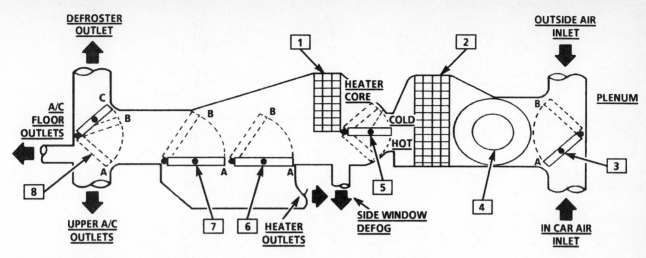

■ FIGURE 11-37

Heating and air conditioning system airflow control system. 1) Heater core; 2) A/C evaporator; 3) outside/inside air circulation door; 4) blower; 5) air temperature mix valve; 6) rear mode door; 7) front mode door; 8) defrost door. (Courtesy of General Motors Corporation.)

6.   *Cycling clutch switch:* controls compressor operation **(Figure 11–49).**

7.   *Self-test feature:* supplies the technician with error codes for diagnostic purposes.

8.   *Vacuum fluorescent display panel:* displays temperature and mode information.

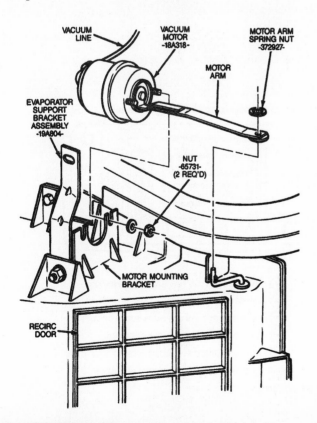

■ FIGURE 11-38

Vacuum motor-controlled airflow control door detail. (Courtesy of Ford Motor Company.)

9.   *Condenser fan:* many air conditioning systems have an electric motor driven condenser fan to ensure good air movement through the condenser even when stopped in traffic. The condenser fan runs only when the compressor runs. The electronic control assembly controls the fan through a fan relay.

A/C Pressure Transducer (Typical)

The A/C pressure transducer senses refrigerant pressure in the discharge line of the R134a system. Its pressure range is from 0 to 500 psi (0 to 72.5 kPa). It performs the following functions:

1.   Sends information to the Powertrain Control Module (Computer).

2.   Replaces the low pressure cut out switch, high pressure cutout switch, and the fan control switch.

3.   It is an analog to digital sensor with a 0–5 volt range.

4.   Provides output voltage to the PCM as a signal to turn the compressor clutch on or off. If system pressure is too high or too low the clutch is turned off.

5.   Its input signal is used by the PCM to control cooling fan operation.

The PCM checks this sensor signal every 23 milliseconds. If system pressure is greater than 430 psi (62.3 kPa) the compressor clutch relay is deactivated. The same is true when system pressure drops below 32 psi (4.6 kPa).

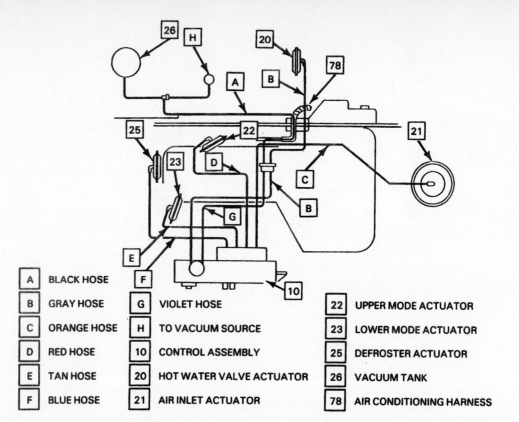

■ FIGURE 11–39
Vacuum control circuit.
(Courtesy of General
Motors Corporation.)

A	BLACK HOSE				
B	GRAY HOSE	G	VIOLET HOSE	22	UPPER MODE ACTUATOR
C	ORANGE HOSE	H	TO VACUUM SOURCE	23	LOWER MODE ACTUATOR
D	RED HOSE	10	CONTROL ASSEMBLY	25	DEFROSTER ACTUATOR
E	TAN HOSE	20	HOT WATER VALVE ACTUATOR	26	VACUUM TANK
F	BLUE HOSE	21	AIR INLET ACTUATOR	78	AIR CONDITIONING HARNESS

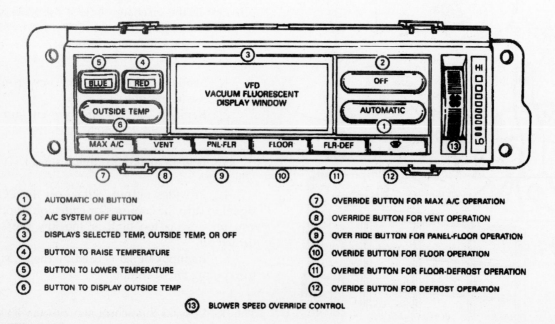

①	AUTOMATIC ON BUTTON	⑦	OVERRIDE BUTTON FOR MAX A/C OPERATION
②	A/C SYSTEM OFF BUTTON	⑧	OVERRIDE BUTTON FOR VENT OPERATION
③	DISPLAYS SELECTED TEMP, OUTSIDE TEMP, OR OFF	⑨	OVER RIDE BUTTON FOR PANEL-FLOOR OPERATION
④	BUTTON TO RAISE TEMPERATURE	⑩	OVERIDE BUTTON FOR FLOOR OPERATION
⑤	BUTTON TO LOWER TEMPERATURE	⑪	OVERRIDE BUTTON FOR FLOOR-DEFROST OPERATION
⑥	BUTTON TO DISPLAY OUTSIDE TEMP	⑫	OVERIDE BUTTON FOR DEFROST OPERATION

⑬ BLOWER SPEED OVERRIDE CONTROL

■ FIGURE 11–40
Instrument panel control assembly for electronic automatic temperature
control system. (Courtesy of Ford Motor Company.)

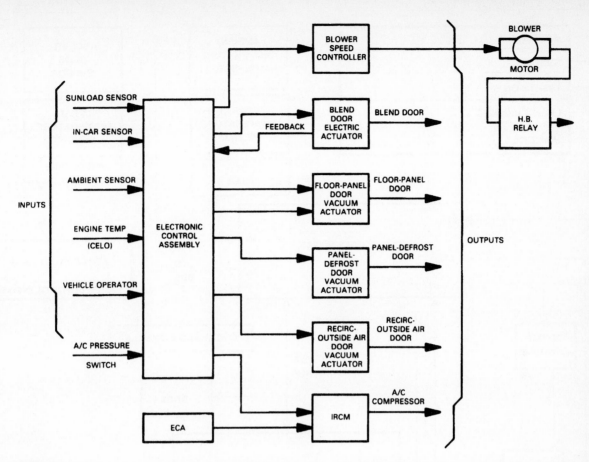

■ FIGURE 11-41

Block diagram of automatic temperature control system inputs and outputs for body control computer. (Courtesy of Chrysler Corporation.)

■ HEATING SYSTEM PROBLEMS

Heating system problems include: not enough heat, poor windshield defrosting, or too much heat.

Causes of insufficient heat include:

1. Obstructed heater air outlets. Remove the obstruction.

2. Mode door inoperative or binding. Check door actuator operation (vacuum or electric) for binding condition through entire range of movement.

3. Temperature control door inoperative or binding. Check the same as for mode door in item 2.

4. Heater blower motor inoperative. Check for burned out fuse, faulty relay, faulty switch, poor motor ground connection, or faulty motor.

5. Defective temperature control cable or switch. Check cable connections and adjustment, check switch continuity through all switch positions.

6. Coolant flow control valve faulty. Check flow control valve operation.

7. Air circulation blocked by objects under front seats. Remove objects.

8. Engine coolant temperature too low. Use test thermometer to test coolant temperature, thermostat operation, and temperature range.

9. Coolant flow through heater core restricted. Check coolant flow through heater core.

Causes of poor windshield defrosting include:

1. Defroster outlets restricted. Remove obstruction.

2. Temperature control door binding or inoperative. Check as in item 2 above.

3. Mode control door binding or inoperative. Check as in item 2 above.

4. Blower motor faulty. Check as above.

5. Coolant temperature too low. Check as above.

Causes of too much heat include:

1. Temperature control door binding or inoperative. Check as above.

2. Coolant flow control valve faulty. Check as above.

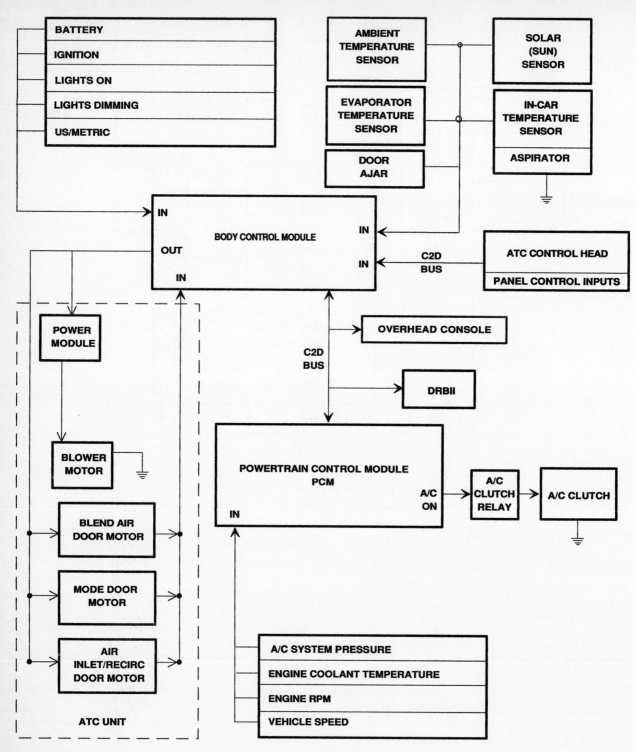

- FIGURE 11–42

Block diagram of automatic temperature control system showing relationship between body control computer and powertrain control module. (Courtesy of Chrysler Corporation.)

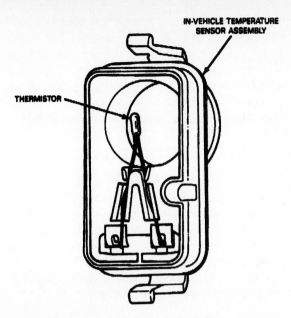

■ FIGURE 11–43
In-car temperature sensor. (Courtesy of Ford Motor Company.)

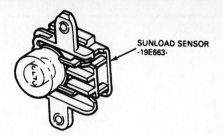

■ FIGURE 11–45
Solar sensor contains photovoltaic cell that is sensitive to sunlight. (Courtesy of Ford Motor Company.)

3. Temperature control cable disconnected or binding.

■ HEATING SYSTEM DIAGNOSIS AND SERVICE

Airflow Control Doors

Airflow control doors are vacuum motor or electric motor actuated. Problems with vacuum motor air door operation usually consist of disconnected or leaking vacuum lines or a faulty vacuum motor. Vacuum motors operation can be checked with a hand

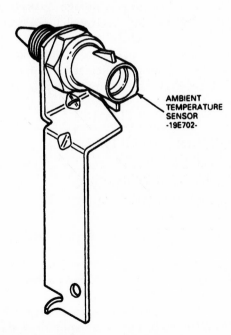

■ FIGURE 11–44
Ambient temperature sensor. (Courtesy of Ford Motor Company.)

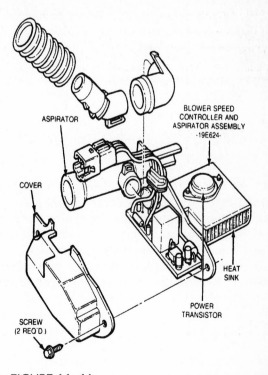

■ FIGURE 11–46
Blower speed control assembly is computer controlled and infinitely variable through a variable ground to the blower motor. (Courtesy of Ford Motor Company.)

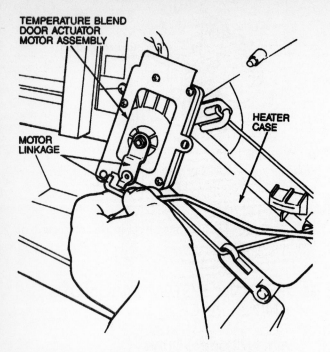

■   FIGURE 11–47
Electric blend door actuator and linkage. (Courtesy of Ford Motor Company.)

vacuum pump. A faulty vacuum motor must be replaced. Vacuum lines must be properly routed and not pinched.

Electrically operated airflow door problems usually consist of poor connections, a blown fuse, or a faulty electric motor. Motor operation can be checked by ensuring that there is a good ground and then applying specified voltage to the motor with a jumper wire. Electrical connections must be clean and tight.

Checking Coolant Flow Through the Heater

With the engine running at operating temperature and the heater temperature control set at maximum heat, feel the inlet and outlet hoses near the heater core. They should feel very warm and nearly the same temperature. If the heater outlet hose is not nearly as warm as the inlet hose, the heater core is restricted. Reverse flushing the heater core with the hoses disconnected may remove the restriction. It will also demonstrate whether water flows freely through the core **(Figure 11–50).** If reverse flushing does not result in good flow, the heater core must be removed for cleaning at a radiator shop.

Check the operation of the heater flow control valve (if so equipped). With the engine at operating temperature and the heater at maximum heat, feel the hoses on each side of the valve. They should both be very warm. If the outlet side is much cooler,

the valve is restricted. Check valve operation by applying vacuum to the valve with a hand vacuum pump. With vacuum applied, the valve should open. If not, replace the valve. Heater core coolant leaks usually show up as leaks on the carpet floor. A leaking heater core must be removed, cleaned, pressure tested **(Figure 11–51),** and repaired or replaced.

Blower Motor Tests

Apply battery voltage in turn to each blower motor electrical input terminal. The motor should run at different speeds as voltage is applied to different terminals. If the motor does not run, check the motor ground connection. Use a jumper wire and connect it from the motor ground to a good vehicle ground. If the motor does not run with a good ground and voltage applied, replace the motor.

Blower Motor Circuit Tests

Fuse Check–Ignition in Run Position

1.   If the blower motor does not operate, check the blower/heater fuse. Replace the fuse if burned out.
2.   The battery side of the fuse should have battery voltage. If not, the circuit between the ignition switch and fuse is open. Repair the circuit.
3.   The battery side of the blower switch should have battery voltage. If not, there is an open circuit between the fuse and switch. Repair the circuit.
4.   Check for battery voltage at each output terminal on the switch in each switch position. If not there, replace the switch.
5.   Check the operation of the high speed blower relay (if equipped). Replace if faulty.
6.   Check wiring continuity. Repair or replace as necessary.

■   FEDERAL REGULATIONS CONCERNING A/C SYSTEM SERVICE (Courtesy of Chrysler Corporation)

Prohibitions

No person repairing motor vehicle air conditioning systems shall do so without properly using approved equipment. This person must also be properly trained and certified as required by this regulation.

The refrigerant recycling equipment must be approved by an independent standards testing organization, itself approved by the EPA. The EPA will maintain a list of approved equipment by manufacturer and model.

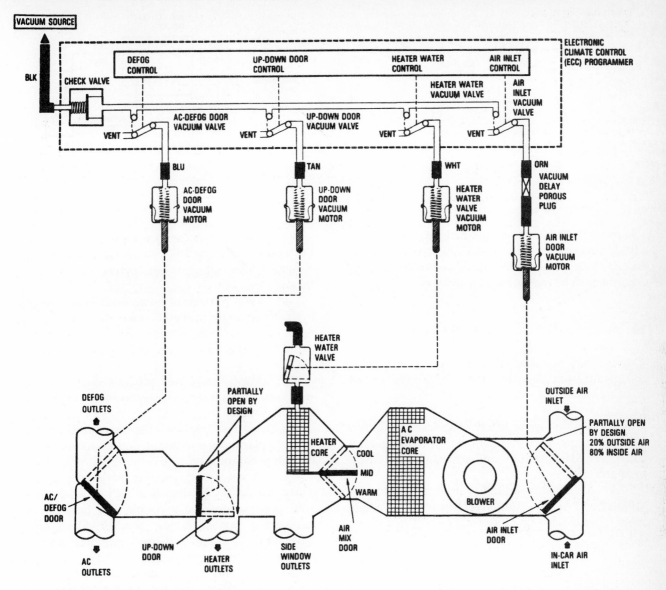

■ FIGURE 11–48
Electronic automatic temperature control vacuum actuators and mode doors.
(Courtesy of General Motors Corporation.)

Technician Training and Certification

All technician training and certification programs must be approved by the EPA. Besides training, a certification test must be given that addresses the following; the recommended service procedures for the containment of refrigerant, extraction and recycle equipment, and the standard of purity for refrigerant. Also, it must provide for new developments such as the new **hydroflourocarbon (HFC)** refrigerant (R-134a). The test must also cover the environmental consequences of refrigerant release and the adverse effects of stratosphere ozone layer depletion. It must also include the requirements of the Clean Air Act Amendments pertaining to motor vehicle air conditioning systems.

The test must be sent to an independent testing authority for grading. The test must be completed honestly by each technician and must provide a way to verify the identification of the person taking the test. Each technician must be given proof of certification such as a certificate or wallet card. Each certification program must provide a unique number to each technician certified.

Certification and Record Keeping Requirements

All technicians servicing motor vehicle air conditioning systems must be certified and use approved equipment.

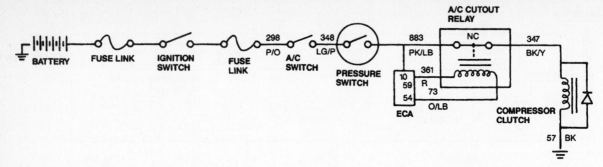

■ FIGURE 11–49
Compressor clutch electrical circuit. (Courtesy of Ford Motor Company.)

Records must be maintained on vehicles serviced, amount of refrigerant purchased, current record of technician certification, and other data. All records must be maintained for three years.

■ A/C SERVICE PRECAUTIONS

Extreme care must be taken to prevent any liquid refrigerant from contacting the skin or eyes. Instant freezing will result.

1. Always wear safety goggles and gloves when working with refrigerants. A/C refrigerants can freeze skin instantly and permanently damage eyesight.
2. Avoid discharging refrigerant into the atmosphere. Always use refrigerant recovery equipment when discharging the system.

3. Never try to service lines or fittings until the system is completely discharged and depressurized. Wipe fittings clean before disconnecting them.
4. Keep refrigerant away from heat. Pressure in the refrigerant container increases dangerously with excessive temperatures. The container may explode. Never allow refrigerant to exceed 125° F (52° C).
5. Always seal any disconnected openings with a cap or plug immediately to avoid contaminating the system.
6. Always replace the accumulator–drier when replacing a refrigerant line, evaporator, condenser, or compressor.
7. *Do not mix refrigerant or lubricant types. They are not compatible.* Mixing them will seriously affect A/C performance and parts life. Use only the recommended hoses, fittings, service valves, seals, refrigerant, lubricant, and test equipment specified for the vehicle being serviced.
8. Use only the recommended hoses, lines, fittings, and other parts for the system being serviced. They are not the same for R134A systems as those for R12 systems.

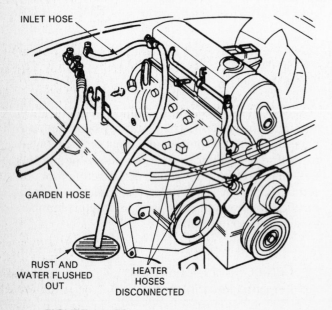

■ FIGURE 11–50
Reverse flushing a heater core. (Courtesy of Ford Motor Company.)

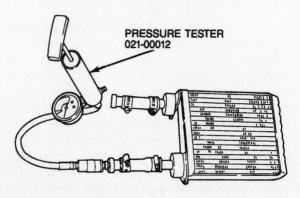

■ FIGURE 11–51
Leak testing a heater core with a pressure tester. (Courtesy of Ford Motor Company.)

9. Use only the recommended discharging, evacuating, recovery recycling and charging equipment specified for each refrigeration system. R12 equipment for R12 systems and R134a equipment for R134a systems. Systems and equipment are not to be interchanged.

■ INSPECTING THE SYSTEM

The first thing to do is to check the operation of the system in all its modes and blower positions. Start the engine and warm it up to operating temperature, then check the operation of the heating and air conditioning systems. This will tell you whether the system heats, cools, and delivers air from the outlets. Then look for problems in the following areas.

1. Compressor drive belt loose or missing.
2. Compressor clutch not engaging.
3. Loose, damaged, or disconnected electrical wiring or connectors.
4. Damaged, kinked, leaking, or disconnected vacuum lines.
5. Leaks around refrigerant lines or fittings. Look for wetness or accumulation of dirt indicating wetness. Use an electronic leak detector to ensure that no leaks are present while the system is operating.
6. Airflow through condenser restricted with leaves, mud, or dirt.
7. Inoperative blower motor. No air discharge from outlets.
8. Airflow control doors not functioning.
9. Sight glass. Should be clear. Foam or bubbles indicate low refrigerant. Oil streaks may indicate low refrigerant (**Figure 11–52**). Low refrigerant

indicates leakage. (Note: not all vehicles have a sight glass.)
10. Refrigerant line temperatures. The high-side or compressor discharge line should be warm or hot during A/C operation. The low-side or suction line should be cool or cold. If not, there is a refrigerant system problem. If the high-side line is hot and the low-side line is cold but the A/C is not working, the problem is not in the refrigeration system but in the control system or air distribution system.
11. Compressor seal leakage. Examine this area closely for any sign of leakage. Use an electronic leak detector with the system operating.
12. Compressor mounting brackets. Check for any looseness or cracks.
13. If preliminary inspection indicates that air output is a problem, the blower motor and its electrical circuit should be tested and repaired.

■ COMPUTER-CONTROLLED SELF-DIAGNOSIS

The computer-controlled A/C system self-diagnosis function can be used to identify A/C problems. Follow the service manual directions to activate the self-diagnosis mode. Use a computer scanner. If a fault exists, a fault code will be displayed. Check the service manual to interpret the fault code. The fault code may indicate a sensor, output device vacuum line, or connecting wire to be at fault (**Figures 11–53 and 11–54**). The faulty component must be tested to verify the failure. Wiring or vacuum problems must be corrected and faulty sensors or output devices replaced. If the fault code indicates a refrigeration

■ FIGURE 11–52
Typical sight glass conditions and their causes. (Courtesy of Chrysler Corporation.)

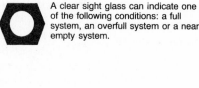

1. **Clear**

A clear sight glass can indicate one of the following conditions: a full system, an overfull system or a near empty system.

3. **Oil Streaks**

Oil streaks across the glass indicate there is no liquid R-12 in the system.

2. **Bubbles**

Bubbles, whether large or small, indicate air or moisture is trapped in the system.

(Occasional bubbles during clutch cycling is normal.)

(Cool temperatures may require restricting air flow through the condenser to bring up system pressure for proper diagnosis (refer to service manual for additional information).

4. **Foam**

Foam indicates a low charge

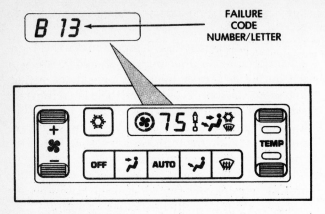

FAILURE CODE NUMBER/LETTER

■ FIGURE 11–53
Fault code typical for automatic temperature control system. This fault code indicates a clutch cycle signal problem. (Courtesy of Chrysler Corporation.)

system problem, the system must be tested like any other A/C refrigeration system.

Sensor Testing

Electronic A/C system input sensor resistance can be tested with an ohmmeter. The procedure is to heat the sensor and test its resistance at various specified temperatures. **Figure 11–55** shows typical resistance values for an evaporator thermal sensor and air inlet sensor.

If the preceding inspection and tests indicate that further tests are required, the practice generally is to performance test the air conditioning system. The procedure usually includes the following steps.

1. Connect the manifold pressure gauges and refrigerant recovery equipment to the refrigeration system.
2. Take a static pressure reading.
3. Performance test the system with the engine running.
4. Inspect the system for refrigerant leaks.
5. Discharge and recover the refrigerant.
6. Repair or replace faulty components and replace the receiver–dryer.
7. Evacuate the refrigerant system.
8. Charge the refrigeration system to the specified level.
9. Add refrigerant oil as needed.

■ SERVICE VALVE TYPES

Service valves and ports provide the means for connecting the pressure gauges to the refrigeration system for diagnosing, recovering, evacuating, and

charging the system. There are two service valves: a high-side valve and a low-side valve.

There are two kinds of service valves used in R12 systems: the Schraeder type and the three-position type. The Schraeder type is a valve with a spring to hold it in the closed position, similar to a tire valve. The pressure gauge hoses have valve stem depressors that push the valves open when they are connected to the service port **(Figure 11–56).** The three-position valves are opened and closed manually by turning the valve stem in or out. When the valve is backseated (full-in position), the service port is closed. When the valve is front seated (full-out position), the service port is open to the compressor. To backseat the valve, turn it counterclockwise. To front seat the valve, turn it clockwise. When the valve is in the midway position the service port is open to the pressure gauges **(Figure 11–57).**

Refrigerant 12 systems use a male type adapter. The service ports in R134a sytems use quick disconnect fittings with sealing caps that screw *into* the service ports not *onto* them. The outside dimensions of the service ports are the opposite of R-12 systems. The high side service port is larger than the low side service port, and a quick connect coupter is used to service R-134a systems. An industry standard has been established for the height of the valve depressor to make all R-134a service ports the same **(Figure 11–58).**

A safety feature designed into the quick connect service ports prevents the release of refrigerant. The refrigerant cannot be released from the discharge or suction side port until the knob is adjusted to activate the valve depressor.

The high side service port on R-134a systems is larger than the low side port.

■ CHECKING THE SIGHT GLASS

On systems equipped with a sight glass check to see if it is clear or if bubbles, oil streaks, or foam are evident. The sight glass may be in the refrigerant line or in the top of the receiver–dryer. The engine must be running with the A/C on for this check. (Compare the results with the conditions shown in **Figure 11–52.**)

■ REFRIGERANT RECOVERY AND RECYCLING

SAFETY CAUTION: *A/C refrigerants are not all the same.* The long-time refrigerant standby R12 is being legislated out of existence worldwide due to its

At "—DRB—" press:

4) SELECT SYSTEM

9) LH CLIMATE CONTROL

      bus test
      module info

1) SYSTEM TEST

    1) Partial Chg Test
    2) A/C On to BCM

2) READ FAULTS

    1) Engine
    2) Body
    3) ATC Ctl Head*

3) STATE DISPLAY

    1) Module Info
    2) Sensors
    3) Inputs/Outputs
    4) Monitors
    5) Custom Disp

4) ACTUATORS

    CLIMATE ACTUATORS

    1) A/C Clutch Rly
    2) Eng RPM
    3) Lo Spd FC Rly
    4) Hi Spd FC Rly
    5) ATC Hi Blw Rly*
    6) In-Car Aspiratr*
    7) More Actuators
        1) Temp Door*
        2) Mode Door*
        3) Recirc Door*
        4) Rr Win Def
        5) VF Disp Seg*
        6) Disp Sequence*

5) ADJUSTMENTS

    1) Reset BCM
    2) Recal ATC Doors*
    3) Reset ATC Head*
    4) Reset ATC & BCM*

*ATC EQUIPPED ONLY

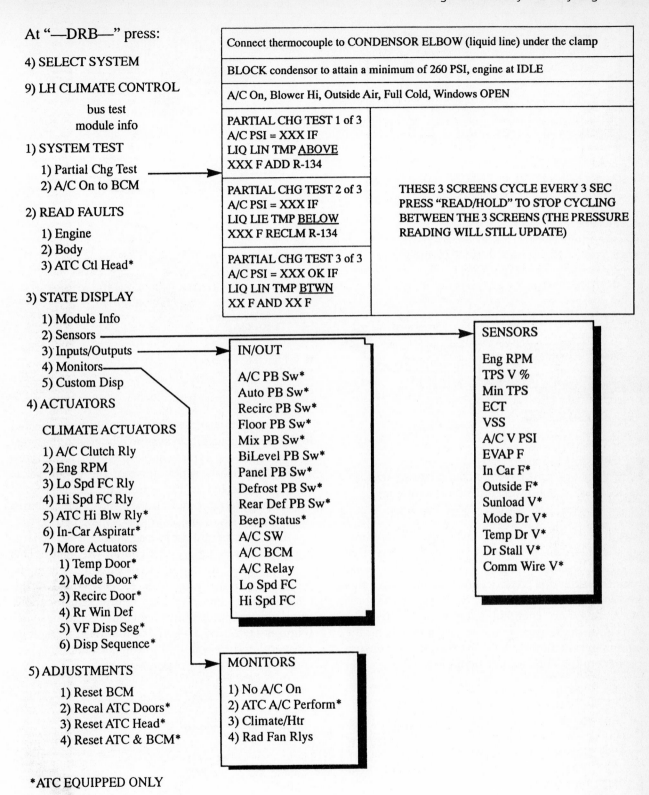

Connect thermocouple to CONDENSOR ELBOW (liquid line) under the clamp

BLOCK condensor to attain a minimum of 260 PSI, engine at IDLE

A/C On, Blower Hi, Outside Air, Full Cold, Windows OPEN

PARTIAL CHG TEST 1 of 3
A/C PSI = XXX IF
LIQ LIN TMP <u>ABOVE</u>
XXX F ADD R-134

PARTIAL CHG TEST 2 of 3
A/C PSI = XXX IF
LIQ LIE TMP <u>BELOW</u>
XXX F RECLM R-134

PARTIAL CHG TEST 3 of 3
A/C PSI = XXX OK IF
LIQ LIN TMP <u>BTWN</u>
XX F AND XX F

THESE 3 SCREENS CYCLE EVERY 3 SEC
PRESS "READ/HOLD" TO STOP CYCLING
BETWEEN THE 3 SCREENS (THE PRESSURE
READING WILL STILL UPDATE)

SENSORS

Eng RPM
TPS V %
Min TPS
ECT
VSS
A/C V PSI
EVAP F
In Car F*
Outside F*
Sunload V*
Mode Dr V*
Temp Dr V*
Dr Stall V*
Comm Wire V*

IN/OUT

A/C PB Sw*
Auto PB Sw*
Recirc PB Sw*
Floor PB Sw*
Mix PB Sw*
BiLevel PB Sw*
Panel PB Sw*
Defrost PB Sw*
Rear Def PB Sw*
Beep Status*
A/C SW
A/C BCM
A/C Relay
Lo Spd FC
Hi Spd FC

MONITORS

1) No A/C On
2) ATC A/C Perform*
3) Climate/Htr
4) Rad Fan Rlys

■   FIGURE 11–54

Typical diagnostic procedure for R134a automatic temperature control system using scan tool (DRB-11). (Courtesy of Chrysler Corporation.)

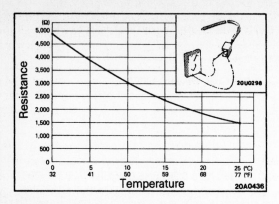

■ FIGURE 11–55
Typical resistance values for an evaporator thermal sensor and air inlet sensor at various temperatures. (Courtesy of Chrysler Corporation.)

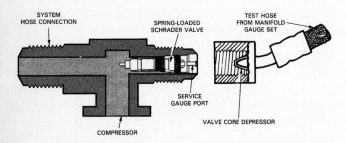

■ FIGURE 11–56
Manifold gauge hose has valve core depressor to open service valve. (Courtesy of Ford Motor Company.)

harmful effects on the ozone layer. New refrigerants such as 134A are being used in current production models. These new refrigerants should not be mixed with the older R12. A/C technicians must take this into account when using A/C discharging, recovery, evacuating and charging equipment. Follow the directions in the appropriate service manual and the equipment manufacturer's instructions to ensure proper equipment and A/C operation.

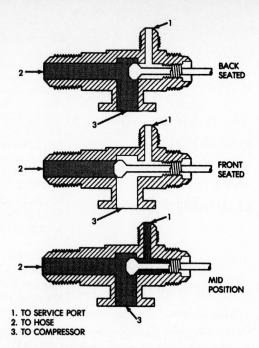

1. TO SERVICE PORT
2. TO HOSE
3. TO COMPRESSOR

■ FIGURE 11–57
Stem-type service valve position. (Courtesy of Chrysler Corporation.)

A refrigerant recovery unit should be connected to the A/C refrigeration system along with the pressure gauge set. A typical hookup is shown in **Figure 11–63.** The yellow center hose of the gauge set is usually connected to the refrigerant recovery unit. Discharging refrigerant into the atmosphere is harmful to the earth's ozone layer and is illegal.

Used refrigerant recovered during the discharging process can be recycled and used again. This requires that all moisture and other contaminants be removed from the refrigerant. To recycle used refrigerant, follow the recycling equipment manufacturer's instructions. Equipment and procedures vary **(Figures 11–59 and 11–60).** The following refrigerant recovery and recycling information appears here courtesy of Chrysler Corporation.

■ FIGURE 11–58
Service port cross section for R134a refrigeration systems. (Courtesy of Chrysler Corporation.)

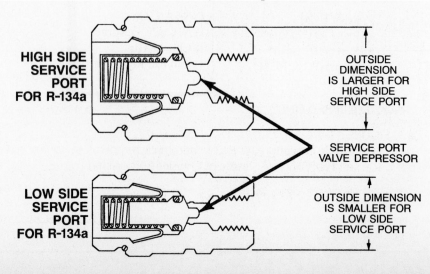

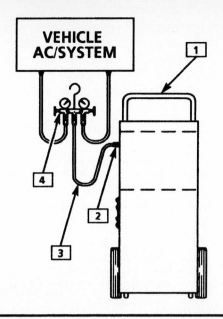

1 REFRIGERANT RECOVERY AND RECYCLING STATION

2 STATION LEFT

3 YELLOW HOSE

4 MANIFOLD GAUGE SET

■ FIGURE 11–59
Modern refrigerant charging and recycling station. (Courtesy of Sun Electric Corporation.)

SAE Service Procedure Standards

The Society of Automotive Engineers (SAE) has established standards that cover the Recommended Service Procedures (SAE J1989 and J2211), Specifications for Recovery and Recycling Equipment (SAE J1990 and J2210), and purity requirement of Recovered and Recycled Refrigerant (SAE J1991 and J2099). Although these standards may cover different phases of service and recovery procedures, *safety* is the most important issue. You must be sure that you and others are protected from injury by following the procedures exactly, without taking any shortcuts.

The standards that most apply to you are J1989 and J2211. They establish guidelines for use of recovery/recycling equipment for servicing automotive air conditioning systems.

Whenever you service air conditioning systems or operate recovery/recycling equipment always do the following: wear safety goggles and gloves, follow common shop safety practices, and follow all manufacturers' instructions for equipment operation. In addition, remember:

- Never use a disposable refrigerant tank for storing reclaimed refrigerant.
- Never transfer refrigerant into another tank unless it is approved by the Department of Transportation (DOT).
- Never fill a storage tank to more than 60% of its gross weight rating.
- Never handle any chemical, including refrigerant, without first consulting the Material Safety Data Sheet (MSDS) which accompanies it.
- Never attempt to use any equipment until you are fully trained.
- Never service the recovery/recycling equipment (other than routine filter changes) without first consulting with authorized service personnel.
- Never use electrical equipment that has switches mounted closer than 18 inches to the floor, and never perform refrigerant service in a shop that receives less than four complete air changes per hour.
- Never use extension cords that are worn, frayed, or have a lighter gauge than 14 AWG or that are any longer than absolutely necessary.
- Never use extension cords that don't have three wires (grounded).
- Never use a pigtail-type grounding adapter to circumvent the ground circuit of an extension cord.

NOTE: Check manufacturers recommended service and calibration procedures for all test equipment and gauges. All equipment must perform to specifications in order to provide accurate test results.

Connect the recovery unit service hoses to the system service ports. These hoses must have shutoff valves within 12 inches of the service ends. If the equipment has quick disconnect hoses, make sure they operate properly.

Operate the recovery equipment according to the manufacturers' recommended procedure.

Start the recovery process and remove the refrigerant from the vehicle. Operate the unit until the sys-

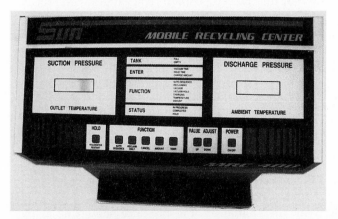

■ FIGURE 11–60
Refrigerant charging and recycling station control panel. (Courtesy of Sun Electric Corporation.)

tem pressure has been reduced to a vacuum. Shut off the recovery unit for at least five minutes and make sure there is no refrigerant remaining in the system. If the system still has pressure, operate the recovery equipment again. Repeat the operation until the system vacuum remains stable for two minutes.

Close the valves in the service lines and remove the lines. Proceed with the repair or service.

Close the valves before removing the hoses from the system to prevent refrigerant from venting to the atmosphere. Attach the gauge set hoses to the reclamation equipment first, under the following conditions: When the manifold gauge set is disconnected from the system, when the center hose is moved to another device which cannot accept refrigerant pressure.

Procedure For Stored Portable Auxiliary Containers

To determine if a recycled refrigerant container has air in it, store the container at 65°F (18° C) for 12 hours, out of direct sunlight.

Install a calibrated pressure gauge, with 1 psig divisions on the container. Measure the pressure.

Measure the temperature of the air with a calibrated thermometer within 4 inches of the container.

Compare the container pressure and air temperature to determine if the container exceeds the pressure limits shown in the chart. If the container pressure is less than the chart values and has been recycled, the air limit has not been exceeded and the refrigerant may be used.

If the pressure is greater than the range and the container has recycled material, slowly vent a small amount of vapor from the top of the container into the recycling equipment. Do not vent if the pressure is less than the pressure on the chart.

If the container still exceeds the pressures on the chart, the complete contents of the container should be recycled.

Recycled Refrigerant Storage

Recycled refrigerants should not be stored in disposable refrigerant containers. New refrigerant is sold in these disposable containers. Use only DOT CFR Title 49 or UL approved storage containers for recycled refrigerant. Any container of recycled refrigerant that has been stored or transferred must be checked as described in "Recycled Refrigerant Checking Procedure."

Transferring Recycled Refrigerant To Portable Containers

When external portable containers are used for transfer, the container must be evacuated to at least 27 inches of vacuum (75 mm Hg absolute pressure)

before transferring of the recycled refrigerant. External portable containers must meet DOT and UL standards. To prevent over filling, the safe filling level must be controlled by weight and must not exceed 60% of the gross weight rating of the container.

Disposal of Refrigerant Containers

All refrigerant must be removed and reclaimed before any refrigerant container is discarded. Attach the container to the recovery unit and remove the remaining refrigerant. When the container pressure has been reduced to a vacuum, close the container valve. Mark the container "EMPTY" and prepare it for disposal.

■ CONNECTING THE PRESSURE GAUGE SET

The pressure gauge set consists of two pressure gauges, a manifold, two control valves, and three hoses (Figures 11–61 to 11–63). The low-pressure gauge is used to test low-side (suction) pressure. The blue hose is connected to the low-pressure side. The high-pressure gauge is used to test high-side (discharge) pressure. The red hose is connected to the high-pressure side. The center yellow hose is used for discharging, evacuating, and charging the system.

Remove the protective caps from the service valve gauge ports and valve stems with the engine stopped. Close both of the hand valves on the gauge manifold set. Do not open these valves at any time during pressure and performance tests. Connect the blue (low-side) hose to the compressor suction service valve gauge port (low side). Connect the red high-pressure gauge hose to the discharge service valve gauge port (high side). Adapters may be required (Figure 11–64).

Set both the service valve stems to the mid-position or the cracked position. The gauges will indicate high- and low-side pressure, respectively. Purge any air from the high-side test hose by opening the high-side hand valve on the manifold for 3 to 5 seconds (the center connection on the manifold must be open). Purge any air from the low-side test hose by opening the low-side hand valve on the manifold for 3 to 5 seconds (the center connection on the manifold must be open).

■ STATIC PRESSURE READING

With the engine off, the pressure should be at the specified level. (See service manual for specifications.) If the pressure is too low, some of the refrigerant has leaked out. In this case the leak must be

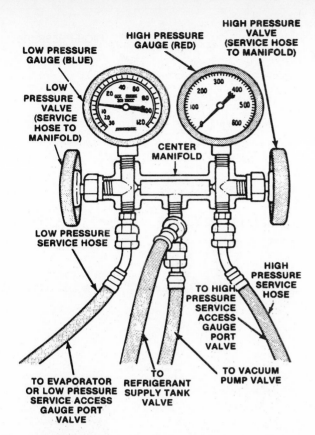

LOW PRESSURE GAUGE (BLUE)

HIGH PRESSURE GAUGE (RED)

HIGH PRESSURE VALVE (SERVICE HOSE TO MANIFOLD)

LOW PRESSURE VALVE (SERVICE HOSE TO MANIFOLD)

CENTER MANIFOLD

LOW PRESSURE SERVICE HOSE

HIGH PRESSURE SERVICE HOSE

TO HIGH PRESSURE SERVICE ACCESS GAUGE PORT VALVE

TO EVAPORATOR OR LOW PRESSURE SERVICE ACCESS GAUGE PORT VALVE

TO REFRIGERANT SUPPLY TANK VALVE

TO VACUUM PUMP VALVE

■ FIGURE 11–61

Manifold gauge set and hose connections. Gauges must be closed while making connections to prevent escape of refrigerant. (Courtesy of Ford Motor Company.)

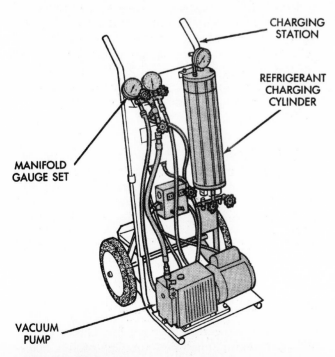

CHARGING STATION

REFRIGERANT CHARGING CYLINDER

MANIFOLD GAUGE SET

VACUUM PUMP

■ FIGURE 11–62

Refrigerant charging station. (Courtesy of Chrysler Corporation.)

repaired and the refrigerant added before making any running tests.

■ PERFORMANCE TESTS

Performance testing is done with the pressure gauges connected and the engine running. The following steps are typical.

1. Close all the car windows and doors.
2. Start the engine and run it at about 2000 rpm.
3. Set the A/C at maximum cooling and run the engine for about 10 minutes to stabilize system pressures.
4. Place a test thermometer in one of the dash air outlets to test air discharge temperatures **(Figure 11–65)**. Place another test thermometer in front of the condenser to test ambient temperature. These temperatures are required for system analysis.
5. Note the gauge readings after pressures have stabilized. Compare the pressure readings with specifications in the service manual. Be sure to take into account the type of refrigerant used (R12 or R134a), the ambient temperature and air discharge temperature readings. Humidity and A/C system design are also factors affecting system pressure readings. See **Figure 11–66** for typical examples of test conditions and results. For interpretation of gauge readings see **Figure 11–67.**

■ PARTIAL CHARGE TEST FOR FIXED ORIFICE SYSTEM

The following method may be used on fixed orifice A/C systems. This method uses the temperature of the lines going into and out of the evaporator, the outside temperature reading and the high pressure gauge readings.

To perform this test, you will need one or two VOMs with thermocouples, or a digital thermometer which will monitor temperature at two locations and compute the difference **(Figure 11–68).** You also need a high pressure gauge.

Attach the high pressure gauge to the high pressure service port. Make sure that the gauge set side valves are closed. Attach the temperature probes to the evaporator inlet and outlet tubes just in front of the quick connect fitting. If you have only one probe, attach it to the inlet.

With the engine and air conditioning running record the temperatures and the pressure reading. If you have only one probe, measure and record the temperature at the inlet and then move the probe to the outlet and measure and record that temperature. Allow the reading to stabilize and record the tem-

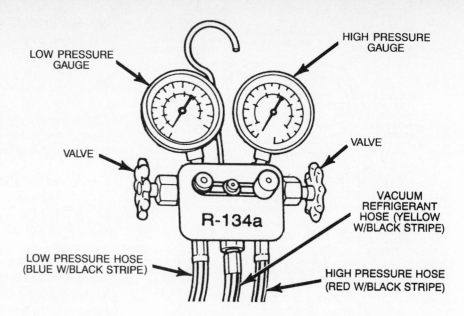

■ FIGURE 11–63
Pressure gauge set component identification (top) and hookup (bottom) with scan tool for R134a air conditioning system performance test. (Courtesy of Chrysler Corporation.)

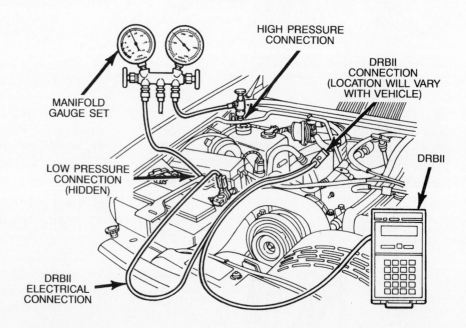

perature. If you are not using a computing type instrument, compute the difference between the two temperature readings.

Compare the pressure reading to the charts in the Service Manual. If the reading is low or normal, the system may be undercharged. If the system is undercharged, add the amount of refrigerant indicated on the appropriate temperature differential chart.

If the pressure reading is higher than normal, troubleshoot the system. Use the temperature readings to help you troubleshoot the system.

If the difference in temperature is higher than normal the problem is probably poor compressor performance or a restriction in the system.

If the difference in temperature is normal or low, the problem is probably with the radiator viscous fan or an overcharged system. After correcting any problems, perform a performance test and check your repair.

■ PARTIAL CHARGE TEST FOR H VALVE SYSTEMS

Sub-cooling is the measurement in degrees above the liquid saturation temperature. Sub-cooling takes place in the condenser. The refrigerant must be completely liquid when it reaches the expansion valve. If

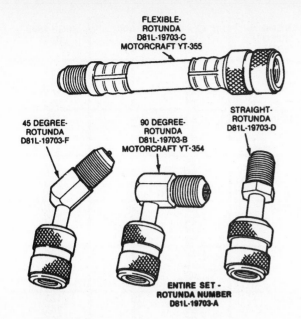

FLEXIBLE-
ROTUNDA
D81L-19703-C
MOTORCRAFT YT-355

45 DEGREE-
ROTUNDA
D81L-19703-F

90 DEGREE-
ROTUNDA
D81L-19703-B
MOTORCRAFT YT-354

STRAIGHT-
ROTUNDA
D81L-19703-D

ENTIRE SET -
ROTUNDA NUMBER
D81L-19703-A

■ FIGURE 11–64
High-pressure service port gauge adapters. (Courtesy of Ford Motor Company.)

it is not, it means that the system is partially discharged. When the system is properly charged, there should be a 10°F to 25°F sub-cooling temperature. Sub-cooling can be determined by measuring high pressure and liquid line temperature.

Refer to **Figure 11–69** which shows the saturation line. This saturation line indicates the point at which all of the vapor has condensed into a fluid at a given temperature and pressure. Any measurements that intersect below the dashed line indicate an over charge and any measurements that intersect above the solid line indicate a low charge.

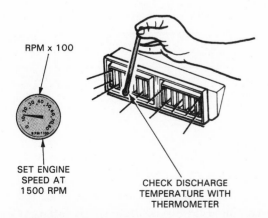

RPM x 100

SET ENGINE
SPEED AT
1500 RPM

CHECK DISCHARGE
TEMPERATURE WITH
THERMOMETER

■ FIGURE 11–65
Checking air discharge temperature at specified engine speed. (Courtesy of Chrysler Corporation.)

■ EXPANSION VALVE (H VALVE) DIAGNOSIS (TYPICAL)

The "H" Valve should be tested at an ambient temperature of 70 to 85°F. This test requires a manifold gauge set and a CO_2 canister.

1. Close the vehicle windows and operate the engine at 1000 rpm.
2. Set the A/C controls to A/C, HIGH Blower, and temperature control lever to full heat position.
3. Use a jumper wire and bypass the low pressure cutoff switch.
4. Disconnect and plug the water valve vacuum (gray) hose, if equipped.
5. Locate and remove both vacuum lines at the recirculating air door actuator and install the light green line where the dark green line had been.
6. Operate the system for at least five minutes to obtain partial stabilization and sufficient heat to load the system. The pressure at the discharge service port should reach 140 to 240 psig. If this pressure cannot be reached, check the system charge level.
7. Spray liquid CO_2 on the control head of the "H" Valve for a minimum of 30 seconds. Completely cover the head. The compressor suction pressure must drop below 15 inches of vacuum. If not, the "H" Valve is stuck open and should be replaced.
8. Remove the CO_2 and watch the compressor suction pressure; it should stabilize at 140 to 240 psig after temporarily rising to a higher pressure. Any "H" Valve that does not produce this response is stuck open and should be replaced.
9. Set the engine speed to 1000 rpm and set the blower speed to high. The evaporator suction pressure should be 20 to 30 psig. If the compressor discharge is higher than 240 psig, check for a restricted discharge line, overheating radiator, air in the system, or an inoperative electric fan.
10. Connect the wires, water valve, vacuum hose, recirculating air door and set the temperature control to COOL. (Courtesy of Chrysler Corporation.)

■ CHECKING FOR REFRIGERANT LEAKS

The refrigeration system should be checked for possible refrigerant leaks. **Figure 11–70** shows areas of possible leaks. Several methods may be used to determine if leakage is present.

RELATIVE HUMIDITY (%)	AMBIENT AIR TEMP		LOW SIDE PSIG	ENGINE SPEED (RPM)	CENTER DUCT AIR TEMPERATURE		HIGH SIDE PSIG
	°F	°C			°F	°C	
20	70	21	29	2000	40	4	150
	80	27	29		44	7	190
	90	32	30		48	9	245
	100	38	31		57	14	305
30	70	21	29	2000	42	6	150
	80	27	30		47	8	205
	90	32	31		51	11	265
	100	38	32		61	16	325
40	70	21	29	2000	45	7	165
	80	27	30		49	9	215
	90	32	32		55	13	280
	100	38	39		65	18	345
50	70	21	30	2000	47	8	180
	80	27	32		53	12	235
	90	32	34		59	15	295
	100	38	40		69	21	350
60	70	21	30	2000	48	9	180
	80	27	33		56	13	240
	90	32	36		63	17	300
	100	38	43		73	23	360
70	70	21	30	2000	50	10	185
	80	27	34		58	14	245
	90	32	38		65	18	305
	100	38	44		75	24	365
80	70	21	30	2000	50	10	190
	80	27	34		59	15	250
	90	32	39		67	19	310
90	70	21	30	2000	50	10	200
	80	27	36		62	17	265
	90	32	42		71	22	330

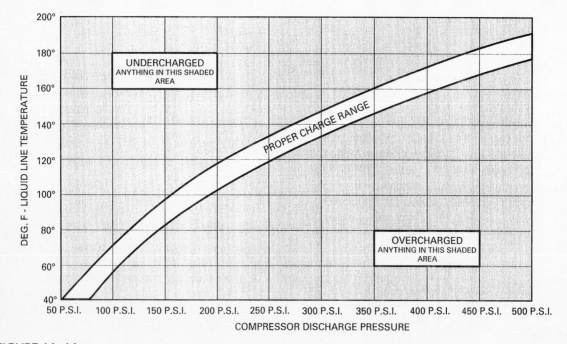

■   FIGURE 11–66

Typical A/C system performance data. (Courtesy of General Motors Corporation.)

1. *Electronic leak detector.* An electronic leak detector uses a sensor to probe suspected areas. A sound or light signal is produced when leakage is detected. The probe is moved very slowly over suspected areas. About 1 inch per second is typical. This is the best method for leak testing **(Figure 11–71).**

2. *Bubble solution.* A liquid bubble solution is applied to the suspected area. Bubbles or foam are formed in the applied solution where leakage exists.

3. *Dye leak detector.* A red dye leak detector solution is mixed with the refrigerant or refrigerant oil. The brightly colored solution will appear where leakage occurs.

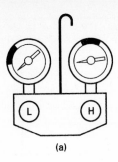

(a)

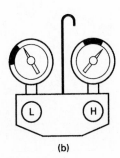

(b)

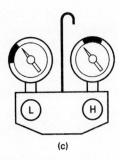

(c)

■ FIGURE 11–67
With a good understanding of A/C system operation, gauge readings can be interpreted to identify problems such as those shown: (A) low charge, faulty thermostatic switch, faulty expansion valve, high-side restriction; (B) overcharged, restricted airflow through condenser, engine running too hot, too much refrigerant oil; (C) compressor internal leak, faulty expansion valve, low-side restriction. (Courtesy of F T Enterprises.)

■ DISCHARGING AND RECOVERING THE REFRIGERANT

1. Following the equipment manufacturer's instructions, connect the recycling station to the vehicle A/C system using a manifold gauge set or a charging station (see **Figures 11–59** to **11–63).**

2. Verify that there is refrigerant in the vehicle A/C system by testing for positive system pressure. Do not try to recover refrigerant if there is no pressure in the system.

3. Set the recovery station to the running mode.

4. Crack open the gauge valves slightly to allow refrigerant to escape slowly.

5. Press the start or power switch to begin the recovery process. (Be sure to follow the manufacturer's instructions; some start switches must be held for a few seconds to start the recovery.) Remove all the refrigerant.

■ VACUUM LEAK TESTING THE SYSTEM

1. When all refrigerant has been recovered, the A/C system should go into a slight vacuum, as indicated on the manifold or charging station gauge. On some recycling stations, the pump will shut off automatically by a low-pressure switch. On others, you may have to shut the pump off manually.

2. Allow the vehicle A/C system to remain closed for about 2 minutes. Observe the system vacuum level as shown on the gauge. If the pressure does not rise, disconnect the recycling station hose(s).

3. If the system pressure rises, repeat steps 4, 5, and 6 until the vacuum level remains stable for 2 minutes.

4. Perform required service operations on the A/C system.

5. The amount of oil removed during the recovery process must be measured, and the same amount of clean oil must be added to the vehicle A/C system. If the system is ruptured most or all of the refrigerant oil may have been lost. Follow the equipment manufacturer's instructions for measuring the amount of oil removed from the vehicle A/C system.

6. When the recycling station tank has reached its full capacity, it will be indicated by a gauge or a "full" lamp. On most stations the power will be shut off automatically when tank capacity is reached.

■ CORRECTING REFRIGERANT LEAKS

Refrigerant may leak from refrigerant lines or fittings, switch or valve connections, the front compressor seal, receiver–drier, evaporator, or condenser. Leaking refrigerant lines must be replaced. A leaking receiver–drier, evaporator, or condenser must be replaced. Leaking fittings may be loose and simply require tightening to stop the leak. Fittings should be tightened to specified torque and not over- or undertightened. Many fittings and line connections have O-ring seals that can be replaced to correct a leak. O-ring seals must be lubricated

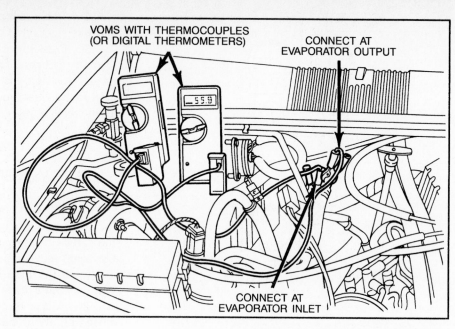

■ FIGURE 11–68
To check the refrigerant charge in a fixed orifice system, two digital thermometers may be used. Connect one to the evaporator inlet and the other to the evaporator outlet. Use the evaporator inlet temperature, evaporator outlet temperature, and the high pressure readings and compare to temperature/pressure chart in service manual. (Courtesy of Chrysler Corporation.)

with refrigerant oil before assembly. A leaking front compressor seal must be replaced to correct the problem.

■ COMPRESSOR EXTERNAL LEAK TEST

A compressor external leak test may require compressor removal and the removal of the compressor clutch. Refer to the service manual for instructions. The general test procedure is as follows.

1. Install pressure test adapters on the compressor.

2. Connect the high- and low-pressure gauges to the adapters **(Figure 11–72)**.

3. Close the gauge valves.

4. Turn the compressor shaft about 10 turns to distribute oil in the compressor.

5. Connect the center hose of the gauge set to a refrigerant drum in the upright position.

6. Open the low- and high-pressure gauge valves.

7. Open the valve on the refrigerant drum and allow refrigerant vapor to flow into the compressor.

8. Use a leak detector to check for leaks at the compressor head seal, front head seal, shaft seal, joint seal, and around the compressor cylinder bolts.

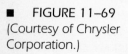

■ FIGURE 11–69
(Courtesy of Chrysler Corporation.)

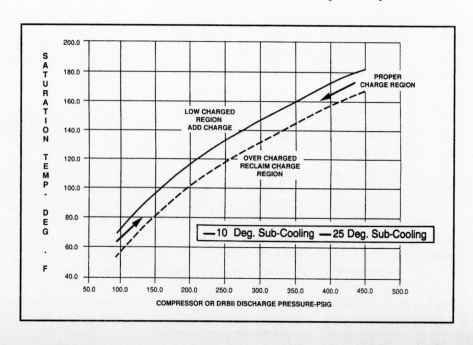

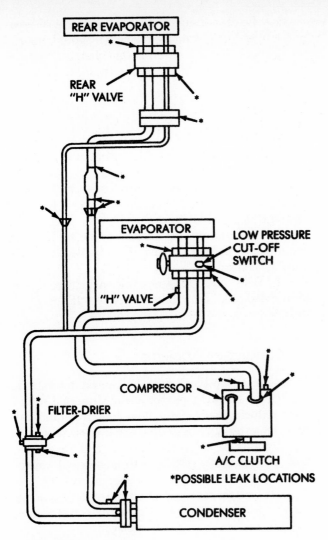

■ FIGURE 11–70
Typical refrigeration system leak points. (Courtesy of Chrysler Corporation.)

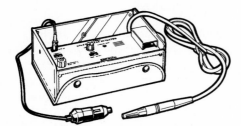

■ FIGURE 11–71
Electronic leak detector for R12 and R134a systems. Can be switched to type of system to be tested. Operates on 12V DC power. (Courtesy of General Motors Corporation.)

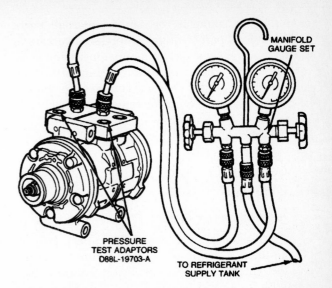

■ FIGURE 11–72
Compressor external leak test hookup. With refrigerant vapor in compressor, use a leak detector to check for external leaks. (Courtesy of Ford Motor Company.)

9. Repair any leaks as outlined in the service manual. Some leaks require only the replacement of a seal, washer, or O-ring without compressor disassembly. Others may require compressor overhaul or replacement.

■ REFRIGERATION SYSTEM PROBLEMS

Receiver–Drier–Accumulator Problems

Other than leaking refrigerant hose replacement, receiver–drier replacement is probably most common. When the receiver–drier or accumulator becomes restricted or dirty, it must be replaced. The receiver–drier should be replaced if any of the following apply.

1. Moisture is found in the system.
2. The system has been left open (lines or fittings disconnected) for over an hour.
3. The receiver–drier is restricted.
4. The system has a leak and has been operating with a partial charge.
5. The sight glass is cloudy, indicating moisture or contamination.

Compressor Problems

Compressor problems include abnormal noise, a leaking front seal, or magnetic clutch failure. A noisy compressor may be caused by loose or incorrect mounting attachments or faulty internal parts. Faulty internal parts require compressor overhaul or replacement. Follow service manual instructions for compressor overhaul. A leaking compressor shaft seal must be replaced. On some compressors this can be done without compressor removal. Special tools are required for seal removal and installation. Follow the procedures in the service manual.

Compressor Clutch Diagnosis (Typical)

A/C Compressor Clutch

1. Place a jumper wire from battery positive post to the A/C compressor clutch connector terminal; the clutch should engage. If not, go to the next step with the jumper installed.
2. Place a wire from the clutch coil frame to chassis ground; the clutch should engage. If not, repair the clutch coil ground or replace the coil. Coil resistance can be checked with an ohmmeter (**Figure 11–73**).

Low-Pressure Switch

Turn the ignition control to MAX cool.

1. The A/C low-pressure switch connector terminal should show battery voltage. If not, proceed to thermostatic control tests.

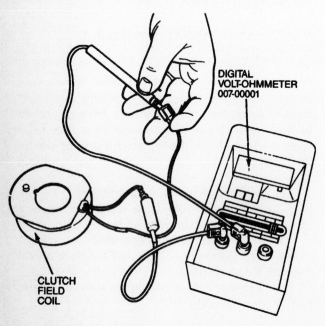

■   FIGURE 11–73
Compressor clutch coil resistance test. If resistance does not meet specifications, replace the coil. (Courtesy of Ford Motor Company.)

2. Place a jumper wire across the A/C low-pressure switch terminals; the clutch should engage. If not, check the system refrigerant charge. If the system is properly charged, replace the A/C low-pressure switch.

Thermostatic Control

Turn the ignition switch to RUN, A/C blower switch to ON, and thermostatic control to MAX cool.

1. The thermostatic control connector terminal should show battery voltage. If not, repair the open from the blower switch.
2. The thermostatic control connector terminal should show battery voltage. If not, replace the thermostatic control.
3. The A/C low-pressure switch connector terminal should show battery voltage. If not, repair the open from the thermostatic control.

Condenser Problems

A condenser problem may be caused by external restrictions blocking proper airflow, internal restrictions reducing refrigerant flow, or refrigerant leakage. An externally restricted condenser should be thoroughly cleaned with shop air and/or a water hose. An internally restricted condenser will cause a higher than normal pressure reading on the high side. Ice or frost may collect on the outside of a partially restricted condenser. An internally restricted or leaking condenser is usually replaced.

Expansion Valve Problems

A restriction can build up in the fixed orifice tube or the expansion valve filter. The expansion valve may fail to operate because of sensor bulb failure or leakage.

Orifice Tube Removal and Installation

The refrigeration system must be discharged before replacing the orifice tube. Typical orifice tube replacement is as follows (**Figure 11–74**).

1. Disconnect the liquid inlet line from the evaporator.
2. Pour a small amount of refrigerant oil into the inlet tube to lubricate the O-rings and orifice tube.
3. Install the orifice remover tool with the two tangs on the fixed orifice tube.

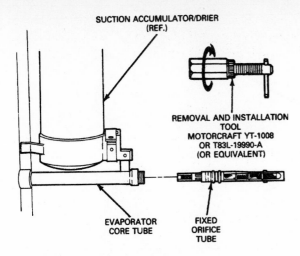

■ FIGURE 11–74

Typical fixed orifice tube replacement. (Courtesy of Ford Motor Company.)

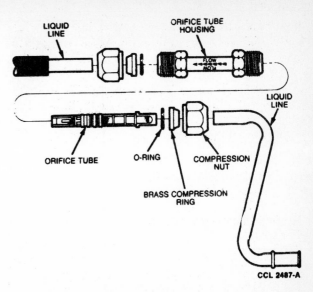

■ FIGURE 11–75

In-line orifice tube replacement requires cutting section containing old tube out of line and replacing it with an orifice tube service kit. (Courtesy of Ford Motor Company.)

PRO TIP

Do not twist or rotate the orifice tube in the evaporator core tube, as this could result in the tube breaking off.

---

4. Hold the T handle of the tool to keep it from turning and turn the nut on the tool down against the core tube until the orifice tube is pulled out of the tube.

If the orifice tube breaks during removal, it can be removed with a special broken orifice tube remover tool. This tool works much like a spiral broken stud remover.

To install the orifice tube:

1. Lubricate the O-rings with refrigerant oil.
2. Position the orifice tube in the orifice tube removal tool and insert the tube into the evaporator inlet tube until it is fully seated against the stop.
3. Remove the tool from the orifice tube.
4. Using a new O-ring lubricated with refrigerant oil, connect the refrigerant liquid line to the evaporator core tube.

In some applications the section of the evaporator core inlet tube containing the orifice tube must be cut out and an orifice tube repair kit containing a new orifice tube installed **(Figure 11–75)**. Follow the service manual directions for replacement.

■ REFRIGERATION SYSTEM PARTS REPLACEMENT

When inspection and test procedures indicate that a refrigeration system component is faulty, it must be replaced or repaired. The variety of system and component designs makes it essential to refer to the appropriate service manual for special procedures and special tools that may be required. When replacing a faulty refrigeration system component that requires disconnecting refrigerant lines, some general precautions must be observed.

1. Never use parts, oil, or refrigerant designed for R12 systems in R134A systems or vice versa. They are not compatible and can cause serious damage to the system if interchanged. Spring lock refrigerant line couplings are shown in **Figure 11–76.**
2. Never replace a refrigeration system part without first discharging the system completely. An exception to this rule is that in some cases the A/C compressor can be isolated from the system using the pressure gauges. Follow service manual procedures to isolate the compressor and replace it.
3. Always wipe fittings and connections clean before disconnecting them.
4. Always cap all disconnected fittings and lines immediately to prevent the entry of air, moisture, and dirt.
5. Leave protective caps in place on new parts until ready to make connections.

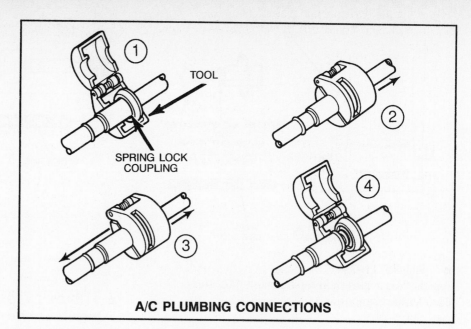

A/C PLUMBING CONNECTIONS

■ FIGURE 11–76
The spring lock coupling is a refrigerant line coupling held together by a garter spring inside a circular cage. When the coupling is connected, the flared end of the female fitting slips behind the garter spring inside the cage of the male fitting. The garter spring and cage prevent the flared end of the female fitting from pulling out of the cage. (Courtesy of Chrysler Corporation.)

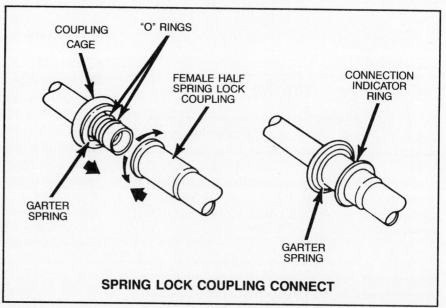

SPRING LOCK COUPLING CONNECT

6. Use new O-rings properly lubricated with refrigerant oil wherever used.

7. Tighten all connections, lines, and fittings to the specified torque.

8. After repairs are completed, evacuate the system, leak test the system using the vacuum drop method, and charge the system with the correct amount of refrigerant.

9. Performance test the system as described earlier.

■ EVACUATING THE REFRIGERATION SYSTEM

The refrigeration system should be evacuated any time that it has been opened or discharged. The following procedure is typical. Refer to the service manual for the actual procedure.

1. Connect the manifold gauge set as outlined earlier.

2. Make sure that both manifold gauge valves are turned all the way to the right (closed).

3. Make sure that the center hose connection at the manifold gauge is tight.

4. Connect the manifold gauge set center hose to a vacuum pump.

5. Open the manifold gauge set valves and start the vacuum pump.

6. Evacuate the system with vacuum pump until the low-pressure gauge reads as close to 30 in. Hg (100 kPa) as possible. Continue to operate the vacuum pump for 15 minutes. If part of the system has been replaced, continue to operate the vacuum pump for another 20 to 30 minutes.

7. When evacuation of the system is complete, close the manifold gauge set valves and turn the vacuum pump off.

8. Observe the low-pressure gauge for 5 minutes to ensure that system vacuum is held. If vacuum is held, charge the system. If vacuum is not held for 5 minutes, leak test the system, repair the leaks, and evacuate the system again.

PRO TIP

A badly moisture-contaminated system may have to be evacuated and charged three or four times to remove all moisture from the system.

■ VACUUM DROP LEAK TESTING THE EVAPORATOR AND CONDENSER

Vacuum drop leak testing can be done on the entire refrigeration system or on individual components. Special fittings are required to connect the charging station to the evaporator or condenser **(Figure 11–77)**. First test the entire system, and if it does not hold vacuum, test the components separately to isolate the problem. The procedure is to evacuate the system or component (as described earlier) until specified vacuum is obtained. Next close the manifold gauge valves and turn the vacuum motor off. Wait for at least 5 minutes. If the system or component holds vacuum, there are no leaks. If vacuum is not held, repair or replace the leaking component.

■ CHARGING THE REFRIGERATION SYSTEM

The amount of refrigerant used to charge the system is critical to proper performance. Either an under-

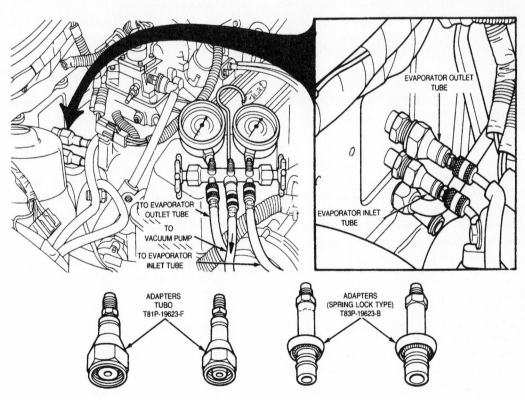

■ FIGURE 11–77
Evaporator core and condenser core can be leak tested using the vacuum drop method and appropriate test gauge adapters. Simply apply specified vacuum to the unit being tested, wait the specified time, and note whether there is a drop in vacuum. (Courtesy of Ford Motor Company.)

charge or an overcharge will reduce system performance. Some vehicle manufacturers do not recommend the use of small refrigerant cans since the charge level cannot accurately be controlled. A charging station or charging cylinder is the recommended method. The following charging procedure is typical.

1. With manifold gauge set valves closed, disconnect the vacuum pump from manifold gauge set.

2. Connect the center hose of manifold gauge set to a refrigerant charging cylinder. If a charging station is used, follow the manufacturer's instructions.

3. Disconnect the wire harness connector from the clutch cycling pressure switch and install a jumper wire across two terminals of the connector.

4. Open the manifold gauge set low-side valve to allow refrigerant to enter system. Keep the refrigerant cylinder in an upright position.

5. When no more refrigerant is being drawn into the system, start the engine and set the control assembly for MAX A/C and HI blower. Continue to add refrigerant to the system until the specified weight of refrigerant is in system. Then close the manifold gauge low-pressure valve and refrigerant supply valve.

6. Remove the jumper wire from the clutch cycling pressure switch. Attach the connector to the pressure switch.

7. Operate system until pressures stabilize to verify normal operation and system pressures.

8. In high ambient temperatures, it may be necessary to operate a high-volume fan positioned to blow air through radiator and condenser. This will aid in cooling engine and prevent excessive refrigerant system pressures.

9. When charging is completed and system operating pressures are normal, disconnect the manifold gauge set from the vehicle. Install protective caps on service gauge port valves. Disconnect jumper wire from the cycling clutch switch.

■ ADDING REFRIGERANT OIL

The refrigeration system must contain the specified amount of refrigerant oil for efficient operation and long life. Before checking the oil level, operate the A/C system for at least 10 minutes. On some systems the oil level can be checked with a dipstick. On others the amount of oil removed during discharging must be measured and an equivalent amount of new oil added. On still other systems the service manual specifies the amount of refrigerant oil to add for each component that is replaced. In one example

when an accumulator is replaced, 3.5 fluid ounces of oil must be added. The variety and size of A/C components on different vehicles require that instructions on the oil level checking procedure and the amount of refrigerant oil to be added must be obtained from the appropriate service manual. Never use oil specified for R12 systems in systems using R134A or vice-versa. Using the wrong oil will cause A/C performance problems and parts failure.

Review Questions

1. The heating system provides heat from the _____ _____ system to provide heat to the interior of the vehicle.

2. Interior heating system controls may be _____ or _____.

3. The automotive air conditioning system _____ _____ _____ and circulates the air in the vehicle.

4. Computer-controlled air conditioning systems are fully automatic. True or False.

5. R12 refrigerant has CFC containing _____ and _____ which are harmful to the earth's ozone layer.

6. R134A has been developed and is used in A.C. systems as it is less harmful to the _____ _____.

7. R12 and R134A refrigerants are interchangeable. True or False.

8. When a vapor is pressurized it gives off heat as it's changed to a _____.

9. As pressure is lowered to a predetermined psi on R12 or R134A it changes to a vapor, therefore takes in _____.

10. A _____ _____ is used to engage and disengage the compressor drive pulley.

11. Special oil must be used for the R12 and R134A A.C. systems. True or False.

12. The same lubricating oil may be used with R12 and R134A refrigerant. True or False.

13. Pressure on the refrigerant is increased in the condenser so it will change from _____ to a _____ dissipating heat.

14. The purpose of the evaporator is to _____ _____ from the vehicles' interior.

15. The purpose of the expansion valve is to control _____ pressure.

16. The receiver–drier has a _____ to remove any moisture from the system.

17. Refrigerant hose lines and fittings must be compatible to the type of refrigerant used. True or False.

18. Service valves are provided on the A.C. system so _____ _____ can be connected.

19. Heating system problems could include not sufficient _____, poor _____ _____, or too much _____.

20. Airflow-controlled doors are controlled by either a _____ or _____ motor.

21. All technicians servicing motor vehicle air conditioning systems must be _____ and use approved _____.

22. All technicians must maintain records on vehicles serviced and keep them for _____ _____.

23. Any refrigerant that contacts the skin or eye will cause instant _____.

24. Be sure to use only the recommended parts for refrigerant R134A or R12 as the parts are different. True or False.

25. On computer-controlled A.C. systems _____ _____ _____ can be used to identify problems.

26. Refrigerant equipment must be used to avoid any refrigerant entering the _____.

27. Static pressure testing an A.C. unit must be done with the engine off. True or False.

28. When testing for R12 leakage with a flame tester, should the flame come in contact with R12 leakage it changes to _____ _____.

29. The amount of refrigerant used to recharge the system is critical to _____ _____.

30. Special refrigerant oil for either the R12 or the R134A system must be used in the correct amount to avoid _____.

Test Questions

1. Temperature control in the heating system is achieved by
   a. mixing cold and hot coolant in the heater core
   b. mixing heated and non-heated air
   c. controlling the condenser
   d. controlling the evaporator

2. The intensity of heat is measured in
   a. British Thermal Units
   b. degrees; Fahrenheit or Celsius
   c. calories
   d. watts

3. Latent heat is
   a. sensible heat
   b. hidden heat
   c. measured with a thermometer
   d. visible heat

4. Technician A says an automatic heating and ventilating system uses a pressure relief valve in the passenger compartment. Technician B says a pressure relief valve is only used on a liquid cooling system. Who is right?

a. technician A
b. technician B
c. both are right
d. both are wrong

5. Which A/C components separate the high-pressure side from the low-pressure side?
   a. the evaporator and condenser
   b. the condenser and expansion valve
   c. the compressor and expansion valve
   d. the receiver–dryer and expansion valve

6. The condenser changes
   a. high-pressure vapor into low-pressure liquid
   b. high-pressure vapor into high-pressure liquid
   c. low-pressure vapor into low-pressure liquid
   d. high-pressure liquid into low-pressure liquid

7. The automotive air conditioning system
   a. adds humidity and cleans the air
   b. removes humidity and cleans the air
   c. does not change humidity
   d. does not clean air

8. On computer-controlled A/C systems perform a visual inspection first, then
   a. connect a pressure gauge set to test A/C performance
   b. take a static pressure reading
   c. discharge the A/C system
   d. activate the on-board self diagnosis

9. There are two kinds of A/C service valves, which are
   a. three-position and Schraeder
   b. two-position and Schraeder
   c. variable displacement and Schraeder
   d. mono port and Schraeder

10. Refrigerant 12 (R12) should not be discharged into the atmosphere because it damages the
    a. azone layer
    b. ozone layer
    c. uzone layer
    d. ezone layer

11. To check a compressor magnetic clutch connect a jumper wire from the battery
    a. negative post to the clutch connector terminal
    b. positive post to the PDA valve
    c. positive post to the clutch connector terminal
    d. negative post to the temperature control

12. To prevent an R12 refrigerant container from bursting, the temperature of storage should not exceed
    a. 40 degrees F
    b. 72 degrees F
    c. 90 degrees F
    d. 125 degrees F

13. Extreme compressor noise could be caused by
    a. clutch electric short
    b. clutch slipping

    c. defective ambient temperature switch

    d. high system pressures

14. With the air conditioning system operating, insert a thermometer into the evaporator with the tip touching the coil. The temperature should be approximately
    a. 35 degrees F
    b. 55 degrees F
    c. 72 degrees F
    d. 25 degrees F

15. Which of the following leak detection methods indicates a leak by a red-colored stain?
    a. Halide
    b. Dytel
    c. Flame
    d. Electronic

16. The purpose of the receiver–drier is to
    a. dry the refrigerant only
    b. filter the refrigerant only
    c. dry and filter the refrigerant
    d. cool the refrigerant

17. The purpose of the expansion valve is to
    a. control the compressor pressure
    b. control the POA valve
    c. make sure the evaporator stays at −20 degrees Fahrenheit
    d. meter the refrigerant into the evaporator

18. What is the function of the evaporator in the air conditioning unit?
    a. to remove heat from the refrigerant
    b. to absorb heat from the passenger compartment
    c. to absorb moisture from the refrigerant
    d. to change the refrigerant from a gas to a liquid

19. The air conditioning system is designed to cool,
    a. clean, dry, and circulate the air
    b. dry, and circulate the air
    c. clean, and circulate the air
    d. and circulate the air

20. Some of the sensors used in electronic A/C systems are
    a. in-car temperature sensor, solar sensor, speed sensor
    b. solar sensor, blend door position sensor, ambient temperature sensor
    c. speed sensor, ambient temperature sensor, solar sensor
    d. solar sensor, defrost door actuator, blend door position sensor

21. When working with refrigerants always wear safety
    a. shoes
    b. glasses
    c. headgear
    d. all of the above

22. To test heater blower motor operation
    a. remove it and test it with an ohmmeter
    b. apply battery voltage to the switch
    c. apply battery voltage to the temperature control terminals
    d. apply battery voltage to each motor input terminal

23. Low heat output from the heater may be caused by
    a. low ambient temperatures
    b. heater core restricted internally
    c. antifreeze level too high
    d. none of the above

24. A sight glass is used to indicate
    a. excessive refrigerant
    b. system overheating
    c. low refrigerant level
    d. low oil level

25. The condenser and evaporator can be leak tested using the
    a. voltage drop method
    b. current drop method
    c. fluid drop method
    d. vacuum drop method

Lighting, Instrumentation, and Power Accessories Diagnosis and Service

INTRODUCTION

This chapter discusses typical automotive lighting, instrumentation, body control computer, and power accessory systems. The number and types of systems vary considerably between different makes and models, and within vehicle price range. Typical diagnostic and service procedures are included in this chapter.

LEARNING OBJECTIVES

After completing this chapter, you should be able to:
- Describe the operation of the various lighting systems.
- Aim headlamps properly.
- Diagnose and repair lighting system problems.
- Describe the operation of dash panel instruments.
- Diagnose and repair speedometer problems.
- Describe windshield wiper operation.
- Replace windshield wiper blades.
- Diagnose windshield wiper problems.
- Describe power seat and power window operation.
- Describe power door lock operation.
- Describe speed control operation.
- Diagnose speed control problems.
- Describe horn operation.
- Describe typical body computer control system functions.
- Describe basic air bag system operation and service.

TERMS YOU SHOULD KNOW

Look for these terms as you study this chapter and learn what they mean.

headlamp	speedometer
light switch	odometer
dimmer switch	electronic instruments
high beam	printed circuit board
low beam	vacuum fluorescent
filament	display
automatic dimmer	voice alert system
halogen bulb	windshield wipers
headlight aiming	wiper motor
tail lamp	wiper arm
park lamp	wiper blade
brake lamp	wiper blade refill
side marker lamp	windshield washer
license lamp	power windows
signal lights	power seats
flasher	power door locks
brake lights	speed control
brake warning light	horns
bimetal gauge	theft deterrent system
thermal gauge	body control computer
balanced coil gauge	air bag module
magnetic gauge	crash sensor
warning lights	safing sensor
charge indicators	

■ HEADLAMP SYSTEMS

The headlamp system includes two or four headlamps, a light switch, dimmer switch, fuses or circuit breaker, related wiring, and the battery **(Figure 12–1).** Related lights include the tail lights, park lights, side marker lights, and instrument panel lights. Concealed headlamps have an electric or vacuum motor to operate the headlamp doors.

The rotary, push/pull headlamp switch has two positions. The first position turns on the parking, side marker, tail, license, and instrument panel lights. The second position turns on all of these and the headlamps. Turning the switch knob operates a rheostat to control the brightness of the instrument panel lights **(Figure 12–2).** Other switch designs are also used.

The dimmer switch has a high-beam and a low-beam function. A high-beam indicator light in the instrument panel lights up in the high-beam mode. Some systems have a light-sensitive automatic dimmer switch. The light sensor produces a small current when exposed to light from oncoming headlamps. This small current operates a relay to dim the headlamps. When there are no approaching lights, the system reverts to high beam.

Cars have either two or four headlamps. In the two-headlamp system each lamp has two filaments,

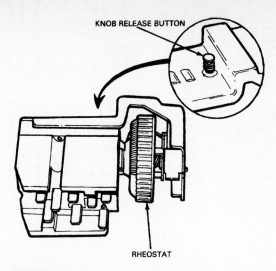

■ FIGURE 12–2

Headlamp switch with dash light dimmer rheostat. (Courtesy of Ford Motor Company.)

one high beam and one low beam. In the four-headlamp system, two lamps each have one low-beam filament. The other two each have two filaments, one high and one low beam **(Figures 12–3** and **12–4).** Sealed-beam headlamps are made from glass or plastic. They may be rectangular, round, or aerodynamic in shape **(Figure 12–5).** Composite headlamps

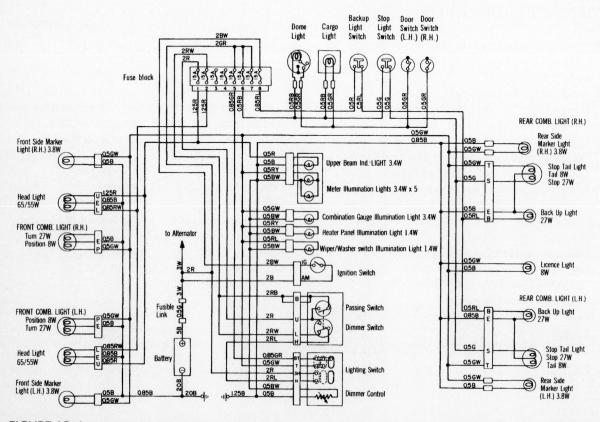

■ FIGURE 12–1

Typical lighting system wiring diagram. (Courtesy of Chrysler Corporation.)

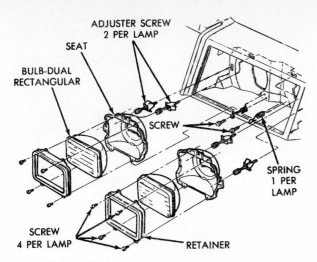

Dual-headlamp system mounting detail. (Courtesy of Chrysler Corporation.)

may contain the headlamp, side marker, and park lamp in a single unit.

Halogen Headlamps

Halogen headlamps have a small inner bulb enclosing a tungsten filament and a small amount of halogen vapor. This results in a brighter light, a longer lasting bulb, and no bulb blackening. Halogen headlamps are either sealed-beam units or are designed with a replaceable halogen bulb (**Figures 12–6** and **12–7**).

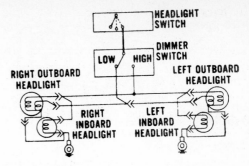

■ FIGURE 12–4
Typical four-headlamp system electrical circuit. (Courtesy of Ford Motor Co. of Canada Ltd.)

Headlamp Delay System

A headlamp delay system keeps the headlights on for a short period of time to provide lights to occupants leaving the vehicle in the dark. The system uses a time-delay relay to keep the lights on after switching off the ignition first and then switching the headlamp switch off.

Automatic Headlamp System

An automatic headlamp system turns the headlamps on automatically when natural light falls below a certain level. It turns the headlamps off automatically when natural light reaches a certain level of brightness. The system uses a photocell sensor and amplifier, a headlamp control relay, and a time-delay control relay with an on/off switch. The system is

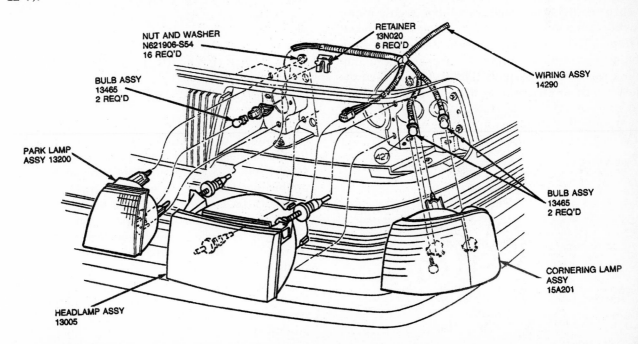

■ FIGURE 12–5
Aerodynamic headlamp, park, and cornering lamp. (Courtesy of Ford Motor Company.)

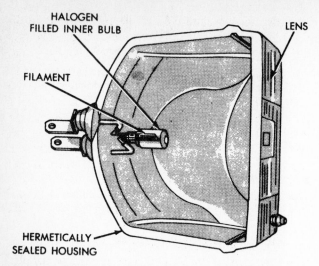

■ FIGURE 12–6
Halogen sealed-beam headlamp. (Courtesy of Chrysler
Corporation.)

connected in parallel with the normal headlamp
control system.

Concealed Headlamps

Some cars are equipped with headlamps that are
concealed when they are switched off. Two methods
are used to provide this feature: headlamp doors
and retracting headlamps. Headlamp doors are positioned in front of the headlamps when they are off.
When the lights are switched on, an electric motor
swings the doors out of the way to expose the headlamps. The headlamps remain stationary. With
retracting headlamps the headlamp and headlamp
door move as an assembly **(Figure 12–8)**. When the
headlamps are switched on, they swing into position
to provide light on the road. When the lights are
switched off, they retract to provide a smooth body

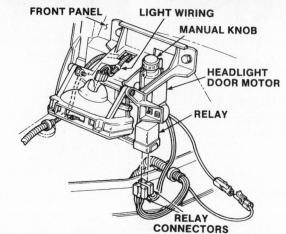

■ FIGURE 12–8
Retractable headlamp system. (Courtesy of General
Motors Corporation.)

surface and conceal the headlamps. Both systems are
provided with a manual method of exposing the
headlamps in case of failure of the system to expose
the headlamps.

■ OTHER EXTERIOR LIGHTS

Tail, Park, and Brake Lights

Tail lamp bulbs are usually double filament types—
one filament for the tail lamp function and the other
for the turn signal and brake light function **(Figure
12–9)**. Front park lamp bulbs are also usually of the
double-filament type, serving both park and signal
functions. License lamp and side marker bulbs are
normally   single-filament   types.   Single-filament
bulbs may be single- or double-contact types. Single-
contact types are grounded through the bulb base,
while double-contact, single-filament types have two
wires—one live and the other a ground. Double-
filament bulbs have two contacts and two wire connections to them if grounded through the base. If not
grounded through the base of the bulb, a two-
filament bulb has three contacts and three wires connected to it. Bulb sockets are spring loaded to provide good electrical contact with bulb contacts. A

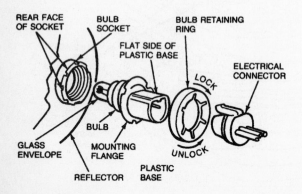

■ FIGURE 12–7
Halogen headlamp bulb mounting detail. (Courtesy
of Ford Motor Company.)

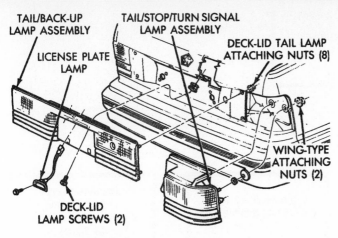

■ FIGURE 12–9
Typical rear lighting components. (Courtesy of Chrysler Corporation.)

typical side marker and cornering light circuit is illustrated in **Figure 12–10.**

Directional Signal Lights

When the ignition switch is in the *on* position, and the signal light switch mounted on the steering column is operated, the front and rear signal lights on the same side flash *on* and *off* to indicate the intention to turn. If so equipped, the side marker lamps

will also flash *on* and *off* and the cornering light on the same side will be in the *on* mode. When the signal light switch is moved to the opposite position, the lights on the opposite side of the vehicle will operate similarly. A signal indicator light on the instrument panel also flashes.

The turn signal switch is mounted in a housing at the upper end of the steering column below the steering wheel. A turn signal actuating plate is mounted to a pivot and contacts the turn signal switch. This switch is integral with a wire harness and a multiple connector **(Figure 12–11).** A canceling cam assembly fits over the steering shaft and the cam turns with the steering wheel.

When the signal lever is in either turn position, a projection on the canceling cam contacts a spring on the actuating plate once per revolution of the steering wheel. Rotation of the steering wheel and cam in one direction does not move the actuating plate; rotation in the other direction causes the actuating plate to be pushed back to neutral position, thereby providing automatic canceling after a turn. See **Figure 12–12** for turn signal problem diagnosis.

Hazard Warning Lights

The hazard warning system, when turned on, causes all turn signal lights to flash simultaneously. This system makes use of the regular turn signal wiring and light bulbs but has a separate supply wire, flasher unit, and off/on switch. This makes it possible to operate the system even though the ignition switch and doors are locked. The system is activated

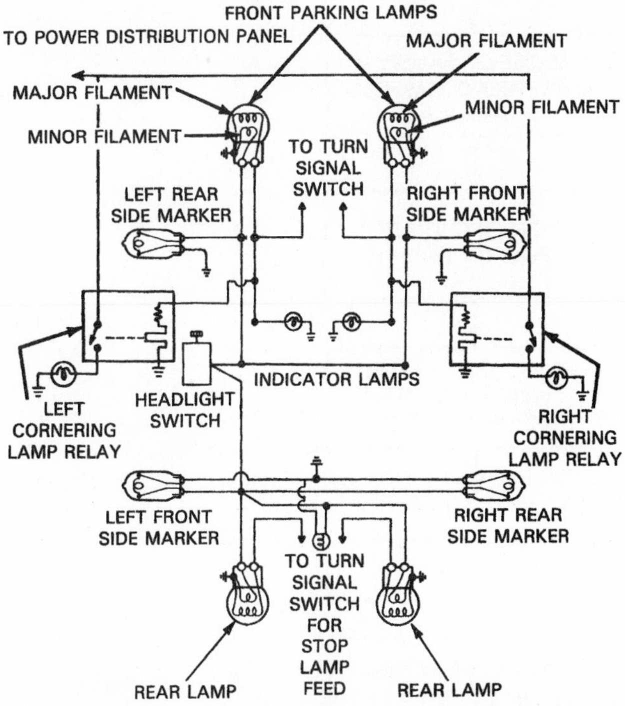

■ FIGURE 12–10
Park, turn signal, and cornering lamp wiring diagram. (Courtesy of Ford Motor Company.)

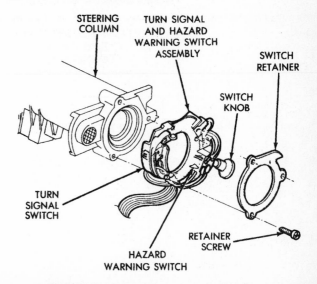

■ FIGURE 12–11
Typical turn signal switch and wiring harness mounted in steering column. (Courtesy of Chrysler Corporation.)

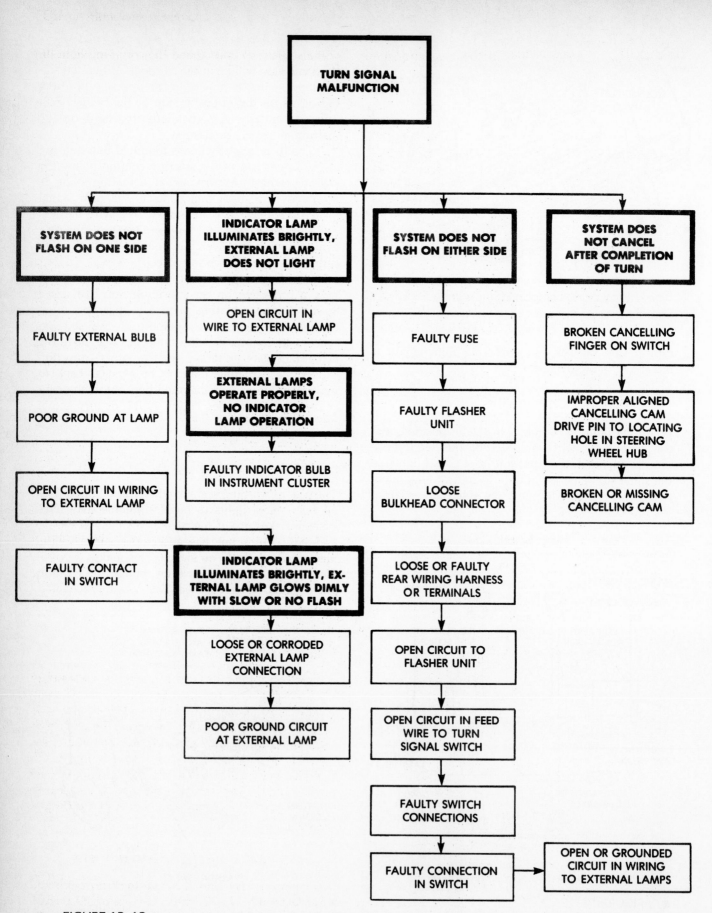

■ FIGURE 12–12
Turn signal flasher diagnosis. (Courtesy of Chrysler Corporation.)

by pushing in on the switch knob usually located on the steering column.

Flasher Operation

A simple light-duty flasher consists of a bimetal strip with a heating coil and a contact point plus a stationary contact point. The contact points are normally in a closed position. When the turn signal switch is turned on, electricity heats up the bimetal strip by means of the heating coil. The heated bimetal strip bends, opening the contact points, which interrupts current to the signal lights. The lack of current allows the bimetal strip to cool and straighten, which closes the contact points to complete the circuit to the signal lights. This sequence is rapidly repeated causing the lights to flash.

A heavy-duty flasher normally uses an electromagnet to operate one or more sets of contacts to cause front and side signal lights to flash alternately in some cases. The normally open contact points are closed by the action of the electromagnet. Closing the contacts energizes a second winding which is reverse wound, causing the electromagnet to operate in reverse and open the points once again. The cycle is rapidly repeated as long as the primary current is being supplied to the flasher **(Figure 12–13)**.

Brake Lights

Each rear lamp assembly has a tail, stop, and direction signal light. The taillights are controlled by the light switch. The brake lights are controlled by a mechanical switch mounted on the brake pedal bracket. This spring-loaded switch makes contact whenever the brake pedal is applied. When the brake pedal is released, it depresses the switch plunger to open the contacts and turn the brake lights off. The direction signal switch is in the circuit, so the brake lights may be flashing or constant, depending on the position of the switch. The high-

level center-mounted brake light is also controlled by the brake light switch.

Brake Warning Light

The brake warning light will light with the ignition in the *on* position, when the parking brake is depressed, or when there is a difference in pressure between the two hydraulic brake circuits. The light will also light, serving as a bulb check, when the key is turned to the start position.

Backup Lights

Most cars are equipped with two single-filament-lamp backup light assemblies. The lights are actuated when the ignition switch is in the *on* position and only when the transmission selector lever is positioned in reverse. A backup light switch is actuated either by shift linkage on the steering column or by the shift mechanism in the transmission, depending on design.

Auxiliary Lights

Auxiliary lights include fog, driving, passing, spot, and work lights. They may be original-equipment-manufacturer installed at the factory or aftermarket installed in the service shop. Regulations governing the installation and use of these lights differ in various jurisdictions. Follow government regulations and the instructions that come with the lights for proper installation.

■ HEADLAMP AND BULB SERVICE

Bulb Types

A variety of bulb designs and shapes are used in cars today. Bulbs may be single or double filament, single or double contact, grounded through the bulb base, or grounded through the wiring. Bulbs may be held in place by a spring and dowels that fit in holes in the bulb socket; the dowels may be in line or off-set, by a wedge fit in the socket. Double end bayonet bulbs may fit between two flat spring contacts or between a pair of spring contacts at each end **(Figure 12–14)**.

Headlamp and Bulb Replacement

To replace a headlamp, remove the trim piece and the retaining ring. Unplug the wiring connector. Plug the new headlamp into the connector and position the headlamp in the headlamp body. Make sure

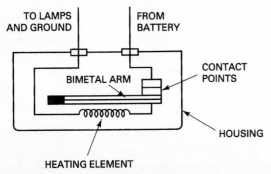

■ **FIGURE 12–13**
Basic flasher schematic. (Courtesy of F T Enterprises.)

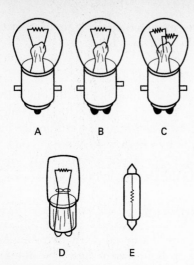

■ FIGURE 12–14

Different bulb designs: (A) single filament, single contact, base ground; (B) single filament, double contact, offset dowels, wiring ground; (C) double filament, double contact, base ground; (D) single filament, wedge base, double end bayonet. (Courtesy of F T Enterprises.)

that it remains fully seated as you install the retaining ring. Install the trim piece. To replace a halogen bulb, grasp it only by its plastic base. Do not touch the bulb glass since this can cause high heat concentration and possible bulb failure. Insert the bulb into the headlamp body and lock it in place with the bulb retainer. Turn the retainer to the fully locked position and plug in the electrical connector. Other light bulbs are replaced as shown in **Figure 12–15.**

Aiming the Headlights

To aim the headlights the car should be on a level floor, have proper tire inflation pressures, have the spare tire and jack in place, and have no additional weight on board. Headlights can be aimed with aiming equipment or by using a shop wall.

Headlight aiming equipment comes with several adapters to fit different headlamp shapes. Headlights are aimed in pairs, one on each side when using some types of aiming equipment. Aiming equipment and procedures vary, so follow the equipment manufacturer's instructions **(Figures 12–16 to 12–19).** To adjust headlights using a shop wall, vertical and horizontal lines are drawn on the wall at specified height and spacing. The car must be at the specified distance from the wall **(Figure 12–20).** Refer to the service manual for measurement specifications.

Some cars have a built-in headlight aiming system that includes a bubble level, adjusting screws,

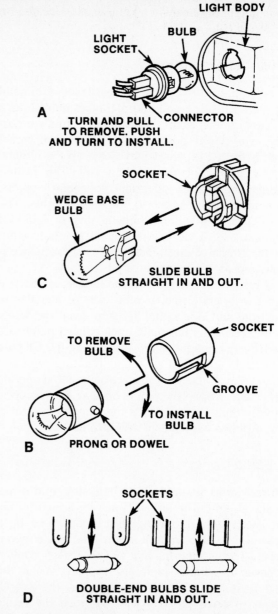

■ FIGURE 12–15

Typical bulb replacement methods. (Courtesy of Nissan Corp.)

and aiming gauge. The bubble level is calibrated first to compensate for a shop floor that is not level. Then the vertical and horizontal adjustments are made. The adjustments are correct when the gauge arrow aligns with the specified line on the gauge **(Figure 12–21).**

Headlights must be aimed to meet government regulations. Improperly aimed headlights are a hazard to oncoming drivers if aimed too high and provide poor lighting to the driver if aimed too low or off to one side.

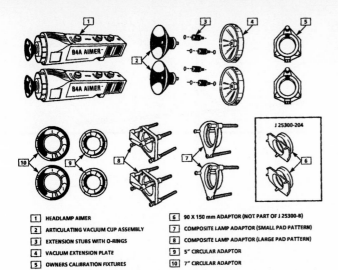

FIGURE 12-16
Headlamp aiming equipment with a variety of adapters to fit different headlamp shapes. (Courtesy of General Motors Corporation.)

1 HEADLAMP AIMER	6 90 X 150 mm ADAPTOR (NOT PART OF J 25300-8)
2 ARTICULATING VACUUM CUP ASSEMBLY	7 COMPOSITE LAMP ADAPTOR (SMALL PAD PATTERN)
3 EXTENSION STUBS WITH O-RINGS	8 COMPOSITE LAMP ADAPTOR (LARGE PAD PATTERN)
4 VACUUM EXTENSION PLATE	9 5" CIRCULAR ADAPTOR
5 OWNERS CALIBRATION FIXTURES	10 7" CIRCULAR ADAPTOR

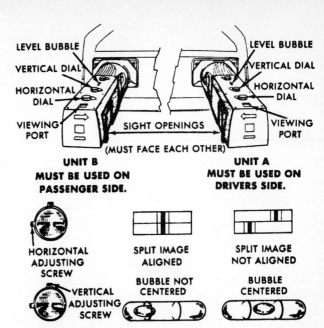

FIGURE 12-18
Headlights are adjusted vertically and horizontally to specifications prescribed by law. Horizontal adjustment is achieved by aligning split image in viewer on each unit. Vertical adjustment is achieved by centering level bubble on each unit. Procedure varies with type of equipment used. (Courtesy of Chrysler Corporation.)

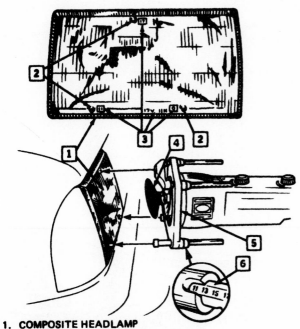

1. **COMPOSITE HEADLAMP**
2. **HEADLAMP AIMING PADS**
3. **ADJUSTMENT (ADAPTER) SETTINGS FOUND NEAR PAD OR ON AN OUTSIDE EDGE**
4. **UNIVERSAL HEADLAMP AIMER WITH ARTICULATING SUCTION CUP INSTALLED**
5. **UNIVERSAL ADAPTER ASSEMBLY**
6. **ADJUSTMENT ROD SETTINGS**

FIGURE 12-17
Headlamp aimer mounting on composite aerodynamic headlamp. (Courtesy of General Motors Corporation.)

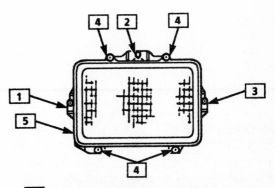

1	RIGHT HORIZONTAL ADJUSTMENT SCREW
2	VERTICAL ADJUSTMENT SCREW
3	LEFT HORIZONTAL ADJUSTMENT SCREW
4	RETAINING RING SCREWS
5	RETAINING RING

FIGURE 12-19
Identification of headlamp adjusting screws and retaining screws. (Courtesy of General Motors Corporation.)

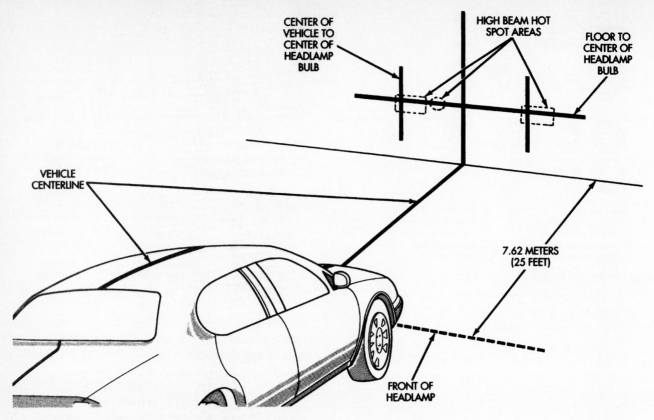

■ FIGURE 12–20
Headlight aiming using a wall marked with lines at specified spacing. The car must be at the specified distance from the wall. (Courtesy of Chrysler Corporation.)

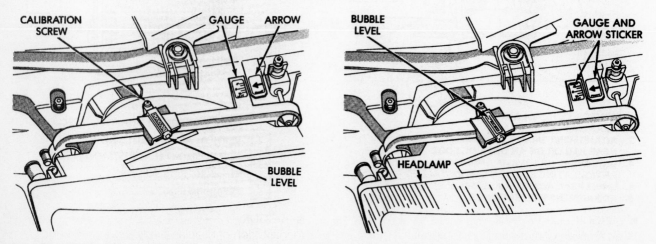

■ FIGURE 12–21
Built-in headlamp aiming system. (Courtesy of Chrysler Corporation.)

■ INSTRUMENTATION, GAUGES, AND INDICATOR LIGHTS

Instrument panel gauges, lights, and meters are provided to monitor the operation of most of the systems on the automobile. Gauges or indicator lights monitor such items as fuel level, engine coolant temperatures, engine oil pressure, and intake manifold vacuum. Indicator lights are used to warn of low fluid levels, brake failure, and light failure. The advantage of indicator lights is that they are more readily noticed than gauge readings. Vehicle speed is indicated by a gauge or by a digital display. Power for all instruments is supplied through the ignition switch.

Bimetal or Thermal Gauges

The bimetal gauge operates on the principle of the difference in expansion of two dissimilar metals in a flat bar with a heating coil wound around it. The heating coil is connected electrically, through a variable resistance sending unit, to ground. As a change in heat or pressure changes the resistance value of the sending unit, a varying level of current is applied to the heating coil around the bimetal strip in the gauge. The free end of the bimetal strip is linked to a gauge pointer. As the bimetal strip bends with the increased or decreased heat, the indicator moves up scale or down **(Figure 12–22).** This type of gauge is often used with a bimetallic constant voltage regulator that maintains gauge voltage at approximately 5 V. Full battery voltage should never be applied to gauges using the voltage regulator. **(Figures 12–22 and 12–23).**

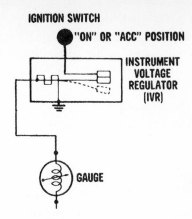

■ FIGURE 12–23
Instrument voltage regulator. (Courtesy of Ford Motor Company.)

Balanced Coil or Magnetic Gauges

The balanced coil or magnetic gauge operates on the principle of magnetism. Two magnetic coils, with a pivoting-needle-type indicator mounted between the coils, are the major parts of this gauge. One coil winding is calibrated to provide a fixed resistance and, therefore, a fixed magnetic force acting on the needle. The other coil is connected in series with a variable resistance to ground. The variable resistance causes the magnetic strength of the other coil to vary with the resistance of the sending unit. The difference in magnetic strength between the two coils determines the position of the needle on the gauge **(Figure 12–24).**

Indicator Warning Lights

Indicator lights are connected in series, through a switch or variable-resistance-type sending unit or sensor, to ground. When the switch or resistance value in the sending unit allows the circuit to be

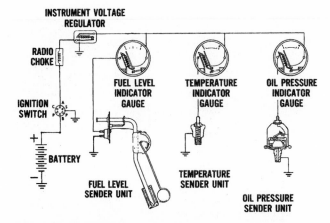

■ FIGURE 12–22
Typical bimetal-type gauge system. (Courtesy of Ford Motor Co. of Canada Ltd.)

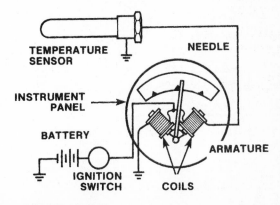

■ FIGURE 12–24
Balanced coil magnetic gauge schematic. (Courtesy of Ford Motor Company.)

completed to ground, the indicator light goes on. Coolant temperature, low charge rate, low fuel level, low oil pressure, and the like use indicator lamp systems on many vehicles **(Figure 12–25)**.

Charge Indicator

The ammeter is used to indicate current to, or out of, the battery. When more current is being used than the charging system is able to provide, the extra current is provided by the battery, and the ammeter needle will read on the minus (–) side. Whenever the battery is not fully charged and the charging system produces more current than is required for vehicle operation, the battery is being charged and the ammeter will read on the plus (+) side. If the battery is fully charged and the charging system is able to provide current to charge the battery, the voltage regulator reduces charging system output, and the ammeter indicator points to zero or midscale (no charge and no discharge).

A conventional ammeter must be connected in series between the battery and alternator to indicate the rate of current into and out of the battery. Since the ammeter must be mounted in the instrument panel, this would require heavy wiring to and from the ammeter. To avoid this problem, a specially calibrated voltmeter is used instead to indicate charge and discharge. Since the voltmeter is connected in parallel, it can be used to indicate the voltage drop across a special resistance wire connected between the battery and alternator. The voltmeter in the instrument panel indicates charging system voltage when the engine is running.

■ MECHANICAL SPEEDOMETER AND ODOMETER SERVICE

The mechanical speedometer incorporates both a speed indicating mechanism and an odometer to record total mileage **(Figures 12–26 and 12–27)**. A flexible cable, which enters the speedometer driven gear in the front drive wheel, or the transmission on one end and the speedometer head at the other, rotates both mechanisms whenever the transmission main shaft, propeller shaft, and wheels rotate. On some cruise-control-equipped cars, there are two cables: one from the transmission to the cruise control regulator, and the other from the regulator to the speedometer head.

The speedometer head has a needle indicator mounted on a small shaft with a coiled hair spring connected to the needle to hold it at zero when the car

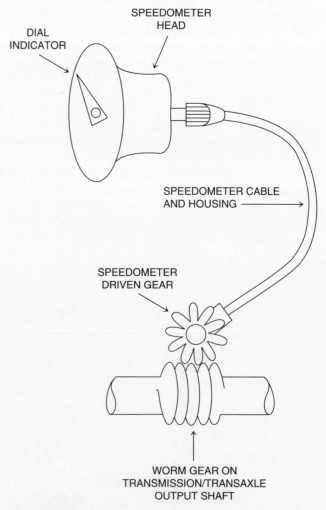

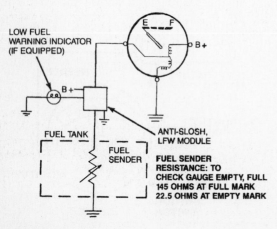

■ FIGURE 12–25
Fuel gauge schematic with low-fuel indicator light. (Courtesy of Ford Motor Company.)

■ FIGURE 12–26
Worm gear on transmission/transaxle output shaft drives speedometer gear and cable. Cable and housing are connected to speedometer head.

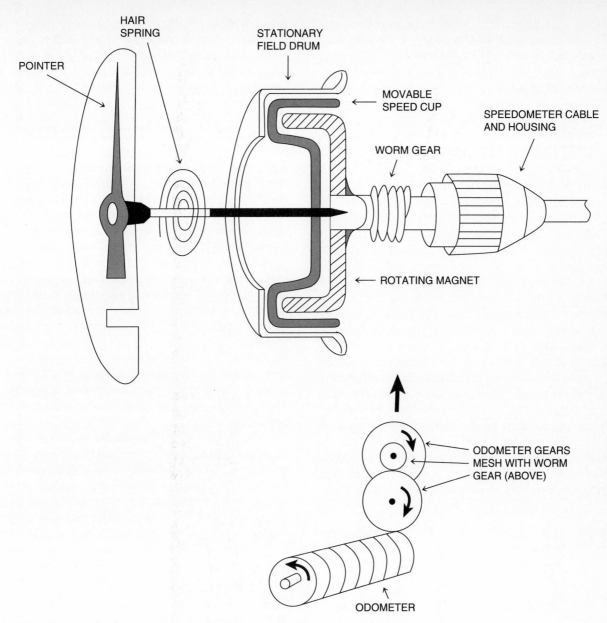

■   FIGURE 12–27
Speedometer head cross section (top) and odometer (bottom). Worm gear drives odometer gears and numbered odometer wheels to indicate distance travelled.

is stopped. A small drum, also attached to the indicator needle shaft, reacts to a magnet rotating inside the drum when driven by the speedometer cable. The faster the magnet spins, the farther the drum moves in response to the magnetism produced and against spring tension. Speedometers are calibrated to accurately indicate road speed when matched with proper wheel and tire size, as well as speedometer drive gear size. Federal, state, and local laws require speedometer accuracy standards to be met. Federal law requires that the odometer, in any replacement speedometer, must register the same mileage as that registered in the removed speedometer.

The odometer is driven by a series of gears from a worm gear cut on the magnet shaft. The odometer discs are so geared that as any one disc finishes a complete revolution, the next disc to left is turned one-tenth of a revolution.

Mechanical Speedometer Problems

Most mechanical speedometer problems—noise and erratic operation—result from lack of lubrication or from cable and housing distortion. Sharp bends or kinks in housing or cable usually require cable and housing replacement. If a cable is broken, the cause (usually a damaged, kinked, or misrouted housing) should be determined and corrected. Both cable and housing should be replaced. Only the recommended lubricant (such as white lube) should be used on speedometer cables.

■ ELECTRONIC SPEEDOMETER/ODOMETER

The electronic speedometer and odometer rely on input signals from the vehicle speed sensor mounted on the transmission/transaxle output shaft **(Figure 12–28)**. This sensor also provides information to other systems such as cruise control, automatic transmission/transaxle shift controls, automatic ride control, and the engine control computer. The speed sensor generates electric pulses that are sent to the computer. The computer converts these pulse signals to output signals to drive the electric speedometer head. The speedometer displays the vehicle speed in digital form or by the position of a needle on a dial. Vehicle speed is indicated in both forward and reverse travel. The odometer displays the total distance travelled based on the total number of output pulses produced by the vehicle speed sensor as calculated by the computer. The speed sensor can be tested with a digital voltmeter by rotating the sensor driver and noting the voltage pulses. The electrical wiring can be checked for continuity with an ohm-

meter. If these two items are not at fault the problem is likely in the speedometer head which must be replaced if faulty. The speed sensor is not at fault if other systems using speed sensor signals are not affected.

■ BODY CONTROL COMPUTER

The body control computer controls a number of electrical and electronic body devices. Among these are dash light brightness, intermittent wipers, low fuel level indicator, engine temperature warning light, low windshield washer fluid level warning, low engine oil pressure warning, low engine oil level warning, door ajar warning, trunk open warning, seat belt warning, air bag warning, automatic door locking, power door lock prevention with key in ignition, lamp outage warning (for headlights, brake lamps, signal lamps, tail lamps), key in ignition warning, low brake fluid level warning, antilock brake warning, park brake on warning, theft deterrent system, check gauge dash lamp, headlamp door control, trip information display, fuel consumption display, radio and tape deck sound system control, and others.

The body control computer may be separate from the engine control computer or it may be part of a larger chassis control computer that serves both functions. It operates in the same manner as other automotive computers. Inputs are processed by the computer and output signals operate output devices. See Chapter 4 for details on computer operation. Input devices include switches and sensors. Output devices include solenoids, switches, relays, and motors.

■ ELECTRONIC INSTRUMENT SYSTEM

A major difference between the electronic instrument panel and the analog-instrument panel is the manner in which information is sensed and displayed **(Figures 12–29 to 12–31)**. Sensors provide information to the computer. The computer activates the various instrument panel displays.

Displays consist of a system of light bars, graphs, or digital gauges. The instrument panel portion of the system normally operates trouble free. Problems with sending units and wiring connections are usually the cause of malfunctions.

A great variety of convenience features are provided with electronic instrument panels. Some of these features include fuel consumption rate indicators, distance vehicle is able to travel with remaining

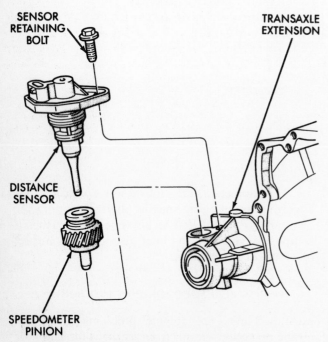

■ FIGURE 12–28
Distance sensor detail. (Courtesy of Chrysler Corporation.)

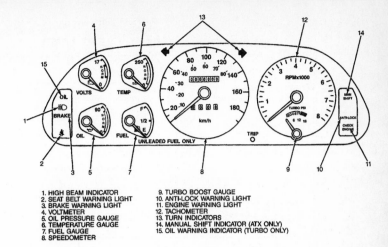

■ FIGURE 12–29
Typical analog instrument panel. (Courtesy of
Ford Motor Company.)

1. HIGH BEAM INDICATOR
2. SEAT BELT WARNING LIGHT
3. BRAKE WARNING LIGHT
4. VOLTMETER
5. OIL PRESSURE GAUGE
6. TEMPERATURE GAUGE
7. FUEL GAUGE
8. SPEEDOMETER

9. TURBO BOOST GAUGE
10. ANTI-LOCK WARNING LIGHT
11. ENGINE WARNING LIGHT
12. TACHOMETER
13. TURN INDICATORS
14. MANUAL SHIFT INDICATOR (ATX ONLY)
15. OIL WARNING INDICATOR (TURBO ONLY)

fuel indicators, monitors of various fluid levels in the vehicle, light-out warning systems, and many others, depending on design. Replacement of any gauges or instruments normally requires removal of the entire instrument cluster or panel before access to individual gauges is possible.

Vacuum Fluorescent Display

A vacuum fluorescent display (VFD) system generates its light similar to a TV picture tube. A colored light is produced as a result of free electrons from a heated filament striking a phosphorus material (Figure 12–32). The display characters are formed as a result of the shape of the anode segments on the glass faceplate. A computer selects the set of segments that are to display any particular message. Sensors provide the input information to the instrument panel computer.

Light-Emitting Diode Display

A light-emitting diode (LED) uses semiconductor material that emits a colored light when electrical current is applied to it. The LED display is made up of segments of small dots arranged to form numbers or letters when energized.

Windshield Hologram Display

Some cars are equipped with a "heads up" display in the upper portion of the windshield. Functions include vehicle speed, signal indication, and other vehicle operating data. The system is similar to that used in high-performance jet aircraft. The driver need not look away from the road to monitor vehicle operation. The display is a hologram which is produced on a film in the windshield that is illuminated by light from behind the display. Sensors provide

■ FIGURE 12–30
Analog gauge wiring schematic.
(Courtesy of Chrysler Corporation.)

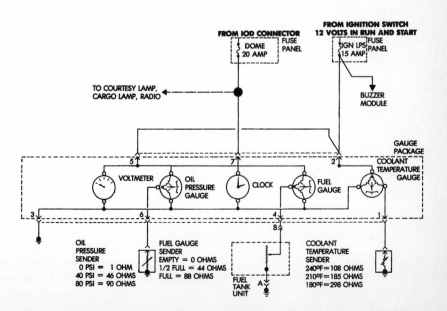

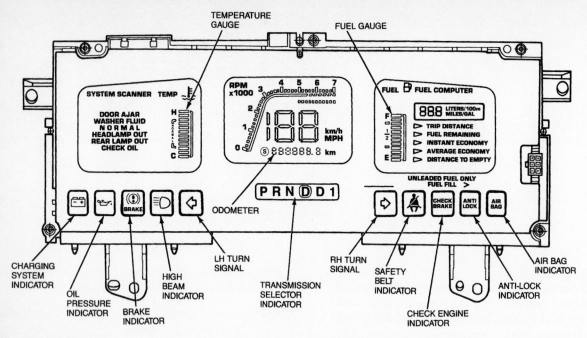

■ FIGURE 12–31
Electronic instrument panel with digital, lamp, and message displays.
(Courtesy of Ford Motor Company.)

the input information to a control module that determines the segments to be illuminated in the windshield.

Voice Alert System

This system uses a computer voice synthesizer to provide a number of short voice alert messages. A volume control is provided to adjust to the desired volume. An on/off switch allows the system to be turned on or off as desired. Visual indicators on the instrument panel indicate any particular alert messages, tones, or bells, whether the voice alert is on or off **(Figure 12–33)**.

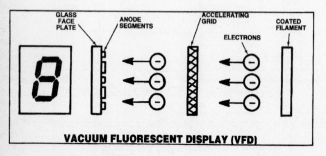

■ FIGURE 12–32
Vacuum fluorescent display operation. (Courtesy of Chrysler Corporation.)

■ POWER ACCESSORIES

Many automobile accessories are power operated to reduce the effort required to operate the device. Power is supplied by the vehicle electrical system through an operating switch to one or more electric motors. Some of the more common of these power accessories are discussed here. Most of them rely on the operation of the permanent magnet type of electric motor.

■ WINDSHIELD WIPER OPERATION AND SERVICE

The typical wiper system consists of a permanent-magnet rotary motor, wiper arms and blades mounted on a pivot shaft—one at each side of the windshield—and an operating linkage connecting the pivot shafts to the electric motor **(Figure 12–34)**. The most common motors are the two-speed and the variable-speed types. A gearbox provides speed reduction. The gearbox is usually part of, or attached to, the motor housing. A two-speed or variable-speed switch provides operator control. A windshield-washer switch is also usually incorporated into the wiper switch. Some switches are provided with an intermittent switch function pro-

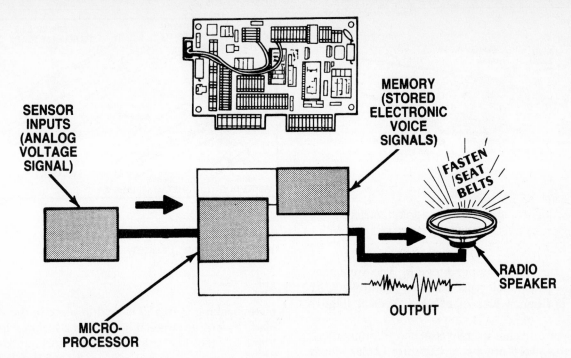

■   FIGURE 12–33
Voice alert system. (Courtesy of Chrysler Corporation.)

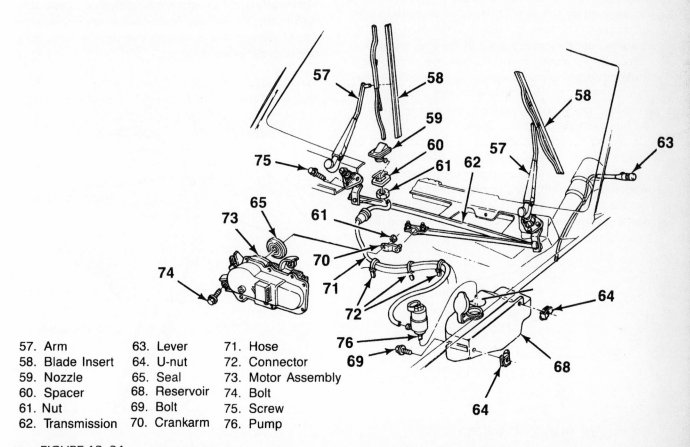

57. Arm	63. Lever	71. Hose
58. Blade Insert	64. U-nut	72. Connector
59. Nozzle	65. Seal	73. Motor Assembly
60. Spacer	68. Reservoir	74. Bolt
61. Nut	69. Bolt	75. Screw
62. Transmission	70. Crankarm	76. Pump

■   FIGURE 12–34
Windshield wiper and washer system components. (Courtesy of General
Motors Corporation.)

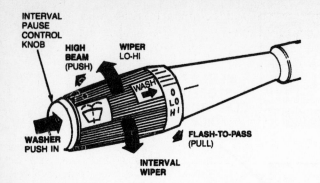

■ FIGURE 12–35
Wiper/washer control switch located on multifunction lever. (Courtesy of Ford Motor Company.)

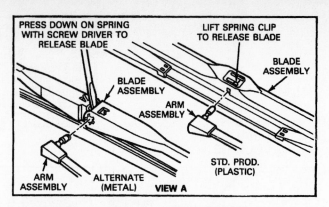

■ FIGURE 12–37
Removing metal (left) and plastic (right) wiper blades from wiper arms. (Courtesy of Ford Motor Company.)

viding wipe–pause–wipe intervals. The frequency of wipe–pause intervals can be controlled by switch position, which operates a rheostat **(Figure 12–35)**.

Wiper arms are usually attached through a lock device to splined pivot shafts **(Figure 12–36)**. Wiper arms must be properly positioned on splined pivot shafts to ensure a proper wiping pattern on the windshield as well as correct parking position. To remove wiper arms, the locking device must be released while the arm is removed from the shaft. Installation requires proper positioning—pushing the arm onto the pivot shaft and the lock snaps into place. Wiper arms pivot against the windshield under spring pressure to ensure wiper element pressure against the glass. Wiper blades can be lifted from the glass surface against this spring pressure for blade or element replacement.

Wiper blades are attached to the wiper arm by one of several different spring lock designs **(Figure 12–37)**. Removal requires releasing the spring lock device. Installation usually requires only engaging the blade and pushing it into place until the lock snaps into place. The rubber wiping element has a

metal backing strip and is held in place in the wiper blade by means of metal hooks and a locking device. Removal requires release of the locking device which allows sliding the wiper element from the wiper blade **(Figure 12–38)**. Installation requires only sliding the element between the retaining hooks until the element locks into place. Wiper blades and arms should not be distorted in any way during this procedure. Rear window wipers are similar in design and operation but usually have only one wiper arm and blade.

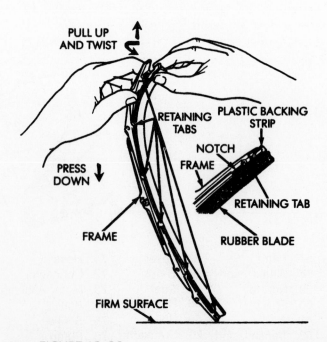

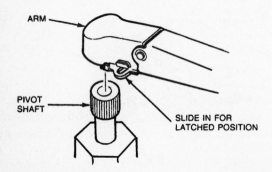

■ FIGURE 12–36
Typical wiper arm to pivot shaft mounting. (Courtesy of Ford Motor Company.)

■ FIGURE 12–38
Removing a wiper blade rubber element. (Courtesy of Chrysler Corporation.)

■ WINDSHIELD WASHER OPERATION AND SERVICE

This system consists of a fluid reservoir, fluid hoses and nozzles, an electric motor-driven pump, and a control switch. Washer systems are used on both front and rear windows. Each system operates independent of the other.

When the switch is turned on, the electric pump forces fluid through the hoses and nozzles onto the window glass. Nozzles are aimed to provide precise spray patterns for maximum effectiveness. Nozzles are usually adjustable to allow aiming. System operation relies on the use of clean fluid to prevent clogging of nozzles. Special washer fluid with nonsmear detergent should be used rather than water. In freezing weather, windshield washer antifreeze must be used to prevent freeze-up of the system. Faulty components must be replaced including the motor and pump assembly. Problems usually result from incorrectly aimed nozzles, use of incorrect fluid, clogged nozzles, poor electrical connections, and the like.

Wiper/Washer Electrical Service

See **Figure 12–39** for typical windshield wiper and washer problem diagnosis.

Locate the applicable wiring diagram in the service manual and follow it when testing the system **(Figure 12–40).** Check whether power is present at the wiper motor electrical connection. If there is no power, check the fuses, connections, wiring, and switch. If power is present at the wiper motor, the motor ground should be checked. If the ground is good and the motor does not run, the motor or gear drive is at fault. A faulty motor is normally replaced. Worn or damaged gears are sometimes repaired by replacing the faulty components **(Figure 12–41).** Check the windshield washer system in the same manner. A faulty washer motor must be replaced **(Figure 12–42).**

Power Windows

Power windows are controlled by a single switch at each of the windows as well as a master set of switches at the driver's position. The master set allows the driver to operate all windows from one position **(Figures 12–43** and **12–44).**

The switches control a reversible electric motor at each window. The electric motor drives the window regulator mechanism forward or reverse, providing up-and-down window movement.

System operation relies on properly adjusted windows and window channels to ensure freedom of movement in the channels without excessive friction or binding. Electric motor operation relies on proper system voltage ensured by good electrical connections and switch operation.

Power Seats

Four-, six-, and eight-way power seats are used on many vehicles. Adjustment is provided in up to six different directions: up, down, forward, back, tilt forward, and tilt rearward **(Figure 12–45).** Four-way systems do not provide tilt adjustments.

The typical six-way power seat consists of a three-armature reversible motor (actually, three motors in one), a control switch assembly, rack and pinion assemblies located in the seat tracks, and cables connecting the pinions to the motor assembly.

The horizontal drive consists of a rack and pinion on each track. The pinion housing and motor is attached to the movable section of the track. When the switch is actuated, the front armature is energized, and the horizontal drive units are activated. The seat is then moved forward or rearward by the pinion gears traveling in a rack in each lower track section.

In the vertical drive, worm gear planetary reducers and sector gear mechanisms are utilized. The drive units are located in the front and rear of the transmission case. When the switch is actuated, the center and rear armatures are simultaneously energized and the vertical drive units are activated. The seat is then moved up or down by the sector gears.

When the front tilt switch is actuated, the center armature drives the front vertical worm gear and moves the seat to the desired position. When the rear tilt switch is actuated, the rear armature drives the rear vertical worm gear and moves the seat to the desired position. The power seat circuit is usually protected by a 30-A circuit breaker. The circuit breaker is mounted in the fuse panel.

The transmission is serviced as a unit. The motor assembly, which contains three armatures, is serviced only as an assembly. The flexible shafts are serviced individually and can be removed by removing the securing clamps. The switch and housing assembly is serviceable separately.

System operation is dependent on the free movement of the seat through the full travel distances—up, down, forward, and back—without excessive friction or interference from articles placed under the seat. Electrical operation is relatively trouble free and is dependent on good electrical connections and proper switch function.

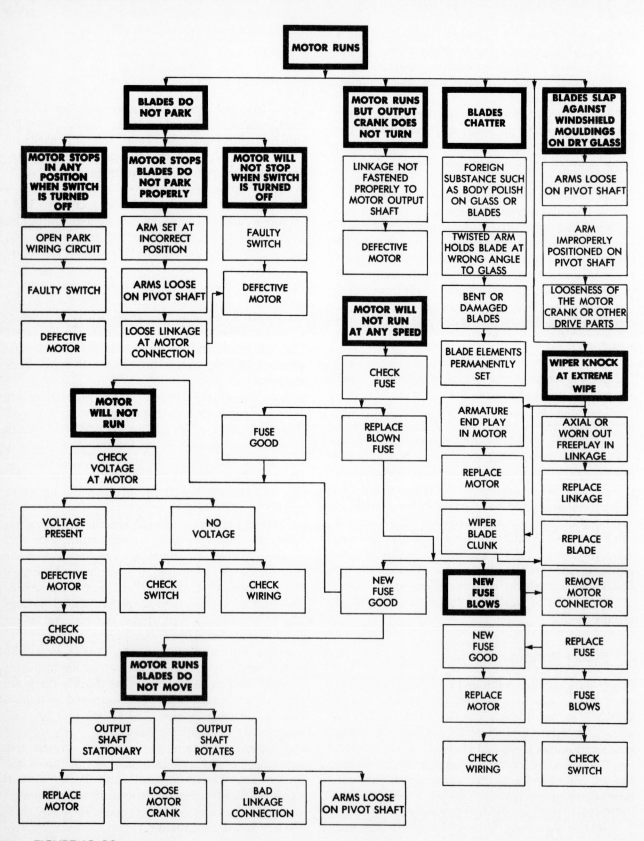

Windshield wiper motor diagnosis. (Courtesy of Chrysler Corporation.)

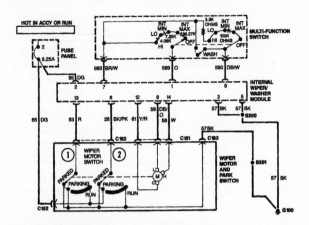

■ FIGURE 12–40
Windshield wiper electrical circuit. (Courtesy of General Motors Corporation.)

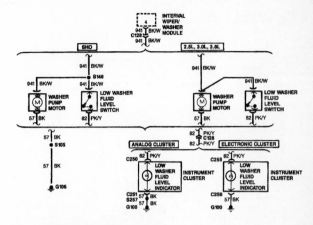

■ FIGURE 12–42
Windshield washer electrical circuit. (Courtesy of General Motors Corporation.)

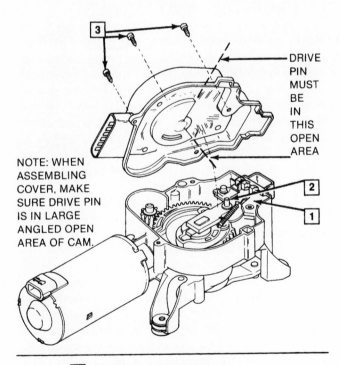

	WIPER IN PARK POSITION
1	WIPER IN PARK POSITION
2	DRIVE PIN
3	SCREW — 2 N·m (18 LB. IN.)

■ FIGURE 12–41
Wiper motor cover assembly. (Courtesy of General Motors Corporation.)

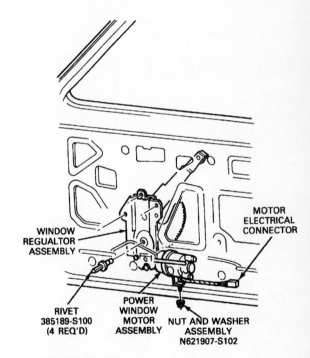

■ FIGURE 12–43
Power window motor and regulator. (Courtesy of Ford Motor Company.)

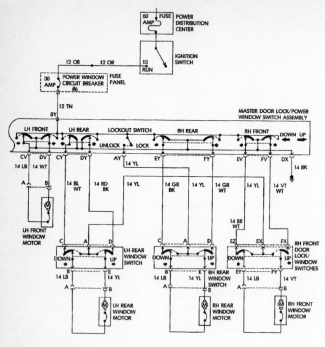

■ FIGURE 12–44

Power window electrical diagram. (Courtesy of Chrysler Corporation.)

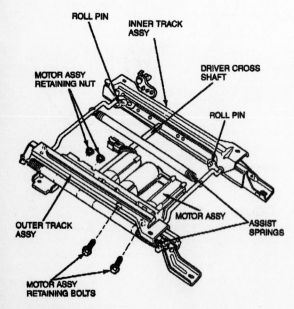

■ FIGURE 12–45

Power seat track and motor assembly. (Courtesy of Ford Motor Company.)

Power Door Locks

A switch-operated, two-position electric solenoid actuator is typically used in each door to electrically operate the door-locking mechanism **(Figure 12–46)**. Usually, each door can be locked and unlocked individually, with either front door switch operating all four door locks. This allows the driver or the passenger to lock or unlock all four doors with one switch. Doors may also be unlocked individually. If the electric locking mechanism fails, the manual system still works normally. Automatic power door locks lock automatically when vehicle speed reaches about 5 mph (8 km/h). A vehicle speed sensor signals the body computer and triggers the locking mechanism. Other powered accessories include electric trunk or deck lid release, power radio antenna, electric fuel door or cap lock, power outside mirrors, clocks, remote keyless entry, and the like.

■ ELECTRIC MOTOR DRIVEN AND SOLENOID OPERATED POWER ACCESSORIES DIAGNOSIS AND SERVICE

Power windows, power seats, and power antennas are all operated by electric motors. Power door locks and power deck lid releases are solenoid operated. When any of these systems fail the general procedure for problem diagnosis is similar and involves inspecting and testing the following as described in Chapter 3.

1. Voltage supply to the control switch(es).
2. Switch operation.
3. Relay operation (where applicable).
4. Voltage supply to the motor or solenoid with the switch in the on position.
5. Wiring harness and ground connections.
6. Motor or solenoid operation.

To determine whether the output device (motor or solenoid) or the control circuit is at fault disconnect the wiring harness at the motor or solenoid. Using a jumper wire apply battery voltage to the input terminal of the motor or solenoid. If the motor or solenoid operates normally the control circuit (switch or wiring harness) is at fault. Check for continuity through the switch and wiring harness. If the motor or solenoid does not operate when voltage is applied with a jumper wire there may be a poor ground connection between the motor or solenoid and ground, or the motor or solenoid may be at fault. Use a jumper wire to provide a good ground and repeat the test. If the motor or solenoid does not operate it

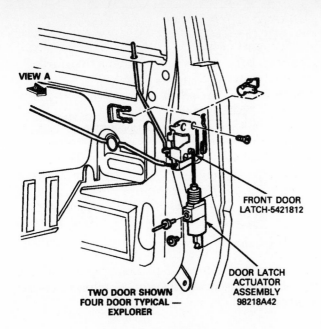

VIEW A

FRONT DOOR
LATCH-5421812

DOOR LATCH
ACTUATOR
ASSEMBLY
98218A42

**TWO DOOR SHOWN
FOUR DOOR TYPICAL —
EXPLORER**

■ MECHANICAL SPEED CONTROL OPERATION AND SERVICE

A speed control system provides the means to maintain a desired driving speed without maintaining throttle position by foot pressure on the accelerator pedal **(Figures 12–47 to 12–50).** Some variation in selected speed is normal when driving uphill or downhill. Most systems provide a "resume speed" function which causes the vehicle to resume the preselected speed on the driver's demand after the system has been disengaged. The system is disengaged by depressing the brake or clutch pedal. Speed is resumed when the resume speed switch is activated.

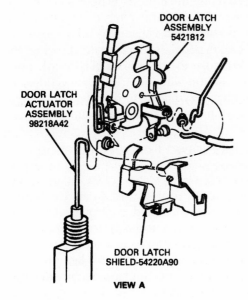

DOOR LATCH
ASSEMBLY
5421812

DOOR LATCH
ACTUATOR
ASSEMBLY
98218A42

DOOR LATCH
SHIELD-54220A90

VIEW A

■ **FIGURE 12–46**
Power door lock detail. (Courtesy of Ford Motor Company.)

must be replaced. To test a relay disconnect the input wiring harness and apply specified voltage to the relay input terminal with a jumper wire and test relay output with a test light. If the test light lights up when voltage is applied to the relay, the relay is good. If it does not light up the relay must be replaced. See Chapter 3 for more detail on electrical system testing.

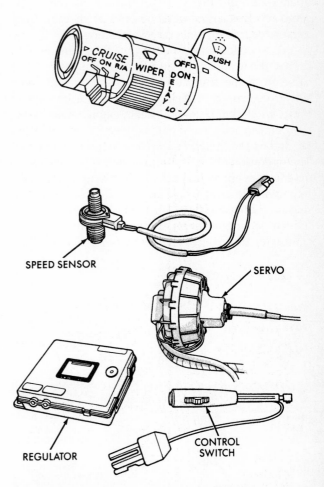

SPEED SENSOR

SERVO

REGULATOR

CONTROL
SWITCH

■ **FIGURE 12–47**
Vacuum servo-type speed control components. Switch at top is more accurate diagram than switch at bottom. (Courtesy of Chrysler Corporation.)

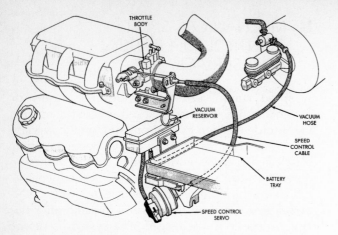

FIGURE 12–48

Underhood arrangement of vacuum servo speed control components. (Courtesy of Chrysler Corporation.)

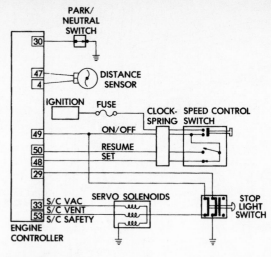

FIGURE 12–50

Speed control electrical diagram. (Courtesy of Chrysler Corporation.)

The system typically uses engine vacuum to operate a servo that controls throttle position. The servo receives a controlled amount of vacuum from a transducer to regulate throttle position.

A speedometer cable from the transmission drives the transducer, and a second speedometer cable from the transducer drives the speedometer. The cruise control transducer contains a low speed limit switch that prevents system engagement below a minimum speed—ranging between 25 and 40 mph (40 and 64 km/h) depending on the transducer used. The operation of the transducer unit is controlled by an engagement switch button. To disengage the system, two release switches are provided. An electrical release switch mounted on the brake pedal bracket (clutch pedal bracket on cars equipped with manual transaxle) disengages the system electrically when

the brake pedal (or clutch pedal) is depressed. A vacuum release valve, mounted on the brake pedal bracket, vents controlled vacuum to the atmosphere when the brake pedal is depressed, allowing the servo unit to return the throttle quickly to idle position. Good vacuum and electrical connections, as well as proper servo-cable-to-throttle adjustment, are required for proper system operation.

Electronic Speed Control Operation and Service

The electronic speed control uses an electronic control module. Driver-operated control switches are similar to those on nonelectronic systems. Closer control within 1 mph (1.6 km/h) is achieved with this unit. The mechanical analog system is less precise in its control and in its speed-increase adjustment. A vacuum-operated servomotor is used to provide throttle adjustment. The servomotor is electronically controlled. A speed sensor is mounted in line with the speedometer cable and provides 8000 magnetic pulses per mile to the microprocessor. Three vacuum solenoids typically control the system:

1. *Supply solenoid:* when energized, supplies vacuum to the servomotor to increase throttle opening.

2. *Vent solenoid:* when energized, holds vacuum in the servo or dumps vacuum to increase speed or to maintain constant speed. The supply solenoid and the vent solenoid are microprocessor controlled.

3. *Dump solenoid:* operates independently from the other two solenoids; is operated directly by the brake switch to dump vacuum when the brake is

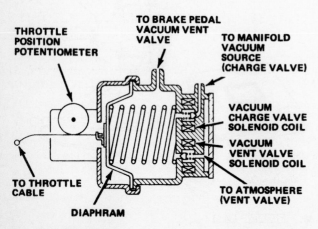

FIGURE 12–49

Details of speed control servo assembly. (Courtesy of Chrysler Corporation.)

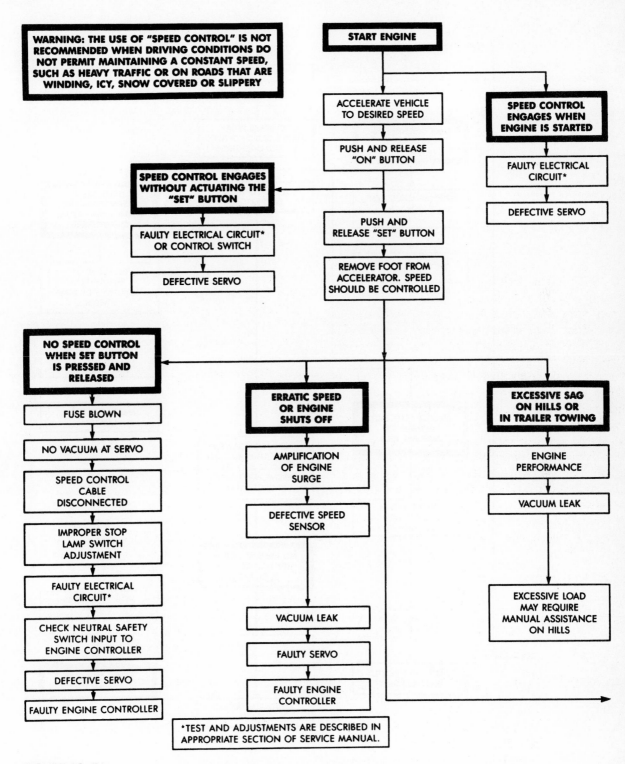

■   FIGURE 12–51
Speed control diagnosis. (Courtesy of Chrysler Corporation.)

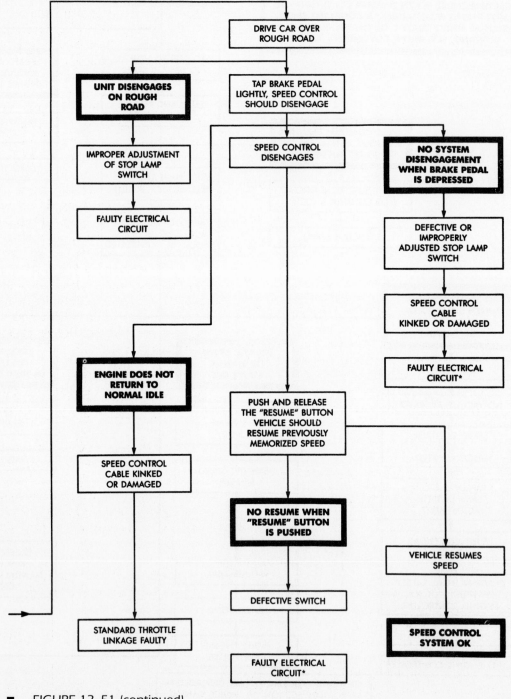

■   FIGURE 12–51 (continued)
Speed control diagnosis. (Courtesy of Chrysler Corporation.)

applied. When the system is off, the supply solenoid is closed and the other two solenoids are open.

A vacuum reservoir is used to allow system operation when engine intake vacuum is low, as in hill climbing.

Computer-Controlled Speed Control

The computer-controlled speed control system consists of the following components:

1. *Control module:* consists of the electronic controller and stepper motor. The controller monitors vehicle speed from speed sensor output signals processed by the speed sensor buffer and sent to the controller. The controller also receives information from the driver-operated mode switch.
2. *Mode control switch:* part of the multifunction switch mounted on the steering column. It has driver-selected ON, OFF, RESUME/ACCELERATE, and SET/COAST positions.
3. *Speed sensor:* provides vehicle speed information to the speed sensor buffer. It is a magnetic pulse generator driven by the transmission output shaft.
4. *Speed sensor buffer:* receives speed sensor signals, processes and amplifies the signal, and sends it to the control module.
5. *Brake release switches:* a torque converter clutch cruise control switch and a stoplight switch, mounted on the brake pedal mounting bracket, cut off current to the control module to deactivate the speed control when the brakes are applied.
6. *Electric wiring harness:* connects the speed control to the vehicle's electrical system and the speed control components to each other.

On-Vehicle Service

See **Figure 12–51** for typical speed control problem diagnosis.

If the speed control does not disengage when the brakes are applied, the brake release switch may be faulty or out of adjustment. Test the switch and replace if faulty. Adjust the switch to ensure speed control cutout when the brakes are applied.

If the mode control switch is faulty, the complete multifunction switch must be replaced. It cannot be serviced. If the speed control module is faulty, it must be replaced as an assembly. Test the speed sensor output signal. It should put out evenly spaced voltage fluctuations when turned by hand. Replace the sensor if faulty. See **Figure 12–52** for an example of a speed control tester and its capability.

■ HORN OPERATION AND SERVICE

Automotive horn operation makes use of an electromagnet, a set of points, a vibrator diaphragm, and a spiral sound amplifier or trumpet **(Figure 12–53)**. Battery current energizes the electromagnet when the horn button or switch is depressed. The electromagnet attracts a metal disc, moving it slightly toward the electromagnet against spring measure. The metal disc is connected to the sound-producing diaphragm. As the disc is attracted to the electromagnet, the points are opened; this deenergizes the magnet and the diaphragm returns to its normal position, closing the points once again. This sequence of events is repeated very rapidly as long as the horn button is being depressed. The vibrating action of the diaphragm produces the sound which is amplified by the spiral trumpet. In most cases, a horn relay is used to reduce the current carried by the horn operating switch. The distance the diaphragm can move is adjustable on most horns and adjustment must be maintained within narrow limits in either direction for good sound, and proper operation in all ambient temperatures. See **Figure 12–54** for typical horn diagnosis and service.

■ THEFT DETERRENT SYSTEM OPERATION AND SERVICE

A theft deterrent system is designed to discourage theft by causing the car horns to sound and the lights to flash when the car is tampered with in any way. The fuel system is also disabled on many newer cars. Any of a series of tamper switches mounted in strategic locations can set off the alarm system if the car is tampered with by attempting to gain entry to the passenger, engine, or trunk compartments **(Figure 12–55.)** See **Figure 12–56** for typical theft deterrent system diagnosis and service.

■ AIR BAG SYSTEM OPERATION AND SERVICE

Air bags are used to provide additional safety in the event of a collision. Air bags are also known as supplemental inflatable restraint (SIR) devices. On the driver's side the air bag module is located in the center of the steering wheel. On the passenger side it is located in the dash panel. Due to the greater distance between the passenger and the module the passenger side air bag is of much greater capacity.

Speed Control Tester

The speed control system can be operated and diagnosed using the Rotunda Speed Control Tester 007-00013 or equivalent. The tester works on vehicles with all combinations of control switches, transmissions, speedometers (electronic and mechanical), brakes, and clutches. With three modes of operation: Automatic, Single Scan, and Scan Probe, the technician can pinpoint any failure including wiring, vacuum hoses, switches and servo. The tester includes an instruction manual with its own specially developed diagnostic tree charts for identifying any failed or marginal component in the speed control system.

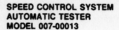

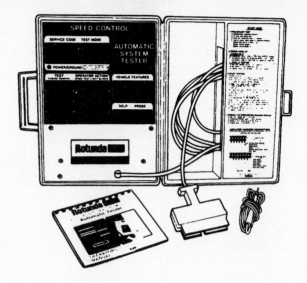

■ FIGURE 12–52

Speed control system tester. (Courtesy of Ford Motor Company.)

The air bag system consists of the air bag module, the electrical system, the knee bolster, and the indicator lamp **(Figures 12–57** and **12–58)**. When the ignition switch is turned on, the indicator lamp lights up for about 8 seconds. During this time the diagnostic circuit checks the operating integrity of

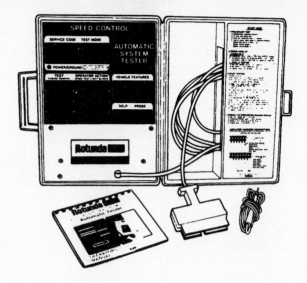

■ FIGURE 12–53

Typical dual horn mounting. (Courtesy of Ford Motor Co. of Canada Ltd.)

the system and charges a backup power capacitor. Backup power is needed in case the car battery is destroyed on impact. When the indicator lamp goes out, the operational integrity of the system is verified and the backup power capacitor is fully charged. System integrity is monitored continuously during vehicle operation. In the event of failure of any system component, the indicator lamp will light up or flash on and off repeatedly. If the lamp fails to light when the ignition is first turned on the system is in need of service.

When an impact force on the vehicle is great enough, the crash sensors activate the inflaters and fill the air bags completely with nitrogen gas. The air bags pop out of their modules during initial activation, creating a cushion between the driver and the steering wheel and between the passenger and the dash panel **(Figure 12–59)**. Knee bolsters prevent the driver and passenger from sliding underneath the air bags.

There are as many as five sensors in the air bag system **(Figure 12–60)**. Two are located at the radiator support, one at each front fender and one at the cowl in the passenger compartment. A safing sensor is connected in series with the sensors. At least two sensors must be activated to cause air bag deployment, a safing sensor and one front impact sensor **(Figure 12–61)**. The safing sensor is designed to verify the severity and direction of the impact before deployment takes place. It takes about $\frac{1}{25}$ of a second for inflation to be completed, after which they deflate immediately.

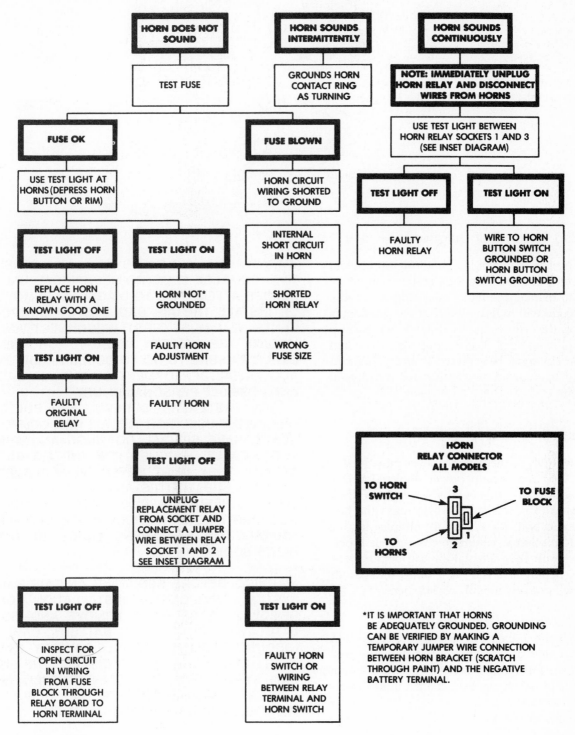

FIGURE 12–54
(Courtesy of Chrysler Corporation.)

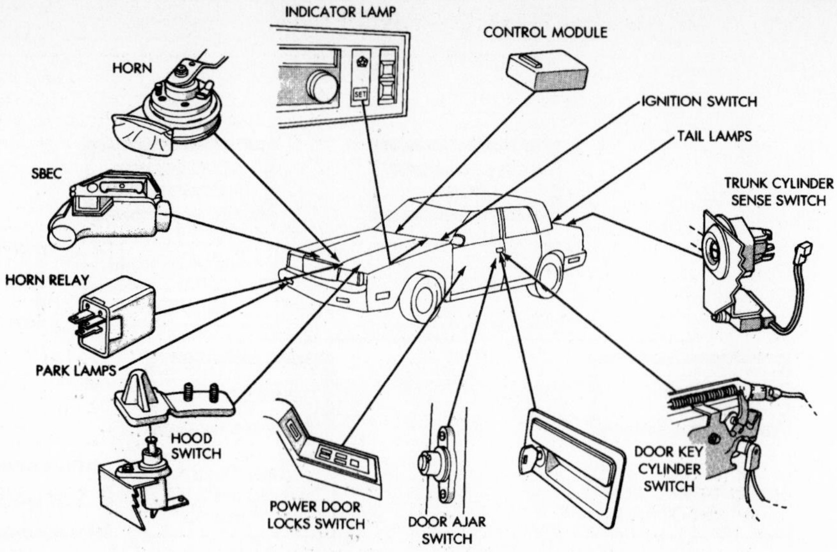

■ **FIGURE 12–55**
Typical theft deterrent system.
(Courtesy of Chrysler Corporation.)

Air Bag System Self Diagnosis

When the air bag indicator lamp indicates a problem in the system, the self-diagnosis system should be activated to display the fault codes **(Figure 12–62)**. The fault code will indicate whether the problem is in a sensor, the wiring, the module, or the backup power supply system. These components are not serviceable but must be replaced if faulty. Refer to the service manual for procedures for component replacement.

Air Bag Service Precautions

SAFETY CAUTION: The battery power must be disconnected and the backup power depleted before any air bag system component is serviced. To dissipate the backup power supply, disconnect the battery cable and wait for at least 10 minutes for the capacitor to discharge. Failure to observe this procedure may result in accidental air bag deployment. Accidental deployment can cause injury and results in needless and costly module replacement.

1.   Always wear safety glasses.
2.   When handling a deployed air bag module, wear gloves and avoid skin contact with the bag. The by-product resulting from deployment is irritating to the skin. Wash any skin contact immediately with soap and water.
3.   When carrying a live air bag module, make sure that the bag and trim cover are pointing away from your body. Accidental deployment can cause injury.
4.   When placing a live air bag module down on a bench or other surface, face the bag side of the module up to reduce module motion in case of accidental deployment.

WARNING: THE AIR BAG SYSTEM IS A SENSITIVE, COMPLEX ELECTRO-MECHANICAL UNIT. BEFORE ATTEMPTING TO DIAGNOSE, REMOVE OR INSTALL THE AIR BAG SYSTEM COMPONENTS YOU MUST FIRST DISCONNECT AND ISOLATE THE BATTERY NEGATIVE (GROUND) CABLE. FAILURE TO DO SO COULD RESULT IN ACCIDENTAL DEPLOYMENT OF THE AIR BAG AND POSSIBLE PERSONAL INJURY.

THE FASTENERS, SCREWS, AND BOLTS, ORIGINALLY USED FOR THE AIR BAG COMPONENTS, HAVE SPECIAL COATINGS AND ARE SPECIFICALLY DESIGNED FOR THE AIR BAG SYSTEM. THEY MUST NEVER BE REPLACED WITH ANY SUBSTITUTES. ANYTIME A NEW FASTENER IS NEEDED, REPLACE WITH THE CORRECT FASTENERS PROVIDED IN THE SERVICE PACKAGE OR FASTENERS LISTED IN THE PARTS BOOKS.

WARNING: BEFORE BEGINNING ANY AIR BAG SYSTEM COMPONENT INSTALLATION OR REMOVAL PROCEDURES. REMOVE AND ISOLATE THE NEGATIVE (-) BATTERY CABLE (GROUND) FROM THE VEHICLE BATTERY. THIS IS THE ONLY SURE WAY TO DISABLE THE AIR BAG SYSTEM. FAILURE TO DO THIS COULD RESULT IN ACCIDENTAL AIR BAG DEPLOYMENT AND POSSIBLE PERSONAL INJURY.

These warnings appear here through the courtesy of Chrysler Corporation and they are typical of the precautions that must be observed when servicing electrical components of steering columns equipped with air bags.

1. ARMING / DISARMING RELATIONSHIP

Trouble symptom	Cause	Check method	Remedy
The system is not armed (The SECURITY light doesn't illuminate, and the alarm doesn't function.) (The central door locking system functions normally. If the central locking system does not function normally, refer to P.8-306.	Damaged or disconnected wiring of ECU power supply circuit	Check by using check chart P.8-303.	Replace the sub fusible link No. ①, ⑥ or repair the harness.
	Damaged or disconnected wiring of door switch input circuit	Check by using check chart P.8-305.	Repair the harness or replace the door switch.
The arming procedures are followed, but the SECURITY light does not illuminate. (There is an alarm, however, when an alarm test is conducted after about 20 seconds have passed.)	Damaged or disconnected wiring of SECURITY light activation circuit	Check by using check chart P.8-309.	Replace the fuse No. ⑲ or repair the harness.
	Blown SECURITY light bulb		Replace the bulb.
	Malfunction of the ECU	—	Replace the ECU.
The alarm sounds in error when, while the system is armed, a door or the liftgate is unlocked by using the key.	Damaged or disconnected wiring of a door key cylinder and the liftgate unlock switch input circuit.	If input checks P.8-300 indicate a malfunction, check by using check chart P.8-307.	Repair the harness replace a door key cylinder and the liftgate unlock switch.
	Malfunction of a door key cylinder and the liftgate unlock switch		
	Malfunction of the ECU	—	Replace the ECU.

2. ACTIVATION / DEACTIVATION RELATIONSHIP

Trouble symptom	Cause	Check method	Remedy
There is no alarm when, as an alarm test, a door is opened without using the key. (The arming and disarming are normal, and the alarm is activated when the liftgate or hood is opened.)	Damaged or disconnected wiring of door switch (all doors) input circuit	If input checks P.8-300 indicate a malfunction, check by using check chart P.8-305.	Repair the harness or replace the door switch.
	Malfunction of the door switch		
	Malfunction of the ECU	—	Replace the ECU.
There is no alarm when, as an alarm test, the liftgate is opened without using the key. (The alarm is activated, however, by opening a door or the hood.)	Damaged or disconnected wiring of liftgate switch input circuit	If input checks P.8-300 indicate a malfunction, check by using check chart P.8-308.	Repair the harness or replace the liftgate switch.
	Malfunction of the liftgate switch		
	Malfunction of the ECU	—	Replace the ECU.
There is no alarm when, as an alarm test the hood is opened from within the vehicle. (The alarm is activated, however, by opening a door or the liftgate.)	Damaged or disconnected wiring of hood switch input circuit	If input checks P.8-300 indicate a malfunction, check by using check chart P.8-304.	Repair the harness or replace the hood switch.
	Malfunction of the hood switch		
	Malfunction of the ECU	—	Replace the ECU.

■   FIGURE 12–56
(Courtesy of Chrysler Corporation.)

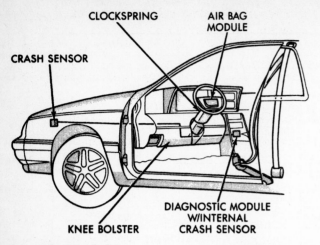

■ FIGURE 12–57

Basic layout of air bag system. (Courtesy of Chrysler Corporation.)

1	DEPLOYED AIR BAG
2	KNEE BOLSTER
3	SAFETY BELT

■ FIGURE 12–59

Air bag deployed. (Courtesy of General Motors Corporation.)

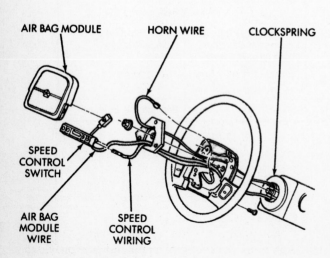

■ FIGURE 12–58

Air bag module and electrical connections. (Courtesy of Chrysler Corporation.)

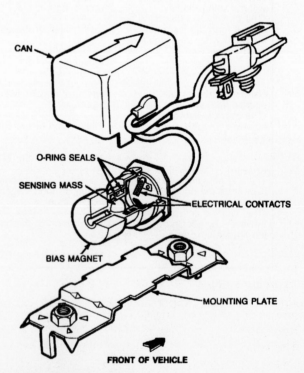

■ FIGURE 12–60

Air bag crash sensor has a sensing mass (ball or roller) that moves forward to close electrical contacts to activate inflater on vehicle impact. (Courtesy of Ford Motor Company.)

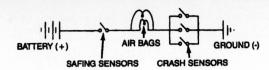

■ FIGURE 12–61
Air bag firing circuit diagram. (Courtesy of Ford Motor Company.)

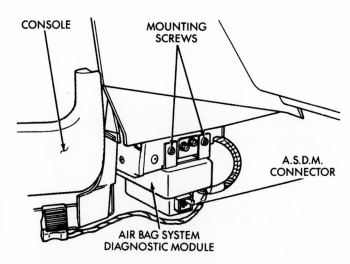

■ FIGURE 12–62
Air bag diagnostic module location. (Courtesy of Chrysler Corporation.)

Review Questions

1. Halogen headlamps have a small inner bulb enclosing a tungsten filament and a small amount of _____.
2. An automatic headlight system uses a _____ _____ to trigger the system.
3. Taillight bulbs are usually of the _____ filament type.
4. Brake lights are controlled by a _____ _____ when the brakes are applied.
5. Bulbs may be _____ or _____ filament.
6. Headlights must be properly aimed to meet _____ _____.
7. Power for all instrumentation is applied through the _____ switch.
8. The balanced coil or magnetic gauge operates on the principle of _____.
9. The Federal law requires that should an odometer or a speedometer be removed for repair or replacement it must be reinstalled with the same mileage as when it was removed. True or False.

10. With an electronic instrument system, _____ supply information to the _____ which activates the various instrument panel displays.
11. Windshield wiper arms must be properly positioned _____ _____ shafts.
12. Windshield washers use an _____ _____ to supply fluid to the windshield.
13. Power windows have switches that control a _____ _____ _____ which moves the window up or down.
14. Power door locks are operated by a two-position _____ _____.
15. A speed control system typically uses engine _____ to operate a _____ that controls throttle position.
16. If the speed control does not disengage when the brake is applied, the _____ _____ is out of _____.
17. It takes ⅟₂₅ of a second for an air bag to become inflated. True or False.

Test Questions

1. The candlepower of a conventional headlamp is about
   a. 750
   b. 7500
   c. 75000
   d. 75
2. a headlamp circuit may use
   a. 2 lamps
   b. 4 lamps
   c. either a) or b)
   d. neither a) nor b)
3. A 4-lamp circuit has
   a. single filament lamps
   b. double filament lamps
   c. both a) and b)
   d. neither a) nor b)
4. The beam of a headlamp may be
   a. symmetrical
   b. asymmetrical
   c. both a) and b)
   d. neither a) nor b)
5. Vertical headlight aiming adjustment is achieved by
   a. a focusing screw
   b. an adjustment screw at the top
   c. an adjustment screw at the side
   d. an adjustment screw at the bottom
6. Automatic canceling of signal lights is provided by
   a. the signal lever
   b. the canceling cam

c. turning in the direction being signaled
d. a photo cell

7. Lighting system problems are *not* the result of
a. a blown fuse
b. tight connections
c. burned out bulbs
d. a poor electrical path

8. The heat of current flow is used in
a. bimetallic gauges
b. electromagnetic gauges
c. solid state gauges
d. mechanical gauges

9. The 2-coil movement is used in a
a. bimetallic gauge
b. electromagnetic gauge
c. solid-state gauge
d. mechanical gauge

10. The indicator needle on a speedometer is held to the zero position by
a. magnetic force
b. the weight of the needle
c. the speedometer cable
d. a coiled spring

11. A digital readout is often used in a
a. bimetallic gauge
b. electromagnetic gauge
c. solid-state gauge
d. mechanical gauge

12. A car's headlamps are dim at idle. Technician A says the condition can be caused by too much resistance in the lamp ground circuit. Technician B says the condition can be caused by low charging system voltage. Who is right?
a. technician A
b. technician B
c. both are right
d. both are wrong

13. Windshield wiper problems may be
a. mechanical
b. electrical
c. both a) and b)
d. neither a) nor b)

14. A windshield washer system may have a problem in
a. pump
b. delivery system
c. both a) and b)
d. neither a) nor b)

15. Power windows are driven by
a. motors
b. solenoids
c. capacitors
d. relays

16. Power door locks are powered by
a. hydraulics
b. solenoids
c. resistors
d. relays

17. The electropneumatic speed control system uses the following major components
a. electric motor, switch, solenoid, gear system
b. switch, solenoid, servo, electric motor
c. solenoid, electric motor, speed sensor, switch
d. speed sensor, servo, switch, solenoid

18. Horns are adjusted to a specific
a. wattage
b. voltage
c. current draw
d. none of the above

19. The abbreviation SIR refers to
a. supplemental instrumentation regulation
b. supplemental internal regulation
c. supplemental inflatable restraint
d. supplemental interior restraint

Appendix

English–metric equivalents

Fractions	Decimal Inch	Metric mm	Fractions	Decimal Inch	Metric mm
1/64	.015625	.397	33/64	.515625	13.097
1/32	.03125	.794	17/32	.53125	13.494
3/64	.046875	1.191	35/64	.546875	13.891
1/16	.0625	1.588	9/16	.5625	14.288
5/64	.078125	1.984	37/64	.578125	14.684
3/32	.09375	2.381	19/32	.59375	15.081
7/64	.109375	2.778	39/64	.609375	15.478
1/8	.125	3.175	5/8	.625	15.875
9/64	.140625	3.572	41/64	.640625	16.272
5/32	.15625	3.969	21/32	.65625	16.669
11/64	.171875	4.366	43/64	.671875	17.066
3/16	.1875	4.763	11/16	.6875	17.463
13/64	.203125	5.159	45/64	.703125	17.859
7/32	.21875	5.556	23/32	.71875	18.256
15/64	.234375	5.953	47/64	.734375	18.653
1/4	.250	6.35	3/4	.750	19.05
17/64	.265625	6.747	49/64	.765625	19.447
9/32	.28125	7.144	25/32	.78125	19.844
19/64	.296875	7.54	51/64	.796875	20.241
5/16	.3125	7.938	13/16	.8125	20.638
21/64	.328125	8.334	53/64	.828125	21.034
11/32	.34375	8.731	27/32	.84375	21.431
23/64	.359375	9.128	55/64	.859375	21.828
3/8	.375	9.525	7/8	.875	22.225
25/64	.390625	9.922	57/64	.890625	22.622
13/32	.40625	10.319	29/32	.90625	23.019
27/64	.421875	10.716	59/64	.921875	23.416
7/16	.4375	11.113	15/16	.9375	23.813
29/64	.453125	11.509	61/64	.953125	24.209
15/32	.46875	11.906	31/32	.96875	24.606
31/64	.484375	12.303	63/64	.984375	25.003
1/2	.500	12.7	1	1.00	25.4

Source: Ford of Canada.

Torque conversion

Newton metres (N-m)	Pound-feet (lb-ft)	Pound-feet (lb-ft)	Newton metres (N-m)
1	0.7376	1	1.356
2	1.5	2	2.7
3	2.2	3	4.0
4	3.0	4	5.4
5	3.7	5	6.8
6	4.4	6	8.1
7	5.2	7	9.5
8	5.9	8	10.8
9	6.6	9	12.2
10	7.4	10	13.6
15	11.1	15	20.3
20	14.8	20	27.1
25	18.4	25	33.9
30	22.1	30	40.7
35	25.8	35	47.5
40	29.5	40	54.2
50	36.9	45	61.0
60	44.3	50	67.8
70	51.6	55	74.6
80	59.0	60	81.4
90	66.4	65	88.1
100	73.8	70	94.9
110	81.1	75	101.7
120	88.5	80	108.5
130	95.9	90	122.0
140	103.3	100	135.6
150	110.6	110	149.1
160	118.0	120	162.7
170	125.4	130	176.3
180	132.8	140	189.8
190	140.1	150	203.4
200	147.5	160	216.9
225	166.0	170	230.5
250	184.4	180	244.0

Source: Ford of Canada.

Decimal equivalents and tap drill sizes

Drill size	Decimal	Tap size	Drill size	Decimal	Tap Size	Drill size	Decimal	Tap size
1/64	.0156		20	.1610		T	.3580	
1/32	.0312		19	.1660		23/64	.3594	
60	.0400		18	.1695		U	.3680	7/16-14
59	.0410		11/64	.1719		3/8	.3750	
58	.0420		17	.1730		V	.3770	
57	.0430		16	.1770	12–24	W	.3860	
56	.0465		15	.1800		25/64	.3906	7/16-20
3/64	.0469	0-80	14	.1820	12-28	X	.3970	
55	.0520		13	.1850	12-32	Y	.4040	
54	.0550	1-56	3/16	.1875		13/32	.4062	
53	.0595	1-64, 72	12	.1890		Z	.4130	
1/16	.0625		11	.1910		27/64	.4219	1/2-13
52	.0635		10	.1935		7/16	.4375	
51	.0670		9	.1960		29/64	.4531	1/2-20
50	.0700	2-56, 64	8	.1990		15/32	.4687	
49	.0730		7	.2010	1/4-20	31/64	.4844	9/16-12
48	.0760		13/64	.2031		1/2	.5000	
5/64	.0781		6	.2040		33/64	.5156	9/16-18
47	.0785	3-48	5	.2055		17/32	.5312	5/8-11
46	.0810		4	.2090		35/64	.5469	
45	.0820	3-56, 4-32	3	.2130	1/4-28	9/16	.5625	
44	.0860		7/32	.2187		37/64	.5781	5/8-18
43	.0890	4-36	2	.2210		19/32	.5937	11/16-11
42	.0935	4-40	1	.2280		39/64	.6094	
3/32	.0937	4-48	A	.2340		5/8	.6250	11/16-16
41	.0960		15/64	.2344		41/64	.6406	
40	.0980		B	.2380		21/32	.6562	3/4-10
39	.0995		C	.2420		43/64	.6719	
38	.1015	5-40	D	.2460		11/16	.6875	3/4-16
37	.1040	5-44	E, 1/4	.2500		45/64	.7031	
36	.1065	6-32	F	.2570	5/16-18	23/32	.7187	
7/64	.1093		G	.2610		47/64	.7344	
35	.1100		17/64	.2656		3/4	.7500	
34	.1110	6-36	H	.2660		49/64	.7656	7/8-9
33	.1130	6-40	I	.2720	5/16-24	25/32	.7812	
32	.1160		J	.2770		51/64	.7969	
31	.1200		K	.2810		13/16	.8125	7/8-14
1/8	.1250		9/32	.2812		53/64	.8281	
30	.1285		L	.2900		27/32	.8437	
29	.1360	8-32, 36	M	.2950		55/64	.8594	
28	.1405	8-40	19/64	.2968		7/8	.8750	1-8
9/64	.1406		N	.3020		57/64	.8906	
27	.1440		5/16	.3125	3/8-16	29/32	.9062	
26	.1470		O	.3160		59/64	.9219	
25	.1495	10-24	P	.3230		15/16	.9375	1-12, 14
24	.1520		21/64	.3281		61/64	.9531	
23	.1540		Q	.3320	3/8-24	31/32	.9687	
5/32	.1562		R	.3390		63/64	.9844	
22	.1570	10-30	11/32	.3437		1	1.000	
21	.1590	10-32	S	.3480				

Pipe thread sizes

Thread	Drill	Thread	Drill
1/8-27	R	1 1/2-11 1/2	1 47/64
1/4-18	7/16	2-11 1/2	2 7/32
3/8-18	37/64	2 1/2-8	2 5/8
1/2-14	23/32	3-8	3 1/4
3/4-14	59/64	3 1/2-8	3 3/4
1-11 1/2	1 5/32	4-8	4 1/4
1 1/4-11 1/2	1 1/2		

Source: Frank J. Thiessen and Davis Dales, *Diesel Fundamentals*, 2nd Ed. (Englewood Cliffs, NJ: Prentice-Hall, Inc., 1986), p. 680.

English–metric conversion

Description	Multiply	By	For Metric Equivalent
ACCELERATION	foot/sec^2	0.304 8	metre/sec^2(m/s^2)
	inch/sec^2	0.025 4	metre/sec^2
TORQUE	pound-inch	0.112 98	newton-meters (N-m)
	pound-foot	1.355 8	newton-meters
POWER	horsepower	0.746	kilowatts (kw)
PRESSURE or STRESS	inches of water	0.2488	kilopascals (kPa)
	pounds/sq. in.	6.895	kilopascals (kPa)
ENERGY or WORK	BTU	1.055.	joules (J)
	foot-pound	1.355 8	joules (J)
	kilowatt-hour	3 600 000.	joules (J = one W's)
		or 3.6×10^6	
LIGHT	foot candle	10.76	lumens/meter^2 (lm/m^2)
FUEL PERFORMANCE	miles/gal	0.425 1	kilometers/liter (km/l)
	gal/mile	2.352 7	liters/kilometer (l/km)
VELOCITY	miles/hour	1.609 3	kilometers/hr. (km/h)
LENGTH	inch	25.4	millimeters (mm)
	foot	0.304 8	meters (m)
	yard	0.914 4	meters (m)
	mile	1.609	kilometers (km)
AREA	inch^2	645.2	millimeters^2 (mm^2)
		6.45	centimeters^2 (cm^2)
	foot^2	0.092 9	meters^2 (m^2)
	yard^2	0.8361	meters^2
VOLUME	inch^3	16 387.	mm^3
	inch^3	16. 387	cm^3
	quart	0. 016 4	liters (1)
	quart	0. 946 4	liters
	gallon	3. 785 4	liters
	yard^3	0. 764 6	meters^3 (m^3)
MASS	pound	0.453 6	kilograms (kg)
	ton	907.18	kilograms (kg)
	ton	0.90718	tonne
FORCE	kilogram	9.807	newtons (N)
	ounce	0.278 0	newtons
	pound	4.448	newtons
TEMPERATURE	degree Farenheit	0.556 (°F −32)	degree Celsius (°C)

Source: Ford of Canada.

■ SAE J1930 Standard Abbreviations

Technicians everywhere have been faced with a great variety of different terms and abbreviations for electrical and electronics components. This has largely resulted from a lack of standard terminology and vehicle manufacturers' efforts to be unique. Different manufacturers have often used different names and abbreviations for the same part. For example an engine control computer might be called an engine controller, an engine control computer, or a powertrain control computer. An oxygen sensor could be called an O$_2$ sensor, or an exhaust gas sensor. The SAE Standard J1930 attempts to correct this situation by standardizing electronics terminology and abbreviations. Vehicle manufacturers have adopted this terminology for use since the 1993 model year for use in their service literature. Unfortunately this does not change the situation in service manuals for prior models which will be used for some years to come. This book therefore uses a similar variety of terms and explains their function. In addition, the applicable terms from the SAE J1930 Standard are listed here.

SAE J1930 Abbreviation	Standard Name
ACL	Air Cleaner
AP	Accelerator Pedal
B+	Battery Positive Voltage
BARO	Barometric Pressure Sensor
CAC	Charge Air Cooler (intercooler, aftercooler)
CFC	Coolant Fan Control
CFI	Continuous Fuel Injection
CL	Closed Loop
CLS	Closed Loop System
CMP	Camshaft Position (sensor)
COLS	Coolant Level Sensor
CPS	Crankshaft Position Sensor
CTP	Closed Throttle Position
DLC	Data Link Connector
DLI	Distributorless Ignition
DTC	Diagnostic Trouble Codes
DTM	Diagnostic Test Mode
EC	Engine Control
ECTS	Engine Coolant Temperature Sensor
EEPROM	Electrically Erasable Programmable Read Only Memory
EFE	Early Fuel Evaporation
EGR	Exhaust Gas Recirculation
EGRC	EGR Function Control
EGRS	EGR Sensor
EGRT	EGR Temperature
EGRV	Exhaust Gas Recirculation Valve
EI	Electronic Ignition
EM	Engine Modification
EVAP	Evaporative Emission Control
FF	Flexible Fuel
FPR	Fuel Pump Relay
GEN	Generator
GND	Ground
HO$_2$S	Heated Oxygen Sensor
IACV	Idle Air Control Valve
IAT	Intake Air Temperature
IATS	Intake Air Temperature Sensor

SAE J1930 Abbreviation	Standard Name
IC	Ignition Control
ICM	Ignition Control Module
IFSS	Inertia Fuel Shutoff Switch
ISC	Idle Speed Control
KS	Knock Sensor
MAF	Mass Airflow Sensor
MAP	Manifold Absolute Pressure
MFI	Multipoint (electronic) Fuel Injection
MIL	Malfunction Indicator Lamp
MVS	Manifold Vacuum Sensor
NVRM	Non-volatile Random-access Memory (Keep Alive Memory)
O_2S	Oxygen Sensor
OBD	On-board Diagnostics
OC	Oxidation Catalyst
OL	Open Loop
PAIR	Pulsed Secondary Air
PCM	Powertrain Control Module
PROM	Programmable Read Only Memory
RAM	Random Access Memory
RM	Relay Module
ROM	Read Only Memory
SABFV	Secondary Air Antibackfire Valve
SABV	Secondary Air Bypass Valve
SASV	Secondary Air Switching Valve
SC	Supercharger
SCB	Supercharger Bypass
SMPI	Sequential Multipoint Electronic Fuel Injection
SRI	Service Reminder Indicator
ST	Scan Tool
TB	Throttle Body
TBI	Throttle Body Electronic Fuel Injection
TC	Turbocharger
TPS	Throttle Position Sensor
TVV	Thermal Vacuum Valve
TWC	Three-Way Catalyst
TWC+OC	Two-Way Catalyst Plus Oxidation Catalyst
VAF	Volume Air Flow
VSS	Vehicle Speed Sensor
WOTS	Wide Open Throttle Switch
WUOC	Warm-Up Oxidation Catalyst
WUTWC	Warm-Up Three Way Catalyst

Answer Keys

■ INTRODUCTION

Review Questions

1. move
2. atmospheric pressure
3. controlled
4. pressure, down
5. intake, compression, power, exhaust
6. cylinder
7. bore, stroke
8. power, fuel consumption
9. 180, crankshaft
10. 60
11. true
12. start, running
13. quickly, perform
14. temperature, humidity

Test Questions

1. b, 2. a, 3. c, 4. b, 5. d, 6. c, 7. a, 8. a, 9. d, 10. c.

■ Chapter 1

Review Questions

1. stroke
2. 14.7
3. intake, compression, power, exhaust
4. 15 parts, 1 part
5. torque
6. pounds per square inch
7. mercury
8. vacuum
9. work
10. power
11. theoretical power
12. friction
13. volumetric efficiency
14. vehicle performance
15. engine, chasses
16. volatility, antiknock quality, deposit control
17. preignition
18. antiknock quality

Test Questions

1.	A	8.	C
2.	B	9.	B
3.	D	10.	B
4.	B	11.	B
5.	B	12.	D
6.	C	13.	C
7.	A	14.	D

■ Chapter 2

Review Questions

1. engine systems
2. preignition
3. excessive clearance
4. piston to cylinder   wall clearance
5. unburned fuel
6. True
7. True
8. cylinders   power
9. 25KV,   40KV
10. blown   head gasket
11. False
12. True

Test Questions

1.	A	10.	C
2.	C	11.	D
3.	C	12.	C
4.	C	13.	A
5.	A	14.	D
6.	C	15.	B
7.	B	16.	C
8.	A	17.	D
9.	D	18.	D

■ Chapter 3

Review Questions

1. electrical, electronic devices
2. doubles
3. open, close
4. True
5. True
6. stepper motor
7. electrical current
8. True
9. wire, carbon
10. active passive
11. electron flow
12. electomotive force
13. watts
14. True
15. open
16. ammeter

Test Questions

1.	B	9.	B
2.	B	10.	B
3.	A	11.	A
4.	C	12.	A
5.	B	13.	C
6.	C	14.	C
7.	C	15.	D
8.	B		

■ Chapter 4

Review Questions

1. True
2. ignition fuel injection
3. application release
4. input, processing output
5. random access memory

6. read only memory
7. variable resistor
8. pressure vacuum
9. exhaust gases
10. True
11. malfunctioning
12. diagnostic connector
13. metal ground
14. generate
15. voltage signals
16. output voltage

Test Questions

1.	A	8.	D
2.	C	9.	D
3.	A	10.	A
4.	B	11.	A
5.	A	12.	D
6.	B	13.	D
7.	A	14.	A

■ Chapter 5

Review Questions

1. True
2. sulfuric acid, water
3. 125° F (516° C)
4. distilled water
5. electrical mechanical
6. starting motor
7. neutral switch
8. ground cable
9. False
10. True
11. current draw
12. True
13. armature is grounded
14. mechanical power
15. polarity
16. True
17. voltage current
18. wear damage

Test Questions

1.	A	8.	D
2.	B	9.	C
3.	A	10.	A
4.	A	11.	B
5.	B	12.	A
6.	B	13.	B
7.	A	14.	B

15. D
16. A
17. A

18. B
19. A
20. B

Chapter 6

Review Questions

1. low voltage,   high voltage
2. 40,000
3. primary circuit
4. distribute spark
5. coil
6. ohmmeter
7. centrifugal, vacuum
8. turning distributor
9. timing light
10. resistance, ohmmeter
11. hot   damage threads
12. wire gauge
13. ohmmeter
14. replaced with a known good module
15. fault code

Test Questions

1. B
2. A
3. B
4. C
5. C
6. B
7. C

8. A
9. D
10. A
11. B
12. D
13. A
14. A

Chapter 7

Review Questions

1. carburetor
2. throttle body, port
3. performance   economy   emissions
4. 25 to 80   psi   (172 to 550 kPa)
5. True
6. pressure,   volume and leak down
7. pressure,   volume and vacuum
8. False
9. True
10. computer
11. fault code chart
12. enrich
13. True
14. False
15. ohmmeter
16. pressure

Test Questions

1. D
2. D
3. A
4. A
5. C
6. A
7. A
8. C
9. A

10. A
11. D
12. C
13. D
14. B
15. C
16. B
17. D
18. D

Chapter 8

Review Questions

1. proper combustion
2. filter element
3. positive, crankcase ventilation
4. exhaust   driven
5. True
6. engine   power   output
7. wastegate
8. air compressor
9. boost
10. reduced
11. catalytic
12. intake   manifold
13. True
14. True
15. blocked

Test Questions

1. C
2. A
3. C
4. B
5. C
6. A
7. C

8. C
9. A
10. D
11. B
12. C
13. A
14. C

Chapter 9

Review Questions

1. crankcase vapors, fuel evaporation and exhaust
2. hydrocarbons,   nitrogen oxides and sunlight
3. harder
4. mixture
5. exhaust gas recirculation
6. fault codes
7. harmful pollutants
8. parts per million

9. percent
10. hydrocarbons
11. True
12. replaced
13. closed
14. HC   CO and NO
15. overheat
16. True
17. high volume,   low pressure
18. True

Test Questions

1.	D	9.	A
2.	C	10.	D
3.	A	11.	B
4.	D	12.	A
5.	D	13.	B
6.	A	14.	B
7.	A	15.	A
8.	A		

■ Chapter 10

Review Questions

1. efficient operating temperature
2. liquid air
3. False
4. belt   electric motor
5. boiling point
6. freeze   boiling point
7. hydrometer
8. voltmeter
9. True
10. pressure tested
11. temperature switch
12. False (must be replaced)
13. True
14. coolant reserve tank

Test Questions

1.	D	7.	C
2.	A	8.	D
3.	C	9.	D
4.	A	10.	D
5.	C	11.	A
6.	D	12.	C

■ Chapter 11

Review Questions

1. engine coolant
2. manual automatic
3. cleans   dehumidifies
4. True
5. chlorine   fluorine
6. ozone layer
7. False
8. Liquid
9. heat
10. magnetic clutch
11. True
12. False
13. vapor to a liquid
14. absorb heat
15. evaporator
16. desiccant
17. True
18. test gauges
19. heat, windshield defrosting,   heat
20. vacuum   equipment
21. certified   equipment
22. three years
23. freezing
24. True
25. self-diagnosis function
26. atmosphere
27. True
28. phosgene gas
29. proper performance
30. parts failure

Test Questions

1.	B	14.	D
2.	B	15.	B
3.	B	16.	C
4.	B	17.	A
5.	C	18.	B
6.	B	19.	C
7.	B	20.	D
8.	C	21.	D
9.	D	22.	A
10.	B	23.	B
11.	A	24.	C
12.	B	25.	D
13.	B		

■ Chapter 12

Review Questions

1. halogen vapor
2. photo system
3. double
4. mechanical switch
5. single   double
6. government regulations
7. ignition
8. magnetism
9. True
10. sensors   computer
11. splined   pivot
12. electric pump
13. reversible electric motor
14. electric solenoid
15. vacuum
16. release switch   adjustment
17. True

Test Questions

1. C
2. C
3. C
4. C
5. B
6. B
7. B
8. A
9. B
10. D
11. C
12. B
13. C
14. C
15. A
16. B
17. D
18. C
19. C

Index